SCIENCE INTERACTIONS

Course 2

GLENCOE
McGraw-Hill

New York, New York   Columbus, Ohio   Mission Hills, California   Peoria, Illinois

Science Interactions

Student Edition

Teacher Wraparound Edition

Science Discovery Activities

Teacher Classroom Resources

Laboratory Manual: SE

Laboratory Manual: TAE

Study Guide: SE

Study Guide: TE

Transparency Package

Performance Assessment

Performance Assessment in Middle School Science

Computer Test Bank: IBM, Apple, Macintosh Versions

Spanish Resources

English/Spanish Audiocassettes

Science and Technology Videodisc Series

Integrated Science Videodisc Program

Series and Cover Design: DECODE, Inc.
Design and Production: DECODE, Inc.

Send all inquiries to:
GLENCOE DIVISION
Macmillan/McGraw-Hill
936 Eastwind Drive
Westerville, OH 43081

ISBN 0-02-826804-0

Printed in the United States of America

2 3 4 5 6 7 8 9 10 VH/LH 00 99 98 97 96 95 94

Authors

Bill Aldridge, M.S.
Executive Director
National Science Teachers Association
Arlington, Virginia

Russell Aiuto, Ph.D.
Senior Project Officer
Council of Independent Colleges
Washington, DC

Albert Kaskel, M.Ed.
Biology Teacher, Emeritus
Evanston Township High School
Evanston, Illinois

Jack Ballinger, Ed.D.
Professor of Chemistry
St. Louis Community College at Florissant Valley
St. Louis, Missouri

Craig Kramer, M.A.
Physics Teacher
Bexley High School
Bexley, Ohio

Anne Barefoot, A.G.C.
Physics and Chemistry Teacher, Emeritus
Whiteville High School
Whiteville, North Carolina

Edward Ortleb, A.G.C.
Science Supervisor
St. Louis Board of Education
St. Louis, Missouri

Linda Crow, Ed.D.
Assistant Professor
Baylor College of Medicine
Houston, Texas

Susan Snyder, M.S.
Earth Science Teacher
Jones Middle School
Upper Arlington, Ohio

Ralph M. Feather, Jr., M.Ed.
Science Department Chair
Derry Area School District
Derry, Pennsylvania

Paul W. Zitzewitz, Ph.D.
Professor of Physics
University of Michigan-Dearborn
Dearborn, Michigan

Consultants

Chemistry

Richard J. Merrill
Director,
Project Physical Science
Associate Director, Institute
for Chemical Education
University of California
Berkeley, California

Robert W. Parry, Ph.D.
Dist. Professor of Chemistry
University of Utah
Salt Lake City, Utah

Earth Science

Allan A. Ekdale, Ph.D.
Professor of Geology
University of Utah
Salt Lake City, Utah

Janifer Mayden
Aerospace Education Specialist
NASA
Washington, DC

James B. Phipps, Ph.D.
Professor of Geology
and Oceanography
Gray's Harbor College
Aberdeen, Washington

Life Science

Mary D. Coyne, Ph.D.
Professor of Biological Sciences
Wellesley College
Wellesley, Massachusetts

Joe W. Crim, Ph.D.
Associate Professor of Zoology
University of Georgia
Athens, Georgia

Richard D. Storey, Ph.D.
Associate Professor of Biology
Colorado College
Colorado Springs, Colorado

Physics

David Haase, Ph.D.
Professor of Physics
North Carolina State University
North Carolina

Patrick Hamill, Ph.D.
Professor of Physics
San Jose State University
San Jose, California

Middle School Science

Garland E. Johnson
Science and Education Consultant
Fresno, California

Barbara Sitzman
Chatsworth High School
Tarzana, California

Multicultural

Thomas Custer
Coordinator of Science
Anne Arundel County Schools
Annapolis, Maryland

Francisco Hernandez
Science Department Chair
John B. Hood Middle School
Dallas, Texas

Carol T. Mitchell
Instructor
Elementary Science Methods
College of Teacher Education
University of Omaha at Omaha
Omaha, Nebraska

Karen Muir, Ph.D.
Lead Instructor
Department of Social and
Behavioral Sciences
Columbus State
Community College
Columbus, Ohio

Reading

Elizabeth Gray, Ph.D.
Reading Specialist
Heath City Schools
Heath, Ohio
Adjunct Professor
Otterbein College
Westerville, Ohio

Timothy Heron, Ph.D.
Professor, Department
of Educational
Services & Research
The Ohio State University
Columbus, Ohio

Barbara Pettegrew, Ph.D.
Director of Reading
Study Center
Assistant Professor of Education
Otterbein College
Westerville, Ohio

LEP

Ross M. Arnold
Magnet School Coordinator
Van Nuys Junior High
Van Nuys, California

Linda E. Heckenberg
Director
Eisenhower Program
Van Nuys, California

**Harold Frederick
Robertson, Jr.**
Science Resource Teacher
LAUSD Science Materials Center
Van Nuys, California

Safety

Robert Tatz, Ph.D.
Instructional Lab Supervisor
Department of Chemistry
The Ohio State University
Columbus, Ohio

Reviewers

Lillian Valeria Jordan Alston
Science Consultant
Institute of Government
University of North Carolina
Chapel Hill, North Carolina

Janet P. Bailey
Science Teacher
East Wake Middle School
Youngsville, North Carolina

Jamie Barnes
Science Teacher
Prescott Middle School
Prescott, Arizona

Betty Bordelon
Science Teacher
Haynes Middle School
Metairie, Louisiana

James Carbaugh
Science Teacher
Greencastle Middle School
Greencastle, Pennsylvania

Elberta Casey
8th Grade Earth Science Teacher
Crawford Middle School
Lexington, Kentucky

Linda Culpeper
Science Department Chairperson
Piedmont Open Middle School
Charlotte, North Carolina

Nancy Donohue
General Science Teacher
Emerson Junior High School
Yonkers, New York

Susan Duhaime
5th/6th Grade Science Teacher
Assistant Principal
St. Anthony School
Manchester, New Hampshire

Ken Eiseman
Science Supervisor
West Chester Area School District
West Chester, Pennsylvania

Mel Fuller
Professor of Science Education
Department of Teacher Education
University of Arkansas
at Little Rock
Little Rock, Arkansas

Janet Grush
7th Grade Science/Math Teacher
Wirth Middle School
Cahokia, Illinois

Joanne Hardy
7th Grade Science/Social
Studies/Language Arts Teacher
Memorial Middle School
Conyers, Georgia

Nancy J. Hopkins
Gifted/Talented Coordinating
Teacher for Middle School Science
Morrill Elementary
San Antonio, Texas

Amy Jacobs
7th Grade Life Science Teacher
Morton Middle School
Lexington, Kentucky

Rebecca King
Chemistry Teacher
New Hanover High School
Wilmington, North Carolina

Ken Krause
Science Teacher
Harriet Tubman Middle School
Portland, Oregon

Martha Sculley Lai
Science Teacher
Department Chairperson
Highland High School
Medina, Ohio

William Lavinghousez
MAGNET Program Director
Ronald McNair MAGNET School
Cocoa, Florida

Norman Mankins
Science Specialist (Curriculum)
Canton City Schools
Canton, Ohio

John Maxwell
7th Grade Life Science Teacher
Claremont Middle School
Claremont, New Hampshire

Fred J. Mayberry
Earth/Life Science Teacher
Department Chairperson
Vernon Junior High School
Harlingen, Texas

Michael Parry
Science Supervisor
Boyerstown Area School District
Boyerstown, Pennsylvania

Lola Perritt
Science Specialist
Instructional Resource Center
Little Rock, Arkansas

Chuck Porrazzo
Science Department Chairperson
Bronx Career Technical
Assistance Center
Junior High 145
New York, New York

James Stewart
Life Science Teacher
W. E. Greiner Middle School
Dallas, Texas

James Todd
7th/8th Grade Science Teacher
East Hardin Middle School
Glendale, Kentucky

Deborah Tully
8th Grade Earth Science Teacher
Department Chairperson
Winburn Middle School
Lexington, Kentucky

Marianne Wilson
Science-Health-Drug
Coordinator
Pulaski County Special Schools
Sherwood, Arkansas

SCIENCE INTERACTIONS
CONTENTS OVERVIEW
Course 2

UNIT
5

SCIENCE INTERACTIONS
TABLE OF CONTENTS
Course 2

UNIT 1 — Forces in Action   18

Chapter 2   Forces in Earth   52

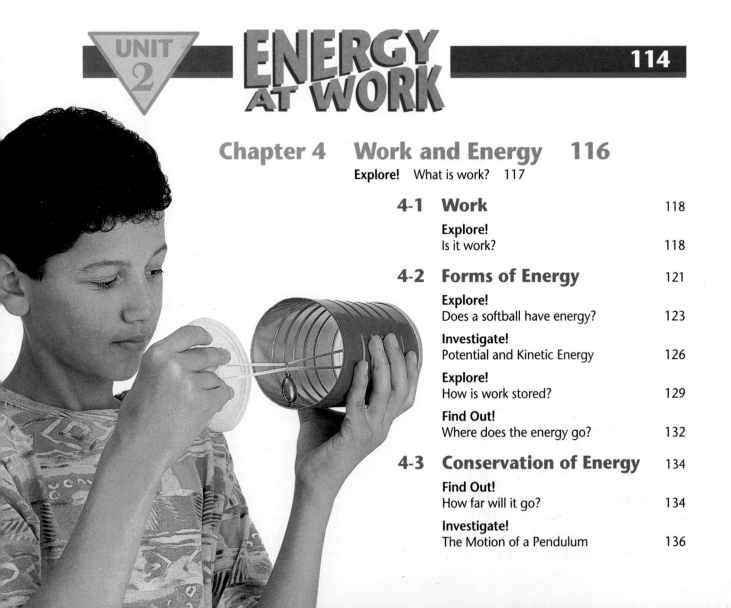

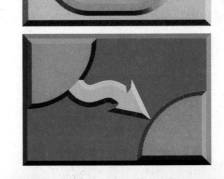

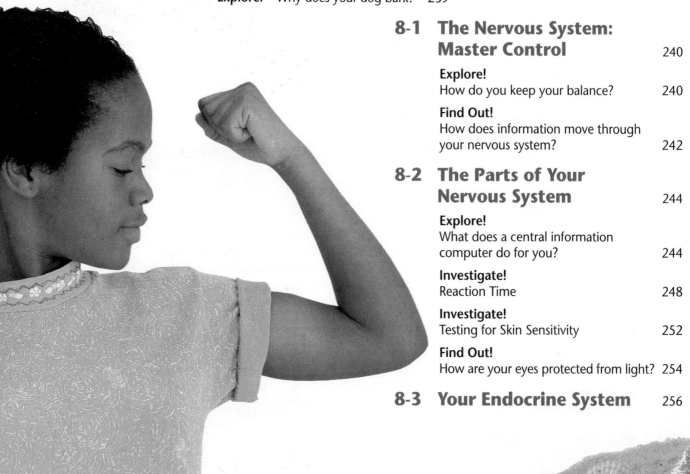

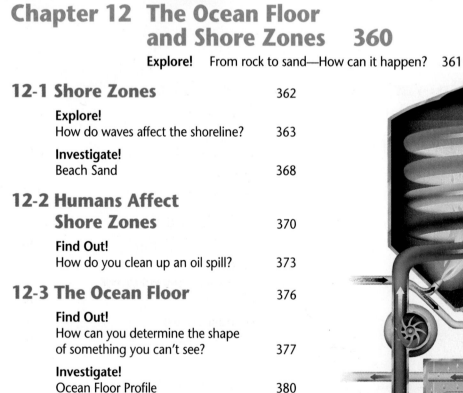

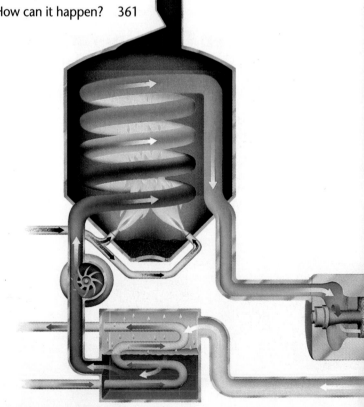

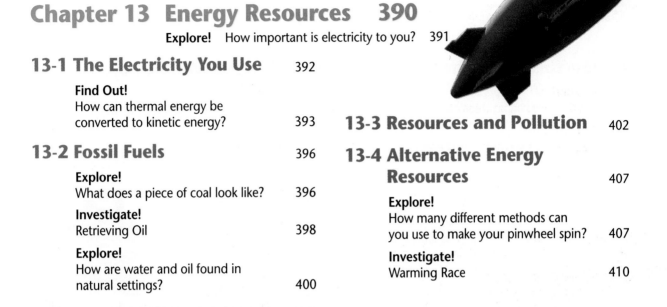

UNIT 4 **Air: Molecules in Motion** **422**

Contents **xvii**

UNIT 5

Life at the Cellular Level

512

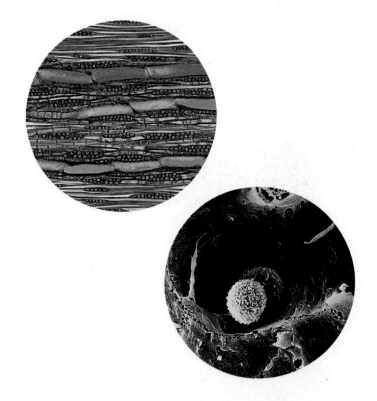

SCIENCE CONNECTIONS

Have you ever noticed that you really can't talk about earthquakes without mentioning forces? How is one science related to another? Expand your view of science through A CLOSER LOOK and Science Connections features in each chapter.

Earth Science

Life Science

Physics and Chemistry

A CLOSER LOOK

SCIENCE CONNECTIONS

Science is something that refuses to stay locked away in a laboratory. In both the Science and Society and the Technology features, you'll learn how science impacts the world you live in today. You may also be asked to think about science-related questions that will affect your life fifty years from now.

Science and Society

Technology Connection

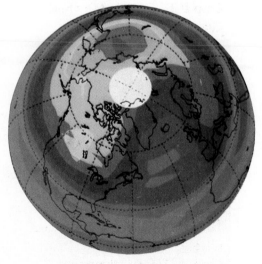

CROSS-CURRICULUM CONNECTIONS

With the EXPAND YOUR VIEW features at the end of each chapter, you'll quickly become aware that science is an important part of every subject you'll ever encounter in school. Read these features to learn how science has affected history, health, and your buying power.

Consumer Connection

Health CONNECTION

HISTORY CONNECTION

Literature Connection / Leisure connection

CROSS-CURRICULUM
CONNECTIONS

What makes this thing work? What do you have to do to become a scientist? In HOW IT WORKS, learn that the workings of most ordinary everyday things are based on scientific principles. Through TEENS IN SCIENCE, you'll find out that you don't have to wear a lab coat to make science happen.

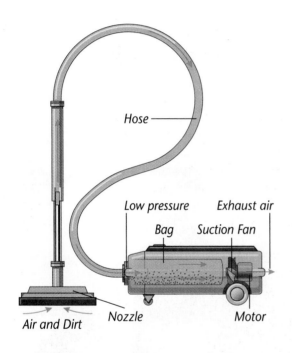

Hose

Low pressure   Exhaust air

Bag   Suction Fan

Air and Dirt   Nozzle   Motor

Teens in SCIENCE

HOW IT WORKS

SCIENCE:
A Tool for Solving Problems

What good is science, anyway? Can everyone use science, or is it reserved for trained scientists? How can it help in your life today? How can scientific methods help you plan ahead or make tough decisions?

Follow Philip, Sachi, Lena, and the rest of their science class as they explore building a city on the moon and learn how to put science to work in their lives. The tools and methods they use can help you answer important questions in your own life, in school and out of school—even if you don't consider yourself a "real scientist."

Who Can Use Science?

"I don't have time to help plan a city on the moon!" Philip told Lena and Sachi. They were standing in the hallway after their science class. "I need every spare second to practice for the track meet this Friday!"

Sachi frowned. "I'd rather finish writing my story. This girl is adopted, and she thinks that her gym teacher is her real mother …"

"What if we end up living on the moon?" Lena interrupted. "Remember what Ms. Howard said? The first people to live on the moon might be in middle school or junior high school right now."

"She didn't mean me," Sachi said. "I'm a writer, not a scientist!"

Lena nodded. "You know, Rachel Carson didn't want to take a science course. She started out as a writer."

"You mean Rachel Carson, the person who wrote *Silent Spring*? She was always a writer!" Sachi said.

"Yes, she always was a writer," Lena agreed, "but she was a scientist, too. Because she was such a good writer and she understood science so well, she helped millions of people learn about pesticides and pollution."

Philip thought for a minute. "My track coach said he studied physics in college to figure out how we could cut down wind resistance when we run. So I guess he uses science, too. I wonder how many other people use science in their work."

Explore! ACTIVITY

How does science contribute to other studies?

Georges Seurat and Rachel Carson, whose works are shown on this page, are just two people who combined science with other fields to produce beautiful paintings and writings. How does science contribute to other parts of life?

What To Do

1. Research a person, living or in the past, who combined science with another field, such as cooking, playing a sport, farming, writing, or another of your own choosing.

2. Make a poster or write a short biography or skit that tells how that person used science to help improve other areas of life. When you're through, display your work.

La Bec du Hoc, a landscape painting by Georges Seurat

3. Observe your classmates' posters and writings. *In your Journal*, describe how science contributed to improving other fields.

How Do We Find Out?

The next day at school, the science class began to plan its city on the moon. "Cities don't just happen," Ms. Howard pointed out, "especially on the moon. What are some things a city needs?"

"A swimming pool and a video store!" offered Philip.

Ms. Howard smiled. "Let's call that 'recreation.'" After everyone called out ideas, the class narrowed the list to these areas: food, water, air, clothing, housing, transportation, health care, recreation, and waste control/removal.

"Our city will be expensive to build," Ms. Howard pointed out. "We'll also have to get supplies from Earth to keep it going after it's built. How are we going to pay for this? Hold a bake sale?"

Alberto said, "We need to find or make something on the moon that people on Earth will buy so we can get money to pay for supplies."

"Or maybe we could offer some special service people want, but can't get anywhere else," Sachi suggested.

Ms. Howard nodded and added "product/service" to the list on the chalkboard. Lena couldn't help wondering what people living on the moon could make and sell. Wasn't the moon just dust and craters?

"Let's recall what we KNOW about the moon." Ms. Howard tacked up a list of statistics.

Facts About the Moon
Distance from Earth: 384,403 km
Diameter: 3,476 km (.27 times Earth)
Revolution around Earth: 29 days, 12 hours, 44 minutes
Rotation on axis: 27 days, 7 hours, 43 minutes
Temperature: 127° C day; -173° C night
Atmosphere: Ultra thin: neon, hydrogen, helium, argon
Surface gravity: 0.17 times Earth (1/6 of Earth's)
Surface: silicate crust

■ Asking a Question

Ms. Howard showed them a form. "This Flex Your Brain chart will help us use what we know to find out what we want to know. What else do we need to know about the moon before we can start planning?" she asked.

Hands went up. As the class suggested questions to be answered, Ms. Howard wrote the questions down.

"If the atmosphere is thin, does that mean there's no ozone layer?" Michelle asked.

"Is there anything on the moon we could use as a building material?" Mieko asked. "Or does everything have to be shipped from Earth?"

Then Lena asked, "Is it always night on one side of the moon and day on the other? I can't remember."

"It's always dark on one side," Philip told her. "So we have to put our city on the 'day' side."

Ms. Howard stopped writing. "I see some puzzled faces. Does everyone agree with Philip? How can we find out if the moon has a dark side? We can't experiment with the sun and moon, so what else could we do? Let's use the Flex Your Brain chart to develop some ideas." The class completed the form and developed one way to investigate whether or not the moon has a dark side.

Find Out! ACTIVITY

A Look at the "Dark Side"

Construct a model to find out if the moon has a dark side. You'll need a globe or large ball (Earth), a small ball (moon), a flashlight (sun), and a sticker.

What To Do

1. Put the sticker on the "equator" of the moon ball.
2. Shine the flashlight on Earth.
3. Then, move the moon slowly around Earth to represent its one-month orbit. Remember, as the moon orbits, it must also rotate on its axis. The moon's orbit around Earth and one rotation take about the same length of time.
4. Watch how long the "sun" shines on the sticker as the moon orbits Earth and rotates on its axis.
5. Record your observations and the answers to the following questions *in your Journal.*

Conclude and Apply

1. Does the moon have a "dark side"?
2. How long is one "day" on the moon, according to your model?
3. How did constructing this model help you answer the question "Does the moon have a dark side?"

■ Planning an Approach

After the class used a model to figure out whether the moon had a dark side or not, they listed more questions. Then, everyone divided into groups to start planning.

Philip thought about joining the Recreation Group. That group would examine how the moon's gravity and other conditions would affect the games we play on Earth. For example, what might happen if you bunted a baseball on the moon? The group could rewrite the rules for a game—or invent a new game, taking into account the conditions on the moon.

But Philip, who was always hungry, decided to volunteer for the Food Group instead. This group would investigate the kinds of food that could be grown on the moon. It would study how conditions on the moon might affect the growth of plants. The group would also figure out how much it would cost to bring food from Earth.

Sachi chose the Waste Control/ Removal Group. This group would explore which materials could be reused, which could be recycled, and which had to be thrown away. The group's aim was to conserve materials

and avoid polluting their new city.

Lena wanted to be in the Product/Service Group. She was curious about what the moon could have that people on Earth would want. After all, how many samples of moon rock would anyone buy?

Each group began by brainstorming a list of questions. They chose some of the questions from the class list. Then, they added more things they needed to know in order to plan their own aspect of the city. Each group had a week to select a question from its list and try to find an answer, using the "Flex Your Brain" chart to plan a scientific approach.

■ **Experimenting**

At the end of the week, the groups shared what they had learned. The Food Group shared first. Philip reported that the group members—Alberto, Michelle, and himself—already were fairly sure seeds could be transported to the moon safely. In fact, a science class at the school had grown great-tasting tomatoes from seeds that had spent six years in space aboard NASA's Long Duration Exposure Facility (LDEF).

"But," Michelle told the class, "even starting with healthy seeds, we thought the moon's long night might kill most plants. So we thought that plants on the moon would probably be grown in artificially controlled light. We wondered how many hours of light would produce the best plants."

"So we set up an experiment," Alberto explained. "We gave some plants a short day, some a 14-hour 'summer' day, and some an extra-long day. We also left some plants in the light all the time, to see how they grew."

After the Food Group explained the results of its experiment, Michelle laughed. "Now we know how many hours of light make the plants grow fastest, but there are a lot of other questions we need to answer before we're ready to feed a city!"

How will your garden grow?

Try developing your own experiment to test the same problem the food group faced.

What To Do

1. First, set up three different schedules for the amount of light each group of plants will receive. One group of plants should be a "control" and follow a normal Earth daylight schedule.

2. Predict which schedule will result in best plant growth. Your prediction will be the hypothesis, or suggested solution, for this experiment.

3. Now, design an experiment to test your hypothesis. Remember, you are only testing the effects of light, so be certain that all the other conditions, or variables, of the experiment are the same for all groups.

4. Get your design approved by your teacher and conduct your experiment.

Conclude and Apply

1. *In your Journal*, write a summary of your experiment. Include your hypothesis, which is your suggested answer to the problem, how you tested your hypothesis and the results of your experiment. Also tell how you evaluated your results. For example, how did you define and evaluate "best growth"?

2. Why is a control important in an experiment?

■ More Experimenting

Sachi told the class that the Waste Control/Removal Group—Kareem, Jeff, and herself—had begun by discussing its goals. "Pollution is the main thing," Kareem said. "We sure don't want to turn the moon into a garbage pit. We thought about setting up an ecosystem that would recycle everything."

"We didn't know much about recycling," Jeff said. "So we became scientists." He smiled, "We also set up an experiment!"

"We did the experiment with paper," Sachi explained. "We wanted to see whether it was easier to reuse paper, recycle it, or make new paper. We thought we could use what we learned about paper to control other waste materials on the moon, too.

"Our hypothesis (the answer we expected) was that reusing paper would be the easiest, recycling it would be harder, and making new paper would be the hardest. We already knew how to reuse paper— just turn it over and write on the other side.

"To make

Two "Amateur" Scientists at Work

Gregor Mendel, who defined the laws of heredity, was an amateur scientist. He studied science on his own, took college science courses, and taught science in a high school.

Mendel began to experiment on plants in his own garden. His careful experimentation led him to understand how characteristics such as tallness and color are passed from one plant to another.

Valentina Tereshkova spent her early years working in a tire factory and in a cotton mill in the Soviet Union. Inspired by cosmonaut Yuri Gagarin, Valentina Tereshkova wrote to the Soviet government and asked to be part of its space program.

Tereshkova was selected and received one year of training. (When she started, her only qualifications were her great interest in the program and her skill in parachuting.) However, her interest and dedication led her to learn all of the mechanics and physics that went into piloting a space capsule.

On June 16, 1963, she became the sixth cosmonaut and the first woman in space, orbiting Earth for three days. That was longer than any of the six U.S. astronauts who had flown, up to that time.

new paper, you have to cut down trees in the forest. That's much harder than reusing paper and wouldn't work on the moon, for sure. Our group didn't know much about recycling paper, the middle part of our hypothesis, so we decided to test that part by finding out how hard it is to recycle paper."

Paper, the Second Time Around

Follow these directions to make one sheet of recycled paper by hand. Machines recycle paper in factories, of course. This activity will show you what's involved in the process.

Problem
Is it easier to reuse, recycle, or make new paper?

Materials
2 pages of newspaper, torn into small squares

2 to 3 cups of water

blender

2 tablespoons of white glue

dishpan

one leg of an old pair of pantyhose

electric iron

clothes hanger

Safety Precautions

Do not take the lid off of the blender while it is operating. Do not get your hands near the blender blades.

What To Do

1 Carefully untwist the clothes hanger and form it into a 6-inch square (see photo **A**).

2 Carefully slip the wire square inside the pantyhose, trying not to snag the hose (see photo **B**). Make sure the hose is tight and flat. Tie each end of the hose into a knot.

3 Put some torn paper and water into the blender. Close the lid and turn it on high. Add more paper and water until the paper disappears and the mixture turns into a large ball of pulp. Then, let the blender run for two more minutes.

4 Put about 4 inches of water in the dishpan and add the glue.

5 Add the pulp to the water and mix well.

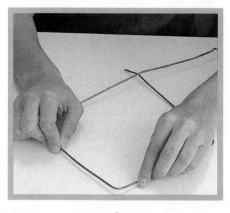

A   B   C

6 Stir the water. Quickly slip the wire frame under the pulp and rest it at the bottom of the dishpan. Then lift the frame slowly as you count to 20.

7 Let the paper on the frame dry completely. (You might put the frame in the sun.) When the paper is totally dry, gently peel it off the frame (see photo **C**).

8 Use the iron on the hottest setting to steam your paper flat. When the paper dries again, it's ready to use!

Analyzing

1. Compare the amount of energy that goes into recycling paper to reusing one sheet of paper.

2. Which process would be more energy efficient?

You can create handmade paper in a variety of textures and colors using not only newspaper, but materials such as flowers, grasses, food coloring, even lint from the clothes dryer!

Concluding and Applying

3. If you did this experiment again, do you think you would come to the same conclusions?

4. When would you choose to use an experiment rather than a model?

5. Why is an experimental method sometimes used in science?

6. Did this experiment raise any questions that were not answered? What questions? How would you go about finding an answer to those questions?

7. Going Further Redesign the experiment to make it more accurate or more measurable. For instance, can you figure out a way to measure how much effort each of the three different paper treatments used?

■ Analyzing Data

Sachi, Kareem, and Jeff held up the sheets of recycled paper they had made. "So you see," Sachi said, "our hypothesis was right. It's easy to reuse paper, and it's harder to recycle it. But it would be hardest to make new paper, especially when you'd have to transport trees to the moon!" she added.

"So we recommend that all paper on the moon be reused and then recycled," Jeff told the class. "But our Waste Control/ Removal Group still has a lot more materials to experiment with before we're ready to help set up an ecosystem in our city!"

The Product/Service Group shared next. "Lewis, Mieko,

and I had a little trouble getting started," Lena told the class. "The first time we met, we just stared at one another. No one could think of anything to make on the moon and sell on Earth. We even started to think that maybe a bake sale was a good idea!"

Everyone laughed. Then Mieko said, "We finally realized we had to

find some way to take advantage of the conditions on the moon, so we listed ways the moon is different from Earth. Here are some ways we thought of, along with questions we needed to answer." She taped a newsprint list on the wall. The list is shown on the right.

"Then," Lewis explained, "we thought about the problem a different way. We listed the different things we value here on Earth and tried to pick ones that might be produced more cheaply or easily on the moon."

"What we finally realized," Lena told the class, "was that we had a lot more questions than answers. We needed to choose a question or two and figure out some way to get the answers. So each of us picked one possible way to make money on the moon and wrote a proposal explaining how we could find out if our idea was practical."

Ways to Take Advantage of Moon Conditions

1. **The moon has lower gravity than Earth.** What does that mean for space vehicles taking off from the moon's surface? What products could be produced more easily if gravity weren't pulling on them? Heavy things? Delicate things? Things that must be a certain shape?

2. **The moon has almost no atmosphere.** How could we take advantage of that? No atmosphere means no humidity. What about making computer parts and other things that are affected by dampness in the air? (The moon also has a dusty surface that might wreck computer parts!)

3. **The moon might have different minerals than Earth has.** Maybe the moon has valuable minerals that could be mined and sold. Or maybe certain minerals in the moon's crust would make plants grow super-fast. (The minerals might also be useful as building materials on the moon.)

4. **The moon and Earth are in different positions in space.** How could we use the moon's position to offer a service to space vehicles or astronomers?

Paying for the Moon

You need to pay for your moon city. You need a product—but what? How could you find a product or service to sell on the moon?

What To Do

1. With a partner, brainstorm some ways a moon colony might make money.

2. Choose one of your ideas to be a hypothesis. A hypothesis is a suggested or possible solution to a problem. In this case the problem is paying for a space colony.

3. Design a way to test your hypothesis and see whether your solution is possible and practical. You won't perform your test, so don't worry about what equipment you'll need to perform it.

4. Here are some of the ways you could test your hypothesis:

    Make a model Create a scale model of what you're proposing and see if it works. Or make a computer model of a process, taking into account the conditions on the moon.

    Experiment Try what you're proposing under different conditions and see which condition works best.

    Observe Go to the moon and look for valuable minerals. Or record the conditions and process needed to manufacture something here on Earth and consider whether they are practical for the moon.

5. Now, write a proposal for your research plan. Start with the problem and your suggested solution. Then explain how you'll test your hypothesis and determine whether your solution makes sense. Create a poster to convince your classmates that your research is reasonable and should be funded.

6. After each group presents its poster and answers questions from the class, vote for the idea that seems most likely to lead to a profitable product. Summarize your classmates' ideas and the reasons for your own vote *in your Journal*. Did some ideas seem more "scientific" than others? What do you think makes good scientific research?

■ Using Science Processes Every Day

After the groups shared, Ms. Howard asked the class for their impressions of the moon project so far.

Kareem laughed. "I think we need a lot more planning before we can start packing for the moon! Our groups have more questions than answers!"

Ms. Howard smiled. "Often good scientific research will answer one question only to come up with several new, unanswered questions."

Sachi said, "But I've thought of a way to use a scientific approach in my writing. See, in this story an adopted girl is trying to find her mother. She carefully observes everyone around her and starts gathering information. . . ."

In this chapter, you've learned some of the ways scientists try to solve problems. You'll use these processes as you study this book and continue to discover what science is about. But you can also use scientific approaches as you try to solve problems in your everyday life.

REVIEWING MAIN IDEAS

Review the statements below about the big ideas presented in this chapter, and try to answer the questions.

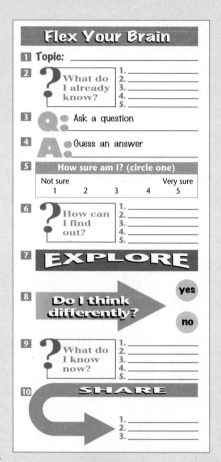

Flex Your Brain

1. **Topic:** _____

2. ? **What do I already know?**
   1. _____
   2. _____
   3. _____
   4. _____
   5. _____

3. **Q:** Ask a question
   _____

4. **A:** Guess an answer
   _____

5. **How sure am I? (circle one)**

Not sure				Very sure
1	2	3	4	5

6. ? **How can I find out?**
   1. _____
   2. _____
   3. _____
   4. _____
   5. _____

7. **EXPLORE**

8. **Do I think differently?** → yes / no

9. ? **What do I know now?**
   1. _____
   2. _____
   3. _____
   4. _____
   5. _____

10. **SHARE**
    1. _____
    2. _____
    3. _____

1 There are many ways to approach a problem scientifically and the first important step in each is to define the question you are investigating. *How does the "Flex Your Brain" approach help you define the question you wish to research?*

2 Scientists use observation, models, and controlled experiments, among other methods to help find the answers to scientific questions. *When is it most appropriate to use a model to help you find the answer to a question?*

3 Ordinary people use science and scientific methods in their everyday work. *List three ways in which an artist or a musician can use science or scientific methods in their work.*

CHAPTER REVIEW

Understanding Ideas

Answer the following questions in your Journal *using complete sentences.*

1. List three activities you do every day that you could do better if you had a scientific understanding of how that activity was done. Explain

2. Describe one way in which to develop a scientific question to investigate.

3. Why is saying what you know about a problem helpful in asking new questions about the problem?

Critical Thinking

Use your understanding of the concepts developed in the chapter to answer each of the following questions.

1. If you wished to study the motion of atoms, which scientific method would you use? Explain.

2. Grena Phacops is a scientist who wants to study communities of clams. What scientific method might she employ? Why?

3. People in the town of Persimmon Gap are concerned about possible pollution from farm water runoff. They want to know the effects of runoff on algae growth in Persimmon Pond. What scientific method should they use? Why?

4. How does using a model differ from designing a controlled experiment? How are they similar?

5. Why is asking the right question such an important part of any scientific method?

Problem Solving

Read the following problem and discuss your answer in a brief paragraph.

Rachelle knows that long-term space travel causes calcium-loss from bone tissue in astronauts. She also knows that this is related to very low gravity conditions that astronauts experience in space. She is concerned that long-term exposure to the low gravity of the moon might have a similar effect. She comes to you and asks you for help in finding out whether or not this is true. Help Rachelle choose an appropriate scientific method and plan an investigation that will help her find the answer.

Forces in Action

Everywhere—around you, within you, within Earth itself—forces make things move. Though you may not be aware of them, you depend on forces to get things done and to keep you alive. Sometimes you can observe the disastrous effects of forces unleashed within Earth. Plunge in and become aware of how forces shape your life.

Try It!

The weight of air in our atmosphere produces a force on all things on the surface of Earth. How can you observe this force?

What To Do

1. Lay a meterstick on a table with 45 cm extending over the edge.

2. Place a large sheet of newspaper over the part of the meterstick on the table.

3. Now quickly push down on the free end of the meterstick extending over the edge of the table. What do you feel? How might air pressure be related to what you feel?

Try It Again

After you've learned more about forces, try this activity again and explain your observations.

CHAPTER 1

FORCES & PRESSURE

Did you ever wonder...

✓ **Why a revolving door continues to turn after the last person has left?**

✓ **Why snowshoes help you walk on top of snow?**

✓ **Why you float in water?**

Before you begin to study forces, think about these questions and answer them *in your Journal*. When you finish the chapter, compare your Journal write-up with what you have learned.

A tightrope walker moves across a rope high overhead. Dogs stand on trotting horses. Elephants perform amazing feats of balance. Jugglers spin their rings, and clowns keep everyone laughing. You can't decide where to look first. You're afraid you'll miss something if you look away for a second.

As amazing as these circus acts are, they're all based on basic principles of motion. These same principles apply to things that go on around you each day. For example, the grocery cart you push continues to roll down the aisle by itself. You slam your locker door, and it flies back at you.

▶ **In this chapter, you'll learn the laws of motion. You'll also see what makes objects move, and what makes them change their motion. Start your exploration on the next page.**

Why doesn't the penny move?

Have you ever seen a magician pull a tablecloth from a table and leave all the items on the table standing? Here's your chance to do a similar sort of trick.

What To Do

1. Lay an index card over the top of a glass or beaker.

2. Place a penny on the card, centered over the glass.

3. With a flick of your finger, give the card a quick horizontal push. What happens?

4. Wad up a small piece of paper to about the size of a marble.

5. Place it on the card and flick the card away. What happens?

6. *In your Journal*, record your observations and your explanation for the differences you saw.

Force and Motion

Section Objectives

- Relate inertia to mass.
- Identify the forces acting when objects interact.
- Describe and use Newton's First Law of Motion.

Key Terms

inertia, force

Keep on Moving

Picture yourself in a car on your way to the grocery store. You're waiting at a stoplight. When the light turns green, the car moves forward. You feel like you're being pushed back into the seat. When the car slows to a stop, you feel pushed forward. And when the car turns a corner, you feel as if you're being pushed outward. What's happening to make you feel as if something is pushing you?

■ Velocity, Acceleration, and Motion

You may have already learned about velocity and acceleration. Velocity is how fast an object is going in a given direction. Acceleration is a change in either the speed of an object or its direction of travel.

When you travel in a car, you may feel pushes and pulls as a result of speeding up, slowing down, or turning a sharp curve. Where do these

Figure 1-1

A Velocity tells the direction and speed of an object. A car's velocity may be stated, "30 miles per hour, East." When an object changes its velocity—starts to move, stops, changes speed, or changes direction—it accelerates.

B In the diagram below, the arrows indicate the direction of movement—blue for the car and orange for the driver. When the car turns, the driver feels pushed in the direction opposite to the turn. What is really happening is that the car changes direction and the driver continues to move straight.

feelings come from? Examine **Figure 1-1** to discover more about your motion in a car.

■ Inertia

When you experience pushes and pulls associated with acceleration, something very simple is happening. You continue the motion, or lack of motion, that you had before the acceleration began.

The tendency to resist changes in motion is **inertia**. The Explore activity at the beginning of the chapter showed an example of inertia. Both the card and the coin were at rest until you flicked the card and caused it to accelerate horizontally. Why didn't the coin accelerate with the card?

The property of inertia can give you useful information about objects. Investigate how on the following pages!

C As the car speeds up, the driver, for a moment, keeps moving at the previous speed. The driver feels pushed back into the seat. Actually, the back of the seat catches up and pushes against the slower-moving driver.

D Once the velocities of car and driver are the same, the driver feels no push or pull until the car again accelerates.

E If the car stops suddenly, the driver feels pushed forward. Even though the forward motion of the car stops, the forward motion of the passenger continues. What might happen if you were on a slippery seat with no back and you suddenly accelerated forward?

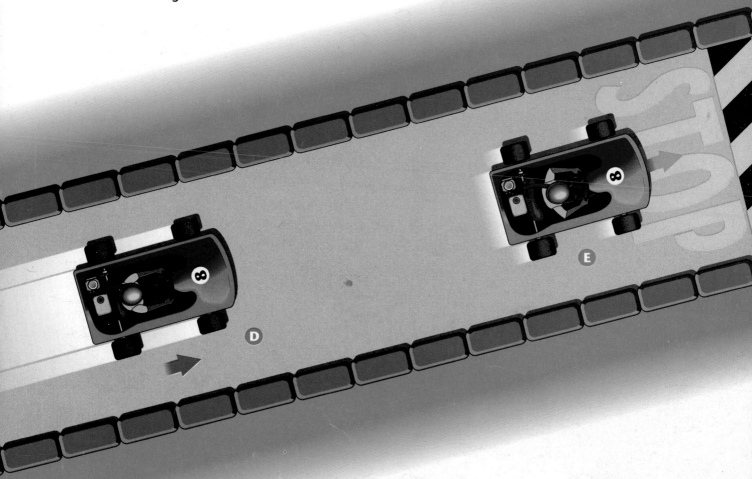

Measuring Inertial Mass

You can find the mass of an object by measuring the way an object speeds up or slows down, and comparing that with the way known masses speed up or slow down.

Problem

How can you find the mass of an object anywhere in the universe without a laboratory balance or a force of gravity?

Materials

inertial balance	pan balance
clamp	second timer
heavy rubber bands	graph paper
object of unknown mass	assorted marked masses

Safety Precautions

Be careful handling the inertial balance. Metal may have sharp edges.

What To Do

1 Copy the data table *into your Journal.*

2 Clamp one end of the inertial balance to the table (see photo **A**).

3 Place enough masses on the outer platform to make a total of 1 kg, including the platform itself. Secure these with heavy rubber bands (see photo **B**).

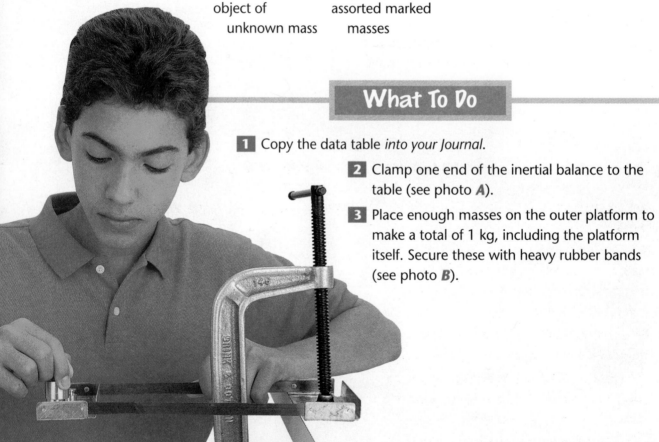

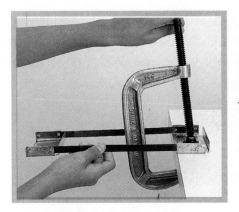

A

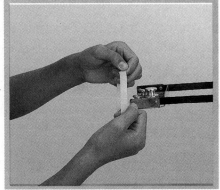

B

4 Pull the outer platform sideways and let go. What happens? Measure the time for 10 complete back-and-forth cycles. Record your data and observations *in your Journal.*

5 Repeat Steps 3 and 4 two more times, with total masses of 0.5 kg and 2 kg.

6 Attach the unknown mass to the platform and measure the time for 10 complete cycles. Record.

Data and Observations

Mass	Time For 10 Cycles	Period
0.5 kg		
1 kg		
2 kg		
Unknown mass		

Analyzing

1. The period of a cycle is the time it takes for one complete back-and-forth motion. *Calculate* the period for each of your four masses.

2. *Plot a graph* of the results with three known masses. Plot period on the horizontal axis and mass on the vertical axis. Connect the points with a smooth curve.

3. Find the period of the unknown mass on the graph. *Predict* what the mass should be.

4. Subtract the mass of the platform from the mass you predicted. This will give you the mass of the unknown object.

5. *Measure* the unknown mass on a pan balance to check your results.

Concluding and Applying

6. What trends do you observe in the relationship between the mass and the period?

7. How did your prediction compare with the actual mass?

8. A period of 0.75 seconds on this inertial balance would indicate how much mass?

9. **Going Further** What would be the period of an object with a mass of 5 kg?

Mass and Inertia

While doing the Investigate activity you may have noticed that mass is more than how much matter an object has. Mass is also a measure of an object's inertia—how much it resists changes in motion. Let's find out more about the inertia of objects as they interact.

Find Out! ACTIVITY

What factors affect the acceleration of objects?

You know that mass and inertia are related. How does mass relate to acceleration?

What To Do

1. Team up with another student who is either much lighter or much heavier than you are. Find two rolling chairs.

2. You sit in one and have your partner sit in the other.

3. Bring your chairs close together. Place your palms against those of your partner. Then push each other away.

4. Which chair moves away with the greater final velocity? Which chair is given the greater acceleration? How does the direction of your acceleration compare with that of your partner?

5. Record your observations and the answers to these questions *in your Journal.*

6. Repeat this activity while both of you are pushing and then when only one of you is pushing.

Conclude and Apply

1. Are there any differences in the resulting accelerations for these different ways of pushing each other?

2. How does the acceleration of each chair compare with how heavy each of you is?

3. Turn your chair around and let your partner push on the back of your chair, rather than pushing against your hands. How is what you experience different from when you pushed hand to hand?

4. What causes you to accelerate in this case?

You've already learned that objects with large mass have greater inertia than objects with small mass. In the Find Out activity you discovered that objects with large mass accelerate less than objects with small mass when acted on by the same force. From this information you can conclude that objects with great inertia (large mass) have a great resistance to acceleration.

■ Newton's First Law

If you had done the Find Out activity on a surface that had no resistance to motion, how would your motion have been affected? Would you have gone farther? As it turns out, under those conditions, you might go on forever.

As a result of a thought experiment, Galileo concluded that objects at rest remain at rest and objects in motion remain in motion. Sir Isaac Newton agreed, except when objects are acted on by a push or pull. Newton's First Law of Motion is that an object remains in motion or at rest unless acted on by a push or pull. One example of this law is that a soccer ball sitting on flat ground will not begin to roll until you apply a push by kicking it.

Figure 1-2

You need a lot of force to start a big truck moving, but less force to start to move a small car. This is due to the relationship between the mass of an object and its inertia.

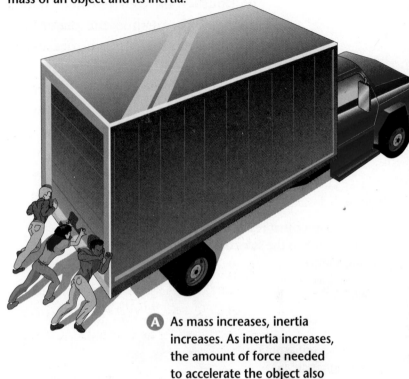

A As mass increases, inertia increases. As inertia increases, the amount of force needed to accelerate the object also increases.

B The opposite is also true. As an object's mass decreases, its inertia decreases, and the force needed to cause it to accelerate decreases.

C When an object accelerates, its velocity changes. To change velocity, a force must act on an object. Which of the three vehicles pictured will require the most force to start moving? To stop moving? Why?

Interactions That Push or Pull

When you sat in the rolling chair and pushed on your partner's hands, each of you pushed the other. You both accelerated in opposite directions. In each case the person with less mass (less inertia) experienced greater acceleration. A push or pull is commonly referred to as a **force**. Let's see how forces are involved in motion.

Figure 1-3

Friction is a force that resists motion between two objects in contact, such as the soles of a runner's shoes and the running surface.

A Ice does not produce enough friction between itself and the shoe soles for the runner to get a firm, controlled push-off.

B A sticky surface produces too much friction for efficient running.

C A dry surface produces the right amount of friction between shoe soles and surface for efficient running.

When you pushed your classmate in the rolling chair, what caused you to accelerate—the force you used to push, or the force your classmate exerted on you? Can you push on yourself and make your body speed up? No, something else must push on you. When you walk on the floor, it is the floor pushing back on your feet that makes you move. You must have a force pushing on you, and then you will accelerate in the direction of that force. So, when you pushed your classmate and he or she pushed back, it was the force he or she exerted on you that caused the acceleration.

■ Friction

Earlier in the chapter, you thought about what would happen if you were in a car with a slippery plastic seat and no seat back. Let's take that one step further. Imagine a block of ice on a flatbed truck.

The truck is at rest and the block of ice is right behind the driver. What will happen when the truck starts up? What force is needed for the ice to accelerate with the truck? There must be an interaction between the ice and the truck bed. That interaction is friction. Friction is necessary when we want one object to accelerate with another one, as with the ice on the flatbed truck. At other times, when we want something to keep moving, friction slows it down. But is friction a force—a push or a pull? Let's find out.

Is friction a force?

Friction is an important aspect of everyday life. What might be some important aspects of friction?

What To Do

1. Place a sheet of plain white paper on a flat surface.

2. Set a 20-g mass on the paper about 7 cm from one end.

3. Grip the other end of the paper and give it a smooth, quick pull.

4. Now repeat the procedure replacing the white paper with a sheet of coarse sandpaper, rough side up.

5. Record your observations *in your Journal.*

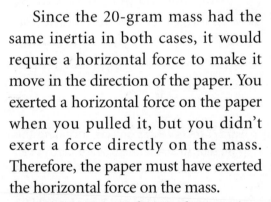

Conclude and Apply

1. Compare and contrast what happens to the 20-g mass with each piece of paper.

2. Use Newton's First Law of Motion to explain your observations.

Since the 20-gram mass had the same inertia in both cases, it would require a horizontal force to make it move in the direction of the paper. You exerted a horizontal force on the paper when you pulled it, but you didn't exert a force directly on the mass. Therefore, the paper must have exerted the horizontal force on the mass.

Friction is a force that resists motion between two objects in contact. The force of friction between the paper and the weight was not large, so the weight slid off the paper. However, the force of friction resisted motion between the sandpaper and the weight. As a result, the weight moved with the sandpaper.

What if there were no friction? Your feet wouldn't be able to grip the ground. You wouldn't accelerate unless something bumped into you and started you going. Once you were moving, you'd keep moving at a constant speed in the same direction until you interacted with something else.

■ Gravity

Another force that results from the interactions of two objects is gravity. Like friction, gravitational interaction is so common that you usually ignore it. You know that free-falling objects accelerate downward at about 9.8 meters per second per second (9.8 m/s^2). This acceleration is due to gravitational force, which pulls you toward Earth's center.

When a meteor is falling, Earth exerts a force that accelerates the meteor downward. Does the meteor cause Earth to accelerate upward, too?

You can see that if the mass of the object you are interacting with is

DID YOU KNOW?

In the English system, the pound is the unit of force and the unit of acceleration is feet/second². What is the unit of mass? Believe it or not, it's called a slug! One slug = 14.6 kg.

1 kg

Figure 1-4

Ⓐ All objects exert a gravitational force that pulls on surrounding objects. For example, as Earth pulls a 1 kilogram meteor toward its center, the meteor, at the same instant, pulls Earth toward the meteor's center.

Acceleration
9.8 m/s²

Acceleration
0.000 000 000 000 000 000 000 001 6 m/s²

6,000,000,000,000,000,000,000,000 kg

much larger than your own mass, the object's acceleration would be so small you couldn't even measure it. In the same way, the gravitational interaction between the meteor and Earth, shown in **Figure 1-4**, is such that only the meteor appears to accelerate.

As objects fall, more massive objects are more strongly attracted to Earth, and for that reason you would expect them to fall more quickly. On the other hand, they are also harder to accelerate. Their inertia reduces their acceleration by exactly as much as their greater attraction increases it. As a result objects fall at the same rate unless air resistance slows them down, as in the case of a feather or a single flat sheet of paper.

In the next section, we'll discover how mass, force, and acceleration are related. They are a part of everything you do and everything that happens around you.

Ⓑ Earth's mass causes objects, including the meteor to accelerate toward Earth's center at about 9.8 meters per second per second. The meteor causes Earth to accelerate toward it at about 0.000 000 000 000 000 000 000 001 6 meters per second per second. Because the accelerations are so different, only the acceleration of the meteor can be observed.

check your UNDERSTANDING

1. What determines an object's inertia?
2. Describe two forces that don't depend upon physical contact.
3. Briefly state and give an example of Newton's First Law of Motion.
4. **Apply** Describe two activities where you need frictional forces and two where you would like smaller frictional forces.

How Forces Act on Objects

Acceleration, Mass, and Force

You know that if you throw a ball harder it moves faster. From your experience, you also know that a car is more difficult to push than a bicycle. How is the force you use related to an object's acceleration? Suppose you have two objects and each object can move. What kind of relationship might exist between the acceleration and forces of the two objects?

Isaac Newton was one of the first to describe it. His observations led him to develop his second law of motion. You can investigate this law for yourself in the activity that follows.

Section Objectives

- Describe the relationships between force, mass, and acceleration.
- Use Newton's second law to predict acceleration.
- Identify pairs of forces.
- Describe the difference between balanced forces and action-reaction forces.

Key Terms

newton, balanced forces, weight, action force, reaction force

Figure 1-5

Ⓐ At any given time several forces may act upon an object. When there is an unbalanced force in one direction, the object accelerates.

Ⓑ In these pictures the same soccer ball is kicked with different forces. Which of the following is the same in both pictures: the mass, the force, the acceleration? Which is different? What is the result?

Acceleration and Mass

You know that velocity is the rate of change of position and that acceleration is the rate of change in velocity. Now find out how acceleration is related to mass.

Problem

What is the relationship between the mass and acceleration of an object?

Materials

balance with 5 kg capacity
masses of 1 kg and less
masking tape
spring carts
2 books
meterstick

What To Do

1. Copy the data table *into your Journal.*

2. Measure and record the mass of Cart 1.

3. Place masses on Cart 2 until its total mass is double that of Cart 1. Tape the masses to the cart.

4. Attach the two carts and place them on the floor. Place a piece of tape even with the front wheels of each cart. Place a book one meter away from each cart (see photo **A**).

5. Release the carts and *observe* the position of Cart 2 when Cart 1 hits the book. Be sure to hold the books in place (see photo **A**).

6. *Predict* what starting position will allow the carts to hit the books at the same time.

A

Data and Observations

	Mass of cart 1, kg	Mass of cart 2 + masses, kg	Distance, m Cart 1	Cart 2	Ratio of masses	Ratio of distances
Trial 1						
Trial 2						

7 Move the carts to the predicted position and repeat Steps 4 and 5. Remember to move the tapes. Repeat Step 7, until the two carts stop at the same time. *Measure* and record the distance that each cart traveled.

8 Add more masses to Cart 2 so that it has three times the mass of Cart 1. Repeat Steps 4–7.

Analyzing

1. Complete the table by calculating the ratio of the distance travelled by Cart 1 to the distance traveled by Cart 2 for each set of masses.

2. How do these distance ratios *compare* to the ratio of the masses?

3. What happened to the acceleration of Cart 2 as the mass increased?

Concluding and Applying

4. What force produces acceleration? Is it the same for both carts?

5. **Going Further** If you added more masses to Cart 2, until it had four times the mass of Cart 1, what would you *predict* would happen to the distance traveled by Cart 2? How would it have compared to the distance traveled by Cart 1?

Figure 1-6

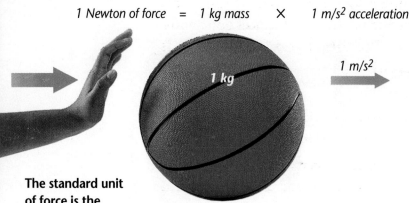

1 Newton of force = 1 kg mass × 1 m/s² acceleration

1 kg

1 m/s²

The standard unit of force is the newton. One newton is equal to the amount of force required to accelerate a mass of 1 kilogram at 1 meter per second per second.

■ Force and Newton's Second Law of Motion

If you had been able to measure the acceleration, the mass, and the force applied to each of the two carts in the Investigate activity, you'd have seen that the initial force applied to each cart was the same and the product of the mass and the acceleration was the same. Newton made similar observations and concluded that the force on an object equals the mass of the object times the acceleration of the object. This is Newton's Second Law of Motion. It can be written as an equation:

$$\text{Force} = \text{Mass} \times \text{Acceleration}.$$

Force is mass times acceleration. In other words, a force causes a mass to accelerate. In what unit do we measure force? You know that mass is measured in kilograms and acceleration in meters per second squared

Centripetal Force

When you swing a mass on the end of a string, the mass whirls around with uniform circular motion. The speed of the mass may be constant, but the velocity is always changing because the direction is changing. Therefore, you can say that the mass is accelerating. Newton's second law tells you that in order for a mass to accelerate, a force must act upon it. What forces act upon an object in uniform circular motion to keep it accelerating?

Look at the print on the next page that shows an example of uniform circular motion. When the gaucho lets go, the bola moves away in a straight line.

The only thing that keeps it moving in a circle is the force acting toward the center of the circle—the pull that the person exerts on the bola.

Satellites and Centripetal Force

If a satellite were in orbit and Earth's gravity were suddenly shut off, what would happen to the satellite? Because of its inertia, it would move off in a straight line. The force of gravity keeps pulling it back in. At any point on the circle, you could think of the path of the satellite as a tiny straight line. To change the direction, there must be a force acting toward

(m/s^2). The unit of force is therefore,

$$kilogram \times meter/second^2$$

The unit of force is also called a **newton**, abbreviated N. In the English system, the unit of force is the pound.

■ Balanced Forces

When does an object accelerate? Hold a book steady on the palm of your hand. What forces are acting? Earth exerts a downward force on the book, and your hand exerts an upward force on the book. Both forces act on the same object, but in opposite directions. Are the forces equal? If they weren't, the book would be accelerating.

But the forces are balanced. **Balanced forces** means that the forces acting on an object cancel one another. The effect is as if no force is acting.

■ Unbalanced Forces and Acceleration

What happens when forces are not balanced? If you increase your upward force against the book, it moves. Objects accelerate only when they are acted upon by unbalanced forces, that is, when there is a greater force acting on an object in some direction. An unbalanced force produces a change in motion.

the center of the circle—in this case, toward Earth. This is centripetal force.

Centripetal force is the force exerted to keep an object moving in a circle. An object traveling in a circle is constantly accelerating toward the center of the circle.

What Do You Think?

Explain how gravity is a centripetal force for objects in orbit around a planet. Think about the direction that gravity pulls with respect to the center of a planet.

South American gauchos used bolas as a tool to hunt animals.

Weight As Force

Up until now you've studied motion and some of the effects of forces on motions. You've seen that if you know the mass of an object and the acceleration of the object, you can calculate the force on the object. But is there any way to directly measure a force? Let's explore.

Explore! ACTIVITY

How can forces be measured?

What To Do

1. Hang a 1-kg mass from the hook of a spring balance that is calibrated in newtons.

2. What causes the spring to stretch? How much force does the mass exert on the spring?

3. Record your observations and answers *in your Journal*.

You discovered that a 1-kg mass exerts a downward force of 9.8 N. How does this happen? The force due to gravity accelerates the mass downward at 9.8 m/s² and the mass, in turn, pulls the spring downward. If the spring did not exert an equal opposing force, the mass would continue to accelerate downward.

When you jump off a step onto the floor, you accelerate downward at the rate of 9.8 m/s². When you reach the ground you stop because the floor exerts an equal force upward on your feet. Earth still pulls on you with the same force. The gravitational force on you or any object is called **weight**.

Weight is calculated by multiplying the acceleration due to gravity by the mass of the object. In the Explore you used a one-kilogram mass. Its weight is:

Force (N) = mass (kg) $\times$ acceleration (m/s²)

9.8 N = 1 kg $\times$ 9.8 m/s²

The force exerted on the 1-kg mass is actually its weight, measured in newtons. When the force being measured is gravitational force, force and weight are equivalent.

Action and Reaction Forces

In all of the interactions we have seen so far, there are always two equal and opposite forces involved. The forces are always equal in size but opposite in direction.

Whenever you push on something, that force is called an **action force**. The force that pushes back on you occurs at exactly the same moment and it is called the **reaction force**. Action and reaction forces always occur in pairs and they always act on different objects. Newton's Third Law of Motion states that for every action force there is an equal and opposite reaction force. These forces occur at exactly the same time. An action force does not produce a reaction force a split second later; they always occur together.

Every day, we see hundreds of examples of the third law in action. When you press lightly on a wall, the wall presses lightly back. A car is set in motion by the push of the ground on the tires as the tires push back on the ground. As you walk, you push on the ground and the ground pushes back. See **Figure 1-7** for another example.

SKILLBUILDER

Recognizing Cause and Effect

When using a high-pressure hose, why is it necessary for fire-fighters to grip the hose strongly and plant their feet firmly? If you need help, refer to the **Skill Handbook** on page 643.

Figure 1-7

Forces always occur in pairs. Whenever a force is applied to an object there is an equal and opposite force applied to another object.

A The equal and opposite actions or forces happen exactly at the same moment. There is no time lag between them.

B The woman's head exerts an upward force on the bundle that is exactly equal to the downward force the bundle exerts on the woman's head.

Figure 1-8

If every action force produces an equal and opposite reaction force, how do objects ever get moving?

A Think about the last time you went bowling. You picked up the ball from the return rack and carried it to the starting point.

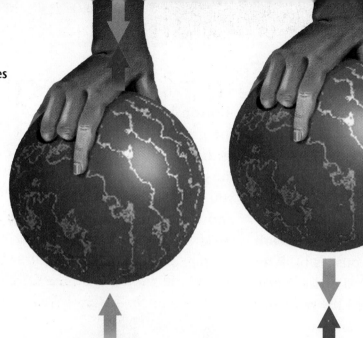

Direction of acceleration

B When the ball was hanging beside you, motionless, there were two sets of action-reaction forces acting on it. Your hand pulled on the ball exactly as much as the ball pulled on your hand. The ball pulled on the Earth exactly as much as Earth pulled on the ball. The force of your hand on the ball and Earth on the ball were balanced so there was no acceleration.

C So, how could you raise the ball to get ready to bowl? When you raised the ball, the same two pairs of action-reaction forces were acting on the ball, but the action-reaction pair between your hand and the ball was much greater than the pair between Earth and the ball. The forces acting on the ball were unbalanced and the ball accelerated upward.

■ **Action and Reaction: An Example**

You've already seen that an object must be acted on by unbalanced forces in order to accelerate. If action-reaction forces are always balanced, how can anything ever move? Look at **Figure 1-8**, which describes the forces acting on a bowling ball.

Forces always come in pairs. When one object exerts a force on a second, the second exerts an equal and opposite force on the first. This is Newton's Third Law of Motion.

check your UNDERSTANDING

1. Write a short paragraph explaining how the following words are related: force, weight, newton, pound.
2. A 10-kg object collides with a 30-kg object. As a result, the 10-kg object accelerates at 60 m/s². What would be the acceleration of the 30-kg object?
3. When you push a door closed, you're exerting a force on the door. Where is the equal and opposite force and what is it pushing on?
4. **Apply** When a stuntperson jumps from a height, he or she lands on a large bag filled with air. What is the purpose of this bag in terms of what you learned in this section?

1-3 Pressure and Buoyancy

Area and Force

In a previous section, you measured the force exerted by a 1-kg mass and found that it was 9.8 N. If you set the mass on the table, does it still exert the same force? What if you hammered the mass into a flat plate—would the force change? You can start to explore the relationship of the force exerted to the area that the force acts on by doing the activity below.

Explore! ACTIVITY

How are weight and pressure related?

What To Do

1. Place a sheet of graph paper lined 1 inch by 1 inch on the floor and cover it with a sheet of carbon paper.

2. Place the tip of a crutch on the carbon paper and lean your full weight on the crutch. This should make an impression showing the surface area of the crutch tip.

3. Find your weight.

4. From the impression, estimate what area the crutch covered.

5. Divide your weight by this surface area to find the force per square inch.

6. Have a much heavier person stand on one foot on the carbon paper and graph paper underneath. Trace the outline of the shoe.

7. Use this person's weight and divide it by this area.

8. How do the numbers you calculated differ? Which push had greater force per square inch? Which push had greater pressure? Answer the question *in your Journal.*

Section Objectives

■ Calculate pressure from a given force and surface area.

■ Explain how objects can float in a liquid.

■ Interpret and use Archimedes' Principle.

Key Terms

pressure
buoyant force

■ Pressure

In the activity, when you divided the weight of an object by the surface area the object occupied, you were finding pressure. **Pressure** is defined as the weight or force acting on each unit of area. The equation is:

(Pressure) = (Force/Area on which the force acts)

Look at **Figure 1-9** to get an idea of practical applications of the concept of pressure.

Figure 1-9

When you reduce the area on which a force acts, you can get a lot of pressure from a small force. Think about a needle. Suppose its point has a surface of 0.001 square inches. How much pressure will that needle exert if you push on it with just 1 pound of pressure? Divide 1 by 0.001 and you get 1000 pounds per square inch. You can see, then, why doctors and people who sew would want very sharp needles for stitching up wounds and clothes.

The snowshoe measures 36 inches long and 18 inches wide.

The boot measures 10 inches long and 3 inches wide.

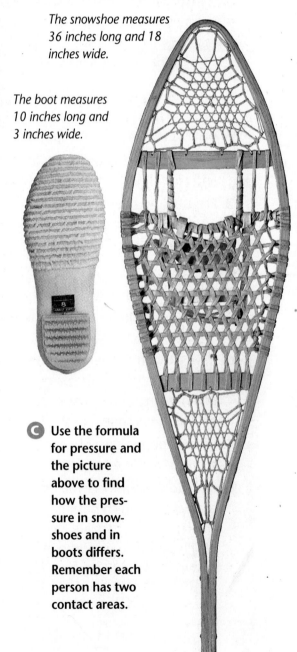

A The surface of snow can support a certain amount of weight without cracking, breaking, or crushing. This ability to resist pressure is measured in number of pounds per square inch.

The two walkers shown both weigh 100 pounds. The one wearing boots crushes the snow and sinks with each step. The one with snowshoes walks along on top of the snow.

B By wearing snowshoes, the girl has spread her weight over a larger area of the snow. By spreading her weight over a larger area, she has limited the force she exerts on the snow in any square inch. The snow supports her weight, and she glides along without sinking.

C Use the formula for pressure and the picture above to find how the pressure in snowshoes and in boots differs. Remember each person has two contact areas.

It's Different with Fluids

What do you think exerts more pressure—10 cm of water on the bottom of a coffee can, or the same depth of water on the bottom of a wading pool? Or does it make any difference?

Find Out! ACTIVITY

What is the relationship of fluid depth to pressure?

If you've ever been in a pool and gone to the bottom, you've experienced one effect of water pressure. How does the pressure relate to the depth of the water? You probably know from experience, but use this activity to confirm your observations.

What To Do

1. Weigh three or four graduated cylinders of different diameters. If you don't have graduated cylinders, you may use cans or glasses, but they must have vertical sides.

2. Record the weights.

3. Fill each container with water to the same height from the base.

4. Weigh the containers again.

5. Subtract the weights of the empty containers from the weights of the filled containers. This gives you the weight of each column of water.

6. If you are using a circular container, measure the inside diameter of each container. Divide each diameter by 2 to get the radius. Multiply the radius by itself, and then multiply that number by 3.14. That gives you the cross-sectional area of each cylinder. Otherwise calculate the rectangular or square cross-sectional area.

7. Divide the weight of each column of water by its container's cross-sectional area. This tells you how much pressure the water exerts on the bottom of its cylinder.

Conclude and Apply

1. How do the pressures compare?

2. If you had a 30-foot vertical pipe filled with water, how do you think the pressure on the bottom of that pipe would compare with the pressure at the bottom of a 30-foot deep lake?

Figure 1-10

The column of water above the top hole is short, so the water is pushed out with a small force. The column of water above the bottom hole is taller and therefore heavier, so the water is pushed out with greater force.

When you did the Find Out activity, you saw that the pressure at the bottom of a container of water depends only on the height of the water. For liquids other than water the same rule holds true; however, the pressures in other liquids would be different from the pressure in water.

But what about pressure other than at the bottom of a column of liquid? A fluid is any substance that does not have a definite shape. Liquids and gases are fluids. Does fluid exert pressure in any direction other than down? Your experience tells you the answer. If you fill a paper cup with water and poke a hole halfway down the cup's side, what happens? Water flows from the hole. So there must be sideways pressure forcing the water out.

If you could move a pressure detector around in any container of fluid, you'd find that the fluid exerts pressure in all directions.

Life Science CONNECTION

Buoyancy in Fishes

For fish that stay more or less at a certain level, the pressure on their bodies is always about the same. Some fish, however, migrate upward or downward in the water. They may, for example, remain on the bottom during the day but swim upward at night to feed. They have to be able to compensate for the change in pressure on their bodies. Through time, bony fish evolved an adaptation that made compensating for pressure possible. The same adaptation makes it possible for the fish to adjust its buoyancy.

An Adaptation for Buoyancy

The swim bladder is a sac-like structure that holds air. This organ helps a fish adjust its buoyancy by changing the

Why You Float

So far you've seen how water pressure depends on the depth of the water. You've also seen that water exerts pressure not only on the bottom of a container but in all directions. Now think about another more familiar occurrence that involves water. Why do you float in a body of water?

Imagine yourself in a swimming pool, pond, lake, or the ocean. You know that something about the water allows you to float. You know that you can easily lift friends in the water, even if you could barely budge them on land. Why is that?

Let's first examine the question in a smaller body of water. We'll move from the swimming pool to the bathtub. When you sit in your tub, the water level rises. That's no surprise. After all, you added something to the water: yourself. How much do you think the water rises?

When you float in the pool, the water doesn't rise by an amount equal to the volume of your entire body. Your entire body isn't under the water. How much does it rise, then? What determines just how far your body sinks into the water? Let's find out.

Swim bladder

amount of gas in the bladder. More gas in the bladder increases the volume of the fish. The fish then displaces just the amount of water needed to keep it buoyant.

Coping with Pressure Changes

As a fish swims upward or downward in the water, the pressure on it changes. The swim bladder helps it react to the changes. The bladder is equipped with two separate organs. One organ allows additional gas from the blood to seep into the swim bladder as it is needed. The other organ removes excess gas from the bladder and returns it to the blood. These organs help a fish maintain buoyancy as depth increases.

The swim bladder makes it possible for a fish to swim at different depths in the water. The ability to swim at different depths allows fish to search for food at any depth.

What Do You Think?

How does the swim bladder help fish survive? A diver does not have a swim bladder. How does a diver overcome the buoyant force on the body at different depths?

How much water does an object displace?

You know that in order for an object to float, some force must be acting upon it. But what? As you do the activity, remember that weight is a measure of force.

What To Do

1. Fill a beaker to the brim.
2. Put a pan underneath it so that you can catch any water that overflows.
3. Using a spring scale, weigh an object dense enough to sink in the beaker. Record its weight.

4. Leaving the object attached to the spring scale, suspend the object in the water so that it is completely beneath the surface, but not touching the bottom. Use the figure as a guide. Some water will overflow into the pan below.
5. Use the spring scale to determine the object's weight while in the water.
6. Weigh a small can with a wire handle.
7. Transfer as much of the water that overflowed from the beaker into the can as possible. Weigh the can again. Subtract to find the weight of the water.

Conclude and Apply

1. How much weight did the object lose when you submerged it in water?
2. What is the relationship between the weight of the water that overflowed and the weight the object lost?

■ Archimedes' Principle

As you saw in the Find Out activity, when an object is immersed in water, it pushes aside some amount of water. The weight of the object is reduced by the weight of the water that is pushed aside. This relationship was discovered by the Greek mathematician Archimedes in the third century B.C.E. Archimedes' Principle says that the weight of water displaced by an object is equal to the amount of weight lost by the object. The greater the weight of water you displace, the

more your weight is reduced.

But hold on. What's this about losing weight? Water doesn't get rid of gravity, does it? No, but it can lift you up as much as gravity pulls you down. If you lose 40 pounds while standing in a pool, the water is exerting an upward force of 40 pounds on you. This force is called the **buoyant force.** When something is pushed upward by fluid, that's known as buoyancy. All objects experience buoyancy, whether they're more or less dense than the fluid they're in.

Figure 1-11

(A) According to Archimedes' Principle, when an object is immersed in water, its weight, while in the water, is reduced by an amount equal to the weight of the water the object is displacing, or moving aside.

(B) The reduction in weight during immersion is due to the upward force of water, called buoyant force. Just as gravity pulls you down, water pushes you up. Water pushes you up with a force equal to the weight of the water you displace.

Because your weight is a measure of the force with which gravity is pulling you downward, your weight in water is reduced by the amount of the buoyant force, which pushes you upward.

(C) When buoyant force pushes up on an object with force that is equal to the weight of the object, the object floats.

We began this chapter by considering the many different kinds of motion and force present in a variety of circus acts. Can you understand now how, regardless of how amazing these acts seem, they are all based on a few basic laws developed by Isaac Newton several hundred years ago?

check your UNDERSTANDING

1. Describe what happens to the pressure exerted by a force as the area that the force acts on increases.

2. How does the diameter of a column of water affect the pressure at the bottom of the column?

3. Explain why a block of wood can float in water and a block of metal of equal volume cannot.

4. **Apply** If you step into a pool and displace 50 pounds of water, how much weight have you lost?

Science and Society

Deep-Sea Submersibles

Alvin is a lightweight, self-propelled vehicle that travels underwater with a crew of three to five persons.

Alvin is lowered into the water, carrying a weight that will help it descend to the bottom. This saves the pilot from turning on the vertical thrusters, which could be used to maneuver the vessel downward. The thrusters run on batteries, and batteries must be conserved for horizontal travel when the vessel is in deep waters near the ocean floor.

Submersibles and Buoyancy

To make small changes in buoyancy while underwater, some submersibles have spheres filled with air and oil. The oil can be pumped into flexible bags on the outside of the vessel. The bags make the vessel as buoyant as the pilot wants, depending on how much oil is pumped into the bags. The more oil in the bags, the greater upward push the vessel receives from the water displaced. When a submersible is ready to ascend, however, using the oil bags is not enough to get it to the top. The pilot must also drop the weight that helped it descend. Then the submersible becomes positively buoyant and rises to the surface.

Discoveries in the Galápagos Rift

In 1977, the crew aboard Alvin descended to the ocean floor to study the hot springs at the Galápagos Rift in the Pacific Ocean. Imagine their surprise when they found a complex community of living things two kilometers below the surface, where not even the faintest light could reach! They had come across a whole new food web on the ocean floor—one that did not depend on plants that convert energy from the sun into chemical energy!

Submersibles like Alvin have made it possible for us to increase our knowledge and understanding of both the ocean and life at great ocean depths. Because of Alvin, we are now aware of an entire ocean community that can survive without light!

What Do You Think?

Think about how submersibles may affect people's lives in the future. It may be possible that at an underwater resort, you could hire a submersible.

How might such widespread use of submersibles affect wildlife in deep-sea habitats? In what way might people enjoy this experience without harming fragile habitats?

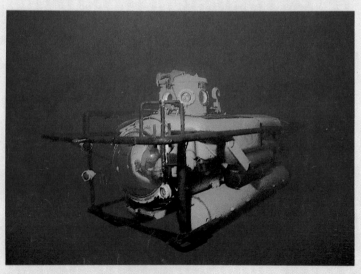

HISTORY CONNECTION

A Royal Solution

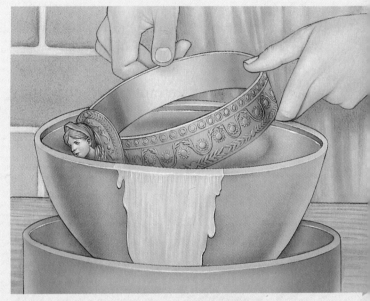

Have you ever tried to figure out a difficult puzzle? If so, you know how it holds your attention until you think of a solution. That's what happened to Archimedes, the Greek mathematician you read about in connection with buoyancy. Legend has it that King Hiero II of Sicily ordered a gold crown to be made. When the crown was delivered, the king suspected that the gold had been mixed with silver. Archimedes was asked to find out whether the crown was made of pure gold.

A Volume Puzzle

Archimedes was puzzled about how he could do this. He could weigh the crown and then find a gold piece that weighed the same as the crown. If both the gold piece and the crown had the same volume, he could be certain that the crown was pure gold. If the crown had a larger volume than the gold piece, he could be sure that silver had been mixed with the gold. He based his strategy on the fact that, for equal volumes, silver weighs less than gold. But, there was a problem. Even though Archimedes was a mathematician, he had no idea how to find the volume of the crown. How could he measure such an irregular object?

Discovering Displacement

One day, as he sank into a bathtub filled with water, Archimedes noticed that water spilled over the top of the tub. He realized that his body had displaced some of the water in the tub. He reasoned that the volume of the water that spilled over was equal to the space that his body took up.

Archimedes submerged the crown and collected the water the crown displaced. He measured the volume of the displaced water because he knew it equaled the volume of the crown. Archimedes had the solution to his problem. He proved that the crown was made of a mixture of gold and silver. He concluded that the man who had made the crown had tried to cheat the king.

You Try It!

Find and compare the volume of five objects of irregular shape by measuring the volume of water each displaces when submerged.

Technology Connection

Transducers in Your Life

You may not have heard of the word transducer before, but you've certainly used gadgets that contain them. A transducer is a device that converts one form of signal into another form. When you speak into a telephone, a transducer converts one kind of information—sound, or variations in air pressure—into another kind of information—electrical signals. The electrical signals are carried over wires to another place, where they are then converted back to sound.

Motion into Signals

A transducer can convert motion to electrical signals, or vice versa. The fuel gauge in an automobile is an example. The transducer is mounted on the fuel tank. A float moves up and down as the amount of fuel changes. The motion of the float is converted to an electrical signal that is transmitted by a wire to the gauge on the dashboard.

Many of the instruments used in laboratories have transducers. In this chapter, you have measured force, pressure, and acceleration. Some instruments can convert a measurement of a mechanical quantity, such as force, to an equivalent electrical signal. This happens when you weigh something on an electronic scale.

Useful Tools From Transducers

When machine parts are cast in metal, it's important that the mold be held together by a large enough force. If the force is less than needed, the part that is cast will be defective. A force transducer indicates on a gauge how much force is being exerted.

Your blood pressure can be measured using a blood-pressure transducer, such as the one shown on this page. Because of the pumping action of the heart, blood pressure pulsates. The transducer keeps track of these pulsations and converts them into an accurate and fast record of the blood pressure.

A transducer that measures acceleration is used in designing safe containers for the shipment of fragile objects. A table to which a delicate instrument is attached is raised or lowered abruptly to determine the amount of acceleration the instrument can tolerate before it malfunctions.

What Do You Think?

Transducers work by changing signals from one form to another. How is an electric switch a transducer? In what ways, other than those mentioned, might transducers be used?

eview the statements below about the big ideas presented in this chapter, and try to answer the questions. Then, re-read your answers to the Did You Ever Wonder questions at the beginning of the chapter. *In your Journal*, write a paragraph about how your understanding of the big ideas in the chapter has changed.

1 Objects in motion continue moving in a straight line at the same speed and objects at rest remain at rest unless the objects are acted upon by an unbalanced force. This tendency is called inertia. *Use inertia to explain why protection, such as a seat belt or a helmet, is important in situations where sudden stops may occur.*

2 When objects interact, the mass times the acceleration of the objects is equal to the force of the interaction (F=ma). *Why is the acceleration of a tennis ball toward Earth so much greater than the acceleration of Earth toward the tennis ball?*

1 kg

3 Forces always occur in action-reaction pairs, and these forces are always equal in strength and opposite in direction. *List a pair of action-reaction forces that involve the rope during a tug-of-war with a friend. List a pair of forces also involving the rope that are not action-reaction.*

4 Pressure is equal to force divided by the surface area over which the force acts. *You have a cube of metal that keeps falling through the snow. What would you do to the metal to get it to rest on top of the snow?*

5 The buoyant force (upward force fluids exert on all objects) is equal to the weight of the fluid displaced by an object. *If the buoyant force is equal to the weight of the fluid displaced by an object, why don't rocks float?*

Using Key Science Terms

action force
balanced force
buoyant force
force
inertia

newton
pressure
reaction force
weight

Answer the following questions using what you know about the science terms.

1. Describe the difference between weight and mass.
2. How is inertia related to mass?
3. Give an example of something you do every day that demonstrates action and reaction forces.
4. Contrast balanced and unbalanced forces.
5. Distinguish between force and pressure.
6. Write the appropriate unit each quantity is measured in: force, mass, acceleration, weight, and pressure.
7. How is buoyant force related to weight?

Understanding Ideas

Answer the following questions in your Journal using complete sentences.

1. What forces act on a picture hanging on a wall to cause it to fall?
2. What amount of force would have to be applied to a 10-kg object to make it accelerate 40 m/s^2?
3. If two bats are swung with equal acceleration by two batters, and bat A is 1 kg heavier than bat B, which bat will make a tossed ball travel further? Why?

4. Which measurement, your weight or your mass, would be the same when taken on Earth and on the moon?

Developing Skills

Use your understanding of the concepts developed in this chapter to answer each of the following questions.

1. **Concept Mapping** Using the following terms and phrases, complete the concept map about Newton's Laws of Motion: *force, tendency to remain in motion or still, mass × acceleration, equal and opposite reaction forces.*

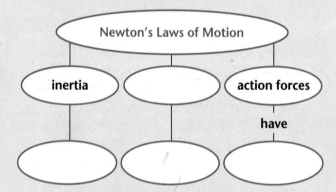

2. **Predicting** Use the information acquired by doing the Investigate activity on page 24 to predict what the period would be if a 2.5 kg mass were placed on the outer platform.
3. **Comparing and Contrasting** Repeat the Explore activity on page 39 using different types of shoes. Use football cleats, clogs, tennis shoes, mid-size heels, and western boots. Find the pressure exerted by each shoe. Compare the results of the different shoes. What can you conclude from the comparison of different shoes?

Critical Thinking

Use your understanding of the concepts developed in the chapter to answer each of the following questions.

1. How can an object be moving if there is no unbalanced force acting on it?
2. How can an object's weight change even though it contains the same mass?
3. The photographs show pictures of two similar cargo ships taken at two different times. What can you tell about the cargo ships from the pictures? Explain your reasoning.

Problem Solving

Read the following problem and discuss your answers in a brief paragraph.

"Newton was wrong and I can prove it!" declared Denton McQuarrel. He took two magnets—one big one and one little one—and he pushed their north poles together. "According to Newton," he said, "each magnet experiences equal force. Watch what happens." He held one of the magnets in place on the table as he let go of the other. "All I had to do was hold one magnet in place, and Newton's law doesn't work any more. The magnet I held in place didn't move at all." What's wrong with McQuarrel's argument?

CONNECTING IDEAS

Discuss each of the following in a brief paragraph.

1. **Theme—Systems and Interactions** Describe the two pairs of forces that are acting when you pick up your books. Why do the books move in an upward direction?
2. **Theme—Stability and Change** Use tug-of-war to explain how forces can be balanced and unbalanced.
3. **History Connection** Describe how you would show that an irregularly shaped piece of metal was pure silver.
4. **Life Science Connection** Sharks must swim constantly to maintain their position in the water. If sharks had swim bladders in their bodies, how would this affect their daily lives?
5. **Science and Society** How are submersibles used to help scientists describe and collect information about ocean depths?

CHAPTER 2

FORCES IN EARTH

San Andreas Fault

Did you ever wonder...

✓ **What causes the ground to shake during an earthquake?**

✓ **How scientists know the exact spot where an earthquake begins?**

✓ **Why there are different shapes of volcanoes?**

Before you begin to study forces in Earth, think about these questions and answer them *in your Journal.* When you finish the chapter, compare your Journal write-up with what you have learned.

*Y*ou've probably heard about the San Andreas fault, pictured below. Over time, tremendous forces inside Earth exert so much pressure on the rocks along the San Andreas Fault that they move.

Sometimes this movement is gradual. Rocks on both sides of the fault may slowly move past each other as these forces are exerted on them. But if the rocks aren't free to move, pressure builds up. When the rocks finally break free, the movement may be sudden and violent—an earthquake! You can feel the earthquake if you are not too far away from the moving rocks and if the vibrations they produce are strong enough.

▶ *In the activity on the next page, explore how forces inside Earth can affect the rocks within Earth.*

Explore! ACTIVITY

How do forces inside Earth affect rock layers?

What To Do

1. Place three rectangular layers of different-colored clay on top of one another.

2. Now place your hands on opposite ends of the clay. Slowly push your hands together, compressing the clay.

3. What happens? Draw a picture to show what happened to the clay.

4. Now place three layers of clay on top of one another as before.

5. With your hands on the opposite ends of the clay, gradually pull the clay apart. What happens?

6. Finally, *in your Journal*, draw a picture to show what you observed.

What Causes Earthquakes?

Section Objectives

- Explain how earth-quakes result from the buildup of pressure inside Earth.
- Describe the forces inside Earth that result in faults.
- Compare and contrast normal, reverse, and strike-slip faults.

Key Terms
fault

Pressure

Have you ever felt an earthquake? Feeling the ground move and seeing things fall off shelves can be scary. A great deal of pressure inside Earth is released as a result of an earthquake. This pressure built up as a result of force on the rocks underground. You learned in Chapter 1 that pressure is force acting on an area. In the following activity, you'll apply pressure to different objects by bending and stretching them.

Find Out! ACTIVITY

How do different objects react when they are bent or stretched?

How does pressure affect everyday items? What can this tell you about how pressure affects rocks in Earth?

What To Do

1. Use a paper clip to hold two sheets of paper together. Remove the paper clip. Has it changed? Repeat this procedure with 5, 20, and 50 sheets of paper. Did the clip change its shape at any point?

2. Now measure the length of a balloon. Stretch the balloon so that it's 1.5 times its original length.

Stop stretching and measure it. Now stretch the balloon farther, so that after releasing it, it won't return to its original length. Measure the length.

3. Without breaking a pencil, can you make it flex by pushing up on it with your thumbs?

Conclude and Apply

1. What happened to the paper clip and the balloon when they were bent or stretched too far? Why did the objects react this way?

2. What would happen if the pencil were bent too far? Record your answers *in your Journal.*

As you learned in the Find Out activity, objects will stretch and bend only so much. Bending and stretching are ways to apply pressure to objects. There is a limit to how much pressure a paper clip, a pencil, a balloon, or some other object can withstand and still return to its original shape. This limit is called the elastic limit. Once the elastic limit is passed, a substance will remain bent or stretched out of shape, or it will break.

Pressure in Rock Layers

Layers of rock behave in much the same way when pressure inside Earth bends or stretches them too far. Just as with the paper clip, balloon, and pencil, forces applied to rocks can cause them to fold or stretch without permanent change, but only up to a point. The rocks will remain folded or will break once their elastic limit is passed. Rocks that have been folded look like those shown in **Figure 2-1B**. When rocks break, they produce vibrations that travel throughout Earth. These vibrations are called earthquakes.

Figure 2-1

A The shape and position of rock layers indicate the pressure the rock has experienced. These rocks at Glen Canyon in Arizona are still flat and horizontal. Therefore, you know that pressures on the rock have been less than the elastic limit of the rock.

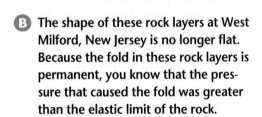

B The shape of these rock layers at West Milford, New Jersey is no longer flat. Because the fold in these rock layers is permanent, you know that the pressure that caused the fold was greater than the elastic limit of the rock.

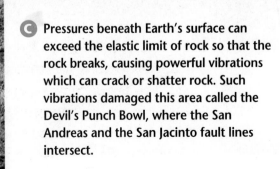

C Pressures beneath Earth's surface can exceed the elastic limit of rock so that the rock breaks, causing powerful vibrations which can crack or shatter rock. Such vibrations damaged this area called the Devil's Punch Bowl, where the San Andreas and the San Jacinto fault lines intersect.

Finding Fault

Sequencing

Arrange these events that lead up to an earthquake in correct order. If you need help, refer to the **Skill Handbook** on page 636.

rocks undergo pressure
earthquake
elastic limit exceeded
rocks bend and stretch
rocks break and move

When rocks break under pressure, they may move. A fracture within Earth where rock movement occurs is called a **fault**. At the beginning of this chapter, you read about the San Andreas Fault. The rocks on one side of this fault move at a different speed from the rocks on the other side of the fault.

Faults can be found very near the surface, as in the case of the San Andreas Fault, or they can be found deep beneath Earth's surface. Regardless of where faults are found, they are always caused by forces within Earth that push the rocks together (compression), pull the rocks apart (tension), or cause the rocks to slide past each other (shearing).

Movement along faults can result in dramatic changes on Earth's surface. **Figure 2-3** on pages 58-59 illustrates the different types of faults and some of the land features that result from these faults.

Passing the Limit

Elasticity exists in both natural objects and those made by humans. Trees, for example, may look straight and stiff, but what happens when strong winds blow through a forest? Do all the trees snap and fall over? Of course not. Trees change their shape, bending when the force of the wind strikes them, then returning to normal when the wind stops.

Hurricane Force

But what happens during a hurricane? If the wind is too strong, the force becomes too great for tree trunks and branches, and they pass their elastic limit and break. The same thing happens when you break a stick. If you bend it gently and then let go, it springs back to its original shape. But if you exert too much pressure, you force the stick beyond its elastic limit, and it snaps in two.

What Happens?

What actually happens when objects pass their elastic limit? As you bend a stick, the energy you exert is stored inside. When you let go, that energy is

Figure 2-2

Faults along the surface are easily-observed evidence of the powerful forces at work deep within Earth.

released as the stick springs back into its original shape. Push too hard, and the energy is released as the stick breaks. This release of energy is called elastic rebound.

If you blow into a balloon, you exert a force that pushes the walls of the balloon out. If you continue to inflate the balloon, it will explode when the balloon wall becomes too weak to store the energy. It will reach its elastic limit and release the stored energy, resulting in a pop. The release of energy in the pop is the elastic rebound.

If a car tire were inflated beyond its elastic limit, the resulting explosion would be much greater than that of a balloon bursting. That's because the tire could store much more energy before reaching its elastic limit.

Earthquake!

When different forces are exerted on rocks inside Earth, the rocks, like the balloon, can store energy—up to a point. But eventually the forces are too great, and the rocks reach their elastic limit. They break. And what happens next? An earthquake! As the rocks pass their elastic limit, energy is released, causing seismic waves to travel out in all directions from the focus of the earthquake.

What Do You Think?

Can you think of examples of objects around you in which energy is stored? Look for objects in your classroom that have not yet reached their elastic limit.

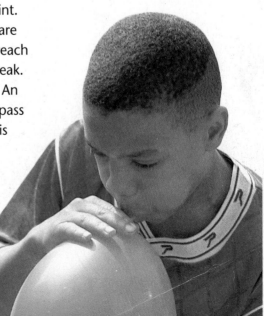

Figure 2-3

In the Explore activity at the beginning of this chapter, you used tension to pull clay apart and compression to push clay together. Rock layers experience tension, compression, and a third type of force called shearing. You can start to explore movement along a fault in the activity below.

Normal fault

Force

A When rock moves along a fracture caused by tension forces, the break is called a normal fault. Rock above the fault moves downward in relation to the rock below the fault surface. Normal faults can form mountains such as the Sierra Nevada which borders California on the east.

Explore! ACTIVITY

How do rocks at a strike-slip fault move past each other?

What To Do

1. Glue sandpaper to the narrow side of two 2 inch × 4 inch blocks of wood. Use just enough glue to make it stick.

(Don't use too much glue.) Press the sandpaper covered edges together to help set the glue and hold the sandpaper in place.

2. Now flip the blocks over so that the sides without sandpaper are together on a desk or table. Push them past each other in different directions so that the side of one block rubs against the side of the other.

3. After the glue has dried, place the sandpaper sides together and push them past each other in different directions so they rub together.

4. *In your Journal*, describe the differences between pushing the smooth surfaces of the blocks past each other and pushing the rough surfaces of the blocks past each other.

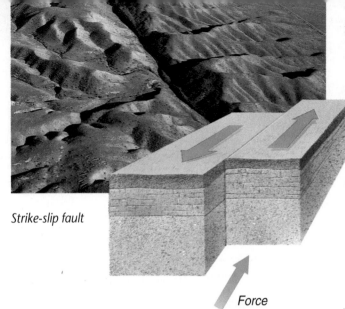

Reverse fault

Strike-slip fault

Force ← → Force

B When compression forces break rock, the rock above the fault surface moves upward in relation to the rock below the fault surface. The mountains shown make up part of the Himalayas separating India and China, and contain many reverse faults.

C Shearing forces push on rock in opposite horizontal directions. When strong enough, these forces split rock and create strike-slip faults such as California's San Andreas Fault. Movement along faults is usually short and sudden but can be slow and steady.

Why is it important to know about faults? Think back to the Explore activity in which you studied how rocks move past each other at strike-slip faults. Suppose the blocks you used were really rocks on either side of the San Andreas Fault. Do you think the rocks would slide past each other at a constant rate? What would happen if the irregular surfaces of the rocks snagged, but shearing forces inside Earth continued to push them? Pressure would build up, and the elastic limit of the rocks would be exceeded. Then rocks along the fault surface would break and move. An earthquake might result.

Most earthquakes are the result of faulting in Earth's rocks. Earthquakes occur as a result of all three types of faults. In the next section you'll find out how scientists locate earthquakes.

check your UNDERSTANDING

1. Explain how earthquakes can result from the buildup of pressure inside Earth.
2. What happens when compression forces are exerted on rock layers? Tension forces? Shearing forces?
3. How do strike-slip faults differ from reverse and normal faults?
4. **Apply** A stream flows through an area where there are many faults. The stream takes a sharp turn to the left, flows for a short distance, and then takes a sharp turn to the right. It flows straight beyond that. How can you explain the stream's sharp turns? Draw diagrams to explain your answers.

2-2 Shake and Quake

Section Objectives

■ Compare and contrast primary, secondary, and surface waves.

■ Explain how an earthquake's epicenter is located by using seismic wave information.

Key Terms

seismic waves
focus
epicenter

Seismic Waves

Have you ever played with a coiled-spring toy? If so, you probably know how it behaves going down stairs. You may also have used a coiled spring to study how waves travel through matter. Such a coil can help you get an idea of how vibrations travel as waves through Earth after an earthquake has occurred at a fault. Do the following activity to help you understand more about earthquake waves.

Explore! ACTIVITY

How can a coiled spring be used to demonstrate two types of earthquake waves?

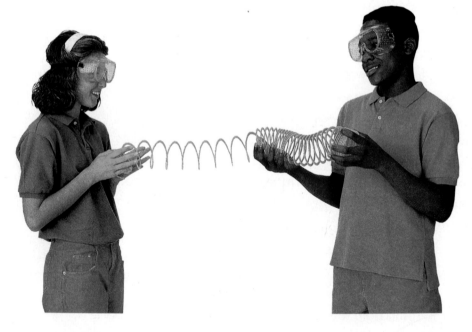

What To Do

1. Stretch a coiled spring between another person and yourself.

2. Squeeze 4 or 5 coils together and then release the squeezed portion. What happens?

3. Now move one end of the spring up and down quickly. *In your Journal,* record your observation of how the wire in the spring moves.

When you let go of the squeezed spring, you created a compression wave. Matter that is squeezed and stretched has a compression wave traveling through it.

The second wave you created was a transverse wave. A transverse wave causes matter to move at right angles to the direction that the wave is moving.

Earthquakes generate waves that are similar to the waves you made with the coiled spring. Such waves are called **seismic waves**. The point in Earth's interior where seismic waves originate is the **focus** of the earthquake. The focus can be between 5 and 700 kilometers below the surface. Seismic waves travel outward through Earth in all directions from the focus. Scientists use an instrument called a seismograph to detect the waves. Seismographs can detect seismic waves that originated as far away as the other side of Earth. In this Find Out activity, you will graph two seismic waves to compare how fast they travel.

Find Out! ACTIVITY

Which is faster, a compression wave or a transverse wave?

The table shows when either a compression wave or a transverse wave arrived at a seismograph station at some distance from an earthquake. Assume that the earthquake occurred at precisely 4:00 P.M. The times given in the table are hour, minutes, and seconds. So a time of 4:06:30 indicates that the wave arrived at a station 6 minutes and 30 seconds after the earthquake occurred.

What To Do

1. Make a graph comparing the distance from the earthquake focus and the time it took for the waves to travel there.

2. How many lines will you plot on your graph? Answer the questions below *in your Journal.*

Conclude and Apply

1. Based on your graph, which is faster—a compression wave or a transverse wave?

2. Do the waves remain the same distance apart as they travel?

3. Do they grow closer together or farther apart over time?

4. How could you use your graph to fill in the missing arrival times?

5. Use your observations to tell why compression waves are called primary waves and transverse waves are called secondary waves.

Compression and Transverse Waves		
Distance from focus (km)	Time of Arrival (Hr:Min:Sec)	
	Compression wave	Transverse wave
250	4:01:00	—
500	—	4:03:00
1000	4:02:30	—
1750	4:04:00	—
2000	—	4:07:30
3000	—	4:10:15
4500	4:08:00	—
5000	—	4:15:00
6000	4:09:30	—
6500	—	4:18:00
7250	4:11:00	—
8000	4:11:45	—
8250	—	4:21:15
9000	4:12:30	—
9500	—	4:22:45

Primary and secondary waves can be detected at Earth's surface by a seismograph. But remember that primary and secondary waves originate from an earthquake's focus and generally travel through Earth's interior. The point on Earth's surface directly above the focus is the **epicenter**. When seismic waves from the focus of an earthquake reach the epicenter, they generate surface waves. These surface waves travel outward from the epicenter the way ripples on a pond's surface travel outward when you throw a stone in. Surface waves travel more slowly than secondary and primary waves and they cause the greatest damage. You can see the directions of motion of all three kinds of seismic waves in **Figure 2-4**.

Figure 2-4

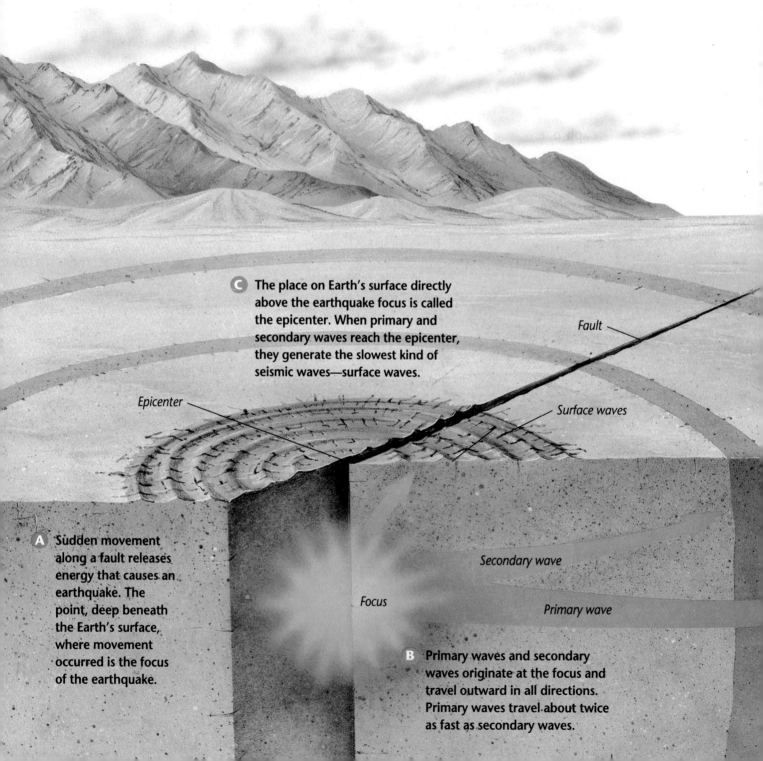

C The place on Earth's surface directly above the earthquake focus is called the epicenter. When primary and secondary waves reach the epicenter, they generate the slowest kind of seismic waves—surface waves.

Fault

Epicenter

Surface waves

A Sudden movement along a fault releases energy that causes an earthquake. The point, deep beneath the Earth's surface, where movement occurred is the focus of the earthquake.

Focus

Secondary wave

Primary wave

B Primary waves and secondary waves originate at the focus and travel outward in all directions. Primary waves travel about twice as fast as secondary waves.

Locating an Epicenter

As you discovered, seismic waves don't travel through Earth at the same speed. **Figure 2-5** shows how far primary and secondary waves travel in a certain amount of time. You can use the graph to determine how far away an epicenter is from a seismograph station. Say your seismograph detects a primary seismic wave at precisely 3:00 P.M. At 3:06 and 30 seconds, the secondary wave arrives. Find the place on the graph where the two curved lines are separated by 6 minutes and 30 seconds. Where on the graph does this occur? It occurs at the 5000-kilometer mark. How far away is your seismograph station from the earthquake epicenter?

Based on your calculations, you can say that an earthquake occurred about 5000 kilometers from your seismograph station. But can you say in which direction? So far, you don't have enough information to answer that question. Can you think of a way to determine the exact location of the epicenter? Do the following Investigate activity to see if you're right.

D Surface waves travel outward from the epicenter along Earth's surface much the way ripples travel outward from a stone thrown into a pond.

Figure 2-5

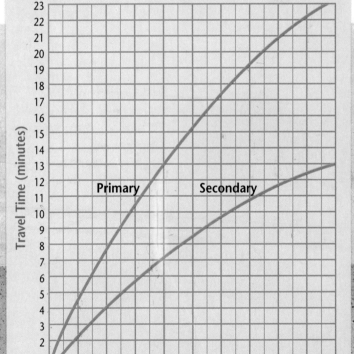

Primary and Secondary Waves

Primary

Secondary

Travel Time (minutes)

Epicenter Distance (km)

Where's the Epicenter?

You know that primary waves travel faster than secondary waves and therefore arrive at a seismograph station first. In the following activity, you'll locate epicenters using the arrival times of these waves.

Problem
How are epicenters located?

Materials
paper	Figure 2-5
string	metric ruler
globe	water-soluble
	marker or chalk

What To Do

1. Copy the data table on the next page *into your Journal.*

2. Determine the difference in arrival times between the primary and secondary waves at each station for each earthquake in the table on page 65.

3. *Interpret the graph* in Figure 2-5 to determine the distance in kilometers of each seismograph from the epicenter of each earthquake. Record these data. An example has been done for you.

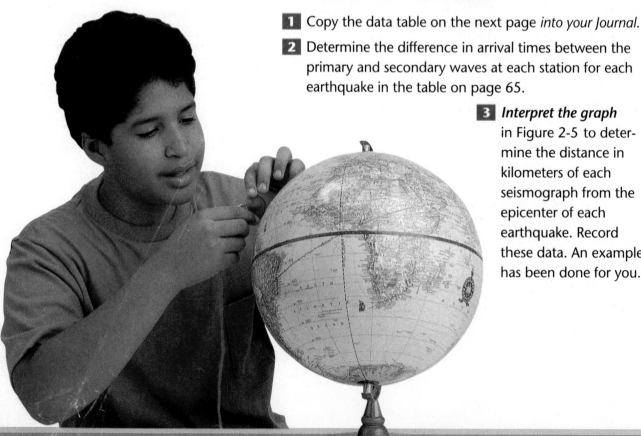

Data and Observations

Earthquake	Calculated distance from epicenter (km) for each seismograph location				
	(1)	(2)	(3)	(4)	(5)
A					
B				9750	

A

4 Using the string, *measure* the circumference of the globe by using the ruler to measure the length of string needed to circle the globe (see photo **A**). Determine a scale of centimeters of string to kilometers on the surface of Earth (Earth's circumference = 40 000 km).

5 For each earthquake, A and B, place one end of the string at each seismic station location. Use the marker or chalk to draw a circle with a radius equal to the distance to the epicenter of the earthquake.

Wave Arrival Times

Location of Seismograph	Wave	Earthquake A	Earthquake B
(1) New York	P	2:24:05 PM	1:19:00 PM
	S	2:28:55 PM	1:24:40 PM
(2) Seattle	P	2:24:40 PM	1:14:37 PM
	S	2:30:00 PM	1:16:52 PM
(3) Rio de Janeiro	P	2:29:00 PM	——
	S	2:38:05 PM	——
(4) Paris	P	2:30:15 PM	1:24:05 PM
	S	2:40:15 PM	1:34:05 PM
(5) Tokyo	P	——	1:23:30 PM
	S	——	1:33:05 PM

Analyzing

1. The epicenter is the point at which all the circles intersect. What is the location of the epicenter of each earthquake?

2. Compare the distance of a seismograph from the earthquake with the difference in arrival times of the waves. How are these data related?

Concluding and Applying

3. What is the minimum number of seismograph stations needed to locate an epicenter accurately?

4. Going Further What information would only two seismograph stations give you in regard to the location of an epicenter? Make a drawing to show what information two stations would provide about the epicenter.

Visualizing Waves

Figure 2-6

A Primary waves cause alternating compression (pushing together) and stretching (pulling apart) in rock, in the direction of the wave. Primary waves cause back-forth, rocking movements on Earth's surface.

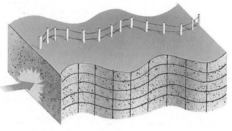

B Secondary waves cause rock to vibrate at right angles to the direction of the wave. This shearing motion causes side-to-side movements on Earth's surface.

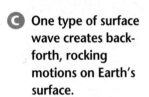

C One type of surface wave creates back-forth, rocking motions on Earth's surface.

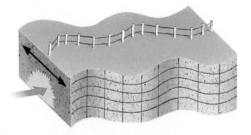

D A second type of surface wave creates up-down, and rolling motions on the surface.

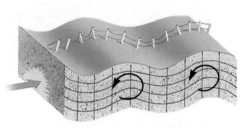

Primary and secondary waves are used to determine the location of an earthquake's epicenter. However, these waves don't usually cause major damage at the surface. When you think of an earthquake, you probably think of shaking ground and crumbling buildings. Surface waves are responsible for most of this destruction.

Figure 2-6 shows the effects of earthquake waves. You can see why surface waves cause the most damage. The waves cause one part of a building to move up, while another part moves down. At the same time, the building moves from side to side. In some areas of the United States, Japan, and elsewhere in the world, many buildings are constructed so that they can better withstand vibrations caused by surface waves.

Thus far, you've learned how forces inside Earth can send seismic waves through Earth and along its surface, and how seismologists use these waves to locate the epicenter of an earthquake. In the next section, you will find out how forces inside Earth can cause volcanoes to erupt.

check your UNDERSTANDING

1. Compare the origins of the three kinds of seismic waves. Which originate at an earthquake's focus? Which originate at an earthquake's epicenter?
2. What do you think would happen to a row of evenly spaced utility poles as a surface wave travels along the row?
3. **Apply** If all seismic waves traveled at the same speed, could the epicenter be located? Explain.

Volcanic Eruptions

What Causes Volcanoes to Erupt?

You've learned that earthquakes occur along faults such as the San Andreas Fault shown in the picture at the beginning of this chapter. Volcanoes and earthquakes often occur in the same regions. In fact, the movement of magma and volcanic eruptions may trigger some earthquakes.

Although heat and pressure within Earth can cause rocks to melt and form magma, some rocks deep inside Earth are already melted. Others are so hot that only a small rise in temperature or slight change in pressure is needed to melt them and form magma.

What causes magma to rise toward the surface and erupt to form a volcano? You can see how this process takes place if you do the following activity.

Explore! ACTIVITY

How does magma move?

What To Do

1. Turn a closed bottle of cold syrup upside down.
2. Observe what happens. Record your observations *in your Journal.*
3. What causes the bubbles to rise? Which is less dense—the syrup or the air?

Magma rises toward Earth's surface for the same reason that air bubbles in syrup rise. Less-dense materials are pushed upward by denser materials. Magma is less dense than the rocks around it, so it's pushed up by the denser material and rises toward the surface.

When magma reaches Earth's surface, it flows out through openings called **vents**. This event is called an eruption, and at this point, magma is called lava. Lava flows out, cools, and forms layers of volcanic rock around the vent. Volcanic material may pile up around the vent to form a cone. How does the type of magma determine the type of eruption that occurs and the kind of volcanic cone that forms?

Figure 2-7

Ⓐ Some volcanoes erupt with such violent explosions that the sound is heard thousands of miles away and the force of the blast blows away great chunks of the volcano. The Arenal volcano in Costa Rica erupted with violence in July 1991.

Ⓑ By comparison, some other volcanoes erupt rather quietly. Melted rock boils out of one or more openings in the Earth and flows steadily outward, until it cools. Mount Kilauea, in Hawaii, had such a history of frequent but relatively quiet eruptions that it was chosen as the site of a permanent volcanic observatory in 1912.

Plate Tectonics

Are there earthquakes and volcanic eruptions near where you live? Scientists have developed a theory called *plate tectonics* that explains how and where earthquakes and volcanic eruptions occur.

According to the theory of plate tectonics, Earth's outer layer is made of many rigid pieces, called plates, that move around on the denser plastic-like rock forming the layer beneath.

When Plates Collide

When plates move toward each other, they collide and the edge of one plate can slip underneath the edge of the other. The collision can cause earthquakes along the meeting edges. The portion of the plate that slips underneath begins to melt in the great heat of the mantle. This newly melted material is less dense than the rock of the mantle, so the newly melted material is forced upward and may flow through the crust in places, causing volcanic eruptions.

What kind of volcanic eruptions occur where plates are colliding? You already know that the newly melted material is less dense than mantle material. So you might expect the newly melted material to contain lots of dissolved gases—and you'd be right. Magma

Types of Eruptions

Gases such as water vapor and carbon dioxide are trapped in magma. Surrounding rock puts pressure on magma when it is deep underground. Under pressure, magma can contain many dissolved gases. But when the magma is pushed toward the surface, the pressure on it decreases. Magma under low pressure cannot hold as much gas. As a result, the gas begins to escape as the magma nears Earth's surface in an explosive blast. Gases in thin, fluid magma escape in a quiet way because they are released gradually before pressure builds up.

Some magma contains a lot of the compound silica. Silica-rich magma tends to be very thick. In fact, it can be so thick that it clogs a volcanic vent. Magma that is trapped below the clogged vent and the gases within the magma are under even greater pressure than before. Eruptions of volcanoes with silica-rich magma are usually very explosive. The magma itself often explodes into dust, ash, and rock fragments. When low-silica magma reaches the surface, it tends to flow from a vent in a much less explosive manner.

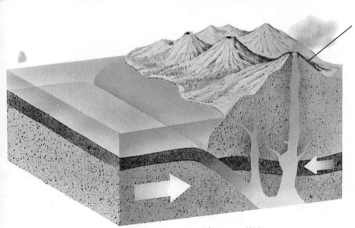

Volcano

Plates colliding

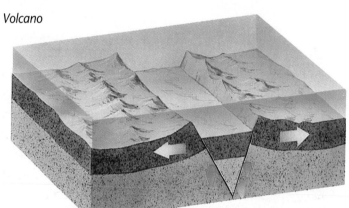

Plates pulling apart

containing much gas under pressure causes explosive eruptions that hurl dust, ash, and rock fragments.

When Plates Pull Apart

As plates move away from each other, magma located a few kilometers below the surface rises to fill the gap. There isn't much stress on the plates here, so earthquakes are not as violent as they are where plates come together. The volcanic eruptions here tend to flow easily rather than exploding, partly because the magma from the deep mantle is very fluid and contains few dissolved gases.

You Try It!

Find a world map and locate the selected eruptions from the table on page 73. Which volcanoes would you say are located where plates are colliding? Which ones seem to be where plates are pulling apart?

Forms of Volcanoes

Figure 2-8

Magma

Shield volcano

The form of volcano that is produced is determined by the nature of its eruption. If the eruption is quiet, a gently sloping shield volcano is produced, like the one shown in **Figure 2-8A**. If the eruption is explosive, a steep-sloped cinder cone is produced, like the one shown in **Figure 2-8B**. Sometimes, however, eruptions alternate between quiet and explosive. Then a composite cone volcano is produced, like the one shown in **Figure 2-8C**.

A When hot, thin lava flows without violent explosions out of one or more vents and then cools and hardens, it builds into a gentle slope. The result is a shield volcano, such as this one at Mauna Loa in Hawaii.

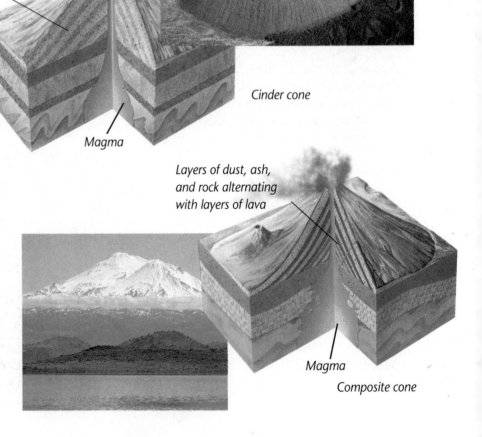

Steep sides

Dust, ash, and rock layers

Magma

Cinder cone

B When volcanic ash and slightly cooled lava are forced out of a single vent during an explosive eruption, they fall back to Earth. The ash and cooled lava form the steep slope of a cinder cone around the vent. Parícutin in Mexico, pictured in the photograph, is a cinder cone.

Layers of dust, ash, and rock alternating with layers of lava

C If a volcano throws out flowing lava, hardened lava, and chunks of ash, a composite cone, such as Mt. Shasta in California shown here, is formed. Because the layers of lava cover and protect the layers of loose materials from erosion, composite cones build into steep-sided towering mountains.

Magma

Composite cone

Volcanoes and Humans

Volcanoes affect people's lives all over the world. On November 13, 1985, Nevado del Ruiz erupted explosively, killing nearly 23,000 people in Armero, Colombia. On May 26, 1991, Mount Unzen in Japan erupted explosively after having been dormant for about 200 years. Soon after, the eruptions of Mount Pinatubo in the Philippines killed nearly 900 people during the month of June 1991.

Figure 2-9

Ⓐ Before its eruption in the spring of 1980, Mount St. Helens's snow-capped cone was a magnificent sight and a favorite of many people.

Ⓑ In March of 1980, Mount St. Helens began a series of explosive eruptions that triggered fires and flooding. Hundreds of tons of volcanic ash fell. More than 60 people lost their lives. Thousands of large animals including deer, elk, and bear, and all the birds and small mammals in the area also died. Crops were ruined. The local timber industry was wiped out.

Ⓒ Within 10 days of the eruption, fresh deer tracks were found in the ash on Mt. St. Helens. Within a month, fireweed was blooming at a nearby lake. Today, Mount St. Helens continues its comeback.

Visions of Volcanoes

You've learned that not all volcanoes are the same. Some erupt explosively, with little or no lava. Others erupt nonexplosively with runny lava. You have also learned that certain properties of magma can affect the type of eruption and the form of the volcano that will develop.

Problem

How could you *interpret data* to show the relationship between the properties of magma and volcano type?

Materials

paper   pencil

What To Do

1 Use the data on the *Selected Volcanoes* table on the next page to fill in 3 charts like the one below.

2 Classify volcanoes by the type of volcano on the first chart, the eruptive force on the second chart, and the ability of magma to flow on the third chart. The first two volcanoes have been classified for you.

Data and Observations

| | Water-Vapor Content of Magma | |
	Low	High
Silica Content of Magma — High	composite (1)	cinder (2)
Silica Content of Magma — Low		

	Selected Volcanoes				
Volcano and Location	Magma Content		Type of Volcano	Eruptive Force	Ability of Magma to Flow
	Silica	Water Vapor			
(1) Etna, Italy	high	low	composite	moderate	medium
(2) Tambora, Indonesia	high	high	cinder	high	low
(3) Krakatoa, Indonesia	high	high	cinder	high	low
(4) Pélee, Martinique	high	high	cinder	high	low
(5) Vesuvius, Italy	high	low	composite	moderate	medium
(6) Lassen, California	high	low	composite	moderate	low
(7) Mauna Loa, Hawaii	low	low	shield	low	high
(8) Parícutin, Mexico	high	low	cinder	moderate	medium
(9) Surtsey, Iceland	low	low	shield	moderate	high
(10) Kelut, Indonesia	high	high	cinder	high	low
(11) Arenal, Costa Rica	high	low	cinder	high	low
(12) Helgafell, Iceland	low	high	shield	moderate	medium
(13) Saint Helens, WA	high	high	composite	high	medium
(14) Laki, Iceland	low	low	shield	moderate	medium
(15) Kilauea Iki, Hawaii	low	low	shield	low	high

3 Be sure to number your volcanoes so you can identify them in all three charts. Use the same numbers that are given in the table.

4 Record any similarities or differences you observe in your classifications *in your Journal.*

Analyzing

1. Which eruptions are the most explosive—eruptions with high silica content or low silica content?

2. Which eruptions are the most common to shield volcanoes—low force, moderate force, or high force eruptions?

3. Which eruption contained low silica and a high water-vapor content? Why might this type of eruption be rarer than the others?

Concluding and Applying

4. *Determine the effect* the silica content and water-vapor content of magma seem to have on its ability to flow.

5. Which of the two variables (silica or water-vapor content) would you *infer* has the greater effect on the eruptive force of a particular volcano?

6. **Going Further** What relationship appears to exist between the silica and water-vapor content of the magma and the type of volcano that is produced?

Figure 2-10

A The eruption of Mount Pinatubo in June 1991 caused destruction and the death of nearly 900 people in the Philippines. The eruption released a cloud of ash and millions of tons of sulfur dioxide gas. The immediate effects of volcanoes are always negative and often devastating. But when viewed over a long span of years, volcanoes also have a positive side.

Connect to...

Life Science

A volcanic eruption can cause a lot of destruction to trees, plants and animals. Within a short time, however, new plants are seen in the area. How is a stable ecosystem formed after a volcanic eruption? Make a poster that shows the steps involved in rebuilding the ecosystem.

B The long range positive effects of volcanoes include the production of sulfur and other mineral deposits. Rocks formed by lava are used in construction of roads. Volcanic ash, once it has time to break down, increases soil fertility. The Canary Islanders pictured here are harvesting onions grown in fertile lava soil.

In this chapter, you have explored the causes of earthquakes and the different types of volcanoes. You will probably read and hear in the news about earthquakes and volcanoes throughout your life. These naturally occurring events are interesting to everyone!

check your UNDERSTANDING

1. What characteristic of magma causes it to be forced upward to Earth's surface and eventually erupt?

2. Some volcanic eruptions are quiet, yet others are explosive. What causes this difference?

3. **Apply** A large body of magma is forced upward close to the surface under what has been flat land, but the magma has no vent to reach the surface. How do you think the magma would affect the land? Why?

Science and Society

Preparing Buildings for Earthquakes

Experts know where earthquakes are most likely to occur, but they don't know when the quakes will happen. If they could predict earthquakes, buildings could be evacuated and lives saved.

While experts are trying to better predict the *when* of earthquakes, others are building earthquake-resistant buildings or modifying older buildings to help them survive earthquakes.

Constructing for Safety

For example, an earthquake safety commission in Japan is working closely with construction companies to determine what features help make a building earthquake safe. They've designed and built the small-scale structures you see in the picture to the right for use in earthquake trials. At each step, the building is fitted with a design feature, then vibrated with the force of a powerful earthquake to test its effectiveness. Note the second structure from the left.

The National Center for Earthquake Engineering Research (NCEER) in Buffalo, New York has undertaken a similar project.

Active Controls

NCEER has also worked with Japanese engineers to build an experimental earthquake-resistant building in Tokyo. The six-story building contains an active system for controlling a building's response to tremors. A computer system in the building tells giant pistons, which move up and down, to shift the level of different areas of the building to counterbalance earthquake waves.

This building is considered strong enough to withstand earthquakes common to Tokyo. Researchers study the effectiveness of the computerized active system during the small earthquakes that occur there every year.

Passive Controls

A much more common approach to stabilizing buildings during earthquakes is through passive control systems. For example, a building sitting on a huge cushion-like foundation might ride out an earthquake relatively well. This is called a passive system because the cushion is always responding, not waiting like an active system.

"A lot of people feel that a dumb (passive) building that performs well is much preferable to a smart (active) building that may have something go wrong with it," says Professor James D. Jirsa, a structural engineer specializing in earthquake-resistant buildings.

Dr. Jirsa explains that passive and active systems are usually added to already existing buildings to prepare them for future earthquakes. New buildings can be built more earthquake resistant in the first place.

Construction Problems

One of the biggest problems in constructing and modifying buildings for earthquake resistance is that each earthquake is different and experts can't always predict the earthquake's strength or its duration. So experts can't be absolutely certain how a building will respond to the next earthquake.

Engineers also have to decide whether to construct buildings that only protect people from injuries or that protect people and contents. Buildings designed to protect only people may move during an earthquake, but they won't collapse. The movement of the building, however, might cause the contents of the building to fall or break. Buildings that protect people and contents are more expensive but may be

necessary when computers, medical equipment, and communications are involved.

Earthquake Education

In addition to efforts to prevent human injury and building damage through earthquake-resistant construction, engineers agree there is another extremely important way people can try to protect themselves—education.

"A very important part of this whole thing is education," says Dr. T.T. Soong of NCEER. "People should take precautions so that lives can be saved. One can have earthquake drills, very much like fire drills, so that people can be in safe places when the earthquake strikes."

What Do You Think?

Does your city have earthquake codes for new buildings? Does it have special requirements for existing buildings? How long have such codes existed in your area?

Technology Connection

Seismic Waves and the Search for Oil

As you learned in this chapter, earthquakes generate seismic waves, which help determine exactly where an earthquake took place.

With explosive devices, geologists can create their own seismic waves and use them in the difficult search for oil beneath the ocean floor. Oil formed millions of years ago from the remains of marine plants and animals deep inside Earth. Today, much of that oil is contained in reservoir rocks—porous rocks with many tiny holes that trap oil. The reservoir rocks themselves are concealed by faults, folds, and other specific rock formations.

beneath the sea. The waves travel down, then bounce back off the different underground rock layers.

Seismic waves travel at different speeds, depending on the kinds of rock through which they're passing. By measuring how long it takes the waves to return to the surface, geologists can map out a cross section of the rock layers.

Using these maps, as well as their knowledge of the area and other drilling sites, seismologists can then estimate where oil might be found. As you may have guessed, no one can be sure they'll find oil until they actually drill into the rocks and collect samples. Drilling is expensive. These maps help limit the possibilities and save money in the search for oil.

Using Waves To Find Oil

Geologists look beneath the ocean for the right combination of reservoir rocks and protective layers, which point to the possibility of trapped oil. To do this, they cause explosions, which send seismic waves into the rocks

What Do You Think?

Look up the words *seismology* and *geology* in the dictionary. Why do you think the search for oil in the rocks beneath the sea is being done by seismologists and geologists?

Circulation

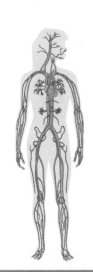

Did you ever wonder...

✓ **What keeps blood moving through your body?**

✓ **Whether all animals have the same kind of heart and circulation?**

✓ **How blood pressure affects blood vessels?**

Before you begin to study about circulation, think about these questions and answer them *in your Journal*. When you finish the chapter, compare your first Journal write-up with what you have learned.

Taking a trip to an unfamiliar city requires a good road map to guide you along endless miles of intersecting highways, like those in the photograph below. There are routes or "arteries" that take you into the "heart" of the city or out to specific streets in the suburbs. There are one-way streets, traffic jams, slow ups, and even the occasional accident. Living organisms have something like a highway system through which needed materials move.

Are there things like one-way streets in living organisms? Are there ever any slow ups? Are there ever accidents as materials are transported in organisms?

▶ ***In the following activity, begin to develop an idea of what circulation is like by using a city map.***

Explore! ACTIVITY

How many ways can you get from one place to another in a city?

Many big cities now have a beltway around them and usually have one or more interstate highways.

What To Do

1. Obtain a map that shows the streets, interstate roads, and a beltway around a large city.

2. Study the map to find the center or "heart" of the city. Use the map key to identify roads that are interstates and roads that are state and county routes.

3. *In your Journal*, plan a route from the heart of your city to a street out in the suburbs. Describe the different types of streets you would take. Are they all the same size? How does the final street compare in size with the one you started out on downtown?

4. *In your Journal*, describe two ways to get from the east side to the west side of the city. State the advantages and disadvantages of both routes.

5. If the city represented a human body, what would the center of town represent? What would the suburbs represent?

Circulatory Systems

Section Objectives

In this section, you will

- Explain the role of a circulatory system in animals.
- Compare and contrast open and closed circulatory systems.
- Describe the path of blood through the heart, lungs, and body.
- Compare and contrast arteries, veins, and capillaries.

Key Terms

arteries
veins
capillaries

Getting What You Need to Live

In the living world, there are organisms of all different sizes and shapes. But whether they are one cell in size or trillions of cells in size, whether they live in a puddle or an apartment building, living organisms all circulate similar things throughout their bodies to stay alive.

You may never have thought about the differences between small and large organisms. However, size makes a big difference in how different organisms have their needs supplied. Those organisms that are one cell in size or only a few cells thick have very different kinds of problems from larger organisms like yourself. Try the following activity to learn about what might take place as materials circulate in a one-celled organism.

Explore! ACTIVITY

How can you make a model of circulation in a one-celled organism?

Even one-celled organisms depend on having nutrients available to all the parts of their bodies.

What To Do

1. Place a spoonful of honey on a paper plate.
2. Add one drop of food coloring at the edge of the blob of honey.
3. Gently tilt the paper plate to make the honey flow in different directions. Observe what happens to the food coloring.
4. *In your Journal*, describe what happens to the drop of food coloring as the honey flows in different directions.
5. Think of the blob of honey as a one-celled organism. *In your Journal*, describe how materials are distributed throughout the organism.
6. How efficient do you think this method is for distributing materials in an organism's body?

Patterns of Circulation

A little one-celled organism, such as the blob of honey represented, has only a thin barrier between the inside and outside of its body. One-celled organisms are usually found completely immersed in water. Nutrients and oxygen are right there to move into the body. Once inside, these substances flow or stream through the liquid that makes up most of the organism's body. As the organism uses up these substances, wastes are produced and move out.

■ Open and Closed Systems

How do nutrients and oxygen reach all the body parts in larger organisms? In the chapter opening exercise, you plotted a route from the center of a city to the suburbs. You may have first moved along a four-lane highway, then onto a county road, and finally along a narrow street. Your body is similar in that it has blood vessels of various sizes going to all body parts.

The circulatory systems of complex animals are of two types, open and closed. Learn about open and closed systems in **Figure 3-1**.

Figure 3-1

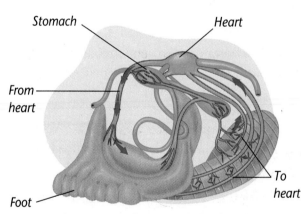

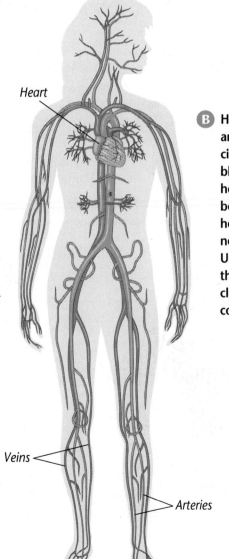

A Clams are examples of animals that have an open circulatory system. Clam hearts pump blood through blood vessels that lead to open spaces within the body. Blood washes through these spaces, and supplies body organs with a bath of nutrients and oxygen. The blood then collects in larger vessels. These vessels are squeezed by the movement of the animal, thereby moving blood back toward the heart.

B Humans are examples of animals with a closed circulatory system. The blood is pumped by a heart to all the cells of the body and back to the heart through a closed network of blood vessels. Unlike an open system, the blood vessels in the closed system are directly connected to one another.

The Heart and Blood Vessels

What is a heart? How important is your heart for circulation? If blood moved through your body just by the action of some body muscles, how fast do you think it would move? Your heart is a two-pump system made up of a special type of muscle found only in your heart. This muscle started to contract about 45 days after you were conceived. Now it contracts at a rate of about 72 beats per minute. Each beat exerts pressure on a fluid enclosed in blood vessels. Use a model in the following activity to see how the two pumps of the human heart compare.

Find Out! ACTIVITY

What are the parts of the heart?

Sometimes, it is easier to learn about some structures, such as hearts, by looking at a model.

What To Do

1. Obtain a model of the human heart that you can open.
2. Look at all the external and internal features shown on the model.
3. Find the two upper chambers. These are the atria. Examine them from the outside and the inside.
4. Next, locate the two lower chambers, the ventricles, and examine them.

Conclude and Apply

1. *In your Journal*, describe any differences you observed between the atria and the ventricles. What hint does the structure of each side give you about the work each side does?
2. Each side of the human heart is a pump. Explain what parts make up each pump.

■ Blood Vessels

Did you notice what looked like large and small tubes attached to the model heart? These tubes represent blood vessels. There are three types of blood vessels in the body. **Arteries** are blood vessels that carry blood away from the heart—to the lungs or to the body. **Veins** are vessels that transport blood back to the heart from the lungs or body. The smallest vessels, called **capillaries**, form an extensive network of vessels in the body organs, connecting arteries to veins.

Technology Connection

Seismic Waves and the Search for Oil

As you learned in this chapter, earthquakes generate seismic waves, which help determine exactly where an earthquake took place.

With explosive devices, geologists can create their own seismic waves and use them in the difficult search for oil beneath the ocean floor. Oil formed millions of years ago from the remains of marine plants and animals deep inside Earth. Today, much of that oil is contained in reservoir rocks—porous rocks with many tiny holes that trap oil. The reservoir rocks themselves are concealed by faults, folds, and other specific rock formations.

Using Waves To Find Oil

Geologists look beneath the ocean for the right combination of reservoir rocks and protective layers, which point to the possibility of trapped oil. To do this, they cause explosions, which send seismic waves into the rocks beneath the sea. The waves travel down, then bounce back off the different underground rock layers.

Seismic waves travel at different speeds, depending on the kinds of rock through which they're passing. By measuring how long it takes the waves to return to the surface, geologists can map out a cross section of the rock layers.

Using these maps, as well as their knowledge of the area and other drilling sites, seismologists can then estimate where oil might be found. As you may have guessed, no one can be sure they'll find oil until they actually drill into the rocks and collect samples. Drilling is expensive. These maps help limit the possibilities and save money in the search for oil.

What Do You Think?

Look up the words *seismology* and *geology* in the dictionary. Why do you think the search for oil in the rocks beneath the sea is being done by seismologists and geologists?

Geography Connection

Climates of the Himalayas

The Himalayas, the world's tallest mountain range, stretch for over 2400 kilometers in Asia. The mountains began forming millions of years ago, when India began colliding with Central Asia.

Weather

Can you guess what kind of weather these mountains might have? Cold and snowy? Right! Warm and wet? Right! Hot and dry? Right again. The Himalayan climate varies greatly from place to place due to altitude and levels of rainfall.

Mt. Everest, the highest mountain in the world, reaches more than 8800 meters above sea level. From that height down to about 4900 meters, the bitterly cold Himalayas are not inhabited by people. The lower Himalayas, from near sea level up to about 2200 meters, have a moist, warm climate that supports dense forests and animal life. A variety of vegetation is able to grow up to about 4900 meters, where the vegetation then becomes scarce. Crops, such as tea and rice, are generally not grown above 3500 meters.

The People of the Himalayas

The people of the Himalayas have adapted to their varied surroundings. Most are farmers, and therefore live below 3500 meters. In fact, they live mainly in fertile valleys, which are the best areas for farming. In areas that receive plenty of rainfall, people cultivate rice. Other regions produce fruit, vegetables, grain, and timber.

Himalayan animal life also varies depending on the altitude. High in the mountains you'll find bears, snow leopards, and eagles. Lower down there are wolves, wild pigs, and goats. On the lower slopes are many of the animals we associate with India, such as tigers, elephants, and rhinos.

You Try It!

Find a topographic map of your state. Locate major cities on the map and look up climatic information about them in an almanac. How does the map help you understand the average annual temperatures and rainfall in the cities you selected?

Afghanistan

China

Nepal

Bhutan

HIMALAYAS

Pakistan

Myanmar

India

Bangladesh

ARABIAN SEA

Bay of Bengal

30°

10°

70°

90°

Sri Lanka

Review the statements below about the big ideas presented in this chapter, and try to answer the questions. Then, re-read your answers to the Did You Ever Wonder questions at the beginning of the chapter. *In your Journal*, write a paragraph about how your understanding of the big ideas in the chapter has changed.

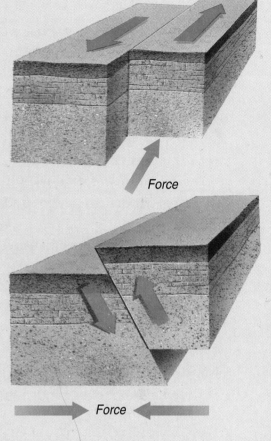

Force

Force

1 Forces within Earth cause faults and earthquakes. *Describe three types of faults and the forces they are associated with.*

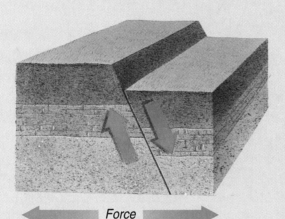

Force

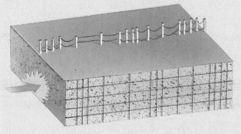

2 Earthquakes generate seismic waves—primary, secondary, and surface waves—that travel outward from the epicenter. *Which seismic waves cause the greatest destruction? Why?*

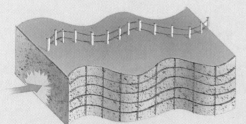

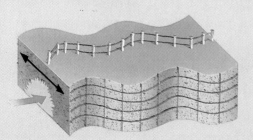

3 Volcanoes form from the eruption of magma onto Earth's surface. *Why does magma rise to Earth's surface?*

Using Key Science Terms

epicenter   seismic waves
fault   vent
focus

Answer the following questions using what you know about the science terms.

1. Distinguish between the focus and the epicenter of an earthquake.
2. Describe what you might find in the area of a vent.
3. What is the relationship between seismic waves and faults?

Understanding Ideas

Answer the following questions in your Journal *using complete sentences.*

1. At what point does magma turn into lava?
2. Describe what type of magma makes a volcano erupt nonexplosively, and what type makes an explosive eruption.
3. When rocks are compressed and released before their elastic limit is reached, how will the shape of the rocks be affected?
4. What differentiates the three types of seismic waves?
5. Describe how volcanoes and earthquakes are alike.
6. Why do many earthquakes occur in the same regions as many volcanoes?

Developing Skills

Use your understanding of the concepts developed in each section to answer each of the following questions.

1. **Sequencing** Outline the process of a volcanic eruption.
2. **Observing and Inferring** Repeat the Explore activity on page 53 to model the clay by compression and tension so that the bottom layer of clay is seen at the surface. Infer how this could happen in rocks on Earth.
3. **Concept Map** Complete the concept map about earthquakes using the following terms: *earthquakes, faults, normal, strike-slip, tremendous pressure.*

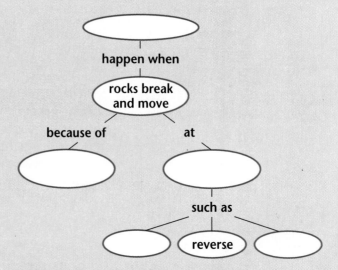

4. **Forming a Hypothesis** Refer to the Explore activity on page 67. Hypothesize what effect thinner syrup would have on the air bubbles. Add water to the syrup and mix. What do you observe? What hypothesis would you make about thinner magma of a volcano?

Critical Thinking

Use your understanding of the concepts developed in this chapter to answer each of the following questions.

1. The data table shows some travel times of two waves from an earthquake. Classify each time as belonging to the primary or the secondary wave. How do you know?

Distance from Earthquake (km)	Time (minutes)
1500	5.0
2000	2.5
5000	14.0
5500	7.0
8600	11.0
10000	23.5

2. In an area around an active volcano, you discover piles of ash, cinders, and rocks. A geologist tells you that the rocks are volcanic rocks. What can you infer about the form of the volcano and the kind of eruptions it undergoes?

3. Do you think it is possible for tension forces and compression forces to be acting on the same rock layer? Explain.

Problem Solving

Read the following problem and discuss your answers in a brief paragraph.

Scientists want a reliable approach to predicting earthquakes. Both seismographs and satellites detect motion. Seismographs detect seismic waves. Satellites send signals that are picked up by radio receivers on Earth. When a radio receiver moves just a few centimeters, it can be detected.

1. Would seismographs be useful for predicting earthquakes? Why or why not?

2. Where could scientists place radio receivers to help detect rock movement that may lead to an earthquake?

CONNECTING IDEAS

Discuss each of the following in a brief paragraph.

1. **Theme—Systems and Interactions** Explain the force behind each type of fault.

2. **Theme—Scale and Structure** In what ways do layers of rock behave when forces inside Earth bend or stretch them too far?

3. **Theme—Systems and Interactions** How do less-dense materials react when they are trapped within denser materials? How is this principle related to volcanic activity?

4. **Technology Connection** Different seismic waves travel at different speeds. What other factor affects the speed at which a wave travels? How do geologists use this information to locate oil?

5. **Physics Connection** What do rocks store and release as forces act upon them? Explain.

CHAPTER 3

Circulation

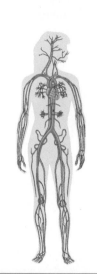

✓ **What keeps blood moving through your body?**

✓ **Whether all animals have the same kind of heart and circulation?**

✓ **How blood pressure affects blood vessels?**

Before you begin to study about circulation, think about these questions and answer them *in your Journal.* When you finish the chapter, compare your first Journal write-up with what you have learned.

Taking a trip to an unfamiliar city requires a good road map to guide you along endless miles of intersecting highways, like those in the photograph below. There are routes or "arteries" that take you into the "heart" of the city or out to specific streets in the suburbs. There are one-way streets, traffic jams, slow ups, and even the occasional accident. Living organisms have something like a highway system through which needed materials move.

Are there things like one-way streets in living organisms? Are there ever any slow ups? Are there ever accidents as materials are transported in organisms?

▶ *In the following activity, begin to develop an idea of what circulation is like by using a city map.*

Blood Flow Through the Heart

As you observed on the model, each side of your heart has an atrium and a ventricle. In an office building, an atrium is an area that people enter before going off to individual offices. Each atrium in the heart is an area where blood first enters the heart before being sent to body parts. The job of each ventricle is to pump blood out of the heart. Just as you enter some buildings through one particular door and leave by another, blood always enters the heart through an atrium and leaves through a ventricle. Follow the pathway of blood through the heart shown in **Figure 3-2.**

Heart

Figure 3-2

During a single heartbeat, both atria contract at the same time, then relax. Then both ventricles contract at the same time and then relax.

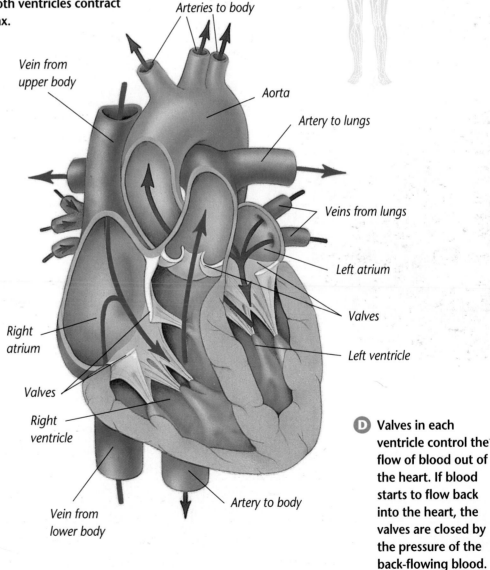

A The right side of the heart receives oxygen-poor blood (represented by blue arrows) from the body and pumps it to the lungs, where it picks up oxygen.

B The left side receives oxygen-rich blood (represented by dark red arrows) from the lungs and pumps it to the body cells.

C On the diagram, find the valves that separate the atria from the ventricles. These valves open in only one direction. What can you say about the direction of blood flow between an atrium and a ventricle?

D Valves in each ventricle control the flow of blood out of the heart. If blood starts to flow back into the heart, the valves are closed by the pressure of the back-flowing blood.

Arteries to body

Vein from upper body

Aorta

Artery to lungs

Veins from lungs

Left atrium

Valves

Left ventricle

Right atrium

Valves

Right ventricle

Vein from lower body

Artery to body

Heart Valves

As you noticed in **Figure 3-2** valves keep blood flowing only in one direction through the heart. But valves can tell you more about the heart. Do the following activity to find out more about heart valves.

Find Out! ACTIVITY

What makes heart sounds?

What To Do

1. Put together a simple stethoscope using a y-shaped tube, a funnel, and three pieces of flexible tubing.

2. Using your stethoscope, listen to your heart for about 30 seconds.

Conclude and Apply

1. *In your Journal*, describe the sounds your heart valves make.

2. What might be the disadvantage of faulty valves?

A Valve Job

Because heart disease remains the number one killer of people in the United States, much research goes on to find ways to prevent heart attack, high blood pressure, and coronary artery problems. Each part of the heart is subject to some sort of problem, including the valves of the heart.

Valve Disorders

The purpose of valves in the heart is to prevent backward flow of blood. Healthy valves make specific sounds when they close. When something happens to damage a valve, a murmur is heard. A murmur is often a swishing sound that is heard as blood slips back through a faulty valve. The sound is different from the normal snap-shut sound "lub-dup," of a healthy valve. Blood flow is slowed from the heart. This means that the heart muscle has to work harder. It often becomes larger to accomplish that work.

There are several diseases that cause heart valve problems. One of the best documented causes of valve problems is rheumatic heart disease in which the valves become scarred as a result of inflammation.

Blood Flow Through the Body

When blood leaves the left ventricle, it travels first through arteries, then capillaries, and finally veins as in **Figure 3-3**, before it returns to your heart.

Figure 3-3

A After leaving the left ventricle, the aorta branches into smaller and smaller arteries that carry blood to every part of the body.

B Eventually, in body tissues, these arteries become smaller and smaller until they are microscopic, thin-walled capillaries through which oxygen and waste products pass easily.

C Blood carrying waste products from body cells travels back to the heart by way of veins.

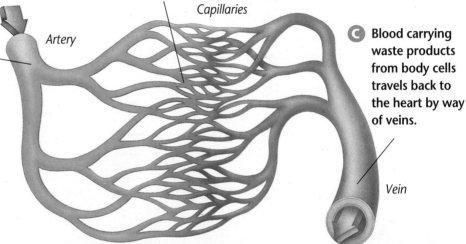

Artery

Capillaries

Vein

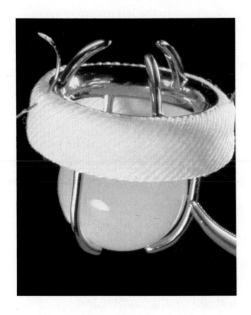

The cage-ball valve above consists of a tiny stainless steel cage that encloses a heat-treated carbon ball. Once sewn into the heart, the valve allows blood to pass in only one direction.

Some damaged valves, such as the one leading out to the aorta, can be replaced by valves from pig hearts. Others are replaced with a mechanical model.

Ball in the Cage

Does the above title sound like some kind of game? It's actually a description of a heart valve—not a natural valve, but a mechanical replacement valve.

The ball-and-cage valve is a perfect name for this replacement valve. Look at the photograph. In it, you'll see that the valve consists of a small cage with a ball inside. When the ventricle contracts, the ball moves up within the cage. This action closes the valve and blood leaves the heart. Once all the blood is out, the ventricle relaxes, and the ball falls back to its open position, allowing blood to flow into the ventricle from the atrium.

Because the valve is ball-shaped, fluids flow past it easily resulting in little wear on moving parts.

You Try It!

The ball-and-cage valve was the first replacement valve invented. Find out more about open heart surgery and different types of replacement valves.

Blood and Breathing

Capillaries in lungs

Heart

Why does blood travel to your lungs? Just as you wash clothes before you wear them again, your blood isn't sent on another trip through your body until the carbon dioxide from your cells has been removed and oxygen has been resupplied. How is this accomplished?

Blood rich with carbon dioxide flows from the right atrium to the right ventricle. From there, it is pumped to your lungs. There it is exposed to oxygen as it flows through capillaries around millions of small thin-walled sacs containing air that you've breathed in. Follow this pathway in **Figure 3-4**.

Figure 3-4

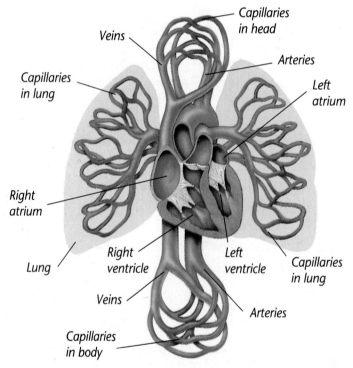

Capillaries in head

Veins

Arteries

Capillaries in lung

Left atrium

Right atrium

Lung

Right ventricle

Left ventricle

Capillaries in lung

Veins

Arteries

Capillaries in body

A Blood returning to the heart is loaded with carbon dioxide that the cells of the body have produced.

B When the right ventricle contracts, it forces the blood, rich with carbon dioxide, through an artery to the lungs. In the lungs, the carbon dioxide is exchanged for oxygen, and the carbon dioxide is then exhaled.

C Replenished with oxygen, the blood returns to the left atrium, then into the left ventricle. When the heart contracts, it pumps the now oxygen-rich blood out to cells throughout the body.

check your UNDERSTANDING

1. Diagram the pathway of blood through the human heart.
2. Compare the three types of blood vessels.
3. Describe the structural similarities and differences between an open and a closed circulatory system.
4. Discuss whether a closed circulatory system is more efficient at delivering oxygen and nutrients to cells than an open circulatory system.
5. **Apply** Fish have gills lined with capillaries. Water contains dissolved oxygen. Explain what you think happens when water flows over the blood supply in fish gills.

A System Under Pressure

With Every Beat of Your Heart

What happens when you put air in a bike tire? Does the air pour in as a continuous stream? Or do you have to apply pressure, let up, then apply pressure again? Is blood in your body pumped by your heart in the same way you pump air into a bicycle tire or is the force continuous? Think about this question as you do the following Explore activity.

Section Objectives

In this section, you will

- Explain what causes pulse.
- Explain how blood moves through your body under pressure.
- Compare the structural adaptations of blood vessels.
- Compare the circulatory systems of fish, birds, amphibians, and mammals.

Key Terms

pulse
blood pressure

Explore! ACTIVITY

How can you feel and measure heart rate?

What To Do

1. Place your fingers on your neck between your ear and your Adam's apple.

2. Push gently and move your fingers around until you feel a strong beat. What you are feeling is blood as it pulses through your carotid artery.

3. Count the number of beats you feel for 15 seconds. Then multiply that number by four. This number is your heart rate for one minute.

4. *In your Journal*, record your heart rate and complete the following statement: If the left ventricle of my heart exerts pressure on the blood each time my heart beats, then I feel my heartbeat in my neck because….

Both air in a tire and blood are classified as fluids. Both air in a tire and blood in vessels are in confined spaces. When pressure is placed on or released from a fluid in a closed space, then all the fluid in the system feels the pressure.

In the Explore activity, you felt the walls of an artery expand each time the left ventricle contracted. You felt your blood apply more, then less pressure on the walls of that artery. The rhythmic expansion and contraction of an artery is your **pulse**. Pulse is also your heartbeat. Find out if you are the only organism with a pulse.

Pulse! Pulse! Who's Got a Pulse?

You've learned that you have a closed circulatory system in which you can measure a pulse. In this activity, find out how to measure pulse in another animal with a closed system.

Problem

How can you determine an earthworm's pulse, and how does it compare with your own?

Materials

live earthworm
paper towels
clock or watch
  with second hand

Petri dish with cover
medicine dropper
water at room
  temperature

Safety Precautions

Always be careful with live animals and return them safely to an assigned container.

What To Do

As you begin this investigation, here are some things to keep in mind.

1 Place the live earthworm in a Petri dish that has been lined with a moist paper towel (see photo **A**). Keep the earthworm moist by periodically dripping water on it, but don't flood the worm.

2 Look for the blood vessel along the top surface of the earthworm (see illustration **B**). Carefully observe the vessel. Describe what you see.

3 Determine a safe method for counting an earthworm's pulse. Record this number in the data table.

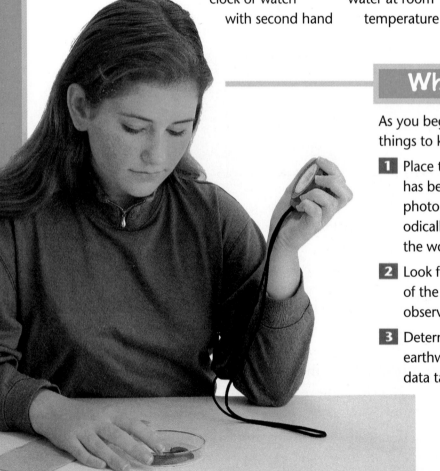

A

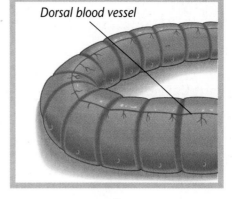

Dorsal blood vessel

B

4 Repeat Step 3 three times. Record all calculations in the data table.

5 *Calculate* an average pulse for one minute for the earthworm. Record your result.

6 Find your pulse rate for one minute as in the last Explore on page 91.

Data and Observations		
Worm Pulse Rate		
	15 seconds	1 minute
1		
2		
3		
4		
Total		
Average		

Analyzing

1. What was the average pulse rate for one minute for your earthworm?

2. What was your pulse rate for one minute?

3. How does the earthworm's pulse rate compare with your own?

4. Why was it important to repeat your measurements and determine an average?

Concluding and Applying

5. What conclusion can you draw about body activity and pulse rates?

6. Going Further Is the range of pulse rates of male students in your class the same as that for female students? *Hypothesize* whether they might be different and design an experiment to test your hypothesis.

When Fluids Are Under Pressure

Your pulse rate tells you the rate of your heartbeat. With every beat of your heart, blood is pushed through the blood vessels in your circulatory system. What happens to the blood and the vessels when this takes place?

 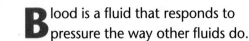

Find Out! ACTIVITY

What happens to a liquid under pressure?

Blood is a fluid that responds to pressure the way other fluids do.

What To Do

1. Fill a plastic squeeze bottle with water.
2. Fit a bendable plastic straw or rubber tubing into a stopper.
3. Put the stopper into the water-filled bottle.
4. Hold the bottle and direct the open end of the tube into a sink. Then squeeze the bottle rhythmically. Try different pressures.

Conclude and Apply

1. *In your Journal,* describe what happened to the bottle when you squeezed it.
2. How did the stream of water respond to differing pressures?

Connect to...

Physics

Many systems make use of Pascal's Principle. Find out what hydraulic lifts are and what they are used for. How is a hydraulic lift similar to your circulatory system?

Each time you squeezed the bottle, you applied a force that pushed the water out of the bottle into the tubing. Between squeezes, when you weren't exerting a force, the water didn't move out. Your hand acted as a pump to move water out of the bottle. How does this activity relate to the heart as it contracts and relaxes during a heartbeat?

Your heart is a pump that moves blood through the blood vessels of your body with pressure that rises and falls. Like the rhythmic squeezing of the water bottle, each time your heart beats, it exerts a force on your blood and pushes it along. What happens to blood vessels when the heart applies and releases pressure?

■ Pascal's Principle

If you have ever squeezed a water-filled balloon, you know that the walls push out in all directions. A water-filled balloon illustrates Pascal's Principle. Pascal's Principle states that any change in pressure applied to a fluid in a confined space is sent unchanged throughout that fluid. What does this mean for your blood and blood vessels?

Blood: A Fluid Under Pressure

Blood exerts pressure against the walls of the blood vessels in which it is confined. The pressure blood exerts against the inner walls of blood vessels is called **blood pressure**.

■ Variations in Pressure

While there is pressure on blood in arteries, capillaries, and veins, it is usually measured in arteries where it is highest. When the left ventricle contracts, it rapidly forces blood under the highest pressure into your aorta. The aorta expands and swells, then contracts, forcing the blood along down the artery.

The graph in **Figure 3-5** shows how blood pressure changes as it travels from the aorta. By the time it enters the right atrium, its pressure is almost zero. How does the body handle these differences in blood pressure?

■ The Walls of Blood Vessels

The walls of arteries and veins have structural differences that tell you something about how they respond to changes in blood pressure. Arteries have thick, muscular walls that stretch and contract a little each time your heart pumps blood into them. Arteries exert and withstand great pressure. Veins, on the other hand, have thinner and more elastic walls. Blood in veins and capillaries does not exert such great pressure.

In the next Investigate, you can learn about differences in these vessels.

Figure 3-5

The force of blood flowing through your circulatory system puts pressure on the walls of all your blood vessels—arteries, capillaries, and veins.

A This graph shows how the force of your blood puts less and less pressure on the walls of your blood vessels as it makes its round-trip journey from the heart and back to the heart.

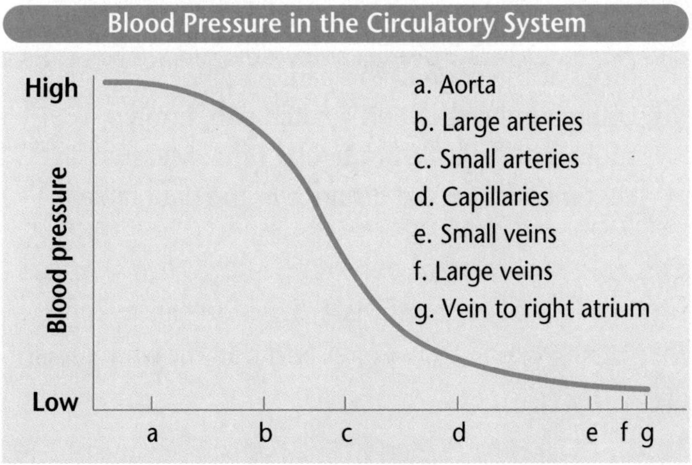

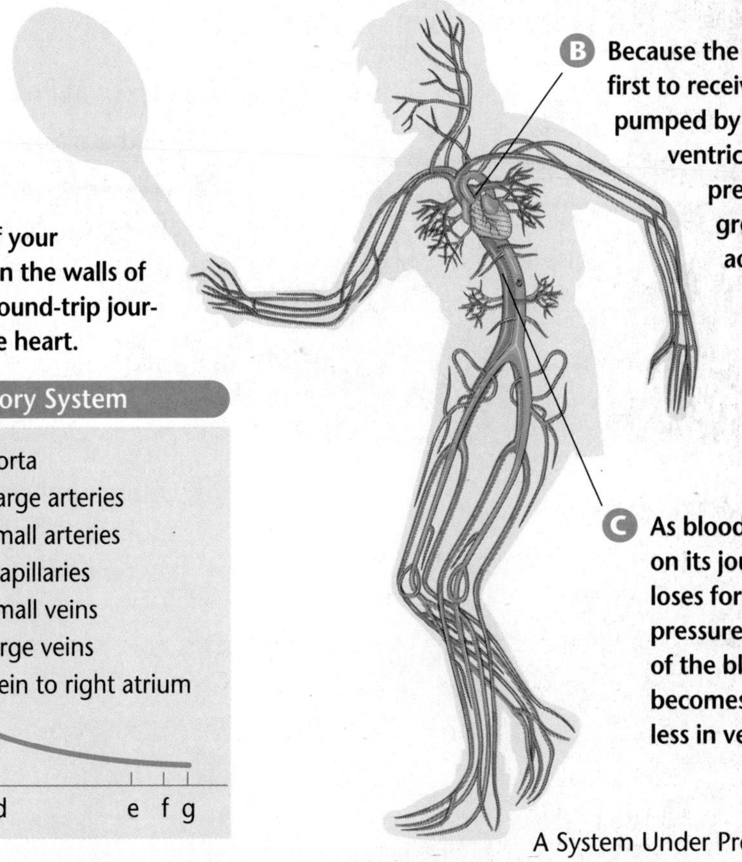

B Because the aorta is the first to receive blood pumped by the left ventricle, blood pressure is greatest on the aorta walls.

C As blood continues on its journey, it loses force. The pressure on the walls of the blood vessels becomes less and less in veins.

Blood Pressure in the Circulatory System

a. Aorta
b. Large arteries
c. Small arteries
d. Capillaries
e. Small veins
f. Large veins
g. Vein to right atrium

Blood Pressure

You've learned that blood travels throughout the circulatory system under pressure. In this activity, use a model to find out how the blood pressure in arteries and veins compares.

Problem
Is blood pressure in arteries and veins the same?

Materials
plastic squeeze bottle
water
two-holed rubber stopper
pan or sink
meterstick
glass or hard plastic tubing
flexible plastic tubing

Safety Precautions

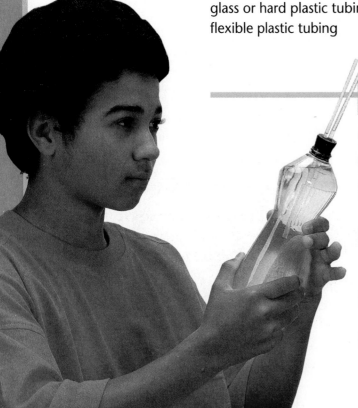

What To Do

1. *In your Journal*, make a copy of the data table.
2. Fill the plastic squeeze bottle with water.
3. Insert the rubber stopper and tube assembly into the plastic bottle.
4. *Predict* from which tube the water will squirt farther when you squeeze the bottle. One tube is hard, and one tube is flexible.
5. Lay the bottle on its side with the ends of the tubes at the edge of the pan.
6. Using a meterstick and a catch pan, firmly squeeze the plastic bottle one time. Measure, in centimeters. Record distance in the data table.

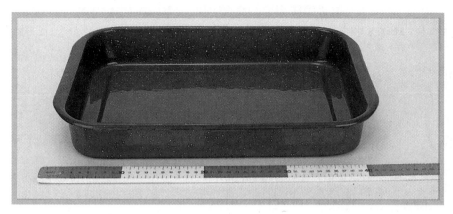

A

6 Repeat Steps 2 through 5 two more times, using the same amount of force each time.

7 *Calculate* the average distance water squirted from each tube. (Add the three distances and divide the total by 3.) Record this in the data table.

Data and Observations		
Trial	Distance Water Squirts (cm)	
	Hard tube	Flexible tube
1		
2		
3		
Total		
Average		

Analyzing

1. Which tube squirted water further?

2. What body organ does the plastic bottle represent?

3. What body liquid does the water represent?

4. Which tube was under higher pressure?

5. Which tube was under lower pressure?

Concluding and Applying

6. The walls of arteries are more muscular, but less elastic, than veins. Which tube represents an artery, and which represents a vein?

7. Based upon this model *compare and contrast* blood pressure in arteries and veins.

8. **Going Further** How might blood pressure in arteries and veins compare if both had the same wall structure?

Going Against Gravity

Have you ever wondered how blood gets from your feet to your heart? It has to move against the force of gravity, doesn't it? In Chapter 1, you learned that there is a gravitational force that pulls things toward Earth. Because of gravity and because pressure is lower in veins, blood can collect in veins and enlarge them. Without help, the blood in veins wouldn't make it back to the heart. How does blood return to the heart?

Valves in Veins

Blood in veins receives some help from one-way valves, similar to the valves in your heart. As you can see in **Figure 3-6**, the one-way valves in your veins stop the blood from flowing backward. If there is a backward movement of blood, the pressure of the blood itself closes the valves. The veins in your legs contain the greatest number of valves. How is this helpful?

Muscle Power

Blood in veins also receives help getting back to the heart from the skeletal muscles in your body as they contract. When the muscles surround-

Physics CONNECTION

The Physics of Blood Pressure Measurement

A sphygmomanometer and a stethoscope are used to measure blood pressure.

Have you ever had your blood pressure measured? If so, then you've had the cuff of an instrument called a *sphygmomanometer* (sfig moh muh NAHM uh ter) wrapped around your upper arm. The prefix *sphygmo-* comes from the Greek word *sphygmos*, meaning pulse. A manometer is a tube partly filled with a liquid such as mercury. Mercury is used to measure gas pressure. How does a sphygmomanometer work?

Taking Blood Pressure

To take blood pressure, the rubber bulb is squeezed until the air pressure inside the cuff is greater than the blood pressure inside the arm artery. As you would guess, when this happens the artery walls collapse, temporarily stopping the flow of blood.

Then the air pressure inside the cuff is slowly reduced by allowing the cuff to deflate. When air pressure becomes less than blood pressure inside the artery, blood surges through the artery again in a pulsating fashion. The pressure at which ing veins contract, they exert pressure on the veins and push blood along toward the heart.

Figure 3-6

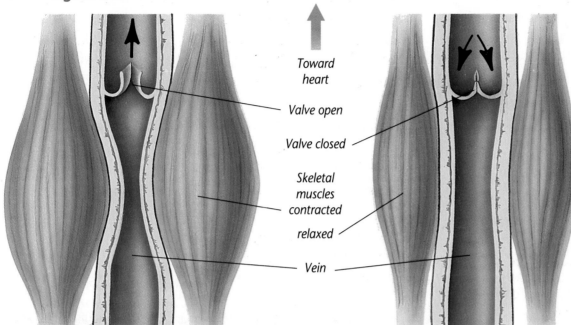

Toward heart

Valve open

Valve closed

Skeletal muscles
contracted
relaxed

Vein

When muscles surrounding veins contract, they squeeze the veins, forcing the blood within to move forward. One-way valves keep the blood moving to the heart.

blood flow resumes is called the systolic pressure. It is the pressure exerted when the left ventricle contracts.

As the pressure in the cuff is further reduced, blood moves through the artery freely. The pressure at which blood can move through the artery is the diastolic pressure.

As you can see from this procedure, blood pressure is not really being measured—air pressure inside the cuff is measured! Blood pressure is measured only indirectly.

Healthy Signs

In a healthy young person, systolic pressure is about 110-120 mm Hg, and diastolic pressure is about 70-80 mm Hg. What does this mean? Hg is the symbol for the element mercury. Millimeters of mercury refers to the pressure needed to

raise a column of mercury up to a certain level. Therefore, normal systolic blood pressure raises a column of mercury 120 mm, and normal diastolic blood pressure raises a column of mercury 80 mm.

What Do You Think?

Find out why mercury is used and not water or some other fluid. How is mercury different from most other fluids?

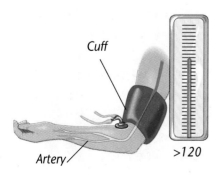

Cuff

Artery

>120

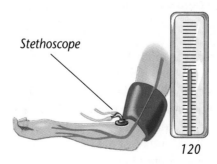

Stethoscope

120

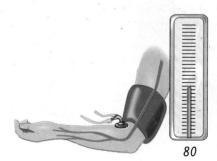

80

Blood Pressure in Other Closed Systems

As you recall from Section 3-1, reptiles, fish, amphibians, and mammals all have closed circulatory systems where a heart pumps blood through a continuous loop of blood vessels. But not all closed circulatory systems are the same. There are differences in the structure of the heart and blood vessels among these animals. These differences tell you something about the lifestyle of the organism and its needs. These differences also affect blood pressure and the efficiency with which oxygen and nutrients are supplied to cells.

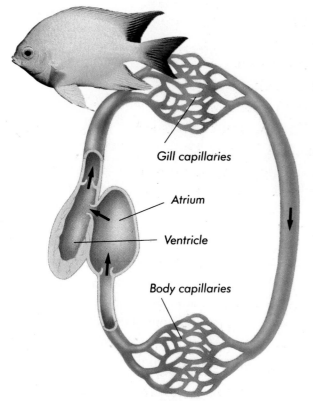

Gill capillaries

Atrium

Ventricle

Body capillaries

Figure 3-7

Fish hearts have only two chambers, an atrium and a ventricle. The atrium is the pumping chamber. Blood pumped by a fish's ventricle flows through a single loop with two capillary networks before it returns to the heart.

A Blood carrying carbon dioxide is pumped from the ventricle and travels through the network of capillaries at the gills. Here the blood releases carbon dioxide and picks up oxygen from the water.

B The blood, now rich with oxygen, continues to the second network of capillaries, which supplies the body cells. Here blood leaves oxygen and nutrients and picks up carbon dioxide and wastes from the body cells. The blood returns and a new cycle begins.

Figure 3-8

The circulatory system of frogs and most other amphibians is powered by a heart with three chambers—two atria that collect blood and a ventricle that is the main pumping organ.

A The left atrium receives blood rich with oxygen from the lungs, and the right atrium receives blood rich with carbon dioxide from the body cells.

B Blood from both atria empty into the ventricle. The ventricle contracts and sends blood in two directions. Even though the atria share the same ventricle, most of the oxygen-rich blood moves on to the body and most of the oxygen-poor blood flows to the lungs.

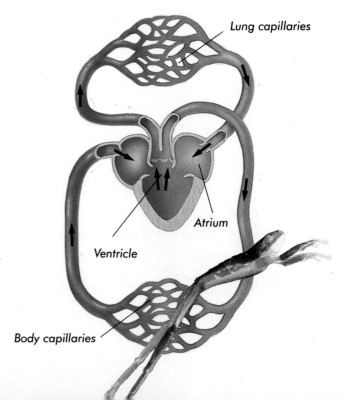

Lung capillaries

Atrium

Ventricle

Body capillaries

Figure 3-9

Birds have a four-chambered heart that works just as your four-chambered heart works. The two sides of the heart are entirely separate. There is no mixing of blood. The right side of the heart pumps blood only to the lungs, and the left side of the heart pumps blood only to the body.

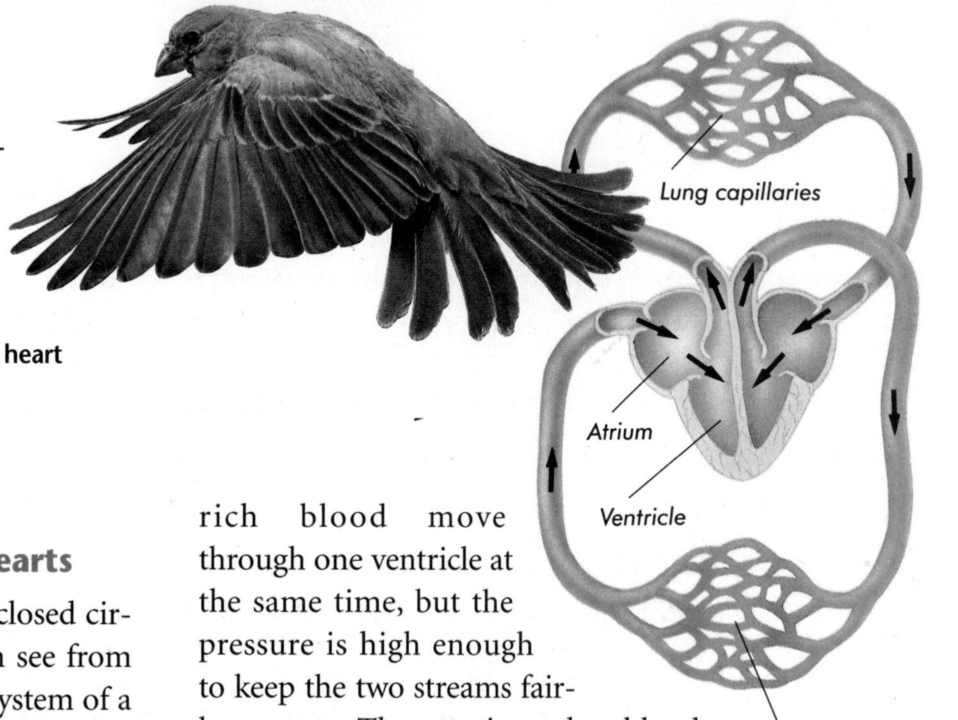

Lung capillaries

Atrium

Ventricle

Body capillaries

■ Two- and Three-Chambered Hearts

Fish have a very simple closed circulatory system. As you can see from **Figure 3-7**, the circulatory system of a fish consists of a two-chambered heart and a single loop of blood vessels. In a fish, pressure builds as blood moves into the atrium by suction, and then into the ventricle. Once the ventricle contracts, pressure drops and the body receives blood under low pressure. Blood pressure drops off as blood moves into the numerous narrow capillaries in the gills. Blood moves slowly as it passes to the body organs in these animals who have low energy requirements. **Figure 3-8** shows circulation in amphibians such as frogs. Oxygen-poor and oxygen-rich blood move through one ventricle at the same time, but the pressure is high enough to keep the two streams fairly separate. The one time when blood does mix in a frog is when the animal is submerged. Then, oxygen tends to move into the blood through its skin, not through its lungs.

■ Four-Chambered Hearts

In birds and in mammals like yourself, not only is blood kept separate in the heart because the ventricles are separated, but there are pressure differences as well. Blood moving to the lungs is at a very low pressure, while blood moving out to the body is under a much higher pressure.

check your UNDERSTANDING

1. Explain how the force of gravity and lower blood pressure are handled in veins.
2. If you receive a serious injury and cut a vein, the blood would flow out smoothly. How would you expect blood to flow out of a cut artery? Explain your answer.
3. Diagram the hearts of fish, amphibians, and birds. Label the following: atria, ventricles, direction of blood flow and pressure differences.
4. **Apply** Explain how the functions of lungs and gills are related.

Disorders in Circulation

3-3

Section Objectives
In this section, you will

- Describe the role of fatty deposits in heart disease.
- Relate lifestyles to high blood pressure.

Key Terms
atherosclerosis
hypertension

Circulation to the Heart

The term *heart disease* is used to describe any of the health problems that affect the heart. Your heart functions all your life to keep your body supplied with nutrients and oxygen, but what keeps the heart muscle itself functioning? How do your heart cells get the oxygen and nutrients they need? What happens when these materials aren't supplied?

Figure 3-10A shows blood is supplied to the heart by several coronary arteries.

Heart disease can occur when problems arise in the coronary vessels. One leading cause of heart disease is **atherosclerosis** (a thuh roh skluh ROH suhs), a condition in which fatty deposits and calcium build up inside the coronary arteries. **Figure 3-10B-D** shows the progressive stages of atherosclerosis in a coronary artery.

As heart muscle tissue dies, scar tissue forms. The ability of the heart muscle to contract and relax is severely affected.

Figure 3-10

A Like the rest of the body, the heart receives the oxygen and nutrients it needs and rids itself of waste by way of blood flowing through blood vessels. On the diagram, you can see the coronary arteries, which nourish the heart.

B This cross section of a healthy coronary artery shows a clear, wide-open pathway through which blood easily flows.

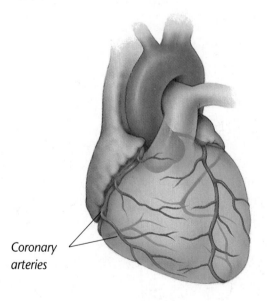

Coronary arteries

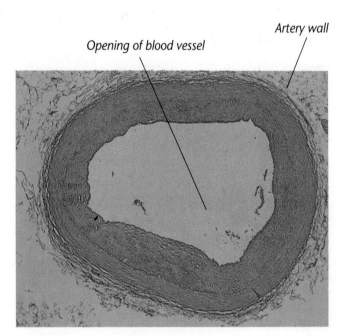

Artery wall

Opening of blood vessel

Find Out! ACTIVITY

What happens to liquid flow in a clogged tube?

Model a blocked artery to show its effect on blood flow.

What To Do

1. Insert a dropper full of mineral oil into a piece of plastic tubing.
2. Squeeze the oil through the tube.
3. Observe how much oil comes out the tube.
4. Next, refill the dropper and squeeze oil through a piece of plastic tubing that has been clogged with cotton.

5. How much oil comes out of the clogged tube?

Conclude and Apply

1. *In your Journal*, explain how the addition of the cotton to the tube changed the way oil flowed through the tube.
2. How does this activity demonstrate what takes place when arteries become clogged?
3. What differences in pressure did you notice in the squeeze bulb?

As you observed in this activity, clogging the plastic tube with cotton severely restricted the flow of oil through it. In the same manner, fatty deposits clog arteries so that blood is restricted from flowing. When this occurs, the heart muscle cells begin to die.

C Here the blood-flow pathway has been narrowed by a buildup of fatty deposits. Blood flow is slowed. The heart muscle does not get enough oxygen and nutrients to do its work. The muscle begins to die.

D If the deposit continues to build, blood flow through the artery may stop. The person will suffer a heart attack.

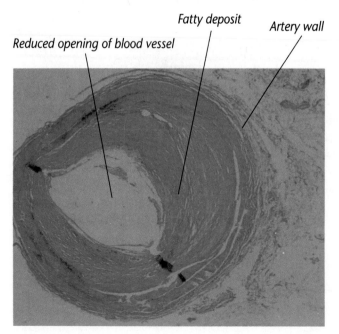

Reduced opening of blood vessel
Fatty deposit
Artery wall

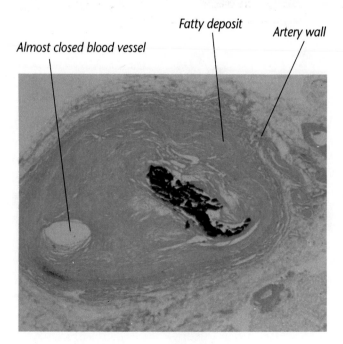

Almost closed blood vessel
Fatty deposit
Artery wall

When Heart Rates Change

Heart rates and blood pressure change for many reasons. Occasional increases in blood pressure are normal. During strenuous activity, your heart beats faster and your breathing rate increases, thus increasing oxygen delivery to your body cells. This increased heart rate is absolutely necessary if your circulatory system is to be able to pick up and deliver the additional oxygen. These activities also increase your blood pressure for a short time. After resting awhile, heart rate and blood pressure in a healthy person return to normal.

■ Hypertension

In some people, however, blood pressure remains high after exercise, or even without exercise. A disorder of the circulatory system when blood pressure is higher than normal is known as **hypertension**, or high blood pressure.

Although the exact causes of most hypertension are not known, diets high in fat or sodium are linked to it. One known cause of hypertension is atherosclerosis. Clogged arteries cause the pressure within a blood vessel to increase by reducing the elasticity of the artery walls and narrowing the pathway of blood flow. This extra pressure puts a strain on the heart, which has to beat faster in an attempt to keep oxygen-rich blood flowing to the body tissues. Many people suffer from hypertension—as many as 50 million people in the United States. However, many of them are never aware of it. Why is high blood pressure dangerous? The extra pressure exerted on your blood vessels is transferred to the organs of your body, and they begin to suffer damage over time.

Figure 3-11

While skating, the blood pressure of these rollerbladers is higher than usual. Blood pressure varies in relationship to activity. If you bike, swim, or shovel heavy snow, your muscle cells use up oxygen at a faster rate than when you are resting.

Your muscle cells require an increased oxygen-rich blood supply. In response to this need for more oxygen, your heart beats faster. When your heart beats faster, your blood pressure temporarily goes up.

Be Good to Your Heart

One of the best things you can do for your circulatory system is to exercise regularly. But not all exercise is the same. To benefit your circulation, you need to regularly participate in walking or aerobic exercises, such as running, swimming, bicycling, or cross-country skiing. Aerobic exercises promote the efficient use of oxygen by your body. When you exercise, your lungs take in more oxygen, and your heart muscle becomes stronger. It then pumps more blood with each beat. This, in turn, allows your heart rate to decrease while still sending the same amount of oxygen-containing blood into your arteries.

Figure 3-12

A Doing regular aerobic exercise such as cycling over a period of several weeks increases your heart's ability to pump blood. Your heart, even at rest, will send out more blood with each contraction.

The increased flow of blood to the heart provides more oxygen. The heart is able to beat at a slower rate and still send the body cells all the oxygen-rich blood they need.

B For exercise to be both safe and effective, it should raise and keep your heartbeat rate to a level that ranges between 70 percent and 85 percent of your maximum heartbeat rate. A rate lower than 70 percent will not help you develop a fit heart and lungs. A higher rate can be dangerous to your heart. Use the chart to calculate your target pulse range during exercise.

How to Find Your Heart Rate Range

1. Subtract your age from 220 to find your maximum heart rate.
   For example, if you are 12 years old,
   220 − 12 = 208.
2. Multiply your maximum heart rate by 0.85 to find the top of your range.
   208 × 0.85 = 177
3. Multiply your maximum heart rate by 0.70 to find the bottom of your range.
   208 × 0.70 = 146

check your UNDERSTANDING

1. What are the risk factors of heart disease?
2. Explain how atherosclerosis can lead to hypertension.
3. **Apply** How can the risk factors of heart disease be turned around or prevented?

Science and Society

Changing a Nation's Lifestyle

In 1980, a United States Department of Health and Human Services report recommended that people in the United States cut back on the fat and fatty foods they consume in order to reduce their cholesterol levels and reduce the risk of heart attack.

A Country on the Move

Because aerobic exercise was found to lower cholesterol levels, some Americans have changed the way they exercise and how much they exercise. Many people participate in programs that involve brisk walking, running, bicycling, and swimming, as well as the familiar dance-type aerobics. The Bicycling Institute of America, a group that monitors and promotes the sport of bicycling in the United States, estimates that in 1990 there were 25 million adults bicycling regularly (at least once a week) compared to only 10 million in 1983.

It's Never Too Late

Ruth Anderson, pictured here, is a living example of the fact that it's never too late to begin new ways of moving. Ruth, a nuclear chemist, began running at age 44. She won the women's division for her age group of the first marathon she competed in. Physical and mental endurance have enabled her to participate in nearly 100 marathons and compete in numerous ultramarathons.

CAREER connection

Dieticians plan menus and supervise food preparation using the principles of good nutrition. They deal with dietetics—the relationship between food and health. Dieticians work in hospitals, schools, restaurants, and the food services of businesses. They have a bachelor's degree and have studied nutrition, foods, institution management, biology, and chemistry.

What Do You Think?

Find out how many people you know actually participate in regular exercise. Survey people to find out why some people resist regular exercise.

HISTORY CONNECTION

"Sewed Up His Heart"

"Sewed Up His Heart" was the newspaper headline on the day in 1893 that Dr. Daniel Hale Williams performed the world's first open-heart surgery. Williams (1856-1931) believed he had no other choice but to operate when a man with a severe knife wound to the chest was brought into Chicago's Provident Hospital.

Surgical Breakthrough

Williams's surgery involved cutting and suturing the pericardium—the sac that surrounds the heart. This marked the first time a surgeon had ever entered the chest cavity. The risk of infection while the chest cavity was open during surgery was great. Williams's patient recovered completely.

It would be many years before open-heart surgery became common. Over the next fifty years, fewer than ten of these operations were recorded. The first woman to operate on the heart was Dr. Myra Logan (1908-1977), an

African American physician at Harlem Hospital in New York.

In addition to their surgical achievements, Drs. Williams and Logan made important contributions toward advancing medical practices for African Americans. Dr. Williams had founded Provident Hospital in 1891. Provident started one of the first training programs in the country for minority nurses and successfully treated the sick and injured of Chicago for nearly a century.

Dr. Logan graduated from New York Medical College in 1933. In the course of her medical career, she researched the early detection of breast cancer and pioneered the idea of group practice so that patients could benefit from a variety of services in one place.

You Try It!

Write and design a pamphlet directed toward increasing student awareness of preventive heart health.

HOW IT WORKS

How Does Water Move in a Plant?

Most of the water that moves about in a plant is supplied through the roots of the plant. Have you ever wondered how water gets to the top of a tree? You have learned that your body has certain adaptations that assist blood in its movement against gravity. What adaptations do plants have that enable water to move upward?

Vessels in Plants

Water and nutrients move about in plants for the same reasons that blood circulates in an animal body. Raw materials and food need to be supplied to the cells in the roots, stems, and leaves of a plant just as your arms, legs, and internal organs are supplied with the materials they need. However, if you were to dissect a plant stem, you wouldn't find a heart, nor would you find arteries, capillaries, and veins. You would find that plants do contain a system of transport vessels called xylem and phloem. Xylem is a type of tissue in plants that carries water and nutrients from roots to leaves. Phloem is a type of tissue that carries food made in leaves to other parts of the plant.

The Basic Plan

The basic plan for the movement of water in plants is that water moves up through xylem cells in the stem and out of the plant through openings in the leaves called stomata. The water molecules stick together in the xylem in a continuous threadlike stream such as in the diagram to the left. Water loss is controlled by the stomata, which close up as temperature rises and at night. Water movement up the stem is then slowed.

You Try It!

Make a model to demonstrate how water moves up in a plant. Roll a piece of paper toweling and dip it into about 2 cm of water. *In your Journal*, describe how water moves in the paper towel. What happens to the water when it reaches the far end of the paper towel? How is this model an example of how water moves in a plant?

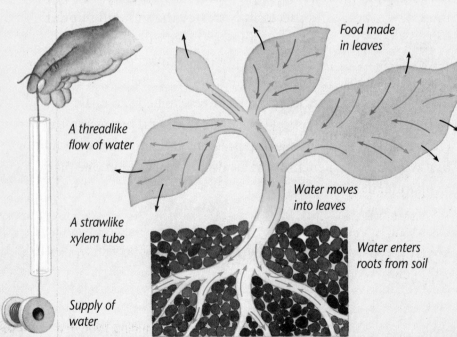

A threadlike flow of water

A strawlike xylem tube

Supply of water

Food made in leaves

Water moves into leaves

Water enters roots from soil

Teens in SCIENCE

Chill Out—It's Good For You

Your teacher has placed the final exam face-down on your desk. You've studied for weeks and feel confident that you will do well. So why does your heart begin to beat a little faster as you turn the test over?

The Stress Factor

According to 16-year-old high school junior Tamika Walker, the answer is stress.

"Some people think that teenagers don't feel stress as deeply as adults. But that's just not true," Tamika said. To prove her point, Tamika conducted a survey to measure the level of stress reported by classmates at her high school in Currie, North Carolina. She wrote and distributed a questionnaire asking the teenagers to rate their stress levels under different types of situations, both positive and negative.

Results Based on Data

"The results of the survey showed that there is a lot of stress in most teenagers' lives. Of course, big things like a divorce or a death in the family scored the highest. But I was surprised to discover that even smaller events, like getting a bad grade on a test or losing a textbook, scored high."

Tamika also researched the physical effects of stress. "It's a chain of events," she explained. "Stress affects hormones, which in turn affect the pituitary gland, which eventually begins to wear down a person's immune system. That's why some people get sick when they are under a lot of stress. In fact, my survey showed that kids who had high stress scores also had the highest numbers of sick days. I think that it's time that someone started teaching kids how important it is to learn how to relax."

Sharing the Results

Tamika entered her report in a regional science fair. Tamika's report was the most widely read exhibit in the fair. "It makes me feel good to know that so many kids took the time to look over the report," Tamika said. "It's time for us to begin learning everything we can about our bodies. After all, the more we know, the better we are likely to feel."

You Try It!

Design a survey to test whether stressful factors are responsible for absenteeism on a certain day of the week.

Review the statements below about the big ideas presented in this chapter, and try to answer the questions. Then, re-read your answers to the Did You Ever Wonder questions at the beginning of the chapter. *In your Journal*, write a paragraph about how your understanding of the big ideas in the chapter has changed.

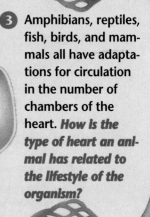

① Circulatory systems deliver nutrients and oxygen to body cells and remove wastes, such as carbon dioxide. *What does this statement tell you about the importance of a healthy heart?*

② Both open and closed circulatory systems exist in animal groups. Circulation and body structures that take in oxygen are usually closely related. *Name three organs that take up oxygen in various organisms.*

③ Amphibians, reptiles, fish, birds, and mammals all have adaptations for circulation in the number of chambers of the heart. *How is the type of heart an animal has related to the lifestyle of the organism?*

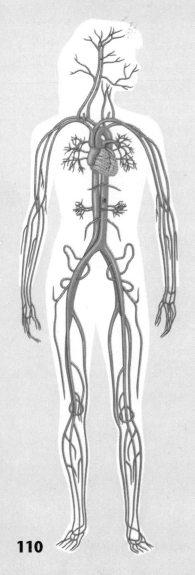

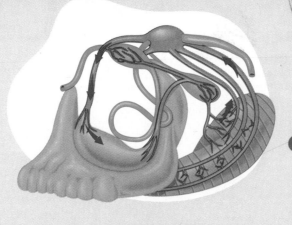

④ Diseases resulting in clogged arteries, such as the one shown below, also affect body organs. *Why would damaged blood vessels affect the rest of the body systems?*

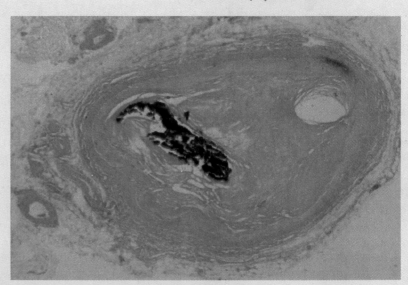

Using Key Science Terms

artery   hypertension
atherosclerosis   pulse
blood pressure   vein
capillary

Answer the following questions using what you know about the science terms.

1. Explain the difference between arteries, veins, and capillaries.
2. How is hypertension related to the circulation of blood?
3. How does atherosclerosis affect arteries?
4. Describe what causes the pulse felt in various parts of your body.
5. How is blood pressure different in arteries and veins?

Understanding Ideas

Answer the following questions in your Journal *using complete sentences.*

1. Compare and contrast open and closed circulatory systems.
2. What is the relationship between oxygen and blood?
3. Why is hypertension a serious health problem?
4. How does availability of oxygen in the blood of an animal with a three-chambered heart differ from the availability of oxygen in the blood of an animal with a four-chambered heart?
5. Ventricles have thicker walls than atria. What does this adaptation tell you about the work each type of chamber does?

Developing Skills

Use your understanding of the concepts developed in each chapter to answer each of the following questions.

1. **Concept Map** Complete the following spider concept map on the circulatory system.

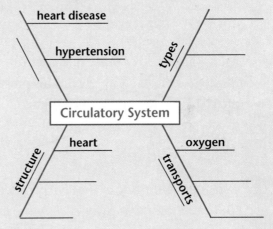

2. **Design an Experiment** Refer to the Investigate on page 92 to design an experiment to increase an earthworm's heart rate.
3. **Predicting** Take your at-rest pulse as in the Explore activity on page 91. If your health permits, run in place for two minutes. Check to see how long it takes the pulse to return to the at-rest rate. Then predict how long it would take to return to the at-rest rate if you ran for three minutes.
4. **Making and Using Graphs** Research the pulse rates of several different animals, including the earthworm from the Investigate on page 92. Make a bar graph to compare these different pulse rates.
5. **Making and Using Graphs** The graph on the next page shows the pulse rate of a boy before, during, and after bicycling. When did the pulse rate increase most rapidly?

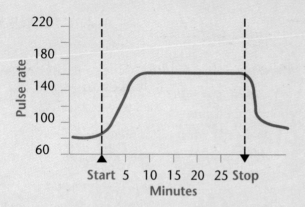

What was the boy's pulse rate after fifteen minutes of bicycling? How did his pulse rate change when he stopped biking?

Critical Thinking

Use your understanding of the concepts developed in the chapter to answer each of the following questions.

1. If a person becomes dehydrated, the lack of fluids decreases the volume of blood in the body. How would dehydration affect blood pressure and heart rate?
2. Larger, active organisms, like yourself, require oxygen to release energy for movement. Why is a closed circulatory system under pressure?
3. Imagine that you are designing an artificial heart. What three factors will your artificial heart have to have or do in order to work well in the body?
4. Doctors often recommend massage of the legs for people who cannot move about as a result of illness or injury. How is massage beneficial to circulation?

Problem Solving

Read the following problem and discuss your answers in a brief paragraph.

A special device that attaches to your wrist can be used to constantly measure your pulse rate and display the number like a digital clock. If you were to wear one of these devices for 24 hours, when do you think you would find your pulse rate the lowest? When would your pulse rate be the highest? Why would your pulse rate change during a 24-hour period?

CONNECTING IDEAS

Discuss each of the following in a brief paragraph.

1. **Theme—Scale and Structure** Explain how a narrowed blood vessel affects the pressure of blood within it.
2. **Theme—Systems and Interactions** Using your knowledge of the force of gravity, explain the importance of the valves in the circulation of blood in your legs.
3. **A Closer Look** Suggest some benefits of using an artificial valve instead of one from another organism.
4. **Physics Connection** Explain how a sphygmomanometer works.
5. **How It Works** Describe an adaptation that plants have for conserving water.

Forces in Action

In this unit, you investigated forces producing motions and changes of motion. You learned about Newton's Laws of Motion and how everyday events, such as picking up a bowling ball, are affected by the laws of motion.

You learned how these same kinds of forces within Earth produce earthquakes and volcanic activity. You also learned that forces within your body cause movement of blood and that water moves up through a plant under force.

Try the exercises and activity that follow. They will challenge you to use and apply some of the ideas you learned in this unit.

CONNECTING IDEAS

1. Sometimes when you are in the car, on an elevator, or on a ride at an amusement park your stomach "drops" as you go down a hill. Explain why that might happen.

2. Why do movements of only two meters along the San Andreas fault cause such great forces to be generated that the ground can vibrate for many miles around?

Exploring Further ACTIVITY

Going Up? How does water move up in a plant?

What To Do

1. Obtain a hand lens and a stalk of celery with leaves. Make sure that it has been in a glass of water with blue or red food coloring for several hours.

2. Where do you see color in the stalk? What does this tell you about where water circulates in a plant?

3. Do leaves have anything to do with how water moves up in plants? Design an experiment to show what happens to the movement of water through a plant (a) in light, (b) in the dark, (c) if the leaves are cut off, and (d) if you coat the leaves with something.

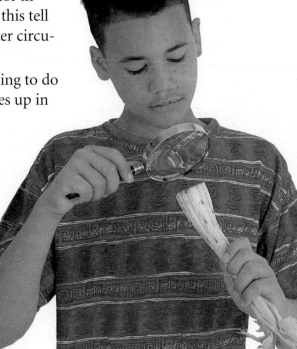

UNIT 2

ENERGY AT WORK

Where would you be without energy? No work would get done and no play either. In fact, nothing would happen. As you might guess, energy is vital to everything that happens in the world around you. This unit will help you understand the energy connection.

114

Try It!

You know that you need energy to do work. But did you k[n]... you can invent devices to help make work easier? What might be some of the advantages of devices that make work easier? What might be some of the disadvantages?

What To Do

1. Suppose your textbook drops to the floor beside a table. Think of some different ways you could raise the book from the floor to the table. Obviously you could simply reach down and pick it up.

2. Suppose your textbook were too heavy to pick up. Diagram three ways you could raise the book to the table without lifting it directly with your hands.

3. Test one of your ideas.

Try It Again

After you've learned more about work, energy, and machines in this unit, identify any simple machines in your diagrams.

CHAPTER 4

Work and Energy

✓ If a football could store energy?

✓ Where energy goes after you use it?

✓ Why a ball bounces lower each time it hits the floor?

Before you begin to study work and energy, think about these questions and answer them *in your Journal*. When you finish the chapter, compare your Journal write-up with what you have learned.

When you hear the words work and energy, what do you think of? You might say that work is what you do at school or at a job. If you take books home with you, you call it homework. But when do you think that you're not working?

When you're enjoying some sport or activity, it's usually too much fun to be called work. For most of us, work consists of the things we have to do. The things that we do for our own pleasure we call recreation or play.

What about energy? What is energy? You might say that you're full of energy. Television advertisements tell you that a certain food will give you energy. It takes energy to do just about anything. What's the relationship between work and energy?

▶ *In the activity on the next page, begin to explore what makes work work!*

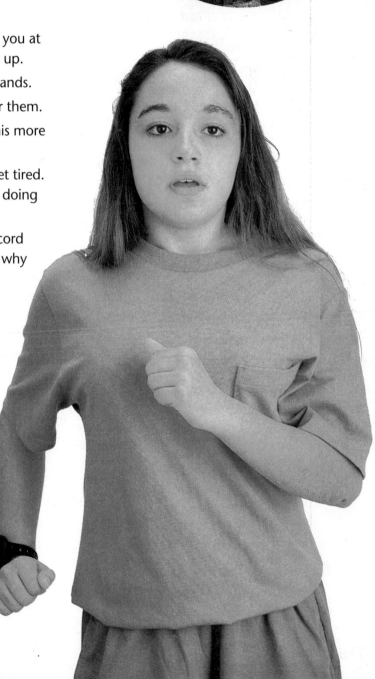

What is work?

Believe it or not, both weeding the garden and playing basketball are work! What makes some activities work? Are all activities work? Have you done work every time your muscles get tired? Begin to explore work with the activity below.

What To Do

1. Stand up and hold your arms out in front of you at waist level, with your hands together, palms up.

2. Have a classmate stack two books on your hands.

3. Raise the books to shoulder level, then lower them.

4. Now try raising them above your head. Is this more work than raising them to shoulder level?

5. Hold the books at shoulder level until you get tired. Are you exerting force? Do you think you're doing work on the books?

6. *In your Journal,* answer the questions and record your observations. Also record your ideas of why some activities are work and others aren't.

Work

Section Objectives

- Define work.
- Calculate work done on an object.

Key Terms

work

Work, Force, and Motion

In the Explore at the beginning of the chapter, you lifted books and then held them still. Were both of these actions work? Let's explore again.

Explore! ACTIVITY

Is it work?

What To Do

1. Put several books into a backpack and place it on the floor.

2. Now, pick it up and put it on the table. Did that action take energy? Do you think you did work on the backpack?

3. Now, hold your hands out in front of you and have another student hand you the backpack. Hold it in place for 10 to 20 seconds. Did you use energy? Did you do work on the backpack?

4. Record your observations and answers *in your Journal.* Also write a paragraph using this activity to explain what you think work means.

What was the difference between the two actions in the Explore activity you just did? In the first, there was motion. You moved the backpack from the floor to the table. In the second, there was no motion. You held the backpack in one position.

What did the actions have in common? For both actions you used energy, and you exerted an upward force on the pack.

In the first case, there was both force and motion. In the second case, there was force but no motion. For work to be done on an object, both force and motion must be present. If there is force but no motion, there is no work. If there is motion but no force, there is no work. See **Figure 4-1** for an example of this.

Figure 4-1

When the girl releases the flying disk she stops doing work on the disk.

Defining Work

In the Explore activity, you transferred energy to the backpack as you picked it up. In scientific terms, **work** is energy transferred through both force and motion. Since there was no motion when you held the backpack steady, no work was done.

For work to be done, one more condition must be met. There must be force, there must be motion, and the motion must be in the direction of the force. **Figure 4-3** shows you when an action can be considered work. When you pick up an object, you exert an upward force, and the object moves in an upward direction. This is work. If you then carry the object across the room while holding it level, you are still exerting an upward force, but the movement is at right angles to that force. In scientific terms, no work is

Figure 4-2

Ⓐ These people are rushing to their jobs. Scientifically speaking, they are already working.

Ⓑ Their muscles exert an upward force to climb the stairs. Force and motion in the direction of the force are required for an action to be called work.

Figure 4-3

Ⓐ Sothila pushed a box of old records forward. The box slid along the floor straight in front of him all the way across the room. As he pushed, did Sothila do work on the box? Why?

Ⓑ Sothila bent down, grabbed hold of the box and lifted it from the floor. As he lifted, did he do work on this box? Why?

Ⓒ Holding the box level, Sothila carried it across the room. Did he do work on the box? Why?

SKILLBUILDER

Comparing and Contrasting

Compare and contrast the everyday meaning of the word *work* and the scientific definition of that term. Give examples of work in the everyday sense that would not be considered work in the scientific sense. If you need help, refer to the **Skill Handbook** on page 642.

done on the object as you walk.

Work is done when an object moves while there is a force acting in the direction of motion. The amount of work done is found by multiplying the force times the distance

that the object moves. The mathematical formula is:

$$W = F \times d$$

W means work done, F means force in the direction of motion, and d means distance moved.

When force is expressed in newtons (N), and distance in meters (m), the unit for work is the newton·meter (N·m). The N·m is also called a joule (J). One joule is the work done when a force of one newton acts through a distance of one meter.

Here's an example of how to calculate work. A student's backpack weighs 10 N. She lifts it from the floor to a table 0.75 m high. How much work is done on the backpack of books?

$$W = F \times d$$
$$W = 10\ N \times 0.75\ m$$
$$W = 7.5\ N\cdot m\ or\ 7.5\ J$$

We've said that work is transferring energy through motion. If a machine uses fuel and does work, it loses energy. Where does that energy go? What forms does it take? As you can see, there's much more to learn about energy and its relationship to work and motion.

Figure 4-4

Amad lifted a stack of books that weigh 40 N from the floor to a shelf 1.75 m high. How much work did Amad do on the books? You can find the answer by using the equation Work = Force × distance.

check your UNDERSTANDING

1. If you went outside and pushed against the school building as hard as you could for five minutes, how much work would you do? Explain your answer.

2. While performing a chin-up, Carlos raises himself 0.8 m. If Carlos weighs 600 N, how much work does he do? If Carlos holds the chin-up for 10 seconds before letting himself down, how much more work does he do?

3. **Apply** Jill is doing chin-ups on the same bar as Carlos. Jill weighs only 400 N. Compare the amount of work Jill does in doing 10 chin-ups to the work Carlos does in doing 10 chin-ups.

4-2 ◆ Forms of Energy

Energy of Motion: Kinetic Energy

Look at **Figure 4-5** that shows a sailing iceboat with steel runners. Imagine that a wind pushes on the sail in one direction with a constant force of 400 N. When a constant, unbalanced force pushes on an object, what happens?

You learned in Chapter 1 that a force causes an object to accelerate. The longer the force acts, the faster the iceboat will be going. Say that the iceboat travels 20 m before the wind stops blowing. The wind accelerated

the iceboat by doing (20 m × 400 N) = 8000 joules of work ($F \times d = W$).

What was the difference in the iceboat after the work was done? Before the work was done, the iceboat was at rest. Energy was transferred from the wind to the iceboat. Work resulted in the iceboat gaining speed.

Section Objectives
- Describe how work can produce kinetic energy, potential energy, and thermal energy.
- Specify that energy is transferred when work is done.

Key Terms

kinetic energy
potential energy

Figure 4-5

Iceboats travel on energy from wind. Iceboats can skim across ice at speeds greater than 160 km per hour.

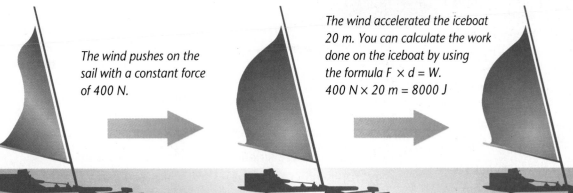

The wind pushes on the sail with a constant force of 400 N.

The wind accelerated the iceboat 20 m. You can calculate the work done on the iceboat by using the formula F × d = W.
400 N × 20 m = 8000 J

A A calm has left this iceboat at rest.

B A gust of wind blowing with a force of 400 N comes up from behind the iceboat. The sail catches the wind and the iceboat accelerates. The iceboat travels 20 m.

C The wind transferred energy to the iceboat by doing work on it. As the iceboat moved, it gained kinetic energy—the energy of motion.

You could say that the iceboat is given energy of motion. This energy of motion is called **kinetic energy**. You can see common activities that involve kinetic energy in **Figures 4-6** and **4-7**.

The kinetic energy of a moving object may be calculated using a formula. It is

$$E_k = \frac{1}{2}mv^2$$

where E_k is kinetic energy in joules, m is mass in kg, and v is velocity in m/s. Kinetic energy is measured in the same unit as work—joules. The How Do We Know explains how this equation is derived. The amount of kinetic energy an object possesses can't be greater than the amount of work that was done on the object. You'll see why later in the chapter.

Figure 4-6

A The baseball has a mass of 0.15 kg. Kesia sends the ball flying by using the bat to do work on it. The speed of the ball as it leaves Kesia's bat is 20 m/s. To calculate the kinetic energy of the moving ball, apply the formula $E_k = \frac{1}{2}mv^2$.

B Start by substituting numbers for the symbols. You know the mass of the ball is 0.15 kg. The formula also calls for the ball's velocity, which is a measure of speed in a given direction. Because direction is not important here, you can use the ball's speed: 20 m/s.

C Now work the formula. Start by calculating the square of the velocity. Remember that the little dot means multiply.

$E_k = \frac{1}{2}mv^2 = \frac{1}{2} \cdot (0.15 \text{ kg}) \cdot (20 \text{ m/s})^2$
$E_k = \frac{1}{2} \cdot (0.15 \text{ kg}) \cdot (400 \text{ m}^2/\text{s}^2)$
$E_k = \frac{1}{2} \cdot 60 \text{ kg} \cdot \text{m}^2/\text{s}^2$
$E_k = 30 \text{ J}$

Figure 4-7

When it is moving down toward a nail, a hammerhead has a lot of kinetic energy. Once the head hits the nail, the hammer stops and no longer has any kinetic energy. Where does the energy go?

How Do We Know?

Kinetic Energy Equation

Where did the equation for kinetic energy come from? It comes from quantities that you are already familiar with. The work done on an object can appear as the object's kinetic energy. You'll remember that work equals force times distance ($W=Fd$). You also know that force equals mass times acceleration ($F=ma$) and distance equals the average velocity times time ($d=vt$). Finally, you know that acceleration is a change in velocity with time. You can combine all these relationships mathematically to get the equation for kinetic energy: $E_k=\frac{1}{2}mv^2$.

Energy of Position: Potential Energy

It's fairly easy to tell that a moving object has energy. But how can you tell if an object has energy when it isn't moving?

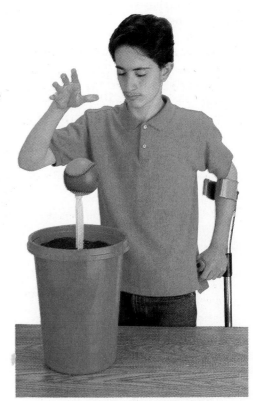

Explore! ACTIVITY

Does a softball have energy?

How can you tell if an object at rest has energy? You can explore this question in the activity.

What To Do

1. Hold a softball in your hand. Does it have any kinetic energy? Does it have any other kind of energy that you can tell?

2. Press a tent stake about halfway into a bucket of dirt.

3. Hold the softball about 1 m above the stake. What kind of energy will the ball have when you drop it?

4. Drop the ball onto the stake. How did the ball transfer its energy? Did the ball's energy perform work?

5. Lift the ball back up to about 1 m. Does the ball have the ability to do work, to produce change now? Does the ball have energy? If so, where did the energy come from?

6. Record your observations and answers *in your Journal.*

When you held the ball above the stake, it looked the same as it did on the ground. There was no obvious change in the ball and there was nothing to indicate that there was any energy in the ball. But as you saw, when you released the ball, it began to move toward Earth. The ball gained kinetic energy. Where did the energy come from? The only change in the ball was a change in its location. Energy was stored in the ball because of its position above the ground. Stored energy is called **potential energy**. **Figure 4-8** shows one example of potential energy in nature.

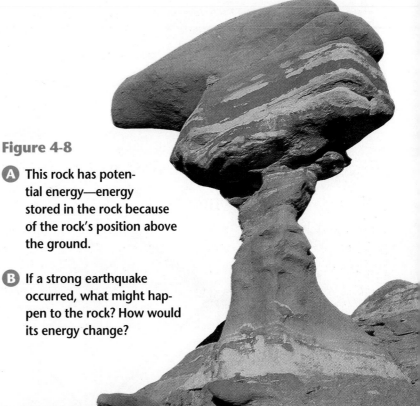

Figure 4-8

Ⓐ This rock has potential energy—energy stored in the rock because of the rock's position above the ground.

Ⓑ If a strong earthquake occurred, what might happen to the rock? How would its energy change?

■ Gravitational Potential Energy

In the Explore activity you did, where did the potential energy come from? Originally, the ball was on the ground. Did the ball have any potential energy when it was there? When you lifted the ball against the force of gravity, you did work against gravity and transferred some of your energy to the ball. The energy you transferred was stored in the ball as potential energy because of the ball's position above the ground. This kind of stored energy is gravitational potential energy. The force of gravity was able to act on the ball when you released it, increasing the ball's speed until it reached the ground. As the ball fell, the kinetic energy increased and the potential energy decreased. Just before the ball hit the stake, almost all of the ball's energy was kinetic. That kinetic energy did the work of driving the stake into the ground.

As you may have guessed, the higher you lift an object, the more potential energy it gains. Also, the more an object weighs, the more potential energy it gains as it is lifted. In each case, the ball will be capable of doing more work when it falls. Another way to think of this is that you must do work to lift the object

Figure 4-9

At some time, work was done on the roller coaster car to get it to the top of the hill. The work done is stored in the coaster car as gravitational potential energy.

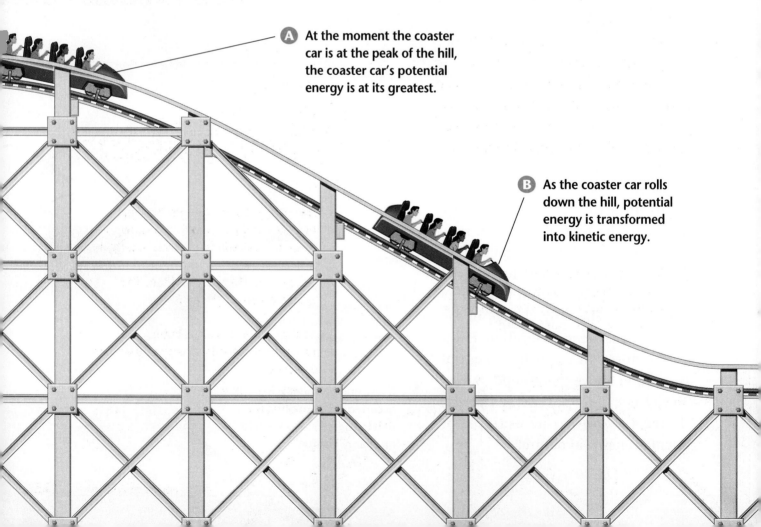

A At the moment the coaster car is at the peak of the hill, the coaster car's potential energy is at its greatest.

B As the coaster car rolls down the hill, potential energy is transformed into kinetic energy.

against gravity. The object then possesses the energy you used to do that work and, in turn, can do work as it falls back to Earth.

A roller coaster car at the top of a hill, as shown in **Figure 4-9**, is a great example of gravitational potential energy.

■ Calculating Gravitational Potential Energy

Gravitational potential energy is the work done in lifting something against the force of gravity. Work equals $F \times d$. When you lift something, the force you use–F–must equal the weight of the object. Therefore, gravitational potential energy–E_p–is given by:

$$E_p = W \times h,$$

where W is the object's weight and h is the distance lifted.

What is the relationship between the potential energy stored in a car at the top of a hill and the kinetic energy that it has when it reaches the bottom of the hill? Let's investigate this relationship in the following activity.

Figure 4-11

Which water slide would you climb to the top of if you wanted to gain the most gravitational potential energy? If a friend weighing 40 newtons more than you climbed the same slide, would his potential energy at the top of the slide be the same as yours? Why?

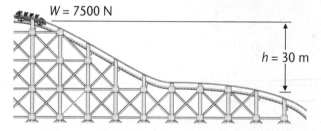

Figure 4-10

Ⓐ When using SI units, the gravitational potential energy of an object is expressed in joules. Gravitational potential energy is equal to the weight of the object multiplied by the height the object is lifted. The formula is stated $E_p = W \times h$.

Ⓑ Use the formula to calculate the gravitational potential energy of the roller coaster car.

$E_p = W \times h = 7500 \text{ N} \times 30 \text{ m}$
$E_p = 225\,000 \text{ J}$

Ⓒ Even though it doesn't fall straight down toward Earth, the coaster car is being affected by gravity. Gravity is pulling the coaster car down, not forward.

Potential and Kinetic Energy

How can you measure and compare the potential and kinetic energy of a vehicle?

Problem
What is the relationship between the potential energy of an object and the kinetic energy of the same object? What can you use to calculate potential energy? How do you calculate kinetic energy?

Materials

20-N spring scale	meterstick
stopwatch	1.0- to 2.0-m ramp
masking tape	1.0-kg mass
cart	several books

What To Do

1 Use the materials listed above or your own materials to develop a way to calculate both the kinetic energy of an object and the potential energy of that same object. Present your plan to your teacher before you do it. If necessary, use your teacher's comments to revise your plan. Once you have an approved plan for making your comparison, record your plan *in your Journal* and carry out the experiment. You may want to keep a couple of things in mind as you make up your plan:

- What's the formula for kinetic energy?
- How will you calculate velocity?
- How will you keep track of the data?
- How will you convert mass to weight to calculate potential energy?

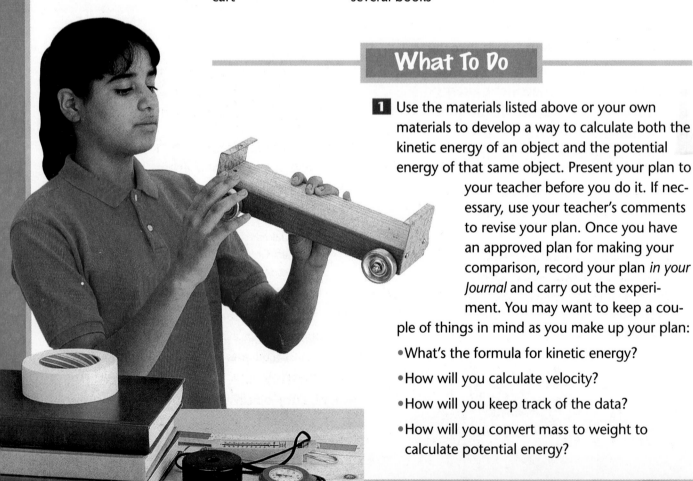

The Soap Box Derby got its name long ago when many of the race cars were built from wooden soap boxes. Derby race cars have no motors. Drivers rely solely on the conversion of gravitational potential energy to kinetic energy to bring their cars down the race-course hill.

2 Remember that all measurements must be in units of meters, m/s, and kg.

3 Your design should include multiple trials to show that whatever you observe holds true under varying conditions.

Analyzing

1. *Construct a graph* or table that summarizes the data from your experiment.

2. *Calculate* the potential energy and the kinetic energy of each object in each of your trials.

3. Make a bar graph that shows the relationship between the kinetic energy and the potential energy in each trial.

Concluding and Applying

4. *Interpret* your data to describe the relationship between the potential energy of an object and the kinetic energy of the same object.

5. Redesign your experiment to achieve greater accuracy in your measurements and your calculations. If possible, test your improvements.

6. Make a poster that summarizes your results and explains the relationship of potential energy to kinetic energy.

7. **Going Further** *Predict* how increasing the weight of the object you used would affect its velocity, its potential energy, and its kinetic energy. Test your prediction.

■ Potential to Kinetic

As you did the Investigate, you may have found that the kinetic energy you were able to calculate was a bit less than the potential energy. Is this what you would have predicted? Why might this be so?

The work you put into the cart to raise it to the top of the ramp is stored in the cart as gravitational potential energy. As the car rolls down the ramp, gravity accelerates it, turning the potential energy into kinetic energy—motion. When the cart leaves the ramp, does it have any potential energy left? Where is that energy now? If you had been able to do this Investigate on a friction-free surface, what do you think the relationship between the potential energy at the top of the ramp and the kinetic energy at the bottom would have been? Later in this chapter, you'll learn what happened to the energy the cart lost by going down the ramp.

■ Elastic Potential Energy

Simply by looking around, you can see many things in your environment that possess gravitational potential energy. Is gravitational potential energy the only way to store work? Can you think of any other ways in which work done on an object can be stored? Let's explore.

Energetic Toy

Your baby sister is playing with her favorite roll-back toy. If you watch closely, you'll notice that this toy demonstrates how energy can be converted from one form to another. Let's build such a toy so we can take a better look.

Materials

one-pound coffee can
2 plastic coffee can lids
heavy rubber band—folded length about 17 cm
lead fishing weight, about 2.5 cm long

What To Do

1. Remove both ends from the coffee can. Beware of sharp edges!

2. With a skewer or the tip of a scissors, poke two holes in each lid, about 2.5 cm apart. Make the holes just large enough so that the rubber band can pass through them.

3. Cut the rubber band at one end. From the inside of one lid, thread the rubber band up through one hole and back down through the other. Even the ends.

Explore! ACTIVITY

How is work stored?

Can you think of any other ways to store work? What happens when you wind the propeller on a toy plane driven by a rubber band? Is energy stored? Explore another way of storing energy.

What To Do

1. Hold a 20-N spring scale flat on the table. Grasp the hook and pull it until the scale reads about 10 N.

2. Have another student measure the distance you moved the hook in centimeters.

3. Now, release the hook. What happens?

4. Where was this work after you stopped pulling? Did kinetic energy increase? Potential energy? Record your answers and observations *in your Journal.*

---

4 Stretching the rubber band slightly, attach the fishing weight to both ends of the rubber band. You may run the rubber band ends through the loop of the weight or tie the weight to both pieces with string.

5 Place the lid and rubber band assembly on the can.

6 Feed each end of the rubber band through the holes on the other lid and tie the ends together. Attach the second lid.

You Try It!

Place the toy on a smooth surface and push. What happens? How would you explain this motion? Make a list of the energy changes, beginning with your push. Be sure to state whether the energy is kinetic or potential and which type of potential energy is involved. Why does the toy eventually stop?

Figure 4-12

A The football player does work on the football by kicking it. When his foot connects with the ball, kinetic energy is transferred from his foot to the ball.

B The energy the ball receives is stored as elastic potential energy in the flattening of the ball.

C As the ball springs back to its original shape and moves away from the foot, the ball's elastic potential energy is converted to kinetic energy.

Because the scale didn't move after you did the work in the Explore activity, the work did not produce kinetic energy. However, you didn't lift the scale so it can't be gravitational potential energy. The energy is stored in the spring. When you released the hook, the scale popped back to its original setting. The spring had stored the energy you put in, and that energy showed itself as motion—kinetic energy—when you released it. This kind of stored energy is called elastic potential energy.

■ Everyday Examples of Elastic Potential Energy

In **Figure 4-12**, you can see an example of elastic potential energy in a football kick. Energy is stored as elastic potential energy when work causes an object to be stretched or twisted, or if its shape is changed, as in the objects in **Figures 4-13, 4-14, 4-15,** and **4-16.** The object must be capable of going back to its original shape in order to store energy in this way. Rubber bands, trampolines, the spring in a wind-up toy, and diving boards are other examples of objects that can store elastic potential energy.

Figure 4-13

A Because the spring in this wind-up toy can go back to its original shape after it is tightened, the spring can store elastic potential energy.

B A loose spring has no elastic potential energy. A tightly wound spring has great elastic potential energy. Where did the energy in the tightly wound spring come from?

Figure 4-14

The propeller of this model plane is attached to a long rubber band. Winding the propeller allows the rubber band to store elastic potential energy as it twists. What will happen when the propeller is let loose? Why?

Is Energy Used Up?

When you drop a tennis ball or golf ball from several feet above the floor, the ball bounces. Actually, it bounces several times, each time a little lower. The potential energy stored in the ball, because of its position above the ground, is converted to kinetic energy as it falls. When the ball hits the ground, it is compressed, storing the energy as elastic potential energy.

When the ball regains its shape, that potential energy does work on the ball, increasing its velocity in an upward direction. But why doesn't it bounce as high? Where did the energy go? Let's find out.

Figure 4-16

The spring on a jack-in-the-box gains elastic potential energy when you compress it. By closing the lid, you keep the spring compressed. What happens to Jack's elastic potential energy when you release the lid?

Figure 4-15

Ⓐ As the ball falls, the potential energy it gained from its position is converted to kinetic energy.

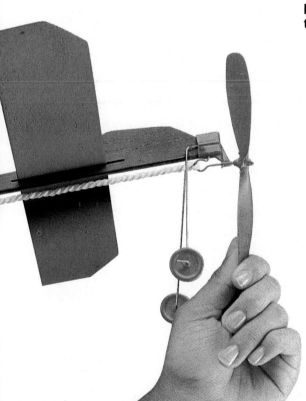

Ⓑ When the ball hits the ground, it flattens slightly. Most of the energy of motion is stored as elastic potential energy as the ball flattens.

Ⓒ When the ball regains its shape, its elastic potential energy does work on the ball. The ball accelerates upward, converting its elastic potential energy to kinetic energy.

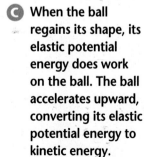

Where does the energy go?

If objects did not transfer energy, they would never come to a halt. But objects do stop, so where does the energy go?

What To Do

1. Attach a 20-N spring scale to the end of a shallow box.
2. Place several books in the box.
3. Pull the box with a steady force 1 m across the table or floor. Record the force needed.
4. Now pull the box with a steady force 1 m across a rug or other rough surface at the same speed you used on the table. Record your measurements and observations *in your Journal*.

Conclude and Apply

1. Calculate the amount of work done in each case. Compare these values. Why do you think you had to do more work in one case than the other?
2. The work you did transferred energy from you to the box and books. Where is that energy now?

Figure 4-17

Ⓐ Sonia gained gravitational potential energy by climbing the rope. As she slides down the rope, her potential energy is converted into kinetic energy.

Ⓑ Some of the kinetic energy is transferred to the rope in the form of thermal energy. What evidence will Sonia have that this transfer is taking place?

■ Where the Energy Goes

If you had put your hand on the bottom of the box immediately after you'd finished dragging it, you probably would have noticed that the box was a bit warmer than it was before. The surface over which you dragged it would also be warmer. This difference in temperature is so small that you might not be able to feel it, but here's an easy way to demonstrate what happens.

Rub your hands together rapidly. What happens to your hands? You're doing work, and the work shows itself in warming your hands. We'd say that the work done shows itself as thermal energy. For another example of this, see **Figure 4-17**.

When you drop a tennis ball, the ball strikes the ground and some of the energy is changed to thermal energy. The floor and the ball get a little warmer. That energy is no longer available to move the ball.

Think back to the Investigate you did with the cart. The kinetic energy of the rolling cart was less than the potential energy of the cart at the top of the ramp. Where did that energy go? The floor and the wheels of the cart warmed up. Some of the kinetic energy was converted to thermal energy.

■ **Energy from Work**

You've seen that doing work on an object can give different results. When you throw a softball, it gains kinetic energy. When you lift the ball, you increase its gravitational potential energy. When you hit the softball with a bat, it compresses and stores the work as elastic potential energy. When you roll the softball across the floor, it will eventually stop. The energy isn't used up or lost—it's present as thermal energy in the ball and floor.

In the next section, we'll track work and energy through several different situations.

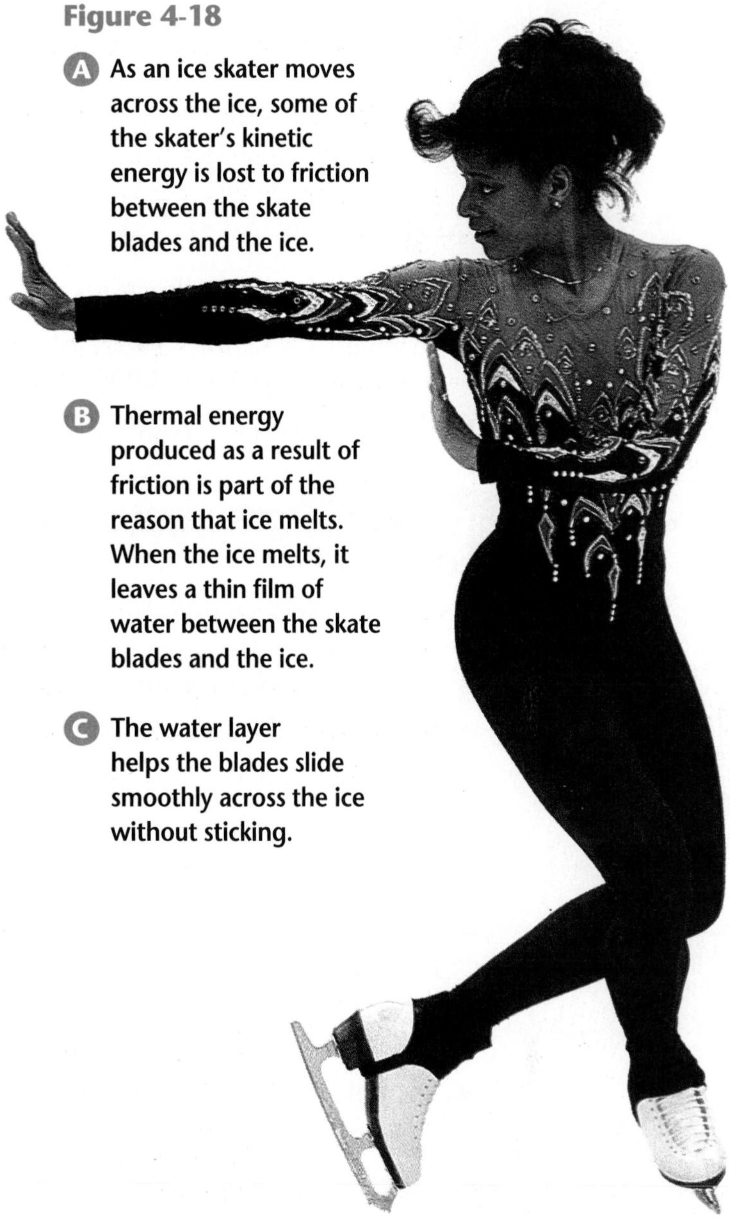

Figure 4-18

Ⓐ As an ice skater moves across the ice, some of the skater's kinetic energy is lost to friction between the skate blades and the ice.

Ⓑ Thermal energy produced as a result of friction is part of the reason that ice melts. When the ice melts, it leaves a thin film of water between the skate blades and the ice.

Ⓒ The water layer helps the blades slide smoothly across the ice without sticking.

check your UNDERSTANDING

1. Give two examples where work done on an object produces kinetic energy.
2. A 15 kg model plane flies horizontally at 2.5 m/s. Calculate its kinetic energy.
3. Which of the following is an example of work producing potential energy? Explain.
   a. putting on your hat
   b. carrying a box across the room
   c. hitting a golf ball with a club
4. **Apply** You pick up a beanbag from the table and lift it over your head. Then you drop it to the floor. Discuss the work done and changes in energy that take place during these actions.

4-3 Conservation of Energy

Section Objectives

■ Describe how energy changes from one form to another.

■ Understand and apply the law of conservation of energy.

Key Terms

law of conservation of energy

Energy on the Move

When you do work on an object, such as throwing, hitting, or rolling a ball, you are transferring energy from yourself to that object—the ball. You already know some ways in which energy can be transferred. Let's find out other ways in which you can transfer energy to move an object.

Find Out! ACTIVITY

How far will it go?

What's the best way to make something move? How can you give the most energy to an object? Experiment to find out!

What To Do

1. Obtain a set of materials, including a marble, foam cup, grooved ruler, balloon, tape, and wood splint or tongue depressor.

2. Use these objects to transfer energy in such a way that your marble travels the greatest distance when you release it. You may not throw the marble. You must simply let it go from wherever your starting point is.

3. Try to demonstrate as many different types of energy transfer as you can.

Conclude and Apply

1. What was the best way to make your marble move?

2. In terms of energy, why did your marble eventually stop moving?

3. Write a paragraph *in your Journal* to describe the kinetic and potential energy present in the system you constructed. Also describe any energy changes that took place.

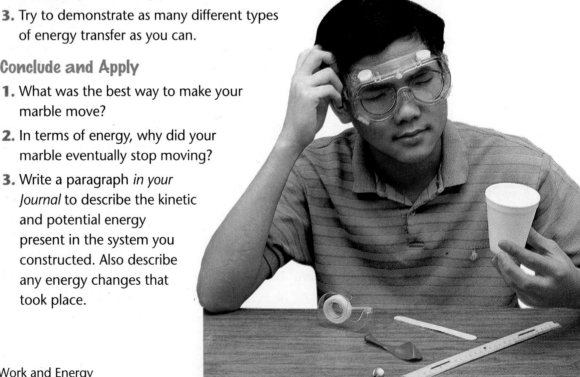

Energy Is Like Money

You can think about energy transfers as being similar to money exchanges. How? Examine the diagram on this page to start making your comparison.

Figure 4-19

The transfer of energy can be compared to the transfer of money among people.

A You have twenty dollars in your pocket. The money has buying power, but for now you are not using that power. You could call the money in your pocket potential money. It has the potential to buy, just as potential energy has the potential to cause action.

B You spend two dollars for a magazine. By putting your money into action, you change its potential buying power to kinetic buying power. Those two dollars now belong to the person who sold you the magazine.

C You transfer five of your potential dollars to a friend. He goes to a store and converts those potential dollars into kinetic dollars when he exchanges them for a gift for his sister.

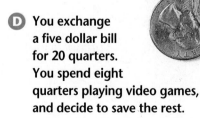

D You exchange a five dollar bill for 20 quarters. You spend eight quarters playing video games, and decide to save the rest.

E Your money has changed form and moved from person to person, but the original twenty dollars still exist. No more. No less. Like the money, energy also neither increases nor decreases. Energy changes form and moves from object to object, but the original amount of energy stays the same.

You've seen that energy occurs in several forms and can be changed from one form to another. Try another activity to see if you can keep track of the energy of an object as it goes through a number of changes.

The Motion of a Pendulum

What kinds of energy transfers take place in the motion of a pendulum?

Problem

What happens to the energy of a pendulum?

Materials

ring stand	cross arm
right-angle clamp	support rod and clamp
masking tape	2-hole rubber
2 metersticks	stopper, medium
	100 cm of string

What To Do

1. Copy the data table *into your Journal*.

2. Set up the apparatus as shown, omitting the cross arm at this time.

3. Use the masking tape to mark the center of the stopper. Use this line to measure heights above the tabletop.

4. Pull the stopper to one side. Measure the height of the stopper above the table (see photo **A**). Record the measurement.

Data and Observations

Trial	Starting Height	Ending Height
1		
2		
3		
4		
5		
6		

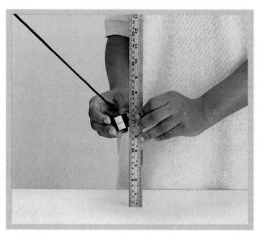

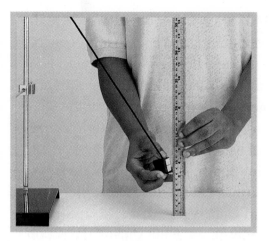

A   **B**

5 Release the stopper and let it swing. Observe carefully and measure the greatest height the stopper reaches just before it begins its return swing. Record.

6 Repeat Steps 4 and 5 twice, each time starting the stopper at a greater height.

7 Repeat Steps 4 through 6 with the cross arm in place (see photo **B**). Begin the first swing below the cross arm, the second level with the cross arm, and the third above it. Record all data and observations *in your Journal*.

Analyzing

1. For a single swing without the cross arm, is the ending height of the stopper exactly the same as its starting height? Explain.

2. What is the highest point that the stopper will reach when it hits the cross arm?

3. Write or draw the sequence of changes in kinetic and potential energy of the stopper at various points on its arc.

Concluding and Applying

4. If you could calculate the maximum potential energy and kinetic energy of the stopper, what would you infer about their relationship?

5. What caused the string to wrap completely around the cross arm?

6. Going Further Could a roller coaster be built with its highest point on one of the middle hills? Explain.

The Law of Conservation of Energy

Connect to...

Life Science

All living things need a constant supply of energy to live. Use what you know about energy conversions to explain where the energy from food goes even when you aren't active.

If there were no friction where the pendulum is tied and no loss of energy to the air, the pendulum would continue to swing forever. The potential energy you put in by lifting the stopper would change to kinetic energy and back to potential energy over and over again. When you include the thermal energy lost to friction, you find that when you add up all the energy at any point during the action, the total amount of energy remains the same. It is conserved as it changes from one form to another. This is called the **law of conservation of energy**. This law says that energy can't be created out of nothing, nor can it be destroyed. Energy may be changed to other forms or transferred to other objects, but the total energy remains unchanged. Energy is conserved.

Why did your pendulum wrap itself around the cross arm when you started it above the level of the cross arm? As the kinetic energy at the bottom of the swing was converted back into potential energy, the stopper had enough energy to reach nearly the same height as where it started.

Earth Science CONNECTION

To Jupiter and Beyond

In the recent past, we've sent uncrewed probes to Mercury, Venus, and Mars. After these missions had been accomplished, scientists wanted to send similar probes to investigate the far planets of the solar system. To achieve this goal, they designed two space probes.

Voyage of the Century

The twin uncrewed space probes *Voyager 1* and *Voyager 2* traveled to Jupiter, Saturn, Uranus, and Neptune. Through the transmissions they beamed to Earth, the world had the incredible experience of riding along and seeing sights never before possible.

By June of 1989, *Voyager 2* had traveled more than 2.8 billion miles to reach Neptune. When the probe gave us our

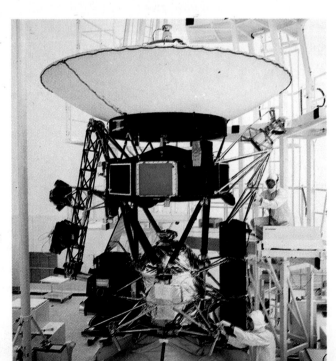

A prototype Voyager space-craft is shown as it successfully passes vibration testing in 1977.

Figure 4-20

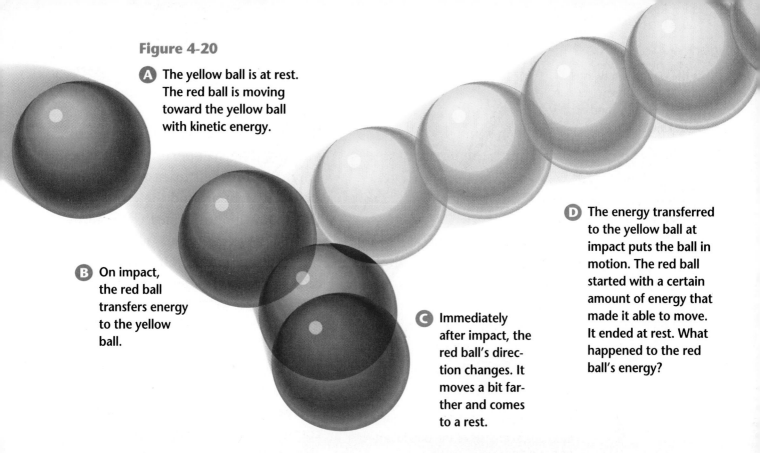

A The yellow ball is at rest. The red ball is moving toward the yellow ball with kinetic energy.

B On impact, the red ball transfers energy to the yellow ball.

C Immediately after impact, the red ball's direction changes. It moves a bit farther and comes to a rest.

D The energy transferred to the yellow ball at impact puts the ball in motion. The red ball started with a certain amount of energy that made it able to move. It ended at rest. What happened to the red ball's energy?

first look at this planet, *Voyager 2* was traveling at a speed greater than when it had left Earth nearly 12 years earlier. A photo of Neptune taken by *Voyager* is shown here.

Riding the Slingshot Effect

How do space probes such as *Voyager* get the energy they need for space travel? Space scientists use a slingshot effect to provide additional kinetic energy to space probes. This effect reduces the amount of fuel the probes must carry.

As a probe comes near a planet, it experiences the gravitational pull of the planet. As a result, potential energy is converted to kinetic energy. The probe speeds up and reaches its greatest speed as it moves behind the planet.

Behind the planet, the probe's path then takes it away from the surface. The kinetic energy is again changed to potential energy. However, the probe's path leaving the planet is a different shape than the path of the probe approaching the planet. Not all of the kinetic energy it gains is needed to pull it away from the planet's surface. Therefore, the probe has more

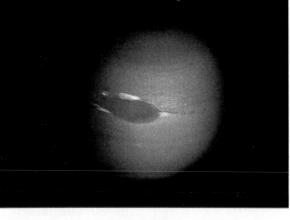

kinetic energy when it leaves the planet than it had when it approached the planet.

What Do You Think?

What are the advantages of using the slingshot effect? What other source of energy is present in space? How might the probes use this energy instead of providing their own fuel?

Figure 4-21

A As the pendulum swings downward, it loses potential energy and gains kinetic energy. As the pendulum swings upward, it loses kinetic energy and gains potential energy.

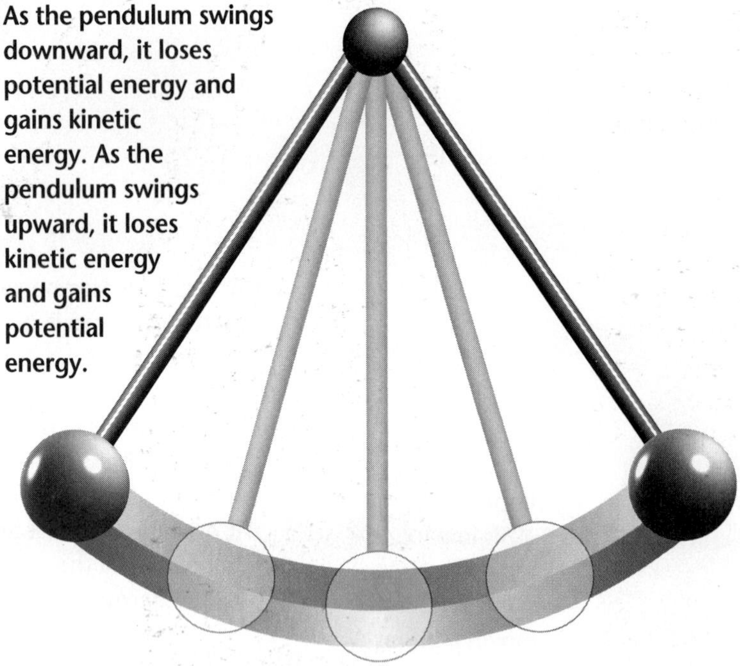

B At every point in the swing, the total mechanical energy of the pendulum (K.E. + P.E.) is the same. Energy is converted from one form to the other, but is never lost from the system.

But the cross arm blocked it. Because the stopper hadn't completely converted its kinetic energy into potential energy, it still had kinetic energy left. Kinetic energy is the energy of motion. The stopper moved in the only direction left open to it by the string. It went around the cross arm. Eventually, motion ended when all of the stopper's energy had been changed into thermal energy. Other examples of energy conversions are present in **Figures 4-21, 4-22, 4-23,** and **4-24.**

■ Conservation and Forms of Energy

There are no cases in which energy appears or disappears without coming from or ending up somewhere else. Whenever energy seems to disappear, scientists have found another form of energy. Some other forms are electrical, electromagnetic, and

Figure 4-22

A At the top of a hill, the roller coaster car has almost no kinetic energy. It has only potential energy.

B As the car rushes downhill, its potential energy is decreasing. At the same time, the car's kinetic energy is increasing.

C The instant the car begins climbing the next hill, the car's kinetic energy begins to decrease and its potential energy begins to increase.

D At the top of the hill, the car's kinetic energy has been converted to potential energy. Again, it has almost no kinetic energy at this point. At what point in its trip is the car's kinetic energy largest?

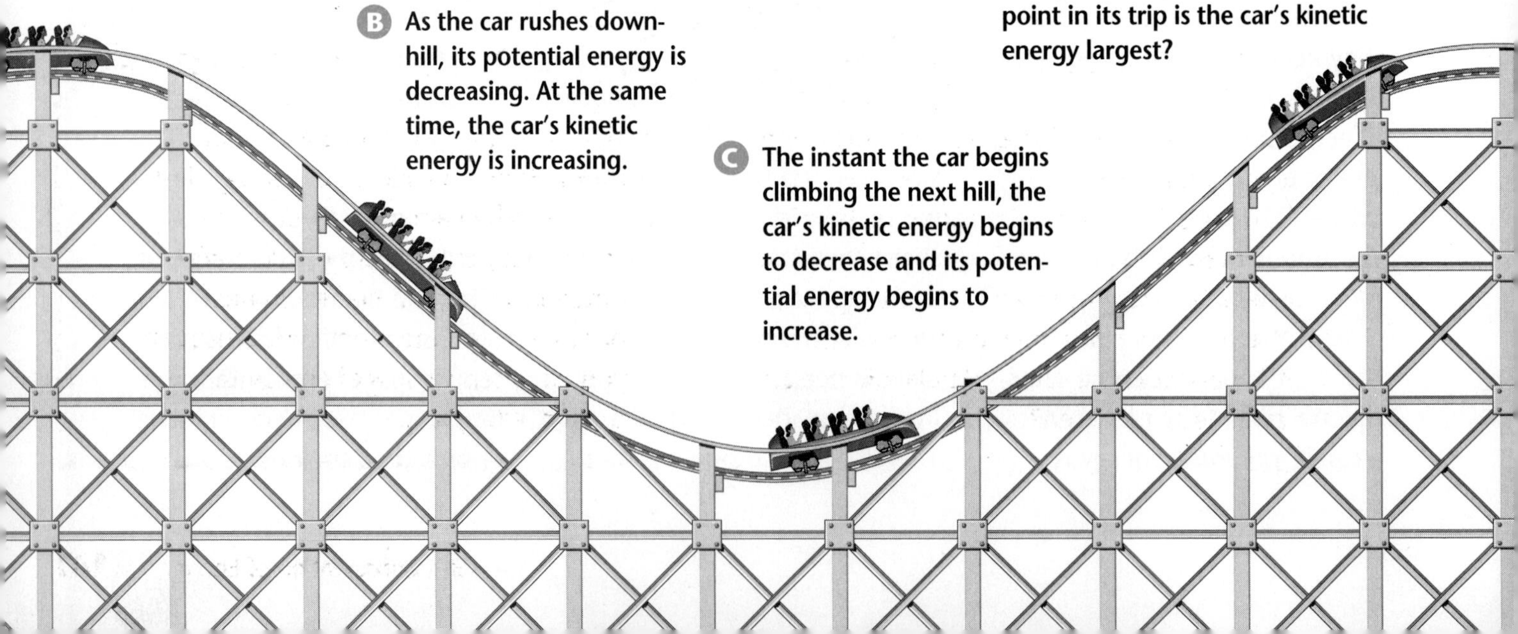

Figure 4-23

(A) When a diver's weight bends a diving board downward, the board gains elastic potential energy.

(B) When the board springs back to its original shape, the elastic potential energy is converted to kinetic energy. The board's kinetic energy is transferred to the diver. The diver moves upward.

Figure 4-24

(A) The kinetic energy of a pole vaulter is stored as elastic potential in the bending of the pole.

(B) As the pole straightens, the elastic potential energy is converted to kinetic energy, and the vaulter is lifted.

nuclear energy. Although we still use these terms, scientists now believe that there are only two basic kinds of energy. Regardless of where the energy comes from, it can be described as kinetic or potential. For example, what we have been calling thermal energy is another combination of kinetic and potential energy. You will learn more about this kind of energy in Chapter 6.

check your UNDERSTANDING

1. Give one example for each of the following energy changes:
   a. gravitational potential energy to kinetic energy
   b. kinetic energy to elastic potential energy
2. You are riding your bike on a level surface. Why do you have to keep pedaling to maintain the same speed?
3. Trace the energy changes as a heavy rock rolls down a hill. Is any energy lost?
4. **Apply** When a machine burns fuel to do a job, only part of the chemical potential energy in the fuel comes out as work on the other end. What can you do to reduce loss of energy to thermal energy?

Technology Connection

The Search for Perpetual Motion

One idea that has fascinated inventors is the idea of a perpetual motion machine. This is a machine that, once set in motion, continues with no additional energy required. With the energy shortages in many parts of the world, this would be a wonderful accomplishment. But scientists know that this is impossible.

What's Wrong with Moving Forever?

The law of conservation of energy states that energy can neither be created nor destroyed—it can only be transformed into another form of energy. In other words, you can't get something from nothing. But what if energy could somehow be recaptured and used over and over? One example of such a machine is a battery that powers a motor that runs a generator that recharges the battery. It sounds good, but why would such a machine not continue forever?

There are moving parts in the device mentioned above. As parts of machines move against one another, the friction produces thermal energy that ends up being distributed through the particles in the air.

Some would say that people who try to invent perpetual motion machines are foolish and are ignoring the laws of science. Do you think that this is necessarily true? What, if anything, might these people accomplish?

What Do You Think?

Here's another idea for a perpetual motion machine. Can you find the problem with it? Remember that this is only an idea for a perpetual motion machine. This machine was not necessarily built!

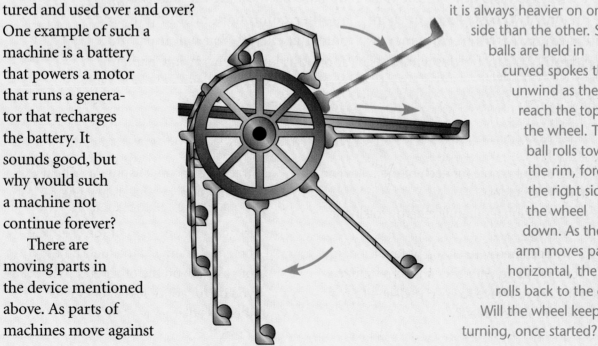

The wheel shown in the diagram is supposed to turn forever because it is always heavier on one side than the other. Steel balls are held in curved spokes that unwind as they reach the top of the wheel. The ball rolls toward the rim, forcing the right side of the wheel down. As the arm moves past horizontal, the ball rolls back to the end. Will the wheel keep turning, once started?

HOW IT WORKS

Vacuum Cleaner

Sometimes "home energy conservation" refers to the use of appliances to conserve human energy. Try telling that to the users of the first vacuum cleaners. One early model, invented around 1908, was made of steel and weighed a hefty 60 pounds. Today's cleaners usually weigh between 6 and 30 pounds, but they work on the same principle as the 1908 model.

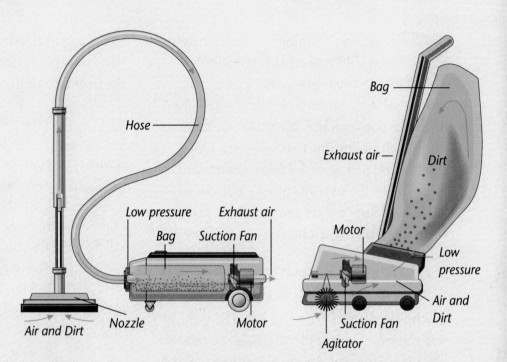

Hose

Low pressure Exhaust air
Bag Suction Fan
Air and Dirt Nozzle Motor

Bag
Exhaust air Dirt
Motor
Low pressure
Air and Dirt
Suction Fan
Agitator

Low-Pressure Cleaning

A fan driven by an electric motor blows air through the unit. The moving air creates an area of low pressure. This reduces pressure inside the bag and hose. Since air pressure is now greater than the pressure at the nozzle, dirt and dust are gathered in the air that rushes in to even out the pressure. The fan forces this dirt-filled air into a bag, where the dust is trapped, and the air is blown out.

Tanks and Uprights

There are two main types of vacuum cleaners—canisters (or tanks) and uprights. A canister vacuum cleaner has a long, flexible hose that ends in a detachable nozzle. Usually a variety of nozzles come with the vacuum cleaner as attachments. The body of this type of cleaner contains a bag and a powerful fan. Dirt is sucked into the bag through the hose.

An upright vacuum cleaner has a small fan in its base. The base of the machine also contains an agitator—a rotating cylinder covered with bristles that loosen dirt. Dirt is sucked upward into a bag attached to the vacuum cleaner's handle. In addition, there are vacuum cleaners that have both a canister unit for strong suction and an agitator in the nozzle.

What Do You Think?

Make a list of some "labor-saving" devices. If labor is work, and work requires energy, are these devices really "savers"? Explain.

HISTORY CONNECTION

What's in a Name?

Can you imagine how a scientist would answer this question? You've learned that in science, names are very important. However, sometimes for convenience, scientists substitute a shorter name for one that is longer. One example is the use of the term joule when referring to the newton meter. Who was Joule, and how did he come to have a unit of work named after him?

James Prescott Joule

James Prescott Joule was an English brewer who lived from 1818 to 1889. His hobby was physics. During the 1840s, he put the law of conservation of energy to a thorough test. He believed that if the law applied to all work and all forms of energy, then it had to be shown that one form of energy could be converted into another, quantitatively.

Energy Conversions

In other words, in energy conversions all energy must be accounted for—no energy should be lost in the process, and no energy created. Joule also measured thermal energy produced by an electric current, the friction of water against glass, and so on. He found that a fixed amount of one kind of energy was converted into a fixed amount of another kind. In fact, energy was neither lost nor created. It is in his honor that we call a unit of work a joule. His ideas were so fundamental to today's understanding of work and energy that most countries use the SI unit joule as the unit of energy.

What Do You Think?

It is common to name scientific quantities after the men and women who have made great contributions to science. In addition to Joule, make a list of other scientists honored in this way.

Imagine that your name is commonly used to describe an important quantity. Describe the quantity you discovered.

HOT-AIR MACHINE.

Review the statements below about the big ideas presented in this chapter, and try to answer the questions. Then, re-read your answers to the Did You Ever Wonder questions at the beginning of the chapter. *In your Journal*, write a paragraph about how your understanding of the big ideas in the chapter has changed.

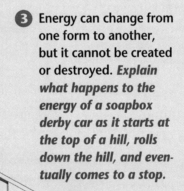

1 Work is energy transferred through force and motion. When a force acts in the direction of motion, work is done. *You pick up a box, transfer it to a cart, push the cart across the room, pick up the box, carry it to a ramp, and push the box down a ramp. Decide when work is being done and when work is not being done. Explain.*

2 Kinetic energy is the energy of motion. Potential energy is the stored energy of position. Although there are many types of energy, all energy exists in these two forms. *List three common examples of both kinetic and potential energy.*

3 Energy can change from one form to another, but it cannot be created or destroyed. *Explain what happens to the energy of a soapbox derby car as it starts at the top of a hill, rolls down the hill, and eventually comes to a stop.*

Using Key Science Terms

kinetic energy   potential energy
law of conservation   work
  of energy

1. How is the definition for work that scientists use different from other definitions?
2. Briefly explain the law of conservation of energy.
3. What is the difference between kinetic energy and potential energy?

Understanding Ideas

Answer the following questions in your Journal using complete sentences.

1. A robin picks up a worm and carries it to her chicks. On what is work being done? How much? What unit is used to measure work?
2. How much work is done when you lift an 18N object 1.5m off the ground?
3. How do velocity and mass affect an object's kinetic energy?
4. How might the potential energy of water behind a dam be increased?
5. What is the gravitational potential energy of an object weighing 6 newtons, lifted 2.5 meters?
6. When a tennis ball sails over a net, what kind of energy does it have? Explain.
7. The gravitational potential energy of an object is 300J. The maximum measured kinetic energy of the object rolling down a ramp is 280J. How do you explain the difference between the two energies?

Developing Skills

Use your understanding of the concepts developed in this chapter to answer each of the following questions.

1. **Concept Mapping** Complete the concept map of energy.

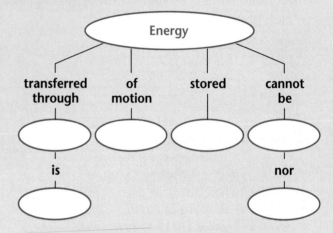

2. **Observing and Inferring** Repeat the Explore activity on page 123 holding the ball 2 meters above the stake. How did the results of this trial differ from the first trial? What caused the difference?
3. **Forming a Hypothesis** If you repeated the Find Out activity on page 132 on a surface of smooth ice, how would the results change?
4. **Making Models** Remake your model from the Find Out activity on page 134 to be the same as the group's whose marble traveled the greatest distance. Will the models work in the same way, so all the marbles travel the same distance? Can your group find a way to increase the distance traveled even more?

Critical Thinking

In your Journal, *answer each of the following questions.*

1. List the examples of kinetic energy, gravitational potential energy, elastic potential energy, and thermal energy found in the picture below.

2. On Monday morning, you see a small weed growing through a crack in the sidewalk. On Thursday, you notice that the weed has grown bigger. How does this prove that the weed has used energy?

3. Which required more work: lifting one 100-N weight 3 m off the ground, or lifting each of three 50-N weights 2 m off the ground?

Problem Solving

Read the following problems and discuss your answers in a brief paragraph.

Jake loves swimming and wants to be a coach. He doesn't see how science can help swimmers.

1. How could the definition of work help him advise a swimmer how to hold his or her hands as he or she strokes through the water?

2. How could an understanding of potential energy and kinetic energy help a diver know when to flex his or her knees and when to leave the board?

CONNECTING IDEAS

Discuss each of the following in a brief paragraph.

1. **Theme—Energy** A dancer lifts a 400-N ballerina 1.4 m off the ground and holds her there for 5 seconds. How much work did he do?

2. **Theme—Stability and Change** In Chapter 1, you learned that opposing forces can cancel each other. Does this mean that their energies also cancel each other? Explain.

3. **A Closer Look** Why did the roll-back toy eventually come to a stop?

4. **Earth Science Connection** What are the advantages of using the slingshot effect in planning and executing the path of space vehicles such as *Voyager*?

5. **How It Works** How can the operation of a vacuum cleaner be compared to using a straw to drink a milkshake?

CHAPTER 5

MACHINES

Did you ever wonder...

✓ How using a crowbar helps you move a large rock?

✓ Why a screwdriver makes it easier to drive a screw into wood?

✓ Why mountain roads twist and turn?

Before you begin to study machines, think about these questions and answer them *in your Journal*. When you finish the chapter, compare your Journal write-up with what you have learned.

T he steep road to the campground curves back and forth as it twists up the mountain. Everyone helps set up camp. You pound tent stakes into the ground with a hammer, while a friend fills water jugs at the outdoor faucet. Two older campers use a crowbar to move a large rock that's in the way of a tent. A counselor is splitting a log with an axe.

It may not seem obvious, but these campers are using several machines. How many can you identify? We use machines to make jobs easier. Can you imagine trying to pound in a nail without a hammer or chop wood without an axe? What if you had to climb the flagpole to get the flag to the top?

▶ *In this chapter, you'll explore some simple machines, and find out how much easier they can make the jobs you do.*

How can a machine make it easier to move an object?

Books may not weigh very much, but how can you make it easier to lift them? Can a machine help?

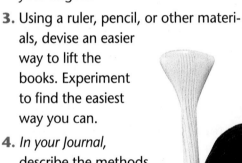

What To Do

1. Stack two books on a flat desk or table.

2. Place your fingertips under the bottom book and lift the books with your fingers.

3. Using a ruler, pencil, or other materials, devise an easier way to lift the books. Experiment to find the easiest way you can.

4. *In your Journal*, describe the methods you used. Do you think your device is a type of machine?

Simple Machines

Making Jobs Easier

Machines make work easier. Think back to the Explore activity at the beginning of the chapter. Although it wasn't very hard to lift the books with your fingertips, the device you invented made the job seem easier. The device you used to move the books was a machine. How does that machine compare to what you usually think of as a machine?

When a machine is used to do work, two kinds of force are involved. The force applied *to* the machine (the force you exert) is called the **effort force**. The force applied *by* the machine is called the **resistance force**. When campers use a crowbar to move a rock, what is the effort force? What is the resistance force?

Although machines make work easier, they do not actually reduce the amount of work that has to be done.

The weight of a rock doesn't change just because you use a crowbar to move it—the same amount of weight has to be moved. How can a machine make work easier if it doesn't reduce the amount of work that has to be done? Let's take a look at the six types of simple machines and find out.

■ Lever

Sitting around the campfire after dark seems like a perfect time for hot chocolate and toasted marshmallows. The hot chocolate can has one of those metal lids that fits tightly into the top. You find a spoon and slip the end of the handle under the edge of the lid. One push on the spoon, and the lid comes right off.

Could you have pried off the lid using just your fingers? Let's explore why it is easier with a spoon.

Figure 5-1

Another example of a common lever that makes work easier is a boat oar. Like the spoon used to open the hot chocolate can, the oar doesn't reduce the amount of work that has to be done, but it does increase the distance over which the force is exerted.

Ⓐ When you use an oar, you exert an effort force on the oar.

Effort force

Fulcrum

Resistance force

Explore! ACTIVITY

How does a lever work?

What To Do

1. Watch carefully as your teacher or classmate uses a spoon handle to pry the lid off a can. *In your Journal*, record how far he or she had to push down on the spoon. How far up does the tip of the spoon handle go to lift the lid? Are these two distances the same or different?

2. Again, watch as your teacher or a classmate pries the lid off the can. Does the spoon handle rest on a part of the can while the lifting is being done?

3. Look at the length of spoon between his or her hand and the can's edge. How does that length compare to the length of spoon between the can's edge and the lid? What direction is the force he or she exerts on the spoon? In which direction does the lid move?

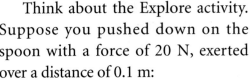

A **lever** is a bar that turns or pivots on a fixed point called a fulcrum. What was the fulcrum for the spoon in the Explore activity? When you use a lever, such as the spoon handle, you exert a small force over a long distance. At the same time, the lever exerts a large resistance force over a short distance. Recall the definition of work you learned in Chapter 4:

    force (N) × distance (m) = work (J)

Think about the Explore activity. Suppose you pushed down on the spoon with a force of 20 N, exerted over a distance of 0.1 m:

    20 N × 0.1 m = 2 J

At the same time, the lever pushed up on the lid with a force of 200 N, over a distance of 0.01 m:

    200 N × 0.01 m = 2 J

In each case, the work done was the same—2 J.

Connect to...
Life Science

Not only do humans *use* levers, but many parts of our bodies *are* levers. Think about how your bones and muscles move in your arm and identify the fulcrum, effort force and resistance force.

B The oar exerts a resistance force on the water.

C The resistance force pushes the boat through the water.

■ Wheel and Axle

There are two water faucets at the campground. It's your turn to fill the water jugs. When you get to the faucets, you find that the handle is broken off of one of them. Which would you use? Why?

Effort force

Resistance force

Figure 5-2

The handle of the water faucet is a wheel. The shaft attached to the center of the faucet wheel is an axle.

The handle of the water faucet, like the knob of a doorknob, is a wheel. Each wheel rotates around its center. The shaft attached to the center of the wheel is an axle. You can think of a **wheel and axle** as a small wheel attached to the center of a larger wheel. The wheel and the axle always rotate together.

We have developed many uses for the wheel and axle. You already know this simple machine makes it easier to move cars, carts, wheelchairs, and wagons. But there are also other, less obvious uses for the wheel and axle. Can you think of any that you use or have seen?

A When you use a wheel and axle, you exert a smaller effort force over a longer distance. The machine exerts a greater resistance force over a shorter distance.

B The bigger a wheel is, the longer the distance you must turn it to move the axle. But as turning distance increases, the amount of effort force needed to turn the wheel decreases. You need less effort force to turn a large wheel than you do to turn a small wheel.

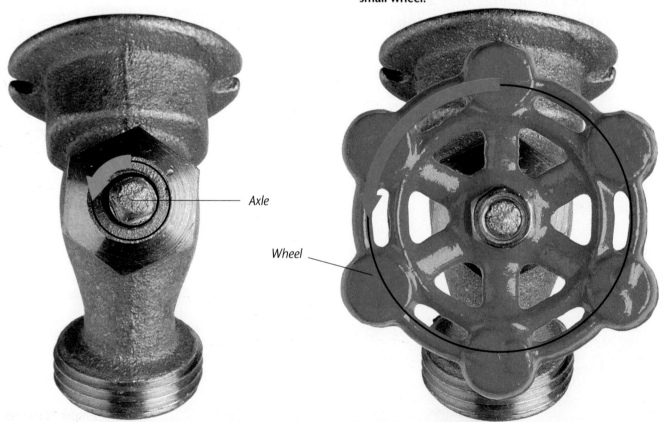

Axle

Wheel

■ Pulley

During a morning walk through camp, you find the ranger is preparing to raise the flag. You help unfold it and the ranger lets you hook the flag to the rope and hoist it up the flagpole. You pull down on one strand of rope while the flag goes up with the other strand. Is this easier than climbing up the flagpole? Have you done any work?

A **pulley** is a wheel that has a rope or chain passing over it. The pulley on the flagpole is the simplest kind of pulley. It's called a single fixed pulley because it's attached to something that doesn't move. Fixed pulleys change the direction of the force that's applied to the object, but not the amount of force. Can the force exerted to get a job done be reduced when a pulley is used? Let's find out.

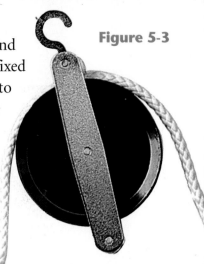

Figure 5-3

Single fixed pulley

Find Out! ACTIVITY

Can a pulley reduce the force you have to exert to get a job done?

What To Do

1. Obtain a brick, spring scale, ring and ring stand, two pieces of string, and a pulley.

2. Tie one piece of string around the brick and lift it using the spring scale. Record the force required to lift the brick.

3. Tie one end of the other piece of string to the ring stand.

4. Place the pulley in the center of that piece of string as shown in the figure.

5. Attach the spring scale to the other end of the string, and hook the brick to the pulley.

6. Pull up on the spring scale. Record *in your Journal* the force required to lift the brick using the pulley. Which requires more effort from you?

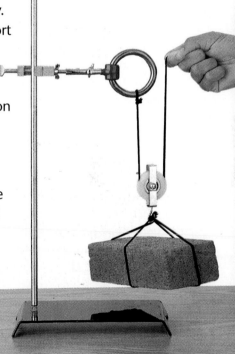

Conclude and Apply

1. How far did you pull up on the free end of the rope?

2. How far did the brick move?

3. Did the pulley reduce the amount of force you had to exert to move the brick?

4. What direction did you have to pull to lift the brick? How does this compare to the flagpole example?

You've just demonstrated how a single movable pulley works. A single movable pulley increases the effect of the effort force and reduces the amount of effort you must exert to get a job done. But a single movable pulley does not change the direction of the force.

■ Inclined Plane

Suppose you need to lift a 100-pound box of camping gear a distance of 3 feet, from the ground into the back of a truck. Lifting the box straight up and into the truck would be difficult. But if you use a board to make a ramp, you could probably push the box up, even though you would have to exert force against the friction between the box and the board.

An **inclined plane** is a ramp or slope that reduces the force you need to exert to lift something. The inclined plane decreases the effort force. Does it change the direction of force?

Look at the diagrams in **Figure 5-4**. Describe the relationship between the length of the ramp and how much easier the job would be.

What are some of the inclined planes you see around you every day? Driveways? Ramps in parking garages? Most buildings with entrances that are above or below sidewalk level have a ramp in addition to steps. The ramp makes the building accessible to people in wheelchairs, and makes it easier for people to use carts to move heavy objects into and out of the building.

Figure 5-4

A Olivia decided to use an inclined plane to help her load boxes of camping gear into the truck. The inclined plane decreases the effort force Olivia needs by increasing the distance through which her effort force is applied. How could Olivia make her job even easier?

B After loading the first box, Olivia replaced the short ramp with a longer one. By making the slope more gradual, Olivia increased the distance she had to push the boxes, but she decreased the effort force she had to exert.

C To get to the mountaintop, the campers drove up a winding mountain road. A mountain road is a type of inclined plane that is used to raise cars up to the top of a mountain, much as Olivia's ramp was used to raise boxes up into the truck. Why do mountain roads take a zigzag course up the mountainside instead of going straight up?

■ Screw

You just learned that a winding mountain road is an inclined plane. Imagine a road that wound around a mountain like a spiral staircase, slowly making its way to the top. Now think of a screw. How could the winding road be compared to a screw? Is the screw a machine? What about the screwdriver used to turn the screw? Let's find out in this next activity.

Find Out! ACTIVITY

Are screwdrivers and screws simple machines?

What To Do

1. Gather a board with a hole drilled partially through it, a screwdriver, and a wood screw.

2. Use the screwdriver to drive the screw part of the way into the hole.

3. Now try using your fingers to turn the screw into the hole. *In your Journal*, record your observations. Can you do it? Do you think you could have finished this task if the screwdriver did not have a handle?

Conclude and Apply

1. Is the screwdriver a simple machine? To decide, you need to compare what it does to what a simple machine can do. Did the screwdriver make the job easier?

2. Did the screwdriver reduce the amount of work that was accomplished?

3. What type of simple machine is the screwdriver? Figure 5-5 may help you decide.

4. What about the screw itself? What type of simple machine is a screw?

Figure 5-5

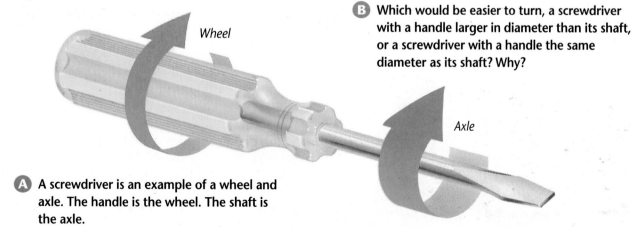

Wheel

Axle

B Which would be easier to turn, a screwdriver with a handle larger in diameter than its shaft, or a screwdriver with a handle the same diameter as its shaft? Why?

A A screwdriver is an example of a wheel and axle. The handle is the wheel. The shaft is the axle.

What about the screw itself? The ridges spiraling around a screw are called threads. As you drove the screw into the board, the threads seemed to pull the screw into the wood. Perhaps this leads you to describe a **screw** as an inclined plane wound around a post. In a way, the spiraling inclined plane helped to lift the wood up around the screw.

Making and Using Tables

Make three columns on a sheet of paper. Label them Simple Machines, Changes Direction, and Changes Force. In the first column, list the six simple machines. In the next two columns, write Yes or No. Then answer these questions. If you need more help, refer to the **Skill Handbook** on page 639.
1. Which machines change the direction of force?
2. Which machines multiply the effort force?
3. Which machines both change the direction of the effort force and increase the force?

Figure 5-6

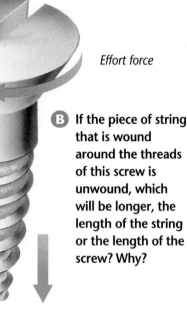

A The threads of a screw change the turning force of a screwdriver into a downward force. It also requires a smaller effort force to drive the screw into the wood, although you have to turn it many times.

Effort force

B If the piece of string that is wound around the threads of this screw is unwound, which will be longer, the length of the string or the length of the screw? Why?

Resistance force

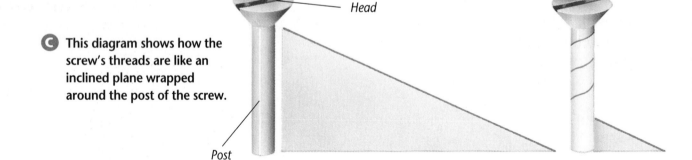

C This diagram shows how the screw's threads are like an inclined plane wrapped around the post of the screw.

Head

Post

D Wood screws, sheet metal screws, and nuts and bolts are all examples of screws. Instead of sharp threads to cut into wood, bolts have rounded threads to match the threads on the inside of the nut. Are tops of bottles and jars screws? What about a lightbulb? Why?

Wood screw

Sheet metal screw

Bolt and nut

Wedge

Once more, think of the campers. In particular, think of the counselor who was splitting logs. Would it be easier to split a log with a baseball bat or with a sharp-edged axe? Why?

Figure 5-7 takes a closer look at an axe. Does it remind you of another simple machine? You can see that each side of the axe blade looks like an inclined plane. The blade of an axe is a wedge. A **wedge** is an inclined plane that uses the sharp, narrow edge to cut through materials.

Chisels, knives, the teeth of saw blades, and many other sharp-bladed tools use the wedge. Can you think of other types of wedges?

Even though the campers were on vacation, there was much work to do. Recall that work is done when a force is exerted to move an object. Luckily, the campers had some simple machines to help them—levers, wheels and axles, pulleys, inclined planes, screws, and wedges. The campers were probably too busy to think about effort or resistance forces. The next time you use a simple machine, try to identify these forces.

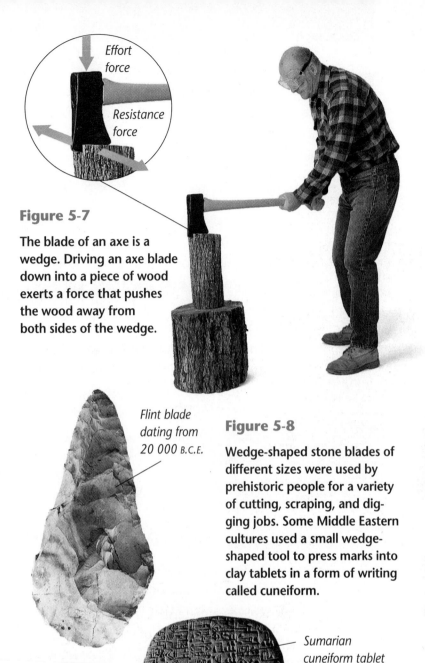

Figure 5-7

The blade of an axe is a wedge. Driving an axe blade down into a piece of wood exerts a force that pushes the wood away from both sides of the wedge.

Flint blade dating from 20 000 B.C.E.

Figure 5-8

Wedge-shaped stone blades of different sizes were used by prehistoric people for a variety of cutting, scraping, and digging jobs. Some Middle Eastern cultures used a small wedge-shaped tool to press marks into clay tablets in a form of writing called cuneiform.

Sumarian cuneiform tablet from 2500 B.C.E.

check your UNDERSTANDING

1. Give one example not given in the text of each kind of simple machine.
2. How do simple machines make it possible for you to exert less force to get a job done?
3. Do any of the simple machines reduce the amount of work that must be done? Explain your answer.
4. **Apply** One counselor built a machine. A camper applied a downward effort force to one end of the machine. The force exerted by the other end of the machine was greater, and the direction of the force was up rather than down. What kind of machine did the counselor build? Explain.

Mechanical Advantage

Section Objectives

- Operationally define mechanical advantage.
- Calculate the mechanical advantage of several machines.

Key Terms

mechanical advantage

How Much Does a Machine Help?

One morning, the counselors returned from gathering firewood. They were covered in mud! They told the story of how the truck got stuck, and after a few unsuccessful attempts to push it out, they decided to jack the truck up and put some logs under the stuck wheel. Unfortunately, they discovered they had left the jack back at camp. They decided to fashion a lever out of a sturdy branch. They found a large log and rolled it near the truck to use as a fulcrum. One of them found two possible branches to use as the lever. One was long while the other was short. Which one should they have used to get the most help from the lever? Try this next activity to find out.

Find Out! ACTIVITY

Can the length of a lever affect the amount of force needed to do work?

What To Do

1. Place a stack of two or three books near the edge of a table.

2. Slide a meterstick under the books so the entire width of the bottom book is resting on the stick, as shown in the figure.

3. Grasp the meterstick at the 30-cm mark. Push up on the meterstick to lift the books. Try again, this time holding the meterstick at the 90-cm mark. Record your observations *in your Journal.*

Conclude and Apply

1. Compare the force you used to lift the books each time. Which time did you need more force to lift the books?

2. How is the distance between the effort force and the fulcrum related to the amount of effort force needed?

Now that you've done the activity, which branch would you have chosen? The counselors decided the long one would give them the most help. After they had lifted the truck and driven it out of the mud, the counselors decided to figure out exactly how much the lever helped them.

They wanted to calculate the mechanical advantage of the machine they used. The **mechanical advantage** (MA) of a machine tells you how much the effort force is multiplied.

Figure 5-9

The branch-lever allows the counselors to lift the truck with less effort force than they would need to exert using just their bodies. The lever provides help with the lifting. But how much help? You can measure the amount of help a machine provides by calculating its mechanical advantage.

You can calculate this by dividing the resistance force by the effort force.

$$MA = \frac{Resistance\ force}{Effort\ force}$$

The larger the mechanical advantage, the more help the machine provides.

Don't forget, a machine does not change the amount of work that is done. It just increases the force on the object.

Calculating the mechanical advantage of a machine can help us make decisions. By comparing the MA of two different machines, we can decide which machine we would need to use to get the job done.

Effort force
500 N

Lever

Fulcrum

Resistance force
2500 N

Ⓐ The mechanical advantage of a machine is the number of times the machine multiplies the effort force. The formula for finding mechanical advantages is:
mechanical advantage
(MA) = resistance force (F_r) divided by effort force (F_e).

$$MA = F_r/F_e$$

Ⓑ The counselors applied an effort force of 500 N to the branch. The branch-lever applied a resistance force of 2500 N to the truck. Calculate the mechanical advantage of the branch-lever.

$$MA = F_r/F_e = MA = 2500\ N/500\ N$$
$$MA = 5$$

Ⓒ The branch-lever multiplied the force exerted by the counselors 5 times. This means the branch-lever made the job of lifting the truck 5 times easier for the counselors.

Figure 5-10

Suppose you did not know the amount of resistance force or effort force. Could you still calculate the MA of a lever? Yes, MA can also be calculated by dividing the length of the effort arm (l_e) by the length of the resistance arm (l_r). The formula for this calculation is $MA = l_e/l_r$.

(A) Apply the formula to determine the mechanical advantage of the branch-lever shown here and the branch-lever on page 161. Which provides the most help with lifting the truck?

Resistance arm: 0.3 m

Effort arm: 1.0 m

Engineers use mechanical advantage as they design machines. They need to know how long to make a lever, or how steep an inclined plane should be to do the job they need done.

But you don't have to be an engineer to use mechanical advantage. Have you ever played on a seesaw with

Efficiency

When you squeeze the brake handles of the bicycle in the picture, the rubber brake pads clamp down against the rim of the tires, using friction to exert a force on the wheels and slow their speed. Friction occurs whenever two substances rub against each other.

Lost Effort

Some of the effort force put into any machine with moving parts is lost to friction. For example, some of the effort force you exert when you pedal a bike is lost to the friction of the pedal gear rubbing against the bicycle chain. The energy used by a machine to work against the force of friction, rather than to do useful work, reduces the efficiency of the machine. Efficiency is a comparison of how much work a machine can do and how much work must be put into the machine. You can figure out the efficiency of a machine by dividing the work output by the work input, then multiplying this by 100.

$$\text{efficiency} = \frac{W_{out}}{W_{in}} \times 100\% = \frac{F_r \times d_r}{F_e \times d_e} \times 100\%$$

Efficiency is usually expressed as a percentage. Low-efficiency machines lose much of the someone who weighed a lot more or less than you? What did you have to do to balance your weights? Most likely, you had to move the seesaw so the heavier person was on the shorter side. You changed the mechanical advantage of the seesaw (which is a lever) by making one of its arms longer than the other. What other situations can you think of when knowing about mechanical advantage would help?

In the Investigate activity that follows, you will discover another use for mechanical advantage.

B What science principle about the relationship between lever length and mechanical advantage do these two examples demonstrate?

Effort arm: 3.0 m

Resistance arm: 0.3 m

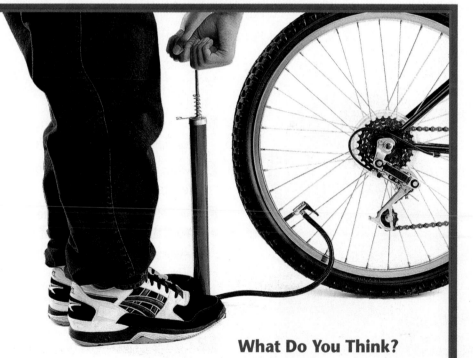

work put into them to work against friction—high-efficiency machines do not. A machine that does no work against friction would have an efficiency of 100 percent. That is, 100 percent of the work put into the machine is used to do useful work. No machine operates at 100 percent efficiency because all machines must work against friction of some kind.

Boosting Efficiency

You can increase the efficiency of a machine by adding a lubricant, such as oil or grease, to the surfaces that rub together. If a bicycle's chain, gears, and other moving parts are cleaned and lubricated periodically, the bicycle will operate more efficiently. Also keeping the tires properly inflated will reduce friction between the road and tires.

What Do You Think?

The efficiency of an automobile is usually expressed in terms of gas mileage. How can changing the engine oil increase the gas mileage of the automobile?

Measuring Mass with Levers

You have seen that mechanical advantage can be calculated using either the forces or the length of the arms. Let's investigate another way that mechanical advantage can be used.

Problem

Can you measure mass with a lever?

Materials

1 sheet of stiff paper,
   20 cm × 28 cm (8 1/2 × 11 in)
3 coins (quarter, dime, and nickel)
balance
metric ruler

What To Do

1 Fold the paper in half lengthwise, then fold it lengthwise again, to make a lever 5 cm wide by 28 cm long.

2 Mark a line 2 cm away from one end of the lever. Label this line resistance.

3 Slide the other end of the lever over the edge of a table until the lever begins to teeter but doesn't fall off. Mark a line across the lever at the point where it crosses the table edge. Mark this line effort.

4 Measure the mass of the lever to the nearest 0.1 g. Write this mass on the effort line.

5 Center a dime on the resistance line.

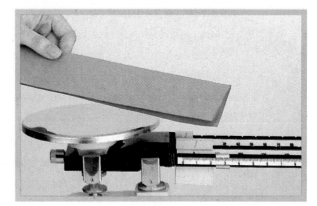

A   **B**

6 Once again, slide the lever over the edge of the desk until it teeters. Mark a line where the lever crosses the table edge and label it fulcrum #1.

7 *Measure* the length of the resistance arm from the center of the dime to the new fulcrum, and the effort arm from the new fulcrum to the effort line. Measure to the nearest 0.1 cm.

8 *Calculate* the MA of the lever. Multiply the MA by the mass of the lever to find the mass of the coin.

9 Repeat Steps 5 through 9 with the nickel and then with the quarter. Mark the fulcrum line #2 for the nickel and #3 for the quarter.

Analyzing

1. Is the total length of the lever a constant or a variable?

2. Describe the length of the effort arm and resistance arm. Identify whether the lengths are constant or variable.

3. *Infer* what provides the effort force.

4. What does it mean if the MA is less than 1?

Concluding and Applying

5. Is it necessary to have the resistance line 2 cm from the end of the lever?

6. Going Further Why can mass units be used in place of force units in this kind of problem?

If you had put two dimes on the resistance point, what would have happened to the fulcrum? What about four dimes? If you had done this Investigate activity with a number of different masses, you could have plotted a graph of the relationship between the length of the effort arm and the mass. This is a direct relationship. As one increases, the other increases, assuming the length of the lever stays constant. Using this relationship, you could find the length of a lever needed to lift different masses. What would happen to the effort force if you moved the fulcrum even closer to the resistance force?

Use another method to calculate the MA of a wheel and axle. The radius of the wheel is the effort arm, and the radius of the axle is the resistance arm. Look at **Figure 5-11** for an example.

Does every machine offer a mechanical advantage? What about a machine that does not increase the force, but only changes the direction of force? Assume you're raising a flag a distance of 10 m to the top of a flagpole. You pull down on 10 m of rope in order to raise the flag 10 m. The effort arm is 10 m long, and the resistance arm is 10 m long. Your effort force moves the same distance as the pulley's resistance force. What is the

Figure 5-11

What kind of simple machine is the ice cream maker? Do you know a formula to calculate its mechanical advantage?

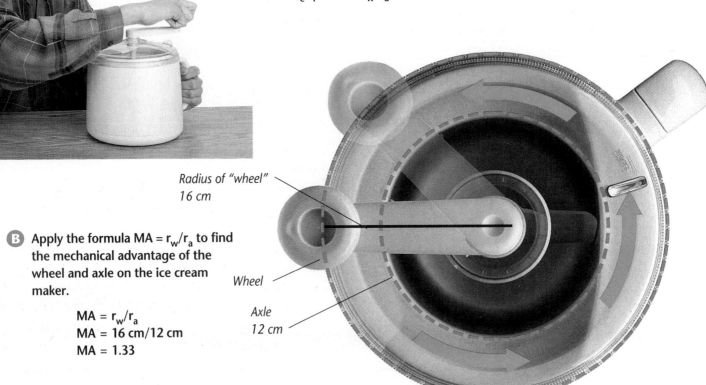

A You used the formula $MA = l_e/l_r$ to calculate the mechanical advantage of a lever. You can also use this formula to calculate the MA of a wheel and axle. In a wheel and axle, the radius of the wheel (r_w) is the effort arm (l_e). The radius of the axle (r_a) is the resistance arm (l_r). Written as an equation,

$$MA = l_e/l_r = MA = r_w/r_a$$

Radius of "wheel" 16 cm

B Apply the formula $MA = r_w/r_a$ to find the mechanical advantage of the wheel and axle on the ice cream maker.

Wheel

$$MA = r_w/r_a$$
$$MA = 16 \text{ cm}/12 \text{ cm}$$
$$MA = 1.33$$

Axle 12 cm

Figure 5-12

A The ropes in pulley systems can be strung in a variety of ways. Some pulleys change direction of the force, but offer no mechanical advantage. Other pulleys multiply the effort force. You can estimate the mechanical advantage of a pulley by counting the number of supporting ropes. A supporting rope is one that leads upward from the load.

MA of the pulley? The fixed pulley has a mechanical advantage of one. It just makes raising the flag more convenient.

Mechanical advantage tells you the ratio between the resistance force and the effort force. The larger the mechanical advantage, the more help the machine is providing. You calculate MA by dividing resistance force by effort force.

You could use this knowledge to explain to the other campers why they wouldn't necessarily need the biggest,

B The single fixed pulley has an MA of 1. The single movable pulley has an MA of 2. What is the MA of the multiple pulley system? From these examples, what can you infer about the relationship between number of supporting ropes and mechanical advantage?

strongest campers to get the truck out of the mud. All they would need is a simple machine with a high mechanical advantage.

check your UNDERSTANDING

1. Define mechanical advantage.
2. An automobile steering wheel with a radius of 40 cm is used to turn the steering column, which has a radius of 4 cm. What is the mechanical advantage of the wheel and axle system?

3. **Apply** Each screwdriver in a set has a handle with a radius that is different from every other screwdriver in the set. The radius of each axle is also different. Which screwdriver would you use to get the greatest mechanical advantage?

Using Machines

5-3

Section Objectives

- Recognize the simple machines that make up a compound machine.
- Describe the relationship between work, power, and time.

Key Terms

compound machine
power

Compound Machines

It's getting close to dinnertime. You hum a favorite song as you put paper plates, mustard, and potato chips on the picnic table. This is the best possible night to pull cooking duty. The menu says chili dogs, so all you have to do to prepare dinner is put a few things on the table and heat up some canned chili. Everyone will roast his or her own hot dog over the campfire. You pull out the can opener and start working on the chili.

Explore! ACTIVITY

What kind of machine is a can opener?

What To Do

1. Using what you know about simple machines, examine a can opener.

2. *In your Journal*, try to describe how it works. What kind of simple machines can you find? Is it a combination of simple machines?

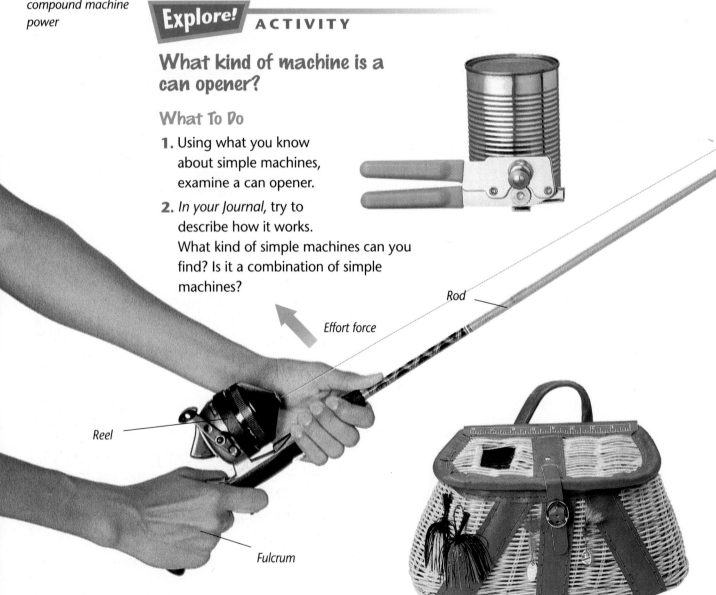

Rod

Effort force

Reel

Fulcrum

166 **Chapter 5** Machines

Figure 5-13

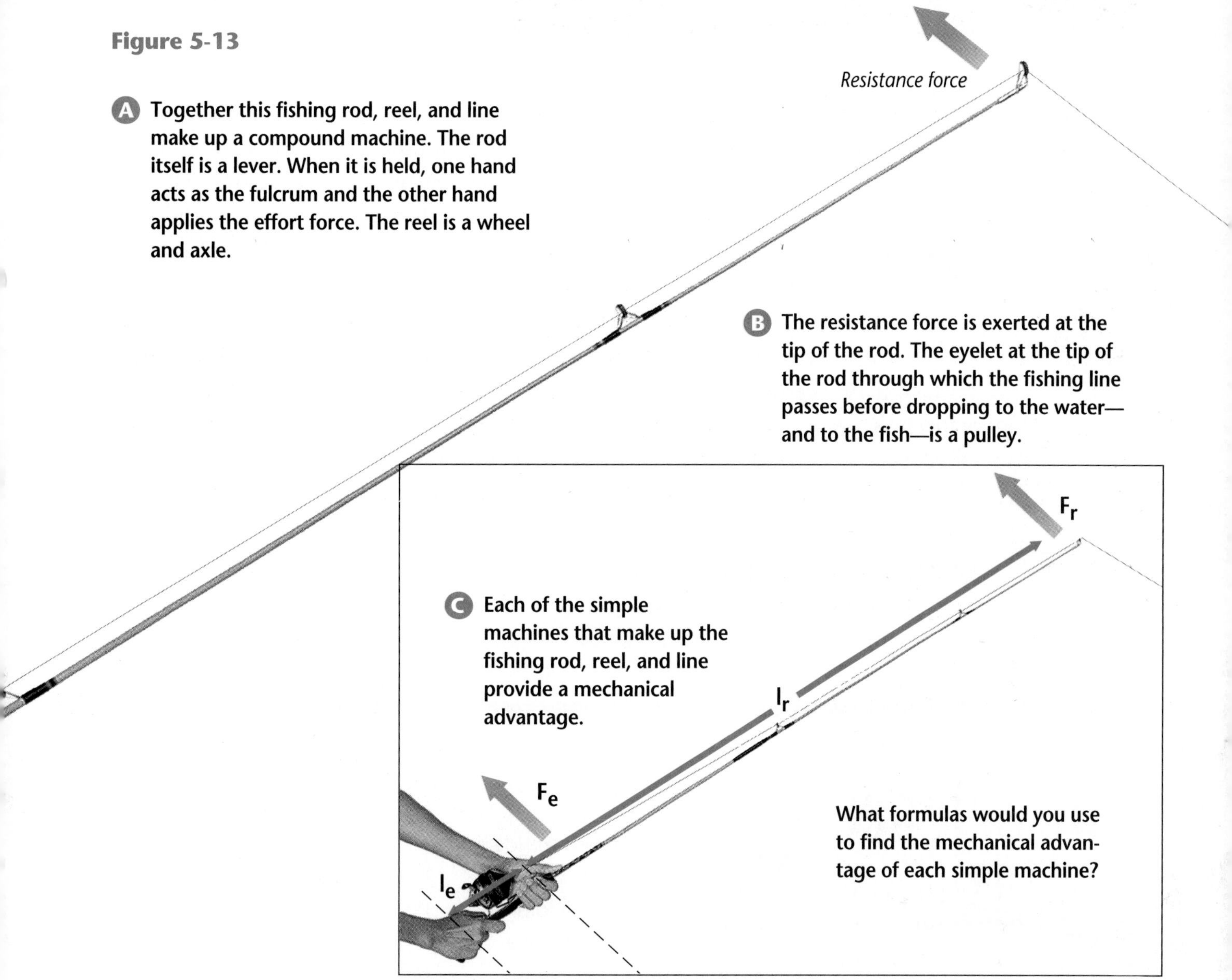

A Together this fishing rod, reel, and line make up a compound machine. The rod itself is a lever. When it is held, one hand acts as the fulcrum and the other hand applies the effort force. The reel is a wheel and axle.

Resistance force

B The resistance force is exerted at the tip of the rod. The eyelet at the tip of the rod through which the fishing line passes before dropping to the water—and to the fish—is a pulley.

C Each of the simple machines that make up the fishing rod, reel, and line provide a mechanical advantage.

F_r

l_r

F_e

l_e

What formulas would you use to find the mechanical advantage of each simple machine?

As you can see, a can opener is actually composed of several simple machines. The handles are two levers that make it easier to fasten the opener onto the edge of a can. The crank is a wheel and axle that turns a toothed wheel. The toothed wheel is called a gear. The first gear turns another gear that moves a circular wedge along the top of the can. The can opener combines the lever, the wheel and axle, and the wedge into a compound machine that makes it easier to open a can.

A **compound machine** is a combination of simple machines that makes it possible to do something one simple machine alone can't do. Can you think of some common compound machines? Look at **Figure 5-13** to see another common compound machine. A fishing rod and reel may look simple, but as far as machines go, it's compound! Before reading on, challenge yourself to identify the simple machines in the fishing rod and reel. If that's too easy, try identifying the machines in a bicycle!

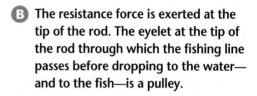
DID YOU KNOW?

The tin can was invented early in the 1800s, but the can opener wasn't invented until more than a hundred years later. At first, people had to use a hammer and chisel to open tin cans!

Power

Sequencing

Make an events chain to show the sequence of how some of the simple machines in a bicycle work together to move the bicycle. Start with the feet applying force to the pedals. If you need help, refer to the **Skill Handbook** on page 636.

You and a friend borrow bikes from the park ranger for the afternoon. You and your friend weigh the same, and your bikes are identical. After pedaling several miles, you begin getting tired. You round a curve and find you're facing a half-mile of steep hill. You manage to pedal all the way up, while your friend has to get off and push the bike. You get to the top of the hill before your friend.

Did you both do the same amount of work? How do you know? Work = force × distance. Since force and distance (the height of the hill) were equal for you and your friend, your work was equal. The only variable was time. You reached the top of the hill first. You did the work faster.

If you divided the amount of work you did by the amount of time to do the work, you would know how much power was used. **Power** is the work done divided by the time interval. The formula for calculating power is

$$\text{power} = \text{work}/\text{time}$$

Life Science CONNECTION

The Machine/Body Interface

Have you ever tried to ride a bike that was the wrong size for you? It probably didn't go very fast, and it may have given you a backache. Or maybe you find that most bikes give you a backache. If so, you need to study ergonomics.

The art and science of making machines suitable for the people who use them is called ergonomics. From computers to office chairs, ergonomics makes many machines more comfortable to use. Applying ergonomic principles to bicycles results in new designs.

Look at the recumbent bicycle shown here. In what ways is it more ergonomically designed than an upright bike?

A Speedy, Comfortable Ride

The first thing people notice about recumbent bikes is the rider's posture. The seat is like a recliner. It gives firm support to

Find Out! ACTIVITY

Can you measure the power of a toy car?

What To Do

1. Place one end of a stiff board on a stack of books to create an inclined plane. Experiment with a wind-up toy car and the steepness of the plane until you find the angle at which the car will travel up the incline at the slowest possible speed.

2. Wind up the car, place it at the bottom of the plane, and then record *in your Journal* the number of seconds it takes to get to the top.

3. Measure the height of the inclined plane in meters. The height is the distance straight up from the floor or table to the top of the incline.

4. Measure the weight of the car in newtons (N). (A kilogram weighs about 9.8 N on Earth's surface.)

5. Multiply the weight of the car by the height of the incline to calculate the work done, in joules (J). Now divide J by the number of seconds it took for the car to climb the incline. Your result is the power of the car. It's expressed in a unit called the watt (W).

Conclude and Apply

What was the power of your toy car?

---

the rider's back and lets him or her make strong forward thrusts to the pedals—so strong that every world land speed and endurance record for human-powered vehicles is held by recumbents.

The biggest advantage of recumbents is their aerodynamic efficiency. In comparison, the rider of an upright bike wastes energy fighting wind drag. Since most of the force a bicycle rider exerts is used to overcome wind resistance, a recumbent can save a lot of energy.

The recumbent rider's nearly reclining position has another benefit, too. It's easier to take deep breaths when you're leaning back than it is when you're crouching over underslung handlebars. Many recumbent bikes have their handlebars below the seat; this helps efficiency by leaving the rider's arms in a natural resting position.

Recumbents can easily be modified for physically challenged riders. For instance, foot pedals can become hand cranks. Paraplegics, amputees, some quadriplegics, and those adapting to the effects of multiple sclerosis or polio can ride modified recumbents and experience speed and maneuverability under their own muscle power.

What Do You Think?

Examine the recumbent bicycle shown here. Compare it to an upright bike in terms of air resistance. Which kind of bike would create more drag and thus lose energy to friction? Think of a way to make the bike with less drag even more streamlined.

Calculating Power

After climbing a long flight of stairs, your heart beats a little faster, your legs may burn, and you probably breathe harder. You don't have to tell your body it just used some power! But does it matter how fast you climb, or how much you weigh?

Problem
What factors determine the power used in walking up a flight of stairs?

Materials
meterstick	flight of stairs
watch with second	bathroom scale
hand or digital	chronometer

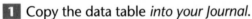

What To Do

1 Copy the data table *into your Journal.*

2 *Measure* the weight, in newtons (N), of a volunteer (see photo *A*). Multiply pounds by 4.45 to get newtons. Record the weight in the table.

3 Measure the vertical height of one step (see photo *B*). Multiply the height of the step by the number of steps. Record the total height of the stairs in the data table.

4 Measure the number of seconds it takes the volunteer to walk up the stairs. Record.

5 *Calculate* the work done, in joules (work = weight × height). Record.

6 *Calculate* the power (work/time) used in walking up the stairs.

7 Repeat for three more volunteers.

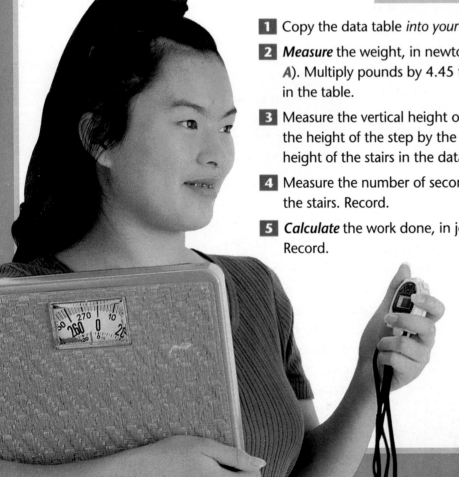

A

B

Data and Observations

Student's Name	Force (N)	Distance (m)	Work (J)	Time (s)	Work/Time (J/s)

Analyzing

1. ***Compare and contrast*** the force exerted by the different people.

2. Which person did the most work? Used the most power?

On Valentine's Day, 1991, Geoff Case and Corliss Spencer led a pack of 133 runners up the 80 flights of the Empire State building, climbing 1,430 steps to the top. The race is an annual event.

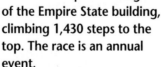

Concluding and Applying

3. Suppose one volunteer walked up the stairs twice. The first time took 10 seconds. The second time took 15 seconds. When did the volunteer use more power?

4. Suppose the heaviest volunteer walked up the stairs much more quickly than the lightest volunteer. ***Predict*** the difference in power used by each person.

5. What determines the amount of power used when walking up the steps?

6. **Going Further** Two volunteers with different weights each decrease their time to climb the stairs from 10 seconds to 8 seconds. Which person has the greater increase in power?

A   What simple machines are examples of a wheel and axle? Does the pulley used to raise the flag offer a mechanical advantage?

B   What simple machine is an example of an inclined plane?

C   How many levers are being used? Where?

Figure 5-14

You've calculated human power, but the same method could be used to calculate the power needed to operate simple and compound machines.

The original campsite scene contained many simple machines. Now, after completing this chapter, you can identify several simple and compound machines. You have determined how much easier these machines can make a task by computing the mechanical advantage. The MA is the ratio of resistance force to effort force.

Finally, you found the power of these machines by dividing the work done by the amount of time it took to do the work. Power = work/time. Now you can compute how much power you use to complete a 3-hour, 5-mile hike up the mountain. What a surprise to find all that work and power at a vacation campsite!

check your UNDERSTANDING

1. Give an example of a compound machine. What are the simple machines that make it up?

2. How are work, power, and time related?

3. **Apply**   How much power does a person weighing 500 N need to climb a 3-m ladder in 5 seconds? How could the same person climb the ladder using less power?

Leisure Connection

Spills, Chills, Waves, and Dunks

You're zooming down a 60-foot-high water slide at speeds of up to 40 miles per hour. You reach the bottom in as little as 15 seconds, but an engineer may have worked on the design of the slide's inclined plane for years. Every bend and twist has been carefully constructed for both speed and safety.

The latest computer technology is used to calculate such factors as the angle of the curves and the lubricating effect of the flowing water. Even the amount of resistance that will be created by your bathing suit is considered.

If your water park has a pool for body surfing and boogie boarding, you can thank a machine for those perfect waves. In the ocean, the wind causes the waves to rise and fall. In a water park, waves are usually created by a computer-operated wave machine. By intermittently pumping air into the pool, the computer generates waves of many sizes and shapes.

You've learned how machines can help to make work easier. The next time you go to a water park, be sure to notice how machines can also work to help you have fun.

You Try It!

Draw the water slide of your dreams. How tall would your slide stand? How long would it take a person to ride it from top to bottom?

Science and Society

Pedal Power!

You've spent months fine-tuning your vehicle. You're all set. At the sound of the starting gun, you jump on your pedals.

Jump on your pedals? That's right. How else do you compete in the International Human Powered Vehicle Association's (IHPVA) Annual Speed Championships?

Most people agree that the bicycle is the most efficient means of transportation on Earth. With its annual races, the IHPVA sets out to prove that bicycles can also be fast. A streamlined bicycle called *Cheetah* set the IHPVA speed record at 68.7 mph. However, a group of high school students in Saginaw, Michigan, just might give the *Cheetah* a run for its money.

On Your Marks ...

The Arthur Hill High School Technology Club was founded by drafting teacher and club advisor, Bruce Isotalo. Members of the club use the principles of compound machines

to design and build human powered vehicles (HPVs), shown in the picture. In 1988, the club signed up to enter its first IHPVA Speed Championships.

Mr. Isotalo recalls how the club created that first HPV, the *da Vinci*. "First, we had to decide what we wanted the vehicle to accomplish. We chose speed as our main goal." To meet their goal, the club members paid

Engineers apply the discoveries of scientists to design, develop, and produce products and systems. Mechanical engineers are unique in the engineering field because they create many of the tools and machines required by other engineers. Mechanical engineers work in industry, business, government service, and universities.

special attention to the *da Vinci's* body design. As you know, when energy is used to overcome friction, efficiency is reduced. With this in mind, the club chose a streamlined body design to allow air to flow smoothly around the *da Vinci*. To keep the weight of the *da Vinci* low, they selected lightweight aluminum as the building material. Once the design had been finalized, it was time to begin the task of transforming the *da Vinci* from an idea into a road-worthy machine. The students worked for months to perfect the wheel-and-axle system in the vehicle's powerful pedaling mechanism.

Get Set ...

The IHPVA Speed Championships were scheduled for August and would be held in Michigan. During summer vacation, many students worked on the *da Vinci* eight hours a day. "We sent out for a lot of pizza that summer," laughs Mr. Isotalo. "But we stuck with it. I think that was one of the greatest things about this project. We learned that there is nothing that can't be accomplished when you put your mind to it."

Go!

On a hot August day in 1989, the *da Vinci* took its place at the starting line of the International Human Powered Vehicle Speed

Championships. The club members watched with pride as the *da Vinci* placed among the top 20 in the sprint event.

In 1990, the Technology Club radically altered the design and the *da Vinci 2* placed third in a grueling 24-hour marathon event. The club continues to explore the potential of human power with a new model every year.

Designing the Future

As engineers, like the students in the Technology Club, push the limits of human power, there may be a day when human-powered vehicles are a common sight on roadways. The dwindling supply of fossil fuels is pushing us towards clean, alternative sources of power. As the IHPVA Annual Speed Championships have shown, many of the shortcomings of alternative power sources can be overcome through innovative design.

What Do You Think?

Imagine what it may be like getting on the school bus and having to pedal your way to school! Think about the possibility of human-powered cars, trains, and school buses. What problems might there be with human-powered transportation? What else could human power be used for besides transportation?

Teens in SCIENCE

Hard Work—the Easy Way to Have Fun

Have you ever been surprised by how much fun you were having while doing a difficult task? For Stephanie Ostler, an original member of the Technology Club, helping to design and build a human powered vehicle was both a challenge and a thrill.

"For me, working on the *da Vinci* was like putting together a puzzle. Only it was harder, because we had to invent each piece of the puzzle first."

With each stage of the *da Vinci's* production, the club members discovered that a new set of problems developed.

"We all worked together to solve problems. Every decision was made by vote.

"By the time summer came, the *da Vinci* was the only thing any of us thought about."

Stephanie did, however, devote some thought to seeing the world around her in a different way.

"I had just gotten my driver's license when I joined the club. At that time, I thought cars were about the greatest thing on Earth. I never really thought about how they affect the environment. After I drove the *da Vinci*, I was really sold on HPVs as an alternative to cars. Not only do they save energy, but they are good exercise, too!"

As the summer drew to an end, Stephanie realized

that the experience of working on the *da Vinci* had an important effect on her. "This may sound weird, but I think one of the best things about the project was completing it. We started out with nothing more than an idea, but we just kept working at it until we had something we could be proud of. I think everybody should explore things they don't know anything about. It really feels good when you figure it out."

The greatest satisfaction, however, was to come on the day of the race.

"I don't think I'll ever forget the race. There we were with inventors and inventions from all over the world. It was awesome."

You Try It!

Even though her HPV did not win the IHPVA Speed Championships, Stephanie is very proud of her work on the *da Vinci*. Which experiences in your life have affected you most? Stephanie Ostler encourages people to try new things. Make a list of some new things you would like to try.

Review the statements below about the big ideas presented in this chapter, and try to answer the questions. Then, re-read your answers to the Did You Ever Wonder questions at the beginning of the chapter. *In your Journal*, write a paragraph about how your understanding of the big ideas in the chapter has changed.

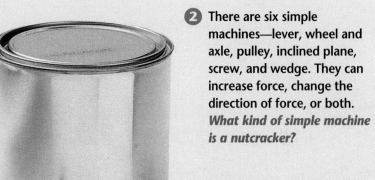

1 Machines make work easier. *What are some machines that make work you need to do easier?*

2 There are six simple machines—lever, wheel and axle, pulley, inclined plane, screw, and wedge. They can increase force, change the direction of force, or both. *What kind of simple machine is a nutcracker?*

3 Machines do not reduce the amount of work that has to be done. *If a machine doesn't change the amount of work that needs to be done, how does it make the work seem easier?*

4 Mechanical advantage (MA) tells you how helpful a machine is in doing a job. MA is the ratio between the resistance force and the effort force. *How can you use knowledge of MA in choosing a machine to do a job?*

5 Power is the work done divided by the time it took to do the work. *Does it require more power to lift a book quickly or to lift the same book the same distance slowly?*

Using Key Science Terms

compound machine	pulley
effort force	resistance force
inclined plane	screw
lever	wedge
mechanical advantage	wheel and axle
power	

For each set of terms below, choose the one term that does not belong and explain why it does not belong.

1. wheel and axle, power, lever
2. watt, power, mechanical advantage
3. wedge, pulley, inclined plane, screw
4. joule, watt, power, newton
5. bicycle, can opener, lever

Understanding Ideas

Answer the following questions in complete sentences.

1. How is a screw an inclined plane?
2. The radius of a bicycle wheel is 35 cm. The gear that is the axle has a radius of 2.0 cm. Find the mechanical advantage.
3. Explain why machines make things easier.
4. Do machines ever increase the amount of work done? Explain your answer.
5. Why doesn't using a pulley on a flagpole increase the force?
6. How is mechanical advantage calculated?
7. Explain why a seesaw works best when the heavier person sits closer to the middle than the lighter person.

Developing Skills

Use your understanding of the concepts developed in this chapter to answer each of the following questions.

1. **Concept Map** Complete the following concept map of simple machines using the following terms: *compound machines, mechanical advantage, resistance force, work.*

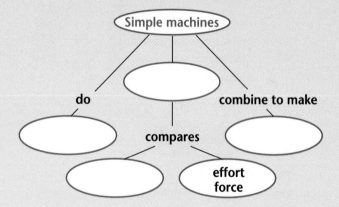

2. **Comparing and Contrasting** Compare and contrast the pulley made in the Find Out activity on page 153 and a pulley on a fishing rod.
3. **Forming a Hypothesis** Form a hypothesis stating why a claw hammer used for removing nails is or is not a simple machine.
4. **Making and Using Graphs** Refer to the Find Out activity on page 169. Graph the measurements of height versus power. First change the height of the ramp several times, and calculate the power each time. What relationship is there between the height and power?
5. **Interpret Data** From the data gathered in the Investigate on page 170, interpret the relationship between force and work.

Critical Thinking

Use your understanding of the concepts developed in the chapter to answer each of the following questions.

50N

350N

1. What is the MA of the axe the woodcutter is using to split the log in the figure?

2. To screw a 5-cm screw into a piece of wood requires turning a screwdriver 15 times. For each turn of the screwdriver, your hand moves 15 cm. What is the MA of the screw?

3. A bricklayer is carrying boxes weighing 400 N up a flight of stairs 10 m high. It takes him 90 seconds. A carpenter is hammering in one nail every 30 seconds. He exerts a force of 500 N over a distance of .05 m. How many watts of power does the bricklayer produce in the 90 seconds it takes him to climb the stairs? How much power does the carpenter produce in 90 seconds?

4. A claw hammer has a mechanical advantage equal to 8. It is used to pull a nail that exerts a force of 2500 N. What is the effort force needed to pull the nail?

Problem Solving

Read the following paragraph and discuss your answers in a brief paragraph.

Suppose you and a friend are pushing boxes of camping gear up a ramp to load them into a van. All the boxes weigh the same, but you push faster than your friend. You can move a box up the ramp from the ground to the van in 30 seconds. It takes your friend 45 seconds.

1. Are you both doing the same amount of work? Explain your answer.

2. Assume the boxes weigh 100 N and the ramp is 1 m high. How many watts of power are you each producing?

CONNECTING IDEAS

Discuss each of the following in a brief paragraph.

1. **Theme—Systems and Interactions** Explain why scissors are a compound machine.

2. **Theme—Systems and Interactions** Explain how a shovel works like a lever.

3. **A Closer Look** Using a ramp 4 meters long, workers apply an effort force of 1250 N to move a 2000 N crate onto a platform 2 meters high. What is the efficiency of the ramp?

4. **Science and Society** What design features did the *da Vinci* bicycle have that allowed it to conserve more energy than a conventional bicycle?

5. **Life Science Connection** Why do you think it is helpful to design some machines to work with the human body?

CHAPTER 6

THERMAL ENERGY

✓ **How temperature scales are created?**

✓ **Why insulation keeps things hot or cold?**

✓ **How an air conditioner or refrigerator works?**

Before you begin to study thermal energy, think about these questions and answer them *in your Journal*. When you finish the chapter, compare your Journal write-up with what you have learned.

We live our lives in climates that range from hot to cold. For many people on Earth, the seasons bring regular changes. Temperatures will vary from hot to mild to cold and then back again.

Hot and cold are things you feel, things your body reacts to. You sweat under a scorching sun and shiver in freezing wind. Before you even go outside, you'll react to the temperature when you read a thermometer. How you dress might depend on what the thermometer tells you about the outside temperature. A cold day means more clothes and a hot day fewer. But what actually is heat? What is temperature? Are they the same thing?

▶ *In the activity on the next page, explore your body's built-in thermometer.*

ACTIVITY

How do we feel "heat"?

Have you ever put your hand in your bath or shower water to make sure it's at a comfortable temperature, or felt your forehead to see if you have a fever? If you have, you were relying on your sense of touch to estimate temperature. But how accurate is your sense of touch?

What To Do

1. Collect a group of familiar objects made of various materials, and place them on a table together, leaving them for several minutes.

2. Use the underside of your wrist to feel which objects feel warmest and which ones feel coldest. This area of your skin is very sensitive to hot and cold objects.

3. *In your Journal,* estimate the temperature of each object.

6-1 Thermal Energy

Section Objectives
- Describe how two objects achieve thermal equilibrium.
- Determine when two objects have the same temperature.
- Use the Celsius temperature scale.

Key Terms

thermal equilibrium

How Do We Know If Something Is Hot or Cold?

You're on the telephone with a friend in another city on a hot summer afternoon. You're both trying to describe how hot it is outside, but neither of you has a thermometer. How could you accurately describe how hot it is?

Like most ideas in science, heat and temperature are connected to our everyday lives. You use your sense of touch to tell you whether something is hot or cold. It can even tell you when one object is hotter or colder than another object. Or can your sense of touch be fooled? In the next activity, you will explore how accurate your sense of touch is for judging the temperature of three containers of water.

Explore! ACTIVITY

Is your sense of touch accurate for judging temperature?

What To Do

1. Fill a pan with lukewarm water. Fill a second pan with cold water and crushed ice. Fill a third pan with very warm water.

2. Now, put one hand into the cold water and the other hand into the warm water. Hold them in the water for 15 seconds.

3. Quickly remove both hands from the water and then put both into the pan of lukewarm water. How do they feel now? Do both hands feel the same way? Can you explain why your hands feel as they do? Record your observations *in your Journal.*

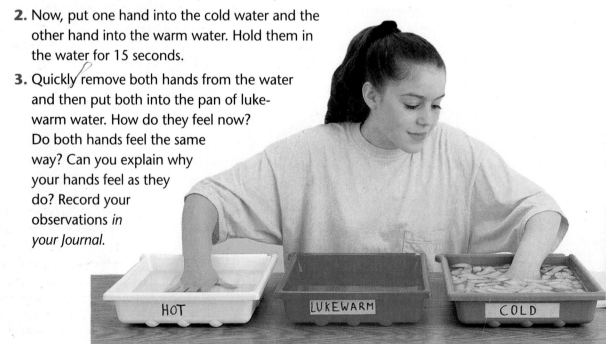

As you've just seen, your sense of touch can be fooled. What does that tell you about your earlier Explore activity with the various objects? If two items feel different, does that really mean that they're at different temperatures? Relying on our sense of touch doesn't help us tell someone else exactly how hot something is. We need a more precise way to indicate temperature.

Around the year 1600, Galileo observed that air takes up more space when it's warm than when it's cold. Galileo used that information in making an instrument to indicate a change in temperature, shown in **Figure 6-1**. About 100 years later, German scientist G. D. Fahrenheit improved Galileo's design by using alcohol or mercury instead of air. Like air, these liquids also take up more space when hot than when cold. But they don't expand as much as air does. Fahrenheit let the liquids expand in a very narrow tube. Why do you suppose he had to do this? Fahrenheit's invention, in **Figure 6-2**, is the thermometer you've used to find the temperature outside or to check your temperature when you're sick.

Figure 6-1

Galileo's thermoscope consisted of a bent column of glass connected to a glass bubble. The column contained liquid. The bubble contained air.

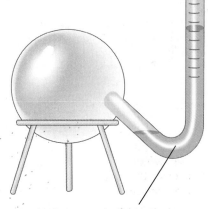

As the room temperature rose, the air in the bubble warmed. The warmed air, needing more room, pushed the liquid up the column.

Figure 6-2

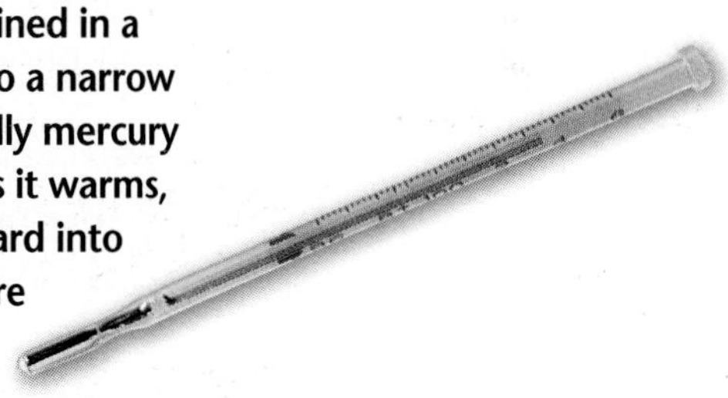

Ⓐ *Liquid-In-Glass Thermometers* consist of a fluid contained in a glass bulb connected to a narrow tube. The liquid—usually mercury or alcohol—expands as it warms, causing it to flow upward into the tube as temperature increases.

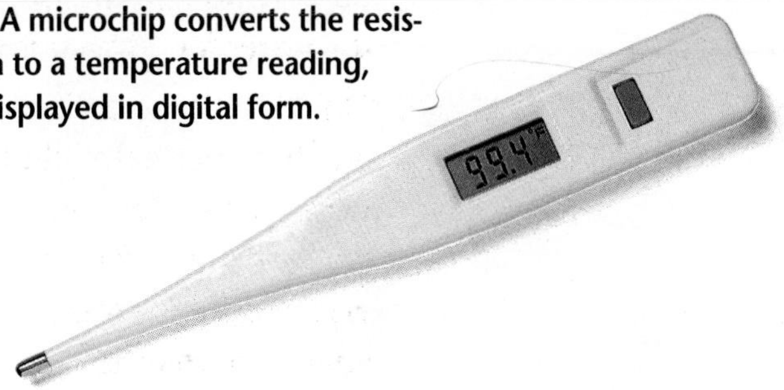

Ⓑ *Thermistor Thermometers* indicate temperature by measuring the resistance of a ceramic bead, called a thermistor, to an electric current. The thermistor's resistance decreases as temperature increases. A microchip converts the resistance data to a temperature reading, which is displayed in digital form.

Ⓒ *Liquid Crystal Thermometers* are made of individual containers, each holding a different type of crystal, which melts and changes color at a specific temperature. The containers are fastened together. As the crystals in each container react to the warmth and cold, color change indicates the temperature.

INVESTIGATE!

How Cold Is It?

Do you remember the last time you had your temperature taken? How long did you have to hold the thermometer under your tongue? Was it several minutes, or did it read your temperature instantly? In this activity you'll investigate the time needed to change the temperature of a container of water.

Problem

What happens to the temperature of warm and cold water when left at room temperature?

Materials

3 thermometers
3 stirring rods
hot plate or heating
 element
ice
paper towels

3 400-mL beakers
300 mL of water
stopwatch or clock
 with second hand
graph paper

Safety Precautions

Do not use mercury thermometers. Use caution when heating water with a hot plate.

What To Do

1 Copy the data table *into your Journal,* extending it to 15 minutes. Work in teams of three. Decide who will be the timekeeper, who will read the thermometers and stir the beakers, and who will record observations.

Data and Observations			
Time	Cold Water (°C)	Warm Water (°C)	Room Temp. Water (°C)
Start			
1 min.			
2 min.			
3 min.			
4 min.			
5 min.			

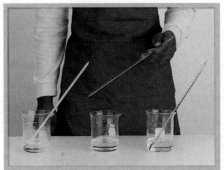

A   B

2 Fill one beaker with the ice and 100 mL of water. Add 100 mL of water to another beaker.

3 Heat 100 mL of water in the third beaker until it's about 70° C.

4 Remove the ice from the first beaker and put a thermometer in each of the three beakers. Record the beginning temperatures of the three beakers of water.

5 *Predict* what will happen to the temperatures of each of the three beakers of water as they sit at room temperature for 15 minutes. Record your predictions *in your Journal*.

6 At one minute intervals, have the timekeeper notify the thermometer reader when to take a reading. The reader should read the temperature of each beaker of water in the same order every minute. Stir the water with a stirring rod between each reading. Continue taking readings for 15 minutes.

7 Make a graph like the one pictured. Using a different color pencil for each beaker, plot the time and temperature data from the cold, lukewarm, and hot water. Connect the points with a curve. Extend the curve to see what might happen if you took readings for a longer time.

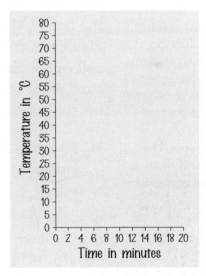

Analyzing

1. What do the extended temperature curves appear to do?

2. How did your predictions compare to the results?

Concluding and Applying

3. *Predict* what would happen if you combined the warm water with the room-temperature water.

4. Going Further What could you do to slow the change in temperature among the beakers? How could you speed it up?

Thermal Equilibrium

Figure 6-3

The glass of water has been in the room long enough for the water temperature to become equal to the temperature of the air in the room. The water and air are in thermal equilibrium.

In the Investigate you just completed, the temperatures of the warm and cold water were changing at every data point. When you extended your graph, however, you could predict when the temperature change would stop. It stopped when it reached the temperature of the air surrounding the water. When two objects are in contact, as the water and air were, and the temperature of one is the same as the temperature of the other, as in **Figure 6-3**, they are said to be in **thermal equilibrium**. We call the temperature of the two objects the equilibrium temperature.

■ Thermal Equilibrium and Energy

You observed that a warm beaker of water will gradually cool off until it reaches thermal equilibrium with the air around it. You might wonder where the warmth goes. Does it just disappear, or does it go somewhere else?

For a clue to help you answer this question, think back to when you were studying work and energy. You pulled a heavy box across a surface, doing work on the box. When you stopped pulling, the box stopped moving so there was no observable kinetic energy. According to the law of conservation of energy, energy cannot be lost, so you looked for where the energy you put into the box went. It hadn't gained potential energy. However, when you felt the bottom of the box, it was warm. You were feeling evidence of another kind of energy, called thermal energy.

This means that when the beaker of warm water cooled, thermal energy was transferred to the surrounding air. A similar thing happened to the cool water. As it warmed, it gained thermal energy from its surroundings.

Figure 6-4

Ⓐ The photographs show two glasses of iced tea. One is just poured, the other has been left for three hours. Which is in thermal equilibrium with the air in the room?

Ⓑ These people are playing in cool water on a very hot day. Will they warm up or cool down? Why?

Temperature Scales

As you wake up one morning, you turn on the radio and the weather reporter says it's 30 degrees outside. Should you put on a sweater or a t-shirt? In order to answer this, you need to know what scale the weather reporter was using to measure the temperature. In the next activity, you will find out how to make a temperature scale.

SKILLBUILDER

Comparing and Contrasting
Compare and contrast the method used to measure temperature in the following thermometers: liquid-in-glass, thermistor, and liquid crystal. If you need help, refer to the **Skill Handbook** on page 642.

Find Out! ACTIVITY

How do you make a temperature scale?

What To Do

1. Prepare a beaker of ice water. Place an unmarked alcohol thermometer in the ice water and put the beaker on a hot plate.

2. Using a stirring rod, stir the mixture as the ice melts and watch the thermometer. What happens to the level of the thermometer while the ice is melting? Mark that level on the thermometer.

3. As the water warms and eventually boils, keep watching the thermometer level. What happens while the water boils? Mark that level, too.

4. Now divide the space between the two points into 20 equal divisions. Mark each division on the thermometer with a fine-point marker and a metric ruler, as shown in the figure. Number each division starting at the melting point mark. Each division is one degree on your scale.

5. Name your scale and use it to measure various objects. *In your Journal,* record these measurements, making sure you identify the scale.

Conclude and Apply

1. How would your measurements be different if there were twice as many divisions on your thermometer?

2. Would the thermometer be as helpful if the divisions were not equal? Why?

Figure 6-5

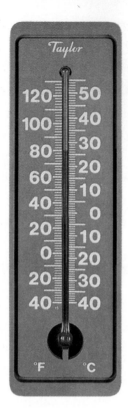

A The Celsius scale, developed by Anders Celsius in 1742, is the most used scale in the world. The melting point of water in Celsius scale is 0°, and the boiling point is 100°.

B Another common scale is one developed by Gabriel Fahrenheit around 1715. The Fahrenheit scale uses 32° as the melting point of water, and 212° as water's boiling point.

C The numbers on the two scales are arranged differently. This thermometer has both scales marked on it. Does the temperature at which water melts or boils actually change from scale to scale?

If both you and your out-of-town friend had a thermometer like the one you made in the Find Out activity, you could tell which city was the hottest. But imagine that the thermometer your friend made had 40 divisions between the melting point and the boiling point. Would it be easy to tell whose city was warmer? Why?

If you look at **Figure 6-5**, you will see two common temperature scales you might be familiar with. One is the Fahrenheit scale and the other is the Celsius scale.

Using the same temperature scale might tell you whose city is warmer, but how did your cities get so hot to

Latent Heat

In the Find Out activity in this chapter you saw that the temperature of ice water didn't change as the ice was melting. Nor did the temperature of boiling water change as the water turned to steam. But you know that thermal energy was being added to the water in each case. Where did the energy go if it didn't result in higher temperatures?

Experiments have shown that it takes about 2260 joules to turn 1 g of water at 100° C to steam at 100° C. The amount of energy required to change the state of a material is known as latent heat. The word latent means hidden. Latent heat got that name because it's not easily seen as a temperature change. Water at 0° C seems as though it has the same amount of thermal energy as ice at 0° C because they both have the same temperature. But water actually has more energy. In the same way, 100° C steam has

begin with? How did the heat outdoors get into your homes? How do you think you could make your homes cooler in the hot weather? Changing things from hot to cold or from cold to hot requires us to look at the concept of transferring thermal energy. You'll explore that in the next section.

check your UNDERSTANDING

1. Suppose you remove a spoon from a cup of hot cocoa. The cocoa has a temperature of 80° C and the room is at 23° C. Sketch a graph of the temperature of the spoon versus time after the spoon is removed from the cocoa.

2. Describe the flow of thermal energy between the spoon and the air when the spoon was the same temperature as the room.

3. Using the Celsius scale, what temperature would be midway between the freezing point and boiling point of water? What are the temperatures of the following: melting ice, boiling water, and room temperature?

4. **Apply** How would the graph you sketched in Question 1 be different if you had measured temperature using the Fahrenheit scale instead of the Celsius scale?

more energy than 100° C water.

Latent heats are the same for freezing as for melting. The same is true for boiling and condensation. You need to add 334 J to 1 gram of ice at 0° C to make it melt, or remove 334 J from 1 gram of water to make it freeze. You must add 2260 J to 1 gram of water at 100° C to make it boil, or remove 2260 J from 1 gram of steam at 100° C to turn it back to water.

You Try It!

In a large beaker, add 200 mL of water to a beaker full of crushed ice. Stir with a stirring rod until the temperature is 0° C. Pour 100 mL of the water only into a second beaker. Pour 100 mL of the water and crushed ice mixture into a third beaker. With a thermometer in each, place both of these beakers on a hot plate and turn it on. Which beaker will reach 20° C first? Record *in your Journal* the temperature of each beaker every 10 seconds. Record how long it takes for each beaker to reach 20° C. How can latent heat explain what you observed?

6-2 Heat and Temperature

Section Objectives

- Describe heat as the transfer of energy.
- Distinguish temperature from heat.
- Give examples of heat transfer by conduction, convection, and radiation.
- Identify materials that reduce heat transfer most effectively.

Key Terms

heat, conduction, convection, radiation

What Is Heat?

You may have heard the expression, "If you can't stand the heat, stay out of the kitchen." In fact, you've probably used the word "heat" many times. But what exactly is heat? Is it the same as temperature?

Heat is related to temperature, but it is not the same as temperature. Temperature measures how much thermal energy there is in an object. **Heat** is the energy transferred from something of higher temperature to something of lower temperature.

When you feel a beaker of warm water, thermal energy is transferred from the water to your skin.

Suppose you place warm water in a cold container. The heat moves from the warm water to the cold container. The transfer of thermal energy will continue until the two objects are in thermal equilibrium.

If heat is energy in transit, how does it move? What is it that takes thermal energy from one place to another? Let's explore.

Explore! ACTIVITY

How does thermal energy transfer from one object to another?

What To Do

1. Gather a wooden spoon, a metal spoon, and a plastic spoon, all about the same length. Stick a bead to the handle of each spoon the same distance from the other end, using a dab of butter.

2. Stand the spoons in a short beaker so that the beads are hanging over the edge of the beaker. If the butter melts, the beads will fall. *In your Journal*, predict the order in which the beads will fall if hot water is added to the beaker.

3. Boil water in another beaker and carefully pour about 5 cm of the hot water into the beaker holding the spoons. Observe the order in which the beads fall. Did other groups get the same results?

From the Explore activity, you could infer that thermal energy traveled from the hot water to the spoons. Did you see any evidence of energy moving from the water to the spoons? If you held a spoon about 10 centimeters above the water, do you think it would get warm?

■ Conduction

In the Explore activity you just completed, you saw that heat was transferred along the spoons. This process—heat moving through a material or from one material to another—is known as **conduction**. That's what happened with the spoons. The heat flowed up the spoon to melt the butter.

In order for thermal energy to transfer by conduction from one object to another, objects must be in physical contact. Conduction transfers heat from a beaker of hot water to the butter via the spoons.

Figure 6-7

Ⓐ The properties of various materials, including their ability to transfer heat are taken into account when designing cooking utensils. Because metals, such as copper and aluminum, are good conductors of heat, they are natural choices for pots and pans.

Ⓑ The metal bottom of the pan transfers thermal energy from the burner to the food. Why are the handles of many pots and pans made of wood?

Figure 6-6

Ⓐ To measure how well various substances transfer heat, you need a standard to measure them against. Silver is a good standard because it conducts heat very well. Silver is given a value of 1.

SILVER
1.00

Ⓑ The ability of other substances to transfer heat is given as a number that compares that substance's ability to conduct heat with the conducting ability of silver.

WOOD
0.01

Ⓒ The ability of wood to conduct heat is only about 0.01 of the conducting ability of silver.

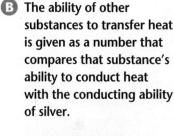

WATER
0.0014

Ⓓ Which is a better conductor of heat: air or water?

AIR
0.00005

Connect to...

Life Science

The amount of wind affects the rate at which heat is lost. It results in cooling a person and can lead to hypothermia. Prepare a short talk to inform your classmates of the symptoms and dangers associated with hypothermia.

■ **Convection**

Liquids and gases are called fluids because they flow. Fluids conduct thermal energy poorly. However, you've seen many cases where thermal energy is transferred by a fluid. When you feel heat from a hair dryer, the heat is contained in the moving air. Warm winds carry heat from one place to another on Earth. Warm ocean currents carry heat from the tropics to cooler northern climates. Warm air is blown through ducts to heat a home. In all of the above examples, something carries heat as it moves from one place to another. A material that carries something else is known as a medium. A fluid such as air or water can be a medium for carrying heat. **Convection** is heat transfer by motion of a heat-carrying medium. Can you think of any other examples where you have seen heat transferred by convection?

You know that the air near the ceiling of a room is generally warmer than the air near the floor. This can be an important thing to remember if you are in a burning building. The warmer smoke will rise to the ceiling, and the cooler air will be found near the floor. That means to avoid the smoke, you can crawl along the floor.

In the next Investigate, you will explore convection using a colored ice cube.

Earth Science CONNECTION

Convection Beneath Your Feet

In Chapter 2 you learned about plate tectonics, the theory that explains how mountains form and why earthquakes and volcanic eruptions occur in some places but not in others. But what makes plate tectonics work? If you look back to pages 68-69, you'll see that Earth's outer crust is made of many rigid pieces, called plates, that move around because they float on the denser molten rock forming the mantle beneath. This denser molten rock is called Earth's mantle. It surrounds the extremely dense core.

The Energy Comes from the Core

The pressure at Earth's center is calculated to be about 3.7 million atmospheres—that is, about 3 700 000 times the surface pressure at sea level. This tremendous pressure makes the core very hot. Heat radiates outward from the core and warms the mantle, which is a putty-like solid.

Since the mantle surrounds the core, the energy heating

Figure 6-8

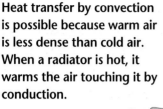

Heat transfer by convection is possible because warm air is less dense than cold air. When a radiator is hot, it warms the air touching it by conduction.

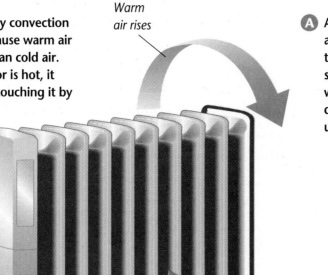

Warm air rises

A As the air warms, it expands and becomes less dense than the surrounding air. The cool surrounding air slides under the warm air. Because it is less dense, the warm air is pushed up above the cold air.

B In time, the cold air is also warmed and is pushed upward by more cold air. The stream of rising warm air is called a convection current.

Cool air replaces the warm air

the mantle comes from underneath. You already know what happens when a fluid is heated from the bottom: convection occurs. As the mantle material warms, it expands, and becomes less dense. It is pushed upward by cooler, denser material flowing in underneath. In the circulation that results, heat is carried upward toward Earth's surface.

The convection currents move slowly, compared to those you can see in a pot of boiling water. Earth's convection currents are estimated to move at less than a few centimeters a year. But slow or not, Earth's convection currents are an important part of the theory of plate tectonics.

What Do You Think?

What might change on Earth's surface if Earth's core cooled down or warmed up a great deal? What changes would appear in the mantle's convection currents? How might life on Earth be different?

Watching Ice Melt

By now you can guess that if you put an ice cube into a glass of water, it will melt. And you can explain why—thermal energy moves from the warm water to the colder ice cube. But you may not be able to explain how the thermal energy moves from the water to the ice cube. Try this next activity to discover how convection transfers heat from one place to another.

Problem

How does convection help an ice cube melt?

Materials

You may want to choose from the following list of materials.

colored ice cubes	tongs
thermometer	250-mL beaker
water	salt
stirring rod	

Safety Precautions

Use caution if using a mercury thermometer.

What To Do

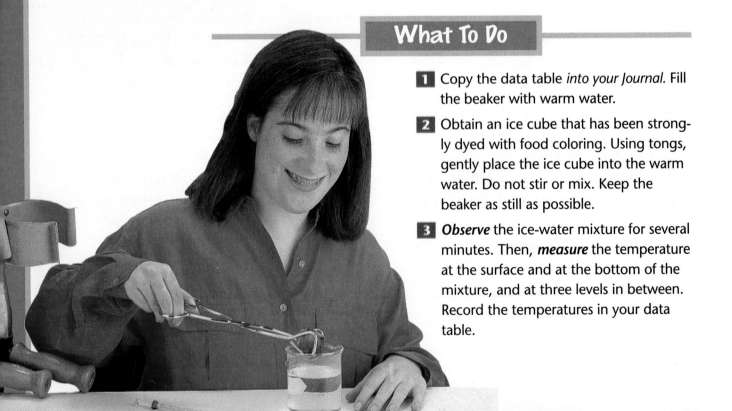

1 Copy the data table *into your Journal.* Fill the beaker with warm water.

2 Obtain an ice cube that has been strongly dyed with food coloring. Using tongs, gently place the ice cube into the warm water. Do not stir or mix. Keep the beaker as still as possible.

3 *Observe* the ice-water mixture for several minutes. Then, *measure* the temperature at the surface and at the bottom of the mixture, and at three levels in between. Record the temperatures in your data table.

As glaciers flow into the sea, huge masses of ice break off. These chunks of broken off glaciers are called icebergs. Convection in the water causes the portion of the iceberg below water to melt much faster than the part above water.

4 Empty the beaker and refill it with warm water. Work with your group to plan a way to reduce the heat transfer through convection. Refer to the definition of convection to help you devise a way.

5 Show your design to your teacher. If you are advised to revise your plan, be sure to check with your teacher again before you begin. Look at all of the safety precautions before you begin. Carry out your plan.

Data and Observations	
Depth	Temp (°C)
Surface	
2 cm	
4 cm	
6 cm	
Bottom	

Analyzing

1. As the ice melts, what happens to the meltwater? What happened to it when you tried to prevent convection?

2. Does the meltwater blend readily with the warm water, or does it tend to remain separate from it?

3. Describe the changes in temperature within the meltwater-warm water mixtures.

Concluding and Applying

4. Infer why convection occurs between the water and meltwater. How did your design interfere with this process?

5. **Going Further** How could you assist the process of convection and make the ice cube melt faster? Refer to the definition of convection to help you think of a way.

Figure 6-9

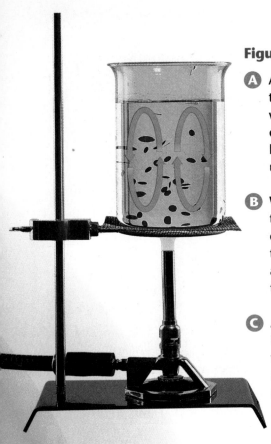

A As water in the bottom of this beaker heats, cold water, which is more dense, flows under the hot water and pushes it upward.

B When the hot water rises to the surface, its thermal energy is transferred to the air. The water cools and moves down toward the bottom of the beaker.

C As the cool water falls, it pushes other hot water up to the surface resulting in a convection current.

Figure 6-10

A Radiant energy from the sun travels 150 million kilometers through mostly empty space to reach Earth.

You can see the same process you saw in the Investigate in a pan of boiling water. **Figure 6-9** shows how convection occurs in a boiling pot. Convection is also a major cause of winds. Sailplanes are gliders that soar on the convection currents in the atmosphere. Many currents in the ocean result from the process of convection. As you can see, convection affects us in many ways.

■ Radiation

Imagine walking outside on a bright, sunny day. As you look up at the sky, you can feel the sun's warmth against your face. But how did the thermal energy from the sun reach your face? How could the heat you feel get across the millions of kilometers of space? In outer space, there is not enough matter to transfer heat through conduction or convection. So

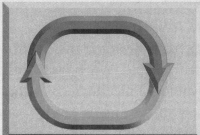

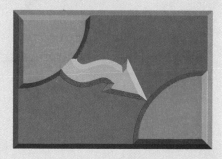

Conduction Conduction is the transfer of thermal energy by two objects in contact.

Examples:
• A pan of food on an electric stove gets warm.
• A spoon in boiling water gets hot.
• A glass of ice water is warmed by the hand holding it.

Conduction can occur in a solid, liquid, or gas.

Convection Convection is the transfer of thermal energy by the movement of matter.

Examples:
• Water boiling in a pot
• Warm air rising above a fire
• Moving air currents causing wind

Convection can occur in a liquid or a gas.

Radiation Radiation is the transfer of thermal energy across a space.

Examples:
• The heat from the sun
• The heat from candles
• The heat that browns marshmallows held near a fire.

Radiation does not require intermediate matter to transfer thermal energy.

B When this energy reaches Earth, some of it is reflected toward space and some is absorbed. Only radiant energy that is absorbed is changed to thermal energy.

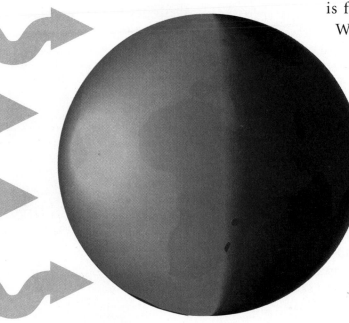

that means the heat gets here another way. That way is called radiation.

Radiation is the transfer of thermal energy across space. No matter is needed for radiant energy to flow as it is for conduction and convection. When you're playing outside on a sunny day, the heat you feel on your face radiated across the vast space between you and the sun.

You've felt also the effects of radiant heat when you put your hand underneath a lighted bulb, or sat next to a campfire. What other examples can you think of that are evidence of radiation?

Minimizing Heat Transfer

Sometimes, you'd rather stop thermal energy from being transferred as it normally would. When it's hot outside, it would be nice to keep the heat out of your room. When you're packing a cold or hot drink to take on an outing, you want to keep it from becoming lukewarm. When you heat your home in winter, you want to keep the energy inside. To do all these things, you need to reduce all three types of thermal energy transfer as much as possible.

You can reduce conduction loss from an object by surrounding it with insulating materials. Because insulators conduct heat very poorly, heat is conducted in or out of an insulated object or room very slowly. Many homes use fiberglass insulation, which contains many pockets of air. Air, as you saw, is a very poor conductor. Containers that keep food hot or cold also use air as a barrier to heat transfer, as shown in **Figure 6-11**.

Heat can't escape from a home by convection unless the air carrying the heat leaves the house. To keep heat inside in winter and outside in

Figure 6-11

A vacuum bottle keeps hot liquids hot or cold liquids cold for several hours. Vacuum bottles are constructed to reduce the rate of all three forms of heat transfer.

Vacuum bottles are made of two glass bottles, one within the other. Glass does not transfer heat well, so heat transfer by conduction is slow.

Most of the air in the space between the two bottles is pumped out and then the bottles are sealed together at the top. There is so little air in the partial vacuum between the bottles that heat transfer by convection or conduction cannot take place.

The sides of the bottles that face each other are coated with a reflecting material, which reflects most of the heat coming from the liquid or from outside air back to its source. The reflecting coating cuts down on heat transfer by radiation.

Figure 6-12

Feathers and layers of fat enable penguins to withstand the cold. An outer layer of oily feathers keeps them waterproof. An inner layer of fluffy down feathers and thick layers of fat act as insulators and keep penguins from losing body heat through conduction.

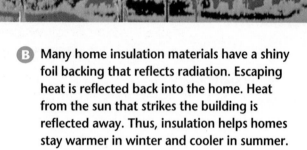

Figure 6-13

Ⓐ The film used in a thermogram records the radiation from thermal energy instead of light. In the photograph, warm temperatures look orange or red. Cooler temperatures are blue or green.

Ⓑ Many home insulation materials have a shiny foil backing that reflects radiation. Escaping heat is reflected back into the home. Heat from the sun that strikes the building is reflected away. Thus, insulation helps homes stay warmer in winter and cooler in summer.

summer, doors and windows need to be well sealed.

This brings us back to the discussion about heat that you and your friend were having on the phone. You should now know where all the thermal energy has come from. But start to think about this: If all this heat you feel is a form of energy, and energy can do work, how much work could the thermal energy in your room do? You'll find out about that in the next section.

check your UNDERSTANDING

1. Describe the transfer of energy as a pan of water is heated to boiling on a gas stove.

2. Explain how a marshmallow can cook even when you hold it next to, but not in a fire.

3. Suppose you needed to keep water hot inside a container for as long as possible. How would you construct the container to meet your goal? Explain your design.

4. Water has a very low thermal conductivity. Yet, when you heat water in a pan, the surface gets hot very fast—even though you're applying the heat to the bottom of the water. Why?

5. **Apply** Which of these materials would best reduce the rate of loss of thermal energy by radiation: iron, wood, or silver? Why?

Making Heat Work

Section Objectives
- Describe how heat can produce work.
- Explain why a heat engine can't be 100 percent efficient.
- Describe how an air conditioner or refrigerator works.

Key Terms
heat engine

Work from Heat

You've already seen heat do work throughout this chapter. Every time you used a thermometer, the transfer of heat did some work on the column of liquid. The energy made the liquid expand as it warmed.

Explore! ACTIVITY

Why is a heat engine inefficient?

What To Do

1. You'll need some help from a teacher or parent for this exercise. Feel the hood of a car.

2. Have the car's driver start the engine and let it run for 5 minutes. Then feel the hood again. What's different?

Figure 6-14

Automobiles run as a result of the transfer of thermal energy in their gasoline engines. Most automobile engines have pistons that move either up and down or back and forth. A part called a crankshaft changes this up-down or back-forth motion to rotary motion, which turns the automobile's wheels. The power to move the pistons comes from the energy released by burning gasoline.

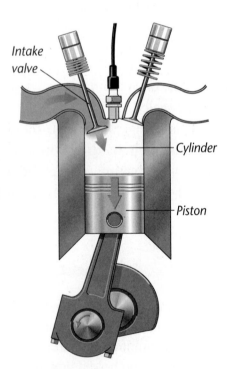

Intake valve

Cylinder

Piston

A *Intake Stroke* The piston moves down the cylinder and draws in the fuel-air mixture— fine droplets of gasoline mixed with air.

What makes heat engines inefficient?

In 1824, the French scientist/engineer Sadi Carnot investigated the amount of work a heat engine produces. He found that even a perfect engine with no friction at all could only use a certain fraction of thermal energy from the fuel. The exact fraction depends upon how much heat the fuel creates and how much the hot exhaust gases can cool in the engine while it runs. But even if the exhaust gases cooled until they were in thermal equilibrium with the surrounding air, there would still be thermal energy left in them. That thermal energy cannot do work because, to make it do so, heat would have to move from a place of lower temperature to a place of higher temperature.

Running on Thermal Energy

One way thermal energy is used to do work is in a car engine. A car engine is an example of a **heat engine.** That's an engine that uses fuel to make thermal energy do work. Heat engines are very inefficient because most of the heat they produce never does work. The heat produced by an engine expands gas, doing work, but it also gets transferred to various engine parts and the air surrounding them. Look at Figure 6-14 to see how a heat engine works. What parts do you think will heat up, wasting thermal energy?

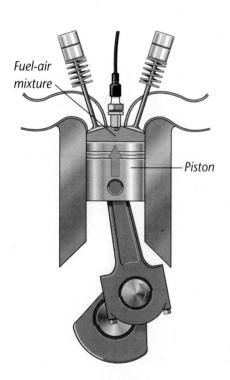

B *Compression Stroke* The piston moves up. The fuel-air mixture is compressed into a smaller space.

Fuel-air mixture

Piston

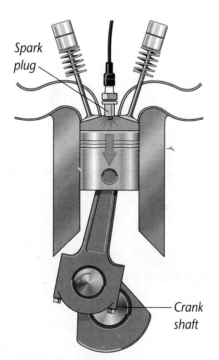

C *Power Stroke* When the piston is almost at the top, a spark ignites the mixture. Hot gases expand, forcing the piston down. Energy is transferred from the piston to the wheels of the automobile.

Spark plug

Crank shaft

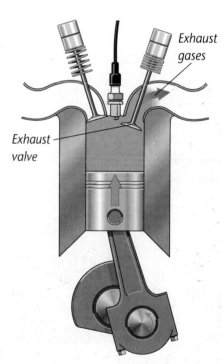

D *Exhaust Stroke* The piston moves up again, compressing and pushing out the waste products left over from burning the fuel-air mixture.

Exhaust gases

Exhaust valve

Keeping Cool with Thermal Energy

Another kind of heat engine is one that makes air cold, such as a refrigerator or air conditioner. Instead of using fuel to produce heat to do work, a refrigerator uses fuel to do work to transfer energy as heat from a lower temperature to a higher temperature. You can examine the basic principles involved in refrigeration by doing the next activity.

Explore! ACTIVITY

How can doing work cool something?

What To Do

1. Fill an eyedropper with alcohol and put a few drops on the inside of your wrist. Record your observations *in your Journal.*

2. Next, inflate an inner tube with an air pump. After the tube is filled, feel the valve. Is it warm or cool? Have you done any work? Let it stand for about 10 minutes. Open the valve and let the air out. Feel the valve again. Is it warm or cool? How might this be helpful in cooling something?

DID YOU KNOW?

Laboratory measurements have shown that the maximum efficiency of gasoline engines is less than 30 percent.

You learned two important properties of fluids that the inventors of refrigerators noticed. The first property is liquids evaporate more as they become warmer. They gain thermal energy from their surroundings. Your wrist cooled when the alcohol gained thermal energy as it evaporated.

The second property has to do with the compression and expansion of air. When air is compressed, it gains thermal energy. When it expands, it loses thermal energy and gets cooler. The work you did while pumping, compressed and warmed the air. When you opened the valve, the expanding air cooled.

Figure 6-15

The icebox was the first home appliance to keep foods cool. By the 1920s, mechanical refrigeration began to replace iceboxes on a large scale.

Figure 6-16

Liquids absorb heat when they vaporize. Refrigerators are designed to take advantage of this property of liquids. The cooling part of a refrigerator is a closed system of tubes in which a cooling liquid, usually Freon 12, is caused to vaporize, to condense back into liquid, and then again to vaporize. This is a continuous cycle.

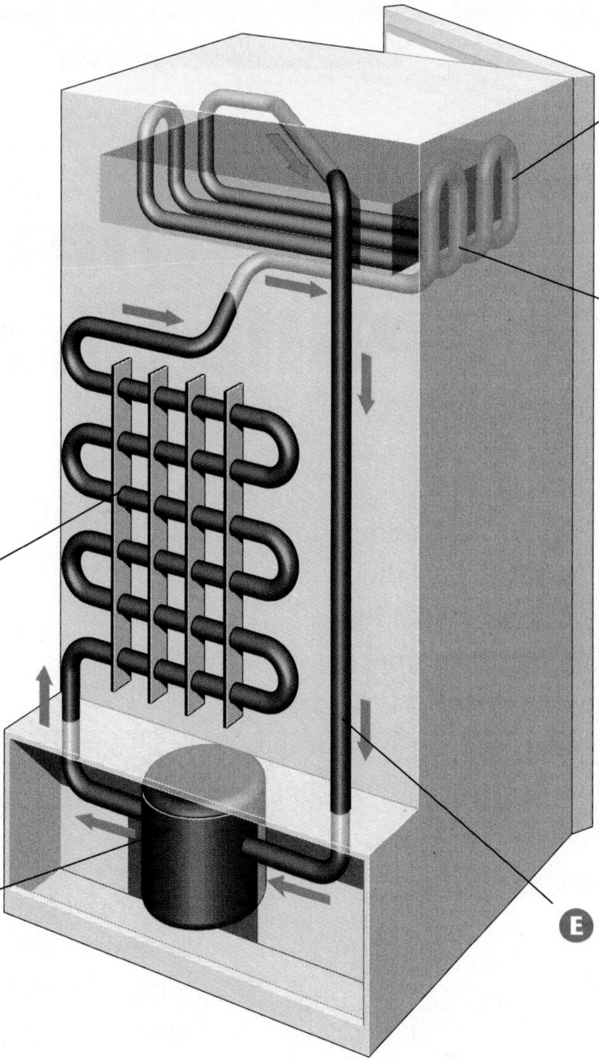

C The liquid is pumped through coils inside the refrigerator.

D The liquid absorbs heat from the food stored in the refrigerator and evaporates, turning back into vapor. This is where the refrigeration takes place.

B The hot vapor moves to the condenser. In the condenser, heat from the vapor is transferred to the surrounding air through the coils along the outside back of the refrigerator. The vapor condenses into a liquid.

A Vapor is compressed by the compressor. Being compressed makes the vapor hot.

E The vapor flows back to the compressor. The cycle begins again.

By the time you and your friend have finished your discussion of heat, the sun has begun to set. You open a window to let cooler air in and the warmer air out. Thermal energy is leaving your room by convection through the open window and—very slowly—by conduction and radiation through the walls and glass. Tomorrow that energy might be almost anywhere. But the sun will return to provide a new supply.

check your UNDERSTANDING

1. Why can heat do work on a piston in a car engine?
2. What prevents heat engines from being perfectly efficient?
3. In an air conditioner or refrigerator, what is the process that actually removes heat from inside the room or refrigerator?
4. **Apply** Could an air conditioner also be used as a heater? Explain what you would have to do and where the heat would come from.

Science *and* Society

Thermal Pollution

Electric power plants use tremendous amounts of water to cool their machines and equipment. Some plants take water from natural bodies of water and return the water once it is used. When used or excess heated water is returned to natural rivers, lakes, or oceans, the higher temperatures may damage the ecology of that water. This dumping of heated water is called thermal pollution.

Power plants are not the only facilities responsible for thermal pollution. Manufacturing plants often use water from a nearby river or lake to cool equipment during the manufacturing process. The warm water is often returned to the river or lake. Researchers have several ways to tell if thermal pollution is occurring. One way relies on satellite photographs taken with temperature-sensitive film. In the photo shown here, red areas are warm. This photograph shows warm water from the Gulf Stream current, not from thermal pollution.

Ecological Impact

Hot, or even warm, water drained into a lake or river, or a section of ocean, may raise the temperature of that body of water by as much as 5° to 11° C. This increased temperature may make it difficult for fish to breathe or to incubate their eggs. Also, over time, this increased temperature can disrupt the total ecosystem of a body of water.

An ecosystem is a community of organisms interacting with one another and with the environment. A self-contained area shared by various animal and plant species is an ecosystem. Microorganisms, plants, and animals found in any body of water occur in groups. Some of these groups are dependent on each other. For example, certain kinds of fish may need to be present to preserve certain species of microorganisms that feed in the water. Heated water can allow the introduction of new organisms, such as species of fish and snails normally associated with areas of warmer water.

In essence, the community changes, the balance of life of various species is disrupted, and the original ecosystem is changed.

Thermal pollution also contributes to eutrophication in a body of water. Eutrophication occurs when an excessive amount of nutrients, such as nitrates and phosphates, enters the water and causes an overgrowth of weeds, algae, and other plant life. The nutrient-rich water overfeeds the fast-growing weeds. If too many weeds and algae develop, they use a large percentage of the oxygen in the water.

Eventually fish and other marine life die from suffocation. The body of water becomes overgrown with unwanted plants, and soon the lake or river changes to a dark murky color. The hydrogen in the water combines with other elements and forms foul-smelling gases. When there is no more oxygen in the water, the remaining algae and unwanted weeds die and decay.

Solutions

Today, most nuclear and fossil fuel power plants have cooling towers like those in the photograph. Heated water is stored in these towers until its temperature is similar to the body of water it is to be returned to. Some facilities send the heated water through sectioned-off rivers or down slow-moving winding creeks, whose angles slow the water and give it time to cool. Other facilities have built their own cooling lakes so that they don't have to rely on natural sources of water for cooling.

You Try It!

Contact a nearby nuclear or fossil fuel power plant. Ask a representative how the plant cools its used water.

Call your local Environmental Protection Agency. Ask to speak to a specialist in water pollution. Ask the specialist how they test water for eutrophication.

CAREER connection

Water quality engineers, such as the one shown below, are trained in biology, chemistry, and engineering. They study the composition of lakes, streams, rivers, and oceans. They observe effects of pollution and seek ways to protect the available water on the planet.

Consumer Connection

Solar Energy for Solar Homes

In our search for thermal energy, the sun has been one of the most obvious sources throughout human history. As the ultimate source of much of the energy found on Earth, the sun's heat can be felt radiating from a dark rock long after dusk.

For thousands of years, people have tried to take advantage of this abundant energy source in everything from heating water for baths, to generating electricity and heating their homes.

Today, solar energy is considered a valuable alternative to dwindling fossil fuel supplies. The challenge in using solar energy, though, is in harnessing the radiation that only strikes Earth during the daylight hours.

Collecting Thermal Energy

The most common kind of solar collector is a flat plate, usually installed on rooftops. It works much like a parked car that sits in the open on a sunny day. The sun's thermal energy radiates through the windows and is absorbed by the car's seat. The thermal energy is then trapped inside and cannot easily pass through the glass window. The solar collector works in a similar way. A shallow, black box with a clear lid sits facing south on the roof of a house. The sunlight passes through the collector and hits a plate. The plate absorbs the radiant energy, which then is temporarily trapped in the collector.

There are basically two types of solar heating systems: active and passive. In an active system, the trapped thermal energy is transferred through convection by either water or air. The water or air is circulated throughout the house with the help of pumps or fans. Excess energy is stored in a water reservoir and used when needed.

In a passive solar system, the sun's thermal energy is collected and absorbed by energy-absorbing masses like walls or water-filled drums. At night, these masses radiate the thermal energy. Through convection, this radiated energy can heat a particular space.

You Try It!

Using a shoe box, some plastic wrap, and other materials you can think of, design your own mini solar collector. How can you collect the most thermal energy with your box? How could you use that energy?

Review the statements below about the big ideas presented in this chapter, and try to answer the questions. Then, re-read your answers to the Did You Ever Wonder questions at the beginning of the chapter. *In your Journal*, write a paragraph about how your understanding of the big ideas in the chapter has changed.

1 All objects contain some amount of thermal energy. Energy transferred as the result of temperature difference is heat. *Explain in terms of temperature, why objects feel warm and cold to our touch.*

HOT   LUKEWARM   COLD

2 Heat always flows from the area of higher temperature to areas of lower temperature. *What happens to a glass of iced tea left in the sun on a warm day?*

3 Thermal energy transfers in three ways. Heat flowing through an object is conduction. Heat carried by a moving fluid is convection. Heat traveling across space is radiation. *Why does blowing on hot food cool it faster?*

4 Thermal energy may be used to do work, as in an engine. *How could you use thermal energy to turn the blades of a propeller?*

Using Key Science Terms

conduction   convection
heat   heat engine
radiation   thermal equilibrium

Use the terms from the list to answer the following questions.

1. What do convection, conduction, and radiation all have in common?
2. Explain the relationship between heat and thermal energy.
3. Explain the relationship of thermal energy to the work of a heat engine.

Understanding Ideas

Complete the following exercise in your Journal using complete sentences.

1. What do we mean when we say that two objects are in thermal equilibrium?
2. Explain why metal cooking pots generally have handles made of nonmetal materials.
3. What are the differences between conduction, convection, and radiation?
4. At one time, many older homes in the southern part of the United States had aluminum roofs. Explain the benefit of this type of roofing using the principle of radiation.
5. Even the best insulation can't completely prevent the transfer of thermal energy. Describe ways insulations are designed to reduce the rate at which heat is lost by conduction, convection, and radiation.

Developing Skills

Use your understanding of the concepts developed in this chapter to answer each of the following questions.

1. **Concept Mapping** Complete the concept map of thermal energy.

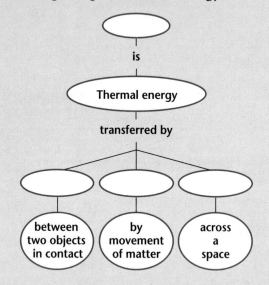

2. **Making and Using Graphs** Repeat the Investigate on pages 184–185 by adding 50 mL of water to the crushed ice instead of 100 mL of water. Chart and graph your data and compare with the original results. Did the addition of the new volume of water decrease or increase the time required to change the temperature of the container of water? Why?
3. **Predicting** Predict what will happen if, on a hot day when the outside temperature is 90° F, you leave all the windows open while the air conditioner is set at 70° F.

Critical Thinking

In your Journal, answer each of the following questions.

1. Examine the photo below. Name at least one place where heat is traveling by conduction, convection, and radiation.
2. Explain this statement: Unless a thermometer is already in thermal equilibrium with the fluid being tested, the act of measuring the temperature either adds or removes thermal energy from the fluid.
3. Before refrigerators were common, many kitchens had an icebox where food was kept cool. The box had one or two shelves in it and a large block of ice was placed at the top of the icebox. The ice block usually weighed 20-30 pounds, and it was often a struggle to place it on top of the box. Why didn't people take it easy and put the ice at the bottom of the icebox?

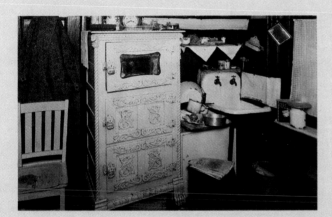

Problem Solving

Read the following problem and discuss your answers in a brief paragraph.

Raphael and his mother are planning to add a new room onto their home. They plan to use a forced-air furnace to heat the new room. Raphael thinks the room will look nicer if the heating vents are near the ceiling, out of sight. His mother says the heating bills will be lower if the vents are in the floor.

1. How does Raphael's mother know the heating bill will be less if the hot-air vents are near the floor?
2. How could Raphael use a ceiling fan to make his plan, with vents at the ceiling, more energy efficient?

CONNECTING IDEAS

Discuss each of the following in a brief paragraph.

1. **Theme—Energy** Anyone who has used ropes much, for any purpose, has heard of rope burn. Explain rope burn in terms of thermal energy.
2. **Theme—Systems and Interactions** How does heat do work on a hot-air balloon?
3. **A Closer Look** Could you use a plastic container that melts at 102° C to boil water? Explain.
4. **Science and Society** What is thermal pollution doing to plant and animal life in rivers and lakes? Are there any ways to keep this from happening?
5. **Consumer Connection** Explain how solar energy can be a valuable alternative to some of our present energy sources.

CHAPTER 7

MOVING THE BODY

Did you ever wonder...

- ✓ Whether bone is alive?
- ✓ Why your knee can't bend backwards?
- ✓ If athletes have more muscles than couch potatoes have?

Before you begin to study bones and muscles, think about these questions and answer them *in your Journal*. When you finish the chapter, compare your Journal write-up with what you have learned.

This is Felípe's first bicycle motocross. His gloved hands clasp the upturned handlebars. His body jets forward, eyes straight ahead. Then, with legs pumping like pistons, Felípe speeds into the turn, leaving his fellow racers in a dusty dirt cloud.

You may not race, or even cycle, but even if listening to music is your favorite hobby, you move. You walk and run, sit and stand, twist and turn. You may have even changed positions while reading this paragraph.

That's what motion is—the process of changing place or position. The kind of movements your body makes depends on the structure of your body, which has more than 200 bones and more than 600 muscles. Muscles move bones. In this chapter, you'll explore the structures that support your body, move it, and give it shape—your body's shapers and movers—bones and muscles.

▶ *In the activity on the next page, explore what happens to your muscles as you bend and straighten your arm.*

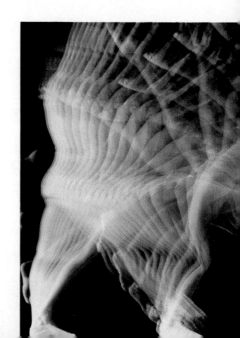

Explore! ACTIVITY

How big is your muscle?

You use your muscles to move your bones, which in turn move you to where you want to go. But did you ever stop to think about how your muscles work—how they get those bones in motion?

What To Do

1. Straighten your arm into a relaxed position. Use a measuring tape to determine the size (diameter) of your upper arm when it is relaxed.

2. Flex your arm by bending it and making a fist. Measure your upper arm again.

3. How did the size of your upper arm change when you flexed your arm?

4. What happened to the muscle to cause this change? Did the muscle actually become larger? Or did it shorten and bunch up?

5. *In your Journal,* write a paragraph about what you think is happening to the muscles in your arm as you straighten and flex your arm.

Living Bones

7-1

Section Objectives
- Identify the major functions of bone.
- Describe bone and its features.

Key Terms
spongy bone, compact bone, bone marrow, cartilage

Your Body's Framework

In the Explore activity on page 211, you observed the changes that took place in your muscle as you straightened and bent your arm. How do these changes in the muscle affect the bones? Before you can answer this question, you need to understand how the bones themselves form a framework for your body. Your skeleton is made up of many different shapes of bones that together support the body and help it move in a coordinated manner.

Even as you read this page, the bones in your neck are being moved so that you can turn your head from side to side. The bones in your neck also perform another important job. Can you guess what it is? They are holding up your head.

Explore! ACTIVITY

How does your skeletal system support your body?

What To Do

1. Using clay and small wooden sticks, build a small model of a tepee.

2. Cover your tepee with tissue paper or fabric. How much of the frame of the model can you see?

3. What is the job of the wooden sticks in your model? What would happen to your model tepee if you removed the sticks?

4. *In your Journal*, write a paragraph about how your body is like the model tepee you built.

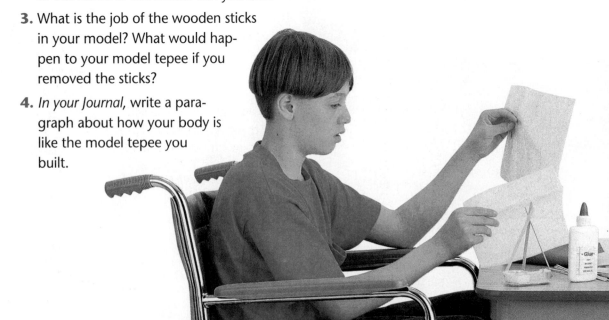

Jobs of Bones

A skeletal system is an amazing structure with many functions. Blood is formed in bone, and the body's supply of calcium and phosphorus is warehoused throughout the skeleton. But the most obvious job of your skeleton is to enable you to have a particular shape that doesn't change, by supporting your body and giving it shape. Bones protect internal organs, such as the brain, heart, and lungs. These organs are surrounded by bone. In Section 7-3, you'll learn that bones also function as the place of attachment for many of the body's muscles.

Figure 7-1

Human and animal skeletal systems can be compared to the internal framework systems that support large structures, such as the Statue of Liberty. For example, if the framework of the statue and a person's skeletal system were removed, the result for each would be the same: both outer coverings would collapse.

Cutaway drawing of the Statue of Liberty

A The Statue of Liberty, pictured at left, is made of more than 300 copper shells, which are bolted to a framework of iron beams. To which body parts can each of these parts of the statue be best compared?

B Bones not only add shape and support, they surround and protect organs such as the brain, heart, and lungs. Without this protection, these organs could be easily injured.

Parts of a Bone

You've seen bones at one time or another. Maybe they were in last night's fried chicken, or you may have watched (and heard) your dog as she chewed on one. You probably know that bones are hard, but did you ever wonder what bones are made of that gives them that hardness?

Find Out! ACTIVITY

What makes bones hard?

To support the weight of your body, bones must be hard. If bones were soft, you would not be able to run, to stand, or even to sit.

What To Do

1. Get two pint jars that have lids. Fill one with vinegar, and the other with water. Label each jar.

2. Put one chicken bone in the jar of vinegar, and another chicken bone in the jar of water. Cover the jars and store them for four days.

3. Predict what will happen to the bones at the end of four days.

4. After four days, remove the bones from their containers and wash them thoroughly. How do the bones feel now? Try bending both bones.

Conclude and Apply

1. Is the bone that was in vinegar different from the bone that was in water?

2. Can you suggest a reason for any changes that took place? Write an explanation for your observations *in your Journal.*

■ Living and Nonliving Parts of Bone

Your bones, like the chicken bones you examined, are unusual because they are made up of both living and nonliving materials. Look at **Figure 7-2** to see the inside and outside parts of a bone. On the outside, a bone is covered by a thin, living membrane called the periosteum. This membrane has many blood vessels in it. The blood vessels are living and carry food and oxygen to the other living parts of bone, which include nerves and bone cells.

You learned that soaking a chicken bone in vinegar makes it flexible. You dissolved something that had made the bone very hard. The nonliving parts of the bone—the minerals calcium and phosphorus—dissolved in the vinegar. What would happen if you were to lose the minerals from your bones? Rickets and osteoporosis are two diseases that result from lack of minerals in bone. Rickets occurs in children and prevents normal bone growth. Bones become bent during development. Osteoporosis occurs mainly in older people. Bone material in people with this disease becomes fragile and breaks easily because the bones lack minerals.

■ Spongy Bone

Do you know what a sponge looks like? Sponges have many little openings in them that hold liquids. One part of a bone looks like a sponge. It's called **spongy bone**. As you see in **Figure 7-2**, spongy bone contains many openings and is found toward the ends of many bones. Unlike a sponge, however, spongy bone is not soft. The fine network of bone you see in the spongy bone is made of minerals and is hard.

■ Compact Bone

You know that calcium and phosphorus are the nonliving parts of bone that make it hard. Compounds of calcium and phosphorus are concentrated in the thick outer layer called **compact bone**. Besides minerals, compact bone also contains living bone material—blood vessels, bone cells, and nerves—and elastic fibers. Elastic fibers keep bone from being too rigid.

■ Bone Marrow

Besides providing support for your body, bones also make blood cells. Have you ever broken a chicken bone? If you have, you may have been

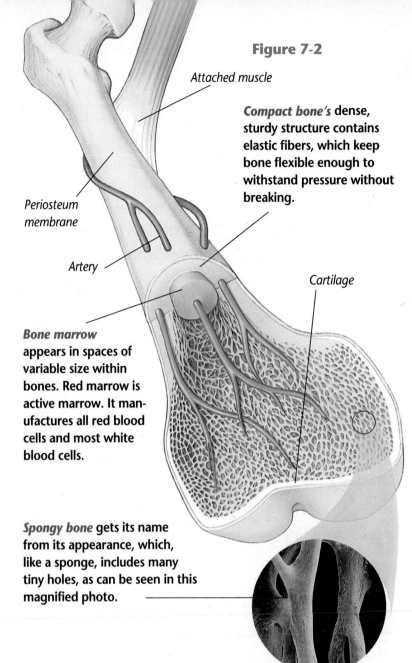

Figure 7-2

Attached muscle

Compact bone's dense, sturdy structure contains elastic fibers, which keep bone flexible enough to withstand pressure without breaking.

Periosteum membrane

Artery

Cartilage

Bone marrow appears in spaces of variable size within bones. Red marrow is active marrow. It manufactures all red blood cells and most white blood cells.

Spongy bone gets its name from its appearance, which, like a sponge, includes many tiny holes, as can be seen in this magnified photo.

surprised to find that the bone was not solid. Many bones have a hollow area or cavity. This space, as well as the spaces in spongy bone, are filled with a gel-like substance called **bone marrow**. Bone marrow, another living part of bone, is red or yellow in color. Yellow marrow is found in the long part of bone and is made mostly of fat. Red marrow is found in spongy bone. New blood cells are made in red marrow.

INVESTIGATE!

Strong Bones

Bones are hard, hollow structures that support your entire weight. You can run, jump, sit, or stand, and your bones will not collapse. Do you ever wonder how bones that are hollow can be so strong? This activity will give you some insight into bone strength.

Problem
How are bones able to support weight?

Materials
several 4 × 6 note cards
cellophane tape
several small books

What To Do

1. Work with your group to develop a model for determining what makes it possible for bones to support so much weight. You may use the materials provided to make your model. You probably will want to develop different kinds of models so that you can compare one with another to see which is stronger (see photos **A** and **B**).

2. *In your Journal*, write a description of the steps you will follow to develop and test your models. Plan a data table to be used in recording your observations.

3. When you have completed your plan, and it has been approved by your teacher, build your models. You may change your original plan, if needed, as you work. Record your observations.

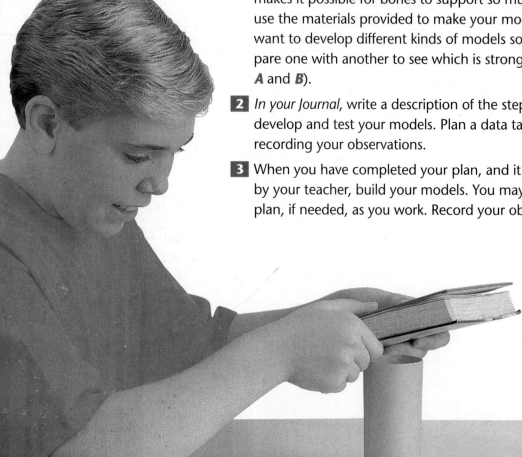

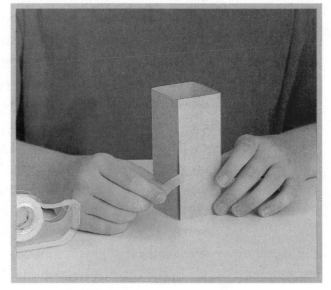

A   B

4 Summarize the procedure you followed in the investigation, and discuss any changes you made to your plan.

5 Using your results, state your conclusions about which model, if any, is the strongest. Make a chart or graph that shows the results of your investigation.

Analyzing

1. Describe the models you developed. Explain why you developed the models as you did.

2. Was one model stronger than another? Which one?

3. How were you able to tell if one model was stronger than another?

Concluding and Applying

4. Compare your models to the structure of bone. Which model was closest to bone in structure?

5. Was the model in question 4 the strongest model? Explain.

6. Going Further Find a lightweight piece of furniture that is supported by one of the shapes you've just tested. Discuss the design of the item, explaining how support is gained through its particular structure.

Compact bone has a strength of about 19,000 — 30,000 lb/in². It would take you and about 200 of your classmates all standing on a single one-inch cube of compact bone to crush it. How does this strength relate to a bone's density?

■ Bone Strength

Healthy bones are hard and flexible, and the arrangement of minerals and fibers in bones gives them great strength. Your bones must be strong to withstand the forces that act on them. Forces that are directed toward an object, such as your body, cause materials in the object to be pressed together. Think of how much force is exerted on your bones when you jump up and down. Forces acting on the body are concentrated at contacts between bones. This action places a lot of pressure on these contact points.

In the Investigate, you made models of bones and discovered one of the

Figure 7-3

To jump upward, you must push against the ground with enough force to overcome the pull of gravity. When you push against the ground, it pushes back with equal force, placing pressure on your bones.

Physics
CONNECTION

Bone Density

The bones of various animals have many similarities, but as you might expect, they also have differences. A cow's bones are strong enough to support the cow as it lumbers across pastures. On the other hand, a finch's bones are light, enabling the finch to flit from tree to tree in search of food. This activity will show you one way in which animals' bones are different.

Measuring Density

For this exercise, you will need to copy the data table. You'll also need water, a balance, a 100-mL graduated cylinder, and bones from a pig, a steer, a turkey, and a chicken. Use the balance to find the mass in grams of a steer bone and record this amount in the data table.

Use the displacement method to determine the volume of the bone. Pour 50 mL of water into the cylinder and

features of bones that give them strength. What was it? Although bones must be strong, they must also be lightweight enough for you to move. The arrangement of materials in spongy bone helps keep your skeleton lightweight because it has many spaces. The spongy nature of the ends of bone also helps you in another way. The ends of bone function as shock absorbers. A shock absorber is anything that absorbs a force and spreads it out over a large area. You may know that many running shoes have cushioned soles and some have air or a soft gel in their soles. These soles are designed to absorb shock. They work like spongy bone works.

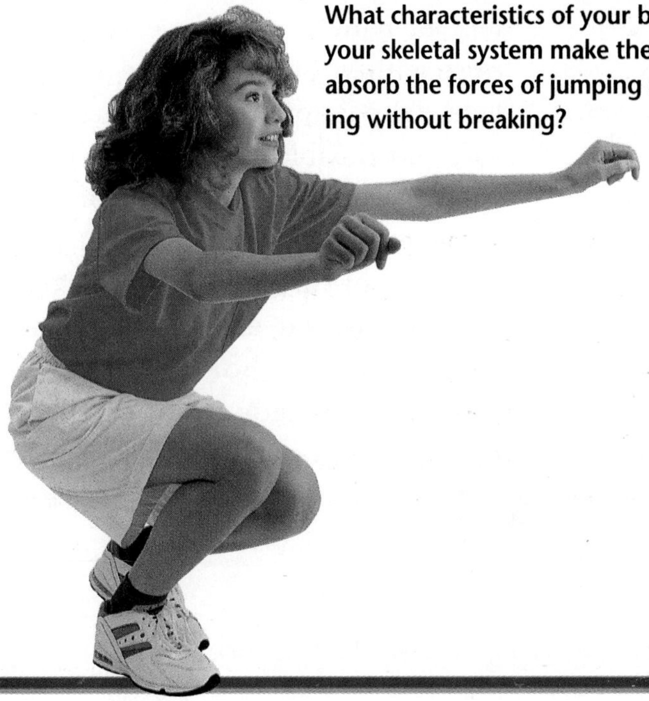

Figure 7-4

Landing from a jump, you hit the ground with considerable force. The ground pushes back with equal force. What characteristics of your bones and your skeletal system make them able to absorb the forces of jumping and landing without breaking?

then add the bone to it. Record the volume of the water plus the bone. Find the volume of the bone by subtracting the volume of water (50 mL) from the water-plus-bone volume reading. Record this amount in your data table. Calculate the density of the bone by dividing its mass by its volume.

Repeat the measurements using the bones of a pig, chicken, and turkey. Record the measurements and find the density of each bone sample. Which kind of bone had the highest density? The lowest?

Why Don't Cows Have Wings?

What makes one bone more or less dense than another? The

Data and Observations				
	Steer	Pig	Chicken	Turkey
Mass				
Water and bone volume				
Bone volume				
Density				

answer lies in the structure of the bone. The bones in a bird's skeleton have numerous air pockets, much like the spongy portion of your own bones. The air pockets make the bone lighter and more buoyant because air is less dense than bone. This lightness helps the bird remain airborne. A cow's skeleton, on the other hand, is made up of solid bones that

lack air spaces. Thus, a cow's bones lack the buoyancy of a bird's bones. Even if a cow had wings, it couldn't fly!

What Do You Think?

Bones from several types of dinosaurs have been found in the United States. How can bone density help researchers determine how large a dinosaur was?

Your Bone Development

Not all parts of your skeletal system are hard. Wiggle the end of your nose with your fingers and feel the external part of your ear. They feel soft and flexible, don't they? These parts of your body are part of your skeleton, but they are not bone. They are made of **cartilage**, a soft, flexible material. In your early development, before you were born, your entire skeleton was made up of cartilage. During development, most of your cartilage was replaced by hard bone.

Look at the X rays of child and adult hands in **Figure 7-5**. Cartilage doesn't show up in the X rays the way hard bone does. Which hands have more cartilage?

Without your skeleton, you would have no body support. Your shape might constantly change, and your internal organs wouldn't be protected against injury. Moving would be a challenge. In the next section, you will explore how your body is able to move.

Figure 7-5

All bone begins as a tough, rubbery substance called cartilage. As a person ages, most of his or her cartilage is gradually replaced by bone. These X-ray pictures of the hands of a two-year-old, an older child, a young adult, and an adult show the gradual replacement of cartilage with bone as people age.

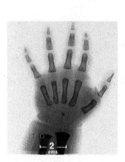
Two-year-old

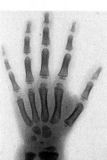
Older child

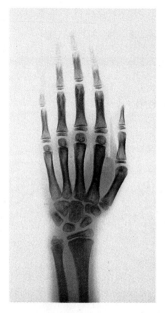
Young adult

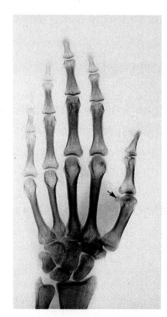
Adult

check your UNDERSTANDING

1. What are three functions of the skeletal system?
2. Why is bone important to your circulatory system?
3. How do compact and spongy bone differ?
4. How is cartilage like compact bone?
5. **Apply** Why do you think certain bones break more easily in an older adult than in a small child?

7-2 Your Body in Motion

The Body in Action

Your body is an amazing collection of bones and muscles, all working together to keep you going. Most of the time you don't think about all the moves you make. But, think of the movements your skeletal system goes through when you turn a page in a book, walk, or throw a ball. When you walk, your leg moves up and down at your hip. Your legs bend at the knee. Your foot bends at the ankle, and your toes bend, too. When you throw a ball, your shoulder twists around. Your arm bends and then straightens as the ball is released. Your wrist also bends, and your fingers straighten. Would any of these actions be possible if your skeleton couldn't move?

Section Objectives

- Compare and contrast types of joints and their movements.
- Describe the functions of ligaments and cartilage in joints.

Key Terms

joints
ligaments

Explore! ACTIVITY

Do you need joints?

What To Do

1. On the hand you write with, use masking tape to tape your thumb and fingers together so that your fingers can't bend and your thumb can't move.

2. Pick up a pencil. How easy was it?

3. Try some other activities. Button your shirt. Tie your shoelaces. Try to write your name. Why is it difficult to do these simple, everyday activities with your fingers taped?

4. *In your Journal,* write a paragraph about how important it is for you to be able to bend your fingers.

Joints

Stand up and move your arm in a circle. Now, bend your elbow and your fingers. You can make a complete circle with your shoulder, but you can't do that with your elbow or fingers. The same is true for your legs. You can move your hip joint in a circle, but you can't do the same with your knee. Body movements are allowed by movable joints, shown in **Figure 7-6**. **Joints** are places in your skeleton where two or more bones meet or are joined together.

Figure 7-6

Match the joint types shown on these two pages with the examples labeled on the baseball player.

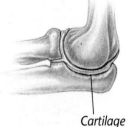

Elbow: hinge

Ⓐ *Hinge joints* move back and forth like the movement of a door hinge. These joints are located at your fingers, toes, elbows, and knees.

Cartilage

Ⓑ *Pivot joints* located at your elbows enable you to twist your lower arms. Pivot joints allow the movement of rotation, or turning on an axis.

Arm: pivot

One Step at a Time

Have you ever heard anyone refer to the human body as a machine? If so, you may have wondered what happens when a part of the body no longer works correctly. You've probably seen automobile mechanics replacing old or worn-out parts. Can human parts be replaced?

Artificial Joints

Yes, thanks to bionics—the science of designing artificial replacements for parts of the human body. Today, the knee is one of the most common parts of the human body to be replaced by an artificial device.

To understand how an artificial knee joint works, you must first understand how a healthy knee joint functions.

How a Real Knee Works

The knee joint, as shown in the X ray, connects the bones in your upper and lower leg. With every step you take, these bones rotate, roll, and glide on each other. Connective tissue, called cartilage, forms a smooth weight-bearing surface between the bones that allows for painless movement. However, with injury or aging, the cartilage begins to wear

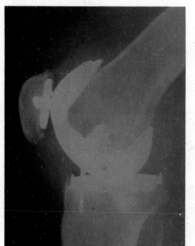

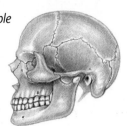

Skull: immovable

C *Immovable joints* are the point at which the bones of the skull come together. Immovable joints allow no range of movement at all.

Vertebrae: gliding

D Vertebrae are small bones that make up your backbone. Vertebrae are separated from one another by disks of cartilage, which allow them to glide over one another at *gliding joints*.

Disk

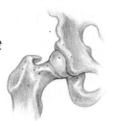

Hip: ball-and-socket

E *Ball-and-socket joints* allow for the greatest range of movement. At these joints, the large round end of one long bone fits into the circular shaped hollow of another bone.

out. Eventually the bones begin to rub together, creating friction and chronic pain.

Technology Takes Us One Step Further

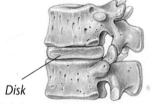

In the late 1960s, bioengineers developed an artificial joint with a wide enough range of movement to replace the knee. Since that time, many designs and materials have been tested. Today, the most common artificial knee joints are made of chrome-cobalt, a hard yet lightweight metal. A plastic material is used to create a durable weight-bearing surface.

Replacing a Joint

Replacing a knee joint requires surgery, in which the artificial joint is fastened to the ends of the bones. One part of the artificial joint has a shaft that is inserted into the upper leg bone. The other half is attached to the lower leg bone and cemented into place. Each half of the joint is coated with a plastic that helps to reduce friction between the two parts of the joint. Joint replacement in other joints, such as the hip, is similar. A shaft is inserted into

the leg bone, and a plastic cup is cemented to the hip socket. Once in place, an artificial hip or knee joint works just like the human joint it replaces.

What Do You Think?

Make a list of body parts in each of these categories:

organs
limbs
senses

Some people think that we are tampering with nature when we use artificial body parts to replace hearts (organs), legs (limbs), or eyes (sense organs). Other people believe that, whenever possible, technology should be used to improve health. What do you think?

How Bones Are Held Together

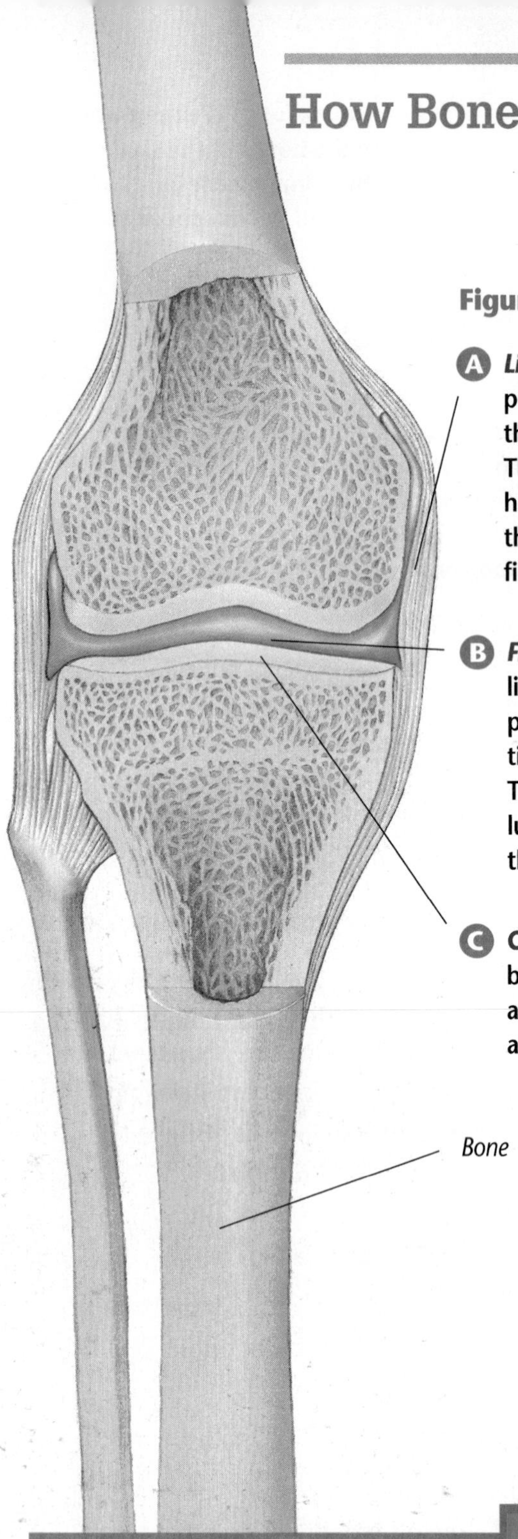

Figure 7-7

Ⓐ *Ligament* If too much pressure is put on a joint, the ligaments may tear. This is called a sprain and happens most often at the knees, ankles, and fingers.

Ⓑ *Fluid* Located under the ligaments are small pouches which contain tiny amounts of fluid. This fluid nourishes and lubricates the surfaces of the joint.

Ⓒ *Cartilage* helps reduce bone-on-bone friction and cushions bones against pressure.

Bone

If bones meet one another at joints, what keeps them from separating or bumping into one another? Bones are held together with very strong bands of tissue called **ligaments**. A fluid, also found in the joint, keeps the joint lubricated. This fluid reduces friction, the force that slows down the motion of surfaces that touch. A thin layer of cartilage over the ends of the bones further reduces friction. Cartilage in healthy joints is like firm, soft plastic, so the bones move smoothly against each other. Because cartilage is flexible, it also acts as a built-in shock absorber in a joint. That helps reduce the effect of forces on the joint by spreading the forces out.

Think about what would happen if you couldn't move your bones. You wouldn't be able to eat, run, pick up things, bend, throw, or do any number of things you probably don't even think about. In this section, you learned how the structure of joints allows for the different movements of your skeleton. In the next section, you will investigate what moves the joints in your body.

check your UNDERSTANDING

1. What makes it possible for you to play the piano? To do sit-ups? Identify the different joints in your body that make these motions possible and the types of joints they are.

2. How can a torn ligament affect movement?

3. Compare ligaments and cartilage in terms of structure and function.

4. **Apply** If a football player tears cartilage in the knee, how might this affect the bones at the knee joint?

7-3 Muscles

Skeletal Motion

Your bones and joints are designed and assembled to fit together like the parts of a motion machine. Your bones and joints have no power to move by themselves. Where does their power come from? Your muscles move your bones and joints and that enables you to slam-dunk a ball, back flip off a diving board, or even run a marathon, if you want to. Together, all your bone-muscle systems are like machines.

Section Objectives

- Describe the three kinds of muscle.
- Explain muscle action and how it results in movement of body parts.

Key Terms

skeletal muscles, tendons, cardiac muscle, smooth muscle

Find Out! ACTIVITY

What are the levers in your body?

In your body, your bones and muscles are arranged to form levers. Recall that a lever is a rigid structure that transmits forces by turning at a point called the fulcrum.

What To Do

1. Rest your elbow, forearm, and hand, palm up, flat on your desk. Lay a heavy book on your hand. Raise your hand, keeping your elbow on the table.

2. You are now using a lever in your body. The book exerts a resistance force that acts downward. Your elbow is the fulcrum. The muscles in your forearm provide the effort force that acts against the resistance force.

3. Now, rest your hand on the table and try to lift the book with your fingers.

Conclude and Apply

1. Why is it more difficult to lift the book with your fingers?

2. *In your Journal,* compare and contrast the leverage provided by your arm and your fingers.

Resistance force

Effort force

Fulcrum

Like all machines, the levers formed by your bones and muscles have mechanical advantage. Mechanical advantage is defined as the number of times a machine multiplies the effort force. The mechanical advantage of your forearm is greater than that of your fingers because your arm is longer and, therefore, creates a greater effort force.

Types of Muscle

Different types of muscle in your body perform different functions. The muscles that move bones are **skeletal muscles**. At movable joints, skeletal muscles are attached to bones by tendons. **Tendons** are strong elastic bands of tissue.

You're most aware of skeletal muscles, probably because you can control the movement of these muscles. But you have two other kinds of muscles, too. The walls of your heart are made of cardiac muscle. **Cardiac muscle** pumps blood through the heart and forces blood through the rest of the body. **Smooth muscle** is found in many places inside your body, such as your stomach and intestines. Food moves through your digestive system by smooth muscle. How much control do you think you have over cardiac and smooth muscle? Compare the three kinds of muscles in **Figure 7-8**.

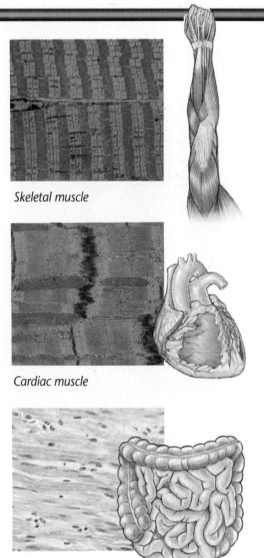

Skeletal muscle

Cardiac muscle

Smooth muscle

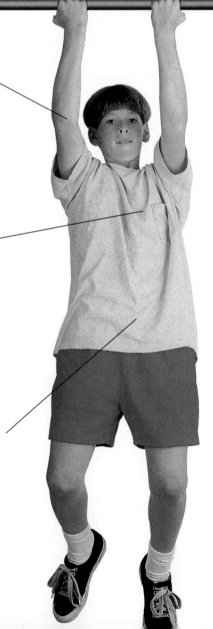

Figure 7-8

A *Skeletal muscle* You decide when to contract or relax skeletal muscles. All outward body movements, like doing a pull-up, are possible because of skeletal muscles.

B *Cardiac muscle* Months before your birth, your cardiac muscle began a pattern of contracting and relaxing that pumped blood to your body cells. Which is the only body organ made of cardiac muscle?

C *Smooth muscles* The movement of food through your intestines and the distribution of blood within your blood vessels are examples of the work of your smooth muscles. Do you control these actions?

Muscle Action

Body movement depends on the action of your muscles. But how do muscles work? Muscles are made up of bundles of long, stringlike structures called fiber that can contract. When a muscle contracts, it gets shorter. In doing so, it pulls on the attached bone. The force of a muscle pulling on a bone moves a body part. Since work is done when a force moves an object a distance, the muscle works when it contracts.

Like all things that do work, your muscles need energy. Fuel of some kind is always needed to obtain the energy to do work.

Glucose is your muscles' main fuel. In your muscles, chemical energy stored in glucose changes to mechanical energy, and your muscles contract.

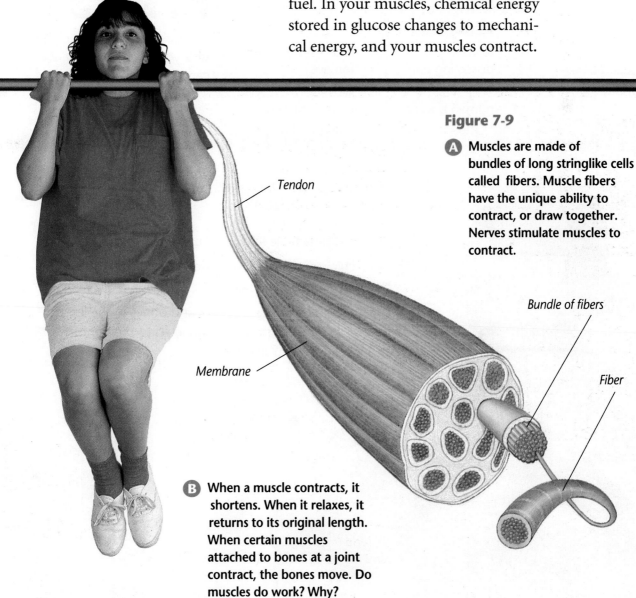

Tendon

Membrane

Figure 7-9

Ⓐ Muscles are made of bundles of long stringlike cells called fibers. Muscle fibers have the unique ability to contract, or draw together. Nerves stimulate muscles to contract.

Bundle of fibers

Fiber

Ⓑ When a muscle contracts, it shortens. When it relaxes, it returns to its original length. When certain muscles attached to bones at a joint contract, the bones move. Do muscles do work? Why?

INVESTIGATE!

Muscles and Bones

Skeletal muscles pull bones at joints. That is how body parts are moved. In this activity, you will observe the relationships among bones, muscles, tendons, and joints.

Problem

How do muscles move bones?

Materials

apron	paper towels
dissecting pan	forceps
scalpel	scissors
human bone and muscle chart	boiled chicken leg and thigh

Safety Precautions

Use care with the scalpel. It can slice your skin as readily as it can slice chicken muscle.

What To Do

1 Copy the data table *into your Journal.*

2 Lay a chicken leg on paper towels in a dissecting pan. Use forceps to remove the skin.

3 Locate and *observe* the muscles and bones in the leg and thigh. How are the muscles connected to the bones? Draw and label what you see.

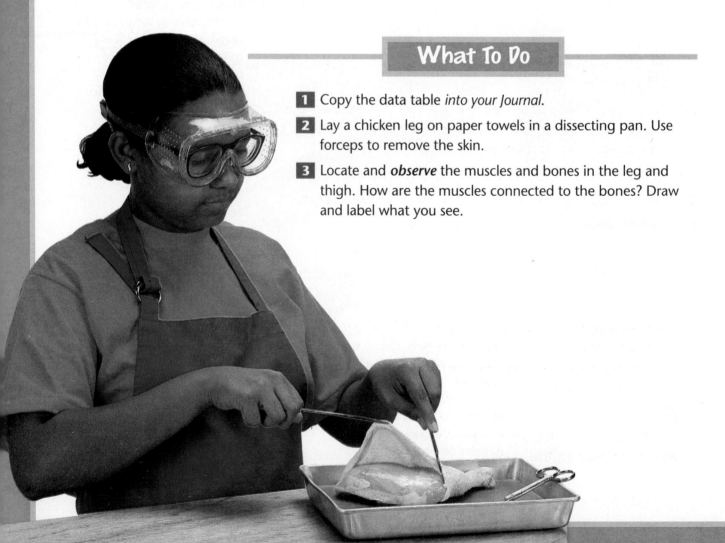

A

Data and Observations	
Body Systems	Body Parts
Muscular	
Skeletal	

4 Bend and straighten the leg and thigh at the joint. *Observe* what happens to the muscles.

5 Use a scalpel and scissors to remove the muscles from the bones (see photo **A**). Locate and *observe* the bones, joints, ligaments, and cartilage. Draw what you see and label these parts.

6 Record the parts of the skeleton and muscle systems that you located.

7 Give all sharp instruments to your teacher for proper disposal.

8 Wash your hands.

Analyzing

1. *Identify* which muscles remain the same length and which shorten when a chicken picks up its leg to walk. *Compare and contrast* their movements.

2. What connects muscles to bones?

3. Did you locate any cartilage or ligaments? Where and how did they appear?

Concluding and Applying

4. What kind of joint is between the thigh bone and the lower leg bone of the chicken?

5. ~~Going Further~~ How is your arm similar to a chicken wing in the way it moves?

Muscles Work Together

In the Investigate, you observed two different muscles bending and straightening a chicken leg. Muscles in your body work in a similar way. Your biceps muscle bends your arm. But how does your arm straighten out?

Find Out! ACTIVITY

How do muscles work together?

To find out how muscles work together, make a model with an index card, a metal fastener, string, and tape.

What To Do

1. Cut an index card lengthwise into two pieces, one for a lower leg bone, and one for a foot. Punch holes in the card as shown.

2. Attach the leg to the foot using a metal fastener as an ankle joint.

3. Cut two 25-centimeter pieces of string and tape one in front and one behind the ankle as shown. Thread one string through each hole at the upper end of the leg.

4. Pull up on the string behind the ankle and observe the action of the foot.

5. Now let go of this string and pull up on the other string.

Conclude and Apply

1. What happens to the foot when you pull up on the string behind the ankle? What happens to the string in front of the ankle?

2. What happens to the foot when you pull up on the string in front of the ankle? What happens to the string behind the ankle?

3. Can both strings be pulled at the same time? Why or why not?

4. What do the strings in your model represent?

5. *In your Journal,* explain what you have demonstrated about the action of muscles.

DID YOU KNOW?

Skeletal muscles are so powerful that if both muscles of a pair that work together were to contract at the same time, they could easily break a bone.

In this chapter, you have explored how muscles work together. When one muscle of a pair contracts, the other muscle relaxes, or returns to its original length. Muscles always work in pairs this way. Because skeletal muscles move bones only when muscles contract, muscles only *pull* bones. Muscles never push on bones.

Bend and straighten your arm a few times to simulate the muscle action shown in **Figure 7-10**. What happens when your biceps contracts? When it relaxes?

You can help your muscles be better coordinated and stronger by using them. Your muscles will become larger or smaller depending on how much you

Figure 7-10

Skeletal muscles work in pairs. When one contracts, its partner relaxes. Your biceps and triceps are classic examples of this teamwork.

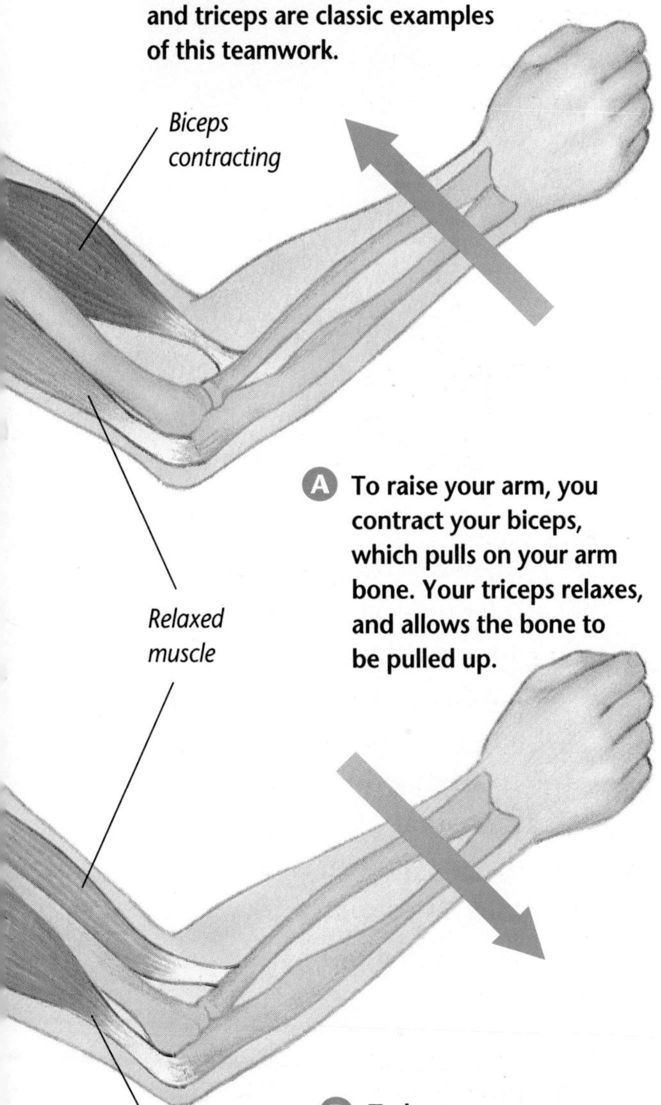

Biceps contracting

Relaxed muscle

A To raise your arm, you contract your biceps, which pulls on your arm bone. Your triceps relaxes, and allows the bone to be pulled up.

Triceps contracting

B To lower your arm, you relax your biceps. Your triceps contracts, and your arm goes down.

use them. Regular exercise increases the size of your muscles as well as their strength. When you exercise, the size of your muscle fibers increases, and this increases your muscles' strength. Exercise also increases muscle tone. *Tone* refers to the state of readiness of your muscles to contract. Muscles are usually slightly contracted so they're ready to go when you need them. Even when you think you aren't moving, some of your muscle fibers are contracting and relaxing to maintain tone. A well-toned body can help you have a better shape and increase your ability to do physical activity. Muscles, along with bones, support and shape your body.

Simple movements you probably take for granted, such as walking, aren't so simple after all. To move the bones and joints required to take just one step can involve the teamwork of up to 200 different muscles from your shoulders to your toes. That's one major reason why it takes a toddler so long to master walking. But once learned, it can be expanded into a variety of movements and activities that can enrich your life.

Concept Mapping

How do your thigh muscles function to bend your leg at the knee? To straighten your leg? Draw a concept map of the sequence of muscle movement. Refer to the diagram of body muscles. If you need help, refer to the **Skill Handbook** on page 637.

check your UNDERSTANDING

1. What do your heart, your stomach, and your thigh muscles have in common? How do they differ?
2. How do your arm muscles function to bend your elbow? To straighten your elbow?
3. How do the muscles in your body attach to the bones?
4. **Apply** Suppose the biceps muscle was removed. What arm movement would not be possible?

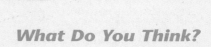

Science *and* Society

Spud Dud!

This afternoon after school, keep track of how much time you spend watching television or playing video games. Do you think this is more or less time than you spent a year ago? Five years ago?

The terms *couch potato* and *spud dud* describe people who spend a lot of their leisure time just sitting.

The couch potato trend is taking its toll on children and teens in the United States. Medical researchers are concerned that, while there is a trend toward physical fitness in adults, young people are less physically fit today than ever before.

Get a Move On

If you sit for a long time, your pulse rate slows, much the way it does when you sleep. When you do get up and move—to get a snack— your system is moving slowly, and so you feel listless.

Muscles that don't get enough exercise lack flexibility. Infrequent or sudden strenuous activity may cause injury. Muscles kept in shape through regular exercise give you the capacity for taking on unexpected activities. Well-developed muscles also use more energy than poorly developed ones, even when you are resting. The result is that you feel more energetic, and you have less chance for fat cell buildup.

Physical activity builds cardiovascular endurance. Cardiovascular endurance is the ability of your heart, lungs, and circulatory system to deliver oxygen to your cells and to take away wastes. To build this endurance, you have to condition your heart and lungs to work more efficiently. Good activities are those that require continuous movement, such as running, swimming, or cycling.

What Do You Think?

Write a description of what you think the world might be like in the year 2020 if everyone became a couch potato today and remained one.

HOW IT WORKS

Robot Arms

Most robot arms used in industry are jointed like the human arm. A typical robot arm may have five or more different movements. Each movement is controlled by a separate power source, usually an electric motor. Motors for these individual movements are controlled by computers. An interface connects the power source, the motors, and the computer. With an intricate electrical circuit, the interface directs power, switching motors on and off, as instructed by the computer.

Nuts and Bolts

A robot arm has a waist (or base), a shoulder, an elbow, and a wrist. You may expect that each of these joints might hold its own motor. However, in most robot arms, especially the smaller ones, the weight of these motors would make efficient movement of the arm difficult. Instead, many robot arms have their motors located near the base. Much like tendons, cords link the motors to the joints they operate. Pulleys are used to hold the cords and ease movement within the sections of the arm.

Electronic Wizardry

Frequently, the motors used to control joint movements are "stepping motors" or "steppers." These motors can turn on and off very rapidly, for quick changes in movement. Extremely fast changes in motion and function happen with step-by-step instructions from the computer. The robot arm can grip, lift, turn, and twist in seconds, much like your own arm.

You Try It!

Imagine that you are designing a robot to assist you with your physical tasks at home. Think about the movements that the robot's arm could make. Then describe which chores the robot could help you accomplish.

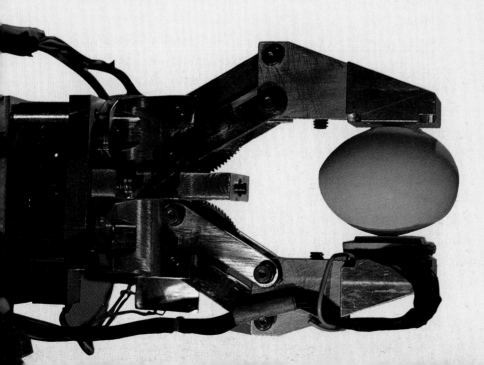

Teens in SCIENCE

Lending a Helping Hand

Have you ever spent a few days in bed because you were ill? If so, you may have been surprised at how quickly muscles in your body began to lose their strength. Imagine how weak you might become if you were bedridden for months!

As a volunteer in a convalescent home, 16-year-old

Jennifer November helps her patients keep their muscle tone. "I start at the hands, moving each finger five times. I'll move on until the entire body has been worked. This motion keeps the muscles from getting contractures or shrinking."

Changing Goals

Jennifer became involved in this work as part of a special vocational education program at her high school in Hacienda Heights, California.

"I had no plans to sign up for the Nursing Assistant Program. In fact, I did it because all the other elective courses were filled. I'd always thought I wanted to be a journalist. But as soon as I got involved in medicine, I knew that I'd found my career. I'm going to nursing school first and then on to become a doctor."

Although Jennifer is very comfortable on the job now, the first few days were tough. "I was frightened. Like most people, I hadn't spent a lot of time with disabled or elderly people. I didn't want to be afraid of them, but I just was. It was confusing. But as soon as I got to know some

of my patients, I found out that we had a lot in common. We're people."

In addition to making new friends, Jennifer has found a good deal of satisfaction in her work. "At first, it seemed like I was the one doing all the helping. But after a while, I realized how much I was being helped. I've learned a lot about life and courage from my patients."

You Try It!

Jennifer describes stumbling into nursing by accident. Write about an unexpected event that had a big impact on your life.

Do you know any disabled or elderly people? Write a brief description of your relationship with them. If you don't have any friends or relatives who fit this description, write about how you might meet such a person.

Review the statements below about the big ideas presented in this chapter, and try to answer the questions. Then, re-read your answers to the Did You Ever Wonder questions at the beginning of the chapter. *In your Journal*, write a paragraph about how your understanding of the big ideas in the chapter has changed.

1 Bone is a vital, living tissue with numerous functions. It gives the body shape and supplies it with minerals. *What are the parts of bone?*

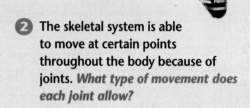

2 The skeletal system is able to move at certain points throughout the body because of joints. *What type of movement does each joint allow?*

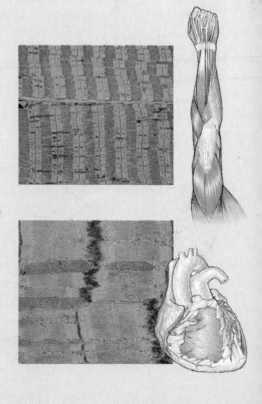

3 Muscle is the tissue in the body that enables the body to move. Different types of muscle tissue move bones, internal organs, and blood. *What are these muscle types and where are they found?*

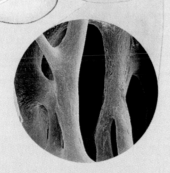

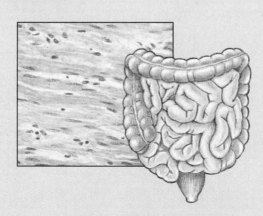

Using Key Science Terms

bone marrow   ligament

cardiac muscle   skeletal muscle

cartilage   smooth muscle

compact bone   spongy bone

joint   tendon

For each set of terms below, choose the one term that does not belong and explain why it does not belong.

1. compact bone, spongy bone, bone marrow, ligament
2. tendon, skeletal muscle, smooth muscle, bone
3. joint, ligament, cardiac muscle, cartilage
4. jaw muscles, hand muscles, skeletal muscles, stomach muscles
5. support, compact bone, bone marrow, skeletal muscles

Understanding Ideas

Answer the following questions in your Journal using complete sentences.

1. How are tendons and ligaments similar? How are they different?
2. List the three types of muscles and an example of where each is found.
3. Describe three functions of bones.
4. Why is it important for muscles to work together in a team?
5. List the types of joints and an example of each.
6. List and describe the living and nonliving parts of bone.
7. What features of bone make it possible for bone to be so strong?

Developing Skills

Use your understanding of the concepts developed in this chapter to answer each of the following questions.

1. **Concept Mapping** Using the following terms, complete the concept map of body movement: *cardiac, compact, joints, muscles, skeletal, smooth, spongy.*

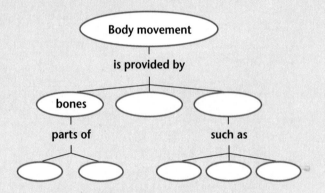

2. **Making Models** Determine what kind of joint the foot model from the Find Out activity on page 230 represents.
3. **Comparing and Contrasting** Thinking about the model you used in the Explore activity on page 212, what are some differences between the model and your body? Now think about your house or apartment. In what ways can the systems or features of that structure be compared to your systems or features?
4. **Predicting** Predict the results of the Find Out activity on page 214 using beef bones rather than chicken bones. Repeat the activity using beef bones and compare your prediction with your results. How do these results compare with those from the original activity?

5. **Observing and Inferring** After doing the Find Out activity on page 225, stand up and bend one of your legs at the knee, keeping your upper leg straight. Where is the fulcrum? Which part of your body provides the effort force? What provides the resistance force?

Critical Thinking

In your Journal, answer each of the following questions.

1. Pick up this book, and then put it down again. What enables you to do both with the same bones and joints in your arm?
2. What is the advantage of having a dome-shaped skull with immovable joints rather than a square skull with gliding joints?
3. Why is there always some movement in your body?
4. How do the foods you eat affect your bones?
5. A bone marrow transplant involves killing the cells in a person's bone marrow and replacing it with bone marrow from a donor. How does a bone marrow transplant help a person with a blood disorder?

Problem Solving

Read the following problem and discuss your answers in a brief paragraph.

On a fossil hunting expedition, Dr. Susman uncovers a remarkable find—an almost complete skeleton of an ape ancestor! Dr. Susman examines the fossil and discovers something important to her research. She finds that the fossil's leg joints are perfectly intact and undamaged. She also finds that the leg joints are similar to those of certain living species of apes. Dr. Susman wants to investigate how the ape ancestor used its legs to move around.

Use your knowledge of the skeletal system to describe what Dr. Susman might do to find out how the leg joints of the fossil worked.

CONNECTING IDEAS

Discuss each of the following in a brief paragraph.

1. **Energy** What forms of energy are involved in a muscle contraction?
2. **Stability and Change** Why does your face turn red when you exercise?
3. **Systems and Interactions** How are your bones and muscles like machines?
4. **Science and Society** Describe some of the benefits of exercise for your muscular system.
5. **How It Works** Compare a robot arm with a human arm. What supplies the energy to move the joints of a robot arm? How is this source of energy similar to that for a human arm?

CHAPTER 8

CONTROLLING THE BODY MACHINE

Did you ever wonder...

✓ How you can walk on a beam without losing your balance?

✓ Why your stomach sometimes growls when you smell food?

✓ Why, if you touch something hot, you pull your hand away before you even think about it?

Before you begin to study about controlling the body machine, think about these questions and answer them *in your Journal*. When you finish the chapter, compare your Journal write-up with what you have learned.

T*he first time I tried to ride a bike, I wondered how anyone could do it. There was so much to remember all at once. Look straight ahead. Pedal. Don't lean sideways. Keep the bike straight. Time after time, the bike and I crash-landed. Then one morning, I got on, pushed away from the curb, and pedaled down to the corner without stopping or falling!"*

Every activity you do requires coordination of bones, joints, and muscles in your body. In this chapter, you'll explore the body systems that control and coordinate most of your behaviors and body processes. You'll examine how these systems work to help you interact with the world around you.

▶ *In the activity on the next page, explore some behaviors of an animal that lives near you or with you.*

Explore! ACTIVITY

Why does your dog bark?

Why do animals do the things they do? Why do some pets run to the kitchen when they hear a can opener? Why do some fish come to the top of the tank when you're about to feed them? Such activities are called behaviors.

What To Do

1. Choose an animal that lives near you or one that you see every day. It can be a pet or an outside animal, such as a bird or squirrel.

2. Observe and record the behaviors of the animal for 30 minutes. Be sure to watch carefully what goes on around the animal.

3. *In your Journal*, record whether the animal did things at random, or whether there seemed to be a pattern to its behaviors.

8-1

The Nervous System: Master Control

Section Objectives

■ Demonstrate the relationship between a stimulus and a response.
■ Describe the function of the nervous system.
■ Diagram the basic structure of a neuron.
■ Explain how impulses travel along nerves.

Key Terms

neuron
synapse

The Role of Your Nervous System

While learning to ride a bike, you probably found yourself a little confused by all the things you had to remember to do all at the same time. As you ride a bike, your body makes adjustments for each of these things. All living organisms are constantly faced with situations in which they have to make adjustments to the changing world around them.

Explore! ACTIVITY

How do you keep your balance?

What To Do

1. Find a long, secured two-by-four board that you can walk across. Make sure the part you are walking on is no wider than your foot. This will be your balance beam.

2. Try walking along your balance beam, slowly at first and then try to walk more quickly.

3. *In your Journal*, record some of the things you have to watch out for on a balance beam. What kinds of body adjustments do you make to keep yourself in balance?

In order to make adjustments to changes around them, living organisms have systems that control all the parts of their bodies. On the balance beam, you probably had to constantly adjust the way you held your body so you wouldn't tumble off. Did you start to tip over or did you lean too far to one side? Maybe you stuck your arms out or bent your knees to keep yourself in balance. Your body has a system that permits you to make these rapid adjustments. The body system that makes adjustments by controlling parts of the body is called your nervous system.

■ Stimuli and Responses

Each behavior you perform during a typical day is the result of the work of your nervous system. A nervous system receives signals, or stimuli, from inside and outside your body. The smell of lunch is a stimulus. The ring of a telephone is also a stimulus. Once your nervous system receives a stimulus, it reacts. The reactions made by your body are called responses. Your stomach growling is a response to the smell of lunch, just as reaching for the telephone is a response to its ring. When you ride a bike or walk on a balance beam, you are faced with stimuli related to balance. You respond by adjusting how your body is held. What stimuli and

Figure 8-1

Your nervous system can be compared to a type of fire department response system. Both receive stimuli, process information, give directions, and respond with action. What part of the fire response system might be compared to your brain?

Ⓐ For the fire department, the heat of a fire, a "stimulus", triggers ...

Ⓑ ... a sprinkler system, which sends a signal to ...

Ⓒ ... the fire department dispatcher. Like your brain, the dispatcher processes the information and makes an appropriate response. The dispatcher gives directions to the appropriate fire vehicles.

Ⓓ The crews of the alerted fire vehicles spring into action to provide a coordinated response to the original stimulus of the fire.

responses did you observe in the animal you watched?

■ How the Nervous System Works

In many ways, your nervous system can be compared to an emergency response system. An example of such a response system is shown in **Figure 8-1** in which a sprinkler system is often used to monitor the safety of buildings.

Like an emergency response system, the job of your nervous system is to receive stimuli, process them, and give directions to various parts of your body so that there is a coordinated response. On an average day, you are bombarded by thousands of stimuli. Your body handles all of these stimuli at the same time, and your body systems respond in a coordinated way. Your nervous system and your endocrine systems are the main systems which control these activities.

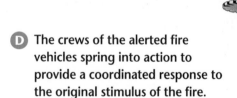

Neurons: Your Body's Relay Team

The sprinkler sends its signal to the fire department using telephone lines. To understand how messages called impulses travel throughout the nervous system, we have to look at the working unit of the nervous system, the **neuron**. Neurons have three main parts—a cell body and branches called dendrites and axons. Each neuron is a separate cell, but neurons usually are grouped together in a bundle called a nerve. **Figure 8-2** demonstrates how impulses are transmitted from one neuron to the next.

Figure 8-2

Dendrites

Axon

Nucleus

Cell body

Cell bodies

Axons and Dendrites

Direction of impulse

A Neurons are made up of dendrites, cell bodies, and axons. Dendrites carry messages, in the form of impulses, toward the cell body. The cell body, which is the largest part, directs the action of the cell. The axon then carries impulses away from the cell body.

Find Out! ACTIVITY

How does information move through your nervous system?

What To Do

1. Out on the track field, or in the school yard, organize a relay team of six students spaced around the track.

2. At the word *Go*, the student at the starting line runs and passes a stick to the second team member.

3. The second team member runs to the next member and passes the stick. The race continues in this fashion until the last team member crosses the finish line.

Conclude and Apply

1. Record *in your Journal* whether the second runner can begin before the first has come along.

2. What enables the second and third to run their parts of the race?

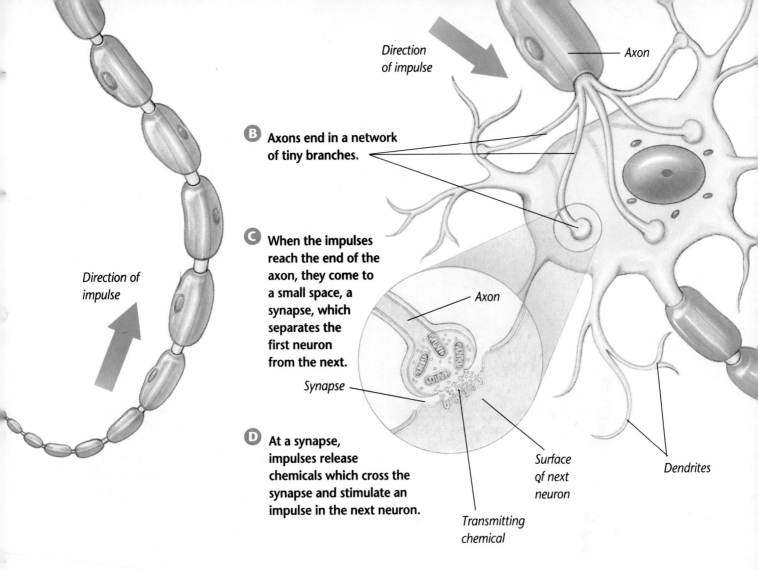

Direction of impulse

Axon

B Axons end in a network of tiny branches.

Direction of impulse

C When the impulses reach the end of the axon, they come to a small space, a synapse, which separates the first neuron from the next.

Synapse

Axon

D At a synapse, impulses release chemicals which cross the synapse and stimulate an impulse in the next neuron.

Surface of next neuron

Dendrites

Transmitting chemical

In your relay race, you never actually touched the next team member. The stick was simply passed to that person. Neurons work in a similar way. As you can see in **Figure 8-2C**, there is a small space called a **synapse** found between the neurons. The impulse from the axon of one neuron causes a chemical to cross the synapse, and an impulse starts in the next neuron.

check your UNDERSTANDING

1. Give an example of a stimulus you encounter every day and your response. What role does your nervous system play in this situation?
2. Diagram two neurons. Include the following: axon, cell body, dendrites, synapse. Show the direction an impulse travels.
3. Neurons never touch one another, so how does an impulse move from one neuron to the next?
4. **Apply** Certain drugs prevent axons from releasing chemicals into a synapse. What effect would drugs like this have on the transmission of an impulse?

8-2 The Parts of Your Nervous System

Section Objectives

- Explain how the cerebrum and cerebellum work together during complex activities.
- Compare and contrast the roles of the central and peripheral nervous systems.
- Trace the pathway of a reflex.

Key Terms

cerebrum, cerebellum, brain stem, spinal cord, reflex

The Central Nervous System

Whether you're sitting alone quietly or playing football, your nervous system receives and acts on many different stimuli all at the same time. Imagine playing football—the clock is running down and you're being chased by opposing team members.

You need to throw the ball! There are so many stimuli. They all seem to happen at once, yet your body responds to all of them. What parts of the nervous system take care of the incoming stimuli? How does your body know what responses to make?

Explore! ACTIVITY

What does a central information computer do for you?

Try the following game to help you understand how your nervous system responds to a stimulus. In this model, you and your classmates will simulate the working of a telephone information service. Students will take turns playing a central computer operator. The operator wins points by either answering science questions or redirecting the caller to where he or she can find the answer.

operator, who will respond to each of the calls.

3. Ten points are awarded for a direct answer and five points are awarded for redirected answers.

4. *In your Journal,* describe how well the operator handled the questions. Were many questions redirected?

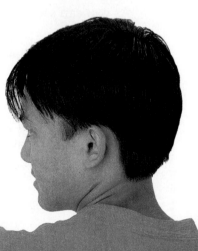

What To Do

1. Choose a classmate to be the operator and others to be callers.

2. Callers will each write one question and pass it to the

The Brain: Operator of the Nervous System

Figure 8-3

Like the central computer operator who receives and processes hundreds of incoming calls a day, your nervous system contains structures that receive and process dozens of stimuli every second. This processing division of your nervous system is called the central nervous system. As shown in **Figure 8-3**, the central nervous system is made up of the brain and the spinal cord.

Your brain, protected by your skull, is divided into three parts, as shown in **Figure 8-4**. The parts are the cerebrum, the cerebellum, and the brain stem, and each has a different function.

wrinkled. Different areas, or centers, in the wrinkled surface of the cerebrum interpret impulses that nerves carry to it from different parts of the body. There is a center for each of your senses, in addition to centers for speech, memory, and for motor activities, which involve muscle movement.

Figure 8-4

One of the three parts of the brain, the cerebrum, carries out complex functions such as memory, thought, and speech. It receives nerve impulses from your skin, eyes, ears, tongue, and nose and changes them into the sensations of touch, sight, sound, taste, and smell. The cerebrum also sends out signals that help control many muscles.

■ The Cerebrum

The **cerebrum** is the largest part of the brain. You may have noticed that the surface of the cerebrum is

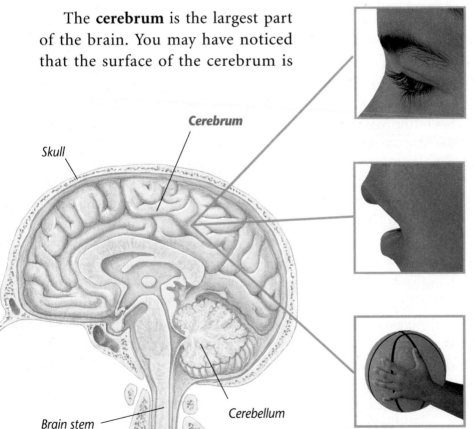

A When playing basketball, nerve impulses from a player's eyes travel to the vision center of the cerebrum. The information is processed and the player recognizes a teammate.

B When the player decides to call out to a teammate, the cerebrum forms the idea and sends nerve impulses to the vocal cords and to the muscles of the tongue and lips to make the player speak.

C When a player wants to pass the ball to a teammate, the motor center of the cerebrum sends out signals to the muscles needed to carry out that action.

■ The Cerebellum

When you ride a bike, the motor center in your cerebrum sends impulses to the muscles. Think for a moment about how many muscles you use when you ride a bike. You can control a bike with ease, even though it requires the coordination and control of many muscles at the same time. How do you know how hard to pedal, where to steer, and how far you should tilt your body to balance?

During complex activities like riding a bike, your **cerebellum** coordinates the actions of all your muscles and maintains balance. The cerebellum is much smaller than the cerebrum. It is located toward the back and bottom of the brain, as shown in **Figure 8-5**. When you're riding a bike, the cerebellum sends messages to the cerebrum that direct and coordinate the activity. The cerebrum then sends out impulses to your muscles.

Your cerebrum and cerebellum work together when you need to move muscles in response to stimuli. For example, if somebody throws a ball toward you in gym class, you may move the muscles in your arms and hands to catch that ball. This type of response must be quick and well timed. In the next Investigate activity, you will explore how quickly your brain causes you to respond to such stimuli.

Mysteries of the Brain

"The brain is the last and greatest biological frontier," says James Watson, the codiscoverer of DNA. He calls the brain "the most complex thing we have yet discovered in our universe."

How Can We Study a Working Brain?

It would help if hair, scalp, skull, and gray matter were all transparent. But they aren't.

Before 1972, what we knew of the brain was learned by studying brain-damaged people. But in 1972 a new technology was introduced. It's called positron emission tomography scanning, or PET scanning.

In a PET scan, the patient's head is surrounded by scanner cameras while he or she sits in something like a dentist's chair. The patient is injected with water containing sugar molecules that have radioactive tracers attached. The patient is given a thought problem, and the cameras record gamma rays being emitted by the radioactive tracers. Where the tracers are found inside the brain shows what part of the brain is working (and using the sugar molecules for fuel) to solve that problem. The computer in the scanner then generates color-coded images of brain activity. Some thought problems researchers

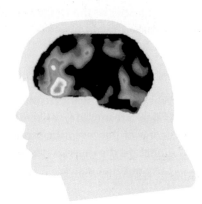

Figure 8-5

When you're riding a bike, your cerebellum sends messages to your cerebrum, which directs the activity. The messages tell your cerebrum in what order and with how much force your arm, hand, and leg muscles need to move for you to ride successfully. Your cerebrum processes the messages and sends out impulses to the appropriate muscles to carry out the needed actions.

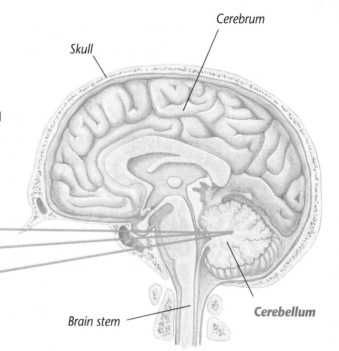

Skull

Cerebrum

Brain stem

Cerebellum

have used include finding words that rhyme, playing a guitar, reading nonsense words, and remembering a fact.

Look at the brain scans accompanying this article. First, picture each of the four images as the left profile of someone's head as shown in the diagram on page 246. Now, compare the colored areas, which indicate brain activity. From the key you can judge whether the brain activity was weak (at the minimum) or strong (maximum).

PET scans also have medical uses. Since tumors grow more rapidly (and metabolize sugar faster) than normal tissue, PET scans can find tumors. Other uses are predicted for the near future.

PET scans are expensive, though. Each scan costs about $1700. The equipment is a big investment for a hospital, too: about $6 to $7 million to build and $1 million a year to run it. A PET setup includes the scanner and its cameras and computer support along with a cyclotron and its radiation shielding. Why a cyclotron? The radioactive tracers injected into the patient decay in just a few minutes so they have to be manufactured on site.

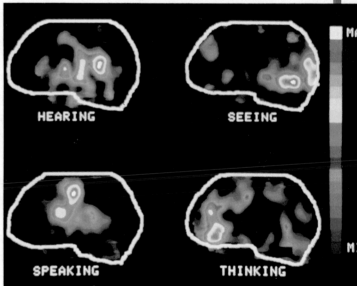

HEARING

SEEING

SPEAKING

THINKING

What Do You Think?

Should every hospital plan to build a PET scanner? In a small group of classmates, discuss the need for PET scanners. Compare the need for PET scanners with other needs hospitals try to meet.

Reaction Time

The time it takes the brain to react to a stimulus is called reaction time. How long is your reaction time? In this investigate activity, you will design methods of measuring reaction time.

Problem

How fast do you react? Is your reaction time the same as your classmates'? Does your reaction time become shorter with practice? Does your writing hand respond faster than your non-writing hand?

Materials

penny   meterstick

What To Do

1 Using the materials provided, work with your group to devise two different methods of measuring individual reaction times. Is the response of one hand quicker than the other? Check out both your writing and your non-writing hand. Find out how fast your classmates' responses are. Do reaction times change with practice?

2 Use a data table to carefully record all your observations.

3 Show your testing designs to your teacher. If you are advised to revise your plan, be sure to check with your teacher again before you begin. Check for all safety concerns. Carry out your plans.

4 You may change your original plan, if needed, as you work.

5 *In your Journal*, summarize the procedures you followed in your investigation, and discuss any changes you made to your plan.

6 Using your results, state your conclusions about reaction times.

Reaction time is critical when playing a sport like basketball. Do you think you can reduce your reaction time by practicing at your sport?

Analyzing

1. *In your Journal*, list the stimulus used in each of your activities.

2. *Compare* and *contrast* your reaction times for each hand. Is there a connection between your response and your writing hand?

3. Did your reaction time improve after a few trials?

Concluding and Applying

4. *Compare* your results with the results of your classmates. Can you *hypothesize* why some people had faster reaction times?

5. Why do you think one of your hands had a quicker reaction time than the other?

6. **Going Further** Do you think it is advantageous for animals to have quick reaction times to stimuli? Explain your answer.

■ The Brain Stem and the Spinal Cord

In the Investigate, you had direct control over the muscles of your hand. Activities that are under your direct control, such as moving arm or leg muscles, are called voluntary activities. But there are many body activities that you do not have control over. Digestion, heartbeat, and breathing, for example, occur without you having to think about them and are called involuntary activities.

Even though involuntary body activities occur without you thinking about them, they are still controlled by a part of your brain, called the **brain stem**. The brain stem is the part of the brain that connects with the spinal cord. The **spinal cord** is a long cord that extends from the brain stem down in the back. It acts like the connection between the brain and parts of the body.

Figure 8-6

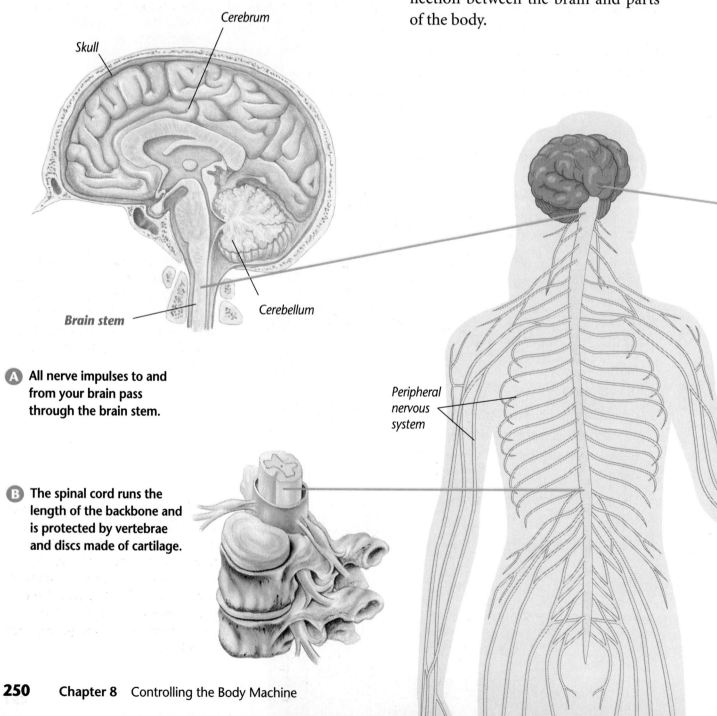

Skull

Cerebrum

Cerebellum

Brain stem

A All nerve impulses to and from your brain pass through the brain stem.

Peripheral nervous system

B The spinal cord runs the length of the backbone and is protected by vertebrae and discs made of cartilage.

The Peripheral Nervous System

Your brain and spinal cord form the central nervous system (CNS). All of the nerves outside the CNS make up the peripheral nervous system. *Peripheral* means to the side and away from. The nerves of the peripheral nervous system, as shown in the **Figure 8-6** body outline, extend to and away from the central nervous system.

Different stimuli are processed in different centers of the cerebrum. The cerebrum sends out impulses along motor nerves to activate muscles. During complex activities, the cerebellum coordinates the speed and timing of muscle action, making the activity run smoothly.

Impulses to and from the central nervous system are carried by the nerves of the peripheral nervous system. Sensory nerves carry impulses from a stimulus to the central nervous system for processing. Motor nerves carry impulses from the central nervous system to activate the muscles of the body. In the following Investigate, you will explore the structures that gather stimuli.

SKILLBUILDER

Making and Using Tables

Make a table of the divisions and functions of the parts of the nervous system. Include the following: central nervous system, cerebrum, cerebellum, brain stem, spinal cord, and peripheral nervous system. If you need help, refer to the **Skill Handbook** on page 639.

Figure 8-7

Ⓐ Sensory neurons carry the impulses from a stimulus to the central nervous system. The sensory neurons of the children send impulses that their cerebrums process to give the children the sensation of smelling the fragrance of the flowers.

Ⓑ The sight and fragrance of the flowers inspire the thought to pick them. The girl's cerebrum stimulates motor neurons to carry impulses from her central nervous system to the muscles of her arm and hand. She reaches out, grasps the flower, and pulls. The flower is picked. Her thought has been put into action.

Testing for Skin Sensitivity

Pressure receptors, scattered throughout your body, permit you to feel the objects you come into contact with. This activity will help you determine the relationship between the sensitivity of your skin and the location, number, and spacing of pressure receptors.

Problem
How sensitive is your skin?

Materials
large paper clip   metric ruler

Safety Precautions

Do not apply heavy pressure when using the paper clip.

What To Do

1 Copy the data table *into your Journal.*

2 Look at the test areas listed in the data table. *Predict* which parts of your arm will be the most sensitive to touch. Record your predictions.

3 Open a large paper clip and bend it into a U shape. Push the two tips of the paper clip together until they are 1 cm apart (see photo **A**).

4 **CAUTION:** *Lightly touch your partner's fingertip with both points of the paper clip. Make sure your partner does not see what you are doing (see photo **B**).*

5 Ask your partner whether one or two points were felt. Record this response in your data table.

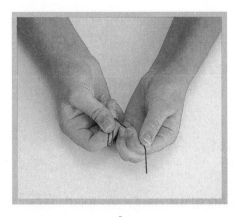

A

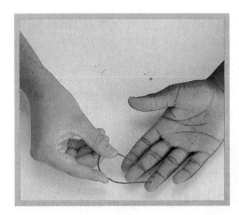

B

6 Fix the paper clip so that the points are farther apart and repeat Steps 2 and 3. Do this for 3 cm, 5 cm, and 7 cm. Record all responses in the data table.

7 Repeat Steps 4 through 6 for each location listed in the data table.

Data and Observations

Distance	Predictions	1 cm	3 cm	5 cm	7 cm
Fingertip					
Palm					
Back of Hand					
Forearm					
Back of Neck					

Analyzing

1. *Interpret* the data in your table to determine which area of your arm was the most sensitive. Which was the least sensitive?

2. *In your Journal,* **compare** the sensitivity of different parts of your arm.

3. How well did your predictions match your results?

Concluding and Applying

4. Can you suggest a reason why it might be beneficial for your fingertips to have many receptors?

5. Can you suggest a reason why your upper arm and neck have fewer receptors than your fingertips?

6. **Going Further** What parts of your body, besides your arm, would you **predict** to be the least sensitive? Explain your predictions.

Reflexes

Sometimes you encounter stimuli in your environment that are so strong they may be harmful to you. How does your nervous system protect you?

Find Out! ACTIVITY

How are your eyes protected from light?

What To Do

1. After your teacher dims the lights in the classroom, lightly tie a blindfold around your partner's head so that the eyes are completely covered. Wait several minutes.
2. Remove the blindfold and quickly shine a flashlight into your partner's right eye for about one second. **CAUTION:** *Do not shine the flashlight any longer than required.*
3. Carefully observe the changes in the pupil of your partner's eye.
4. Repeat the procedure on the left eye. What happens to the pupil?

Conclude and Apply

1. How does the eye respond to the light?
2. Is this a protective response?

Connect to...
Physics

Nerve impulses can travel at speeds of up to 120 kilometers per second in the body. By comparison the speed of electricity is about 300 000 kilometers per second. How many times faster is an electric impulse than a nerve impulse?

Your eyes respond to brightness by controlling the size of the pupil. When you walk around in a dimly lit room, your pupils become larger. As a result, more light enters the eye to strike the retina. If there is a lot of light, such as on a sunny day, your pupils get smaller. The changes in your pupil size happen automatically and involuntarily. You have no control over them. How is this response helpful? Can you identify another response that protects your eyes?

Other parts of your body also respond automatically to stimuli.

Step on a sharp object and you jump instantly! Do you think about your reaction before it happens? An automatic body response to a potentially harmful stimulus, such as a bright light or a hot object, is called a **reflex**. Can you think of some other reflexes that protect you? How are reflexes important for the survival of an organism?

Reflexes must occur very quickly and in the same way each time. These impulses follow the shortest possible pathways through the nervous system and do not involve the brain. These pathways are called "reflex arcs".

Figure 8-8

If you picked up a piece of burning hot pizza, which would happen first: would you yell because of the pain or would you drop the pizza? A reflex arc would be triggered.

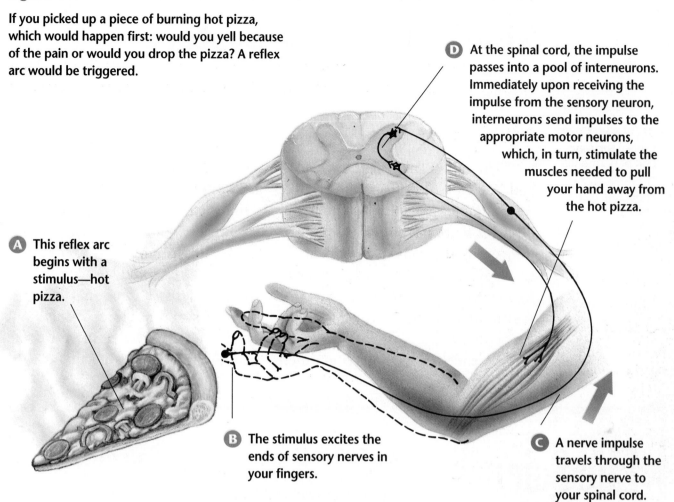

D At the spinal cord, the impulse passes into a pool of interneurons. Immediately upon receiving the impulse from the sensory neuron, interneurons send impulses to the appropriate motor neurons, which, in turn, stimulate the muscles needed to pull your hand away from the hot pizza.

A This reflex arc begins with a stimulus—hot pizza.

B The stimulus excites the ends of sensory nerves in your fingers.

C A nerve impulse travels through the sensory nerve to your spinal cord.

This whole reflex arc can take less than a second to complete. It is completed even before you feel the pain. To be aware of the sensation of pain, nerve impulses must travel up the spinal cord to your brain. This takes a few milliseconds. By the time you're ready to yell about the pain, your hand is safely pulled away.

check your UNDERSTANDING

1. Describe the roles of your cerebrum and cerebellum during a swimming exercise.
2. Describe the path of an impulse associated with lifting your arm. What part of your brain starts this impulse?
3. Describe the role the nerves of your peripheral nervous system play in responding to a stimulus.
4. Discuss some reasons why reflexes are important for the survival of organisms.
5. **Apply** After a severe accident, a person can talk and write, but has to learn to walk all over again. What parts of the nervous system were probably affected by the accident? What parts of the nervous system were not affected?

Your Endocrine System

Section Objectives

- Explain the function of hormones.
- List three endocrine glands and explain the effects of their hormones.
- Explain how the endocrine system is involved in human growth.

Key Terms

hormone
target tissue

Body Control

"The tallest man in the world!" and "the shortest woman in the land!" were commonly seen entertainers in circuses of the past. These people were ordinary persons except for their extraordinary height or lack of height. In most cases, their sizes were the result of a malfunction in their endocrine systems.

The endocrine system is another system for sending messages through the body, but it does not use neurons. This system is made up of tissues throughout the body called ductless glands. A **hormone** is a chemical made by a ductless gland in one part of the body that brings about a change in another part of the body. Hormones are needed in very small quantities and move directly from the

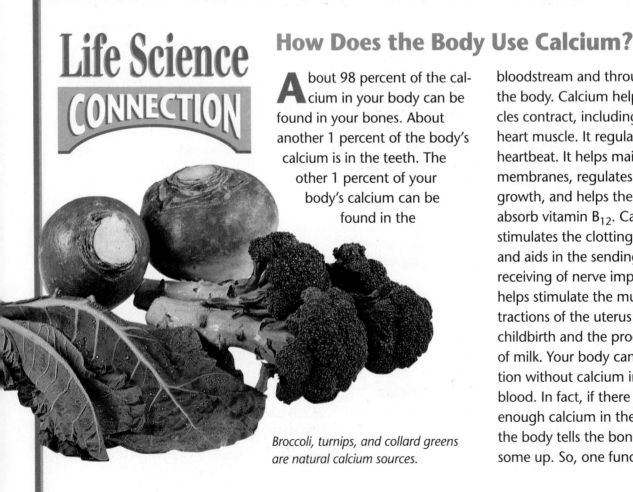

Life Science CONNECTION

How Does the Body Use Calcium?

About 98 percent of the calcium in your body can be found in your bones. About another 1 percent of the body's calcium is in the teeth. The other 1 percent of your body's calcium can be found in the bloodstream and throughout the body. Calcium helps muscles contract, including the heart muscle. It regulates the heartbeat. It helps maintain cell membranes, regulates cell growth, and helps the body absorb vitamin B_{12}. Calcium stimulates the clotting of blood and aids in the sending and receiving of nerve impulses. It helps stimulate the muscle contractions of the uterus during childbirth and the production of milk. Your body can't function without calcium in the blood. In fact, if there isn't enough calcium in the blood, the body tells the bones to give some up. So, one function of

Broccoli, turnips, and collard greens are natural calcium sources.

Figure 8-9

cells of the glands into your bloodstream. The specific tissue affected by a hormone is its **target tissue**. A target tissue may be located far from the gland that makes the hormone. **Figure 8-9** shows where eight endocrine glands are located and what each gland regulates in the body.

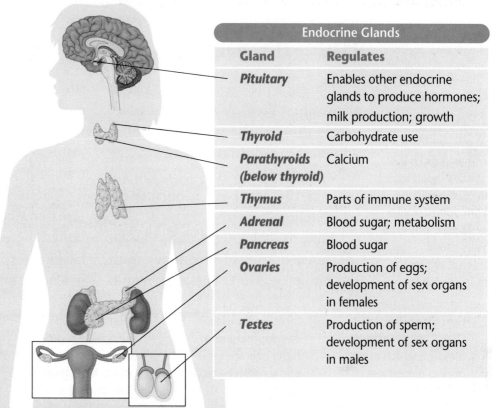

Endocrine Glands	
Gland	**Regulates**
Pituitary	Enables other endocrine glands to produce hormones; milk production; growth
Thyroid	Carbohydrate use
Parathyroids (below thyroid)	Calcium
Thymus	Parts of immune system
Adrenal	Blood sugar; metabolism
Pancreas	Blood sugar
Ovaries	Production of eggs; development of sex organs in females
Testes	Production of sperm; development of sex organs in males

bone tissue is storing calcium for the blood to use.

What Controls Calcium?

Two endocrine glands, the thyroid and the parathyroid, work together to keep levels of calcium in the blood at equilibrium. How does it work?

Eating calcium-rich foods causes a high level of blood calcium. This cues the thyroid to release a hormone that causes calcium to be deposited in the bones and to be excreted in urine from the kidneys.

On the other hand, a low level of blood calcium stimulates the parathyroid gland to secrete a hormone that causes bone to partially dissolve and causes the kidneys to conserve

calcium, not excrete it.

If you regularly avoid eating calcium-rich foods, the result may be weakened bones. Research has found that calcium deficiency may also be a possible cause of high blood pressure and of colon cancer.

You Try It!

Discover which foods are rich in calcium. Then find out the amount of calcium

recommended for your age group. Analyze how much calcium you have ingested in the past three days. Should you make an adjustment to your present diet?

Products such as cheese, milk, and yogurt also provide your body with calcium.

Human Growth

Figure 8-10

In addition to sex organs, which are primary sex characteristics, adult males are distinguished from adult females by specific physical traits called secondary sex characteristics.

During a lifetime, a person passes through stages. A newborn baby grows through infancy, childhood, adolescence, adulthood, and old age followed eventually by death. You are now in the stage of adolescence, which follows puberty.

Puberty is brought about by an increased output of hormones from the pituitary gland. These hormones stimulate the sex organs in both males and females to produce sex hormones. Such development is also influenced by general health, nutrition, and heredity of the individual.

The nervous and endocrine systems control the activities of your body. The effects of hormones often take longer and last longer than those of a nerve impulse.

A One secondary sex characteristic of females, which occurs during puberty, is developed breasts and widened hips.

B Increased muscle development and facial hair are secondary sex characteristics of males.

C Soon after puberty, the female reproductive system becomes active. Menstrual flow, known as a woman's period, repeats about every month.

D Enlargement of the larynx, which at first causes a cracking voice, is a secondary sex characteristic of males.

check your UNDERSTANDING

1. What is the function of a hormone?
2. List three endocrine glands and explain what each gland regulates in the body.
3. What are secondary sex characteristics? Give two examples of such characteristics.
4. **Apply** Why do some adolescents exhibit secondary sex characteristics earlier than others?

Technology Connection

Voice-Activated Computers

Voice-activated computers may someday replace many of the personal computers that require typed instructions.

How Does a Voice-Activated Computer Work?

When you speak, a microphone converts the sounds into electrical signals. The computer stores this information as data in its memory. When you speak into the computer the next time, it compares the new data with the data already in its memory. If the data match, the computer will indicate that it has recognized a word. This process is called voice recognition.

Most voice-activated computers recognize only the voice of a particular operator. Sometimes, even clearly spoken words may confuse it. Because people have different speech patterns, stored data may not match the sounds of an unfamiliar operator.

Who Will Benefit?

Speech pattern characteristics make voice-activated computers a useful choice for security systems that depend on the spoken word. But by far the most exciting application of voice-activated computers is as a tool for the physically challenged. People with limited use of their hands or fingers will be among the first to benefit from the use of voice-activated computers. Voice-activated computers can assist these people in the workplace, as well as at home. In the future, computers may even carry on conversations with their operators, with stored sounds converted into computer-voice sentences.

What Do You Think?

Imagine yourself sitting in front of a voice-activated computer. Your voice has been stored in its memory and is recognized by it. Still, some of the words that the computer has displayed are not the correct words as spoken by you. What do you think might cause this to happen?

Science *and* Society

Alzheimer's Disease

Mrs. Greeley was surprised and confused the other day when she realized she was outside in her nightgown. She couldn't remember coming downstairs or unlocking the door.

Early Symptoms

Every day, scenes like this one take place across the country. These people feel frightened, confused, and ashamed. After accumulating a lifetime of memories, memory has begun to slip away like sand along a beach. These people are experiencing Alzheimer's disease.

Cause of Disease

At the present time, researchers have only a few concrete answers about the cause of Alzheimer's disease. The nervous system uses a chemical called acetylcholine to move impulses from one neuron to the next. In Alzheimer's patients, the brain cells fail to produce this vital chemical. The neurons become inactive, then begin to die. It may be the inactivity that causes neurons to die, but researchers are not sure.

Role of Heredity

Many researchers believe that heredity plays a role in causing the disease. They point to a specific type of chromosomal abnormality in Alzheimer's patients as a probable cause. Statistics also show that children of Alzheimer's patients are more likely to develop the disease themselves.

Who Can Get It?

People with Alzheimer's are generally over 65. However, some people in their 40s have been affected by the disease. It doesn't occur more often in certain ethnic or economic groups, nor has it been linked to the occurrence of any other disease.

Diagnosis

Because some brain cells die, the Alzheimer's patient suffers a loss of mental powers. Although 60 to 70 percent of the patients who suffer a loss of mental powers due to a physical cause have Alzheimer's disease, there is no specific test for it. When other possible causes have been eliminated, Alzheimer's disease is usually diagnosed.

Symptoms

While some patients have occasional periods of full awareness, others have difficulty feeding and dressing themselves. Many Alzheimer's patients suffer severe personality changes, leaving them unable to recognize family members or to control violent outbursts toward these people and other caregivers. The ultimate outcome for all, however, is the eventual loss of physical function, and then death. In the United States each year, Alzheimer's disease takes the lives of more than 100,000 people.

Will There Be a Cure Soon?

Although intensive research has been done only since the early 1970s, much knowledge of the disease has been gained. Still, no real progress toward a cure has yet been made. Drugs that produce the essential acetylcholine have been tested. However, these drugs have been found to cause serious side effects in most patients.

Treatment Drugs

In 1986, test results were published that showed the drug THA produced a significant reduction in symptoms in Alzheimer's patients. The drug was studied by the Food and Drug Administration, the government agency that determines whether drugs work and whether they are safe and can be marketed in the United States.

Some patients were helped greatly by THA. Other patients showed no improvement, and others even suffered a harmful side effect that could cause liver damage. The FDA lowered the legal dosage of the drug to an amount that would

reduce the risk of liver damage. At the lower dosage, however, the drug helped so few people that the FDA decided THA is not an effective treatment for Alzheimer's disease and did not approve the use. Other drugs are being developed and tested.

What Do You Think?

The FDA's decision not to approve the use of THA was very controversial.

1. How do you think Alzheimer's patients and their families would evaluate the possible risk of liver damage against the possible benefit of THA?

2. What do you think about the FDA's decision?

Review the statements below about the big ideas presented in this chapter, and try to answer the questions. Then, re-read your answers to the Did You Ever Wonder questions at the beginning of the chapter. *In your Journal*, write a paragraph about how your understanding of the big ideas in the chapter has changed.

① The neuron is the basic unit of the nervous system. Messages called impulses travel along neurons from dendrites to cell body to axons. *How do neurons help you to respond to changes in your environment?*

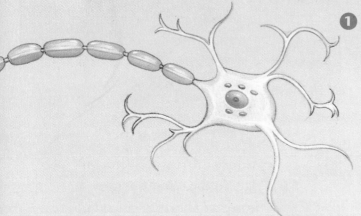

② The central nervous system contains the brain and spinal cord, highly specialized organs containing billions of neurons that control and coordinate body activities. The spinal cord acts as a connection between the brain and the nerves of the body, which make up the peripheral nervous system. *When you tie your shoe, how are the different parts of your nervous system involved?*

③ Reflexes are automatic body responses to potentially harmful stimuli. The pathway of a reflex bypasses the brain. *How are reflexes important for your survival?*

④ Endocrine glands control body activities by secreting hormones directly into the bloodstream. These hormones affect specific tissues throughout the body. *How is the pituitary gland involved in the beginning of puberty?*

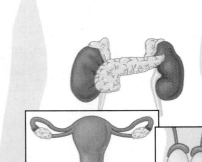

Using Key Science Terms

brain stem   reflex

cerebellum   spinal cord

cerebrum   synapse

hormone   target tissue

neuron

Answer the following questions using what you know about the science terms.

1. Explain the relationship between a neuron and a synapse.
2. Differentiate by function among the three parts of the brain: brain stem, cerebellum, and cerebrum.
3. What is the function of the spinal cord?
4. Describe and give an example of a reflex.
5. How do hormones and target tissues interact?

Understanding Ideas

Answer the following questions in your Journal *using complete sentences.*

1. What role do hormones play in the body?
2. List the part of the nervous system responsible for the following activities.
   walking on a balance beam
   reading a book
   breathing
   playing soccer
   circulating blood through the circulatory system
3. If neurons don't touch each other, how does the impulse continue on its course?
4. Compare your central nervous system to a fire emergency situation. Which part of your CNS acts like the fire dispatcher?

5. Discuss the role of the cerebellum for performing activities involving many skeletal muscles all working at the same time.

Developing Skills

Use your understanding of the concepts developed in this chapter to answer each of the following questions.

1. **Concept Mapping** Using the following events, create an events chain concept map of the nervous system: *central nervous system processes stimulus, response, stimulus, impulse reaches central nervous system, sensory neurons carry impulse, central nervous system sends impulses to appropriate muscles or tissues.*

Initiating event

Event 1

Event 2

Event 3

Event 4

Final outcome

2. **Predicting** Refer to the Explore activity on page 240 and predict ways to improve your balance. Test your prediction.
3. **Comparing and Contrasting** Compare and contrast the two body control systems, the endocrine system and the nervous system, using a table.

Critical Thinking

In your Journal, *answer each of the following questions.*

1. Why is the pituitary gland known as the "master gland"?
2. Why would a person have to learn how to speak again after a serious brain injury?
3. How do feet grow when the gland that controls growth is the pituitary, located in the head?
4. Look at the illustration of the nervous system. Which body parts might be affected if the spinal cord were injured at the area marked "X"—the arm muscles or the leg muscles?

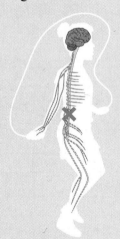

Problem Solving

Read the following problem and discuss your answers in a brief paragraph.

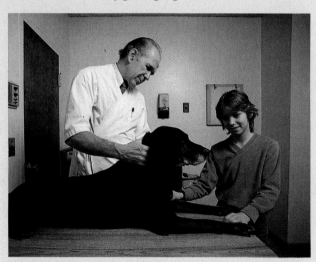

During your dog's visit to the veterinarian's office, the doctor checks your pet's nervous system by testing a reflex that makes the dog's tail wag. During the test, the doctor finds that your dog's tail doesn't wag after the proper stimulus is given. Using your knowledge of the nervous system and skeletal muscles, suggest two reasons your dog's tail-wagging reflex may not have worked.

CONNECTING IDEAS

Discuss each of the following in a brief paragraph.

1. **Theme—Scale and Structure** Describe the parts of a neuron and their function: cell body, axon, and dendrite.

2. **Theme—Systems and Interactions** Describe the functions of the nervous system and how it interacts with other systems.

3. **A Closer Look** Compare a PET (positron emission tomograph) scan to a normal X ray. How does PET technology allow researchers to learn more about the brain?

ENERGY AT WORK

In this unit, you learned that work is done on an object when force is applied and the object is moved in the direction of the force. You also learned that the Law of Conservation of Energy means that work can only be done if energy is put into a system. Systems such as machines or the bones and muscles of your body convert energy into work. Energy for machines may come from various sources, while your body relies on energy from food.

Try the exercises and activity that follow. They will challenge you to use and apply some of the ideas you learned in this unit.

CONNECTING IDEAS

1. As you ride your bike, an animal darts in front of you. You apply the brakes and come to a stop. Explain how your nerves and muscles acted, how machines in your body and bike stopped the bike, and where the bike's energy went.

2. An inventor claims that she can make a car more efficient by using the waste heat from the exhaust pipe. In fact, she says the modified car will be twice as efficient as the original car. Is this possible? Explain.

Exploring Further — ACTIVITY

How can you model your forearm?

What To Do

1. Build a model of your forearm using wood for the bones, a metal hinge for the joint, and cords for muscles.

2. What is the mechanical advantage of your model? How does it compare to that of your arm?

Earth Materials and Resources

In Unit 2, you learned how the human body works as a machine. You compared your arm to a lever as it used energy to perform work. As you study Unit 3, you will learn about Earth's materials and how some of these materials, such as coal and natural gas, can be used to produce energy that is used to do work in machines such as stoves, tape players, and VCRs.

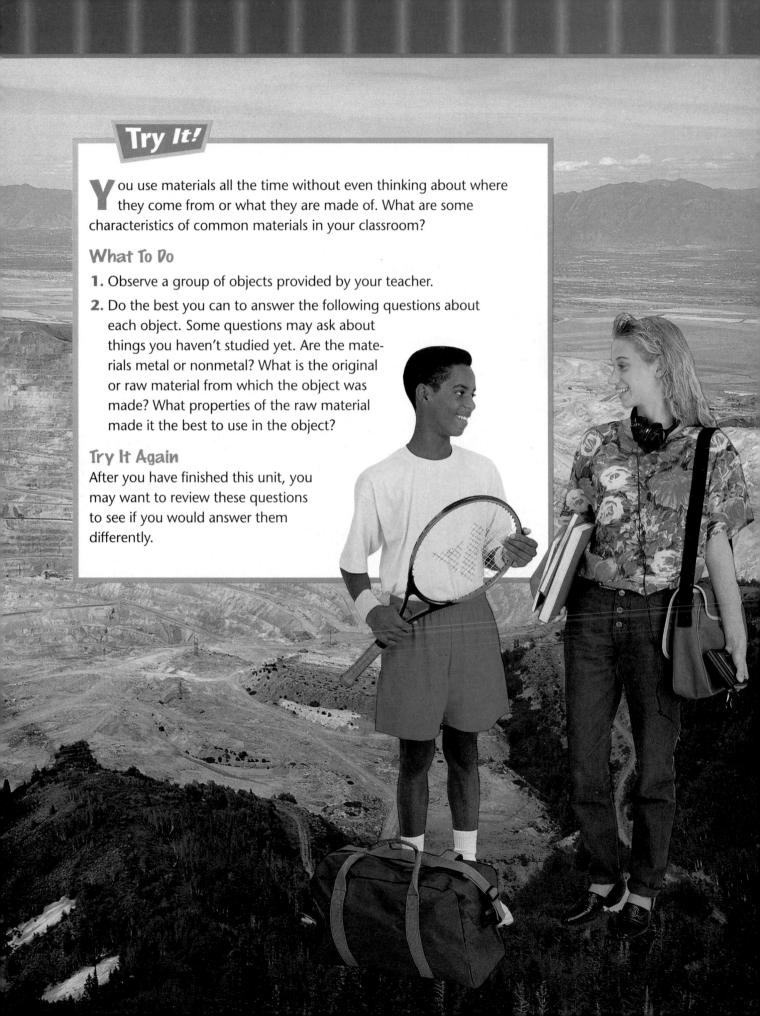

Try It!

You use materials all the time without even thinking about where they come from or what they are made of. What are some characteristics of common materials in your classroom?

What To Do

1. Observe a group of objects provided by your teacher.

2. Do the best you can to answer the following questions about each object. Some questions may ask about things you haven't studied yet. Are the materials metal or nonmetal? What is the original or raw material from which the object was made? What properties of the raw material made it the best to use in the object?

Try It Again

After you have finished this unit, you may want to review these questions to see if you would answer them differently.

CHAPTER 9

DISCOVERING ELEMENTS

Did you ever wonder...

✓ **Why pennies contain copper?**

✓ **What happens to plants and animals after they die?**

✓ **How video games can be so small?**

Before you begin to study about elements, think about these questions and answer them *in your Journal*. When you finish the chapter, compare your Journal write-up with what you have learned.

Omar collects stamps, Yolanda collects shells, and Luis collects model trains. What do you collect? Whether buttons or baseball cards, the objects in your collection are made up of elements or a combination of elements. Coins, for example, may be made up of gold and silver but more likely contain a combination of elements, such as copper, zinc, and nickel. Omar's stamps, Luis' trains, and Yolanda's shells also are made up of combinations of elements.

Everything around you, in fact, everything in the known universe, is made of elements. What are these elements and what combinations do they form? After completing this chapter, you'll think the answer to that question is elementary!

▶ **In the activity on the next page, explore some elements that may be found in your environment.**

Explore! ACTIVITY

What elements are in you and in your environment?

The oceans and the forests, automobiles and clouds, stars and planets, even your body and the air you breathe—all are composed of fewer than 100 different elements. What are these elements?

What To Do

Think about what elements are in your body and your environment.

1. *In your Journal,* make a list of as many elements as you can think of that are found in your body— in your muscles, bones, teeth, and blood.

2. Where in your environment are these elements found?

3. What other elements exist in your environment? Where are they found?

4. *In your Journal,* use your list of elements to suggest why you think each item is an element.

9-1

Discovering Metals

Section Objectives

- Describe the physical properties of a typical metal.
- Compare and contrast the terms *malleable* and *ductile*.
- Explain how the properties of metals determine their uses.

Key Terms

metals, malleable, ductile, coinage metal

Elements

As you have learned, substances are materials that are made up of one kind of matter. Elements, such as sulfur, are the simplest type of substance. An element can't be broken down into anything simpler by ordinary physical or chemical means. Every other form of matter is either a compound, another type of substance that is produced when elements combine, or a mixture.

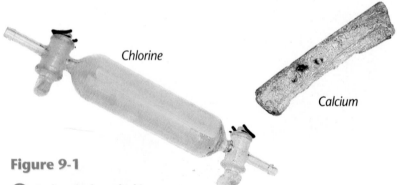

Chlorine

Calcium

Figure 9-1

Ⓐ A chemical symbol is one, two, or three letters, taken from the name of the element it represents. The letter H, for example, stands for the element hydrogen.

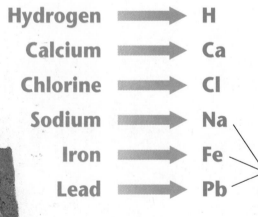

Lead

Hydrogen ➡ H

Calcium ➡ Ca

Chlorine ➡ Cl

Sodium ➡ Na

Iron ➡ Fe

Lead ➡ Pb

■ Symbols

Sometimes, when we want to discuss these elements we use a kind of shorthand. You're already familiar with some shorthand notations. For instance, we use St. to stand for the word street, h to stand for the word hour, L to stand for the word liter, or lb to stand for the word pound.

In a similar type of shorthand, chemical symbols are the abbreviations that stand for the names of different elements. These symbols are needed so that scientists from different countries with different languages can communicate. For example, the element gold will be called different names in different languages, but the chemical symbol for gold is the same all over the world.

Ⓑ The first letter in a symbol is always capitalized. Any other letter is always lowercase. Ca stands for calcium and Cl stands for chlorine. As you can see, two-letter symbols are not always the first two letters of the element.

For some elements, the letters of the symbol come from the Latin, not the English name that is used for the element. Lead, for example is Pb. Iron is Fe.

Explore! ACTIVITY

What element is it?

What To Do

1. Look at the following list of elements and symbols.

Oxygen	Copper	Hg	Zn
Zinc	Aluminum	Al	Au
Nitrogen	Carbon	Ca	N
Gold	Mercury	C	Cu
Magnesium	Calcium	O	Mg

Aluminum

2. Match each symbol listed with the element you think it stands for.

3. Can you think of a reason why symbols aren't always just the first letter of an element name? Record your answer *in your Journal.*

4. Which symbols were the easiest to match to the name of an element? Which were the most difficult? Explain your answer *in your Journal.*

Some of the elements listed in the Explore activity may be unfamiliar to you, and you do not know how they look. Others are easy to picture in your mind. As you picture the familiar elements that were named in the Explore activity, you may notice that each element has its own set of properties. You may notice that some elements differ in color, but some elements have similar colors. You may notice that some are solids, some are gases, and one, mercury, is a liquid at room temperature. Could you use any other properties to place elements into groups?

Explore! ACTIVITY

How can you identify a metal?

What To Do

Examine the element samples provided by your teacher.

1. Separate the elements into two or more groups by using their properties.

2. What properties did you choose? Did other students choose the same properties? How did the properties chosen affect the grouping?

3. In which group would you place gold? Would you place nitrogen in the same group? Explain your answer *in your Journal.*

Properties of Metals

Figure 9-2

A *Luster* When light strikes an object, the object either absorbs or reflects the light. Ability to reflect light is described as the property of luster. Most metals reflect a large amount of the light that strikes them and appear shiny. Silver reflects almost all light that strikes it, and is, for this reason, used as backing for mirrors.

There are several ways you might have grouped your elements in the Explore activity. Although all groups of elements are important, one of the most important groups is **metals**. Picture a metal. What does it look like? How do you know that it's a metal? Is it shiny and hard?

There are several properties that most metals have in common. Many metals are shiny solids. The shine or sheen of an object is called luster. Many metals are **malleable**, that is, they can be hammered or pressed into shape without breaking. Have you ever seen a roll of copper wire? Many metals are also **ductile**, which means that they can be pulled into a wire without breaking. **Figure 9-2 A-E** shows examples of these, and other properties of metals.

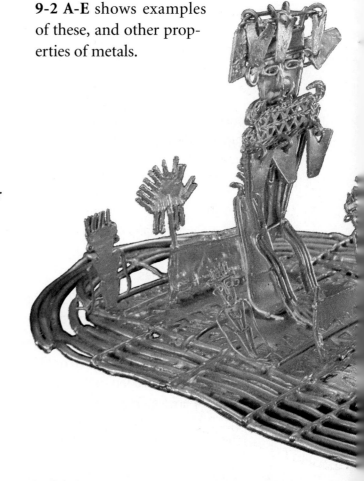

B *Able to be Magnetized* Magnets are metals or rocks that have the ability to attract certain metals—mainly those containing iron. This ability to attract is described as the property of magnetism. A mineral called magnetite is a natural magnet and can attract small iron objects. Three metals— nickel, cobalt, and iron—can be magnetized, or given the property of magnetism. These are the only abundant metals that can be magnetized.

■ How Do Metals Differ?

Not all metals are equally malleable or ductile. There are metals, such as sodium and potassium, soft enough to be cut with a knife!

Metals do not all conduct electricity or heat as well as copper, iron, or aluminum. Metals differ in other properties as well.

Metals such as gold, silver, and copper react less readily and can be found in their natural state in Earth, while other metals, such as sodium and calcium, immediately form compounds when they come in contact with air or water. Sodium and calcium combine so easily with other substances that they are never found as elements in nature.

When metals form compounds, they no longer have properties of metals. Let's see if we can still identify those elements.

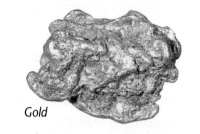

Gold

Iron

E *Color* The colors of many metals are so different from one another that color is one of the properties used to identify specific metals. For example, gold is yellow, iron may be grayish-silver, and copper is reddish-orange.

Copper

C *Malleability* An element that can be hammered or pressed into a thin sheet without breaking is described as being malleable, or as having the property of malleability. Most metals have malleability, but some are more malleable than others. Gold, silver, and copper are highly malleable. This property makes it easy to fashion these metals into intricate shapes.

Gold Muisca raft with figures from Colombia

D *Ductility and Conductivity* A material that can be stretched into a wire without breaking is described as ductile, or having the property of ductility. Most metals that are malleable are also ductile. An ounce of gold can be pulled into a wire more than 46 miles long! Many metals are also good conductors of electricity. Metals that are both ductile and able to conduct electricity are used to carry electrical signals. Copper, which has both properties, is a common material for electrical wire.

Copper wire

Identifying Metals

Centuries ago, the Chinese discovered what happens when a compound containing a metal is heated to a high temperature. The Chinese put this discovery to a use that has been observed for centuries. We still find it exciting today. In this activity, you will discover this novel property of solutions of compounds that contain certain metals.

Problem

How can we identify the presence of certain metals in a solution?

Materials

7 test tubes and rack	wooden splints
7 metal salt solutions	matches
candle or laboratory burner	marking pen
	tweezers

Safety Precautions

During this Investigation, wear goggles and an oven mitt to protect your eyes and skin.

What To Do

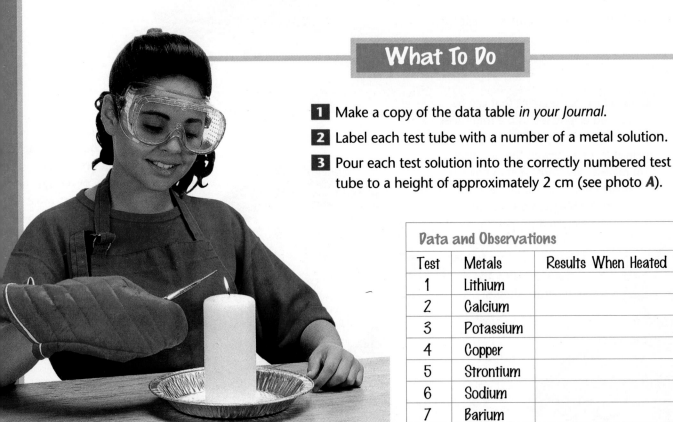

1 Make a copy of the data table *in your Journal.*

2 Label each test tube with a number of a metal solution.

3 Pour each test solution into the correctly numbered test tube to a height of approximately 2 cm (see photo **A**).

Data and Observations		
Test	Metals	Results When Heated
1	Lithium	
2	Calcium	
3	Potassium	
4	Copper	
5	Strontium	
6	Sodium	
7	Barium	

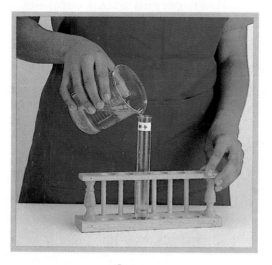

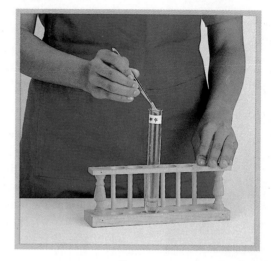

A   B

4 Break several splints into 2-cm length pieces. Drop one piece into each test tube until the splint piece is soaked.

5 Light the candle or laboratory burner. **CAUTION:** *Always be careful when using open flames.*

6 Using tweezers, remove the splint from test tube 1 (see photo *B*) and hold it in the flame.

7 *Observe* and record your observations.

8 Repeat Steps 6 and 7 for each of the other solutions. Be sure to clean the tweezers between solutions. **CAUTION:** *Dispose of all substances as your teacher directs.*

Analyzing

1. What did you *observe* when you heated each of the different solutions?

2. Why is it necessary to clean the tweezers between solutions?

3. *Compare* the colors of the flames to the colors of the solutions.

Concluding and Applying

4. Can you *infer* how the Chinese used this property of metals?

5. If you were given an unknown metal compound solution, how might you identify the metal present?

6. **Going Further** *Predict* what would happen if your test solution were a mixture of the compounds of two metals. Could each metal be identified?

Figure 9-3

Ⓐ When certain metal salts are heated to a high temperature, they produce light of specific colors. For example, strontium salts produce a red flame; sodium salts, yellow; and copper salts, blue-green.

Ⓑ Pyrotechnists, people who make fireworks, use their knowledge of these properties of metal salts to design and make fireworks of various colors. How might scientists use these properties of metals to produce colors to identify unknown metals?

■ Uses of Metals

In the Investigate, you saw that when certain metal compounds are heated, they produce different, characteristic colors. The colors can then be used to identify the metals. Then, you can see how many different roles metals play in your life.

Think of the properties of metals described in this section. What common objects are lustrous, malleable, or ductile? You know from the Investigate that not all substances containing metals look like metals. Your body contains metals. Can you guess where these metals might be found? Where else are metals found?

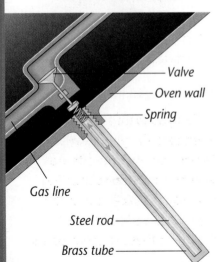

Valve
Oven wall
Spring
Gas line
Steel rod
Brass tube

Thermostats

The temperature in your home is probably regulated by a thermostat. Have you ever looked closely at one? A thermostat is a combination of a thermometer that measures the air temperature in a room and a switch that turns the heating and cooling systems on and off. A modern automated heating and cooling system uses a thermostat to provide safety and comfort and to conserve fuel.

How It Works

A thermostat uses the expansion of metal to maintain the house at a constant temperature. The most common thermostat is a bimetal thermostat. This type uses two layers of metal held together. An increase in the temperature of the room causes each layer to expand at a different rate. The strip (metal layers) bends, closing a switch that controls the heating and cooling systems.

A clock thermostat allows you to change the temperature in your home automatically at certain times of the day. This feature allows you to keep your home at a comfortable temperature when you are there and conserve fuel at other times.

Gas ovens and heaters use a rod thermostat to control the temperature. The control

Metals in Your Body

It may seem strange to think that you have metal in your body. Well, maybe in a tooth filling, but in your bones? Or blood?

■ Calcium

Most of the calcium in your body is in the compound calcium phosphate, which strengthens your bones and teeth. Some calcium is also in your muscles and in the fluid between your body cells. At work in your body, calcium contracts muscles and regulates your heartbeat.

Calcium, along with sodium and

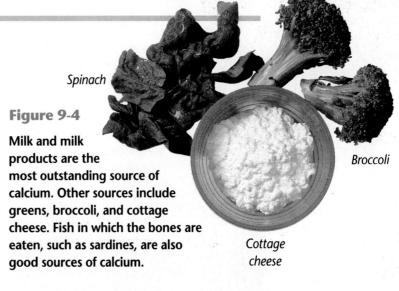

Spinach

Figure 9-4

Milk and milk products are the most outstanding source of calcium. Other sources include greens, broccoli, and cottage cheese. Fish in which the bones are eaten, such as sardines, are also good sources of calcium.

Broccoli

Cottage cheese

potassium, is essential for the proper working of the nervous system. The concentration of these elements as they move in and out of your nerve cells determines what signals are

---

mechanism in this kind of thermostat is attached to a steel rod that sits inside a brass tube. When the temperature increases, the brass tube expands more than the steel rod expands. As the right temperature is reached, a spring closes the valve that controls the gas supply. When the temperature decreases, the brass tube contracts, pushing the rod back so that it opens the valve, allowing gas to flow.

A Part of the Whole

The thermostat is part of an automated system. An automatic furnace heats a home, but the temperature is kept in

Desired temperature

Uncoiled bimetallic strip

Wires to heating system

60 70 80 90

HEAT

50 60 70 80

Mercury

Actual temperature

Dial of thermostat

Switch

Coiled bimetallic strip

check by the thermostat. The thermostat measures temperature in the air and adjusts the heat by switching the furnace on when room temperature is below the desired temperature and off when the room temperature is too warm.

You Try It!

Can you identify all the thermostats in your home? Remember, thermostats are switches that control heating or cooling. Make a list of the appliances and machines in the home that use thermostats.

transmitted from one nerve cell to another. We get sodium from foods that contain sodium chloride, or table salt. Bananas, oranges, and potatoes are good sources of potassium.

■ Iron—The Blood Element

Iron is another metal important to the proper functioning of your body. A small amount of iron is contained in hemoglobin, a substance in red blood cells. When the iron in hemoglobin combines with oxygen from the lungs, blood turns from dark red to very bright red. It is this ability of iron to combine with oxygen that makes it important. The iron in your blood picks up oxygen in your lungs and carries it to the rest of your body.

Figure 9-5

Magnesium is part of the green pigment compound known as chlorophyll. Without magnesium, plants could not produce food for their survival or oxygen for our survival. Magnesium also stimulates the body processes that release energy from food. Whether you are doing something active, such as swimming, or are just resting, your need for energy never stops.

Figure 9-6

When your muscles are working hard, such as when you're doing sit-ups, they require a lot of oxygen. Iron in your blood carries oxygen to your muscles. You can get the iron you need by eating a variety of foods including meats, especially liver; peas; beans; and prunes.

Prunes

Kidney beans

Peas

Metals Dangerous to Your Health

Not all metals are beneficial for your body. Lead and mercury are both metals that can be poisonous to living things. Lead and mercury, called heavy metals, can take the place of iron in your red blood cells. Because they don't have the same ability to carry oxygen through your system as iron does, they can produce some of the same symptoms as anemia.

In ancient Rome, the water pipes were made of lead. Some historians believe that many Romans died from lead poisoning, because the lead contaminated the water as it flowed through the pipes. In fact, the name *plumber* comes from the Latin word for lead, *plumbum*. The symbol for lead is Pb.

At one time, workers who made felt hats treated them with mercury and mercury-containing materials to preserve the felt. Many of these people later went insane because of mercury poisoning. That's where the expression "mad as a hatter" came from.

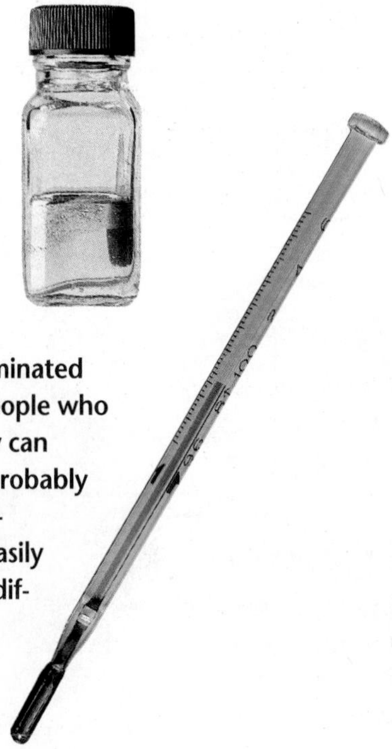

Figure 9-7

Mercury, which can be inhaled or absorbed through the skin and collect in the body, is poisonous. Because mercury compounds have long been used in agriculture and industry, they have contaminated the environment in some places. People who eat fish contaminated with mercury can become ill and may die. You have probably seen mercury in some types of thermometers and barometers. What easily seen property of mercury makes it different from all other metals?

Galena, the principal ore source of lead.

Figure 9-8

Lead particles can enter the body by being breathed in, swallowed, or absorbed through the skin. Lead interferes with the formation of red blood cells and if it builds up in the body may damage the brain and other body organs. Lead is no longer used to make paint, but old paint containing lead still injures thousands of children each year.

Coinage Metals

For centuries, three metals have been widely used as coins. Study **Figure 9-9**. Can you name these metals? If you said copper, silver, and gold, you're right. Together, these are called **coinage metals**.

1897
$5 Gold half-eagle

1922
Peace dollar

Figure 9-9

A The current price of metals has a lot to do with how they are used. For many years gold, silver, and copper were the metals most widely used as coins. As the price of the gold and silver went up, this use of the metals was discontinued in the United States. Gold has not been minted as legal currency since 1933. "Silver" coins, once 90 percent silver, have been minted with no silver at all since 1970. Even the penny, once pure copper, now contains zinc.

1981
Lincoln penny

Copper, silver, and gold are often uncombined in nature and can be mined. They are also malleable and ductile. These metals are easily shaped and stamped into coins. These coins have a denomination imprinted on them, but the actual value may be different. By international agreement, the value of gold and silver is determined by the amount of these metals available in the marketplace.

In addition, silver is used as a backing for mirrors and in photographic film. Silver chloride or silver bromide is used in photographic film and turns dark when exposed to light. That's why film turns dark when it is exposed.

Silver, gold, and copper are not the only elements used in coins. Although there is no silver in new silver money, there is nickel inside the nickel coin you may have in your pocket. Nickels are actually 25 percent nickel and 75 percent copper. Zinc is also used in some pennies.

B Copper is still used as a base for many coins. Sometimes it is mixed with other metals and the coin is minted from the mix. Another way copper is used is as a base coin that is covered with a thin layer of a more expensive metal. The Susan B. Anthony dollar—a copper base covered by nickel—is an example of such a coin.

Copper
Nickel

Aluminum—Jack of All Trades

The most common metal in Earth's crust is aluminum. Aluminum is strong, light, and not easily affected by oxygen or other substances that can destroy many metals. Aluminum is in soft drink cans, in the foil wrap in your kitchen, and may be in the siding you have on your house. Aluminum compounds may be used in medicines, deodorants, pigments, and dyes.

Aluminum alloys, which are homogeneous mixtures of aluminum with another element, are used in many products. Aluminum-lithium alloys provide a strong, lightweight material used in aircraft.

■ Recycling Aluminum

When an aluminum can is recycled, some aluminum ore is conserved. But of equal importance, much less energy is needed to process the recycled can. To produce one aluminum can from ore takes much more electricity than is needed to produce the same can from recycled aluminum.

Look around you. How many of the objects that you can see right now contain metals? They are in the things that you eat, touch, ride in, and wear. Think about how different your life would be without metals.

SKILLBUILDER

Making and Using Tables
Make a table listing six of the metals described in this section. Include column headings for four properties and a heading for uses of each metal. If you need help, refer to the **Skill Handbook** on page 639.

Every month there are about 31 aluminum cans used per person in the United States. 21 of those cans are recycled and the other 10 are just thrown away.

21 cans   10 cans

Figure 9-10

When recycling metal is mentioned, what do you think of? Most people think of aluminum beverage cans, and for good reason. In 1992, 6.8 billion pounds of aluminum were recycled. Of that amount, 2.14 billion pounds came from used beverage cans. That comes to about 253 cans per person, per year.

check your UNDERSTANDING

1. Given a substance, how would you test it to see if it is a metal?
2. Name some elements that are both malleable and ductile.
3. Why would silver be a good coinage metal, while calcium would not?
4. **Apply** Early civilizations used salt, glass, and seashells as coins or money. Why do you think metals have replaced these materials as coins?

Discovering Nonmetals

Section Objectives

■ Describe the physical properties of a nonmetal.

■ Compare and contrast metals and nonmetals.

■ Relate the properties of nonmetals to their uses.

Key Terms

nonmetal

Properties of Nonmetals

In the last section, you grouped several elements together. These elements, metals, usually share properties such as luster, malleability, ductility, and conductivity of heat and electricity. But what about the elements that do not have those properties? Can we observe the properties that these other elements have? How can they be grouped together?

Explore! ACTIVITY

How can you identify nonmetals?

What To Do

1. Think back to the second Explore in Section 9-1 on page 271. If we remove all the metals from the group of elements we examined, we're left with the elements shown in this photo.

2. What properties might you use to describe the elements that are not metals? Write your answer *in your Journal*. Did other students choose the same properties?

3. What other elements can you think of that are not metals? What, if anything, do all these elements have in common?

DID YOU KNOW?

At today's prices, if the human body were reduced to its elements, it would be worth about $3.88.

The elements examined in the Explore activity are called **nonmetals**. Solid nonmetals, such as sulfur and carbon, are dull rather than lustrous. They are brittle and break into pieces instead of being malleable and ductile. Most are poor conductors of heat and electricity. Many nonmetals, such as oxygen and nitrogen, are gases. You might say that most of the properties of nonmetals are just the opposite of most of the properties of metals.

Although there are many more metals than nonmetals, most living material is composed of nonmetallic compounds. Most of your body is made up of compounds of nonmetallic elements.

Common Nonmetals

Many common and important elements are nonmetals. Oxygen, for example, is the most common element in Earth's crust. Most common nonmetals are gases.

■ Hydrogen

Just as metals have properties you could test for, nonmetallic gases, such as hydrogen, have properties you can test for.

  Explore! ACTIVITY

What are some properties of hydrogen?

What To Do

1. Drop a small piece of sanded magnesium ribbon into a test tube containing about an inch of white vinegar.

2. *In your Journal*, record what you observe.

3. When the reaction is going well, put a cork stopper loosely over, not into, the top of the tube.

4. After a few moments, hold the tube at a slant, making sure you aren't pointing it at anyone.

5. Just as you remove the cork, bring a lighted splint to the mouth of the test tube. Record your observations *in your Journal*.

Based on your observations, what are three properties of hydrogen? You probably noticed that it is a colorless, odorless gas that explodes when lit.

Hydrogen is also much less dense than air. Most of the hydrogen on Earth is found in the compound water.

How Do We Know?

What's the universe made of?

How do researchers know that the universe is 99 percent hydrogen? The process of spectroscopy is the chemist's most important tool in identifying what kind of material—and how much of a material—is contained in a sample. You may recall that using spectroscopy is a little like looking at a rainbow. In a rainbow, the colors appear because the light is affected as it passes through the raindrops. In spectroscopy, a researcher can look at light given off by a sample such as stars. The colored bands of light the substance produces can be matched to the colored bands given off by identified substances. The brightness of the colored bands helps researchers know how much of a material is present.

Connect to...

Life Science

Living organisms on Earth contain carbon. Carbon-12 makes up 99 percent of this carbon. Carbon-13 and carbon-14 make up the other 1 percent. What is meant by carbon-12, carbon-13 and carbon-14? Make a poster that explains this and shows the difference between these carbons.

■ Nitrogen

Each breath you take is about 80 percent nitrogen. However, your body can't use nitrogen directly, but uses compounds of nitrogen. Bacteria and plants play a key role in producing nitrogen your body can use. First, bacteria change the nitrogen in the soil into nitrogen compounds. Then plants take in these compounds and change them to proteins that your body can use. This process is called the nitrogen cycle, which you have studied previously.

Although it supports life, nitrogen can produce problems in your environment. Nitrogen compounds from car and truck exhausts react with water in the air to form nitric acid. This contributes to acid rain, which corrodes metal and poisons soil and water in which living organisms exist.

Although, like hydrogen, nitrogen itself is colorless and odorless, nitrogen and hydrogen combine to form a strong-smelling compound, ammonia. Ammonia is found in many household cleaners. Nitrogen makes up a major portion of fertilizers because it promotes plant growth.

■ Carbon

Carbon is found in all things that are living or that lived in the past.

Earth Science CONNECTION

Diamonds and Pencils

Did you know that a diamond and the graphite in your pencil have a lot in common? Diamond is one of the hardest substances known. And yet, if exposed to temperatures exceeding 1830° F, a diamond will turn into graphite—the soft, black material found in a pencil. The pure natural form of carbon we know as a diamond is different from graphite only in the way its crystals formed. Although diamond and graphite are both forms of carbon, their value and use in society are as different as two materials can be.

How Diamonds Formed

Diamonds formed billions of years ago in dying volcanoes. When molten lava in the volcanoes became solid, heat and pressure changed the carbon present into diamond crystals. As Earth's crust and upper mantle moved, volcanic eruptions pushed the diamond deposits closer to the surface. Not all volcanoes contained carbon. For this reason, diamonds formed in only certain regions of the world.

Where are Diamonds Found?

The earliest diamond mine is believed to have been in central

When plants and animals die, they decompose. As layers of soil are deposited on top of them, the pressure produces carbon-containing products, such as coal and petroleum. These fuels are the basic form of energy used in our society.

■ Oxygen

Oxygen is another nonmetal that is necessary for you to survive. Let's investigate some of the properties of this element.

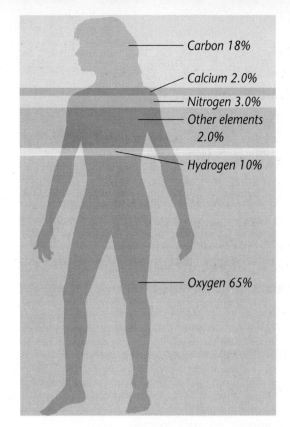

Carbon 18%

Calcium 2.0%

Nitrogen 3.0%

Other elements 2.0%

Hydrogen 10%

Oxygen 65%

Figure 9-11

A Although your body contains several metals, most of it is composed of elements that are nonmetals. This diagram shows the major elements that make up your body. The *Other elements* category contains both metals and nonmetals.

B Calculate the percentage of your body that is made of nonmetals by identifying the metals discussed in the previous section. The remaining elements are nonmetals. How much do the nonmetals add up to?

India. By the early 1700s, mines had been dug in Brazil. Over a century later, young children playing along the Orange River in South Africa discovered a South African diamond. Today, most of the world's diamond production comes from Canada, Australia, Congo, Botswana, and South Africa.

Uses of Diamonds

Of the five tons of diamonds mined yearly, only one ton can be used for jewelry. The most valued diamonds are colorless or pale blue stones and are relatively free of impurities.

Diamonds are useful in industry. Their hardness makes them resistant to chipping or cracking. For this reason, better quali-

ty phonograph needles are tipped with diamonds. Because diamonds do not corrode and are resistant to temperature changes, they are excellent as mechanical parts. For example, hospital and science laboratories use diamond bearings in their machines.

You Try It!

Study a phonograph needle in class. Can you see that the needle is tipped with a diamond crystal? Test the hardness of the diamond by scratching it across an old glass bottle. Can you see why diamonds are very useful in industry?

Preparing and Observing Oxygen

Oxygen makes up about 20 percent of air. It is the most abundant element in Earth's crust. Animals and humans need it for respiration and plants release it as they produce food during photosynthesis. In this Investigate activity, you'll observe some of the important properties of this element.

Problem

What are some of the properties of oxygen?

Materials

test tube	balance
test-tube holder	cork stopper
wooden splint	graduated cylinder
matches	0.5 g cobalt chloride
spatula	

liquid laundry bleach (5% sodium hypochlorite)
5-cm × 5-cm square of notebook paper

Safety Precautions

Wear protective clothing during this investigation. Dispose of substances as directed by your teacher.

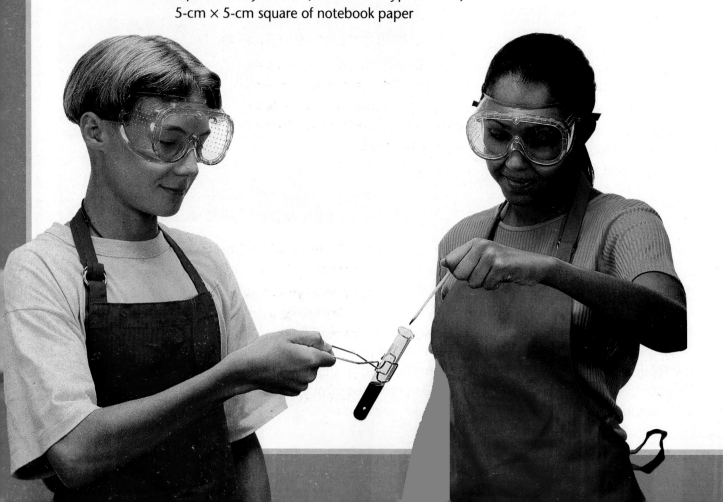

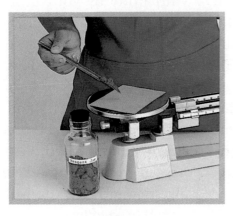
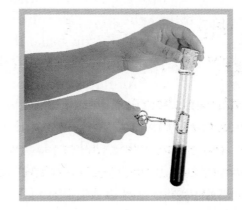

A   *B*

What To Do

1 Measure 20 mL of bleach with the graduated cylinder and pour it into the test tube. **CAUTION:** *Wash your hands thoroughly after working with bleach.*

2 Place the paper on the balance pan. Using the spatula to transfer the cobalt chloride to the paper, measure 0.5 g of cobalt chloride (see photo *A*).

3 Add the cobalt chloride to the test tube and *observe*. Record your observations *in your Journal.*

4 Place the cork stopper loosely over the opening of the tube (see photo *B*).

5 Tilt the tube at a 45° angle. **CAUTION:** *Do not point at anyone.* Be sure you are holding the tube with a test-tube holder as shown in the picture. Remove the stopper. Have your partner light a splint, then blow it out. Then your partner should carefully lower the glowing splint into the mouth of the tube. *Observe,* and record your observations.

Analyzing

1. How did you infer that a gas was being formed in the test tube?

2. What happened when the glowing splint was placed in the tube?

3. What properties of oxygen did you *observe*?

Concluding and Applying

4. *Compare and contrast* the properties of oxygen with those of hydrogen.

5. Why do you think you used a glowing splint rather than a lit one? What property of oxygen does this demonstrate?

6. Going Further Sunlight can also release oxygen from bleach. How are bleach containers designed to stop this?

Oxygen is another colorless, odorless gas. In the Investigate activity, you used a glowing splint rather than a lit one to test the gas. The splint relit, didn't it? How do you make the fire burn more brightly? You fan it, don't you? That circulates more oxygen around the coals. Putting the glowing splint in the oxygen serves the same purpose. Burning takes place in the presence of oxygen, so the more oxygen present, the better the burn.

The oxygen that you inhale in every breath is carried throughout your body by your blood. Unlike nitrogen, which must be changed into useful compounds, your body can use oxygen from the air. This oxygen is used by your body to burn the foods you eat and the fats and carbohydrates you have stored. It does this by slowly combining these foods with oxygen from the blood. In this way, digestion provides you with the energy you need to live.

Oxygen easily combines with many other elements to form compounds called oxides. When the other element is a nonmetal, such as sulfur or nitrogen, the oxide forms a substance called an acid when it is dissolved in water. As you have learned, these acids cause problems in the environment when they fall as acid rain.

Oxygen is the other element present in water. Isn't it interesting that one element that burns explosively (hydrogen) and another that allows things to burn (oxygen) can combine into something that puts out fires—water?

Another form of oxygen is ozone, which is described in **Figure 9-12**.

Figure 9-12

Ⓐ Ozone is a form of oxygen that develops near Earth's surface from the action of sunlight on pollutants, which result from burning gasoline. Ozone damages the leaves of plants, and irritates the human respiratory system.

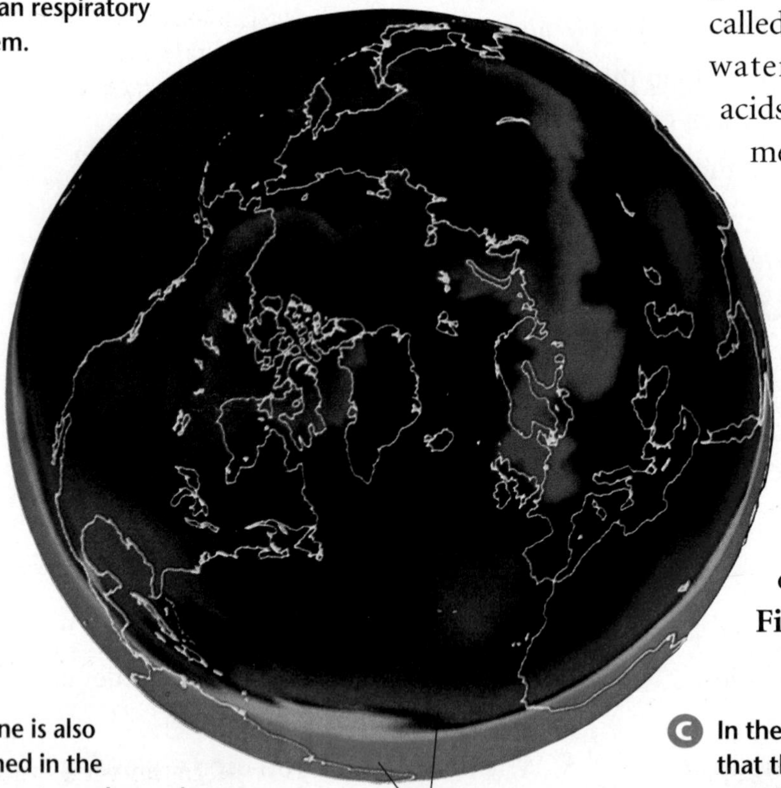

Ⓑ Ozone is also formed in the upper atmosphere when radiation from the sun strikes regular oxygen. The ozone high in the atmosphere is helpful. It forms a layer that protects Earth from harmful rays of the sun that can cause sunburn and skin cancers.

Areas where ozone has decreased are colored blue-purple. Increased ozone areas are red.

Ⓒ In the 1970s, scientists noticed that the protective ozone layer was thinning. Since then they have carefully watched and measured the ozone layer for changes. This image compares ozone amount differences between March 1993 and the average amount for 1979 through 1990.

Other Nonmetals

You have learned from **Figure 9-12** that ozone can harm your lungs. Two other nonmetals that shouldn't be inhaled are fluorine and chlorine.

Chlorine is described in **Figure 9-13A**. Chlorine is a yellow, poisonous gas. You can smell chlorine and observe its yellow color when you open a bottle of laundry bleach. Because chlorine is poisonous, you should never use another cleaner with a chlorine bleach unless you know it is safe to use, such as a laundry detergent. Some cleaners may contain substances that cause bleach to release enough chlorine gas to harm your health.

Figure 9-13B shows a common use of another gas, fluorine. Fluorine also has a strong odor. Its compounds are commonly used to help your teeth stay healthy. Most toothpastes and many water supplies use fluorine compounds because they help prevent tooth decay.

Life on Earth has developed around the elements that are present in the land, sea, and air—our environment. You've explored the properties of metals and nonmetals.

In the next section, you'll explore the properties of elements that are neither metals nor nonmetals.

Figure 9-13

A Because it reacts easily with other substances, chlorine is found in nature in compounds. Chlorine is used as a laundry bleach and a swimming pool disinfectant. Although chlorine as an element is poisonous, there is one chlorine compound that you probably eat every day—sodium chloride, common table salt.

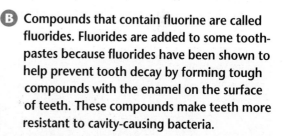

B Compounds that contain fluorine are called fluorides. Fluorides are added to some toothpastes because fluorides have been shown to help prevent tooth decay by forming tough compounds with the enamel on the surface of teeth. These compounds make teeth more resistant to cavity-causing bacteria.

check your UNDERSTANDING

1. If you were given a piece of the element sulfur, how would you test it to see if it is a metal or a nonmetal?
2. Compare and contrast the properties and uses of metals and nonmetals.
3. Many of the nonmetals are gases. How does this observation relate to the most common uses of nonmetals?
4. **Apply** If you wanted to protect a historical document from damage, you might put it in an airtight case. Which of the nonmetals would you choose to replace the air in the case? Explain why you would choose this particular nonmetal.

Understanding Metalloids

Section Objectives
- Distinguish among metals, nonmetals, and metalloids.
- Relate the unique properties of metalloids to their uses.

Key Terms
metalloids

Properties and Examples of Metalloids

What would you call something that was part human and part alien? You'd probably refer to this being as a humanoid, because it has some human characteristics but is not human. In the same way, what would you call an element that had some characteristics of metals and some of nonmetals? Right! A metalloid. As a group, **metalloids** are elements that have properties of both metals and nonmetals. Although the properties of metalloids vary from one element to another, all metalloids show metallic luster. It is the one property all metalloids have in common. Although there are eight metalloids, we'll talk about the two most common ones.

■ Boron

Do you hate scrubbing away the dreaded bathtub ring? Borax, a compound of boron, can be added to laundry products to soften the water so that the minerals in the water don't form soap scum. If you add a little borax to your bathwater, it helps prevent bathtub ring!

Figure 9-14

The major sources of the metalloid boron and boron compounds are mineral deposits from the beds of evaporated lakes and other bodies of water. Boron and its compounds are used in making varied products including cleaning agents, antiseptics, and rocket fuels.

Boron is also found in boric acid, a mild disinfectant that is sometimes used to treat infections. Boron is also used in rocket fuels.

■ Silicon

Although the name may not be familiar, almost everyone has been in contact with silicon. Combined with oxygen, it may be called sand. When sand is melted and allowed to cool, it forms glass. Ordinary glass is melted silicon dioxide with at least one metal, such as sodium, calcium, or aluminum, added.

The element silicon is a perfect example of a metalloid. It comes in shiny gray chunks that look somewhat like a metal. But the chunks are rough and full of little holes—not smooth and dense like many metals. Silicon breaks apart easily, it is not malleable or ductile, but it does conduct an electric current.

Silicon

Figure 9-15

A Silicon makes up about one-fourth of Earth's crust. Silicon and its compounds have many important uses.

B Pure silicon is a semiconductor and is used to make integrated circuits and similar electronic devices.

C The most common compound of silicon is silica, the main ingredient of most sand. Glass, mainly formed from sand, has many important household and industrial uses including optical fibers. Optical fibers are taking the place of copper telephone cables because one tiny optical fiber of glass can transmit more information than a much larger and more expensive copper cable.

D Silica tiles are fixed to the outside of spacecraft to help control the heat the spacecraft generates during its re-entry into the atmosphere.

E The properties of silicon make it possible for scientists to make complex, yet very small electronic devices, such as the experimental robot shown here. Scientists have developed a process to carve entire motors, called micromotors, into tiny flecks of silicon.

If you have any kind of electronic or video game, a calculator, or even a watch that runs on batteries, you are probably carrying around some silicon right now. Because silicon doesn't conduct electricity as well as a metal, it is called a semiconductor. This property makes it important in the computer and electronics industry.

The tiny electronic parts contained in the device in **Figure 9-15B** are based on silicon and other metalloids, such as germanium. Metalloids are used to manufacture items we rely on every day. But are metalloids, like metals and nonmetals, important to your health? The next Explore will help you answer that question.

Explore! ACTIVITY

What elements are in your mineral supplements?

What To Do

1. Examine the label on one or more bottles of mineral tablets.
2. *In your Journal,* write the names of all the elements listed on the label.
3. Classify each element as a metal, a nonmetal, or a metalloid.

From the observations you made in the Explore, you saw that some metalloids, as well as metals and nonmetals, are important to your health and well-being. Silicon, in particular, is needed in very small amounts for proper use of calcium in bones. But no matter what was listed on the label, the ingredients were all elements or contained elements.

Everything within you and outside of you is composed of metals, nonmetals, and metalloids. No matter how complex a substance seems, it is a combination of these approximately 100 elements. From the gold, copper, and iron objects at the beginning of the chapter to the video games and experimental robots at the end, it's an elemental world.

check your UNDERSTANDING

1. Classify each of the following elements as 1) a metal, 2) a nonmetal, or 3) a metalloid: chlorine, carbon, calcium, boron, neon, sodium, aluminum.
2. In addition to metals, which group of elements is likely to contain elements that can conduct electricity?
3. **Apply** The basic component of most small video games is the silicon chip. Why is this component called a chip rather than a wire?

Science *and* Society

Recycling Aluminum

Did you know that the energy saved from recycling one aluminum can could keep a television running for three hours? It requires only five percent of the energy needed to mine aluminum to recycle it.

Aluminum is found in the form of bauxite. Although bauxite is still plentiful, easily mined deposits will disappear one day if we do not recycle the aluminum we use.

Uses of Aluminum

World production of aluminum in 1990 exceeded 17 million metric tons. This lightweight and malleable metal is an excellent conductor and is useful when substituted for heavier, more costly materials.

Aluminum is used in making many cooking utensils. Heat spreads more evenly in aluminum pans. Aluminum foil is used in roofing and insulating homes.

The packaging industry uses about 30 percent of the total United States production of aluminum. Most of that is used for soft drink cans. More than 85 billion cans are produced yearly.

Aluminum as Waste

Aluminum products don't rust and break down. Aluminum combines with the oxygen in air and a thin coat forms over the metal, protecting it from further change.

When aluminum is used and thrown away, it becomes solid waste. Solid waste includes all discarded products that biodegrade slowly or not at all. All materials in aluminum products can be used and reused.

Like some other kinds of industrial waste materials, aluminum can be reused in the manufacturing of new products. After it is separated from other garbage, aluminum can be sold to be melted down and used again.

You Try It!

Find out how recycling programs in your community recycle aluminum and other materials. What other materials does your community recycle?

onsumer onnection

The Prices of Precious Metals

The prices of precious metals, such as gold, silver, and platinum, are listed daily in *The Wall Street Journal* and other major urban newspapers around the country. Under the heading Commodities Futures Prices, readers all over the world can see how these prices change from day to day.

Why Do These Prices Change?

Each day, individuals or groups of people buy and sell these metals. The prices of gold and silver increase when more people wish to buy than sell. Prices go down if more people want to sell than buy. Everyone is affected by these prices.

As Good as Gold

Most of us have seen a gold ring or necklace. Gold has been valued as jewelry for thousands of years. It is also accepted all over the world as currency.

Recently, gold has become an important material in the industrial community. The metal's durability, luster, malleability, and electrical conductivity make it useful in several ways. For example, gold is used to coat

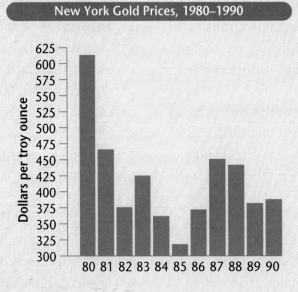

New York Gold Prices, 1980–1990

Dollars per troy ounce

625 600 575 550 525 500 475 450 425 400 375 350 325 300

80 81 82 83 84 85 86 87 88 89 90

windows to reduce heating and cooling costs. It has been used in space equipment to reflect light. And, of course, dentists use gold to repair teeth.

You Try It!

Study the graph on this page. Can you tell which years gold prices increased? Why do you think the price of gold went up during these years? Ask a parent or teacher what might have happened during those years when gold prices increased.

A **metallurgist** is trained in chemistry and engineering. Metallurgists study the way metals are extracted from ore and how they might be used to make different products. An extractive metallurgist explores the ways to remove and refine metal. A production metallurgist would work to develop the metal into some real product.

CAREER connection

HOW IT WORKS

Metalworking in Jewelry

Jewelry is made from a variety of rare and not-so-rare metals and gems. Expensive jewelry is usually made from gold or platinum. Most gold contains some copper, zinc, or silver. Less expensive jewelry is made from bronze or tin. Because consumers like gold, costume jewelry is sometimes given a gold wash or covered with a thin sheet of gold to make it look like pure gold.

The photos show one of the most popular metals used in jewelry today—silver. Most silver jewelry will have other metals mixed in. According to United States law, sterling silver must consist of at least 92.5 percent silver.

Historically, metalworkers made jewelry by hand. Today there are several methods used to make jewelry.

Casting

One frequently used method is called casting. Once a design is developed, a master model, usually made of metal, is formed. A rubber mold is then made of the metal model. Molten wax is poured into the rubber mold, creating a wax model. After completing this process, a second mold is made by dipping the wax model in thinned clay, letting the clay dry, and then baking it in an oven until hard. The melted wax drips through a hole left in the clay. Liquid metal is then poured through the hole, filling up the cavity left by the wax. Once the metal has cooled and hardened, the ceramic mold is cracked open to reveal the cast piece. While the rubber mold can be used a number of times, each wax model can only be used once.

Stamping

In another method called stamping, metal is squeezed between two steel pieces called dies. Stamping and other methods of mass production are used to make huge quantities of inexpensive costume jewelry.

You Try It!

Study some of your family's jewelry at home. Can you tell what kinds of metals were used to make the jewelry?

Technology Connection · Neon Lights

Before fluorescent lights became part of our culture, neon and lamps of other gases were used. The gas tubes weren't practical inside homes and offices because the color of the light is so unlike sunlight. These special gases were best used in creating glowing, lettered signs. Although they are called neon lights, after neon gas, the colored signs contain a number of different gases including helium, argon, krypton, and xenon.

By 1923, neon lights were used in Los Angeles to advertise automobiles. And in the 1970s, artists created a new medium using glass sculptures filled with different noble gases.

How Do These Signs Work?

Electricity passes through a tube that contains one of these gases, causing the gas to glow. The color of the glow depends on the type of gas in the tube. For example, argon gives off a

purple glow, neon gives off a red glow, and krypton gives off a pale violet glow.

Discovery

These gases were discovered late in the 19th century. One reason that they went undiscovered for so long is that they make up a small fraction of Earth's atmosphere.

Noble gases are also difficult to observe. They are colorless, tasteless, odorless, and do not easily combine chemically to make compounds with other elements.

Sources

The chief source of the noble gases is air. To extract noble gases from air, the air is first chilled to a very low temperature, then liquefied. The liquid air is gradually heated. As the air boils, each noble gas separates out.

You Try It!

Look at the neon signs in your community or in a photo. Identify what colors are most common. Why might these colors be used for advertising?

Review the statements below about the big ideas presented in this chapter, and try to answer the questions. Then, re-read your answers to the Did You Ever Wonder questions at the beginning of the chapter. *In your Journal,* write a paragraph about how your understanding of the big ideas in the chapter has changed.

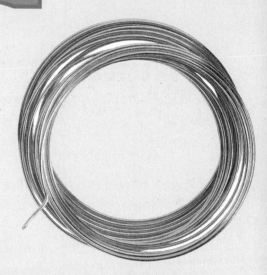

1 All matter is made of elements. Elements can be grouped into metals, nonmetals, or metalloids. *Why must we conserve these resources?*

2 Metallic elements are prized for their luster, hardness, ability to be easily shaped, and ability to conduct heat and electricity. *What properties of a metal make it useful as a material for electrical wiring?*

3 Nonmetals are important ingredients in many common products, such as toothpaste. In addition to these uses, nonmetals form the basis of life cycles and play important roles in the processes of living organisms. *What is the most common nonmetal?*

4 Metalloids have properties of both metals and nonmetals. *How are metalloids used in our daily lives?*

Using Key Science Terms

coinage metal   metalloid

ductile   metal

malleable   nonmetal

For each set of terms below, choose the one term that does not belong and explain why it does not belong.

1. metalloid, ductility, nonmetal, metal
2. brittle, metal, nonmetal, gas
3. conductor, magnetic, malleable, ductile
4. metal, ductile, malleable, nonmetal

Understanding Ideas

Answer the following questions in your Journal using complete sentences.

1. Why were copper, silver, and gold used for coins years ago? Why aren't coins used today made out of silver and gold?
2. Why was hydrogen once used to fill aircrafts, such as blimps? Why isn't hydrogen used anymore?
3. Why do some symbols for elements have more than one letter?
4. How is nitric acid formed from pollutants in the air? What effect does it have on the environment?
5. Why does a fire burn more brightly when air is blown on it?
6. How does mercury differ from other metals?
7. Which of these elements are most likely to have properties similar to those of chlorine? Why?
   a. boron
   b. hydrogen
   c. nitrogen
   d. oxygen
   e. silicon
8. In what ways is silicon like a metal?

Developing Skills

Use your understanding of the concepts developed in this chapter to answer each of the following questions.

1. **Concept Mapping** Using the following terms, create a concept map of the three major groups of elements and their properties: *brittle, dull, elements, good conductors, luster, malleable, metalloids, metals, nonmetals, poor conductors.* Some of the terms may be used more than once.
2. **Design an Experiment** Suppose you just discovered an unknown element. How would you find out if it were a metal or a nonmetal? Refer to the Investigate on page 274 and the Explore activity on page 282.
3. **Comparing and Contrasting** Compare and contrast metals, nonmetals, and metalloids.
4. **Observing and Inferring** Water is added to baking powder and a gas is given off. A lighted match is held in the gas and the flame goes out completely. Is the gas either hydrogen or oxygen? Explain your answer.
5. **Making and Using Graphs** Use the data in Figure 9-11 to make a pie graph.

Critical Thinking

In your Journal, *answer each of the following questions.*

1. Explain the relationship between oxygen and iron in your body.
2. Compare and contrast the properties of the elements sodium and chlorine with those of salt.
3. From the properties shown in the picture, is this element a metal, nonmetal, or metalloid? Explain your answer.

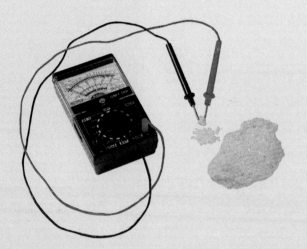

4. What is the most abundant element in your body? In the universe? In Earth's crust? Are they metals or nonmetals?
5. Why is it more useful to divide elements into metals, nonmetals, and metalloids than into solids, liquids, and gases?
6. Describe the relationship between ordinary glass and semiconductors in computers.

Problem Solving

Read the following problem and discuss your answers in a brief paragraph.

You've been hired to design a new fireworks display for the 4th of July. The display must be a flag in red, white, and blue.

1. Which of the flag's colors would be easily made using the metals from the Investigate on page 274? Why?
2. A sodium compound was mixed into your American flag display. What color will be added to the flag?

CONNECTING IDEAS

Discuss each of the following in a brief paragraph.

1. **Theme—Systems and Interactions** How can metals be dangerous to your health?
2. **Theme—Scale and Structure** Why are silver and copper good materials for making electric wires?
3. **How It Works** Explain why more inexpensive costume jewelry is made by stamping than by molding.
4. **Technology Connection** What physical property of matter is used to help collect noble gases from air? Explain the process that is most commonly used.
5. **Earth Science Connection** Describe how diamonds in nature are formed.

CHAPTER 10

MINERALS
AND THEIR USES

Did you ever wonder...

✓ Where gold comes from and why it's so valuable?

✓ Why some stones are called gems and others are called rocks?

✓ How to tell the difference between real gold and "fool's gold"?

Before you begin to study minerals, think about these questions and answer them *in your Journal*. When you finish the chapter, compare your Journal write-up with what you've learned.

Here you are, looking at the museum's display of relics from the tomb of King Tutankhamen—an ancient Egyptian pharaoh. The first thing you notice is the gleaming gold.

You catch your breath a little as you move to the next section of the exhibit. Blue sapphires, red rubies, and green emeralds glisten at you from necklaces and bracelets. Light seems to stream from every point on their surfaces.

Virtually every item on display here is made of minerals. What makes the minerals of King Tut's treasure different from the minerals around you?

▶ *In the activity on the next page, explore what characteristics make some items more valuable than others.*

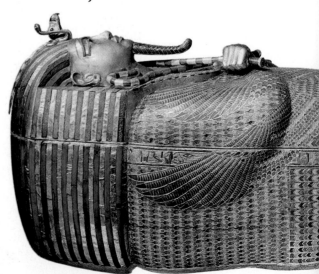

300

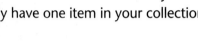

Explore! ACTIVITY

What makes jewels valuable?

Just as a museum director gathers similar items together to make an exhibit, many of us have collections of our own.

Perhaps you have a collection of leaves, shells, or baseball cards. No matter what you collect, you probably have one item in your collection that is special.

What To Do

1. Place the items of your collection around you. *In your Journal*, describe the common characteristics of all the items.

2. Pick out the one special item you have—the "gem" of your collection. Describe what makes it different.

3. Why is your collection important to you? Would it be valuable to others?

Minerals and Their Value

10-1

Section Objectives

- Name four conditions that define minerals.
- Explain how rarity and beauty can affect the value of a particular mineral.

Key Terms

gem

mineral

Quartz

Figure 10-1

When stimulated with an electric charge from a battery, microthin quartz crystal slices vibrate more than 30 000 times each second. Because the vibrations are so regular, they can be used as a measure of time.

Titanium

Figure 10-2

Because of its light weight and great strength, titanium is a favored material for making aircraft frames and engines.

Minerals Can Be Familiar

Without asking anyone, you know that the gold and jewels you see in the museum are worth a good deal of money. You may decide that they are valuable because they are so beautiful. You may also take into account that gold and jewels are rare and hard to find. Even the most beautiful, rare, and costly jewels, however, fall into a broad category of substances. These substances are called minerals.

Minerals are part of your life. Write your name with a pencil, and you use the mineral graphite, which is used in pencil lead. Toss a penny, and you toss the mineral copper, one of several substances used in coin currency.

There are more than 4000 different minerals on Earth. As you can imagine, we have found many uses for

302 Chapter 10 Minerals and Their Uses

them. Some of these uses are shown on this and the following pages. Can you think of other common uses of minerals?

How can you know what substances are minerals? Even though there are thousands of minerals, they all meet several basic conditions. A **mineral** is a naturally occurring, inorganic solid with a definite crystalline structure, and a definite composition. In the following Find Out activity, you'll learn more about the crystalline nature of minerals.

Halite

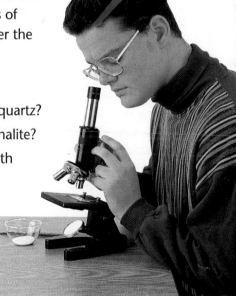

Figure 10-3

When you munch on a salted pretzel, you eat the mineral halite. Halite is also known as rock salt and is the source of common table salt.

Find Out! ACTIVITY

How do minerals look up close?

What To Do

1. Slide a tiny amount of table salt—the mineral halite—under your microscope and separate the granules.

2. Focus on just one granule as you examine the salt under your microscope.

3. Now, examine a quartz sample with evidence of its crystal structure visible on the outside. How does the shape of the quartz crystal compare with the shape of the halite crystal?

4. Count the number of sides each crystal has. Make a sketch of the quartz crystal and of the halite crystal.

5. The diagram below shows the six major crystal systems of minerals. Use it to answer the following questions.

Conclude and Apply

1. Which type of crystal is quartz?

2. Which type of crystal is halite?

3. Examine sugar grains with your microscope. Determine which type of crystal shape they are. Sugar is formed by plants. Is it a mineral?

Cubic

Tetragonal

Hexagonal

Orthorhombic

Monoclinic

Triclinic

How Do We Define Minerals?

Let's look at the conditions that define minerals more closely.

1. Minerals Occur Naturally When salt deposits form by natural processes, the mineral halite is formed. However, salt manufactured by humans is not considered a mineral.

2. Minerals Are Inorganic Minerals are not alive, nor are they formed from anything that ever was alive. For example, coral is formed from skeletons of tiny sea animals, therefore, it is organic. On the other hand, diamonds form deep underground from inorganic matter. A diamond is a mineral, but coral is not.

3. Minerals Have Unique Chemical Compositions A mineral can be an element or a compound. Each type of mineral has a chemical composition that is unique to that mineral. The mineral quartz, for example, is a combination of two elements, silicon and oxygen. Although other minerals may also contain silicon and oxygen, the arrangement and proportion of the elements in quartz are unique to quartz.

Life Science CONNECTION

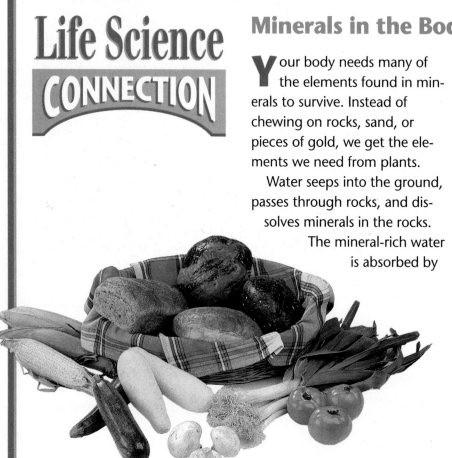

Minerals in the Body

Your body needs many of the elements found in minerals to survive. Instead of chewing on rocks, sand, or pieces of gold, we get the elements we need from plants.

Water seeps into the ground, passes through rocks, and dissolves minerals in the rocks. The mineral-rich water is absorbed by plant roots and carried throughout the plant. The elements in minerals help the plant grow by assisting in photosynthesis and other processes.

The human body needs more than 20 different kinds of elements, but only in very small amounts. Iron, which is found in such minerals as magnetite and pyrite, helps blood carry oxygen throughout our bodies. Calcium, found in calcite and dolomite, helps make bones and teeth strong. Sodium, found in halite, helps regulate water in the body's cells.

The elements needed to form minerals can be recycled. Plants absorb minerals from the

4. Minerals Have Crystalline Structure

The atoms in a mineral are arranged in a regular geometric pattern repeated over and over again. Substances with this kind of inner structure are crystalline.

■ Classifying Minerals

Most minerals are nonmetallic. Graphite, quartz, and halite are all examples of nonmetallic minerals.

However, other substances such as gold, silver, and copper also meet the definition of a mineral. They are also defined as metals. Metals are materials that are used in many different ways. Can you think of a few ways we use metals?

Figure 10-4

Ⓐ Topaz is a naturally occurring inorganic solid. It has a unique chemical composition and a crystal structure. Having these four characteristics qualifies topaz to be classified as a mineral.

Coal

Topaz

Ⓑ Coal is a solid, naturally occurring substance composed of the remains of plants and animals. Is coal a mineral? Why?

soil, then animals eat the plants. When the animals—including humans—die and decompose, they return the elements to the soil. But most of the plants humans eat come from large production farms, where there isn't enough time for this gradual cycle.

Farmers use different methods of returning elements to the soil. Often, organic or inorganic fertilizers are used. Organic fertilizers, often referred to as compost, are fertilizers made from plant and animal remains and waste. Inorganic fertilizers are made from essential elements and minerals that have been extracted from rock.

Crop rotation is another method by which minerals in soil can be preserved or replaced. Farmers rotate the types of crops they plant each year to ensure that the minerals used by one type of crop are replaced the following year by a different crop.

You Try It!

Calcium is the most abundant element in the body, and is found in teeth and bones. Calcium is found in many foods, including whole grains. Read and compare the labels on the foods you eat.

Figure 10-5

People have been combining tin and copper to make bronze objects since 3500 B.C. Is bronze a metal? Is it a mineral? Why?

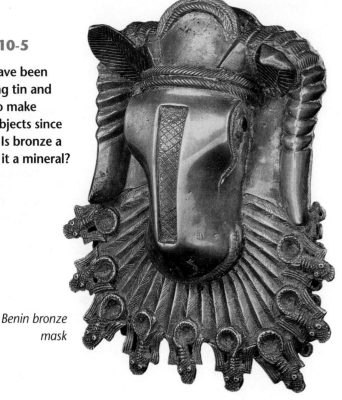

Benin bronze mask

Are all metals minerals? To find the answer to that question, read the caption of **Figure 10-5**.

■ Some Minerals Are Gems

Think back to your visit to the museum at the beginning of the chapter. Why were the minerals on display considered "gems"? A **gem** is a valuable, highly priced mineral that is rare, or is difficult to obtain.

The treasures of the pharaohs are easily identified as gems because they've been cut and polished. But suppose you were seeking gems in their natural form. Would you know what to look for? How could you tell a valuable find from a nonvaluable one? In the next section, you'll learn how we can distinguish one mineral from another.

Figure 10-6

Ⓐ It takes a skilled stonecutter to bring out the sparkle in a gemstone. A stonecutter begins by cutting the mineral crystal in half, and rounding its edges.

Ⓑ The next step is faceting the gemstone on various grinding wheels. Faceting is a process of grinding tiny, polished sides, called facets, into the gemstone.

Ⓒ The number of facets varies according to cut style. The standard brilliant cut, shown here, has 58 facets.

check your UNDERSTANDING

1. What four conditions do minerals satisfy?
2. What factors help determine the value of a mineral?
3. **Apply** Opal is a substance that occurs naturally, is inorganic, and has a unique composition. But opal does not have a definite crystalline structure. Is opal a mineral? Explain your answer.

10-2 Identifying Minerals

Properties of Minerals

Picture a time in history when people left their jobs and families, took all they could carry, and ran off in search of their fortunes. That's what happened during the California Gold Rush.

A gold rush is a mass, rapid migration of people to an area where gold has been discovered. The largest and most famous gold rush in U.S. history began with the discovery of gold in Sutter's Mill in California in 1848.

Suppose you had been living during the 1840s. Would you have been part of the rush for gold? If so, would you have known what to look for? Many people of that day thought they, too, would know gold when they saw it, but they were fooled. The mineral pyrite, or "fool's gold," looks a lot like true gold. There are several simple tests you could have performed to know whether or not you had "struck it rich." You'll learn about one such test in the following Find Out activity.

Section Objectives

- Describe how physical characteristics are used to identify minerals.
- Differentiate between mineral characteristics such as hardness, color, streak, cleavage, and fracture.

Key Terms

streak, hardness, cleavage, fracture

Figure 10-7

Ⓐ The first California gold fields were discovered near present day Sacramento in 1848. Word of the find spread. The gold rush was on! In the following year thousands of people, hoping to get rich, rushed into California.

Gold

Ⓑ The gold rush made a few people very rich. But many were disappointed. Some found too little gold to make a profit. Some found only pyrite, a mineral that looks so similar to what inexperienced prospectors think gold looks like that it is called "fool's gold."

Pyrite

Ⓒ The gold fever faded in a few years, but the social and economic development that it started continued to thrive.

10-2   Identifying Minerals   **307**

Find Out! ACTIVITY

What is a streak test?

Your teacher will give you a piece of unglazed porcelain called a streak plate and several samples of minerals, including pyrite, hematite, and graphite.

What To Do

1. First, run the graphite across the streak plate. This is called streaking the graphite.

2. Look at the color of graphite's streak on the streak plate. How does it compare with the color of the graphite?

3. Before you streak the pyrite and hematite, hypothesize what color they will streak on the streak plate.

4. Now streak the pyrite and hematite. What color are the streaks? How do the streak colors compare with the actual colors?

Conclude and Apply

1. Were you correct in the hypothesis you made before you streaked the pyrite?

2. When streaked, gold leaves a yellow mark. How could you use the streak test to make sure you weren't fooled by "fool's gold"?

■ **Streak**

When a mineral is rubbed across a streak plate, as you did in the Find Out activity, a streak is left behind. The color of a mineral when it is broken up and powdered is called its **streak**. Was the red-brown streak of hematite what you expected to see?

■ **Color**

A mineral's color is another clue to its identity. As you can see from the photos on this page, sulfur and azurite are easy to distinguish based on color alone. But is this always the case? Think back to what you know about gold and pyrite. Are they easy to identify based on color?

Color may give you a clue as to a mineral's identity, but you'll need more information before you can be sure.

Figure 10-8

A Color is one of the first characteristics you notice about a mineral, and it can often give a valuable clue to its identity. Sulfur, for example, has a very distinctive yellow color.

Sulfur

B You could never confuse sulfur with azurite, which is always a shade of blue. The blue of azurite, seen at the right, is the source of the color term azure blue.

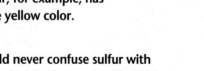

Azurite

Luster

Look at **Figure 10-9**. How do these two minerals differ in appearance? Which of the two would you label as having a "metallic" luster? Which has a nonmetallic luster?

Luster refers to the way in which a mineral reflects light. If you refer to Appendices K and L of your book, you'll see that minerals are divided into two groups based on their luster.

Do you think all minerals with a metallic luster are metals? You may be surprised to learn that they are not. For example, graphite is metallic in luster. Yet, you know that the graphite in your pencil is not a true metal.

Hardness

So far, you've learned that a mineral's color, luster, or streak can help you identify it. Unfortunately, these characteristics sometimes vary among samples of the same mineral. A more useful property you can use to identify a mineral is its hardness.

Galena

Figure 10-9

Ⓐ Minerals with a metallic luster shine like metal. Galena, which is an ore of lead and sometimes of silver, has a bright metallic luster.

Feldspar

Ⓑ The appearance of minerals with a non-metallic luster vary. Feldspar, used in making glass and pottery, has a glossy to pearly appearance. Talc, another mineral with a nonmetallic luster, has a pearly surface.

Yellow sapphire   *Blue sapphire*

Ⓒ A single color alone may not be enough to distinguish one mineral from another. Some minerals come in various colors. Sapphires, shown above, form from the mineral corundum and come in blue, purple, green, pink, and yellow.

How does a scratch test help identify minerals?

Your teacher will give you samples of the three minerals listed in the table.

What To Do

1. Copy the table *in your Journal.*

2. Choose one of the mineral samples and try to scratch the other minerals with it. For example, does calcite scratch quartz? If so, make a check mark in the calcite row where it intersects with the quartz column.

3. Repeat the scratch test for each mineral in the chart.

4. Analyze the completed data table, and sequence the minerals from softest to hardest: 1 = softest, 3 = hardest.

Conclude and Apply

1. Can you scratch any of the minerals with your fingernail?

2. Hypothesize how a scratch test might help you identify pyrite or gold.

3. Describe how you could use a scratch test to determine which minerals are harder than a copper penny.

Data and Observations

	Calcite	Quartz	Talc
Calcite	✕		
Quartz		✕	
Talc			✕

Figure 10-10

The Mohs scale of mineral hardness lists 10 minerals in order of hardness. The softest mineral is 1; the hardest is 10.

The Find Out activity shows one characteristic that helps distinguish one mineral from another. **Hardness** is a measure of how easily a mineral can be scratched. Talc is one of the softest known minerals and can be scratched with your fingernail. If you have ever rubbed talcum powder on your skin, you know how smooth and soft talc can be. In contrast, diamonds are so hard that they are used in sharpening and cutting tools. A diamond

1	2	3	4	5
Talc	Gypsum	Calcite	Fluorite	Apatite

Easily scratched by fingernail.

Can be scratched by fingernail.

Barely can be scratched by copper penny.

Easily scratched with steel knife blade.

Can be scratched by steel knife blade.

can be scratched only by another diamond.

Remember how you sequenced the minerals in the Find Out activity according to hardness? You were working with minerals that had three distinctive hardnesses, so you used a scale of 1 to 3. In a similar way, you can use a scale of 1 to 10 to compare the hardnesses of all minerals. This scale is shown in **Figure 10-10**. The scale is named for the German scientist who devised it, Friedrich Mohs.

■ Cleavage and Fracture

Minerals also differ in the way they break. You might perform this test by tapping a mineral sample against a hard surface. Minerals that break along smooth, flat surfaces have **cleavage**. Mica is a mineral that has perfect cleavage.

Minerals that have curved, rough, or jagged surfaces when they break apart have **fracture**. Quartz is a good example of a mineral with fracture.

Mica

Figure 10-11

Ⓐ Cleavage is the result of the orderly arrangement of the atoms that form the crystals of that mineral. Mica is a mineral that has perfect cleavage.

Ⓑ Barite is another mineral with perfect cleavage. If you examine a barite crystal, you can see the cleavage planes, along which the crystal would split.

Barite

6	7	8	9	10
Feldspar	**Quartz**	**Topaz**	**Corundum**	**Diamond**
Can be scratched by steel knife blade.	*Easily scratches both glass and steel.*	*Scratches quartz.*	*Scratches topaz.*	*Scratches all common materials.*

INVESTIGATE!

Becoming a Mineral Detective

You are now aware of many of the physical properties of minerals. But suppose it was your job to identify samples of minerals. Could you do it? You're about to put your knowledge to work as you uncover the identity of several "mystery" minerals.

Problem

How can mineral identities be determined from tests?

Materials

mineral samples	Mohs scale of
steel file	hardness on
streak plate	pages 310
hand lens	and 311
goggles	5% hydrochloric
apron	acid (HCL) with dropper

Safety Precautions

During this Investigate you will be working with some materials that need to be handled with care.

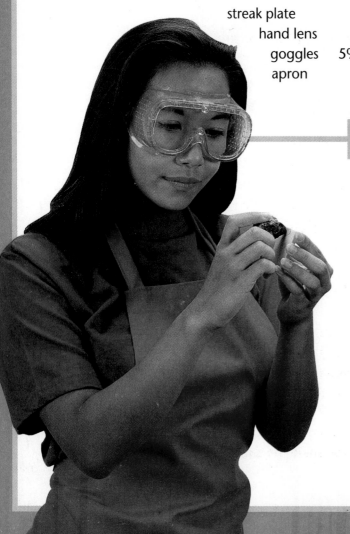

What To Do

1. Examine the materials you have available to you to identify your mineral samples.

2. Determine how each item can be used in this investigation.

3. Construct a data table. Record the characteristics of each sample as you perform various tests on it.

4. **CAUTION:** *Wear your goggles and apron. HCl is an acid and may cause burns. If spills occur, rinse with water and notify your teacher.*

Figure 10-12

Mineralogy is a branch of geology. Mineralogists seek answers to questions such as: How are minerals formed? Where do they occur? What are their chemical and physical properties? What is their composition?

Rose quartz

5 Once you have decided how you will use the materials to identify the samples, obtain your teacher's permission before you go on. DO NOT PERFORM ANY TESTS ON THE SAMPLES WITHOUT YOUR TEACHER'S PERMISSION.

6 Test your mineral samples and fill in your data table.

7 Identify the name of each sample. Refer to the table in Appendix K if you need help.

Analyzing

1. Compare your results with those of another group.

2. Were your methods of testing samples different from the methods of the other groups? How?

3. What mineral samples were you unable to identify? Were other groups unable to identify the same samples?

4. Can you group any of your samples based on the test results? Do any of these groupings have any other properties in common?

Concluding and Applying

5. Which tests were most useful?

6. If you were unable to identify some samples, explain why. Were there tests you needed to perform but were unable to?

7. How many tests should usually be performed before deciding what mineral a given sample is? Why?

8. **Going Further** Pretend you are going on a geological expedition. Your purpose is to determine what minerals are abundant in the area of the expedition. What things will you pack to take along on your expedition? What activities will you be engaged in while you are on the expedition? How will you keep track of your observations? How might you share the data you obtain with others?

Other Properties of Minerals

Some minerals have unique traits that set them apart from other minerals. They have unique and interesting properties. In the following Explore activity, you'll be able to discover one of them.

Explore! ACTIVITY

How do clear minerals compare?

What To Do

1. Your teacher will give you samples of some clear minerals. Place each sample over the print on this page.
2. Describe the appearance of print through each mineral.
3. Which mineral can be identified by the way it changes light passing through it?

Figure 10-13

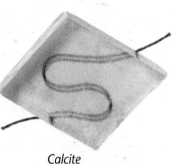

A Light passing through calcite is split into two rays. Each ray produces its own image. When you look at something through calcite you see both images. This unusual property of calcite is called double refraction.

Calcite

B The mineral magnetite is a natural magnet and has the ability to attract small iron and steel objects.

Iron filings

You discovered in the Explore activity that calcite has a unique property. Magnetite is another mineral with its own unique trait. What property of magnetite can help you identify it?

■ Looking Ahead

Since you first started thinking about minerals you've learned that four features set minerals apart from all other substances on Earth. You've probably been wondering where minerals come from and how we collect them. You'll find the answers to your questions in the next section.

check your UNDERSTANDING

1. Name four characteristics that can help distinguish one mineral from another.
2. **Apply** Pretend you're a prospector looking for silver. You find a nugget that you think may be silver. What tests can you use to determine whether you've "struck it rich"?

 **Mineral Formation**

How Minerals Form

As you know, a substance can be classified as a mineral only if it occurs naturally. Yet the photos on this page show human-made "minerals." People were able to produce these synthetic "minerals" by studying the way true minerals formed.

There are two main ways that minerals form. One is from the cooling of magma. As the magma cools, elements in the magma may form minerals. Minerals can also form from elements dissolved in a liquid. When the liquid evaporates, the elements stay behind and may form minerals. When a solution becomes saturated, dissolved material may also precipitate, or start to crystallize, out of solution.

In the next activity, you'll watch crystals form. You will be able to see a process of mineral formation in action.

Section Objectives
■ Examine mineral formation from solution.
■ Describe mineral formation by the cooling of magma.

Figure 10-15

Ⓐ Today synthetic emeralds are common. To produce synthetic emeralds, a powder of the components of emerald is heated with a flux. A flux is a substance that speeds up the process.

Ⓑ The flux melts and the powdered components dissolve. As the mixture cools, crystals form and begin to grow. It takes several months for emerald crystals to grow. Is a synthetic emerald a mineral?

Figure 10-14

Ⓐ In 1988, U.S. astronaut mission specialists George D. Nelson (left) and David C. Hilmers conducted an experiment that involved growing crystals in the zero gravity of space.

Ⓑ The experiment, carried out aboard the space shuttle *Discovery,* was proposed by then high school student Richard Cavoli of Marlboro, N.Y. as part of the Shuttle Student Involvement project.

INVESTIGATE!

Growing Crystals

So far, you've read about "minerals in solution." Still, you may be unsure of what that means. You know something about both minerals and solutions. This activity will help you put the two together and then take them apart again!

Problem

What are two ways that crystals can form from solutions?

Materials

salt solution	sugar solution
large test tube	toothpick
cotton thread	hand lens
1 shallow pan	thermal mitt
test-tube rack	cardboard
table salt	granulated sugar
hot plate	beaker

Safety Precautions

During this investigate you will be handling materials that will be hot.

What To Do

1. Pour the sugar solution into a beaker. Use the hot plate to gently heat the solution.

2. Place the test tube in the test-tube rack. Using a thermal mitt to protect your hand, pour some of the hot sugar solution into the test tube. **CAUTION:** *The liquid is hot. Do not touch the test tube without protecting your hands.*

3. Tie the thread to the middle of the toothpick. Place the thread in the test tube (see photo **A**). Be sure that it does not touch the sides or bottom of the tube. Let the toothpick rest across the top of the test tube.

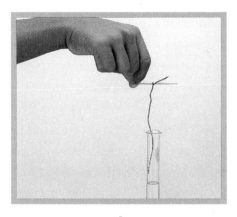

A   **B**   **C**

4 Cover the test tube with a piece of cardboard (see photo **B**). Place the rack containing the test tube in a location where it will not be disturbed.

5 Pour a thin layer of the salt solution into the second shallow pan (see photo **C**).

6 Place the pan in a warm area of the room.

7 Leave both the covered test tube and the shallow pan undisturbed for at least one week.

8 Examine sample grains of table salt and sugar with the hand lens. *Observe* any similarities or differences.

9 At the end of one week, *observe* each solution and see if crystals have formed. Use a hand lens to examine any crystals.

Analyzing

1. *Compare and contrast* the crystals that formed from the salt and sugar solutions. Make a sketch of each type of crystal.

2. *Infer* what happened to the salt water in the shallow pan.

3. Did this same process occur in the test tube? Explain.

Concluding and Applying

4. What caused the formation of crystals in the test tube and in the shallow pan?

5. Are salt and sugar both minerals? Explain your answer.

6. ~~Going Further~~ *Hypothesize* the results of your experiments if you had switched the salt solution with the sugar solution. Explain your hypotheses.

Minerals Form from Water Solution

You may remember from what you've learned about solutions that a given volume of water can dissolve only a certain amount of solid before the water becomes saturated. When the water is saturated, the next teaspoonful of solid will not dissolve.

If the water is hot, you can dissolve even more solid. As the solution cools, crystals form from the solution onto the string. This is what the sugar did in the last activity.

Salt crystals formed from solution because as the water evaporated, the solution left couldn't hold the same amount of salt, and the salt crystals formed.

You read in the first section that many minerals are composed of more than one element. Before they become minerals, however, these elements are in solution. In some cases, this solution forms when elements are dissolved in water. When the water evaporates, the elements may combine in a mineral's characteristic crystal structure. If the mineral has an open space to form, crystals will form that show their crystal shape on the outside. If there is no open space for the mineral to form, the crystals will overlap. When this happens, the elements have still combined in an orderly pattern, but we just cannot see it on the outside of the crystal.

Waterfall containing minerals in solution.

Figure 10-16

A Water carrying minerals in solution sometimes seeps into cracks in rock, which also contains minerals. The water dissolves the minerals contained in the rock.

C Some gold, shown here, is formed in veins. Quartz, copper, sulfur, and galena are other examples of minerals that sometimes form in veins.

B As conditions within the water change, minerals begin to precipitate out of solution. Evaporation of the water can also lead to the formation of minerals out of solution.

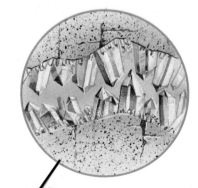

Figure 10-17

A Both rhyolite and granite are formed from the same type of magma, but rhyolite, which forms from rapidly cooling lava, is finer grained.

Rhyolite

B If magma cools slowly, as it is apt to do in Earth's interior, large mineral crystals form. Pegmatites are an example of materials that form with large crystals.

Pegmatite

■ Minerals Form from Cooling Magma

The elements and compounds that make up minerals are also in solution deep below Earth's surface. The solution is magma—the hot, molten material found beneath Earth's crust. When magma moves upward into cooler layers of the planet's interior, it cools. As the magma cools, the elements in magma may combine chemically and form minerals. Again, if there is enough open space, the minerals form large, visible crystal shapes.

The cooling process can be slow or quick. This cooling rate determines crystal size. If magma cools slowly, as it is apt to do in Earth's warm to hot interior, large crystals form. Minerals such as mica, feldspar, and quartz are examples of minerals that often form large crystals. If the magma cools quickly, minerals form as small crystals. Lava, which is magma that reaches Earth's surface, is exposed to air and sometimes water. Lava cools quickly in air, so small mineral crystals form. If lava runs into water, it may cool so quickly that no crystals form at all.

Sometimes flowing magma or lava will fill cracks in surrounding rock.

Figure 10-18

A As hot magma flows, it sometimes fills cracks in surrounding rock. The rock keeps the heat from escaping, and the molten material takes a very long time to cool. The slow cooling time allows deposits of large mineral crystals to form in the cracks. These mineral-filled cracks are called veins. Veins of some gemstones such as ruby, topaz, sapphire, and beryl form this way.

B Veins of beryl crystals are found most often in granite rocks. Pure beryl is colorless, but impurities in the crystals add color. The most common colors of beryl are bluish-green and yellow-green. Emeralds, seen in the photo at the right, are dark green beryl crystals.

1.36 carat cut emerald (not to scale)

Emerald crystal

Retrieving Minerals

You know a lot about minerals and how to identify them. But before you can classify a mineral sample, you have to find one! Where would you look for minerals in their natural state?

Very few of Earth's minerals are found just lying on the ground, "waiting" to be picked up and used. Instead, they occur deep underground, trapped in rocks or soil. To get to these mineral deposits, the overlying rocks and soil must be removed.

There are many methods of removing the unwanted materials and collecting the minerals we desire. Strip mining, open pit mining, and room and pillar mining are just a few of the methods that we use.

Let's take a closer look at some mines. At an open pit mine, the mine is made deeper as the mineral and the rocks

The rock traps the heat from the molten material, causing it to cool very slowly and form large mineral crystals. Veins of some gems and rare minerals form in this way. Some examples are rubies and sapphires which are types of the mineral corundum; and emeralds and aquamarines which are types of the mineral beryl.

Minerals spend much of their existence in rocks. Humans go to great length and expense to extract them from the rocks. In fact, rocks are made of minerals. Rocks are the next group of materials you will investigate as you go on to Chapter 11.

check your UNDERSTANDING

1. What is the connection between evaporation and mineral formation?
2. Describe two ways in which a vein of a mineral may form in a rock.
3. **Apply** A volcano erupts in the middle of the ocean. Lava slips down the sides of its cone and eventually enters the ocean water. Will the mineral crystals formed from the lava be large or small? Explain your answer.

that contain them are hauled away. Usually, terraces are left on the slope of the deep pit. An open-pit copper mine is shown at left.

You may think of a mine as a sort of underground "cave." People dig rooms in the sides of mountains or under flat ground. They then remove the minerals from the walls of the mine. This is what the miner is doing in the photo at the right.

Not long ago, people thought that Earth's mineral supplies would last forever. Today, we know mineral supplies are limited.

Our demand for minerals increases as we find more and more uses for them. The answer

to our mineral needs probably isn't simply to open more mines.

Mines can destroy land, water, and the plants and animals that live nearby. Instead, we must find ways to make mining less destructive.

We also need to use minerals more efficiently.

You Try It!

Think of several ways you can conserve mineral resources, and list them *in your Journal.*

Science and Society

Asbestos Debate

Asbestos has been the subject of debate for nearly 20 years. What is asbestos, and why is it so controversial?

Asbestos is a mineral sometimes found in metamorphic rock. It is a lightweight, fibrous mineral that is white to green in color. The use of asbestos dates back to ancient times, when Egyptians and Romans realized that asbestos was resistant to fire and heat. They wove asbestos into clothing and pressed it into paper.

Asbestos

More recently, asbestos has been used to produce insulation for buildings and water pipes. It is well suited for those uses because asbestos doesn't conduct heat or electricity very well. Since it doesn't burn easily and is resistant to acids, asbestos is used in products such as automobile brakes and fireproof clothing.

As far back as the early 1900s, scientists were concerned with the possible harmful effects of inhaling asbestos fibers. Airborne asbestos fibers are so small they can't be seen without a microscope. Even when asbestos is mixed with other materials, such as cement,

the products can break down over time and release the fibers into the air.

Scientists first realized the dangers of asbestos by studying workers in plants where asbestos products were manufactured. Breathing some types of asbestos fibers can cause asbestosis, a disease that stiffens the lungs and makes breathing difficult. It can also cause lung cancer or cancer of the stomach lining. Sometimes these diseases don't show up until 20 or 30 years after a person has been exposed to asbestos.

The Environmental Protection Agency (EPA) has researched the effects of asbestos for the United States government since the early 1970s. Beginning with a ban on the use of asbestos in public schools in 1973, the EPA

CAREER connection

The **economic geologist** uses a broad knowledge of all areas of geology and applies it to the exploration and development of mineral deposits. Working with other specialists, such as engineers and financial analysts, the economic geologist determines whether and how a mineral or fuel can be developed.

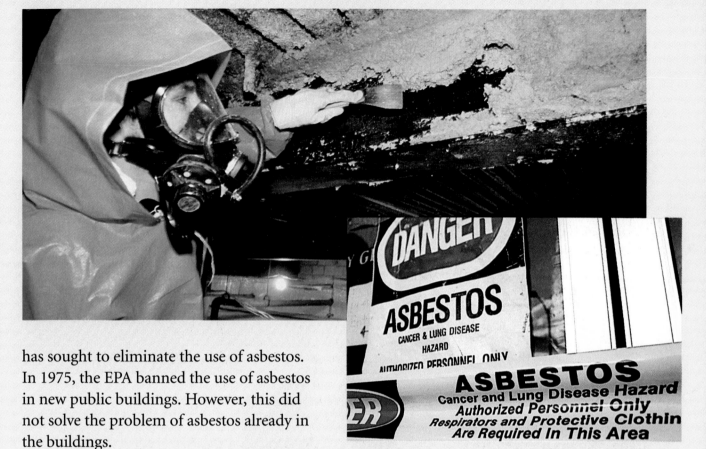

has sought to eliminate the use of asbestos. In 1975, the EPA banned the use of asbestos in new public buildings. However, this did not solve the problem of asbestos already in the buildings.

In 1986, Congress passed the Asbestos Hazardous Emergency Response Act, which directs local school districts to control or remove asbestos from public school buildings. The schools could cover the asbestos with sealants to prevent the fibers from becoming airborne, or could remove the asbestos altogether.

The debate over the government's anti-asbestos activities focuses on two issues. First, some studies show that the removal process may release more fibers into the air than if the asbestos were left in place.

Second, the asbestos industry and product manufacturers are concerned with the costs of eliminating asbestos. They say that substitute materials in the manufacture of products would cost far more in dollars than society would gain in health benefits.

The asbestos industry won a major court victory in the fall of 1991, when a federal appeals court overturned the EPA ban on the use and manufacture of asbestos. The court said that the EPA failed to prove that the dangers of asbestos outweighed the costs of the ban and the possible health effects of removal. The EPA plans to do further research on asbestos, which may set the stage for yet another court battle in the years to come.

What Do You Think?

Research has shown that although asbestos is dangerous to people who mine or manufacture products from it, the risk of dying from exposure is very small. Do you agree with the ruling that the EPA went too far in trying to ban asbestos?

HISTORY CONNECTION

Rewriting Prehistory

From 5000 B.C.E. to 2500 B.C.E., human culture in Europe, Africa, and Asia depended on bronze, a combination of tin and copper, to make everything from tools and weapons to hairpins.

Tablets written by the Assyrians 4000 years ago claim that they were very shrewd traders with their trade partners to the north in Anatolia—present day Turkey. The Anatolians never got to tell their side of the story because they left no written record. However, a Turkish-American archaeologist, Kutlu Aslihan Yener, is writing another chapter in this story based on newly found archaeological evidence.

Her original research involved identifying the sources of lead used in bronze objects. While searching for trade patterns for some of these sources, she made a far greater find in the Taurus Mountains

of Turkey. Dr. Yener first found a cluster of 850 silver mines in a

six-square-mile area. In 1989, further research in this area yielded what she felt was a Bronze Age tin mine.

When the tin mine was found, little tin was left. Dr. Yener knew she would have to find tin oxide to prove that the Taurus mine was actually originally mined for tin. Dr. Yener and her colleagues painstakingly searched for proof for six years before finding Turkish tin. The tin turned out to be burgundy colored rather

than the usual black—one reason it may have been overlooked. As a final piece of evidence, in 1990 Dr. Yener discovered a vast underground city and tin processing center.

Dr. Yener's work has shown that the Bronze Age must have had some complex economic relationships. With competing sources of tin, there were probably trade wars even then.

You Try It!

Many scholars relied upon the Assyrian tablets to give them an accurate picture of Bronze Age trade. Can it be misleading to learn about an event from only one source?

Review the statements below about the big ideas presented in this chapter, and try to answer the questions. Then, re-read your answers to the Did You Ever Wonder questions at the beginning of the chapter. *In your Journal,* write a paragraph about how your understanding of the big ideas in the chapter has changed.

1 All minerals occur naturally, are inorganic, have a unique chemical composition and have a crystalline structure. *Give examples of items that are minerals.*

2 All minerals have characteristics that we can use to help identify them. *What are some of these characteristics? Give an example of each.*

3 Minerals form in several ways. *Describe how minerals form from magma and compare a mineral that cooled quickly to one that formed more slowly.*

Using Key Science Terms

cleavage   hardness

fracture   mineral

gem   streak

Explain the difference between the terms in each of the following sets:

1. mineral, gem
2. cleavage, fracture
3. hardness, streak

Understanding Ideas

Answer the following questions in your Journal using complete sentences.

1. If an enormous diamond mine were discovered, resulting in diamonds becoming common rather than rare, how might diamond usage change?
2. Are all metals minerals? Why or why not? Are all minerals metals? Why or why not?
3. List four characteristics of minerals and how each characteristic is measured or evaluated.
4. What are two ways minerals are formed?
5. If two samples of the same mineral have crystals of different sizes, what does that tell you about the samples?
6. What is the difference between evaporation and precipitation in the formation of minerals from water solutions?
7. What characteristics make a mineral a gem?

Developing Skills

Use your understanding of the concepts developed in this chapter to answer each of the following questions.

1. **Concept Mapping** Complete the concept map of minerals.

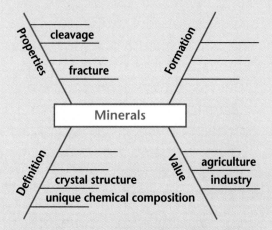

2. **Observing and Inferring** Repeat the crystal system identification activity on page 303 using the mineral calcite. Identify and sketch the crystal system of calcite.
3. **Comparing and Contrasting** Add the mineral fluorite to your data table from the Find Out activity on page 310. Perform the scratch test and make a new list sequencing the minerals. Refer to the Mohs Hardness Scale on pages 310 and 311 to see if your results agree.
4. **Predicting** Predict what would happen if you used a streak plate to test a diamond. What would you expect to see on the streak plate? Why did you make the prediction you did?

Critical Thinking

In your Journal, *answer each of the following questions.*

1. Suppose you decide to enter the mineral mining business. You discover that there are five relatively abundant types of minerals near where you live. In the table, these five are ranked according to their abundance—5 represents the most abundant and 1 represents the least abundant mineral. The table also gives the ease with which they may be extracted—5 represents the most difficult and 1 represents the least difficult.

Mineral	Abundance Ranking	Ease of Extraction
Bauxite	5	2
Hematite	4	1
Halite	3	3
Quartz	2	5
Sphalerite	1	4

With two of your classmates, decide which mineral you would mine and explain why. Keep in mind the fact that the harder a mineral is to extract, the more it will cost to pay for the equipment and labor needed.

2. List at least five ways in which minerals are important to your daily life.
3. Hypothesize what might happen to the value of gold jewelry if someone found an inexpensive way to manufacture gold. What would happen if we found more sources of gold?
4. Hypothesize what might happen to the value of automobiles if someone found an inexpensive way to manufacture or mine the aluminum and iron used in automobiles.

Problem Solving

Read the following problem and discuss your answers in a brief paragraph.

While hiking in the mountains, Helen found a pink rock and a gold rock. She took them home and tested them. The pink one had no metallic luster and broke along a flat, smooth plane. The streak test was colorless. The other rock had a metallic luster and left a black streak. Which minerals did Helen decide her rocks contained? Why?

CONNECTING IDEAS

Discuss each of the following in a brief paragraph.
1. **Theme—Energy** Explain how mineral formation relates to forces inside Earth and thermal energy.
2. **Theme—Scale and Structure** Explain why observing physical properties is important in identifying minerals.

CHAPTER 11

The RoCk Cycle

Did you ever wonder...

✓ **Where rocks come from?**

✓ **What's inside a rock?**

✓ **Why some rocks are smooth and rounded while others have jagged edges?**

✓ **Why there are so many different colors of rock?**

Before you begin to study about the rock cycle, think about these questions and answer them *in your Journal*. When you finish the chapter, compare your Journal write-up with what you have learned.

The Grand Canyon, in northwest Arizona, is 277 miles long, 1 mile deep, and 18 miles wide in some places. When viewed from the bottom near the river, people marvel at how small the great river appears compared to the high wall of rock that rises above it. Isn't it amazing that this extraordinary canyon was formed little by little as the swiftly flowing Colorado River cut into many different rock layers? Here in the Grand Canyon, erosion has exposed many different types of rocks.

The Colorado River begins its journey in the Rocky Mountains, the largest mountain system in North America. Just as layers of rock in the Grand Canyon have been eroded, the peaks of the Rockies have been weathered and eroded to their present form.

▶ ***Let's explore the great variety of Earth's rocks.***

The Grand Canyon, Arizona

How are rocks different?

What To Do

1. Collect eight or nine different rocks from around your school and examine them closely.

2. In what ways are they the same? In what ways are they different? What characteristics could you use to sort them?

3. Try to sort them into three separate groups.

4. Record your answers and observations *in your Journal.*

Mexican agate

Igneous Rocks

11-1

Section Objectives

- Distinguish between a rock and a mineral.
- Explain how igneous rock is formed.
- Identify and classify igneous rocks.

Key Terms

rock, igneous rock, intrusive, extrusive

How Do Igneous Rocks Form?

As viewed from the bottom of the Grand Canyon, rocks form shelves, steep slopes, and sharp cliffs. You may see variations in the rocks along the sidewalk as you are walking to school. You might pick up an unusual rock and wonder why it looks different from most of the other rocks nearby. While most of the rocks are flat and dull, this one is rounded and has shiny black and white pieces in it. You put the interesting rock in your pocket and decide that you'll ask your science teacher about it.

What exactly should you ask your teacher? You might begin by asking, "Why are rocks different from one another?" and "Is this a rock or a mineral?" You would probably also ask, "What kind of rock is this?"

Explore! ACTIVITY

What makes a rock unique?

Y ou've noticed that rocks can be found with many shapes, colors, and textures. These characteristics can be used to classify and name rocks. Examine granite and its minerals to explore how.

What To Do

1. Use a magnifying lens to examine the granite and the mineral grains. *In your Journal*, compare and contrast the small fragments in the rock and the mineral samples.

2. Suppose you were asked to assemble granite using the mineral samples. Which minerals would you use to make pink granite? Which would make gray granite?

3. Now examine a rock that isn't granite. Can you identify any of the minerals that make it up? Are they the same minerals you found in granite?

4. *In your Journal*, define the term *rock* based on your observations.

Figure 11-1

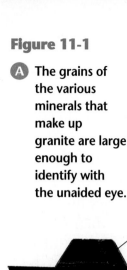

A The grains of the various minerals that make up granite are large enough to identify with the unaided eye.

Mica is found in small amounts.

Quartz is one of the major components.

Feldspar is a major component.

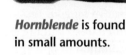

Hornblende is found in small amounts.

B Because the minerals in granite are interlocked with one another, granite does not weather easily. Where have you seen granite used?

In the Explore activity, you discovered that a **rock** is a mixture of one or more minerals. In addition to minerals, rocks can also be a mixture of mineraloids, glass, or organic particles. Often several different minerals are mixed together, which gives a rock its color or texture. In granite, the mineral pieces are large enough to be seen without a microscope. Look at **Figure 11-1**. It shows a photograph of granite and its components.

The photo helps you see that a rock can be made up of different minerals, but how do minerals combine to form granite and other types of rock? The following activity will help you see how minerals crystallize to form rock.

Find Out! ACTIVITY

What happens as a mineral cools?

What To Do

1. Place a small piece of salol (phenyl salicylate) on a microscope slide.

2. Wearing a thermal glove, set the slide on a hot plate for a few seconds—just until the salol melts.

3. Then quickly observe the slide with a magnifying glass or under a microscope.

4. Record your observations *in your Journal*.

Conclude and Apply

1. What is happening to the salol?

2. How is this similar to what happens when an igneous rock forms?

In the Find Out activity, the salol behaved like lava from a volcano or like magma that is trapped below Earth's surface. As the lava or magma cools, it becomes solid, similar to the way fudge candy hardens as it cools. Many crystals of various minerals form from the cooling of lava or magma. The crystals grow together and form solid igneous rock. An **igneous rock** is a rock that formed as molten material cooled.

■ Intrusive Igneous Rocks

When igneous rocks are formed by magma that cools beneath Earth's surface, they are called **intrusive** igneous rocks. Intrusive rocks are found at Earth's surface when rock and soil that once covered them is removed by erosion. They may also be found at the surface when forces in Earth, such as compression or tension, push them to Earth's surface. **Figure 11-2** shows you an example of an intrusive igneous rock and where it might form.

Figure 11-2

Ⓐ *Intrusive Igneous rock* Although formed deep within Earth, it is not uncommon to find intrusive igneous rock on Earth's surface. Forces in Earth, such as compression and tension, push some intrusive igneous rock to the surface. Some other intrusive igneous rock is exposed when erosion removes the rock and soil above it.

Ⓑ All intrusive igneous rocks, including diorite shown here, as well as granite and gabbro, form slowly. Do you expect these rocks to have small or large minerals? Why?

Diorite

Lava flow

Magma (trapped)

■ Extrusive Igneous Rocks

Igneous rocks formed by lava that cools on Earth's surface are called **extrusive** igneous rocks. This lava is exposed to air and moisture, and it cools quickly. Study **Figure 11-2** to learn more about how extrusive igneous rocks form. Observe the size of the minerals of the extrusive igneous rocks. Compare this with the size of the minerals in intrusive igneous rocks.

C *Extrusive igneous rock* Because lava is exposed to cooling air and moisture, minerals in extrusive igneous rock form quickly and are much smaller than minerals in intrusive rock. Most extrusive igneous rock minerals can be seen only through a microscope.

D Rhyolite and andesite are examples of extrusive igneous rock.

Rhyolite

Andesite

Magma

Basalt, the most common extrusive igneous rock, is shown in **Figure 11-3**. Basalt is a common rock of the Hawaiian Islands. The photograph also shows an unusual beach in the Hawaiian Islands that has black sand. Study **Figure 11-3** and try to figure out why the Hawaiian Islands have black sand beaches.

Figure 11-3

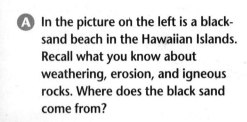

A In the picture on the left is a black-sand beach in the Hawaiian Islands. Recall what you know about weathering, erosion, and igneous rocks. Where does the black sand come from?

B Below is a sample of basalt. Notice that it is made of small, dark mineral grains.

Basalt

Natural Glass

Natural glass forms when thick, slow-flowing lava cools rapidly. One kind of lava that typically forms natural glass is rhyolitic lava. When rhyolitic lava cools on the surface of Earth, it forms crystals. The size of the crystals determines the texture of the igneous rock.

Some scientists compare rhyolitic lava to cold honey. The lava is a thick liquid that flows very slowly. Sometimes rhyolitic lava cools so quickly, crystals do not have time to form. The result is a smooth, glossy volcanic glass called obsidian.

Obsidian

Obsidian is natural glass, sometimes called supercooled liquid. To understand what is meant by *supercooled liquid*, picture a windowpane. Window glass is also considered supercooled liquid. It is smooth and glossy in texture. The difference between window glass and obsidian is that window glass contains no impurities, so it's clear in color.

Obsidian contains metallic impurities, and so is usually black in color. The presence of iron oxide will turn obsidian

Classifying Igneous Rocks

Unless we're near an erupting volcano, we can't actually observe the formation of igneous rocks to see whether they were created below or above Earth's surface. Yet we can identify igneous rocks as either intrusive or extrusive by the size of their crystals. Rocks that have large, visible crystals are called coarse-grained rocks. Rocks that have crystals so small that we cannot see them are referred to as fine-grained rocks. Coarse-grained, fine-grained, glassy, and porous are examples of rock textures.

Igneous rocks can also be identified and grouped by their overall color. Light-colored rocks must be composed of light-colored minerals, such as quartz and some feldspars. Dark-colored rocks are composed of minerals, such as pyroxenes and amphiboles.

SKILLBUILDER

Comparing and Contrasting

Examine samples of obsidian, pumice, and gabbro. In what ways do obsidian and pumice differ from gabbro, another igneous rock? In what ways are they similar? If you need help, refer to the **Skill Handbook** on page 642.

red. Other colors of obsidian are rare. Obsidian is found in abundance where volcanoes erupted in cool areas.

Obsidian for Tools

When obsidian fractures, it breaks into shards that are angular and sharp like a broken windowpane. For this reason, ancient cultures found obsidian useful for arrowheads and knives.

Scientists estimate that humans began making their own glass about 6000 years ago. Some scientists theorize that human-made glass was discovered by accident, when rocks and sand were melted by fire, creating a product similar to nature's own glass. Today's glass is made in a similar way. Sand, soda (sodium oxide) and lime (calcium oxide) are mixed and melted in a furnace.

What Do You Think?

Today, obsidian is often used in surgical instruments. Describe how the properties of obsidian make this rock useful for surgery.

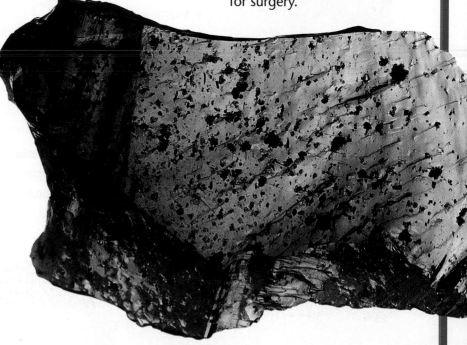

INVESTIGATE!

Interesting Igneous Rocks

Here's your chance to apply what you know about igneous rocks. You've learned how and where they form. You've learned about the characteristics of igneous rocks. Now it's time to get your hands on some of them to see firsthand what they're like.

Problem

One way to study the characteristics of igneous rocks is to think about them like recorded music. That's right, at a compact disc and tape store, music is classified according to its characteristics. You have rock, classical, jazz, soul, and other classifications of music. How could you classify igneous rocks?

Materials

igneous rock samples, A-F
hand lens

What To Do

1. Examine your rock samples. You'll want to look at them with a hand lens, feel the texture, and so on (see photos **A**, **B**, and **C**).

2. Fill out a data table like the one on the next page with your observations. (For texture, use the terms regarding texture you learned on page 335.)

A

B

C

Data and Observations

Rock Sample	Texture	Overall Color	Minerals Visible	Rock Name
A				
B				
C				
D				
E				
F				

3 Now, classify your rocks by placing them in lists. For example, samples A, D, and E might have coarse-grained texture, and B, C, and F might have a fine-grained texture.

4 Make classification lists for texture, color, minerals visible, and whether you think the rock is intrusive or extrusive.

Analyzing

1. Which samples are intrusive? Extrusive?

2. What minerals may be responsible for the color of sample B?

3. Name at least two other igneous rocks that owe their colors to the presence of these minerals.

Concluding and Applying

4. Why do igneous rocks of the same composition sometimes have different sizes of grains?

5. What characteristics help you identify an igneous rock as extrusive or intrusive?

6. **Going Further** How does obsidian differ from most other igneous rocks?

Common Igneous Rocks		
Color	Intrusive (course texture)	Extrusive (fine texture)
Dark	Gabbro	Basalt Scoria
Intermediate	Diorite	Andesite
Light	Granite	Rhyolite Pumice

Figure 11-4   Granite, rhyolite, gabbro, and basalt are individual types of igneous rocks. Use **Figure 11-4** above to describe their characteristics. There are also some igneous rocks that are classified as intermediate in color. They are neither dark nor light in overall color. Diorite and andesite are examples of these intermediate rocks.

Igneous rocks are the most abundant type of rock on Earth. They've been classified to make them easier to identify and to study. By studying all types of rocks, geologists and other scientists have been able to hypothesize how Earth formed. They have been able to determine how mountains such as the Rockies were formed from an upheaval of Earth's crust, and how the rock layers of the Grand Canyon region have accumulated and eroded over millions of years.

check your UNDERSTANDING

1. What is the difference between a rock and a mineral?
2. How do igneous rocks form?
3. Describe the differences between intrusive and extrusive igneous rocks.
4. **Apply** How are granite and rhyolite similar? How are granite and rhyolite different?

Metamorphic Rocks

How Do Metamorphic Rocks Form?

Suppose you discovered that the rock you found on your way to school is an igneous rock. It formed when crystals of one or more minerals grew together as magma or lava cooled. Will the minerals in the rock remain unchanged forever? You know that weathering can change rocks, but are there other ways that rocks can change?

To understand a different way that rocks can change, think about how the contents of your lunch bag might change after it's been in your locker all day. The apple you packed has been resting on your sandwich and cream-filled cake since early this morning. The heat in your locker has turned the cake into a gooey mess. The pressure from the apple has flattened your sandwich. In the following activity, observe what changes occur when pressure is similarly applied to a model of rock layers.

Section Objectives
- Explain how metamorphic rock is formed.
- Identify and classify metamorphic rocks.

Key Terms
metamorphic rock
foliated
nonfoliated

Find Out! ACTIVITY

What can happen to a rock when it is exposed to pressure?

To find out, you'll first need to make a crayon rock using four to six of each color of crayon—red, green, blue, and yellow.

What To Do
1. Use a pencil sharpener to make a pile of crayon shavings on a sheet of aluminum foil. They will represent different minerals in an igneous rock.
2. Fold the edges of the foil toward the middle to enclose the shavings within a rectangular packet.
3. Gently flatten the packet by squeezing it between your palms.
4. Now, unfold the foil packet and examine your rock.

5. Return the crayon rock into its foil packet and see what happens when you squeeze it between two boards using a vise or two C-clamps.

Conclude and Apply
1. How did the crayon rock change?
2. Recall that the individual shavings represent mineral crystals. What do you think would happen to the crayon minerals if heat were applied?

Figure 11-5

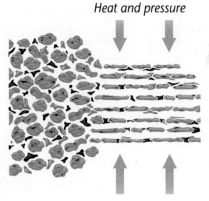

Heat and pressure

Granite

Gneiss

A The weight of overlying rock layers causes pressure on formations of igneous rock deep beneath Earth's surface.

B Look at the diagram above. How has pressure on the igneous rock affected the mineral grains?

C The altered rock is now a metamorphic rock. The gneiss above was produced from granite by this process.

You've seen what happens to minerals in rocks when they're exposed to increases in pressure. **Metamorphic rock** forms when rock is changed by heat or pressure or both. **Figure 11-5** shows what can happen when pressure is applied to the igneous rock granite. The minerals in granite are flattened and form the metamorphic rock gneiss (NICE). What occurs in Earth to change these rocks?

Rocks beneath Earth's surface are under great pressure from overlying rock layers. They are also exposed to

Figure 11-6

Some forms of gneiss originate from igneous rock and result from the process shown above. Other forms of gneiss begin as sedimentary rock and pass through several stages before becoming gneiss.

A *Shale* When the weight of overlying layers exerts pressure on mud containing clay, the weight forces water out of the mud and presses the clay layers together forming solid rock, called shale. Microscopic grains of clay minerals are evenly distributed in shale.

B *Slate* Forces within Earth expose some shale to heat and pressure. The heat and pressure cause the clay minerals in the shale to separate into distinct layers. Once this change takes place, the rock is called slate. The mineral grains in slate are barely visible.

heat from magma. If the heat and pressure are great enough, the rocks melt and magma forms. If the heat and pressure are not great enough to melt the rocks, the mineral grains in the rock may change in size or shape. To better understand how metamorphic rocks can form, do the Explore activity below and then study **Figure 11-6.**

Explore! ACTIVITY

From what do metamorphic rocks form?

Metamorphic rocks can also form from rocks other than igneous rocks. In the following activity, you'll compare metamorphic rocks with nonmetamorphic rocks.

What To Do
Your teacher will provide you with samples of four metamorphic rocks and four nonmetamorphic rocks. Each of the metamorphic rocks formed from one of the nonmetamorphic rocks.

1. For each metamorphic rock, determine which nonmetamorphic rock it might be related to.

2. *In your Journal,* list the characteristics of the four pairs of rocks.

C *Schist* Continuing heat and pressure on slate may cause mineral grains to grow larger or new minerals to form. If this change takes place, the resulting rock is called schist. Mineral grains in schist are much larger than those in slate.

D *Gneiss* As temperature and pressure continue to increase, the minerals will separate into bands and the mineral grains will become large enough to easily identify. When these changes take place, the schist will have changed into gneiss.

Classifying Metamorphic Rocks

Figure 11-7

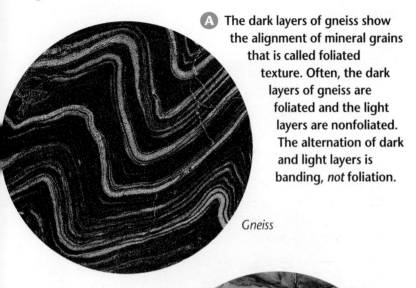

A The dark layers of gneiss show the alignment of mineral grains that is called foliated texture. Often, the dark layers of gneiss are foliated and the light layers are nonfoliated. The alternation of dark and light layers is banding, *not* foliation.

Gneiss

B Compare this photograph of marble with the one of gneiss above. How do the two rocks differ? Marble is an example of a metamorphic rock with a nonfoliated texture.

Marble

In any of the samples you observed in the Explore activity, did the mineral grains flatten and line up in parallel bands? Metamorphic rocks with this kind of **foliated** texture form when minerals in the original rock flatten under pressure.

The metamorphic rock slate forms from the sedimentary rock shale. Under heat and pressure, the minerals in shale become so tightly compacted that water can't pass between them. Slate is easily separated along its foliation layers.

In some metamorphic rocks, the mineral grains change, combine, and rearrange, but they don't form visible bands. This process produces a **nonfoliated** texture. Such rocks don't separate easily into layers. Instead, they fracture into pieces of random size and shape.

So far, we've discovered how two types of rock are formed. Next we'll observe how sedimentary rocks are formed and how some igneous and metamorphic rocks are formed from them. The next section will complete our investigation of different kinds of rock.

check your UNDERSTANDING

1. How do igneous rock and metamorphic rock differ?
2. By what characteristics are metamorphic rocks classified?
3. **Apply** Slate is a metamorphic rock that is sometimes used as building material for roofs. What properties make slate particularly useful for this purpose?

Sedimentary Rocks

How Do Sedimentary Rocks Form?

So far, you've explored two major types of rocks: igneous and metamorphic. In this section, you'll learn about a third type of rock, which is composed of sediments. This rock is called sedimentary rock. Where do sedimentary rocks come from?

You may recall that weathering and erosion are two major processes that change Earth's surface. Weathering breaks rocks or remains of plants and animals into smaller pieces called sediments. Sediments are transported to new locations by the agents of erosion—water, wind, ice, and gravity. Under certain conditions, deposited sediments recombine to form a solid rock called **sedimentary rock**. How do deposited sediments form rock?

Think of an area where layer after layer of sediments are deposited. The pressure from the upper layers pushes down on the lower layers. The sediments compress and form rock. This process is called compaction, and is shown in **Figure 11-8**. How else can sediments form rock? The activity on the next page will help you find out.

Section Objectives
- Explain how sedimentary rock is formed.
- Identify and classify sedimentary rocks.
- Use a diagram of the rock cycle to explain how rocks form and change.

Key Terms
sedimentary rock
rock cycle

Figure 11-8

Compaction During the process of compaction, pressure from overlying layers pushes the sediment layers together. The amount of sediment stays the same, but the grains become more tightly packed.

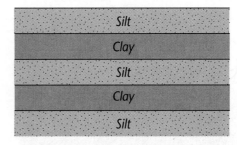

A Sediment accumulates in layers.

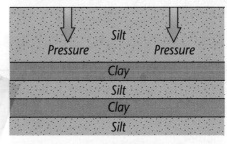

B Pressure from above squeezes the lower layers.

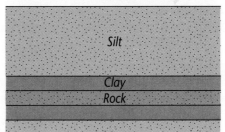

C As pressure continues, the lower layers continue to compact and eventually form rock.

Figure 11-9

The size of the grains in sediment and the kind of sediments determine the type of sedimentary rock that will form. Sandstone is formed from grains of sand up to 2 millimeters across.

Sandstone

Find Out! ACTIVITY

How can sediments become cemented together?

What To Do

1. Fill a paper cup with sand.

2. In a second cup, mix one part white glue and one part water.

3. Poke small holes in the sand-filled cup large enough for the glue solution to drain through, but not large enough for much sand to run out.

4. Suspend the paper cup with the sand over a bowl.

5. Pour the glue solution into the cup and allow it to drain through the sand for several days. Tear away the paper.

6. Record your observations *in your Journal.*

Conclude and Apply

1. How is this block of sand similar to a sedimentary rock?

As you saw in the Find Out activity, cementation is also an important rock-forming process. To get a better idea of how cementation occurs nature and helps to form sedimentary rocks, study **Figure 11-10.**

Figure 11-10

Cementation Cementation is another process that binds sediments tightly and long enough to form sedimentary rock.

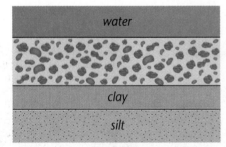

A Layers of sediments accumulate.

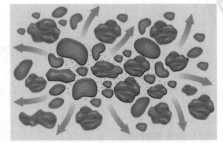

B Water is squeezed out. The mineral deposits that were dissolved in the water remain and crystallize.

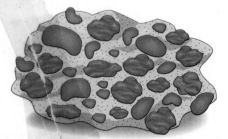

C The crystallization of the minerals cements the sediments together to form rock.

Classifying Sedimentary Rocks

Sedimentary rocks can be composed of any type of weathered and eroded rock material and sometimes even particles from plants and animals. To classify sedimentary rocks, you must look at the sediment they contain, as well as the way in which the rocks were formed.

■ Detrital Sedimentary Rocks

Detrital sedimentary rocks are made of the broken fragments of other rocks. These sediments, which are the solid products of weathering, have been compacted and cemented together.

In some detrital rock, the sediments are large and well rounded. In others, the sediments are large but have sharp angles.

Although not a rock, concrete is made from pebbles and sand grains that have been cemented together. Look at **Figure 11-11**. Notice how similar the concrete sidewalk looks to naturally occurring detrital rock.

Shale is a detrital sedimentary rock that requires no cementation to hold its particles together. Its sediments are clay-sized minerals, which are even smaller than sand-sized particles. Clay-sized sediments can be compacted together by pressure from overlying layers.

Sandstones are another very common detrital sedimentary rock. Look at **Figure 11-12** to learn more about sandstones.

Figure 11-11

People make concrete, a building material, by mixing sand grains, pebbles, and pieces of crushed rock with cement. Conglomerate is made of broken fragments of rock and sometimes of plant and animal remains. Conglomerate occurs naturally and is classified as a sedimentary rock. Look at the photographs. How are concrete and conglomerate alike?

Conglomerate

Sandstone

Figure 11-12

Sandstone is a detrital sedimentary rock formed from sand-sized sediments, usually grains of the minerals quartz and feldspar. The sandstone rock formations shown here were formed from sand deposited in layers in the desert. Judging from the shape of the formations, what was the most likely agent of erosion that shaped the rock?

■ Chemical Sedimentary Rocks

The sediments of detrital sedimentary rocks originate from weathering and are transported as solid particles.

But what happens when weathering causes some of the minerals in rocks to dissolve? Find out what kind of rocks might result from evaporation.

Find Out! ACTIVITY

What can happen to dissolved minerals?

What To Do

1. Dissolve 2 grams of alum in 20 mL of water to make a solution.

2. Pour the solution into a shallow pan and allow it to evaporate. Now look at the bottom of the pan.

Conclude and Apply

1. What do you think happens when ocean water evaporates? Answer the question *in your Journal.*

As you've just observed, some layers of sediment come from minerals that were once chemical compounds dissolved in solution. Chemical compounds become concentrated when the water in seas or lakes evaporates.

These mineral layers can form chemical sedimentary rocks. Rock salt is an example.

Rock salt can form when halite is carried in solution in ocean or lake water. As the water evaporates or

Figure 11-13

A Limestone is an example of sedimentary rock. Limestone makes an excellent building stone because it can be carved easily. The Sphinx and many pyramids in Egypt are made of limestone.

Limestone

other conditions change, the concentration of halite increases until the point of saturation is reached. The halite then precipitates onto the ocean or lake floor, where it may eventually form rock salt.

■ Organic Sedimentary Rocks

Other sedimentary rocks have large amounts of the remains of once-living things, also known as fossils. They are classified as organic sedimentary rocks. One of the most common organic sedimentary rocks is fossil-rich limestone. It is made of the mineral calcite. Fossil-rich limestone consists mostly of the remains of once-living aquatic organisms, together with calcite. Look at **Figure 11-13** to see examples of limestone and how it has been used.

Ocean animals, such as mussels and snails, make their shells from the mineral calcite and a few other minerals. When the animals die, their shells accumulate on the ocean floor. When these shells are compacted and cemented together, layers of sedimentary rock are formed.

Connect to...
Life Science

One of the most common fossils in ancient organic rocks is the brachiopod. Find out what a brachiopod looks like and draw a picture of it. Are any brachiopods living today? If so, where do they live?

B The white cliffs of Dover are thick layers of soft, fine-grained, white organic limestone, commonly called chalk. These chalk cliffs are made mostly of tiny shells and crystals of the mineral calcite.

The Sphinx in Egypt

The white cliffs of Dover in England

There are many types of limestone. This example is called oolitic limestone.

INVESTIGATE!

Very Sedimentary

Now that you've explored three different types of sedimentary rocks, you can use your knowledge and power of observation to identify the unknown sedimentary rocks you'll examine in the following Investigate activity. In this activity, you'll identify and classify sedimentary rocks.

Problem
How can you classify sedimentary rocks?

Materials
dropper water
hand lens goggles
paper towels apron
sedimentary rock 5% hydrochloric
    samples   acid (HCl)
      calcite sample

Safety Precautions

Acid can cause burns and damage clothes; handle it with care. Report any spills to your teacher.

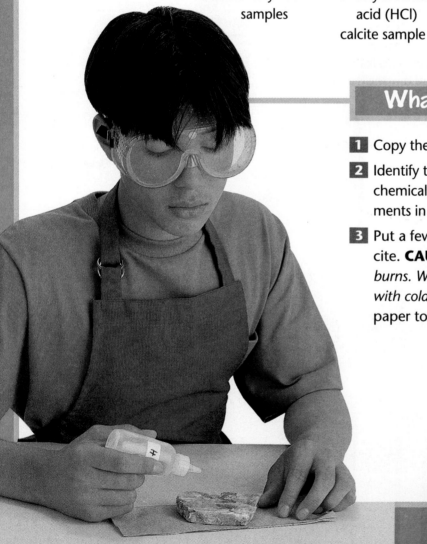

What To Do

1 Copy the data table *into your Journal.*

2 Identify the sediments in each sample as detrital, chemical, or organic. *Classify* the size of the sediments in the rocks.

3 Put a few drops of HCl on your sample of calcite. **CAUTION**: *HCl is an acid and can cause burns. Wear goggles and an apron. Rinse any spill with cold water. Observe* what happens. Use a paper towel to remove remaining acid.

After identifying the ancient sea organisms in this rock, geologists were able to determine that the rock is about 200 million years old.

Data and Observations					
Sample	Sediment Size	Observations	Minerals Present	Detrital, Chemical, or Organic	Rock Name
A					
B					
C					
D					
E					

4 Put a few drops of HCl on each rock sample. Which samples contain calcite?

5 Describe any minerals present.

6 *Classify* your samples. Then, identify each rock.

Analyzing

1. How did examining the sediments help you to identify the detrital rocks?

2. Why did you test the rocks with HCl?

Concluding and Applying

3. Contrast detrital rocks with chemical and organic rocks. How do they differ?

4. Going Further Acid dissolved some minerals in the rock. Explain why this is a weathering process.

Figure 11-14

The Rock Cycle

Figure 11-14 shows how weathering, erosion, compaction, and cementation lead to the formation of sedimentary rock. The processes by which Earth materials change to form different kinds of rocks make up the **rock cycle**. The illustration below shows just one part of the rock cycle.

Ⓐ Weathering and erosion loosen and break down rock. Some rock pieces fall into moving water, such as a river.

Life Science
CONNECTION

Fossil of a mammal-like reptile

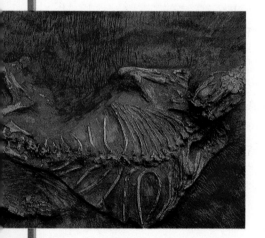

Using Rocks and Fossils to Tell Time

Studying sedimentary rock, such as that exposed in the Grand Canyon, can yield a wealth of information about what has occurred in Earth's past. Geologists use features of the rocks themselves and fossils within the rocks to help understand the history of Earth.

Telling Time with Fossils

Fossils help in many ways, but one of the most important is that they help geologists tell time. Because fossils are the remains or traces of once-living things, they record the features of those living things. You may be aware that living things evolve, or change over time.

Fossils record the changes in characteristics of living things and are therefore physical

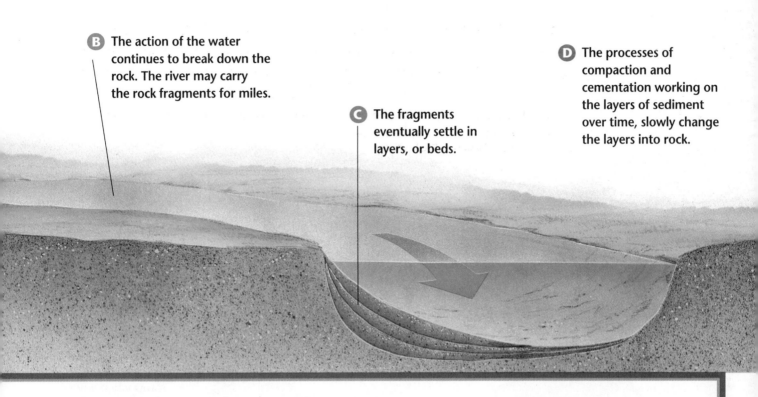

B The action of the water continues to break down the rock. The river may carry the rock fragments for miles.

C The fragments eventually settle in layers, or beds.

D The processes of compaction and cementation working on the layers of sediment over time, slowly change the layers into rock.

evidence of how plants and animals have changed over time. Careful study of fossils can help a scientist determine how animals preserved by fossils were related—whether one was an ancestor or descendant of another.

The Geologic Time Scale

The fossil record shows us how life has evolved during Earth's history. Geologists have used the fossil evidence found in rock layers to construct what is called the geologic time scale. It is simply time divisions with names for the history of Earth.

The Geologic Time Scale is based on the fossil evidence of plants and animals. For example, the trilobite shown here is found in rocks that are between 545—505 million years old. This time in Earth's history is known as the Cambrian period.

What Do You Think?

If you found two fossils that were very similar, but one had a feature that indicated that it had evolved from the other, which one would be the older of the two? If you found a fossil in a layer of flat sedimentary rock and then another fossil in the flat sedimentary rock above the first one, which one probably lived *before* the other?

Trilobite

Figure 11-15

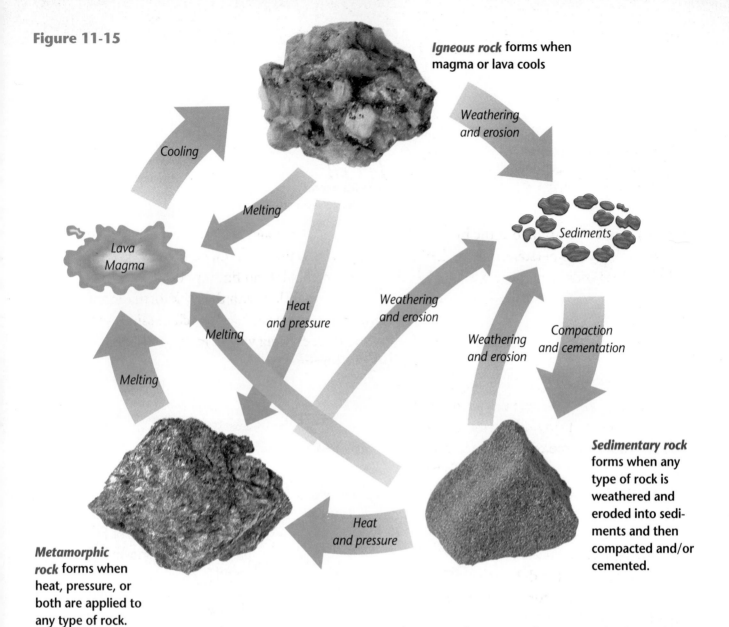

Igneous rock forms when magma or lava cools

Weathering and erosion

Cooling

Melting

Lava Magma

Sediments

Heat and pressure

Weathering and erosion

Melting

Weathering and erosion

Compaction and cementation

Melting

Heat and pressure

Sedimentary rock forms when any type of rock is weathered and eroded into sediments and then compacted and/or cemented.

Metamorphic rock forms when heat, pressure, or both are applied to any type of rock.

In **Figure 11-15**, you can trace the formation of different types of rock. All the rocks you've learned about in this chapter formed through the processes of this cycle. And all the rocks around you, including those used to make buildings, monuments, and even sidewalks, are part of the rock cycle. They are all in a constant state of change.

check your UNDERSTANDING

1. How is sedimentary rock formed?
2. Why can limestone be classified as either a chemical or an organic sedimentary rock?
3. Explain how limestone can change into several other rocks in the rock cycle.
4. **Apply** How can particles or fragments of both granite and slate be found in the same detrital rock?

Collecting Rocks

You can learn about the history of Earth, understand the work of geologists, and uncover fossils while exploring your environment—just by collecting rocks.

Equipment

You'll need a few tools. A geologist's hammer and chisel are available at a hardware or camping store. A sturdy knapsack will carry tools and any specimens you collect. A pocketknife is handy for scraping rocks. To be safe, make certain to have on sturdy boots, a hard hat and safety goggles.

Maps

Most important for the serious collector is a pocket guidebook for collecting and a map of the area in which you'll be collecting, preferably a topographic map. Look for rocks where natural forces have uncovered them. Streams and cliffs are good places to look. You can also look in places where human activity has exposed rock, such as railroad cuts and quarries.

Fossils

You may be lucky enough to uncover fossils to add to your collection. Look for places where sedimentary rock is exposed. Chip away carefully at the rock and try to keep the fossil intact. Fossil collecting is more difficult than finding rocks. But if you become familiar with the rock formations, and are patient in your search, fossil collecting is an exciting way to make your own discoveries.

You Try It!

Marble, granite, and limestone are just some of the common rock materials used for buildings in most towns and cities. If you live in an urban area and can't find a natural place to collect rocks, use a magnifying lens to examine the materials on buildings around you. You can also determine the geological history of your town by learning which rock materials are from the region, and which are imported. Old stone buildings may even have fossils "built" right into them!

Science and Society

Who Owns the Rocks?

Let's say you lean over your back fence and pick up an interesting rock from your friend's yard. Does this rock belong to you or to your friend? Did you know that there are laws to decide questions like this?

Black Gold

Let's say you own a house and the property on which your house is built. You decide to build a swimming pool in your backyard. While digging a hole for your pool, you discover oil right there in your own backyard! The newspaper publishes a story on your lucky find, but you don't really know anything about the oil business. Then the phone starts to ring. People are offering you money in return for the rights to the oil in your yard. What would you do?

Your Rights

In the United States, the law says that if you own the land, you own anything buried beneath that land. If you live in an urban area, chances are that as a landowner you have restricted rights, meaning you can't, for example, just stick an oil well in the middle of a busy city. But many landowners do own the land, the rocks beneath the land, and any mineral deposits found there. Actually, the law says that, in theory, as a landowner, you own your property all the way to the center of Earth.

You could let someone pay you to drill for oil in your backyard. What you are doing is selling the mineral rights to your land. The person who buys your mineral rights can drill for oil, but that person has only bought the rights to the minerals, not to your land.

Law of Capture

As a landowner, you own your land, and the rock formations underneath the ground. But you don't automatically own all the resources—such as gas, oil, and water—on the land or embedded within the rock layers beneath the surface. That's because such resources may shift in position, even when they are located underground. If your neighbor started drilling an oil well and was able to drain the oil from your land through his well, that is legal. It is legal because of the law of capture. This law says that if you stay on your own land but can capture such a resource, it now belongs to you.

The Controversy

The law of capture has become more controversial in this country in recent years because of the growing shortage of fresh water. It is legal for someone to drain water from an underground source on someone else's land. Such an action, however, may leave others without groundwater, and some people don't think this is fair. The law of capture is also an issue now because some oil companies have discovered ways to drain the oil from miles of underground oil fields.

Our government owns thousands of acres of land across the country. When it comes to the question of who should have the right to search rock formations for mineral deposits in these areas, there is disagreement. Environmental groups are opposed to mining and drilling in these areas because of possible environmental damage. Corporations fight for the chance to search for mineral deposits on those properties.

What Do You Think?

The government is considering selling off more of its mineral rights. The oil industry is in favor of more land becoming available for them to use. But some people are opposed to the idea because some of the methods used to extract oil from the ground have caused damage to the surface land.

Environmentalists want the government to keep certain wilderness areas pure and unspoiled. They want the government to find alternative energy sources.

How do you think the government should respond to the oil industry's and environmentalists' requests?

Teens in SCIENCE

Caving Clan

If you ask Mike Bittinger and his dad, Craig, to take you along when they explore caves, they'll ask you to take a little test first. They'll take a wire coat hanger, bend it to form a large circle, and ask you to fit your entire body through it. They want to be sure you can crawl through some tight places.

Spelunking

Cave exploration, or caving, is also known by its technical name—spelunking. Spelunking comes from the word *speleology*, which is the science of caves. Mike, a fourteen-year-old who lives in Austin, Texas, has been caving most of his life. Craig started caving with his father when he was Mike's age.

Cave Formation

Mike and his dad go caving at least once a month. Austin has a lot of caves because of the large volume of underground water and the high acid content in the soil. When the water mixes with the soil, it becomes a mild acid. This acidic water wears away the limestone in Earth's crust, forming caves over thousands of years.

Mike and Craig have explored caves in five states. One thing they don't like to find in caves is other people's garbage. "Mike and I live by the cavers' motto," says Craig, "and we wish everyone else would follow it,

too." The motto says: Take nothing but pictures, leave nothing but footprints, kill nothing but time.

You Try It!

Mike listed the basic rules of caving:

1. Always tell someone where you are going.
2. Always tell someone when you'll be back.
3. Always go with an adult who has a lot of caving experience.
4. Groups of three are best.
5. Always bring three sources of light.
6. Follow the cavers' motto.

Can you explain these rules of caving?

Heat and pressure

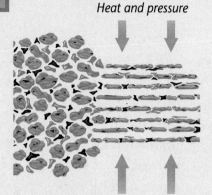

Review the statements below about the big ideas presented in this chapter, and try to answer the questions. Then, re-read your answers to the Did You Ever Wonder questions at the beginning of the chapter. *In your Journal*, write a paragraph about how your understanding of the big ideas in the chapter has changed.

1 Intrusive igneous rocks form below Earth's surface and generally contain large mineral grains. Extrusive igneous rocks form on Earth's surface and generally have small mineral grains. *Explain how a volcano might cause both intrusive and extrusive igneous rocks.*

2 Pressure and heat can change minerals to form metamorphic rock. *Where on Earth is metamorphism most likely to occur: at the surface or deep within the crust? Why?*

3 Weathering breaks rocks and plant and animal remains into small sediments. *Explain the role of weathering in the formation of sedimentary rocks.*

Silt
Clay
Silt
Clay
Silt

⬇ Silt ⬇
Pressure   Pressure
Clay
Silt
Clay
Silt

4 Sediments can be compacted, cemented, or precipitated out of solution to form sedimentary rock. *Describe the formation of rock salt. Is it an example of a detrital, organic, or chemical sedimentary rock? Why?*

5 Rocks can form and change through several processes in the rock cycle. *Explain how the rock cycle shows that "matter can be neither created nor destroyed."*

Using Key Science Terms

extrusive

foliated

igneous rock

intrusive

metamorphic rock

nonfoliated

rock

rock cycle

sedimentary rock

Answer the following questions using what you know about science terms.

1. Compare and contrast foliated and nonfoliated rocks.
2. Distinguish between intrusive igneous rocks and extrusive igneous rocks.
3. Compare and contrast igneous, metamorphic and sedimentary rocks.
4. Describe the relationship between minerals and rocks.
5. What is the rock cycle?

Understanding Ideas

Answer the following questions in your Journal using complete sentences.

1. What is the most abundant type of rock? Why?
2. How are rocks classified? Why is classification of rocks necessary?
3. How are the particles that make up sedimentary rocks held together?
4. What processes work together to form metamorphic rocks?
5. What is needed in order to form sedimentary rocks?
6. In what kind of rocks will fossils normally be found? Why?
7. What characteristics are used to classify sedimentary rocks?

Developing Skills

Use your understanding of the concepts developed in each chapter to answer each of the following questions.

1. **Concept Mapping** Using the following processes, label each arrow to complete the concept map of the rock cycle: *weathering and erosion, compaction and cementation, heat and pressure, melting, cooling.*

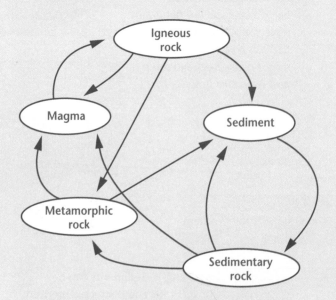

2. **Observing and Inferring** Infer what would have happened if you had allowed the salol in the Find Out activity on page 331 to cool in the refrigerator.
3. **Forming a Hypothesis** Refer to the rocks you observed in the Explore activity on page 341. Form a hypothesis stating why metamorphic rocks do not usually contain fossils.
4. **Forming a Hypothesis** Form a hypothesis explaining why some rock fragments in detrital sedimentary rocks are rounded.

Critical Thinking

In your Journal, *answer each of the following questions.*

1. Describe some effects of heat and pressure on mineral crystals.
2. What might cause intrusive igneous rocks to appear at Earth's surface?
3. How could concrete become part of the rock cycle when it is not a natural rock?
4. Look at the two photographs of igneous rocks. Which is an extrusive igneous rock? Which is an intrusive igneous rock? Explain your answers.

5. Why are metamorphic processes difficult for scientists to study?
6. Why can both sedimentary and metamorphic rocks have bands of colors?

Problem Solving

Read the following problem and discuss your answers in a brief paragraph.

While on a class field trip in the city, you observed rocks used as building materials. In the city square, you noticed flowers arranged in a rock terrace, that is, layers of rock and soil with plants growing among the rock. The rocks were light-colored and contained many small fossils.

Soon your class left the square and entered a historic district with an assortment of buildings. The first building you noticed was light pink with small crystals of quartz that felt gritty to the touch. Continuing down the street, you observed another building with columns. This building was constructed of a light-colored, highly polished rock. Next, you saw a wooden building with a roof made of dark tiles. Some of the tiles had been broken off in layers.

Using what you've learned about rocks, name the rocks that you observed. What rocks or rock-like materials do people use for buildings and other structures?

CONNECTING IDEAS

Discuss each of the following in a brief paragraph.

1. **Theme—Systems and Interactions** What are the processes of the rock cycle that form different types of rocks?
2. **Theme—Scale and Structure** How do igneous rocks form with various colors and textures?
3. **Life Science Connection** Explain how fossils can help "tell time."
4. **Leisure Connection** How can rocks tell us about Earth's history?

CHAPTER 12

THE OCEAN FLOOR AND SHORE ZONES

Did you ever wonder...

✓ **Where beach sand comes from?**

✓ **Why beaches are sometimes closed for health reasons?**

✓ **What land beneath the ocean looks like?**

Before you begin to study about the ocean floor, think about these questions and answer them *in your Journal*. When you finish this chapter, compare your Journal write-up with what you have learned.

*Y*ou've probably seen movies or read books about people living on the ocean floor. In your Journal, describe what an ocean city might be like. In which ocean would you build such a city? Would it matter on which part of the ocean floor you placed it?

Do you think of "oceans" when you hear the word Earth? If you're like many people, you think about forests, mountains, and other landforms. After all, the land is where we live and play. Very few people stop and think that land makes up only about one-fourth of Earth's surface.

Most of the water on Earth is found in the oceans. The oceans affect the climate in your area and around the world. People obtain food from ocean waters, and they use the oceans for recreation. People even misuse the oceans by dumping wastes into them.

▶ ***In the following activity, you'll begin to discover why some shore zones are covered with sand.***

Explore! ACTIVITY

From rock to sand. How can it happen?

When you think of oceans, the beach probably comes to mind. You may be familiar with the sand that's found on many shores, but do you know how the sand arrived there?

What To Do

1. Hold a piece of sandstone in one hand and some sand in the other.

2. Feel the differences and similarities between these two materials.

3. Now rub two pieces of sandstone together. Describe what happens.

4. How do the particles of sandstone compare with the sand? Hypothesize what forces in nature could possibly cause large rock surfaces to become as small as sand.

Shore Zones

12-1

Section Objectives

- Describe how longshore currents form.
- Contrast steep shore zones and flat shore zones.
- List some origins of beach sand.

Key Terms

longshore current

Changing Shore Zones

Imagine yourself sitting on a beach. You hear the gentle surf and watch gulls as they circle around a lighthouse, resting atop rocks and sand dunes yards away from the ocean's edge.

Now look at **Figures 12-1A** and **B**, which show sand disappearing from the beaches along the ocean. Structures cannot stand for very long without special supports along an eroding beach. The sand dunes that the buildings once stood upon are being carried away, bit by bit, by the ocean.

Shore zones constantly change. They change because waves and currents are constantly eroding and depositing sediments along the shore. In the next activity, you will discover how this happens.

Figure 12-1

Waves carry energy. When they hit land, waves release their energy against the shoreline and cause erosion. Much shoreline erosion takes place during storms when strong waves can make dramatic changes in a few hours.

A When the Cape Cod Lighthouse was first erected in 1797, the distance from the tower base to the cliff edge was 155m. By 1903 the forceful energy of waves against the shoreline eroded that distance to 95 m. In 1993 only 35 m of land stood between the tower and the edge of the cliff. If the structure were left as is, and the shore eroded at about the same rate, in what year might the sea claim this historic structure?

ACTIVITY

How do waves affect the shoreline?

In this activity, you will determine whether the angle at which waves strike the shore makes any difference in their effects on the land.

What To Do

1. Pour enough fine sand into one end of a rectangular cake pan to form a small beach.

2. Add water to the pan until it is half full. At the end of the pan away from the sand, move a ruler back and forth on the surface of the water to create a series of waves that move directly parallel toward your beach. Record your observations *in your Journal.*

3. Now change the angle of your ruler to form waves that strike the beach at an angle.

4. In the sand, place a short ruler perpendicular to the beach, as shown.

5. Once again, create waves that strike the beach at an angle. Observe the shape of the beach near the ruler.

Conclude and Apply

1. How did the "groyne" that you constructed with the short ruler affect shore erosion?

2. Describe how building a groyne could protect a house on the shore zone.

B Many people are drawn to the beauty of the sea, and staying at the beach is popular. Wave erosion, however, is a serious threat and destroys many of those homes each year.

Longshore Currents

As you continue with this section, you will be able to apply what happened in your model shoreline in the previous activity to actual events. When a low, gentle wave breaks on the shore, it moves sand onto the beach. At other times, as during a storm, waves remove more sand than they bring in, and the beach is eroded.

In most places, waves approach at a slight angle to the shore. Therefore, the sand is pushed along the beach. A **longshore current** is a flow of ocean water that runs close to the shore and parallel to it. **Figure 12-2** diagrams such a current for you.

Figure 12-2

Waves approaching the shoreline at an angle push water along the shore, causing what is called a longshore current.

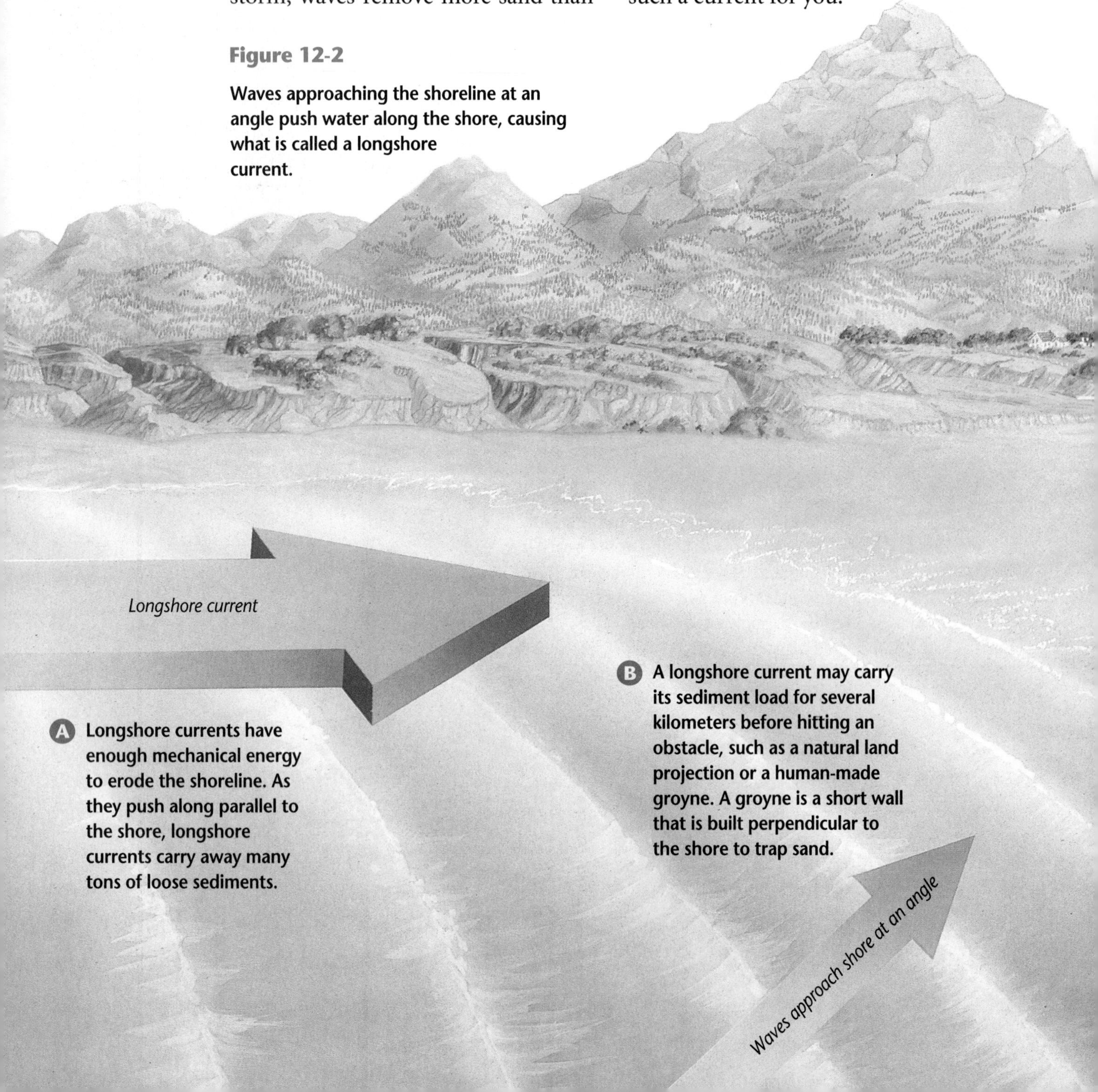

Longshore current

Waves approach shore at an angle

A Longshore currents have enough mechanical energy to erode the shoreline. As they push along parallel to the shore, longshore currents carry away many tons of loose sediments.

B A longshore current may carry its sediment load for several kilometers before hitting an obstacle, such as a natural land projection or a human-made groyne. A groyne is a short wall that is built perpendicular to the shore to trap sand.

Steep Shore Zones

All shore zones are affected by waves. Yet some shore zones are steep and rocky, with little if any beach area.

Rock fragments produced by the waves become sediment. But the constant pounding motion of the water in a steep shore zone prevents most of the sediment from settling at the base of the cliffs. Waves and longshore currents carry it away and deposit it in quieter waters somewhere along the coastline.

Figure 12-3

In steep shore zones, incoming waves smash into cliffs and rocks and give up their energy all at once. Sometimes the waves curl over and collapse on themselves, trapping and compressing air. The compressed air explodes, shooting ocean spray high into the air. The same violent pounding motion that erodes a steep shore zone also prevents most of the eroded sediment from settling there.

D Sediments deposited by a longshore current build up on the up-drift side of a groyne and enlarge the beach. But the groyne cuts off the normal supply of drift sand on its down-drift side. The eroded beach sediments are not replaced, and the shoreline erodes at a faster than normal rate. Would placing groynes close together or far apart best help solve this problem?

Down-drift side

Up-drift side

C When the longshore current hits an obstacle, the current's energy is transferred to the obstacle. With its energy gone, the current slows down and drops its sediment load.

Groyne

Flat Shore Zones

If you like a sandy beach, a flat shore zone is the place for you. Beaches are made of different materials. Some are made up of sand and stones, while others consist of shell fragments. You can find beach fragments ranging in size from fist-sized rocks to grains of sand almost as fine as powder.

Does it surprise you that most beach sand comes from sediment carried to oceans by rivers? Some sand is

Figure 12-4

Beaches extend as far inland as the tides and waves can deposit sediments. Beaches also extend some distance out below the surface of the water.

Ⓐ Beaches are made of various materials. Some, like the beach pictured above, are mostly sand and small stones.

Ⓑ Some beaches are mostly shell fragments and coral skeletons. The beach in Stuart, Florida, pictured below, is made up of shell fragments and sand.

formed as waves weather the rocks, shells, or coral found in the shore zone. Many beach sands contain a lot of quartz.

Other types of sand are made up of organic materials. Warm ocean waters, such as those of the Caribbean Sea, contain abundant marine life. The white beaches of a Caribbean island like Jamaica are made up of many fragments of seashell and coral.

Perhaps the next time you visit the seashore, or see scenes of the shore, you'll stop and think about the type of shore zone you're looking at and some of the factors that formed it. Keep in mind, however, that all shore zones are subject to constant change. In addition to the daily effects of winds, waves, and currents, humans have a great effect on shore zones. You will learn about some of these effects in the next section of this chapter.

C Sometimes you can find a wide variety of sediment fragments on the same beach. The beach in the St. Joseph Peninsula State Park, Panhandle Area, Florida has fragments that range in size from fist-sized rocks to powder-fine grains of sand. Which of the beaches shown on these pages would you most like to spend time on? Why?

check your UNDERSTANDING

1. How do longshore currents form?
2. Contrast the characteristics of a steep or rocky shore zone with those of a flat shore zone.
3. Are all beach sands alike? Explain your answer.

4. **Apply** At a nearby lakeshore, you notice that a long, low wall, just a little above the water's surface, is being built about 100 meters from shore. What effect might this construction have on the lake's shore?

INVESTIGATE!

Beach Sand

You have learned how to identify different types of rocks and minerals by looking for certain characteristics. In this activity, you'll identify the compositions of different beach sands by observing the characteristics of their grains.

Problem

What are some characteristics of beach sand?

Materials

samples of 3 different types of beach sand
stereomicroscope
magnet

What To Do

1. Use the stereomicroscope to observe one of the sand samples. Copy the data table and record your observations of each sample.

2. Place sand grains from one sample in the middle of the circle of the sand gauge shown. Determine the average size of the grains. What does the size of a sand grain tell you about its origin? Explain your answer *in your Journal.*

3. Repeat Steps 1 and 2 for the other two samples.

4. Pour a small amount of sand from one sample into your hand. Describe its roundness as smooth, rough, or sharp. Repeat for the other two samples.

Data and Observations

Sample	Color	Roundness	Grain Size	Texture	Luster	Composition
1						
2						
3						

5 Determine if a magnet will attract grains in any of the samples. What does this property tell you about the sample?

6 Try to classify the types of fragments that make up your samples. What properties can you use to classify the sands?

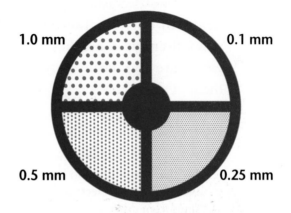

Analyzing

1. Were the grains of a particular sample generally the same size? Explain.

2. Were they generally the same shape?

3. Were all of the grains the same color? What might you imply about the source of the material from which the sand is made?

4. Were all of the particles made of rock, or were other materials found in your beach sand? Explain.

Concluding and Applying

5. Explain why you wouldn't find sand composed mostly of coral along a beach of Lake Superior.

6. How might sand from a rock made mostly of quartz differ from sand eroded from a rock made of a softer mineral?

7. ~~Going Further~~ In Nome, Alaska the beach sand contains gold that was mined during the late 1800s. How would you separate the gold from the rest of the sand particles? Where do you think the gold came from?

Humans Affect Shore Zones

12-2

Section Objectives

- Relate the ways in which human activities pollute shore zones.
- Describe the effects of ocean pollution on sea life.

Key Terms

pollution

Pollution

Imagine going to the beach shown in **Figure 12-5**. You notice a sign has been posted. It states that the beach is closed because waste materials have washed ashore. You may have heard of such an incident on the news. Every year, beaches around the world are spoiled by careless treatment of shore zones.

Shore zones are popular areas. In the United States, three out of every four persons live in a coastal state. Coastal cities and towns are active places. Commercial shipping and fishing are important industries, and factories often line the waterfronts.

Unfortunately, one side effect of these many human activities is

Figure 12-5

Ⓐ Pollution left behind by people along beaches is ugly and can be deadly to wildlife. Plastic objects such as bags, rings from drink six-packs, and toys are especially dangerous.

Ⓑ More than a million seabirds and 100 000 ocean mammals, such as seals and sea otters, are killed each year by plastic garbage in the ocean when they swallow or become entangled in the plastic.

pollution. **Pollution** is unwanted or harmful materials or effects in the environment. Pollution may range from a plastic cup left behind by a picnicker to heat released into the water by a factory or power plant.

Some pollution is just annoying and ugly, such as litter. Yet other types of pollution, such as wastes from factories, homes, and businesses, can cause great harm when they get into streams, lakes, or ocean water. These materials include toxic chemicals and metals from factories along with plastic, paper, and garbage from homes and businesses. This refuse is dumped directly into the sea or in landfills near the shore. Medical wastes, such as used needles and plastic tubes, have washed up onto beaches, where they threaten humans and other animals with disease.

SKILLBUILDER

Recognizing Cause and Effect

You've learned how many human activities are polluting the ocean. As the human population grows, these activities will increase in size and number. Think of ways that you can help prevent pollution. Make a cause-and-effect chart listing the effects of your actions. If you need help, refer to the **Skill Handbook** on page 643.

Figure 12-6

Ⓐ Wastes from industry such as toxic chemicals, paper and plastics, and raw and treated sewage are dumped directly into the sea or in landfills near the shore.

Ⓑ Medical wastes, such as used needles and plastic tubes, have washed up onto beaches, threatening humans and other animals with serious disease.

Some of the most serious cases of ocean and shore zone pollution have been produced by oil spills. Oil spills are usually caused when offshore oil wells leak, oil tankers collide at sea, or accidents occur at oil refineries. Oil is very harmful to living things. It makes breathing and eating very difficult, causing many animals to suffocate or starve.

Figure 12-7

Oil kills animals because it makes breathing and eating difficult, causing many animals to suffocate or starve. Oil coats the feathers of birds, causing the feathers to tangle and stick together. When birds' feathers are affected by oil, the birds cannot fly, float, or keep warm. They soon die.

Life Science CONNECTION

Adaptation of Marine Life in the Rift Zones

It is always dark in the deepest parts of the ocean. There is no sunlight, and the temperature is only a few degrees above freezing. For many years, biologists believed that it was unlikely that any form of life could exist in such an environment. Without sunlight, plants would be unable to carry on photosynthesis. Without plants, there would be no food or oxygen.

Then, in 1979, marine scientists made a startling discovery. In a Pacific Ocean rift zone, 2500 meters under water, they found a thriving colony of bizarre sea creatures. Giant clams the size of footballs were piled on top of one another. Bright red worms, as thick as a person's wrist, were encased in white tubes more than two meters long. Pale, ghost-white crabs that had never been exposed to a ray of sunlight crawled along the rocks.

Ghost-white crabs

Giant clams

How do you clean up an oil spill?

Cleaning up an oil spill presents a problem because of the nature of oil. It floats on the water's surface and forms a sticky coating on everything it touches. The following activity will help you appreciate the difficult job people have in cleaning up an oil spill.

What To Do

1. Place a few small rocks at one end of a shallow baking pan to represent a shoreline.

2. Pour water into the pan until it is half full. Next, pour 10 mL of vegetable oil into the water.

3. Gently slosh the water back and forth to make sure that the rocks are wet.

4. Try using the following materials to clean up the oil: tongue depressors, cotton balls, detergent, paper toweling, and feathers.

Conclude and Apply

1. Describe your efforts to remove the oil from the water and the rocks.

Living Conditions

All of these creatures were living in the vicinity of a hot-water vent—the chimneys of rock that spew forth water heated by magma beneath the ocean floor. The hot water warms the surrounding ocean to temperatures as high as 30° C. The animals cluster around the vent like people huddle around a camp fire on a cold winter night.

Although the vents provide heat, they don't provide sunlight. That left biologists puzzled. How could this community of creatures survive without plants, and how could plants grow without sunlight? In the deepest parts of the ocean, there is a substitute for sunlight. The vents spew forth a foul-smelling gas known as hydrogen sulfide. Through a process called chemosynthesis, some species of bacteria can convert hydrogen sulfide into food and oxygen. Then, deep-sea dwellers feed upon these bacteria, the way animals in shallow waters feed upon green plants.

Tube worms

What Do You Think?

Living off of chemosynthetic bacteria is just one example of how animals have adapted to survive in the ocean. Can you think of other ways marine animals have adapted to life in the ocean?

As you learned in the Find Out, oil pollution isn't easy to clean up. But at least you can see oil. Imagine how difficult it is to clean up harmful materials you can't see. Two examples of such materials are the substances used to kill insects (insecticides) and weeds (herbicides).

When the waters near shore zones become polluted, everyone and everything is affected. Food chains are disrupted, and the oxygen supply in the region is reduced.

Figure 12-8

Sewage Human sewage promotes the growth of some marine organisms, such as algae and plankton. When algae and plankton die, their remains are decomposed by bacteria, which use up large amounts of oxygen from the water. Fish and other organisms that use this oxygen die.

Landfills Rainwater penetrates landfills and picks up a variety of pollutants in dissolved form from the waste. The polluted water seeps into the soil and groundwater, and some makes its way to the ocean.

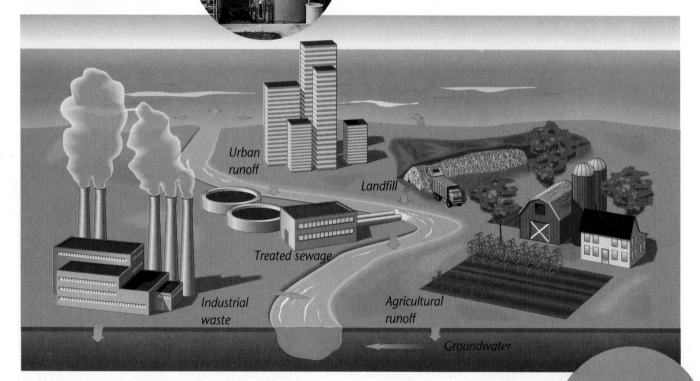

Urban runoff

Landfill

Treated sewage

Industrial waste

Agricultural runoff

Groundwater

Industrial waste The air over many large cities is continually polluted. When rain falls through polluted air, chemicals such as sulfuric acid are washed down upon Earth in the form of acid rain. The pollutants harm plant life and enter streams, rivers, and the ocean.

Agricultural runoff To increase their crop production, farmers use poisonous chemicals applied by crop dusters such as the one in the photograph to the right to kill pests. When rain falls on fields that have been treated with chemicals, the chemicals dissolve and mix with the rainwater. Some poisons seep into the soil and make their way into groundwater and finally to the ocean.

Habitat Destruction

The place where an organism lives is called its habitat. If one part of a habitat is altered or destroyed, all members are affected.

One way people destroy shore habitats is to fill them in. As populations in many flat shore zones grow, the need for more land becomes urgent. Huge areas of coastal wetlands are filled in with soil, rock, construction materials, and even garbage. The newly created land is used for buildings, roads, and airports, while thousands of acres of shore zone habitats have been destroyed.

Thus far in this chapter, you have learned about shore zones and the harmful effects humans can have on these important regions. But the shore zones make up only a small part of Earth's surface. Most of the solid Earth lies beneath the ocean waters, largely unexplored. Many people feel that the ocean basins will become more important as the world's population continues to increase. We certainly will look to the ocean floor for new sources of minerals. You'll learn about the ocean floor in the next section of this chapter.

Figure 12-9

Huge areas of coastal wetlands are filled in with soil, rock, construction materials, and even garbage. The newly created land is used for buildings, roads, and airports. But while making way for people and their needs, thousands of acres of shore zone habitats have been destroyed.

A The Back Bay area of Boston was once a marshy section of the Charles River. For years it was a favorite dumping ground for people living in Boston. In the mid-1800s the Bay was filled in.

B The marshlands and the homes and food of the animal species that lived there are gone. Over the years Boston has added 3000 acres of land by filling in the shallow coastal waters that surround it.

check your UNDERSTANDING

1. Describe some things an individual might do to reduce shore zone pollution.
2. Describe some of the effects of pollution on organisms in and near the shore zone.
3. **Apply** How can planting trees and grass help to preserve a shore zone habitat?

 **The Ocean Floor**

Section Objectives

- Describe some of the methods used to map the ocean floor.
- Name and describe some features of the ocean floor.

Key Terms

continental shelf, abyssal plain, rift zone, mid-ocean ridges

Exploring the Ocean Floor

How do we know what the ocean floor is like? Most of the information comes from making indirect measurements. Humans can't measure features of the ocean floor directly because they can't withstand the very high pressure exerted by the water at great depths. The following Find Out activity will help you to understand how indirect measurements are made. In the following activity, you will attempt to determine the shape of a surface without seeing it. Your teacher will provide you with a sealed shoe box having a series of numbered holes in a straight line along the lid of the box. You will insert a straw into each hole to determine the shape of the ocean-floor model on the bottom of the box. Once the shape has been determined, you will construct a graph to represent the shape of the model in the box.

Figure 12-10

Submersibles and semi-submersibles bring the ocean floor into view.

B In 1985, scientists aboard *Alvin* made a 2.5 hour descent to the ocean floor to explore the *Titanic,* a luxury liner that had lain unseen since it collided with an iceberg and sank in 1912. *Jason Jr.,* a sonar and camera equipped ROV shown below and to the right, explored the inside of the *Titanic* and sent images to the crew of *Alvin.*

A *Alvin,* shown above, is a people-operated submersible, first used in the 1970s. By the late 1980s, remotely operated vehicles (ROVs) with no people aboard were available.

How can you determine the shape of something you can't see?

When exploring something you can't see, you often must use evidence based on indirect observations. This approach is especially true in science, when you have to consider such questions as what the inside of Earth is like or how deep the ocean is.

What To Do

1. First, construct a graph like the one shown here. Make the graph as long as the shoe box. Draw the vertical lines so they line up with the holes in the lid. Mark the vertical scale in centimeters as shown.

2. Place the straw beside a ruler and, starting with zero, mark the straw at 0.5-cm intervals. Label each mark.

3. Now make your measurements. Insert the zero end of the straw into hole 1 until it touches the ocean-floor model on the bottom of the box.

4. Record this measurement on your graph by placing a dot on line 1 at the depth measured.

5. Repeat Steps 3 and 4 for holes 2–10.

6. Connect the points on your graph to produce a side-view drawing of your ocean floor.

Conclude and Apply

1. What do the highest points on your model represent?

2. What do the lowest points represent?

3. Would your graph change if the holes in your box were moved 2 cm to the left or right? How do you know?

Data and Observations

Top of the box (sea level)

Depth (cm): 0 1 2 3 4 5

Hole: 1 2 3 4 5 6 7 8 9 10

C All but the very top of the Plexiglass semi-submersible *Nemo*—invented in the late 1980s—floats below the surface. *Nemo* passengers get a clear view of a reef in the Red Sea, shown right.

Ocean Floor Features

Figure 12-11

Early sailors obtained depth measurements in much the same way as you did in the previous Find Out—they lowered weighted ropes to the ocean floor. They then retrieved and measured the length of the submerged rope.

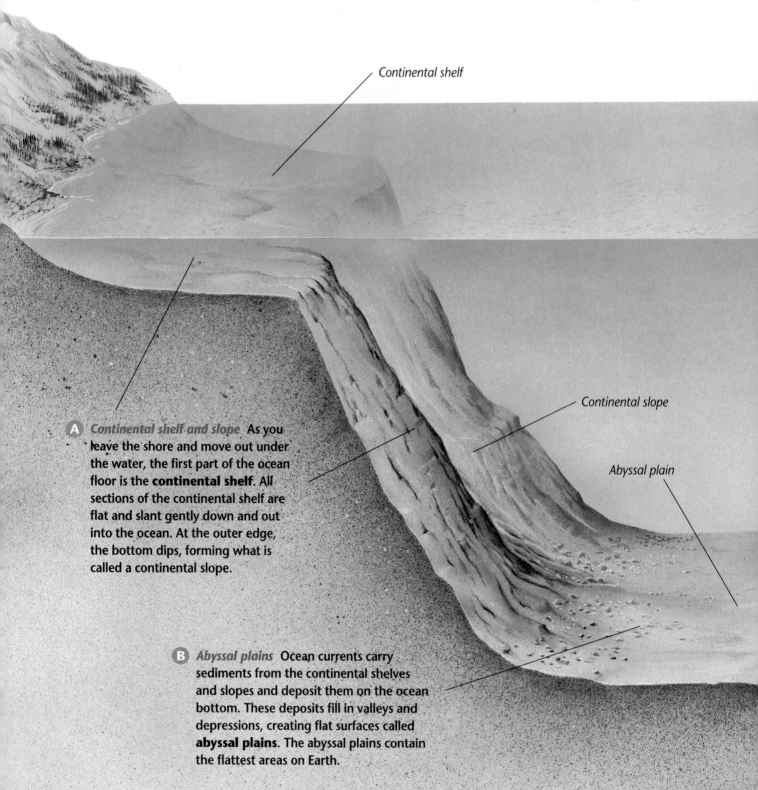

Continental shelf

Continental slope

Abyssal plain

A *Continental shelf and slope* As you leave the shore and move out under the water, the first part of the ocean floor is the **continental shelf**. All sections of the continental shelf are flat and slant gently down and out into the ocean. At the outer edge, the bottom dips, forming what is called a continental slope.

B *Abyssal plains* Ocean currents carry sediments from the continental shelves and slopes and deposit them on the ocean bottom. These deposits fill in valleys and depressions, creating flat surfaces called **abyssal plains**. The abyssal plains contain the flattest areas on Earth.

Today, we use sonar, as shown in **Figure 12-11C**. We've discovered many features on the ocean floor. Some of these geologic structures are shown below. Read the captions of **Figure 12-11** to explore the wonders of the deep world of Earth's oceans.

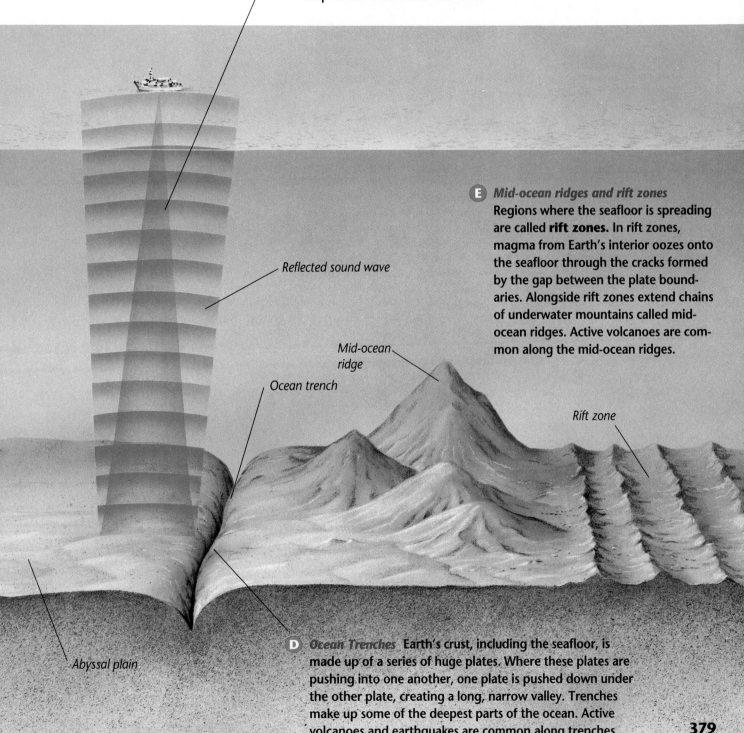

C *Sonar* To map the ocean floor, oceanographers use sonar. They send a beam of sound waves toward the ocean floor. When the sound waves hit the bottom, they bounce back and are received by a recorder on the ship. The recorder measures the time it took for the waves to travel from the ship to the ocean floor and back.

E *Mid-ocean ridges and rift zones* Regions where the seafloor is spreading are called **rift zones.** In rift zones, magma from Earth's interior oozes onto the seafloor through the cracks formed by the gap between the plate boundaries. Alongside rift zones extend chains of underwater mountains called mid-ocean ridges. Active volcanoes are common along the mid-ocean ridges.

Reflected sound wave

Mid-ocean ridge

Ocean trench

Rift zone

Abyssal plain

D *Ocean Trenches* Earth's crust, including the seafloor, is made up of a series of huge plates. Where these plates are pushing into one another, one plate is pushed down under the other plate, creating a long, narrow valley. Trenches make up some of the deepest parts of the ocean. Active volcanoes and earthquakes are common along trenches.

379

Ocean Floor Profile

In this activity, you will construct a profile, or side view, of the features of the ocean floor between New Jersey and Portugal. To make your profile, you will interpret a table of data that were collected by a depth-sounding technique similar to the sonar technique described earlier.

Problem

What does the ocean floor look like?

Materials

graph paper

blue and brown pencils

What To Do

1 Set up a graph as shown.

2 Examine the data listed in the table. This information was collected at 29 locations across the Atlantic Ocean. Each station was along the 39° north latitude line from New Jersey to Portugal.

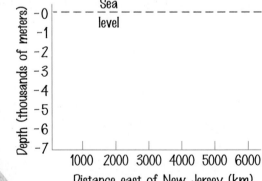

This map shows the mountains, valleys, and plains of Earth—those on dry land as well as those on the ocean floor.

Data and Observations		
Station Number	Distance from New Jersey (km)	Depth to Ocean Floor (m)
1	0	0
2	160	165
3	200	1800
4	500	800
5	800	4600
6	1050	5450
7	1450	5100
8	1800	5300
9	2000	5600
10	2300	4750
11	2400	3500
12	2600	3100
13	3000	4300
14	3200	3900
15	3450	3400
16	3550	2100
17	3600	1330
18	3700	1275
19	3950	1000
20	4000	0
21	4100	1800
22	4350	3650
23	4500	5100
24	5000	5000
25	5300	4200
26	5450	1800
27	5500	920
28	5600	180
29	5650	0

3 Plot each data point listed on the table. Then, connect the points with a line.

4 Color the ocean bottom brown and the water blue.

Analyzing

1. What ocean-floor features would you infer occur between 160 and 1050 km from the coast of New Jersey? Between 2000 and 4500 km? Between 5300 and 5600 km?

2. Would a profile taken across the Atlantic at 39° South latitude be similar to the one at 39° North latitude? Explain.

3. Would you see a similar profile for the Pacific ocean floor compared to the Atlantic? Explain.

Concluding and Applying

4. You have constructed a profile of the ocean floor along the 39° latitude line. If a profile is drawn to represent an accurate scale model of a feature, both the horizontal and vertical scales will be the same. What is the vertical scale of your profile? What is the horizontal scale?

5. ~~Going Further~~ Compare and contrast your profile with the actual ocean floor. See Figure 12-10. How accurate do you think it is? Explain.

Figure 12-12

Some volcanic mountains build from magma bubbling from rift zones in the ocean floor and rise above the surface of the water. The islands near Iceland formed this way. Other islands, such as Hawaii, formed from seafloor volcanoes over hot spots in the ocean floor.

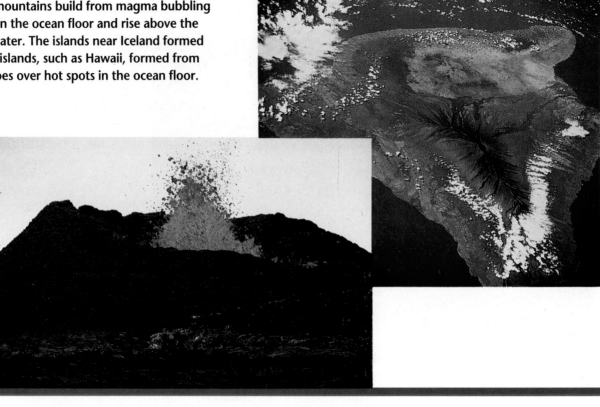

Mining Minerals at the Rift Zones

The year 1848 will always be remembered as the start of the Gold Rush. Hundreds of prospectors—people who search the ground for valuable minerals—headed out west to search for gold in the mountains of California. There may be another gold rush in the

Black plume at a rift zone

twenty-first century, except this time it will be to mine precious metals at the bottom of the ocean. Oceanographers say that a good place to look for metals will be at rift zones, where undersea surveys have already discovered huge amounts of such metals.

Where do they come from? It's a slow process, beginning when seawater passes through cracks in rocks at the rift zone. Beneath the ocean's crust, the seawater encounters magma. The hot seawater mixes with particles of metal in the magma and then rises back up to the surface. The seawater pours out of chimneys of rock standing up

In the activity just completed, you learned that the Atlantic Ocean floor has many interesting features. Now study the map shown in the Investigate. Down the middle of the Atlantic Ocean, you can see a rift zone.

Alongside the rift zones extend chains of underwater mountains called **mid-ocean ridges**. What other geologic features can you identify on the map?

At the beginning of this chapter, you were asked for ideas about living on the ocean floor. If you were asked to plan an ocean city, which part of the ocean floor would you choose?

to 30 meters tall. As it erupts, it forms black plumes. Then the dissolved metal particles in the plumes solidify and sink to the bottom of the ocean.

Mineral-rich nodules similar to those found at rift zones

Mineral Rights

Finding precious metals might not be nearly as troublesome as figuring out who has a right to own them. If a silver deposit is found in the middle of the Atlantic Ocean, which country has a right to claim it?

In an attempt to prevent such disputes, the United Nations drafted a treaty—The Law of the Sea. The treaty states that a nation has a right to minerals found within 370 kilometers of its shoreline. Any metals found beyond that boundary line are "the common heritage of humankind."

What Do You Think?

In 1988, 35 countries had signed the United Nations treaty. Yet, many industrialized countries, such as the United States and Japan, refused to sign. They feel that only countries that participate in undersea mining should have the right to claim any profits. Do you agree? What do you think would be the fairest way to distribute metals found at the bottom of the ocean?

Science and Society

Beach Erosion

Imagine that you take a trip to the ocean. You walk down to the beach and lay down your towel, only to discover that there's no more sand. Everywhere you look, you see nothing but rocks and cobblestones. It's hard to believe that anything as large as a beach can simply vanish. Yet, in some places, longshore currents carry away tons of sand each year.

How does this happen? Waves and currents can cut away at the land that slopes toward the sea, eventually shaping the shoreline into steep cliffs. Land that is eroded in this way may form

a flat underwater terrace. This type of formation permits the waves to pound directly at the base of the cliff. Finally, the overhanging portion above the notch may crumble, and more land is carried out to the sea.

Wave action and other currents can shape the shore in other dramatic ways. They can build up sandbars directly offshore. The sandbars then absorb much of the force of the waves, altering the effects of the waves' impact on the shore. Sandbars, once formed, may show continual and rapid change—eroding at one end and getting longer at the other as the sand particles are deposited differently.

A fierce storm or hurricane may magnify the effects discussed above, by generating huge waves and strong currents. And the effects of a storm are further magnified if it happens to hit when tides are especially high. At such times, homes along the threatened beach may be flooded or destroyed. The day after such a storm, an onlooker can often notice a visible change in the shore's configuration from the day before.

Erosion Control

What would you do if you had a home by the beach, and you found out that your property was eroding away? You might want to build a groyne. Groynes are short walls built at right angles to the shore that trap sand being carried away by longshore currents.

Sometimes, however, human efforts to stop beach erosion can be detrimental. The problem with groynes is that they work too well. They capture so much sand that beaches down-current from the wall are deprived of sand. You would trap sand at your own beach, but meanwhile sand would continue to be eroded from the next beach area down-current.

Some property owners try to minimize the effects of shoreline erosion simply by constructing more groynes similar to the one in the photograph above. On the New Jersey shore more than 300 such walls have already been built. Seen from above, such beaches take on the appearance of a wavy line, with alternating peaks and valleys.

Other communities have decided to stop building groynes altogether. They try to prevent sand erosion through a technique known as beach nourishment. Truckloads of sand are dumped on the beach to replace sand that has been washed away. Unfortunately, beach nourishment is only a temporary solution, and it can be very expensive. In the early 1980s, it cost $65 million to restore 24 kilometers of beach along the shores of Miami.

Other Shore Problems

Beach nourishment can also pose a serious hazard for the environment. In Miami, for instance, coarse quartz sand was replaced with a muddier, softer sand. When the waves broke upon the shore, they picked up a lot of mud, and the water became thick and cloudy. This natural pollution killed many coral reefs.

Another important cause of beach erosion is destruction of coastal vegetation. Plant cover stabilizes sand dunes and helps prevent the loss of beach sand or dirt. Off-road bikers or too many recreational hikers may harm the vegetation. So can real estate development and road building.

The twentieth century has seen more erosion than any other period in recorded history. This is largely because of all the construction that takes place on our beaches. Bulldozers clear away tons of sand every time someone decides to build a hotel, restaurant, or highway. This speeds the process of erosion.

What Do You Think?

Some people think that our government should pass laws that would place restrictions on beach-front construction. What other ways can you think of to halt the process of beach erosion?

Teens in SCIENCE

Rescue Team Is All Wet

Imagine that your telephone has just rung. It's the Pod Squad alerting you to another rescue. Fifteen-year-old Marc D'Anto is a member of a volunteer whale rescue team in Key Largo, Florida. He works with marine biologists and veterinarians.

"To me, the ocean is very exciting. It's a whole new world. Like a real-life video game," Marc says. "I guess Trish and Alex, two pilot whales, are the biggest rescues I've been involved in. Trish weighed close to 1200 pounds and Alex nearly 700 pounds. When we found them, they were floating in shallow water."

The rescuers used a crane and specially made harness to lift the whales to safety. They transported them in a moving van to a nearby canal. "The whales had to be given antibiotics to combat pneumonia. The medication made them sleepy. If we

didn't watch them closely, they would sink."

Marc and other volunteers stayed in the water 24 hours a day to keep the whales afloat. After months of care, both whales were strong enough to be set free.

What Do You Think?

Marc describes the ocean as a "real-life video game". What do you think he means by this?

Literature Connection

A Real Find

Shell collecting is a hobby enjoyed by many people. They like to search the seashore at low tide for shells that wash up at high tide. Empty shells are called dead shells. But sometimes shells are found that are still "alive"—an animal is attached to it and lives inside.

"The Strombus", by Latino author Sylvia C. Peña, is the story of a father and daughter who find a shell on the beach after a hurricane. Read the story to learn how the strombus inside the shell

feels in the ocean during the hurricane and after being washed ashore. Also learn how finding a prized strombus shell, and then realizing the animal is still alive, affects the girl.

What Do You Think?

What do you think about the girl's behavior? How would you have reacted to finding the strombus?

Review the statements below about the big ideas presented in this chapter, and try to answer the questions. Then, re-read your answers to the Did You Ever Wonder questions at the beginning of the chapter. *In your Journal*, write a paragraph about how your understanding of the big ideas in the chapter has changed.

1 Land areas in contact with the ocean are called shore zones. *Compare the characteristics of a steep shore zone, as seen in the picture to the right, to a flat shore zone.*

2 Currents play a major role in shaping shore zones. *Describe how longshore currents move sand and sediment.*

3 Human activities affect life in a shore zone. *How would an oil spill, as seen in the photo above, affect life in a shore zone?*

4 Most of what we know about the ocean floor has come from indirect measurement. *What are some of the ways we indirectly measure the ocean floor?*

Using Key Science Terms

abyssal plain   mid-ocean ridges
continental shelf   pollution
longshore current   rift zone

Using the key science terms, write a brief paragraph describing your understanding of the ocean floor and shore zones.

Understanding Ideas

Answer the following questions in your Journal using complete sentences.

1. Explain how the action of waves against the rock produces interesting and beautiful rock formations in a steep shore zone.
2. What is the difference between the effect of a low gentle wave and a large storm wave on the shore?
3. Define pollution and give examples of several kinds of pollution.
4. What is the difference between the continental shelf and the abyssal plain?
5. Compare the location of rift zones and mid-ocean ridges.
6. Why does beach sand from different beaches vary in size, color and composition?
7. How would a pesticide used on a field far from the coast pollute ocean water?
8. What causes erosion and deposition of beach sand?
9. How does a trench compare to a rift zone?

Developing Skills

Use your understanding of the concepts developed in the chapter to answer each of the following questions.

1. **Concept Mapping** Complete the concept map of shore zones.

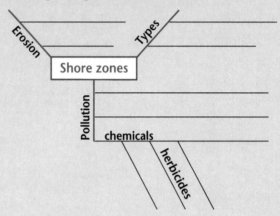

2. **Making and Using Graphs** Using the following information, construct a line graph similar to the one on page 380.

Hole #	Depth (cm)	Hole #	Depth (cm)
1	2 cm	6	3.5 cm
2	2 cm	7	1.5 cm
3	3.5 cm	8	3 cm
4	4 cm	9	1.5 cm
5	5 cm	10	5 cm

3. **Comparing and Contrasting** If the above graph represents a profile of the ocean floor, what can you say about those features as compared to land features?
4. **Observing and Inferring** Refer back to the Find Out activity on page 373. Explain what happened when detergent was used to remove the oil. Would this be an environmentally safe way to remove the oil? Explain why or why not.

Critical Thinking

In your Journal, *answer each of the following questions.*

1. Specialized submarines called submersibles have been developed that can carry people safely to some of the deepest parts of the ocean, where they can make direct observations of the ocean floor. Why don't scientists use these machines to map the ocean floor?

2. The distance "as the crow flies" from North Point to South City is 15 km. The table shows how much coastline lay between the two cities in the years 1894, 1924, 1954, and 1984. What could account for the difference? What do you think the distance might be in 2004?

Distance Between South City and North Point	
Straight Line Distance	15 km
1894	27 km
1924	26 km
1954	22 km
1984	19 km

3. Phosphates are chemicals that contain phosphorous, which is a plant nutrient. Why is it a good idea to use phosphate-free laundry detergents?

Problem Solving

Read the following problem and discuss your answers in a brief paragraph.

Scientists use sound waves produced by sonar to map the ocean floor.

1. In using these waves, what two factors must they know in order to calculate how deep the floor is in a particular place?

2. Sound travels through ocean water at an average speed of about 1500 meters per second. If a sound wave takes 4 seconds to travel from the machine to the ocean floor and back, how deep is the ocean floor at that location?

CONNECTING IDEAS

Discuss each of the following in a brief paragraph.

1. **Theme—Scale and Structure** What kind of rock would most likely be found on the ocean floor near the continental slope? What kind might be found along a rift zone? Explain your answers.

2. **Theme—Systems and Interactions** Explain how the wastewater that leaves your home might pollute a shore zone.

3. **Theme—Systems and Interactions** How might a steep shore zone become a flat zone over time?

4. **Life Science Connection** On what parts of the ocean floor is there probably an adequate amount of sunlight for ocean plants to photosynthesize? What parts may be so deep that only chemosynthesis is possible?

5. **Science and Society** What effect do groynes have on longshore currents and their movement of beach sediment?

CHAPTER 13

ENERGY RESOURCES

Did you ever wonder...

✓ **Where the electricity in your home comes from?**

✓ **How a power plant produces electricity?**

✓ **If we'll ever run out of electricity?**

Before you begin to study energy resources and conservation, think about these questions and answer them *in your Journal*. When you finish the chapter, compare your Journal write-up with what you have learned.

Remember the last time you were without electricity? Perhaps you were camping. What did you do for light at night? How did you cook?

Perhaps your city experienced a power outage. How long did the power failure last? The longer it lasted, the more likely it was to have serious effects, such as food defrosting inside freezers or accidents resulting from traffic lights that didn't work. When the power returned, you and others may have breathed a sigh of relief. Traffic flow could resume normally. Food would not spoil in freezers.

▶ **In this chapter, you'll read the story behind the flick of a switch that brings us electricity. You'll read about power plants. Day and night, power plants provide the electricity that many people have become totally dependent upon.**

A solar furnace in Odeillo, France

Explore! ACTIVITY

How important is electricity to you?

Take a survey to see how electricity is important in your daily life.

What To Do

1. List how you use electricity in your daily activities.

2. Classify the items and activities as things you need (refrigerator), things that make life easier (blow dryer), or things you have or do for fun (TV set).

3. If you didn't have electricity, how would you supply the things you need? What changes would this cause in your lifestyle? Record your answers and observations *in your Journal*.

13-1 The Electricity You Use

Section Objectives

■ Trace the source of the energy that runs appliances.

■ Describe what water and steam do in an electric power plant.

■ Relate the role of generators in producing electricity.

Key Terms

generator

The Source of Electricity

When you wake up in the morning and reach for a lamp or wall switch, you take it for granted the light will come on. You may turn a number of appliances on and off as you get ready for school without thinking about the electricity you're using.

Where does the electricity in your home come from? Imagine jumping through an electrical outlet to see for yourself. Once behind the outlet, you find that you're inside electrical wires. Study **Figure 13-1** to discover where electricity comes from and how it gets to your home.

Figure 13-1

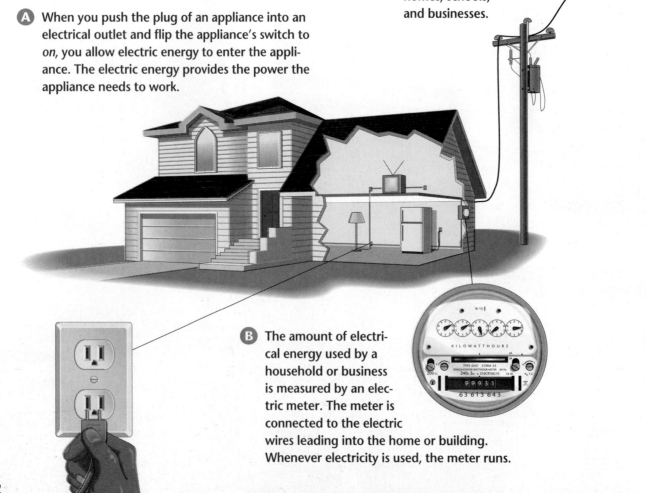

A When you push the plug of an appliance into an electrical outlet and flip the appliance's switch to *on*, you allow electric energy to enter the appliance. The electric energy provides the power the appliance needs to work.

B The amount of electrical energy used by a household or business is measured by an electric meter. The meter is connected to the electric wires leading into the home or building. Whenever electricity is used, the meter runs.

C The wires that supply electricity to the outlets all come together at a fuse box or a breaker box. A transformer, often on a utility pole outside the home, converts high-energy electricity into lower-energy electricity that can be used by homes, schools, and businesses.

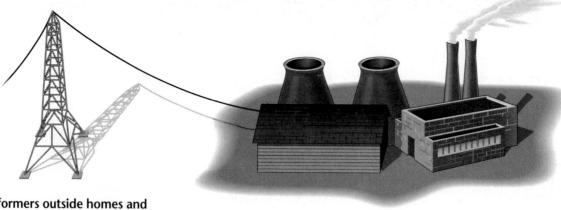

D Transformers outside homes and buildings are connected to wires that eventually lead into even larger lines called transmission lines. Transmission lines carry electric current in a much greater strength.

E Transmission lines receive electricity from the electric power plant where electricity is generated.

After your journey through the outlet to the power plant, you've finally arrived at the source of the electricity. What goes on there? Do this Find Out activity to discover one way electricity is generated.

Find Out! ACTIVITY

How can thermal energy be converted to kinetic energy?

How can thermal energy make things move? You know that if you get your hand too near a heat source, you move rapidly to get away. However, that's not the way it works with mechanical objects.

What To Do

1. Fill a teakettle about three-fourths full with cool water and place it on a burner.

2. Turn on the burner. What happens to the water as energy from the burner is transferred to the kettle? Is the transferred energy still thermal energy?

3. When steam begins coming out of the kettle's opening, hold a pinwheel in the path of the steam and observe.
CAUTION: *Steam causes severe burns. Do not hold your arm, hand, or the pinwheel too near the steam.*

Conclude and Apply

1. What happens to the pinwheel?

2. Explain why the following statement is true: The demonstration you have just done shows that energy changes forms.

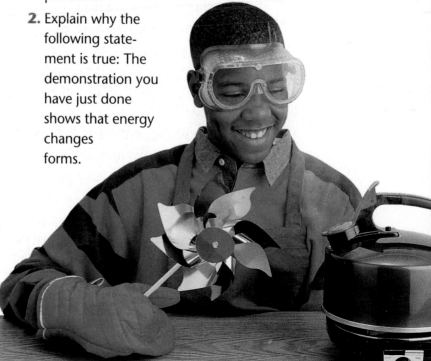

Energy Changes Forms at a Power Plant

Recall that in Chapter 4 you learned about the law of conservation of energy. According to the law of conservation of energy, energy can change form, but it cannot be created or destroyed. The total amount of energy in a system does not change. You worked with the law of conservation of energy as you completed the activity with the teakettle and the pinwheel. You neither created nor destroyed energy. You simply caused it to change form. First you transferred thermal energy from the burner to the water. Steam from the boiling water acted on the blades of your pinwheel, changing thermal energy to mechanical energy.

■ Generating Energy

Electricity can be generated at power plants using the same principles of energy transfer and change as your teakettle and pinwheel. **Figure 13-2** shows some of the equipment at a power plant and how it works.

As you can see, the main steps for generating electricity include boiling water to produce steam, and passing the steam through the blades of a turbine, which causes the axle of a generator to turn. A **generator** is any machine that converts mechanical energy to electrical energy. Most

SKILLBUILDER

Sequencing

Use the information in the text to show the chain of events, or sequence, connecting the burning of coal with turning on a light in your room. Use the light coming on as your final outcome and work backward toward the starting event. If you need help, refer to the **Skill Handbook** on page 636.

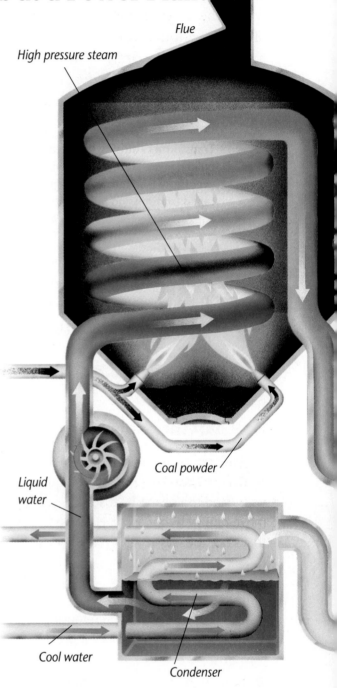

Figure 13-2

Ⓐ The generation of electricity begins with thermal energy. The power plant shown here burns coal in a combustion chamber to create steam. Thermal energy in the combustion chamber causes the water inside the pipes to turn into steam.

Labels on figure: Flue, High pressure steam, Coal powder, Liquid water, Cool water, Condenser generators consist of a coil of wires that rotates within a magnetic field. When the magnetic field of the magnet interacts with the wires, it causes electrons within the wires to move. This movement of electrons is electricity.

You know how important electricity is to our way of life. You found that out when you listed all the activities and appliances that use electricity. A world without electricity might be interesting to imagine in a story. What changes might you need to make in the way you are living if you did not have electricity in your school or community?

B The steam created in the combustion chamber is directed at the turbine. The pressure of the steam turns the blades of the turbine. The blades are connected to a shaft. When the blades turn, the shaft turns. The turning of the shaft is mechanical energy produced by the action of steam on the turbine. What part of the teakettle and pinwheel activity is the turbine like?

C The turning turbine shaft is connected to an electric generator. A simple generator contains a coil of wire that spins through a magnetic field. This rotation of the coil generates electricity. The electricity travels out of the coil and into electrical wires.

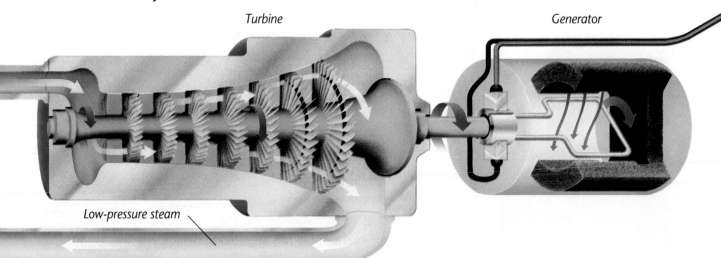

Turbine

Generator

Low-pressure steam

check your UNDERSTANDING

1. How does a blow dryer or other appliance you might use every day at home get the energy to operate?
2. Use the terms water, steam, mechanical energy, and electrical energy to discuss how steam helps generate electricity.
3. What is the relationship between a turbine and a generator in an electric power plant?
4. **Apply** Do you think it would be possible to generate electricity without coal? Explain.

Fossil Fuels

13-2

Section Objectives
- Compare and contrast three different fossil fuels.
- Trace the steps in the formation of fossil fuels.

Key Terms
fossil fuel

The Energy in Coal

A power plant can use any one of a number of different resources for the energy needed to operate turbines and generators. Some power plants, for instance, generate electricity from the force of rushing water or blowing winds. Others generate electricity by burning oil or natural gas. In the United States, more than 57 percent of the electric power plants rely on burning coal. That makes coal very important.

But what is coal made of? How can something like coal generate energy? Do the Explore activity below to begin to investigate the nature of coal.

Explore! ACTIVITY

What does a piece of coal look like?

Where does coal come from? A careful examination of a coal sample may give you some clues.

What To Do

1. Examine a piece of coal under a hand lens. What do you see? What color is the coal?

2. Describe its luster. Are there layers in the sample? Try running your finger or pencil tip along one of them.

3. Now see if you can detect any fossils in the sample. A fossil is any evidence of past life. It might be the imprint of either plant or animal life. If your coal sample has any fossils, decide whether they are remains of plants or of animals.

4. Record your observations and answers to the questions *in your Journal.*

Your examination of coal may have given you some clues as to how coal forms. Coal is a sedimentary rock. The distinguishing feature of coal, however, is that the sediments that form it are the remains of once-living organisms.

Most coal is made up of the remains of plants that captured energy from the sun to make food and to grow. These plant remains retain some of that solar energy in a changed form—chemical potential energy.

Formation of Coal

Much of the coal mined in the United States began forming more than 300 million years ago. Coal started as the remains of plants that died in swampy regions. As time went by, more plants died and sediment covered and compressed the plants. **Figure 13-3** on this page will give you a clearer idea of how the coal mined today formed.

Connect to...

Physics

Trace the energy conversions from the formation of coal from plants to the production of electricity at a coal-burning power plant.

Figure 13-3

1 Swamps formed in lowlands. These swamps had living plants growing in a soil composed almost entirely of decaying organic matter.

2 Through time, layers of sediment covered and compressed the layers of organic matter. The increase in temperature that resulted from increasing depth of the sediment layers changed the organic matter into a soft brown coal called lignite.

3 More layers of sediment piled on top of the lignite and compressed it even further. With the deeper layers, temperature increased further and lignite became bituminous coal.

4 Bituminous coal is the coal used most often to provide thermal energy. Many coal deposits are made up of several layers of coal separated by layers of rock. This is the result of a second coal-producing swamp forming over an old, buried, coal-producing swamp.

5 When layers of bituminous coal were severely compressed and heated by forces within Earth, the layers changed into anthracite coal, the hardest of all coals.

Because of its link with fossil plants from the past, coal is one of several different kinds of fossil fuels. A **fossil fuel** is the remains of ancient plants or animals that you can burn today to produce thermal energy. Other fossil fuels are oil and natural gas. Do the Investigate that follows to discover some difficulties with recovering another type of fossil fuel.

INVESTIGATE!

Retrieving Oil

In this activity, you'll be an oil driller. Your objective is to find methods for pumping out the greatest amount of oil possible.

Problem
What methods can be used to remove the most oil from a reservoir?

Materials
clear plastic bottle with spray pump
clear plastic tubing
100-mL graduated cylinder

1 to 2 cups of small, clean pebbles
liquid detergent
100 mL vegetable oil
100 mL hot water
50 mL cold water
eye dropper

Safety Precautions

Be careful when operating your "oil well" not to spray other people in your class.

What To Do

1. Study the picture. Then, use the plastic pump bottle, plastic tubing, and pebbles to build your oil well. The plastic tubing should be inserted deep into the pebbles (see photo **A**).

2. Pour 100 mL of oil into your well (the plastic bottle). Seal your well.

3. Now, pump as much oil as you can get out of your well into a graduated cylinder. Measure the amount and record the amount in a data table *in your Journal*.

4. Empty the oil out of your graduated cylinder, into the reclaiming bottle your teacher will provide. Rinse your cylinder thoroughly.

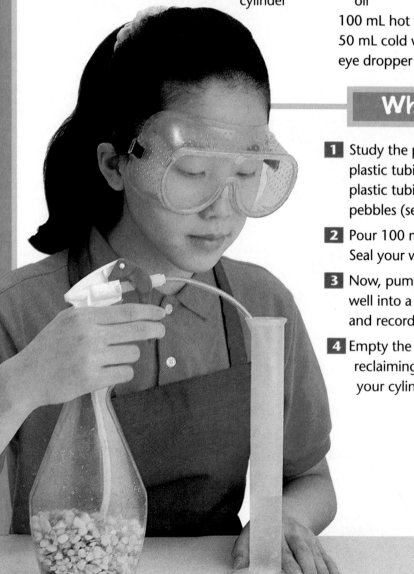

A

B

C

5 Pour 50 mL of cold water into your well (see photo **B**). Observe what happens in the bottle. Again, pump out as much oil as you can. Give the oil and water time to separate in the graduated cylinder. Then, record the amount of oil you recovered. Empty the cylinder. Do not empty this into the reclaiming bottle. Place it in a separate container that your teacher will provide. Rinse your cylinder thoroughly.

6 Using 50 mL of hot water, repeat Step 5.

7 Using 50 mL of hot water and 8 drops of liquid detergent (see photo **C**), repeat Step 5.

This huge oil gusher on May 28, 1923, helped to bring much of the oil boom activity to West Texas. It took 21 months to drill the well, located in Reagan County, Texas, before oil flowed.

Analyzing

1. How many milliliters of oil did you retrieve by pumping alone?

2. What did the oil do when you added the cold water to your well? How much oil did you pump out?

3. How much oil did you pump out using hot water?

4. How much oil did you pump out using hot water and detergent?

Concluding and Applying

5. Tell how you would support this statement: Pumping alone is not adequate for removing all the oil from a well.

6. **Going Further** Predict the results of using detergent alone. Then, try the experiment that way.

Oil and Natural Gas

You probably remember that the other fossil fuels are oil and natural gas. What makes these two energy resources fossil fuels? Both formed millions of years ago from the remains of ancient organisms. Unlike coal, however, which came from land plants, oil and natural gas formed from plants and animals that lived in ancient shallow oceans.

As ancient sea organisms died, their remains settled on the ocean floor. Most organisms decayed. But in some places, they were buried under thick layers of sand and mud. Just as layers of decaying plants were compressed during the formation of coal, so the layers of sediment and partly decayed organisms were compacted over time. Slowly, chemical reactions changed the organisms into oil and natural gas. How are these fuels found within the ground now? The next activity will help answer that question.

Explore! ACTIVITY

How are water and oil found in natural settings?

You may already be aware of how oil and water interact with each other. But what does that tell you about how they're likely to be found in natural settings?

What To Do

1. *In your Journal*, write your prediction of how oil and water might be layered if they are found within the same beds of rock. Which would you be able to pump out of the ground first?

2. Pour equal amounts of water and vegetable oil into a small bottle or jar. Shake the container.

3. Describe the appearance of the mixture. Observe what happens after the container is allowed to rest for a few minutes. What does the oil and water mixture do?

4. What does this tell you about how oil and water interact? What does this model show you about how oil and water are likely to be found in natural settings? Did this model support your prediction?

5. Record your observations and answers *in your Journal*.

Figure 13-4

Ⓐ A petroleum-bearing rock must be porous, (have holes in it) and permeable, (the holes must be connected) so fluids like oil and water can flow through it. Sandstone is porous and permeable, while shale is porous but not permeable. Oil and other fluids can flow through sandstone but not through shale.

Ⓑ The oil and water gather in a pool under the impermeable rock layer. Because oil is less dense than water, oil lies on top of the water. If natural gas is present, it lies on top of the oil.

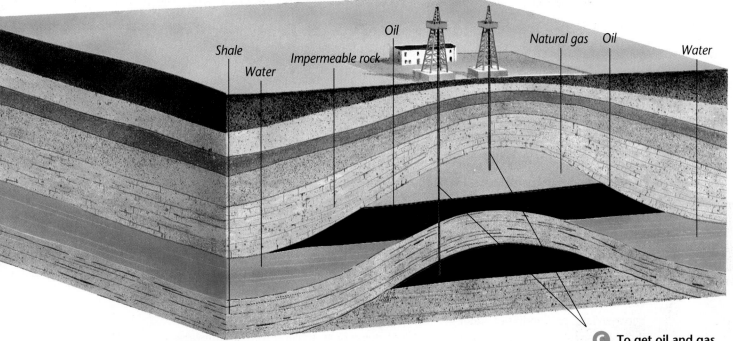

Ⓒ To get oil and gas from the ground, engineers must drill through the rock layers to reach the reservoir.

■ Oil and Natural Gas in Natural Settings

Oil, gas, and water may get squeezed into the spaces of porous sandstone. If there's a space for oil and gas to accumulate, an oil or gas reservoir is formed. See how oil, gas, and water are arranged in **Figure 13-4**. Which is the least dense? How can you tell?

Coal, oil, and natural gas are all important resources for thermal energy and also for generating electricity. But you've seen that fossil fuels can be difficult to obtain. Fossil fuels can also create problems with the environment in a number of different ways. You'll find out about some of these problems next.

check your UNDERSTANDING

1. In what ways are fossil fuels used in the United States?
2. How was the formation of coal like the formation of oil and natural gas? How was it different?
3. **Apply** Natural gas is often taken from the same locations where oil is drilled. Why do you think this is true?

Resources and Pollution

Section Objectives
- Classify energy resources as either renewable or nonrenewable.
- Discuss the environmental effects of burning fossil fuels.

Key Terms
renewable resources
nonrenewable resources

Fossil Fuel: How Much and How Long?

The processes that caused coal to form continue today in some places on Earth. The same is true for the formation of oil and natural gas. This doesn't mean that we'll be able to find all the fossil fuel we need. Fossil fuels are natural resources. A natural resource is anything that occurs naturally that people use. Some natural resources occur in almost endless supplies. Others, such as fossil fuels, do not.

■ Renewable Resources

Natural resources that can be replaced by natural processes in fewer than 100 years are **renewable resources**. For example, think about the sun. It will continue to shine for millions of years. Energy from the sun will continue to warm the planet and provide light for growing plants. Study **Figure 13-5** to learn more about renewable and reusable resources.

Figure 13-5

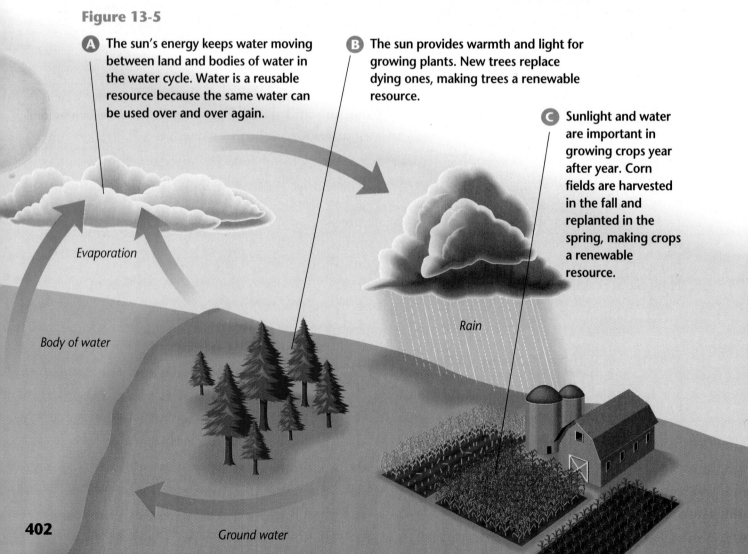

A The sun's energy keeps water moving between land and bodies of water in the water cycle. Water is a reusable resource because the same water can be used over and over again.

B The sun provides warmth and light for growing plants. New trees replace dying ones, making trees a renewable resource.

C Sunlight and water are important in growing crops year after year. Corn fields are harvested in the fall and replanted in the spring, making crops a renewable resource.

Evaporation

Body of water

Rain

Ground water

Nonrenewable Resources

Resources that people use up much faster than nature can replace them are **nonrenewable resources**. A nonrenewable resource is one that may be replaced only over a very long time, or it may never be replaced.

Take coal as an example. It took millions of years for decaying plants to change into a seam of coal. An electric power plant burns the amount of coal in a small seam in a single day. Plants dying in today's swamps won't become coal for millions of years. Our supplies of coal, therefore, are limited. Even so, we may be able to rely longer on coal than on any other fossil fuel.

The United States has a great supply of bituminous coal; however, more than 430 billion tons of it are still in the ground. The United States recovers and burns over 900 million tons of coal each year. Of that 900 million tons, electric power plants burn more than 750 million tons.

Even at this rate of usage, the United States would still have enough coal to last hundreds of years.

Supplies of other fossil fuels are much more limited. The United States and some other countries of the world still have reserves of oil and natural gas. Reserves are places people know of where natural resources are deposited. According to some estimates, all the world's oil reserves could be emptied within the next 25 years if people continue to use oil at current rates.

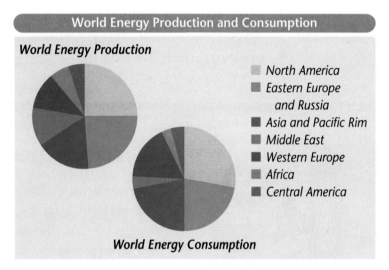

World Energy Production and Consumption

World Energy Production

- North America
- Eastern Europe and Russia
- Asia and Pacific Rim
- Middle East
- Western Europe
- Africa
- Central America

World Energy Consumption

Figure 13-6

A The map below shows the locations of the known oil, gas and coal reserves. Judging from locations marked on the map, what can you infer about distribution of these resources?

B The pie charts above compare the amount of world energy produced with the amount of energy consumed. Which area has the greatest difference between amount produced and amount consumed? Which area uses the most energy?

Key

- Coal reserves
- Oil and natural gas reserves

Burning Fossil Fuels: Costs to Be Paid

DID YOU KNOW?

In one year, burning the coal to light one 100-watt light bulb for 12 hours a day creates more than 900 pounds of carbon dioxide and 8 pounds of sulfur dioxide.

Fossil fuels are available in limited supplies and there may be scarcities in the future. But air pollution is a threat connected with fossil fuels right now.

Most of the air pollution traced to oil comes from burning gasoline, kerosene, and other oil-based fuels used in cars, trucks, and other motor vehicles. Because electric power plants burn so much coal, most of the air pollution traced to coal comes from them. Burning coal gives off nitrous oxide, which is made of nitrogen and oxygen, and carbon dioxide, which is made of carbon and oxygen.

Figure 13-7

A Earth reradiates some heat from the sun back into space in the form of infrared rays. Burning fossil fuels releases gases that absorb infrared rays. Too many of these gases in the atmosphere could work like a greenhouse roof and prevent heat from escaping. Earth's temperature could rise to an uncomfortable and dangerous level.

B Burning high-sulfur coal releases large amounts of the gas sulfur dioxide, which when combined with water vapor in the air, forms acid rain. Acid rain damages plant and animal life as well as buildings.

Electric Expense

The electric company charges your family for the electric energy you use. The company sells energy in units called kilowatt hours (kWh). A kilowatt hour is equal to 1000 watts of power used for one hour.

For example, one 100-watt light bulb left burning for ten hours uses one kilowatt hour of electric energy. If that bulb burns day and night for a month, it uses 72 kilowatt hours of energy.

Reading the Meter

To figure out your monthly bill, an electric company employee comes to your home and reads the electric meter. The meter might have dials like those on the one shown. It works something like a clock. The hands on the dials move to

This electric utility meter is being read electronically. Information from the meter is downloaded to a small hand-held computer which then sends the reading to a larger computer at the electric company.

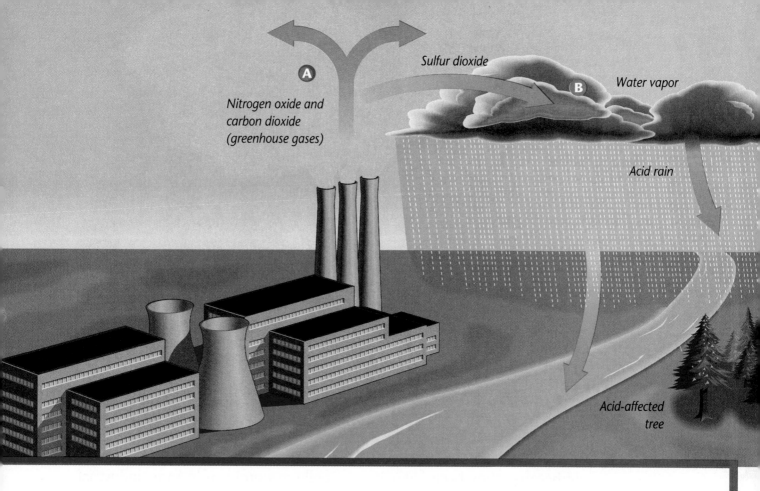

Nitrogen oxide and carbon dioxide (greenhouse gases)

A

Sulfur dioxide

B

Water vapor

Acid rain

Acid-affected tree

measure the amount of electricity used.

Read the meter from left to right. If the needle is between numbers, read the smaller number. This meter reads 18 432 kilowatt hours. It read 17 268 kilowatt hours last month.

The difference between the two readings (18 432 kWh – 17 268 kWh = 1164 kWh) is how much electric energy was used this past month.

In this particular city, using one kilowatt hour of electricity

costs 10.658 cents. Multiplying the cost of one kilowatt hour by the number of kilowatt hours used (10.658 cents per kWh × 1164 kWh) gives the amount of the bill—$124.06.

What Do You Think?

What can you and your family do to reduce your electric bill by $10.00 a month? Do you think you can reduce your bill by $25.00 a month? How?

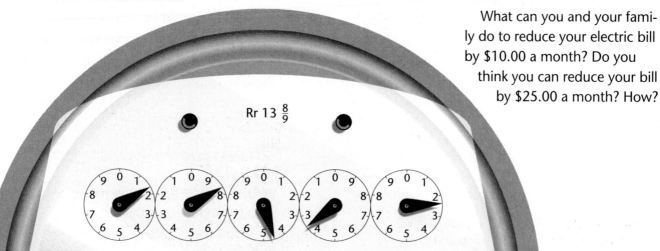

Rr 13 $\frac{8}{9}$

K I L O W A T T H O U R S

2A

2A

F.L. S

LL S

TYPE D45' FORM 25

Figure 13-8

Smokestack scrubbers remove the pollutants from industrial smoke.

A A fan blows the polluted smoke past electrically charged plates.

B The plates give the particles of pollution a positive electric charge.

C The smoke with its positively charged particles of pollution moves past negatively charged plates. The positively charged particles are attracted by and held to the negatively charged plates.

D The smoke, now stripped of its pollutants, is released through the smokestack.

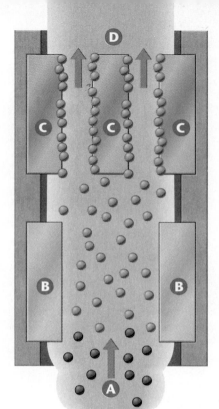

Carbon dioxide and nitrous oxide are both greenhouse gases. They get that name because they keep solar heat from escaping from Earth, much as a greenhouse retains solar heat inside. An accumulation of greenhouse gases may contribute to global warming. You will study more about greenhouse gases and global warming in Chapter 15.

Some coal contains large amounts of sulfur. When high-sulfur coal burns, sulfur dioxide is produced. The sulfur dioxide combines with water vapor in the air to form tiny droplets of acid. These droplets gather together to form acid rain, which is a severe pollution problem in some industrial areas. **Figure 13-8** shows one device that helps remove some pollutants.

Only time will tell what the future of our fossil fuel resources will be. We can be certain, however, that we will always need energy. What qualities would the perfect energy source have? It should be clean, it should be plentiful, and it should be renewable. In the next section, you'll read about several alternatives to fossil fuels that meet these requirements.

check your UNDERSTANDING

1. What makes coal a nonrenewable resource?
2. Why might the burning of fossil fuels be considered a costly practice?
3. **Apply** List several problems that result from burning fossil fuels. What alternatives to fossil fuels can you suggest that would help do away with some of these problems? How can you reduce consumption of fossil fuels?

Alternative Energy Resources

If Not Fossil Fuels, What?

Imagine that you're responsible for developing the power source for a new city. You know you'll have to build a power plant to generate the electricity. You decide not to use fossil fuels as your energy source. But where do you go from there? What alternative sources of energy might you use? The following activity may help you develop some ideas.

Section Objectives
- Describe alternative sources of energy.
- Differentiate among the ways alternative energy resources are used to produce electricity.

Key Terms
hydroelectric
solar cell

Explore! ACTIVITY

How many different methods can you use to make your pinwheel spin?

You know that one way to generate electricity is to cause turbines to spin. Use a pinwheel as a model of a turbine and see how many ways you can make it spin.

What To Do

1. Demonstrate some of the ways you are already aware of.

2. Try this one. Fill a 400-mL beaker with water.

3. Hold the pinwheel over a sink, a bucket, or a pan.

4. Pour the water on the pinwheel, being careful that the water falls into the sink, bucket, or pan. Did you get the pinwheel to turn? Record your observations and answers *in your Journal*.

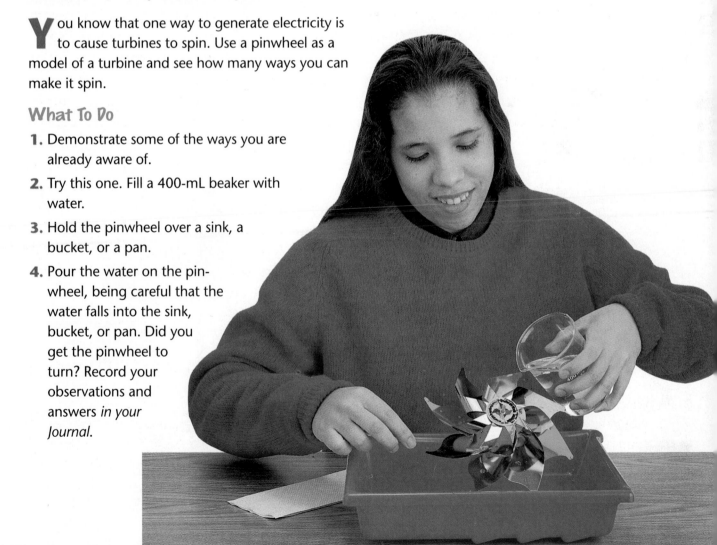

Hydroelectric Energy

Now you've seen that there is more than one way to get a pinwheel to spin. The same must be true of turbines in electric power plants. You might be pleased to discover that a number of alternative sources of energy are already at work generating electricity. One of them is waterpower. Power plants that use waterpower to generate electricity are called **hydroelectric** plants.

People in southern Canada and the eastern United States use the river waters at Niagara Falls to generate electricity for a number of large cities. In other places, where there are no natural waterfalls, people have built concrete dams to produce

Figure 13-9

A Hydroelectric power plants take advantage of the potential energy of water stored behind a dam.

B The stored water is released through gateways into pipes near the base of the dam that lead to the blades of turbines. Because of the weight of the reservoir water above it, the water entering the gateways is under great pressure as it falls to the turbines.

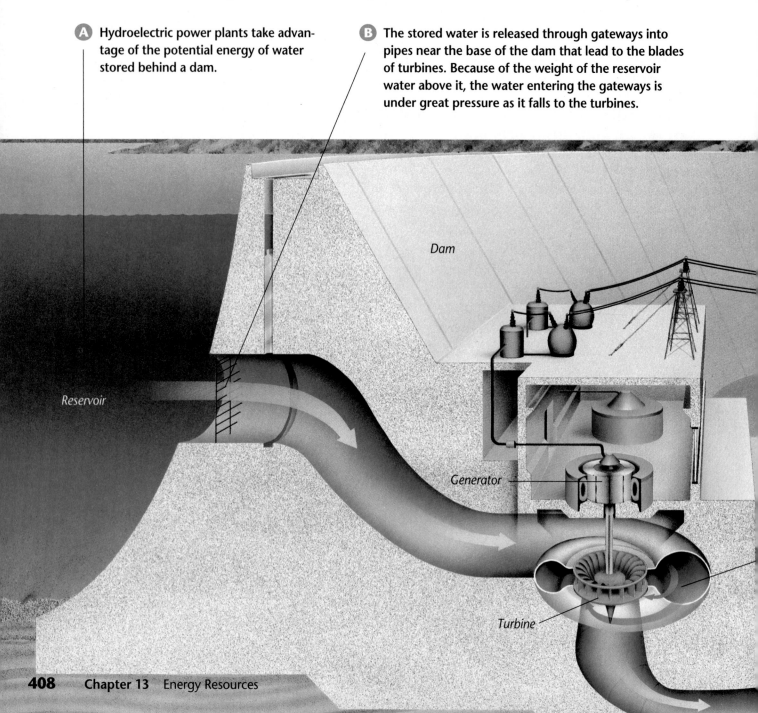

Dam

Reservoir

Generator

Turbine

hydroelectric power. The Shasta Dam, in northern California's Sacramento River, is the tallest structure of its type in the world. What happens to the waters of the Sacramento River behind the dam?

The river water that backs up behind a dam makes up the hydroelectric plant's reservoir. Most reservoirs are the size of lakes. Lake Shasta extends 56 kilometers up the Sacramento River. Now look at **Figure 13-9** of the dam and power plant to find out how a hydroelectric plant generates electricity.

Hydroelectric power is a clean, renewable source of energy. However, the dams that must sometimes be constructed to provide hydroelectric power create lakes that flood and destroy many different ecosystems.

About 6.5 percent of the electricity used in the United States comes from hydroelectric power plants. Hydroelectric power is one source that may meet future energy needs. Do the activity that follows to investigate another possible source.

Figure 13-10

The High Aswan Dam in Egypt, pictured below, is one of the world's largest hydroelectric plants. It gets its power from the Nile River.

Power lines

C The pressure of the water turns the turbines that drive the electrical generators in the plant.

D Power plant operators open or close the gateways in the dam to control when the generators will run and how much electric power they will produce. When does the water have the most potential energy? The most kinetic energy?

Warming Race

Solar energy seems like a perfect solution to our energy problems. Solar energy is nonpolluting, readily available and constantly renewed on Earth's surface. However, solar energy has a number of drawbacks. **In your Journal,** *make a list of some drawbacks that you can think of. Then, do this activity to explore one drawback you may not have thought of.*

Problem

Which will warm water better—solar energy or electrical energy?

Materials

400 mL water	250-mL beaker
hot plate	black plastic
coffee can, painted black	clear plastic shoe box
newspaper (for insulation)	thin plastic foam sheets (for insulation)
clear plastic	tape
rubber bands	aluminum foil
white glue	2 thermometers
bowl	

Safety Precautions

Be cautious around all sources of heat.

What To Do

1 Construct a device that uses the sun's energy to warm water. You will not use all of the materials, and you may find you do not need to use very many of them.

2 At three different times of the day—morning, afternoon, and evening—place your solar heater in the sun to warm 200 mL of water for five minutes. Make certain that you always start with water at the same temperature.

3 *In your Journal*, record the temperature of the water every 30 seconds.

4 Warm 200 mL of water in a beaker on a hot plate for five minutes.

5 *In your Journal*, record the temperature every 30 seconds.

Mana La, the solar-powered car pictured above, is on a test run in Hawaii. Notice the solar collecting panels, which wrap around the top and sides of the vehicle.

Analyzing

1. *In your Journal*, make a table that summarizes the results of all four warming experiments.

2. Graph the results of all of the warming experiments—temperature on the vertical axis, time on the horizontal axis.

3. How do the warming experiments in the solar device compare to each other? Did water reach a higher temperature more quickly at one time of the day than at another?

4. How did the solar energy-device experiments compare to the electric device? With which device did water reach a higher temperature?

Concluding and Applying

5. Expand your graph to predict how long it would take for water warmed by solar energy to reach the same temperature as the water warmed by electric energy.

6. What might be one of the drawbacks to using solar energy to warm water?

7. **Going Further** Redesign your solar device to improve its ability to warm water and try heating 200 mL of water again. Compare your results to the previous experiment's results.

Figure 13-11

Solar Energy

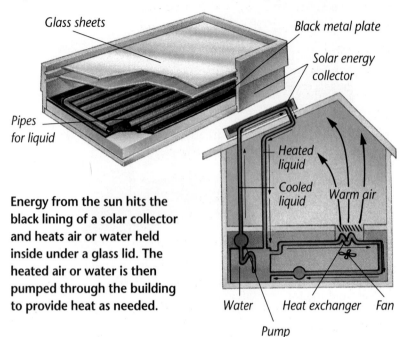

Glass sheets

Black metal plate

Solar energy collector

Pipes for liquid

Heated liquid

Cooled liquid

Warm air

Water

Heat exchanger

Fan

Pump

Energy from the sun hits the black lining of a solar collector and heats air or water held inside under a glass lid. The heated air or water is then pumped through the building to provide heat as needed.

Suppose your new city could find a single source for all its energy needs. This source might be the sun. The sun sends as much energy to Earth's surface in 40 minutes as humans use all around the world in one year. Energy from the sun, called solar energy, is clean and renewable. Look at **Figure 13-11** to see one way in which solar energy can be used.

Another way to use the sun's energy is to concentrate it with mirrors. For example, on pages 390 and 391 is a picture of a towering structure of flat mirrors that stands just outside the town of

Physics CONNECTION

The containment tower at the Palo Verde, Arizona, nuclear power plant

Promises and Problems

Between 5 and 7.5 percent of the electricity in the United States comes from nuclear energy. One kind of nuclear energy is released when atoms of uranium are split apart. The particles move apart at high speed. They collide with other particles and give off thermal energy. The thermal energy causes water to boil, which makes steam to drive a turbine. In this way, electricity is produced.

The Advantages

One kilogram of uranium releases a million times more energy than one kilogram of fossil fuel. Nuclear energy does not release pollutants, such as CO_2 and sulfur emissions, as coal-burning power plants do.

The Disadvantages

However, nuclear energy has its disadvantages. Uranium releases radioactive particles. Therefore, the fuel in nuclear reactors must be handled with extreme care. Even though nuclear power plants are designed to contain radiation, accidents can and have occurred.

Odeillo, France. The mirrors are positioned to focus energy from the sun on one part of the tower. In that tower is a high-temperature laboratory where temperatures can reach 3300° C.

■ Solar Cells

There are other uses for solar energy on a much smaller scale. For example, you may have used a solar calculator. A **solar cell** converts light from the sun into electricity, which powers the calculator. In one type of solar cell, thin layers of silicon, a hard dark-colored element, are sandwiched together and attached to tiny wires. As light strikes the different layers, it causes an electrical current to flow.

Solar cells are efficient because they generate electricity in just one step. Compare that with the number of steps required to produce energy from coal at an electric power plant that uses coal as an energy source.

Solar energy seems like a perfect energy source, doesn't it? But there are some drawbacks. Solar energy is available only when the sun is shining. Solar collectors and cells work less efficiently on cloudy days. They don't work at all at night. And during winter, when days are short, the collectors and cells generate less energy. Finally, although silicon is cheap and plentiful, solar cells are still expensive to make.

Solutions to Some of the Problems?

Even the most safely run nuclear power plant produces radioactive waste. Currently, there is no entirely safe way to store these wastes, which remain dangerous for thousands or millions of years.

Some government officials and scientists have suggested putting the waste in storage areas deep underground, in rural areas away from cities and towns. But others have said there is no way to make sure the storage area won't leak in the thousands of years the waste will remain dangerous.

Some people have suggested that the use of nuclear power should not be expanded until the serious problems connected with it are solved. Others think that nuclear power should continue to be developed and that safety and environmental problems can be solved as they occur.

What Do You Think?

Do you think we should continue to use nuclear power? Would you be willing to live near a nuclear power plant? Why or why not?

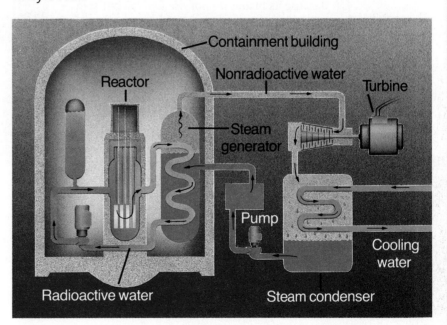

Wind Energy

What source of energy makes a kite soar overhead or a sailboat move on a quiet lake? It's wind power, an energy source that has been used for thousands of years. Egyptians used wind power to propel their sailing barges along the Nile River more than 5000 years ago.

One way to take advantage of the energy in wind is windmills. Today, people use windmills to generate electricity on a large scale. Examine **Figure 13-12** to see a windmill that generates electricity.

Wind energy is another clean and renewable alternative energy source. Like waterpower, it can be used only at certain locations. Winds must reach speeds of about 32 kilometers per hour to turn the blades of windmills. Also, if the winds are not blowing steadily, no electricity is generated.

Now that you've studied energy resources, you know that wise use and planning of resources can supply us with electricity for as long as we need it. As time goes on, we'll continue to use electricity, but the energy resources that generate it will be different from those we now use.

Figure 13-12

The power of the wind is often harnessed by windmills. The turning windmill blades are connected to a turbine, which drives an electrical generator.

A The Darrieus rotor in the photograph is a windmill with a vertical axis. Unlike traditional windmills, the Darrieus can operate in winds from any direction.

B Because its blades do not rise and fall but spin around, gravity does not slow the rotation of the Darrieus's blades. The Darrieus is also easier to maintain because all of its mechanical parts are located on the ground.

check your UNDERSTANDING

1. List the alternative energy resources that are renewable. What makes each of these renewable?

2. Which alternative energy source is not renewable? Explain.

3. **Apply** Do you think solar energy could serve well as an alternative energy resource where you live? What conditions would be needed in an area that wanted to use solar power?

Science and Society

Using Coal Resources

Some coal lies within 200 feet of Earth's surface. To mine this coal, tons of soil and rock lying above the coal must be moved out of the way. It's a simple but dirty process.

First, bulldozers clear off an area and make it level. Then, many small holes are drilled in the rock and soil above the coal. The holes are filled with explosives. The explosives are set off and the rock is shattered. Next, earth movers, some as tall as a 20-story building, clear away the rock and soil, shoving it into massive heaps. The exposed coal is scooped up and loaded into huge trucks. This process is called strip mining.

The Cost of Strip Mining

For over 100 years, huge expanses of land were scarred by strip mining.

Once the coal was removed, the mined areas, looking like landscapes from some barren planet, were abandoned. Abandoned strip mines were more than just an eyesore. Serious environmental problems, including erosion and acid mine drainage, resulted.

Reclaiming the Land

Since 1978, companies that strip-mine in the United States have been required by law to restore the land they disturb. In this process, the open coal pit is leveled, and the rock and soil that were removed to expose the coal are placed back in the leveled pit. Topsoil is replaced and replanted.

The restored area looks better than the abandoned pits, but it isn't as good as new. The process of succession is slow to replace all the natural diversity the ecosystem had before strip mining destroyed it.

Below, a pit mine

Below, a reclaimed strip mine

You Try It

Write a short letter to your local newspaper that outlines some of the problems from mining and burning coal. Suggest ways in which people can conserve energy so that less coal is used.

Technology Connection

Geothermal Energy

An erupting volcano or geyser produces vast amounts of thermal energy. Can we tap into that energy source? If we can, not only will we conserve the fossil fuels we would have burned otherwise, but we might even reduce the volcano's or geyser's destructiveness by giving it another outlet.

Natural Water Heaters

People in Iceland have used hot water and steam from local geysers for hundreds of years to heat their homes and to wash laundry and dishes. Those of us who live farther from naturally boiling springs need to use technology.

Engineers drill a deep well into Earth's crust until they reach a layer of heated rock that surrounds a magma chamber. If the rock is porous, it may already hold water in the form of steam under great pressure. When the drillers tap into the reservoir, steam and hot water rise to Earth's surface where they can be used to turn the blades of turbines. This energy source is called geothermal ("Earth heat") energy. The picture on this page shows a geothermal power plant in Iceland.

Geothermal power plant west of Reykjavik, Iceland

Limitations on Geothermal Sources

All rocks everywhere get hotter as you go deeper into Earth's crust. Then why don't we use geothermal energy everywhere? For one thing, geothermal energy must be found near Earth's surface. Drilling deep wells is expensive and causes pollution.

Geothermal wells release hydrogen sulfide and sulfur-dioxide gas, which are poisonous. Engineers can install industrial scrubbers that keep these gases from polluting the atmosphere, but scrubber technology is expensive.

Another drawback is the water. It may contain toxic elements such as ammonia, boron, mercury, or even radioactive elements.

A geothermal power plant has to plan for safe disposal of cooled wastewater.

What Do You Think?

Yellowstone National Park is a large wilderness area in Wyoming that has numerous geysers and hot springs, sources of geothermal energy. How do you think you would feel about a geothermal power plant being built on the border of Yellowstone National Park? How might the plant affect the park?

HOW IT
W O R K S

Tidewater Power Plants

I t's a simple concept. Find a bay where high tide and low tide vary by more than 10 meters (33 feet). Build a dam across the bay. When the gates are open and the tide is coming in, seawater fills a reservoir behind the dam. Install turbines in the dam. Now, every time the tide comes in or goes out, the turbines are turning and you're making electricity. It's nonpolluting, renewable, and—after the initial construction costs are met—free. The diagram on this page is an example of a tidal power plant that has been operating in France.

So Why Aren't Tidal Power Plants More Common?

The answer to that question is in the fact that the operation of tidal power plants isn't quite that simple.

First, there aren't many bays with such a large tidal range. And when you find one, the shape of the bay may be wrong for storing a large volume of seawater on the landward side.

Second, tidal power plants don't generate much electricity. The water is not under great pressure, as it is at the foot of the huge dams that generate hydroelectric power. Also, of course, the turbines turn (and therefore generate electricity) only part of each day. Still water means still turbines. And unfortunately, we have not yet created a good way to store electricity in large quantities. So an industry or a community that wanted to use tidal power would need other reliable power sources.

What Do You Think?

What other problems can you think of that must be solved before tidal power plants are common? What about such a plant's environmental impact on its own intertidal zones and on currents hundreds of miles down the coast? Discuss the future of tidal power as a group.

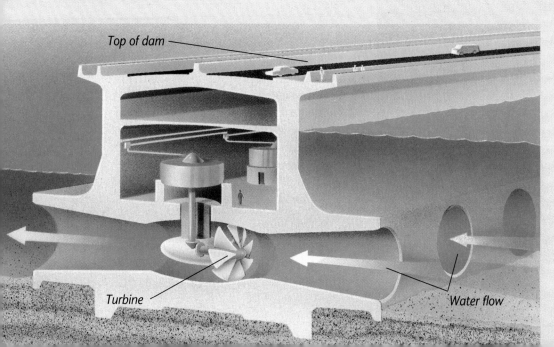

Top of dam

Turbine

Water flow

Review the statements below about the big ideas presented in this chapter, and try to answer the questions. Then, re-read your answers to the Did You Ever Wonder questions at the beginning of the chapter. *In your Journal*, write a paragraph about how your understanding of the big ideas in the chapter has changed.

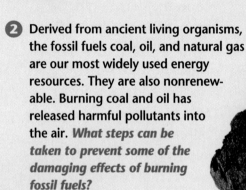

1 Wires transport electricity from generators to our homes, schools, and other places that need electric power. Many power plants have steam turbine generators that rely on coal for fuel. *Describe how a generator produces electricity.*

2 Derived from ancient living organisms, the fossil fuels coal, oil, and natural gas are our most widely used energy resources. They are also nonrenewable. Burning coal and oil has released harmful pollutants into the air. *What steps can be taken to prevent some of the damaging effects of burning fossil fuels?*

3 As fossil fuel supplies dwindle, alternative energy resources become increasingly important. Some of those already being used are hydroelectric, nuclear, solar, wind, and geothermal power. *How is the way hydroelectric plants cause turbines to spin different from the way fossil fuel-burning plants cause turbines to spin?*

Using Key Science Terms

fossil fuel	nonrenewable resource
generator	renewable resource
hydroelectric	solar cell

Answer the following questions using what you know about the science terms.

1. Compare and contrast geothermal power and hydroelectric power.
2. What are fossil fuels and what makes them different from one another?
3. Draw a generator and describe how it works.
4. Compare and contrast nonrenewable and renewable resources.
5. How does a solar cell produce energy?

Understanding Ideas

Answer the following questions in your Journal *using complete sentences.*

1. Why is a corn crop considered a renewable resource?
2. What are greenhouse gases? Why are they called greenhouse gases?
3. How does power production by nuclear plants help reduce air pollution?
4. How does a fossil fuel-burning plant contribute to acid rain?
5. Why are fossil fuels used more often than alternative energy resources?

Developing Skills

Use your understanding of the concepts developed in this chapter to answer each of the following questions.

1. **Concept Mapping** Create a sequence concept map of the formation of coal. You may use the format below or modify it to use in your map.

Initiating event

Event 1

Event 2

Event 3

Final outcome

2. **Sequencing** Outline the steps in the generation and transportation of electricity to your school.
3. **Hypothesizing** Refer to the Explore activity on page 400. Hypothesize what can happen to wildlife as a result of an oil spill.
4. **Designing an Experiment to Test a Hypothesis** Refer to the Explore activity on page 407. Hypothesize what other methods can be used to spin the pinwheel. Design an experiment to test your hypothesis.

Critical Thinking

Use your understanding of the concepts developed in this chapter to answer each of the following questions.

1. You find a fossil in a chunk of coal. Is it more likely to be a coral or a twig? Explain your answer.
2. What geographic limitations do solar, wind, geothermal, hydroelectric, and tidal energy resources have?

3. The diagram below shows one geologist's idea of the place fossil fuels will occupy in human history. What statement is the geologist making about the use of fossil fuels today? What statement is she making about oil in particular? Do you agree or disagree with the geologist's view of the future of fossil fuels?

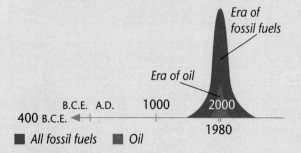

4. Imagine that there's a natural resource called a barghopper. Using barghoppers at the rate of 5000 a year, you've now used up all of the existing barghoppers. Nature still produces barghoppers at the rate of 2000 a year. What change do you make to change the barghopper from a nonrenewable to a renewable resource?

Problem Solving

Read the following problem and discuss your answers in a brief paragraph.

Dmetri lives with his family in a cabin atop a mountain. The cabin is above the tree line, and is so far from the nearest city that there's no electric service and no natural gas. Much of the year, the mountain is covered with snow. During the spring and summer, the snow melts, forming rapidly moving meltwater streams in the nearby valleys.

Consider sources of electricity that could be used in Dmetri's home. List suggestions for Dmetri, telling him what to do to get electricity for his cabin throughout the year.

CONNECTING IDEAS

Discuss each of the following in a brief paragraph.

1. **Theme—Energy** How can coal be used to generate electricity?
2. **Theme—Systems and Interactions** How is oil related to air pollution? How is it related to pollution of the ocean?
3. **Theme—Energy** How is the sun an important source of energy in the fossil fuels used today?
4. **Technology Connection** Why is geothermal energy usually most readily available in regions of frequent volcanic activity?
5. **Science and Society** What environmental effects would you expect from exposing high-sulfur coal to rain? What might happen to local ecosystems if strip mining allowed drainage of water into local streams, lakes, and ponds? Explain your answer.
6. **How Does It Work?** Why aren't there many tidal energy stations operating today?

Earth Materials and Resources

In this unit, you learned how to distinguish among metals, nonmetals, and metalloids. You compared minerals based on properties, such as hardness, luster, and cleavage. You classified rocks as sedimentary, igneous, and metamorphic. You learned how some of Earth's materials can be used as sources of energy.

You also investigated the structure of Earth's oceans and learned about features of Earth's shorelines and the ocean basin floor.

Try the exercises and activity that follow—they will challenge you to use and apply some of the ideas you learned in this unit.

CONNECTING IDEAS

1. Explain why sedimentary rocks will likely form on ocean floors. What types of natural resources would you expect to find within the layers of sedimentary rocks on the ocean floor? Explain your answer.

2. Arrange groups a through d in order from the simplest to the most complex of Earth's structures: a) Rocky Mountains and the Mid-Ocean Ridge; b) silicon, aluminum, and oxygen; c) granite and basalt; and d) quartz, feldspar and mica. Classify each group according to the type of natural resource it represents.

Exploring Further ACTIVITY

Granite: Looking between the grains

What To Do

1. Pretend you could reduce your size to fit between the particles in a piece of granite.

2. Write a story about what you might see in your travels through the rock.

3. Describe the different particle sizes, elements, minerals, crystals, gas molecules, liquids, colors, lusters, or any other properties you might see.

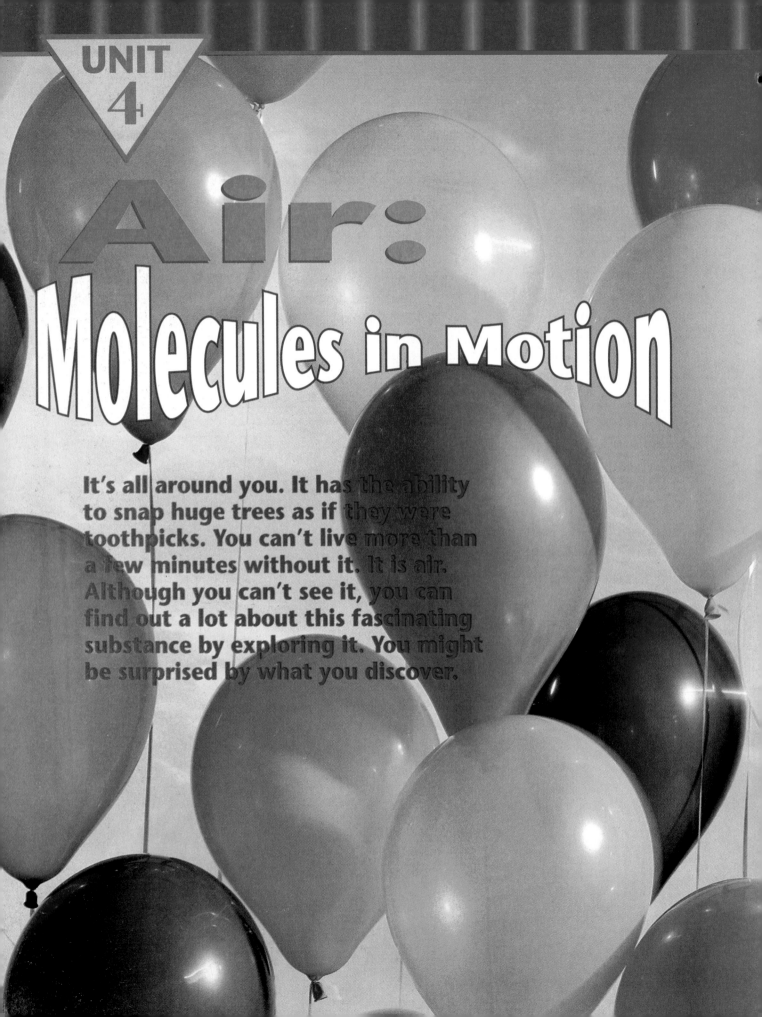

UNIT 4

Air:
Molecules in Motion

It's all around you. It has the ability to snap huge trees as if they were toothpicks. You can't live more than a few minutes without it. It is air. Although you can't see it, you can find out a lot about this fascinating substance by exploring it. You might be surprised by what you discover.

Can you place a paper towel in an aquarium full of water and still keep it dry?

What To Do

1. Half-fill an aquarium with water. Crumple a paper towel and put it in a baby food jar so the towel won't fall out when you turn the jar over. What do you think will happen if you put the upside-down jar in the aquarium? Write your prediction *in your Journal*, then test it.

2. What will happen if you half-fill the jar with water, place a plastic coffee can lid over the jar, and turn it upside down in the aquarium? Record your prediction, then test it.

3. Now, add 30 mL of water to a soft drink can and heat until the water boils. What will happen if you use a thermal mitt to turn the can upside down over the aquarium, placing the rim of the can just below the level of water? Write your prediction, then test it.

Try It Again

After you've learned more about gases, do this activity again and explain your observations.

CHAPTER 14

GASES, ATOMS AND MOLECULES

Did you ever wonder...

✓ **Why you sometimes see remnants of exploded car tires at the side of the road?**

✓ **What's in a balloon?**

✓ **Why a hairspray can feels cold when you use it?**

Before you begin to study gases, atoms, and molecules, think about these questions and answer them *in your Journal*. When you finish the chapter, compare your journal write-up with what you have learned.

magine you are casually riding your bike through the neighborhood. In the alley behind one building, you cannot avoid some broken glass. You hear a loud "Thwop!" and your front tire is flat. As you walk your bike home, you see your older sister at the gas station. She is putting air in her car's tires. You remember that she said the tires squealed when she turned corners and that they probably needed more air. She looks up and sees your plight, and you gratefully accept her offer to drive you home. As you round the corner toward home, you notice the car's tires no longer squeal. You begin to wonder what made the difference.

▶ ***In the next activity, you'll explore a useful and unique property of gases.***

Explore! ACTIVITY

Does air exert pressure?

What To Do

1. Obtain a partially inflated balloon and a box that's smaller than the balloon. Predict *in your Journal* whether the balloon will fit in the box.

2. Try to close the lid. Does the lid stay closed without help?

3. Repeat Steps 1 and 2 using various sizes of boxes. How does the size of the box relate to how easy it is to close the lid?

How Do Gases Behave?

Identifying Properties of Gases

Section Objectives

- Identify the gas phase of matter by its properties.
- Find the relationships involving pressure, volume, and temperature of a gas.

Key Terms

Boyle's law
Charles' law

You know that matter exists in three common physical phases—solid, liquid, and gas. Each phase has its own characteristic properties and behaviors. In this section, you will study gases.

Explore! ACTIVITY

Do gases move?

What To Do

1. With your classmates, arrange chairs facing away from a small table or desk like four equally spaced spokes of a wheel. Everybody except the experimenter should sit in one of the chairs.

2. The experimenter then will put on the small table something that has a strong odor such as a cut orange or an open bottle of perfume. The sitting students are to raise their hands as soon as they can smell whatever is on the table. Which hands are raised first? How long is it before everyone can smell the odor? In what direction does the odor travel?

Vapors from the thing you smelled moved without any help from a fan or any other outside source. **Figure 14-1** reviews this characteristic of gases as well as a few others.

Figure 14-1

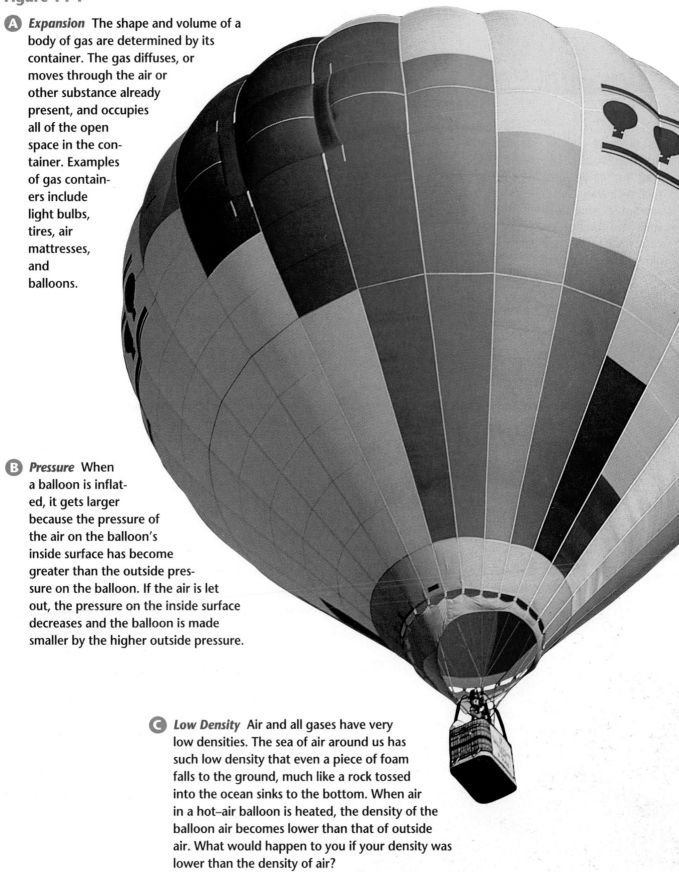

A *Expansion* The shape and volume of a body of gas are determined by its container. The gas diffuses, or moves through the air or other substance already present, and occupies all of the open space in the container. Examples of gas containers include light bulbs, tires, air mattresses, and balloons.

B *Pressure* When a balloon is inflated, it gets larger because the pressure of the air on the balloon's inside surface has become greater than the outside pressure on the balloon. If the air is let out, the pressure on the inside surface decreases and the balloon is made smaller by the higher outside pressure.

C *Low Density* Air and all gases have very low densities. The sea of air around us has such low density that even a piece of foam falls to the ground, much like a rock tossed into the ocean sinks to the bottom. When air in a hot–air balloon is heated, the density of the balloon air becomes lower than that of outside air. What would happen to you if your density was lower than the density of air?

Relating Gas Pressure and Volume

SKILLBUILDER

Observing and Inferring

As you leave your apartment building, you notice a neighbor washing her apartment door with a cleaner containing ammonia. An hour later, you walk into the building and you can smell ammonia cleaner almost everywhere. The smell is strongest near your neighbor's door. State an inference to explain your observations. If you need help, refer to the **Skill Handbook** on page 642.

If you've ever inflated a balloon or a bicycle tire, you may have already noticed a very interesting property of gases. When you pump air into a bicycle tire, you are compressing it. That means you are squeezing the air so it takes up less space. In other words, you are reducing its volume. Unlike water and other liquids, gases can be compressed. As you squeeze or compress a gas such as air, you increase the pressure of the gas. You noticed this when you were trying to stuff a balloon into different boxes in the Explore activity. The smaller the box you attempted to put it in, the harder the gas in the balloon pushed back as you tried to close the lid. The pressure got higher as the volume got smaller. Pressure and volume are two important characteristics of gases. **Figure 14-2** describes other characteristics of gases that are important to understand.

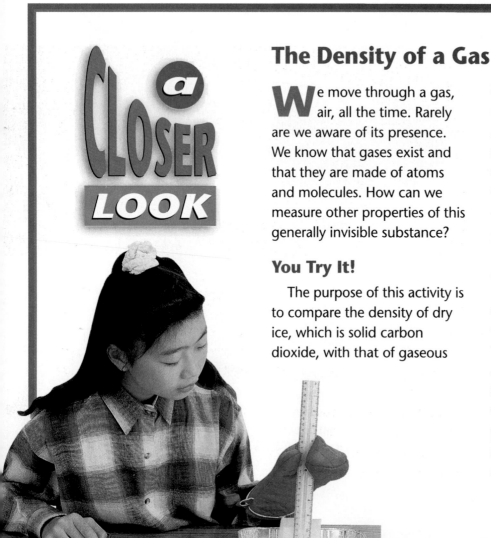

The Density of a Gas

We move through a gas, air, all the time. Rarely are we aware of its presence. We know that gases exist and that they are made of atoms and molecules. How can we measure other properties of this generally invisible substance?

You Try It!

The purpose of this activity is to compare the density of dry ice, which is solid carbon dioxide, with that of gaseous carbon dioxide. Flatten a tall kitchen trash bag so there is no air in it. You will use a cube-shaped piece of dry ice so you can measure its dimensions. **CAUTION:** *Dry ice is very cold and must be handled with extreme care because it could freeze your skin. Do not touch dry ice with your fingers. Always use tongs when handling the dry ice.* Quickly use a balance to find the mass of the dry ice cube. Then, measure its dimensions, and immediately place the dry ice in the large plastic bag. Seal the bag tightly as soon as you put the dry ice in. Try not to let any gaseous carbon dioxide escape.

Figure 14-2

When describing a gas, there are four variables to consider: amount, pressure, volume, and temperature. To find how these four variables are related, choose two at a time to test. While keeping all the other variables constant, make changes in one of the two test variables and measure its effect on the other. This process of controlling the number of variables is called a controlled experiment.

A *Amount*, expressed in g or kg, is the mass of the gas.

B *Volume*, expressed in cubic units, is the amount of space the gas takes up.

C *Temperature* of gas can be measured on a Celsius (°C) or Fahrenheit (°F) scale.

A Amount of air = 0.1g

B Volume of air = 100 cm³

C Temperature of air = 20°C

D Pressure of air = 1 atm

D *Pressure*, often expressed in atmospheres (atm), is related to the force the gas exerts on the objects it touches. The force is equal to the pressure times the area of the object. One atm is equal to 14.7 pounds per square inch.

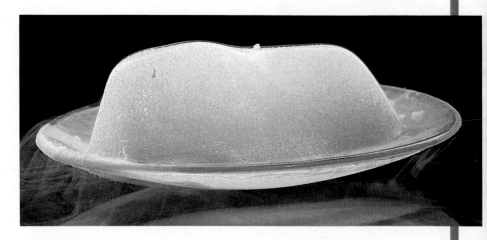

Once the dry ice is sealed in the bag, you may begin your calculations of the volume and density of the dry ice. The volume is equal to the length times the width times the height, or $V = l \times w \times h$. The density is the mass divided by the volume, or $D = M/V$.

While you are doing your calculations, the dry ice will be changing into a gas inside the plastic bag, so the bag will appear to be partially inflated. When you are sure there is no longer any solid dry ice in the bag, put the bag into a shape that is as box-like as possible. When it is in this shape, measure its dimensions as well as you can. Then, calculate the volume and the density. Since the bag is not perfectly box-like, you will not be able to get measurements that are extremely accurate. However, with patience and care, you will get a close approximation. Because little carbon dioxide was allowed to escape, the mass of the dry ice will be about the same as the mass of the gaseous carbon dioxide.

How does the volume of the gaseous carbon dioxide compare with the volume of the dry ice? Is the number of molecules the same in the dry ice and in the gaseous carbon dioxide? Why do the molecules in gaseous carbon dioxide take up more space?

Pressure and Volume

Have you ever wondered why a balloon pops when you step on it? Maybe on television you've seen a scuba diver's bubbles get bigger as the bubbles near the surface. Why do these things happen? In this activity, you'll discover how the pressure and volume of a gas are related.

Problem

How are the pressure and volume of a gas related?

Materials

large air cylinder
   with piston or
   plastic syringe
petroleum jelly

various weights,
   such as bricks or
   books

Safety Precautions

What To Do

Work with your group to *hypothesize* how the pressure and volume of a gas are related. Plan a way to test your hypothesis using an air cylinder. Here are some things that your group should do when using the air cylinder to help you in your investigation.

1 Remove the cap from the air cylinder. Lightly lubricate the plunger of the piston with petroleum jelly. Insert the plunger into the cylinder. Make sure the plunger is snug, but moves easily.

2 Pull the plunger back so that the cylinder contains 30 mL of air. Replace the cap.

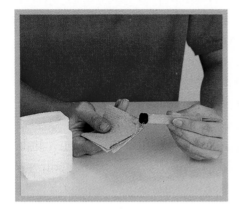

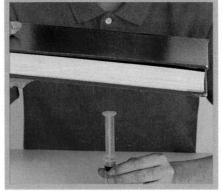

A   B

No. of Weights	Volume of Air			Average Volume
	Trial 1	Trial 2	Trial 3	
1				
2				
3				
4				

Data and Observations

If you moisten two plunger cups and push the ends together, there will be almost no air left in the cups. The difference between the cup pressure and the outside air pressure will create a force so strong that you cannot pull them apart. Try it!

3 Set a weight on the cylinder's platform. Twist the plunger a bit to keep it from sticking. Read the volume of air in mL. Remember that pressure can raise the temperature of a gas, so wait a minute or so for the temperature to return to room temperature.

Show your experimental plan to your teacher. If you are advised to revise your plan, be sure to check with your teacher before you begin. Carry out your plan. Record your data in a table *in your Journal*.

Analyzing

1. *Identify the variables* in your experiment. How were they controlled?

2. Determine the effect of increasing pressure on the volume of a gas.

Concluding and Applying

3. **Going Further** Graph your data, putting pressure on the horizontal axis and volume on the vertical axis. *Interpret* your graph to find the relationship between pressure and volume of an enclosed gas.

Figure 14-3

The diagram below demonstrates Boyle's law. As gas pressure increases, volume decreases, as long as the temperature is constant.

In the Investigate, you found the same result that scientists discovered over 300 years ago. They found that the pressure and volume of a gas are inversely related. What does that mean? It means that when one goes up, the other goes down. For this relationship to be true, the amount of gas in the system and the temperature of the system must be held constant. This relationship is known as Boyle's law. **Boyle's law** can be stated thus: The volume of a certain amount of gas is inversely proportional to the pressure, if the temperature remains constant. The law is illustrated in **Figure 14-3**.

You now have a better understanding of how pressure and volume are related. More important, you have a sense of what it means to carry out a controlled experiment. Boyle's law tells how pressure and volume are related, but it does not tell why. You will learn why later.

1P

P equals pressure

2P

3P

3.0 liters
25°C

1.5 liters
25°C

1 liter
25°C

Earth Science CONNECTION

Research Giants

Have you ever heard of an aerostat? An aerostat is an aircraft that is supported by the buoyancy of a gas that is less dense than air.

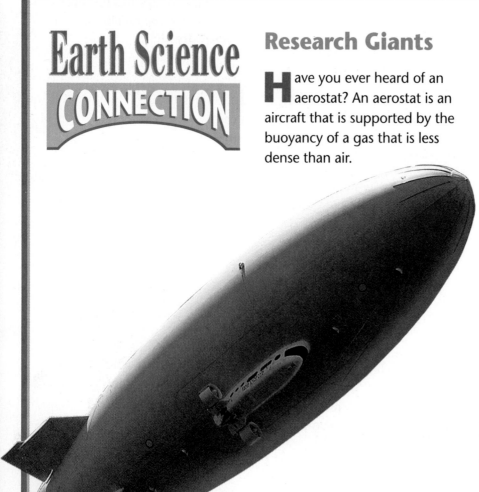

Aerostats include blimps and dirigibles. The simplest kind is the balloon, because it has no means of propulsion or steering. In other words, a balloon just goes wherever the movement of the air takes it.

Basically, a balloon is a large bag that is filled with a gas that is lighter, or less dense, than air, for example, hot air or helium. This large bag displaces a lot of air, and has an upward force on it—called a buoyant force—that is equal to the weight of the displaced air.

These giant balloons can lift a load of instruments higher than a jetliner but lower than an orbiting satellite.

Effect of Temperature on Gas Pressure and Volume

What happens to the tires on your bike in hot weather? They probably get harder. What's going on inside the tire? What happens when you put a balloon over a heat source, like a lamp? It swells and eventually explodes, doesn't it?

What goes on in the bike tire and balloon is the same thing that goes on in the tires on cars and trucks that travel roads and highways. You know that there is air inside the tires. What happens to that air as the tire pounds against the road? The tire heats up because of the friction with the road. As the tire heats up, so does the air inside the tire. If it heats up too much, the tire may explode. How could this happen if no additional air was pumped into the tire? Can you think of any other examples where you have observed a gas change with temperature? How is the volume or pressure of a gas affected by a change in its temperature? Try this next activity to find out what happens.

Connect to...

Life Science

When you breathe, air rushes into and is expelled from your lungs. Explain breathing to your classmates in terms of volume and pressure in the chest cavity and in the air around you.

The volume of helium needed to lift the load could be equal to the volume of a small house on the ground. Once the balloon reaches the altitude it's designed for, the volume of the gas could be the volume of 283 houses.

What kind of information can be obtained by balloons? Balloons carry many different kinds of instruments. Some have telescopes for viewing objects in space. Others collect and analyze the gases in the atmosphere. Still others measure and record temperature, pressure, and the amounts and kinds of radiation from space. Ground-based radar can track balloons to find out about the speed and direction of high-altitude winds.

Information collected in these studies helps scientists understand the makeup and behavior of the gases in our atmosphere. As we learn more about this important part of the environment, we will be able to predict the atmosphere's behavior and to know how we can protect and preserve it.

What Do You Think?

What would be an advantage of taking pictures through telescopes on high-altitude balloons, rather than through ground-based telescopes? What are the disadvantages? In what ways are research balloons different from the multicolored balloon shown on page 427?

How does the volume of a gas depend on its temperature?

What To Do

1. Copy the data table *into your Journal*. Obtain a thermometer and plugged capillary tube from your teacher.

2. Prepare a mixture of crushed ice and water in a deep beaker. Place the thermometer and tube into this beaker. Be sure the air column is below the water level. Wait until the temperature becomes constant and bring the thermometer close to the side of the beaker. Read and record the temperature.

3. Place a ruler in the water next to the tube and record the length of the air column.

4. Replace the ice water with tap water and slowly heat the water. Measure the length of the air column at various temperatures as the water heats to boiling. Record the temperatures and column lengths in the data table.

Conclude and Apply

1. We can assume that the diameter of the tube is constant, so that as the length increases, the volume increases proportionally. Since we're looking for a relationship between temperature and volume, let's use the length of the column in place of the volume to make our calculations easier. Plot a graph with volume (length) on the vertical axis and temperature on the horizontal axis.

2. As the temperature increases, what happens to the volume? What is the relationship between the temperature and volume of a gas?

3. How did you hold the variables of pressure and amount of gas constant in this activity?

Data and Observations					
Temp °C					
Volume represented by length of air columns					

You have discovered that the relationship between the volume of a gas and its pressure is inverse: as one goes up, the other goes down. You have seen that the relationship of the volume and temperature of a gas is direct: as one goes up, so does the other, and vice versa. If you could repeat the Find Out activity, measuring pressure instead of volume, you would find that the relationship between the temperature and pressure of a gas is direct: as one goes up, the other goes up too, and vice versa. These relationships are shown in **Table 14-1**. These relationships were found by careful experiments. In each case, two variables were held constant

Pressure constant

T = temperature

1 liter
T

2.0 liters
2T

3.0 liters
3T

Figure 14-4

This diagram demonstrates Charles' Law. If the pressure on a gas remains constant and the temperature of the gas is increased, the volume of the gas also increases. An everyday example of this law is a cake baking in a hot oven. The increase in temperature causes the bubbles of gas in the dough to expand—the cake rises.

Table 14-1

Boyle's Law	P↑	V↓
	P↓	V↑
Charles' Law	T↑	V↑
	T↓	V↓
Pressure and Temperature	P↑	T↑
	P↓	T↓

Table 14-1 summarizes the relationships between the variables in a gas. Is the relationship between pressure and temperature inversely proportional?

and the other two were allowed to change. The results tell how the gas behaves. But they do not tell why. That will require more investigation.

The relationship between the temperature and volume of a gas is called Charles' law. **Charles' law** can be stated thus: Gases increase or decrease their volume as the temperature rises and falls, provided pressure and amount of gas are held constant. Charles' law is shown in **Figure 14-4**.

If instead of allowing the volume to change, you had just a solid, immovable plug in the capillary tube, what would have happened when you heated the air column?

You have learned some ways in which gases behave, but you haven't explored why they behave that way. In the next section, you will discover what's behind the behavior of gases.

SKILLBUILDER

Making and Using Tables
Use **Table 14-1** to answer the following question. If you need help, refer to the **Skill Handbook** on page 639. What would happen to the volume of a gas if you doubled the pressure and doubled the temperature?

check your UNDERSTANDING

1. Give an example for each of the characteristics of a gas.
2. As you pump more air into a basketball, what happens to the pressure in the ball? What happens to the temperature of the air in the ball?
3. **Apply** One way to fill up a balloon is to blow air into it—increase the inside air pressure. Can you think of another way to expand a balloon?

What Are Gases Made Of?

Section Objectives

- Relate how the behavior of gases can be explained by a particle theory of matter.
- Describe evidence for an atomic theory of matter.

Key Terms

atomic theory of matter

Describing Gases

You've seen huge trailer trucks on the road supported by nothing but the air in the tires. You know air is supporting all that weight. But it's hard to imagine how. Using a model can help.

Explore! ACTIVITY

Can you see air?

No. But you can see what air can do, such as bend trees and blow dust around.

What To Do

1. Push a deflated balloon into an empty soda bottle or flask and stretch the open end of the balloon back over the bottle's mouth, as shown in the picture. Try to blow up the balloon. What happens?

2. Remove the open end of the balloon from the bottle's mouth but keep the balloon in the bottle. Try to blow up the balloon now. What happens?

3. Insert a straw into the bottle between the balloon and the glass. Now, try to blow up the balloon in the bottle. What happens?

No matter how hard you huff and puff, you cannot blow up the balloon—until the straw is put in. But why? Even though you cannot see it, there is air inside the bottle. That air is keeping the balloon from inflating. How can air do this? Well, imagine the bottle filled with sand. What would you have to do to inflate the balloon? You would have to remove some of the sand. Think of the air as tiny sand particles—so small you can't see them. As you tried to inflate the balloon, you squeezed the particles closer and closer together. Like sand, it gets harder and harder to squeeze the particles in air closer together.

The idea that a gas, such as air, is made of particles can explain some of the other properties of gases you have

Figure 14-5

Gas particles are always moving. When air is forced into a deflated balloon, the particles of air spread out and the balloon inflates. The air, like all gases, expands to fill the container it is in.

A Density is the mass of a material within a certain volume. The more mass, the higher the density. Substances with tightly packed particles have a lot of mass and a high density. Air particles, like all gas particles, have a lot of space between them. The spaces between the air particles give air a low density.

B As the particles of hot air move around inside the balloon, they constantly collide with the walls of the balloon. Every time a particle hits something, the particle exerts a force. That force is the pressure of the air. The pressure of any gas is the result of its particles pushing against whatever they touch.

already observed. Look at **Figure 14-5** to see how expansion, low density, and pressure can be explained by particles.

■ **Explaining Pressure and Temperature**

What if gas particles were in motion? Moving gas particles could bang into the walls of a container and cause pressure. The kinetic energy of moving particles is measurable. In fact, the temperature of a gas is proportional to the average kinetic energy of the gas particles. So as temperature increases, both pressure and kinetic energy of the gas increase.

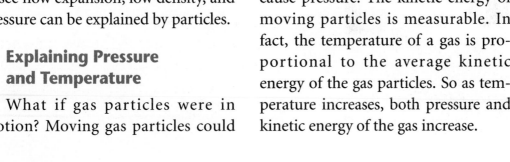

Explore! ACTIVITY

How do gas particles move?

If gas particles are too small to see, how can anyone see them moving? Try this activity to find out.

What To Do

1. Light a flashlight in a darkened room.

Watch the dust specks in the beam of light. Do the specks ever change speed?

2. Set a tray of ice cubes in the light beam and watch the dance of the dust specks now. What happens?

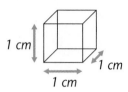

Figure 14-6

Billions of gas particles are in one cubic centimeter of space.

The dust specks you saw were never still. Although dust is not a gas, it seems reasonable to assume that gas particles in the air around the dust are also moving.

The idea that gas particles are in motion could help explain how a gas expands to fill a space. You've probably observed that shortly after a bottle of perfume is opened, the fragrance seems to fill the room, too. The gas particles of the perfume spread rapidly. This suggests that the particles of a gas are in motion. It also suggests that there are relatively large spaces between the gas particles.

So you've seen evidence that tiny gas particles have energy and are constantly moving very rapidly. This can also be used to explain pressure. The particles continually collide with the walls of any container they are in. As each particle of gas strikes the container wall, it exerts a push, or force—like that caused by a baseball hitting a wall. There are billions of gas particles in even a cubic centimeter of space. The push of that many particles adds up to quite a force being exerted.

The air in the soda bottle illustrated this. The air particles in the bottle exerted enough force in their collisions with the surface of the balloon to keep the balloon from inflating in the bottle.

Figure 14-7

A Air does not have to be trapped in a container to exert pressure. The air particles in the atmosphere constantly collide with one another and with different surfaces. Air particles exert pressure on you, on your books, on the floor and ceiling and walls of your classroom—on everything.

B Air exerts pressure on light things, such as feathers, and heavy things, such as rocks. Does air exert a greater pressure on rocks than on feathers?

The Atomic Theory of Matter

It seems that particles could be used to explain what you have observed and to accurately predict the behavior of matter. This is one reason that scientists have theorized that such particles exist and make up all gases, as well as solids and liquids. In fact, they make up your body. What are these particles called? Atoms.

The theory that matter is composed of small particles called atoms is the **atomic theory of matter**. It was first suggested by a Greek named Democritus. An expanded theory building on Democritus' idea of the atom was put forth by the chemist John Dalton. His theory will be explained as the chapter continues.

In the next section, you will examine more about atoms and some of the evidence that has led to the atomic theory of matter.

How Do We Know?

Thinking about atoms

You might wonder how someone living 2000 years ago and without the benefit of experimental testing that we do today could imagine something like the atom.

Early thinkers had to rely on their experience—with rain, snow, and wind; heat and cold; salt water and fresh water; and the lives of animals and plants around them. Lucretius, a Roman poet, helped us understand how Democritus reasoned in these lines about atoms.

... Their nature lies beyond our range of sense,

... Especially since things we can see, often

Conceal their movements, too, when at a distance.

Take grazing sheep on a hill, you know they move,

... Yet all this, far away, is just a blur,

A whiteness resting on a hill of green ...

These ancient philosophers knew that even things they could see would disappear when at a great distance. They reasoned that matter could appear as solid as the flock of sheep on the hillside, if it were made of very tiny particles. Like the sheep, these particles could be moving, and yet that movement would be invisible.

check your UNDERSTANDING

1. How does a particle theory of matter explain diffusion?
2. How does a particle theory of matter explain gas pressure?
3. What evidence do scientists have that gases are made of particles?
4. **Apply** When weather balloons are sent up from Earth, only a small amount of gas is added to the balloon. As the balloon rises, it expands until it appears full. Use the particle theory to explain why this happens to a sealed balloon.

What Is the Atomic Theory of Matter?

Section Objectives
- Describe evidence that pure substances are made up of identical particles.
- Specify what is meant by element, compound, and atom.

Key Terms
atom

Pure Substance—Elements and Compounds

You have seen evidence that there are pure substances. Aluminum metal has certain properties. If you cut aluminum into smaller and smaller pieces by ordinary means, you can never find a piece of this metal that differs from the larger piece. Aluminum is an example of an element.

But aluminum can combine with other elements to form entirely new substances. Is there some pattern in the way elements combine when they form other substances? Let's find out.

Find Out! ACTIVITY

How do hydrogen and oxygen make up water?

You know that hydrogen and oxygen are gases and that they are elements. How much of each gas is needed to make water?

What To Do

1. Partially fill a 250-mL beaker with concentrated washing soda solution. Overfill two test tubes with the same solution. Insert an electrode completely into each test tube.

2. Holding your thumb over the mouth of one test tube, invert it into the beaker. When you let go, there should be no bubble at the top of the tube. Repeat with the second test tube. **CAUTION:** *Wash your hands thoroughly after touching the solution.*

3. Connect the electrodes with alligator clamps to a power supply. What happens?

4. Let the setup run for at least 15 minutes. Use a ruler to measure the amounts of gas collected in the tubes. Record these measurements.

Conclude and Apply

1. What do you notice about the relationship between the volumes of gas in the test tubes?

The gases you collected in your test tubes were hydrogen and oxygen. The proportion should have been very close to, if not exactly, twice as much volume of hydrogen gas as oxygen. Experiments like this show that when you break up water, you always end up with the same volume ratio of hydrogen to oxygen.

Why do you think you ended up with two gases when you separated the water? **Figure 14-8** shows that when you keep dividing a drop of water, you eventually enter a microscopic world of molecules, elements, and atoms.

As you see, the molecules of water can be broken down into different atoms. **Atoms** are the smallest particle of an element. If you had to "build" some water, you would need to use atoms as your building material. Just as a carpenter needs different building materials to construct a house, you need different atoms to "build" water. You'll need two atoms of the element hydrogen and one atom of the element oxygen to build one molecule of water. However, you'll need to build a lot of molecules to end up with even a tiny drop of water!

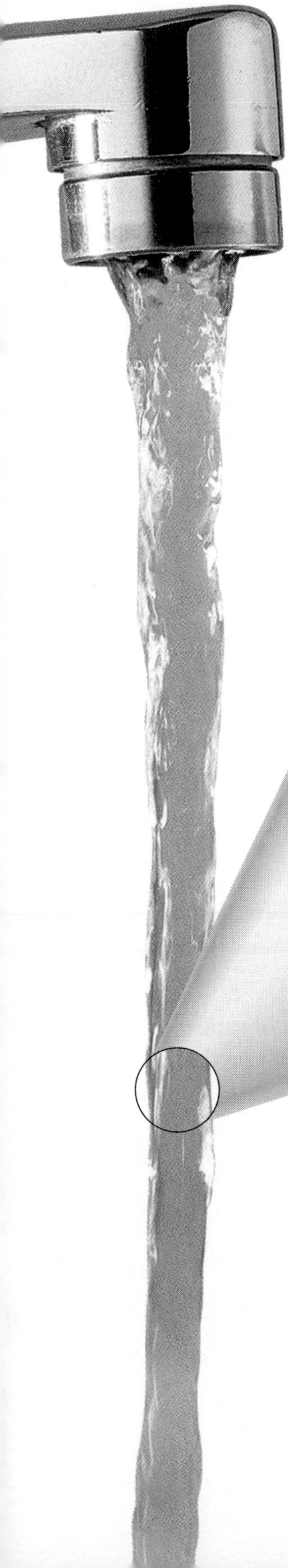

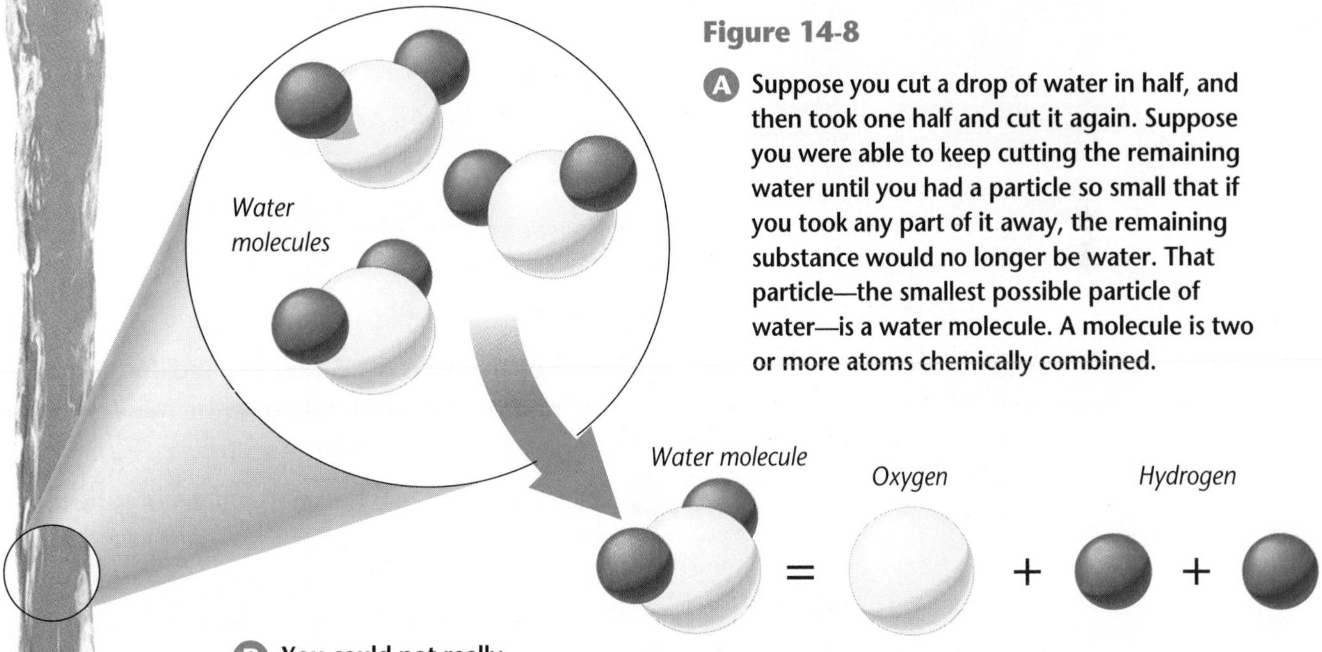

Figure 14-8

Ⓐ Suppose you cut a drop of water in half, and then took one half and cut it again. Suppose you were able to keep cutting the remaining water until you had a particle so small that if you took any part of it away, the remaining substance would no longer be water. That particle—the smallest possible particle of water—is a water molecule. A molecule is two or more atoms chemically combined.

Water molecules

Water molecule   Oxygen   Hydrogen

Ⓑ You could not really break up a molecule of water by cutting, but electric current can separate the molecule into the elements hydrogen and oxygen. Water is therefore a compound of these two elements.

Ⓒ Elements and compounds are both pure substances. Elements cannot be divided into any other pure substance by ordinary chemical means, but compounds can.

Ⓓ The substances into which compounds can be broken are often elements, but may be other compounds. Hydrogen peroxide, for example, is a compound that can be broken down into oxygen—an element—and water, a compound.

An Atomic Model

How do we know that matter is really made of atoms? One way to tell is by making a model. Scientists often use models to test predictions when the thing they want to test happens too fast, or the object is too big or too small to see. In this activity you will use a model to test a prediction based on the atomic theory.

Problem

What is the relationship of the masses of atoms when they combine?

Materials

15 pennies
15 nickels
rubber cement
balance

What To Do

1. Copy the data table *into your Journal.*

2. *Measure* the mass of 15 pennies and 15 nickels (see photo **A**). Record. Measure the mass of eight pennies and eight nickels. Record.

3. Make 6-cent coins by placing a drop of rubber cement on the center of each of the nickels. Press a 1-cent coin on each of the nickels. You now have 15 6-cent combinations (see photo **B**).

4. Measure the mass of the 15 6-cent combinations. Record.

5. Measure the mass of eight 6-cent combinations. Record.

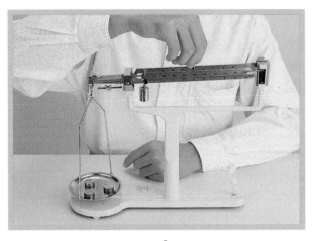

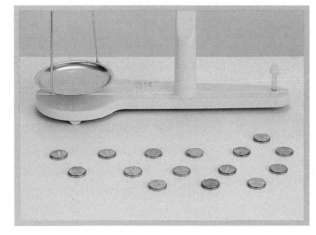

A   **B**

Data and Observations

Mass	15 1¢ Coins	15 5¢ Coins	15 6¢ Coins	15 7¢ Coins
	8 1¢ Coins	8 5¢ Coins	8 6¢ Coins	

Analyzing

1. How does the mass of 15 6-cent combinations compare with the sum of masses of the 15 separate 1-cent and 5-cent combinations? What is the ratio of the total mass of 15 nickels to the total mass of 15 pennies?

2. In Step 2, what is the ratio of the mass of eight 5-cent coins to the mass of eight pennies? *Hypothesize* the ratio of the mass of one 5-cent coin to one 1-cent coin.

Concluding and Applying

3. *Hypothesize* the ratio of the mass of 150 nickels to 150 pennies. What would the mass of 150 6-cent combinations be?

4. Based on the results of this model, how would you expect the masses of elements in a compound to relate?

5. Going Further If you had made 15 7-cent combinations, what would be the mass of the 15 7-cent combinations?

How Do We Know that Matter Is Made of Atoms?

Only recently has technology been available that can get even close to seeing a single atom. So how could anyone tell that matter was made of atoms? In the past, scientists had to rely on other experiments to investigate this. The main evidence for the existence of atoms came from chemical reactions.

■ The Ratios Remain the Same

When you mix a solution, such as a powdered fruit drink, you can make it as strong or weak as you want. You can add a little more or less sugar to suit your tastes, or add more water to weaken the flavor. Without concern for taste, you can add as much of any ingredient you desire, up to the saturation point.

Mixing a solution is not the same as chemically combining them, though. Think back to the Investigate activity you just finished. In order to make a 6-cent combination, how many pennies and nickels did you need? Could you use more nickels and still get a 6-cent combination? If matter is made of atoms, we would expect them to behave similarly to the coin

Figure 14-9

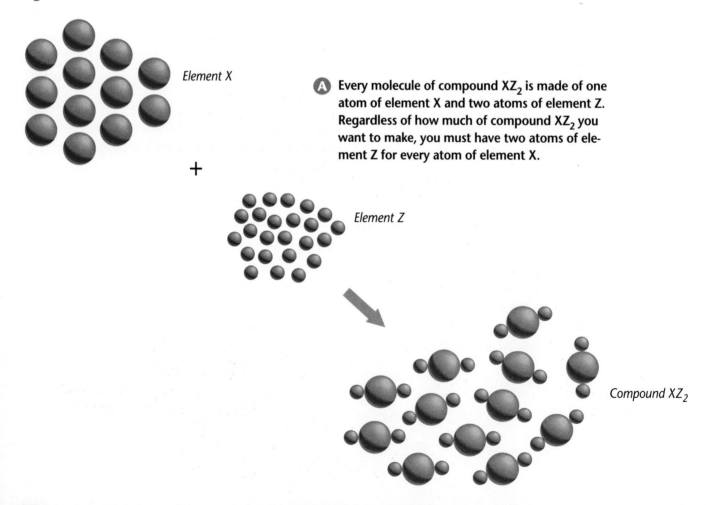

Element X

Element Z

Compound XZ$_2$

Ⓐ Every molecule of compound XZ$_2$ is made of one atom of element X and two atoms of element Z. Regardless of how much of compound XZ$_2$ you want to make, you must have two atoms of element Z for every atom of element X.

model you explored. We would expect the ratios of elements needed to make a compound to be fixed, just like you needed one penny for every nickel to make a 6-cent combination.

To make ordinary table salt, for example, you need one atom of chlorine for every atom of sodium. If you use more sodium, you won't get more salt; you'll just end up with extra sodium. Look at **Figure 14-9** to see how this works.

If we can't see atoms, how do we know this happens? Scientists count on the fact that if matter is made of atoms, then each atom must have a certain mass. That means if you have two piles of an element, and one pile has twice as much mass as the other,

then that pile has twice as many atoms. Mass is something we can measure fairly easily.

So if you add 1 g of sodium to 1.54 g of chlorine, then you will end up with 2.54 g of salt. However, if you add 1.5 g of sodium to 1.54 g of chlorine, you would still get only 2.54 g of salt, but you'd have 0.5 g of sodium left over.

Every compound is made with an exact ratio of elements. For example, you need 2.67 g of oxygen for every 1 g of carbon to make carbon dioxide, never more, never less. No matter how much of a compound you have, the ratio of masses of the elements that make up that compound is always the same.

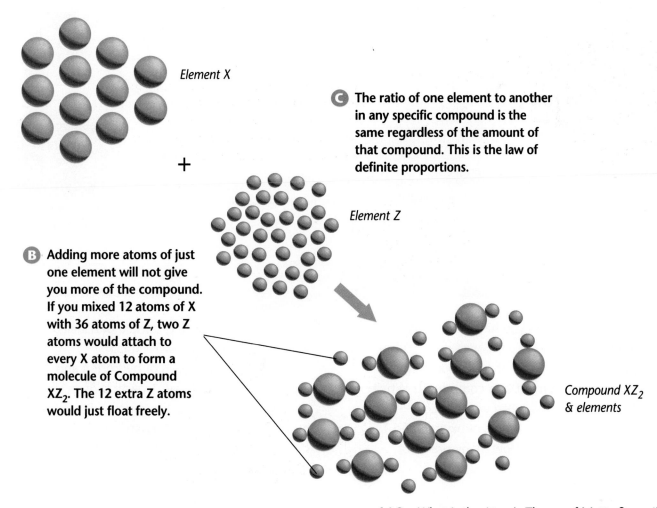

Element X

C The ratio of one element to another in any specific compound is the same regardless of the amount of that compound. This is the law of definite proportions.

Element Z

B Adding more atoms of just one element will not give you more of the compound. If you mixed 12 atoms of X with 36 atoms of Z, two Z atoms would attach to every X atom to form a molecule of Compound XZ_2. The 12 extra Z atoms would just float freely.

Compound XZ_2 & elements

■ Who Developed the Atomic Theory?

When John Dalton analyzed the masses of elements in the early 1800s, he could see the same kind of ratios you observed in the Investigate. He created the model to account for the ratios he observed. This model is called the atomic theory of matter.

Dalton proposed that different elements would be composed of different atoms. Just as pennies are different from nickels, atoms of helium are different from atoms of sodium, and just as pennies are all the same, atoms of helium are the same, too. The atoms of one element would differ in mass from the atoms of another element, just like the mass of a penny is different from the mass of a nickel.

The atomic theory of matter can be summarized in the following statements. Try to explain each in terms of the model you used in the Investigate activity.

1. Matter consists of atoms.
2. All atoms of a given element are identical.
3. Different elements have different atoms.
4. Atoms maintain their mass in chemical reactions.

Figure 14-10

Copper sulfide (CuS) is a compound made by combining 1.98 g of copper with 1 g of sulfur. In other words, for every gram of sulfur, you must add 1.98 grams of copper. If you combined 3.354 g of sulfur with 6.646 g of copper, you would have 10.000 g of copper sulfide.

How much copper would you need to combine with 33.54 g of sulfur to make 100.00 g of CuS?

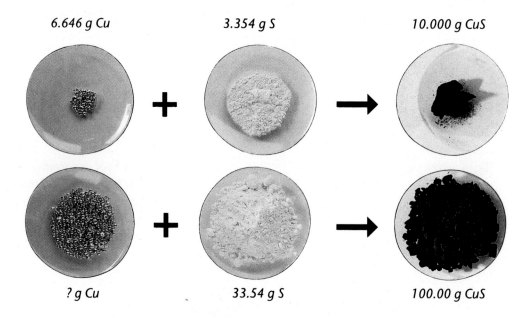

6.646 g Cu   3.354 g S   10.000 g CuS

? g Cu   33.54 g S   100.00 g CuS

check your UNDERSTANDING

1. What evidence do you have that every water molecule is alike?
2. Table salt is made up of sodium and chlorine. Is it an element or a compound? Why?
3. A 9 g sample of distilled water in Los Angeles contains 8 grams of oxygen and 1 gram of hydrogen. How many grams of hydrogen would a 90 g sample of distilled water in London contain? Explain.
4. **Apply** Draw 4 particles of hydrogen and 1 particle of carbon. Draw 1 particle of methane (made up of 1 carbon and 4 hydrogens). Which of the particles that you drew is a molecule? How do you know?

The Gas Laws

Does it seem strange that some of the earliest experiments were done on gases? Most gases are, after all, invisible. How did these early scientists even know they were there?

One of the most important characteristics that a scientist possesses is curiosity. If you hold a glass upside down and push it into a container of water, what happens? If you are a curious person, you might begin to wonder what is in the glass that won't allow the water to enter.

Robert Boyle was very curious about nature. The relationship between pressure and volume that you know as Boyle's law was first published in 1662. But Boyle didn't spend his life working with gases. He went on to study blood circulation, water expansion, color, electricity, the bending of light in transparent objects, as well as the way sound travels in air.

But a scientist doesn't always spend his time doing fancy experiments. Jacques Charles, a French physicist, was another scientist who was interested in how and why things happened. When the French Academy of Science, where Charles worked, decided to experiment with balloon flight, Jacques Charles was given the job of making the hydrogen gas and filling the balloon. He was so fascinated by the idea that, within a month of the first flight, Charles and his brother built their own balloon and flew for 90 minutes. Charles took along several scientific instruments, but managed to show only that air pressure decreased as the balloon rose.

Even though his interest and research in the behavior of gases continued, Charles never published his experiments. However, he explained them to the French chemist, Joseph Gay-Lussac. Gay-Lussac repeated the experiments and published the results in 1802. For this reason, Charles' law is sometimes called Gay-Lussac's law. Gay-Lussac also published results on the pressure-temperature relationship of a gas when the volume is constant. This law completes the circle of laws relating pressure, volume, and temperature of gases.

What Do You Think?

If you were doing an experiment and something unexpected happened, would you just assume you'd done something wrong or would you try to figure out why the unexpected occurred? Why is curiosity an important quality for a scientist to possess?

Breathing Underwater

![Health CONNECTION]

U nlike fish, a person's body has no way to draw oxygen from water. We must take our environment with us when we travel in the depths of the oceans or the vacuum of space. As you know, the pressure on your body due to the mass of air around you is one atmosphere. This is as if a weight of almost 15 pounds is pressing on every square inch of your body. Underwater, the pressure increases due to the added mass of water above you. Every 10 meters adds 1 atmosphere pressure. At a depth of 30 meters, the total pressure on your body would be 4 atm. That's nearly 60 pounds of pressure per square inch!

Pushing Back

The muscles controlling your lungs and diaphragm evolved to work in 1 atm pressure. At a depth of 40 meters, the pressure on your chest would make it impossible to inflate your lungs to breathe, even if you had a supply of air available. In 1943, Jacques-Yves Cousteau and Emile Gagnan invented the SCUBA (Self-Contained Underwater Breathing Apparatus). SCUBA equipment provides air to the lungs at a pressure that matches the underwater environment. Therefore, you can breathe comfortably.

If the pressure in your lungs is increased to match the outside pressure, what happens when you swim toward the surface? Boyle's law tells us that if the amount of a gas remains constant, as the pressure decreases, volume increases. If you went from an outside pressure of 5 atm to a pressure of 1 atm without exhaling, the air would expand to five times

the volume, certainly enough to rupture your lungs.

The Bends

When you breathe air under increased pressure for 30 minutes or longer, more nitrogen from the air dissolves in your blood than normal. As you move up to the surface, the nitrogen becomes less soluble and comes out of your blood as bubbles. This is much like what happens when you release the cap from a soda bottle and you see bubbles of carbon dioxide gas rising in the liquid.

If you rise to the surface too quickly, these bubbles of nitrogen form in joints and muscles and cause pain. If they form in the spinal cord, brain, or lungs, they can cause death. This effect is called "the bends" or decompression sickness. If a diver rises slowly, decreasing the pressure gradually, the nitrogen can be released through the lungs.

What Do You Think?

If SCUBA equipment can provide air at a pressure equal to that underwater, why do people still have to use enclosed diving vessels at depths below 100 m?

Leisure Connection

Cooking Under Pressure

Sometimes, foods are cooked by boiling them in water. The time it takes for them to cook varies depending on factors such as the temperature of the boiling water. But water does not always boil at the same temperature.

The temperature at which water boils depends on the pressure surrounding the water. As the molecules in the air bounce against the surface of the liquid, they exert pressure. The water molecules throughout the liquid must have enough energy to overcome that pressure before they change state from liquid to gas.

Air pressure varies inversely with altitude—that is, the greater the altitude, the less the pressure. For example, the air pressure in Miami, which is very near sea level, is greater than the pressure in Denver, the mile-

high city. Therefore, water boils at a slightly higher temperature in Miami than in Denver.

And so, a cook in Denver must increase cooking times for everything from boiled eggs to baked cakes.

What Do You Think?

A pressure cooker, like the one pictured here, increases the pressure in the pot. What do you think that does to the temperature at which water boils? Will foods cook more quickly or more slowly in a pressure cooker?

Technology Connection

What Is a Vacuum?

Vacuum cleaners, vacuum-sealed containers, vacuum-packed foods—just what is a vacuum?

A vacuum is a space that has no matter in it. There is no such thing as a complete vacuum because no one has ever been able to remove all the air molecules within a given space. Even in the near-vacuum of outer space, it is estimated that there are about 100 molecules of matter in every cubic meter of space.

Why would anyone want to create a vacuum in the first place? Have you ever used a straw to drink from a glass or can? When you draw on the straw, you remove some of the air inside the straw. This produces a lower pressure inside the straw than in the air outside—a partial vacuum. The greater air pressure of the air on the surface of the liquid pushes the liquid up the straw.

How else are partial vacuums used? A vacuum conducts heat poorly, so it's a good insulator. This property is used in devices such as insulating bottles. These bottles contain a double-walled glass container that has had the air removed from between the walls. Thermal energy can't pass through this space from either direction, so the liquid inside stays hot or cold.

You may recall when you studied sound that sound is a result of vibrations of molecules. Because there are no molecules—or atoms—in a vacuum, it does not conduct sound.

Light bulbs contain a partial vacuum and nitrogen or argon gas, which is why a light bulb will pop when it breaks. Since there is little oxygen in the light bulb, the burning filament lasts longer than it would if surrounded by air. You will learn more about this in a later chapter.

One of your favorite uses for a vacuum may be the television. The television tube works because there are very few air molecules in the tube. The beam inside the television tube would never get to the screen if it had to travel through air molecules.

You Try It!

Roll a wax-coated paper straw between your fingers a few times to remove the stiffness. Be sure to leave the straw open. Now press your finger tightly over one end so that no air can enter. Put the other end of the straw in your mouth and suck on it. What happens? Why did this happen?

Review the statements below about the big ideas presented in this chapter, and try to answer the questions. Then, re-read your answers to the Did You Ever Wonder questions at the beginning of the chapter. *In your Journal,* write a paragraph about how your understanding of the big ideas in the chapter has changed.

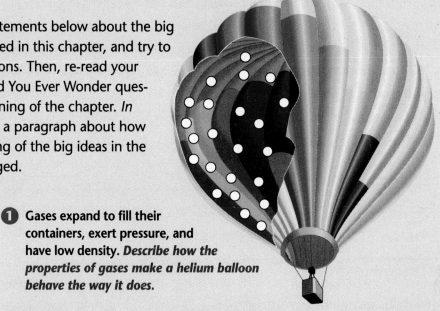

1 Gases expand to fill their containers, exert pressure, and have low density. *Describe how the properties of gases make a helium balloon behave the way it does.*

1P

2P

3P

3.0 liters
25°C

1.5 liters
25°C

1 liter
25°C

2 The temperature, volume, pressure, and amount of a gas are all related. As one changes, so do the others. *Describe how the temperature, volume, amount, and pressure of a gas change as you pump up a bicycle tire.*

3 Elements are made up of particles called atoms. Compounds are made up of atoms that are chemically combined. *What characteristics of gases prove that they are made of particles?*

4 The atomic theory states that matter consists of atoms, all atoms of an element are identical, and different elements have different atoms. *Why is the ratio of masses of elements in a compound always the same?*

Pressure constant

T = temperature

1 liter
T

2.0 liters
2T

3.0 liters
3T

Using Key Science Terms

atom   Boyle's law
atomic theory of matter   Charles' law

In your own words, explain:
1. an atom
2. the atomic theory of matter
3. Boyle's law
4. Charles' law

Understanding Ideas

Answer the following questions in your Journal *using complete sentences.*

1. Suppose you blow up a brown paper lunch bag, you hit it hard, and it explodes. Use what you have learned in this chapter to explain why the bag exploded.
2. How much pressure increase is required to cut the volume of a gas in a balloon to one-third of the original? How much would the pressure of a gas change if its volume were four times greater?
3. What part(s) of the atomic theory of matter help(s) explain why the airship that takes overhead pictures of football games stays inflated?

Developing Skills

Use your understanding of the concepts developed in this chapter to answer each of the following questions.

1. **Recognizing Cause and Effect** Repeat the Explore activity on page 426 with the experimenter using a small hand-held fan to direct the odor toward one group of

students. How do these results compare with the results taken when the air in the classroom was as still as possible?

2. **Concept Mapping** Complete the concept map of gases.

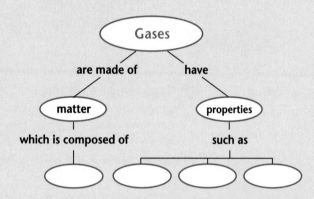

3. **Separating and Controlling Variables** Repeat the Investigate on pages 430-431 without waiting between trials. Which variable have you changed? How do these results compare with the results taken after waiting between trials?
4. **Observing and Inferring** Repeat the Explore activity on page 437, placing the flashlight over very hot water. What happens to the movement of the dust specks you see in the beam of light?

Critical Thinking

In your Journal, *answer each of the following questions.*

1. You have a weak spot in the wall of your bicycle tire. Is your tire more likely to tear on a hot day or a cold day?
2. Compare the piece of bread and the piece of volcanic rock shown in the picture. How may their formations have been similar?

3. The pressure on a gas in a closed container was increased. What can you say about the volume of the gas?

4. You are taking a bouquet of inflated balloons to a friend in the hospital on a winter day with the air temperature near freezing. You blew the balloons up in your house, but by the time you got to the hospital, they appeared shriveled and smaller. Why did this happen? What will happen when you take the balloons into the hospital?

Problem Solving

Read the following problem and discuss your answer in a brief paragraph.

Juan and Sam were camping and a rainstorm during the night got their tent bottom wet. The next day was warm and bright, so Sam left his inflatable air mattress in the sun to dry while they went hiking. When they returned, the mattress had a jagged hole in it and all the air was gone.

Sam thought that an animal had ripped the mattress. How did Juan explain what happened using what he learned in this chapter?

CONNECTING IDEAS

Discuss each of the following in a brief paragraph.

1. **Theme—Systems and Interactions** On TV, the weather map shows a large air mass moving into your area. Its volume is increasing, but its pressure is staying the same. What is happening to its temperature?

2. **Theme—Energy** Explain how gas from digesting food in the intestines can cause a stomachache.

3. **Earth Science Connection** How do aerostats help scientists learn about gases in the atmosphere?

4. **Leisure Connection** Describe how cooking with a pressure cooker might speed up the process of cooking.

5. **Technology Connection** Describe how you are able to drink liquids through a straw.

CHAPTER 15

THE AIR AROUND YOU

Did you ever wonder...

✓ **What the air is made of?**

✓ **Where Earth's air ends and outer space begins?**

✓ **Why the wind blows?**

Before you begin to study the air around you, think about these questions and answer them *in your Journal*. When you finish the chapter, compare your Journal entry with what you've learned.

A rainbow of colors soars overhead. This is a balloon meet. It's your first, and you're quite excited.

"How do they stay afloat?" you wonder. "How can they turn or go up and down without any machinery or wings?"

You remember that last weekend the meet was scheduled but called off because of very high winds. Earlier today, you overheard two of the balloon pilots saying that the air was perfect for a great flight.

You know it's air that enables a balloon to soar through the sky. What properties of air can support the weight of the balloon and the pilot? What properties of air cause the balloon to change altitude or direction?

In this chapter, you will study the properties of air that enable balloons to fly as you learn about one part of Earth, its atmosphere.

▶ *In the following activity, you'll begin your exploration of Earth's atmosphere and its properties.*

Explore! ACTIVITY

Does air have mass?

What To Do

1. Use a pan balance to determine the mass of a completely deflated ball. Record your measurement *in your Journal.*

2. Use a bicycle pump to inflate the ball to its recommended maximum pressure. Predict what you think the mass of the inflated ball is.

3. Use the pan balance to determine the mass of the air-filled ball.

4. Were there any changes in mass? If so, what were they?

5. Finally, *in your Journal,* use your observations to explain any conclusions that you make.

So This Is the Atmosphere

15-1

Section Objectives

■ Describe the composition of the atmosphere.

■ Discuss ways people affect air composition.

Key Terms

atmosphere
smog

Figure 15-1

The atmosphere is the layer of gases hundreds of kilometers thick that surrounds Earth.

What's in the Atmosphere?

It's early morning, and you're getting ready for work. Before you leave, you decide to check the weather report coming over the computer screen. The smog is bad today. Once again, you will need to wear your air-filter mask. Pollution in the atmosphere has raised the temperature, and it could reach 104°F today. You will have to wear clothes designed to keep you cool. The ozone layer is thinner than it was when you were young, so you will have to use strong sunblock lotion to protect your skin from the sun. You sigh and remember attending a balloon rally when you were a teenager. It was on a beautiful day before the atmosphere became so polluted.

Could this be your future? It's one possible future you could face. Your life depends on the air you breathe and the condition of the atmosphere in which you live. The **atmosphere** is the layer of gases hundreds of kilometers thick that surrounds Earth.

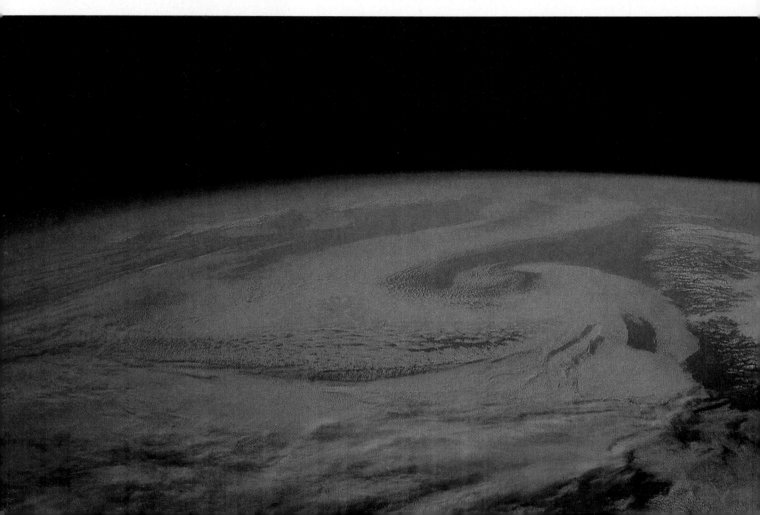

When you think of the atmosphere, you probably think about oxygen, wind, or the air you inhale or exhale. Yet the atmosphere contains more than just gases.

You may be surprised to learn that you breathe in more than you think! What's in the air other than the gases you need to stay alive? Let's find out.

Find Out! ACTIVITY

What solids are in the air around you?

What To Do

1. Smear thin layers of petroleum jelly onto four plastic lids.
2. Place the lids in four outdoor locations around your home and school.
3. After one week, collect the lids. Be sure to mark each one to indicate the location from which it came.
4. Examine each lid with a magnifying glass. *In your Journal,* record the materials you can identify.
5. Sort the solids—large pieces of dust, plant pieces, seeds, insect parts, and so on—taken from each sample site.
6. Place the materials on microscope slides and examine each slide with a microscope.

Conclude and Apply

1. Which of the solids collected could have been a result of human activity?
2. If you collected seeds, do any of them suggest how some plants disperse their seeds?
3. Do you think any of the materials might be harmful to people? Explain your answer. (HINT: Think about people you may know who have allergies.)

From the activity, you may have discovered that some things are more abundant than others in the air. Together, gases, solids, and liquids make up the atmosphere we live in. Each time you take a breath, you breathe in a mixture of these substances. Yet, you're probably most concerned with the oxygen component of Earth's atmosphere. After all, you know that you need oxygen to stay alive. But how much of the air is made of oxygen? It may be less than you think. Other important gas components found in the atmosphere include nitrogen, methane, and carbon dioxide. In the following Investigate, you'll find the answer.

How Much Oxygen Is in the Air?

Steel wool, which is mostly iron, reacts with the oxygen in air. The steel wool will combine with oxygen in a test tube to form rust. This reaction will continue until all of the oxygen has been used. In this activity, you will determine how much oxygen was used, and calculate the percentage of oxygen in the air.

Problem

How can the amount of oxygen in the air be measured?

Safety Precautions

Materials

measuring cup with mL gradations	2 pencils	test-tube clamp	2 rubber bands
	tongs	test tube	metric ruler
	white vinegar	paper towels	beaker
scissors	test-tube stand	water	steel wool

What To Do

1. Copy the data table *into your Journal.* Then, measure the length of the test tube in millimeters, and record it *in your Journal* as well.

2. Mix 30 mL white vinegar with 20 mL of water in the beaker.

3. Unroll a bale of steel wool. Cut a strip that is 2 cm wide and 20 cm long. Soak the steel wool in the vinegar solution for 1 minute (see photo **A**).

4. Using tongs, remove the steel wool from the vinegar solution. Use the tongs to stretch out the strip of steel wool, and dry it thoroughly between two paper towels.

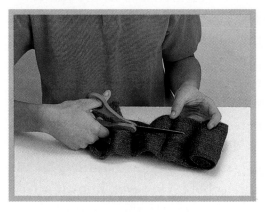

A

B

5 Pour out the vinegar solution, rinse the beaker, and fill it about 2/3 full of water.

6 Using two pencils, push the steel wool into the bottom 2/3 of the test tube, keeping it as loose as possible (see photo **B**).

7 Use rubber bands to attach the ruler to the test tube. Position the tube such that its open end is at about the 0 mm mark.

8 Turn over the test tube and ruler and insert it into the beaker so the opening of the tube is just below the surface of the water. Then, attach the tube to the stand, using the clamp. Readjust the ruler so that the 0 mm mark is at the water line.

9 Observe and record the level of the water in the test tube, in millimeters, every 2 minutes until the water level stops changing.

Data and Observations

Time Elapsed (Minutes)	Water Level (mm)
2	
4	
6	
8	

Analyzing

1. Use this formula to calculate the percentage of oxygen in the air.

$$\frac{\text{final water level (mm)}}{\text{tube length (mm)}} \times 100 = \% \text{ oxygen}$$

2. About what percentage of the air in the test tube was oxygen?

Concluding and Applying

3. Why was it important to stretch the steel wool and pack it loosely before inserting it in the water?

4. Based on your observation, do you think the air is mostly oxygen?

5. ~~Going Further~~ What do you predict will happen to the steel wool after you remove it from the test tube and expose it to air?

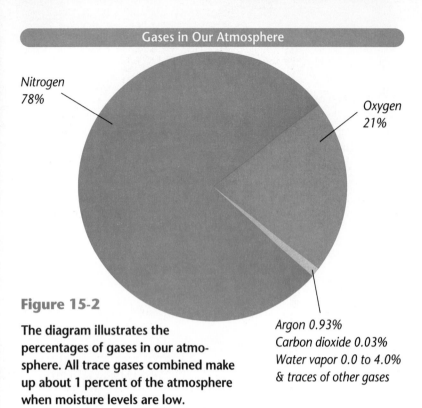

Gases in Our Atmosphere

Nitrogen 78%

Oxygen 21%

Argon 0.93%
Carbon dioxide 0.03%
Water vapor 0.0 to 4.0%
& traces of other gases

Figure 15-2

The diagram illustrates the percentages of gases in our atmosphere. All trace gases combined make up about 1 percent of the atmosphere when moisture levels are low.

From the Investigate activity, you found that oxygen makes up about 20 percent of the gases in the test tube. The gases in the tube are the same as the gases in the atmosphere. Therefore, you've shown that the atmosphere is only about 20 percent oxygen. What gases make up the other 80 percent?

Figure 15-2 shows the percentages of gases that occur naturally in the atmosphere. However, human activities can increase the amount of certain gases while decreasing others.

Burning fossil fuels releases gases into the atmosphere. Sulfur dioxide and nitrous oxides are among them. When these gases build up in the

Life Science CONNECTION

Smog and Our Health

Athletes who train in big cities have to get up early—often before 5 A.M.—for their daily run. Later on, smog levels are too high. Breathing in dirty air during such strenuous activity would be dangerous for the athletes' bodies, as smog is harmful to the heart as well as the lungs.

Too Much Ozone

What exactly makes the air dirty? Two of the worst gases we can breathe in are ozone and carbon monoxide. The ozone layer high up in the atmosphere is crucial to our existence. Ozone, formed from pollutants released into the air we breathe, is a serious pollutant. Breathing in ozone is irritating, causing a burning sensation in your nose and throat. It can give you a headache, make your eyes sting and, if levels are high enough, blur your vision. Ozone can also damage lung tissue, reducing your ability to fight infection, and lead to diseases like pneumonia, chest colds, and bronchitis.

atmosphere, they can result in smog. **Smog** is a type of air pollution that is visible as a smokelike haze. Breathing smog is unhealthy for everyone. Smog can irritate your eyes and damage the tissues of your lungs, making them more susceptible to disease. Smog is also harmful to plants, because it prevents plants from absorbing the carbon dioxide they need.

check your UNDERSTANDING

1. Which gas in the atmosphere is most important to people? Why?
2. Why can driving a car be harmful to the atmosphere?
3. **Apply** Why do you think smog is more likely to form over cities than rural areas?

Cars and Smog

Carbon monoxide, a gas produced when gasoline is burned in a car engine, is absorbed by red blood cells when we breathe in. Red blood cells are supposed to be absorbing oxygen, and are less efficient at this when carbon monoxide gets in the way, so the body receives less oxygen than it needs. Decreased oxygen levels can cause heart trouble and chest pains. This is why, on days when pollution levels are extremely high, the elderly, young children, and people with heart or chest problems are warned to stay indoors and rest.

Low levels of oxygen in the brain can impair coordination

and motor functions. When we exercise, we need even more oxygen than usual to keep our bodies functioning. That's why it's dangerous to exercise when smog levels are high.

You Try It!

There are lots of stories on TV and in the newspapers about pollution. Using newspapers and other resources, find out which areas in the United States are most severely affected by smog.

Structure of the Atmosphere

15-2

Section Objectives

- Describe the structure of Earth's atmosphere.
- Explain what causes atmospheric pressure.

Key Terms

troposphere
ozone

Figure 15-3

All of the clouds, from fluffy, white puffs to gray sheets of storm clouds, appear in the troposphere.

Layers of the Atmosphere

Return for a moment to your future. After breakfast, you leave your home to travel downtown. As you wait with others for public transportation, you join in a discussion about the atmosphere's ozone. An outer layer of ozone shields Earth's life-forms from the sun's harmful rays. You recall that the loss of ozone protection was already a concern when you were a child. Air pollution from human activities in the last half of the 1900s was at the heart of the concern. But what exactly is the ozone and where is it found in the atmosphere?

The atmosphere changes as you move away from Earth's surface. Some layers contain gases that easily absorb energy from the sun, while others do not. As a result, some layers are warmer than others. Based on the temperature differences, we can divide the atmosphere into five layers.

■ Troposphere

You live in the **troposphere**, the layer closest to the ground. The troposphere contains 75 percent of all the gases in the atmosphere as well as dust, ice, and liquid water. Raging thunderstorms, sizzling heat, numbing cold, and all other kinds of weather occur in this layer.

■ Stratosphere

Just above the troposphere is the stratosphere. It is within the stratosphere that the ozone layer is found. Use **Figure 15-4** to locate the ozone layer in the atmosphere. About how far above Earth's surface does it lie? **Ozone** is a gas that absorbs some of the harmful radiation from the sun. As a layer in the atmosphere, ozone acts much like a filter. The ozone layer filters many of the sun's harmful rays, keeping them from reaching the troposphere. Thinning areas and holes in the ozone layer let harmful rays pass on through.

■ Mesosphere and Thermosphere

Beyond the stratosphere are the mesosphere, the thermosphere, and the exosphere. The mesosphere and the thermosphere are useful for radio transmission. The exosphere is the uppermost part of Earth's atmosphere. Beyond it is outer space. Unlike states or countries with defined boundaries, the upper part of the atmosphere has no special ending point. The air just becomes less and less dense until there is no air at all. Where there is no atmosphere at all, outer space begins.

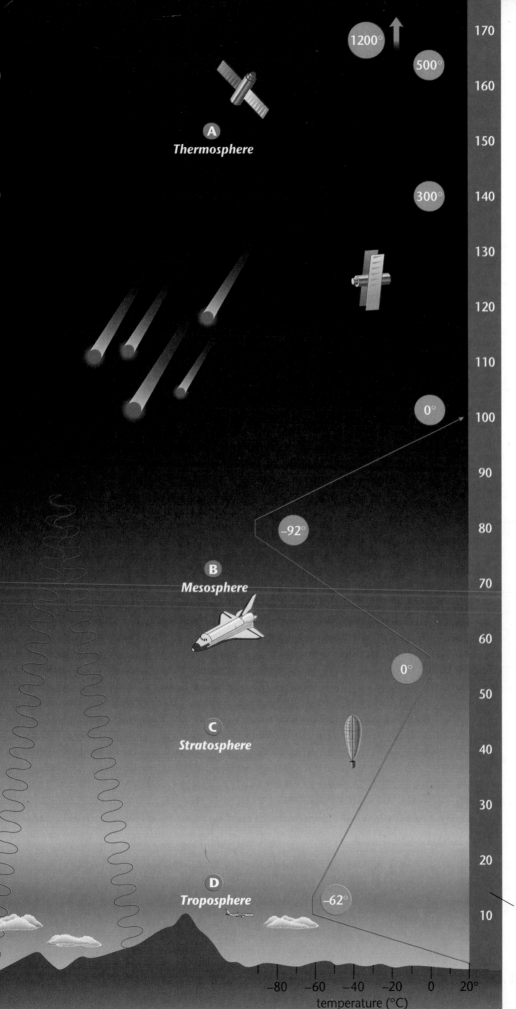

Figure 15-4

The division of Earth's atmosphere into layers is based on temperature differences.

A *Thermosphere* Only a small portion of the thermosphere is shown. This layer extends beyond 500 km in altitude. Beyond the thermosphere is the exosphere, and beyond that is outer space. Temperatures in the thermosphere and exosphere increase rapidly, and may reach 1200° C.

B *Mesosphere* Obstacles on the Earth's surface block radio waves and make long distance transmission at this level impossible. The solution has been to transmit in the obstacle-free mesosphere. The boundary between the mesosphere and thermosphere, called the ionosphere, reflects radio waves back to Earth's surface.

C *Stratosphere* Earth's protective layer of ozone lies within the stratosphere. Weather balloons are flown here and some high-flying jet aircraft travel within the lower stratosphere.

D *Troposphere* The troposphere is the lowest layer of Earth's atmosphere. This is the layer in which we live. It is here where clouds form and weather occurs.

Altitude (km)

Atmospheric Pressure

Why do you suppose clouds are found only near Earth's surface, in the troposphere? Clouds are made of water, which has mass. You know that gravity pulls anything with mass toward Earth's surface. So, you would expect to find most of the water near Earth, rather than in the mesosphere or thermosphere.

In the Explore activity on page 455, you discovered that air also has mass. Earth's gravity pulls the air toward the ground the same as it does water, a stone, or you. Air has weight too, and this weight causes air molecules to push together, producing pressure on each other. We call this air pressure.

Explore! ACTIVITY

Is atmospheric pressure the same in all layers of the atmosphere?

What To Do

1. Use four textbooks to represent layers of the atmosphere.
2. Place a ball of clay on your desk.
3. Place a piece of waxed paper over the clay and a book on top of the waxed paper.
4. Alternate balls of clay, waxed paper, and books until you have a pile of all four books.
5. One by one, remove the books. Note the appearance of the clay.
6. What differences do you see in the four lumps of clay?
7. How would you account for these differences?

Think of your desktop as Earth's surface. The closer the air was to the surface, the more compressed the air became under the weight of the layers pushing down from above. On Earth, air pressure tends to be greatest at sea level. There is more air pressing down from above at sea level than on a mountaintop.

Air pressure doesn't change only if you go up or down in altitude. It can change from hour to hour, right where you live.

You've probably heard weather forecasters use the terms "high-pressure system" or "low-pressure system." You've seen these marked on weather maps as "H" or "L."

Figure 15-5

Scientists and weather forecasters use a type of barometer called an aneroid barograph to measure and record changes in air pressure. A change in air pressure usually indicates a coming change in weather, as seen in the bottom left photo. By analyzing the changes in air pressure, weather forecasters can predict what the weather will be.

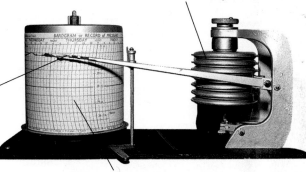

A The measuring part of an aneroid barograph (a type of barometer) is a metal chamber from which almost all of the air has been removed. When air pressure goes up, the chamber contracts. When air pressure goes down, the chamber expands.

B Levers transfer the movement of the chamber to a pen—the recording part of the instrument. The pen moves up and down as the chamber moves in and out.

C The pen's up-and-down movements draw a line on a paper attached to a very slowly turning cylinder. One complete turn of the cylinder might record pressure changes for a week.

The "L" marks the center of a large mass of air with low pressure. Often, a low-pressure system moving into your area means clouds, precipitation, and storms. A high pressure system often means clear weather.

But how do the weather forecasters on television know whether the air pressure is going up or down? As you can see in the figure above, an instrument called a barometer can be used to measure air pressure. The activity on pages 466-467 will help you understand how a barometer works.

check your UNDERSTANDING

1. Tell which layer has each of these characteristics—(a) a raging thunderstorm, (b) a blurred boundary with outer space, (c) a protective ozone layer.

2. What is the pushing together of air molecules?

3. **Apply** Would you expect air pressure to be greater in the thermosphere than in the stratosphere? Why?

The Ups and Downs of Weather

Right now, as you're reading these words, you're experiencing pressure! Air is pressing on you from all sides. Do you think you would notice if a high- or low-pressure air mass were approaching? It's unlikely that your body is sensitive enough to detect the small changes in pressure. Can you construct an instrument that could show you when the air pressure is changing?

Problem

How can a barometer measure atmospheric pressure?

Materials

small coffee can	heavy paper
scissors	drinking straw
transparent tape	metric ruler
rubber band	rubber balloon

What To Do

1 Look at the materials in front of you. How can you use them to construct a barometer?

2 Do you think increasing or decreasing air pressure could cause the metal can to compress or expand? Are changes in air pressure that great?

3 How might a balloon stretched over the can make a more sensitive instrument? (See photo **A**.)

4 You'll need a way to know whether the can and balloon are expanding or compressing with changes in air pressure. Make a gauge to observe this. (See photo **B**.)

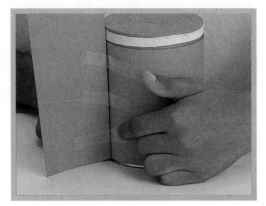

A   **B**

5 Be sure to trim the end of the straw so that it comes to a point.

6 After you've attached the straw to the balloon, place a mark on the paper gauge at the level of the point of the straw.

7 Write "High" above the mark on your paper gauge and "Low" below it.

8 Check that your straw is free to move up and down along the gauge. Make sure you haven't taped it to the gauge. If the straw rubs on the gauge, reposition it.

9 Place your barometer where it can remain undisturbed for two weeks. Observe and measure how far the straw moves from the mark each day. Keep a record of its movements and of the weather conditions each day.

Analyzing

1. Explain how your barometer works.

2. If the atmospheric pressure changed in your area over the week, what was the weather like on the days when it changed?

3. What was the reading on your barometer when the weather was good compared to when the weather was bad?

Concluding and Applying

4. Hypothesize what you might record if your barometer were placed on a mountaintop. What type of readings would you expect in the stratosphere? Why?

5. Going Further Would you predict that the air pressure would be greater at sea level or on a mountaintop if both places had the same air temperature? Why?

15-3

The Air and the Sun

Section Objectives

■ Explain what causes wind.

■ Describe Earth's wind systems.

Key Terms

trade winds
prevailing westerlies

Energy from the Sun

The future workday ends, and you return to your home. You place your dinner in the microwave oven. While waiting for your dinner to cook, you flick on the news scanner and request to see the news about the planetary atmospheric program. The space agency runs the program that is studying the atmospheres of Venus and Mars. The scientists hope to find solutions to Earth's atmospheric problems through the study. The atmosphere on Mars is too thin to support life. As **Figure 15-6** shows, Mars can't hold much of the energy that radiates from the sun. As a result, Mars is a very cold, lifeless planet. Venus is a very hot, lifeless planet. Its atmosphere is so dense that most of the energy coming from the sun changes to heat, is trapped in the atmosphere, and can't escape. On Earth, there's a delicate balance between the amount of radiation that's trapped and the amount that escapes.

Earth's atmosphere and the sun interact to provide an environment that can support life. How do they do this? The sun is the source of most energy on Earth. Energy is transferred from the sun to Earth and heat is transferred from one part of Earth to another.

Figure 15-6

The sun radiates energy to the planets revolving around it. How that radiated energy affects a specific planet depends on that planet's atmosphere.

Ⓐ Most radiation entering Venus's atmosphere is trapped by thick gases and clouds.

You may recall that there are three ways to transfer heat from one object to another—radiation, conduction, and convection. These three processes are also at work in the atmosphere.

■ Heat Transfer Through Radiation

Radiation from the sun travels through space on its way to Earth. As you can see in **Figure 15-7**, some of this radiation is reflected back out into space. However, about 70 percent of it is absorbed.

The radiation from the sun is trapped in Earth's atmosphere in much the same way as heat is trapped in a greenhouse. You can demonstrate this warming effect by doing the next Explore activity.

Figure 15-7

Ⓐ The sun is the source of most energy on Earth.

Ⓑ Three different things happen to the energy Earth receives from the sun. Some energy is reflected back into space, some is absorbed by the atmosphere, and some is absorbed by land and water surfaces.

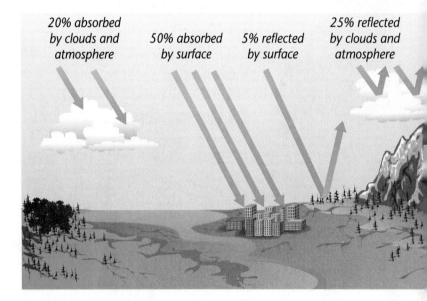

20% absorbed by clouds and atmosphere

50% absorbed by surface

5% reflected by surface

25% reflected by clouds and atmosphere

Ⓑ Earth's atmosphere creates a delicate balance between energy received and energy lost.

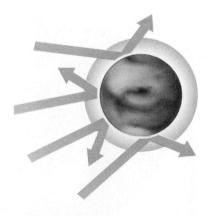

Ⓒ On Mars, a thin atmosphere allows much radiation to escape.

How does a greenhouse trap heat?

To demonstrate how heat is trapped in Earth's atmosphere, you will need a clear plastic storage box and lid.

What To Do

1. Fill the bottom of the storage box with about 3 cm of soil.

2. Insert a stiff piece of cardboard into the soil at about half the length of the box.

3. Use the cardboard as a prop for a thermometer. The bulb of the thermometer should be facing up.

4. Overhead, about 30 cm from the box, place a heat lamp.

5. Do not cover the box with the lid. Turn on the heat lamp and wait 10 minutes.

6. Turn off the heat lamp and read the thermometer. Record the temperature *in your Journal.*

7. Allow the box to return to room temperature. Then, put the lid on it.

8. Turn on the heat lamp and once again wait 10 minutes.

9. Turn off the heat lamp and read the thermometer again. Record the temperature. In which situation was the temperature higher?

Global Warming and the Greenhouse Effect

The greenhouse effect, or the trapping of heat by our atmosphere, has become a serious environmental concern. Some people fear that average temperatures on Earth are rising at an abnormal rate.

It's normal for Earth's average temperatures to rise and fall over time. However, some believe that humans may be rapidly changing the temperatures. Such global warming might melt enough of the polar ice to raise sea levels everywhere. Weather patterns also might shift.

A Greenhouse Without the Green

Carbon dioxide is one of the main gases that causes the greenhouse effect. Pollution caused by human activities adds carbon dioxide to the atmosphere. The worldwide loss of trees and plants has an effect because trees and plants remove carbon dioxide from the air and give off oxygen. Destruction of forest lands has a double impact—less carbon dioxide is taken out of the

Giant tree-fern from the Atlantic rain forest in southern Brazil

■ Conduction Transfer

Heat is also transferred from Earth's surface to the atmosphere by conduction. Conduction is the transfer of heat through a material from a higher temperature to a lower temperature. Have you ever left a metal spoon in a hot pan? If you have, you know that the spoon handle becomes hot. This is an example of conduction.

The atmosphere is not a good conductor of heat. Only air that directly touches hot surfaces, like a hot road, becomes heated by conduction. As the air moves over Earth's surface, it picks up heat from the surface.

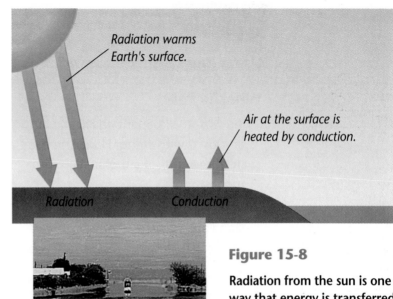

Radiation warms Earth's surface.

Air at the surface is heated by conduction.

Radiation   Conduction

Figure 15-8

Radiation from the sun is one way that energy is transferred to Earth's atmosphere. Heat is also transferred from Earth's surface to the atmosphere by conduction.

---

atmosphere, and more is put into the atmosphere when the forests are burned.

Although global warming is not completely understood, many people feel we should take action to slow it down. What ways can you think of to reduce levels of carbon dioxide?

What Do You Think?

What would happen if global warming were to continue? Would our planet come to resemble another nearby planet of our solar system? Which one?

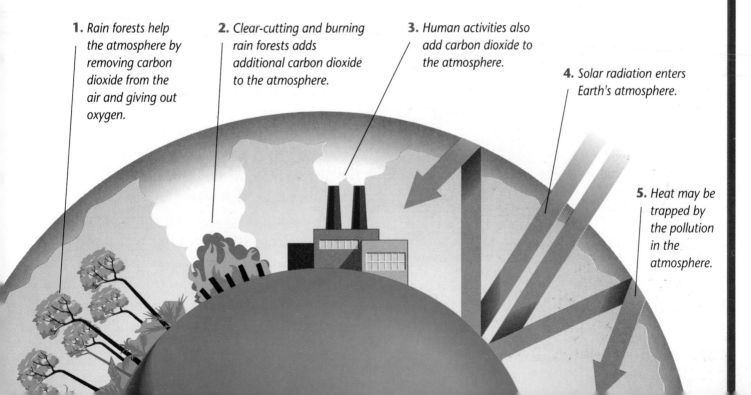

1. Rain forests help the atmosphere by removing carbon dioxide from the air and giving out oxygen.

2. Clear-cutting and burning rain forests adds additional carbon dioxide to the atmosphere.

3. Human activities also add carbon dioxide to the atmosphere.

4. Solar radiation enters Earth's atmosphere.

5. Heat may be trapped by the pollution in the atmosphere.

Find Out! ACTIVITY

Why does hot air move?

What To Do

1. Tie two small paper bags filled with air closed with string. Hang the bags from the ends of a meter stick with more string.

2. Suspend the meter stick on a ring stand and adjust the strings and meter stick until the meter stick is balanced.

3. Place a lamp with a 100-watt bulb below one of the bags. **CAUTION:** *Make sure the bulb is at least 25 cm from the bag so that it does not catch on fire.*

4. Stand back about 1 meter from the bags. Remain very still as you observe what happens. Try not to stir up any air currents.

Conclude and Apply

1. What happened to the suspended bags?

2. Explain the purpose of the lamp in this experiment.

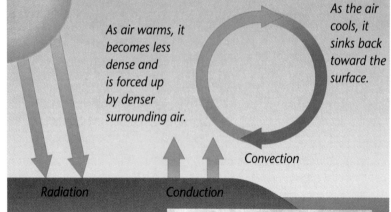

As air warms, it becomes less dense and is forced up by denser surrounding air.

As the air cools, it sinks back toward the surface.

Convection

Radiation   Conduction

Figure 15-9

This up-and-down cycle sets up a convection current of moving air as seen in the photo on the right. What do we call such movement of air?

■ Convection Transfer

When the air inside the bag over the lamp was heated, it became less dense and had less air pressure than the surrounding room air. The pressure in the room air pushed the heated bag upward. As a result, the meter stick tilted. Convection causes movement of air masses in the atmosphere in a similar manner. Convection is the transfer of heat by the movement of an air mass from one place to another. Warm air in the atmosphere is less dense and has less air pressure than cooler air. The cooler, denser air forces the warmer air upward. In the atmosphere, as the warm air is forced upward, it begins to cool and becomes more dense. It can then sink back down to the surface where the newly warmed air is being forced upward. This up-and-down cycle sets up a convection current of moving air we call wind.

Global Winds

Look at how the sun's radiation strikes different places on Earth, shown in **Figure 15-10**. Where are the sun's rays more direct, at the North Pole or at the equator? Because the equator receives so much solar radiation, it is usually warmer than any other place. The unequal heating of places all over Earth results in large, global wind systems. The trade winds and the prevailing westerlies are examples of wind systems that can have a great effect on global climate.

■ Trade Winds

Hotter air over the equatorial area rises and creates low pressure. Staying aloft, the heated air moves toward the poles. Cooler air from the polar regions moves toward the low pressure at the equator. The winds caused by the air sinking and returning to the equator are called **trade winds**.

The trade winds are warm and steady. In the Northern Hemisphere, early ship captains were able to use these winds to help them sail southwest and to explore the Americas. In the Southern Hemisphere, the trade winds would help a sailing ship glide northwest. Even today, airplane pilots use the trade winds to help save fuel. If you travel from Miami, Florida, to Ecuador in a jet, the pilot might ride the trade winds to increase the plane's speed and save fuel.

Figure 15-10

(A) Near the poles, the sun's rays are spread out more than at the equator. So, equal amounts of energy don't heat equally—each square meter of land at the poles receives less energy than each square meter at the equator.

The same amount of energy from the sun must heat a larger area in northern Europe than in central Africa.

Energy from the sun in central Africa is concentrated on a small area.

Equator

(B) Whether near the poles or near the equator, humans have adapted to living in regions where temperatures vary as a result of large global wind systems.

473

■ Prevailing Westerlies

Earth's rotation on its axis affects other air movements. Some of the warm air traveling away from the equator does not cool enough to sink back to the surface. It continues to move toward the North and South poles. At the same time, cold, polar air is moving along the surface of the land toward the equator. Earth's rotation prevents either one of these masses from moving in a straight southerly or northerly direction.

The rotation of Earth deflects air from its north or south path. Between 30° and 60° latitude, the wind is deflected to the east. In the northern hemisphere, it appears to move from a southwestern to a northeastern direction. The winds between 30° and 60° latitude are called the **prevailing westerlies**. The northern prevailing westerlies are responsible for much of the weather movement in the United States and Canada.

■ Local Winds

Within the global patterns, smaller wind systems also exist. Whether you enjoy a bright, sunny day or a cold, rainy one often depends on the wind systems in your local area.

Do you live by a large lake or the sea? If you do, you have probably enjoyed days and nights at the beach. Have you ever noticed that during the daytime a cool breeze seems to blow gently toward the land from the water? Then at nighttime, the cooling breeze blows from the land toward

Figure 15-11

Cold air sinks as the warm air is forced upward, creating trade winds.

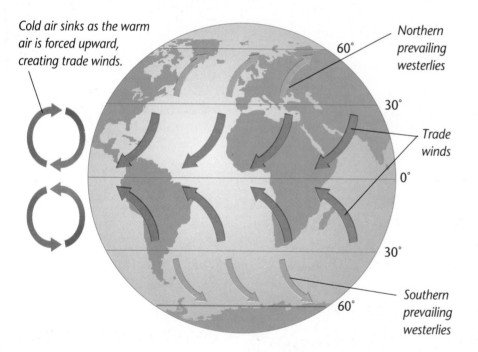

Northern prevailing westerlies

60°

30°

Trade winds

0°

30°

60°

Southern prevailing westerlies

A Warmer air over the equatorial area is less dense and is forced upward, creating low pressure. The warmer air moves toward the poles.

B Cooler air from the polar regions sinks and moves toward the lower pressure at the equator. The air sinking and returning to the equator creates the trade winds.

The northern prevailing westerlies are responsible for much of the weather movement in the United States and Canada.

Airplane pilots often tap into the energy of the trade winds. If you travel from Miami, Florida, to Ecuador in a jet, the pilot might ride the trade winds to increase the plane's speed and save fuel.

Figure 15-12

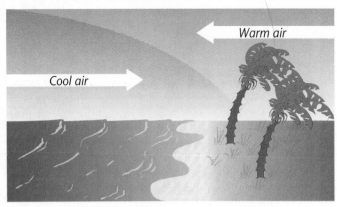

A During the daytime, the water and land absorb most of the sun's radiation. Over the land, much heat is radiated back up into the air above the land. Over the water, the air remains cool.

B Later in the day, the cool, dense air from the sea begins to move on land, forcing the warm air over the land upward. A sea breeze begins to blow from the water to the land.

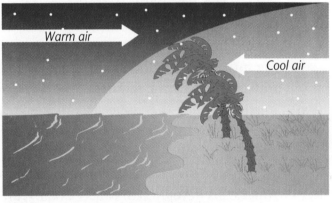

C At night, the heat that had been trapped by the water begins to escape. The air over the sea is heated. Over the land, very little heat is given off, and it is cooler than the sea.

D During the nighttime, the cool air from the land moves toward the sea, forcing the warmer air over the sea upward.

the water. Can you explain why this happens?

Land and sea breezes are only one example of the many wind patterns that can create the weather in local communities. No matter what the locality, however, the air around us makes Earth a special planet in our solar system—the only planet known to have a life-supporting atmosphere.

check your UNDERSTANDING

1. Describe three ways heat is transferred in the atmosphere.
2. Why do weather patterns tend to move from west to east across the United States? Do they move west to east all over the world?
3. **Apply** Why does a cool breeze come from the water during the day and from the land at night?

Science and Society

The Disappearing Ozone Layer

As you'll remember from reading this chapter, the ozone layer is part of the stratosphere—it lies between 10 and 50 kilometers above your head. This layer of ozone gas absorbs some of the sun's radiation that is harmful to living things. The harmful radiation that manages to pass through the ozone layer makes you tan or sunburn—and too much of it can cause skin cancer, as well as other health problems. Currently, as many as 27,000 Americans develop skin cancer every year, and as many as 6000 die from it per year.

To Tan or Not to Tan?

What would happen if something happened to the ozone layer and more of the sun's dangerous radiation reached Earth? There could be a sharp increase in rates of skin cancer in humans and other animals. People who sunbathe would have to be more careful too, as exposure could lead to a very painful sunburn, cancer, or death.

It's a frightening thought—but the ozone layer is already starting to develop holes. In 1986, scientists discovered two holes in the ozone layer—a small hole over the North Pole, and a much larger hole over Antarctica. Since that time, the holes have disappeared, then reappeared at certain times of year. No one is quite sure what's causing the holes, or why they open and close. But most scientists do agree that the holes are gradually getting bigger, and that the ozone layer has become thinner all around Earth.

Chlorofluorocarbons

One of the possible causes of the holes is a group of chemicals called chlorofluorocarbons (CFCs), which destroy ozone. CFCs are used in automobile air conditioners, in some aerosol sprays, in refrigerators, bicycle seats, foam cups, polystyrene egg cartons, and

The Nimbus 7 satellite, as seen on the next page, is used in mapping global ozone distribution.

The two views of the Northern Hemisphere show ozone distribution for February 1992 at the top and February 1993 at the bottom. The darker red indicates a higher ozone concentration.

foam packaging for fast-food containers. We used to think CFCs were ideal for consumer products—they're nonflammable, nontoxic, and decompose very slowly. CFCs enter the atmosphere when these products are manufactured and used.

CFC gases rise slowly from Earth to the ozone layer, where the sun's rays are very powerful. The CFCs break down in the intense heat and release chlorine. It is the free chlorine gas that destroys ozone.

You may have heard that some major fast-food chains converted from using foam packaging to cardboard hamburger containers, in an effort to stop using CFCs. Several countries, including the United States, have introduced laws to restrict the use of CFCs, and some manufacturers have promised to stop CFC production by the year 2000.

Many people think that despite these laws and promises, not enough is being done to get rid of CFCs. It can take up to 150 years for CFCs to decompose, and a further 15 years for the gas to rise to the stratosphere. Some scientists say that even if we stopped using CFCs today, the ozone layer would continue to thin for the next 100 years.

How Can You Help?

Sometimes, looking at a global problem makes us feel helpless because so many things are beyond our immediate control. We feel we can't change laws or influence the policies of international companies. But politicians and businesses can be affected by the way we act. If people stopped buying products containing CFCs, the companies that make them would need to find an alternative—and that process is already starting. Imagine you do some grocery shopping for your family, and you have to buy a box of eggs. If you buy eggs packed in a recycled paper container, instead of in a foam container that contains CFCs, you've made a decision that will help the environment.

What Do You Think?

What conveniences would you be willing to give up if you knew they were destroying the ozone layer?

Teens in SCIENCE

Flying High and Loving It

Have you ever let go of the string holding a helium-filled balloon? Did your balloon shoot straight up like a rocket, or did it seem to drift in the direction of the wind? Having trouble remembering? Just ask 18-year-old commercial hot-air balloon pilot, David Bair. He ought to know.

Earning His Wings

David took his first ride in a hot-air balloon at the age of four. His hometown of Albuquerque, New Mexico is host to an annual festival called the International Hot-Air Balloon Fiesta. "My family met a pilot who had no crew. We volunteered

to help out."

But not all the flights have been smooth. "Navigating is tricky. You don't steer a balloon as you would an airplane."

The Science of Flight

Why is navigating a hot-air balloon so difficult? As you know, if the temperature of a gas is increased, air molecules become more active and they begin to move away from each other. When the heat source in the balloon is turned on, air in the balloon heats up. Molecular action in

the balloon makes air in the balloon less dense than the surrounding air, and the balloon is pushed upward by the colder air. To go down, the heating source is simply turned off. Air in the balloon becomes more dense, and the balloon sinks. Balloon pilots can control the up and down movements of the balloon.

"To move side to side, you have to depend on wind currents. This past summer, I got caught in a severe wind. Even though I kept the balloon at a stable temperature, this wind current tossed my balloon at a speed of 400 feet a minute. Normally, ballooning is very safe, but weather is part of what makes ballooning so exciting."

Review the statements below about the big ideas presented in this chapter, and try to answer the questions. Then, re-read your answers to the Did You Ever Wonder questions at the beginning of the chapter. *In your Journal,* write a paragraph about how your understanding of the big ideas in the chapter has changed.

1 Three major components make up the atmosphere. *Describe these three components.*

2 The atmosphere is made up of several layers. *What are these layers and why is each important?*

3 Heat transfer occurs three ways. *How do each of these three ways affect the atmosphere?*

4 Two of the global wind systems are the trade winds and prevailing westerlies. *Where are these two wind systems located?*

CHAPTER 16

Breathing

Did you ever wonder...

✓ Why you can see your breath on a cold day?

✓ Why you breathe faster when you exercise?

✓ Why a doctor thumps on your chest when you're having an examination?

Before you begin to study the respiratory system, think about these questions and answer them *in your Journal*. When you finish the chapter, compare your Journal write-up with what you have learned.

It's a rainy day. You're relaxing by reading a magazine while your dog is asleep at your feet. As you finish a page, you become aware of a big sigh and the dog's rhythmic breathing. In and out, in and out, he breathes deeply and slowly. Occasionally, he even snores. You're aware of the dog's breathing, but he isn't. Come to think of it, most of the time you're probably not aware of your own breathing. You don't have to be. From the moment you're born until the moment you die, air enters and leaves your body automatically. You don't have to think about it.

Breathing is actually one step in supplying your body with the oxygen it needs. In this chapter, you will discover how and why you and some of the organisms around you breathe. You'll also find out what happens to the air you breathe in. Finally, you will learn about some disorders of the respiratory system.

▶ *In the activity on the next page, explore your breathing patterns and compare them with those of your classmates.*

482

ACTIVITY

What happens when you breathe?

The act of breathing is just doing what comes naturally for most of us. Breathing is actually a complex activity that requires coordination between your respiratory system and your brain (telling your respiratory system what to do). What exactly happens to your respiratory system when you breathe? Try this activity to explore your breathing and how often it takes place.

What To Do

1. Put your hand on your chest. Notice your breathing. Feel your chest move up and down.

2. Take a deep breath. What happens to your rib cage? In which directions does it move?

3. Count your breathing rate for one minute. How does your breathing rate compare with the rates of your classmates?

4. *In your Journal*, write a paragraph describing your observations. What explanation can you offer for why breathing rates vary?

How Do You Breathe?

16-1

Section Objectives

- Compare how different organisms take in oxygen.
- Trace the pathway of air into and out of the lungs.
- Describe the pressure changes that occur within the chest cavity when you breathe.

Key Terms

trachea, gills, lungs, alveoli, diaphragm

How Some Organisms Take In Oxygen

You and a dog have similar respiratory systems. However, while most organisms need oxygen, they don't obtain it the same way.

■ One-celled Organisms

One-celled organisms take in oxygen directly from their watery environment. The figure below shows how oxygen and carbon dioxide move into and out of a paramecium.

■ Complex Organisms

Most complex organisms have specific body structures to take in oxygen and release carbon dioxide. The

Figure 16-1

A One-celled organisms, such as a paramecium, take in oxygen directly from their watery environment. The outer surface of a paramecium is covered by a membrane. Oxygen in the water diffuses into a paramecium's body through the membrane. Likewise, carbon dioxide wastes move out of the body through the membrane.

B Most complex organisms have specific body structures to take in oxygen and release carbon dioxide. Earthworms have capillaries in their skin where carbon dioxide is exchanged for oxygen. An earthworm takes in oxygen from moist soil and releases carbon dioxide waste through its skin.

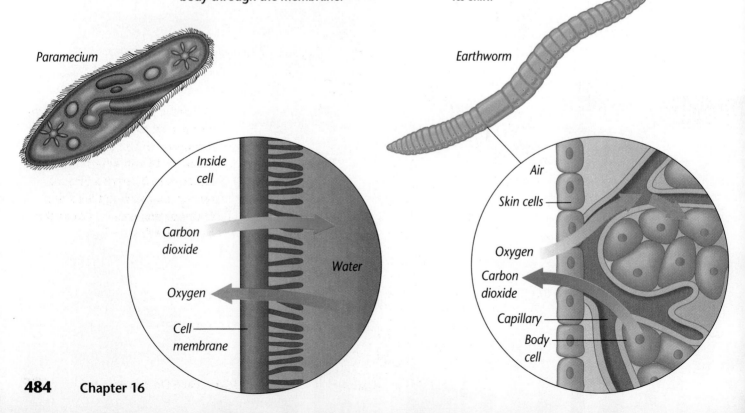

Paramecium

Inside cell

Carbon dioxide

Water

Oxygen

Cell membrane

Earthworm

Air

Skin cells

Oxygen

Carbon dioxide

Capillary

Body cell

figures on these two pages show how grasshoppers and earthworms take in oxygen. The grasshopper's respiratory system is more complex than the earthworm's. The grasshopper has a system of tubes, each called a trachea.

The **trachea** is a passageway through which air travels into and out of the body. But not all complex organisms possess a trachea. In the next activity, you will explore how fish obtain oxygen.

Explore! ACTIVITY

What can you learn by watching a goldfish?

What To Do

1. Observe goldfish in an aquarium. Watch the overall behavior of the fish for several minutes.
2. Note any body parts that move. Which body parts moved while you watched the fish?
3. Did any of the fish's body movements seem to be related to each other?
4. *In your Journal,* describe the fish's movements and explain how they are related to the fish's body functions.

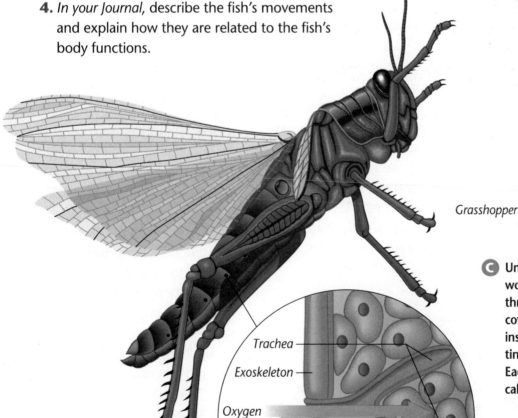

Grasshopper

Trachea
Exoskeleton
Oxygen
Carbon dioxide
Air

C Unlike the paramecium and earthworm, oxygen doesn't diffuse through an insect's outer body covering. Grasshoppers and other insects take in oxygen through tiny openings along their sides. Each opening connects to a tube called a trachea.

■ Gills

Fish have body structures that extract oxygen from the water. When you observed the goldfish in the last activity, you probably noticed the flaps on either side of its head. Beneath these flaps are gills. **Gills** are respiratory structures of some aquatic animals through which oxygen is removed from water.

When a fish opens its mouth, water flows in at the same time as a cover, or flap, over the gills closes. When the mouth closes, the water moves through the mouth, over the gills, and out past the flap that is now opened.

Each gill is made of several spongy structures called gill filaments. Because the filaments are feathery in nature, they provide increased surface area for water to pass over. Tiny capillaries extend throughout each filament. When the water passes over the filaments, oxygen diffuses from the water into the fish's blood as it travels through the capillaries. This oxygen-rich blood is then delivered to all parts of the fish's body. At the same time, carbon dioxide moves from the capillaries of the gills out into the water. The water then flows out of the fish through the opened gill covers. **Figure 16-2** shows a fish's respiratory system.

a CLOSER LOOK

Unusual Breathers

Human beings and many other animals obtain oxygen through breathing with lungs. Have you ever explored some of the ways that animals get the oxygen they need to sustain life? Consider a few of nature's many examples.

Insects

A grasshopper has pairs of small openings called spiracles that lead to thousands of tracheal tubes. Through the spiracles, air travels into the tracheal tubes, then to all cells of the grasshopper's body. By using muscles to squeeze its abdomen, the grasshopper forces air out of the tracheal tubes. When it relaxes these muscles, air enters again, repeating the breathing process.

Mosquito larvae, also known as wrigglers, live in pools of water. Wrigglers swim near the top of the water and poke tiny protruding tubes through to the air. Air enters

Figure 16-2

The main respiratory organs of fish are their gills. The gills contain capillaries.

A When a fish opens its mouth, water flows in. At the same time, a flap over the gills closes.

B When the mouth closes, the flap over the gills opens. Water moves through the mouth, over the gills, and out past the open flap.

C As water moves over the gills, oxygen diffuses from the water into the gill capillaries.

D At the same time, carbon dioxide, a waste gas carried by the circulatory system, moves from the capillaries out into the water.

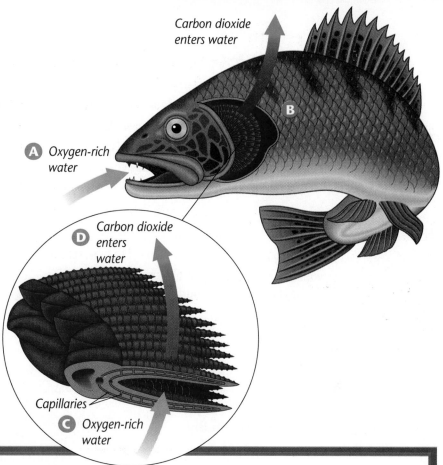

Carbon dioxide enters water

B

A Oxygen-rich water

D Carbon dioxide enters water

Capillaries

C Oxygen-rich water

these tubes and moves to tracheal tubes throughout their bodies.

Some aquatic beetles carry extra oxygen in large bubbles within their thick hairs. When beetles are underwater, oxygen passes from these bubbles to the tracheal tubes leading to all parts of their bodies. The oxygen bubbles also give them added buoyancy for traveling up to the water's surface.

Spiders

Spiders and scorpions have book lungs connected to tracheal tubes. Book lungs look a lot like gills, and they work in a similar way, removing oxygen from air instead of water. Book lungs are a series of thin "plates" full of blood vessels that catch and carry oxygen throughout the animal's body. The European water spider carries bubbles of air within its book lungs to bell-shaped webs that it builds under water. It uses these webs to store oxygen for future use.

You Try It!

Imagine that you are writing a science fiction novel about a creature with an unusual way of getting oxygen. Write a description of what this animal looks like and exactly how it breathes.

Your Pathway for Air

Your body has its own structures through which it receives oxygen and expels carbon dioxide wastes. These structures make up your respiratory system. The major parts of your respiratory system are shown in **Figure 16-3**. Refer to this diagram as you follow the path of air from your nose to your lungs.

Figure 16-3

A Air enters your body through your nostrils and sometimes your mouth. When are you most likely to breathe through your mouth?

B As the air moves past the tissues in your nasal cavity, your body tissues transfer heat and moisture to the air.

C The warmed, moistened air moves to the pharynx, a passageway at the back of your nose and mouth, and then on to the larynx, or voice box.

D A protective flap of tissue called the epiglottis covers the top of the larynx. When you breathe, the epiglottis is open. When you swallow, the epiglottis closes so that food or liquid moves toward your esophagus and not toward your lungs. Why do you think it's important not to talk while eating?

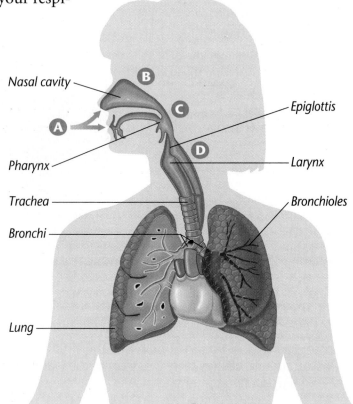

Nasal cavity — **B** — **C** — Epiglottis

A

Pharynx — **D** — Larynx

Trachea — Bronchioles

Bronchi

Lung

Explore! ACTIVITY

What is your trachea like?

What To Do

1. Place your fingers on the front of your neck and gently move them up and down. What do you feel?

2. Turn your head from side to side and continue breathing. How does the structure in your neck help keep you alive?

3. Now, gently cough while keeping your fingers on your neck. What happens when you cough?

4. *In your Journal,* describe the structure and possible function of the structure you felt in your neck.

When you ran your fingers up and down your throat, you felt the top of your trachea. Remember, an insect's trachea carries air in and out of its body. Your trachea is also a passageway for air moving into and out of your body. The rings you felt are C-shaped rings of cartilage that keep the trachea open. What advantage is there to having a trachea that is open all the time?

■ Lungs

At the lower end of the trachea are two short branches called bronchial tubes through which air moves into the lungs. The **lungs**, which are located in the chest cavity, are the main organs of your respiratory system. Here in the lungs, the exchange of oxygen and carbon dioxide takes place.

Within your lungs, the bronchial tubes branch into increasingly smaller and smaller passageways. At the ends of the narrowest tubes are clusters of tiny, thin-walled sacs called **alveoli**, which are shown in **Figure 16-4**. You can get an idea of what a mass of alveoli looks like if you imagine a tight cluster of grapes. Your lungs contain millions of alveoli that are surrounded by capillaries. Just as oxygen and carbon dioxide pass between the gills and capillaries in fish, the exchange of these gases takes place between the alveoli and capillaries in your body. Oxygen and carbon dioxide pass easily, or diffuse, through the thin walls of the alveoli. In addition, the large number of alveoli provides a huge surface area for gases to be exchanged.

Connect to...

Physics

The surface area of your lungs is about 20 times as great as that of your skin. Prepare a talk that tells what this means about how well adapted the body is to take in oxygen.

Figure 16-4

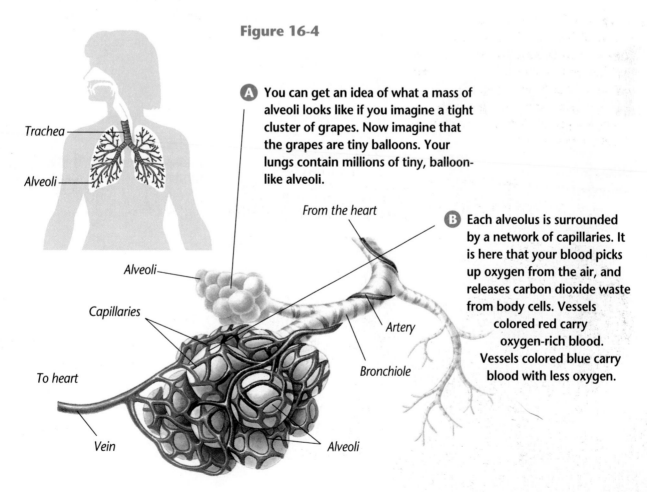

Trachea

Alveoli

A You can get an idea of what a mass of alveoli looks like if you imagine a tight cluster of grapes. Now imagine that the grapes are tiny balloons. Your lungs contain millions of tiny, balloon-like alveoli.

Alveoli

Capillaries

To heart

Vein

From the heart

Artery

Bronchiole

Alveoli

B Each alveolus is surrounded by a network of capillaries. It is here that your blood picks up oxygen from the air, and releases carbon dioxide waste from body cells. Vessels colored red carry oxygen-rich blood. Vessels colored blue carry blood with less oxygen.

Take a Deep Breath

Vital capacity is the largest amount of air your lungs expel after taking the deepest breath you can. In this activity, you will find your vital capacity.

Problem
What is your vital capacity?

Materials
round balloon   metric ruler

What To Do

1 Copy the data table *into your Journal.*

2 Stretch a balloon several times. Take as deep a breath as you can. Exhale into the balloon as much air as possible. Pinch the balloon closed.

3 Measure the diameter of the balloon in centimeters as shown (see photo **A**). Record the data.

4 Repeat Steps 2 and 3 four more times.

Data and Observations		
Trial	Diameter in Centimeters	Vital Capacity in Cubic Centimeters
1		
2		
3		
4		
5		
Total		
Average		

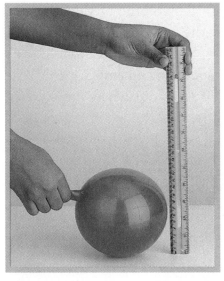

A

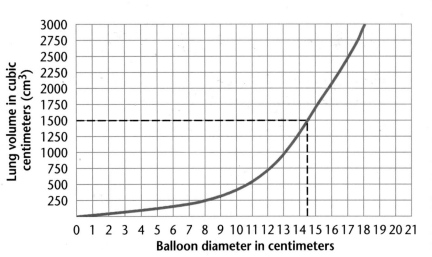

5 Vital capacity is expressed in cubic centimeters. To calculate vital capacity, find the balloon diameter on the horizontal axis of the graph. Follow this number up to the red line and move across to the corresponding capacity. The dashed line on the graph shows an example of how to find vital capacity.

6 Record your vital capacity for each trial.

7 Calculate and record your average vital capacity.

Analyzing

1. What is your vital capacity?

2. Were there differences in the diameters of the balloon during the five trials?

3. How does your average compare with the averages of other class members?

Concluding and Applying

4. How could you improve the accuracy of this activity?

5. Can you infer how this activity could be used to find people who might have a lung disease?

6. **Going Further** Tidal volume is the amount of air that you exhale after drawing a normal breath. Design an experiment to find your tidal volume.

How Air Moves In and Out

You learned in Chapter 14 how gases act under certain conditions. Air is a mixture of gases. It follows the same laws in your lungs as it would in a laboratory. For example, you know that according to Boyle's law, if you decrease the volume of gas in a container, the pressure of the gas will increase. You can demonstrate Boyle's law by squeezing an empty plastic bottle. Air rushes out when you squeeze the bottle, as illustrated in **Figure 16-5**.

Figure 16-5

A If you hold your hand over an open plastic bottle, you feel no flow of air. Why?

B Squeezing the bottle increases the pressure inside the bottle. The air inside the bottle has a higher pressure than the air outside the bottle.

C As you release your grip, the air pressure inside the bottle drops below the air pressure outside the bottle.

A B C

Explore! ACTIVITY

How does your chest size change when you breathe?

What To Do

1. Inhale and use a metric measuring tape to find the size of your own chest. When measuring, place the tape around your chest and directly under your armpits.

2. Measure the size of your chest when you exhale.

3. In your Journal, compare your chest size when inhaling and exhaling. Explain what you think caused the differences in the measurements.

■ The Diaphragm

The size of your chest changes as air moves in and out of your lungs. Like hands on a plastic bottle, something in your chest cavity exerts pressure or relieves pressure on your lungs. These pressure changes are caused by your **diaphragm**, a thin sheet of muscle under your lungs. Follow the events in **Figure 16-6** to see how the pressure changes caused by the diaphragm allow you to inhale and exhale.

You've seen that air pressure is important in helping you to breathe. What happens when you go to the

Figure 16-6

Inhaling

A When you inhale, your diaphragm contracts and muscles pull your ribs upward and outward. These actions increase the size of your chest cavity. Your lungs expand to fill the space.

B Because there is now more room for the air in your lungs, the pressure of that air decreases. The air pressure in your lungs becomes lower than the air pressure outside your body. The higher-pressured outside air rushes in through your nose to fill the low-pressured lungs.

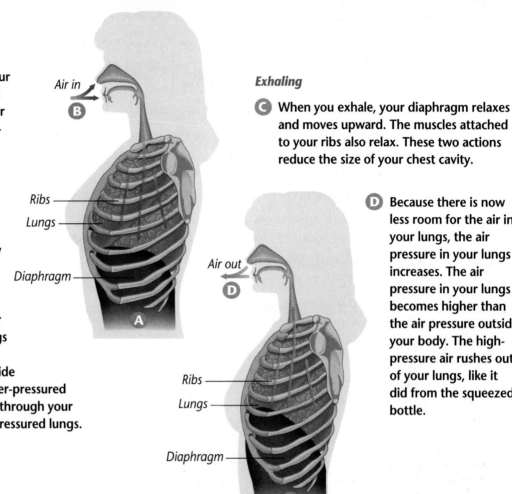

Air in

B

Ribs

Lungs

Diaphragm

A

Air out

D

Ribs

Lungs

Diaphragm

C

Exhaling

C When you exhale, your diaphragm relaxes and moves upward. The muscles attached to your ribs also relax. These two actions reduce the size of your chest cavity.

D Because there is now less room for the air in your lungs, the air pressure in your lungs increases. The air pressure in your lungs becomes higher than the air pressure outside your body. The high-pressure air rushes out of your lungs, like it did from the squeezed bottle.

mountains where the air pressure is lower? You probably find it harder to breathe.

People who live at high altitudes have physical traits that help them breathe at the lower air pressure. The Aymara and Quechua Indians of the Andes Mountains have barrel-shaped chests, strong diaphragms, and large lungs. They also have more capillaries around the alveoli, larger hearts, and more red blood cells. All of these traits deliver oxygen to their body cells and tissues more efficiently.

check your UNDERSTANDING

1. Compare how a paramecium and a fish obtain oxygen.
2. Draw a diagram of the respiratory system indicating the direction of air flow in and out.
3. Explain how air pressure relates to inhalation and exhalation.
4. **Apply** Describe what occurs inside your chest cavity when you blow out the candles on a birthday cake.

The Air You Breathe

16-2

Section Objectives

- Compare air that is inhaled with air that is exhaled.
- Explain cellular respiration and its relationship to gas exchange in your body.

Key Terms

hemoglobin, cellular respiration

How Oxygen Gets To All Parts Of Your Body

Because only 21 percent of the air you inhale is oxygen, your body needs to move a steady supply of air into and out of your lungs. You learned the path air travels into your lungs, but how does your body remove the oxygen it needs?

■ Hemoglobin

Your blood contains an oxygen-binding substance called **hemoglobin**. Hemoglobin is found in the red blood cells and contains iron, which easily bonds with oxygen. **Figures 16-7** and **16-8** show how oxygen moves into the

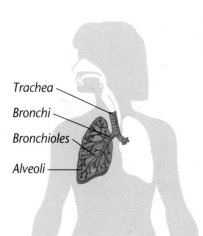

Trachea
Bronchi
Bronchioles
Alveoli

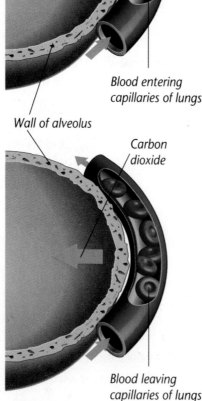

Oxygen

Blood entering capillaries of lungs

Wall of alveolus

Carbon dioxide

Blood leaving capillaries of lungs

Figure 16-7

Ⓐ As blood moves through your capillaries around the alveoli, oxygen diffuses from the alveoli into the capillaries and then into your red blood cells.

Ⓑ Once inside the red blood cells, oxygen binds with molecules of hemoglobin.

Ⓒ After leaving your lungs, the oxygen-rich blood moves to your heart, which pumps blood to the rest of your body.

Figure 16-8

Ⓐ The hemoglobin and oxygen remain bonded as the red blood cells move throughout your body.

Ⓑ As the blood passes body cells that have low amounts of oxygen, the oxygen in the red blood cells is released by the hemoglobin and diffuses from the red blood cells into individual body cells.

Ⓒ At the same time, carbon dioxide wastes diffuse from your body cells into the blood in your capillaries. The carbon dioxide then diffuses from the capillaries into the alveoli and is exhaled from the lungs.

What makes air vital?

In the 1700s, a British chemist, Joseph Priestley, discovered that a mouse couldn't live in a container in which a candle had previously been burned. He reasoned that some substance in the air was destroyed when the candle burned. He also discovered that if he put a mint plant into the container for eight or nine days, and then returned a live mouse to the container, it lived. The substance necessary for life had returned. It was later to be called oxygen.

red blood cells, where it bonds with the hemoglobin. Because of hemoglobin, your blood is able to carry oxygen throughout your body, where it is needed. The heart pumps this oxygen-rich blood to all parts of your body. Then, the oxygen is released by the hemoglobin and taken in by body cells. As oxygen is being released to your body cells, carbon dioxide is being taken up by the blood. About 30 percent of the carbon dioxide attaches itself to passing hemoglobin. The rest travels back to your lungs in plasma, the watery substance in blood.

Once the blood is back in the lungs, the carbon dioxide diffuses from the plasma and red blood cells into the alveoli. Your lungs release this waste gas from your body whenever you exhale.

Find Out! ACTIVITY

What other gas do you exhale?

It's tempting to think of the air you breathe in and out as being made up only of oxygen. Try this experiment to find out if that is true.

What To Do

1. Use a towel to wipe off your hands.
2. Hold the palm of your hand up to your mouth and exhale into it.
3. Feel the palm with your other hand.
4. Then, hold a mirror up to your mouth and breathe onto it. Observe what happens to the mirror.

Conclude and Apply

1. How did your hand feel after you breathed into it?
2. What did you see on the mirror?
3. *In your Journal*, summarize your observations and infer what other gas is released from your body when you exhale.

Comparing Air Inhaled With Air Exhaled

You discovered in the Find Out activity that water vapor is one gas that is evident when you exhale. Where does this water vapor come from? Tissues lining the respiratory system are very moist. When you inhale atmospheric air, it is immediately exposed to these moist tissues, and it becomes more humid. But the amount of water vapor in air is not the only thing to change when you breathe. The amount of carbon dioxide and oxygen gases changes as well, as you can see in **Figure 16-9**. What happens to cause this change in composition of the air you breathe?

Figure 16-9

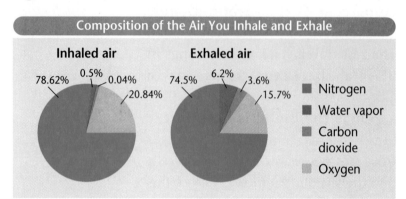

Composition of the Air You Inhale and Exhale

Inhaled air
78.62% 0.5% 0.04%
20.84%

Exhaled air
74.5% 6.2% 3.6%
15.7%

■ Nitrogen
■ Water vapor
■ Carbon dioxide
■ Oxygen

The air you inhale and the air you exhale are different in composition from one another.

Physics CONNECTION

Your Larynx

What kinds of sounds can you make with your voice? You may be able to sing or to imitate the sound of a door creaking, a dog growling, or a bass drum booming. You may have noticed that when you get excited, the pitch of your voice goes up or that when you're depressed, the pitch goes down. Your larynx makes a wide range of sounds possible.

When you speak or sing, air rushing out of your lungs as you exhale vibrates your vocal cords to produce sound. Muscles in your throat control the length and shape of the cords. Loose, relaxed vocal cords produce a low sound. Tightened, stretched cords make higher pitches.

Building a Vocal Cord Model

Try building a model of the vocal cords. Find a metal, plastic, or cardboard tube one inch

When you sing, air moving across your vocal cords causes them to vibrate.

Cellular Respiration

Think about what is needed before machines can run or microwave ovens can cook. Don't these objects need energy to work? Your body needs energy to operate, too. Your body gets this energy from a chemical reaction that happens within individual cells. This process is called cellular respiration. During **cellular respiration**, oxygen combines with stored nutrients in cells to release energy, carbon dioxide, and water. Your respiratory system supplies the oxygen and removes the carbon dioxide produced in this process.

Figure 16-10

The process of respiration is always happening, but the rate at which it happens varies with the types of activities that you do. The more energy you need to carry out an activity, like swimming, the greater your rate of respiration. As your respiration rate increases, your need for oxygen increases. During which activity do you think your need for oxygen would be greater: swimming or walking?

in diameter. Find a rubber stopper for one end of this tube, fitted with a smaller glass or metal tube through its center.

Connect this smaller tube to an air pump. A foot pump, like the one you might use to inflate a bike tire, would be a good choice. Cut two pieces of rubber from toy balloons. Stretch these pieces across opposite sides of the open end of the tube, securing them with tape or rubber bands. Rubber bands may be better, as they will allow you to make alterations more easily. Be sure to leave plenty of width in the pieces of rubber for further alteration.

As you pump air through the tube, the rubber sheets should vibrate—producing sound.

Loosen or tighten the sheets as you wish. Looser sheets should produce a low pitch. Tighter sheets, with the rubber pieces stretched thinner, will produce a higher pitch.

If you have easy access to the materials, construct more than one of these models. You may be able to combine different sounds, or even to play a tune, alternating use of the models or by sounding them at the same times.

You Try It!

See if you can match the pitch of your own speaking or singing voice with that of your model vocal cords. Also,

take note of the effects of different quantities of air on the pitches and volumes of sounds from the model.

INVESTIGATE!

Inhale! Now, Exhale!

You may have noticed that when you exercise or play sports, your breathing rate increases. Is the amount of carbon dioxide you exhale also related to your body's level of activity? You can test for the presence of carbon dioxide in your breath by using chemicals that change color in the presence of carbon dioxide.

Problem

How does exercise affect the amount of carbon dioxide exhaled by the lungs?

Materials

clock or watch with
    second hand
200 mL
    bromothymol
    blue solution

2 drinking straws
2 400-mL beakers
graduated cylinder

Safety Precautions

Be careful not to inhale or swallow bromothymol blue solution.

What To Do

1 In your groups, work together to make a hypothesis about how exercise will affect the amount of carbon dioxide exhaled by the lungs.

2 Use the following information to help you design an experiment to test your hypothesis: bromothymol blue solution turns green and then yellow as carbon dioxide is added to it.

Data and Observations	
Beaker	Time it takes for solution to turn yellow
Beaker A	
Beaker B	

A   **B**   **C**

3 Use the materials listed to design an experiment to test your hypothesis. To test your hypothesis, you may want to look at the amount of time it takes for bromothymol blue to turn yellow under different conditions.

4 Write a description of the steps you will follow to do your experiment. Plan a data table to be used in recording your observations.

5 When you have completed your plan, and it has been approved by your teacher, carry out your experiment. You may change your original plan, if needed, as you work. Record your observations.

6 *In your Journal*, summarize the procedure you followed in the Investigate, and discuss any changes you made to your plan. Using your results, state your conclusions about how exercise affects the amount of carbon dioxide exhaled. Make a chart or graph that shows the results of your investigation.

Analyzing

1. Was there a difference in the amount of carbon dioxide exhaled before and after exercise? How can you tell?

2. What control did you use in your experiment?

Concluding and Applying

3. Why does exercising cause you to breathe faster than usual?

4. What is going on within the cell when you exercise?

5. **Going Further** Design an experiment to see if age is related to the amount of carbon dioxide exhaled. Use the same materials as in this experiment.

Figure 16-11

A When you run, your breathing becomes more rapid and deep to supply the added oxygen your increased rate of respiration requires. An increase in the rate of respiration also results in an increase in the amount of carbon dioxide produced by your body cells.

B When running, and immediately afterward, you exhale more carbon dioxide than usual. Eventually, as you rest, your rate of respiration slows down and your breathing rate returns to its before-exercise rate.

In the Investigate, you explored the relationship between physical activity and the amount of carbon dioxide exhaled. You probably discovered that increased activity caused an increase in the amount of carbon dioxide your body gives off. You know that carbon dioxide is a waste product of cellular respiration. How, then, are breathing and cellular respiration related?

You've learned that breathing—a function of the respiratory system—gets oxygen and carbon dioxide into and out of your body. The circulatory system moves these two gases around within your body. The cells use oxygen and give off carbon dioxide during cellular respiration, which is how your body obtains energy.

Your respiratory system is very efficient, especially when you have clean, fresh air to breathe. What happens if the air is not so fresh and clean? What if a disease prevents the efficient transfer of oxygen to your lungs and body cells? In the next section, you will learn how these problems affect your respiratory system.

check your UNDERSTANDING

1. How does the air you inhale differ from the air you exhale?

2. What role does hemoglobin play in the transfer of oxygen between your lungs and body cells?

3. Why is the amount of water vapor higher in air you exhale than in air you inhale?

4. **Apply** Explain why both your heart rate and breathing rate increase with exercise.

16-3 Disorders of the Respiratory System

Keeping Your Lungs Clean

As you learned, air is a mixture of gases, but it also contains particles of dirt, pollen, dust, and smoke. These pollutants can damage your respiratory system and interrupt the flow of oxygen to your body's cells. Every year thousands of people in the United States die from diseases related to smoking and air pollution.

Your body has some defenses against the particles that mix with the different gases in air. When you inhale, these particles become stuck in a moist lining in the trachea and lungs. This lining is covered with tiny hairlike structures called **cilia**, shown in **Figure 16-12**. Cilia beat in an upward direction, causing a current that carries the particles to the throat, where they are swallowed and disposed of by acid in the stomach. What do you think happens if your cilia stop working?

Lung Disease

When inhaled air contains large amounts of dust, pollen, smoke, or smog particles, cilia lining the respiratory system can be affected. Smoke from cigarettes, for example, temporarily paralyzes cilia, preventing them from performing their sweeping jobs. Particles not swept out by cilia

usually reach the alveoli, where they are engulfed by white blood cells. White blood cells help prevent infections by consuming both dirt and bacteria. However, some substances such as asbestos, a material used for insulation, can't be consumed by white blood cells, and the substance remains in the lungs. In the following activity, you can determine how a classmate's lungs sound.

Section Objectives
- Discuss respiratory disorders and their causes.
- Determine how to keep your lungs healthy.

Key Terms

cilia, asthma, cystic fibrosis, emphysema, lung cancer

Figure 16-12

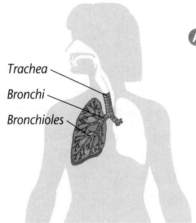

Trachea
Bronchi
Bronchioles

Ⓐ The linings of your nasal passageways, trachea, and lungs are covered with tiny hairlike structures called cilia. Cilia are covered with mucus. They beat toward your pharynx and cause the mucus to move, like a flowing sheet, in that direction.

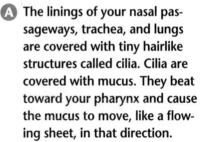

Cilia

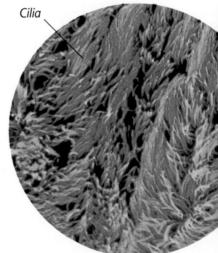

Ⓑ Dust and other particles stick to the mucus and move with it toward the pharynx as fast as one centimeter per minute. At the pharynx, the particles and mucus are swallowed and broken down by acids in your stomach.

Explore! ACTIVITY

What is percussing?

Have you ever gone to a doctor and had him or her thump on your back? This procedure is called percussing. A doctor can tell whether a body part is solid or air-filled by percussing.

What To Do

1. Put one hand flat on your partner's back.
2. Tap the third finger of that hand with the three middle fingers of your other hand. Healthy lungs should make a clear, hollow sound.
3. Pneumonia patients have fluid around their lungs. *In your Journal*, infer how percussing can help a doctor diagnose if a patient's lungs are healthy or filled with fluid.

■ Asthma

Did you ever see a person who was having a difficult time breathing? That person may have been having an asthma attack. **Asthma** is a disorder of the lungs in which there may be shortness of breath, wheezing, or coughing. When a person has an asthma attack, the bronchial tubes become constricted very quickly. As a result, the flow of air to the lungs is reduced. Asthma is often an allergic reaction. An attack can be caused by breathing certain substances, such as plant pollen. Stress and eating certain foods also have been related to the onset of asthma attacks.

■ Cystic Fibrosis

What color are your eyes? Your hair? These traits were passed from your parents to you. They're not harmful—they're what make you you. However, harmful traits also can be passed from parents to their children. One of these traits is a disease called cystic fibrosis (CF). If both parents carry this trait in their genetic make-up, they have a 25 percent chance of passing the trait to a child.

Cystic fibrosis affects the respiratory system by blocking the air passages. Fluid that lines the lungs and air passages thickens. This thickened fluid builds up, blocking the flow of air and causing lung damage. A person with CF coughs, wheezes, suffers from frequent lung infections, and usually dies at a young age. Although some people with CF live into adulthood, there is presently no cure for the disease.

■ Emphysema

Smoking has been shown to cause severe damage to lungs. One disease that is closely linked with smoking is emphysema. **Emphysema** is a disease that occurs when air passageways or alveoli lose their ability to expand and contract. When a person has emphysema, air becomes trapped in the alveoli. Eventually the alveoli stretch and rupture. As a result, the overall surface area of the lungs is decreased. The lungs become scarred, and less oxygen moves into the bloodstream. The amount of oxygen carried by the blood decreases while the amount of carbon dioxide increases, resulting in a shortness of breath. Some people affected with emphysema can't blow out a match or walk up a flight of stairs. Because the heart works harder to supply oxygen to body cells, people who have emphysema often develop heart problems as well.

SKILLBUILDER

Recognizing Cause and Effect

Infer what would happen in your body if you were near a volcano that had erupted and the carbon dioxide level of the surrounding air had risen sharply. If you need help, refer to the **Skill Handbook** on page 643.

Figure 16-13

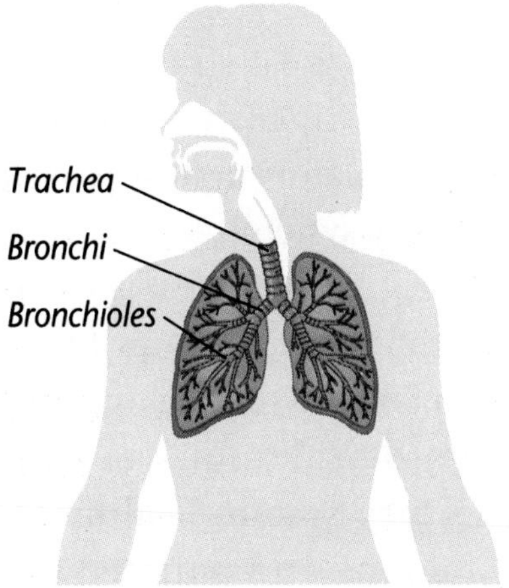

Air Tube Opening
Lining of Air Tube
Mucus

Trachea
Bronchi
Bronchioles

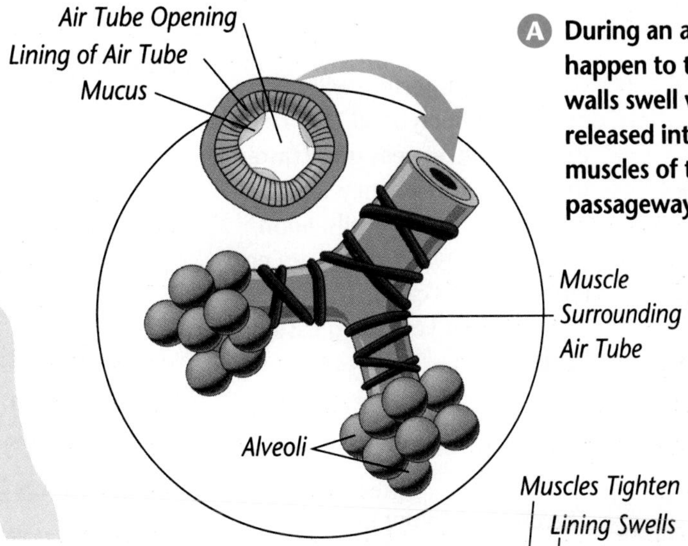

Muscle Surrounding Air Tube

Alveoli

Ⓐ During an asthma attack, three things happen to the bronchial tubes: their walls swell with fluid, thick mucus is released into the tubes, and the smooth muscles of the tubes constrict. The air passageways become very narrow.

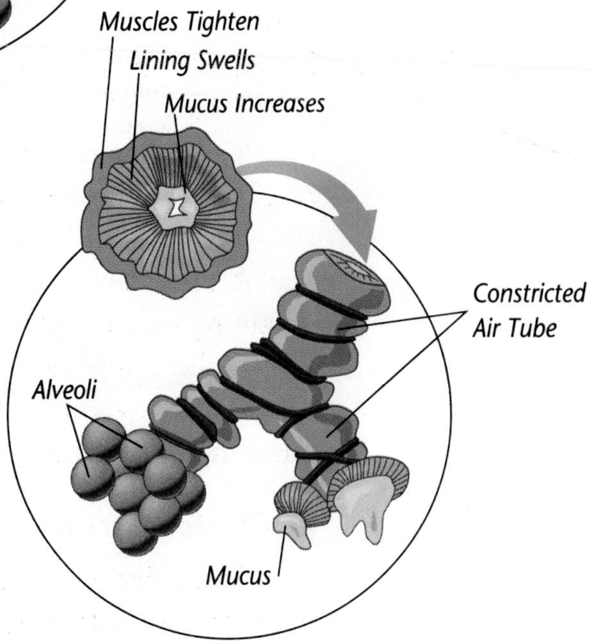

Muscles Tighten
Lining Swells
Mucus Increases

Constricted Air Tube

Ⓑ During exhaling, the smallest bronchial tubes are compressed even more. Most people having an asthma attack can breathe in enough oxygen but cannot breathe out enough carbon dioxide. This diagram shows a cross section of the bronchial tube with some of the alveoli removed to show mucus buildup.

Alveoli

Mucus

■ Lung Cancer

If you were asked which cancer caused the most deaths among men and women in the United States, would you know that the answer is lung cancer? When cilia are damaged, the lungs lose a defense against disease

Figure 16-14

A Healthy lungs have clear bronchial tubes through which air can freely pass. When healthy, the tiny alveoli of the lungs are able to take in a full supply of oxygen and give up their full load of carbon dioxide.

B Cancer cells interfere with the normal function of all lung cells. Because cancer cells grow faster than normal cells, they soon outnumber normal cells. Soon, normal cells weaken and are no longer able to carry out the activities that keep lung tissue healthy.

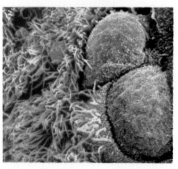

C The cilia in healthy lungs beat continually and strongly to keep the mucus sheet moving toward the pharynx. When cancer invades the lung, the cilia are weakened.

and **lung cancer** can develop. Inhaling the tar in cigarette smoke is the greatest contributing factor to lung cancer. Tar is a black, sticky substance that builds up on the linings of the smoker's mouth, throat, and lungs.

Carbon monoxide is another poisonous substance found in cigarette smoke. You might be familiar with this compound, because it's one of the gases found in car exhaust. When a smoker inhales, carbon monoxide enters the respiratory system. Here, it interferes with the binding of oxygen to hemoglobin. This happens because carbon monoxide binds more easily and more firmly to hemoglobin than oxygen does. Thus, the smoker's body cells receive less oxygen than they need. This puts a great strain on the smoker's heart. Cigarette smoking damages the circulatory system as well as the respiratory system.

Most living things we know of would die without oxygen. Your respiratory system takes in oxygen and gets rid of carbon dioxide. You can keep your respiratory system healthy by avoiding smoking and polluted air. Also, regular exercise helps you increase your body's ability to use oxygen. This makes your breathing more efficient.

check your UNDERSTANDING

1. What two diseases of the respiratory system are linked to smoking?
2. What happens during an asthma attack?
3. How does air quality affect respiration?
4. **Apply** Why are people with respiratory disorders warned to stay indoors on days when air pollution is severe or pollen counts are higher than normal?

Science and Society

Cigarette Ads—Are They a Crime?

Advertising is meant to make you want to buy the product being advertised. But what if the product can be shown to injure the user? Should our government protect us from harming ourselves?

Past and Future Cigarette Ad Bans

The Public Health Cigarette Smoking Act of 1970 banned all advertising of cigarettes on radio and TV in the United States.

One result of the Act was to turn the tobacco companies' attention to the rest of the world. As smoking declines in the U.S., Canada, and Western Europe, markets are expanding elsewhere. In the 1970s and 1980s, global tobacco use rose 75 percent and is still rising. For example, in China, cigarette consumption has risen 500 percent since 1965.

In the United States, tobacco companies have still been able to advertise in magazines and newspapers, on billboards, and by the use of couponing, sales promotion, sampling, store displays, and new packaging. Now it's very likely that the United States and many other countries will soon ban tobacco advertising from all print media. The debate is raging over whether or not banning tobacco ads will have a significant effect on smoking behavior.

The Tobacco Industry

Since 1966, cigarette packages and ads have warned that users were risking their health. That's the same year that one very large tobacco company announced that it was diversifying, or buying into, other less controversial fields. Was it trying to protect its image? Many large tobacco companies now own subsidiaries that make and sell such diverse products as cookies, crackers, canned fruits and vegetables, flour, frozen foods, and even television programs. Millions of people get their paychecks from diversified tobacco companies. If cigarette ads are banned, what would be the effect on the tobacco companies and the companies they own? Could people lose their jobs as the result of such a ban? If, as some people believe, banning tobacco ads would not affect people's decision to smoke, what would be the point?

What Do You Think?

In a small-group discussion, list some effects you would expect if all cigarette ads were banned. Try to decide whether you are for or against such an ad ban.

Technology Connection

Garrett A. Morgan: Gas Mask Inventor

African American inventor Garrett A. Morgan (1877-1963) developed "The Safety Hood" in 1912—the predecessor of the gas mask. A patent was granted to Morgan in 1914 for a device consisting of a hood placed over the head of the user. A tube from the hood featured an inlet opening for air, with the tube long enough to enter a layer of air underneath dense smoke or gas. The tube could be placed beyond the reach of gas fumes and dust, and through it pure air could be furnished to the user. The lower end of the tube was lined with an absorbent material, such as a sponge, that was moistened with water before use. This lining prevented smoke and dust from penetrating the tube and cooled the outside air entering the tube. A separate tube contained a valve for exhaled air.

A Life Saver

The original intent of Morgan's invention was to allow fire fighters to enter fires without suffocating from smoke and gases. Morgan had an opportunity to personally prove the value of his invention following a tunnel explosion in the Cleveland, Ohio, Waterworks. Morgan, his brother, and two volunteers saved several men trapped in the smoke and gas-filled tunnel under Lake Erie from almost certain suffocation. The men entered the burning tunnel wearing Safety Hoods and carried the trapped workers to safety. After 1914, many fire departments across the country were using the Morgan Safety Hood to save lives and property.

During World War I, Morgan's Safety Hood was improved and used as a gas mask by the United States Army. Thousands of lives were saved during this war thanks to Garrett Morgan's invention.

You Try It!

Research the type of "gas masks" used by fire fighters today in resource books at the library. Write a report on how fire fighters' respiration equipment has changed since the time of Morgan's Safety Hood.

HISTORY CONNECTION

Keeping a Nation Healthy

Health problems come from many sources, such as contaminated food or water supplies. Some behaviors encourage ill health, too, as has been shown with smoking and the abuse of other drugs including alcohol. What does an entire country do to protect the health of its people?

Public Health Service

In the United States, the Public Health Service, a division of the Department of Health and Human Services, works to provide services that maintain health, treat illness, and devise methods to prevent the spread of disease. To accomplish these goals, the Public Health Service works on many fronts. It provides educational programs and funding for research. It also provides suggestions for improved health-care delivery systems, and protection of consumers against unsafe food, drugs, and cosmetics.

The Role of the Surgeon General

Within the Public Health Service, the spokesperson for the nation's health is the surgeon general. Most people are familiar with the surgeon general through the health warnings that appear on cigarette packages. The office of surgeon general came into being by an act of Congress in 1870. Its original purpose was to oversee the health care of American sailors. Over time, the duties of the office have expanded beyond the health of sailors so that now the surgeon general has become the advisor and spokesperson for anything that affects the health of anyone in the nation.

Dr. Antonia Novello

In 1990, the first woman and first Hispanic surgeon general was appointed by President Bush, Dr. Antonia Novello. Dr. Novello received her MD from the University of Puerto Rico in 1970 and has specialized in pediatrics

with an emphasis on kidney diseases. Dr. Novello has been on the staff of several large hospitals in the United States and has directed research projects dealing with kidney diseases in children. As surgeon general, Dr. Novello spoke out against advertising that entices children to smoke, but she was also interested in pursuing other health risks that affect children, such as underage drinking and AIDS.

What Do You Think?

Pretend you are a doctor at the public health office in your hometown. You become aware of a pollution site that poses a health threat. Explain how you would go about helping to make people aware of this problem. Whom would you contact? What services would you use?

Review the statements below about the big ideas presented in this chapter, and try to answer the questions. Then, re-read your answers to the Did You Ever Wonder questions at the beginning of the chapter. *In your Journal*, write a paragraph about how your understanding of the big ideas in the chapter has changed.

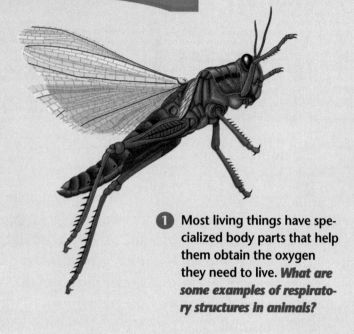

1 Most living things have specialized body parts that help them obtain the oxygen they need to live. *What are some examples of respiratory structures in animals?*

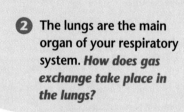

2 The lungs are the main organ of your respiratory system. *How does gas exchange take place in the lungs?*

3 Cellular respiration occurs in the body's cells when oxygen combines with food to release energy and produce carbon dioxide and water. *How is cellular respiration important to your body?*

4 Lung diseases and disorders reduce the amount of oxygen that can be transported to the body's cells. *What are some of the effects of reduced oxygen availability?*

Using Key Science Terms

alveoli	emphysema
asthma	gill
cellular respiration	hemoglobin
cilia	lung
cystic fibrosis	lung cancer
diaphragm	trachea

For each set of terms below, choose the one that does not belong and explain why it does not belong.

1. gills, alveoli, diaphragm, trachea
2. asthma, cellular respiration, emphysema, lung cancer
3. gills, lungs, hemoglobin
4. cystic fibrosis, lung cancer, emphysema
5. Look up hemo (or hem) and globin in the dictionary. Explain why hemoglobin is an appropriate name for the substance it represents.

Understanding Ideas

Answer the following questions in your Journal using complete sentences.

1. In what ways are gill filaments similar to alveoli?
2. Where is hemoglobin found and what are its functions?
3. How do asthma, emphysema, and lung cancer impair the performance of the respiratory system?
4. How do the circulatory system and respiratory system work together?
5. What is the difference between breathing and cellular respiration?

Developing Skills

Use your understanding of the concepts developed in this chapter to answer each of the following questions.

1. **Concept Mapping** Complete the concept map of breathing.

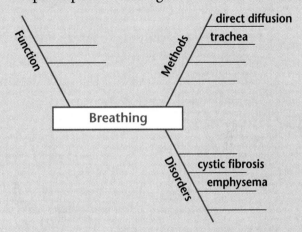

2. **Predicting** Predict what will happen when you repeat the Explore activity on page 483 after running in place for 20 seconds. How does the new number compare with the new numbers of your classmates?

3. **Recognizing Cause and Effect** After performing the Investigate on page 498, hold your nose and use a straw to breathe for 30 seconds. How do you feel? Would you want to run or walk anywhere using the straw to breathe? Why?

4. **Observing and Inferring** After performing the Explore activity on page 488, keep your fingers on your trachea and swallow. What movement did you feel? Recalling the text, what happens when you swallow?

Critical Thinking

In your Journal, *answer each of the following questions.*

1. Explain where the air pressure is greater, inside the chest cavity or outside the body, when you inhale and when you exhale.
2. Why is it an advantage to have cilia in your respiratory system?
3. What is the advantage of the lungs having many masses of air sacs instead of two large sacs?

Problem Solving

Read the following problem and discuss your answers in a brief paragraph.

People who are physically active have a larger lung capacity than those who are less active. The largest possible amount of air that can be exhaled after drawing a deep breath is called the vital capacity. A relationship exists between a person's height and vital capacity. The average adult male's vital capacity is 5000 cm^3, while that of an adult female is 4000 cm^3.

1. To find your calculated vital capacity, multiply your height (in centimeters) by one of the following factors:
   - 20 for females
   - 25 for males
   - 22 for female athletes
   - 29 for male athletes
2. How does your calculated vital capacity compare with the average adult of your sex? What could account for any differences in the figures?
3. Explain how exercise can increase one's vital capacity.
4. How can information about vital capacity be used to evaluate physical fitness?

CONNECTING IDEAS

Discuss each of the following in a brief paragraph.

1. **Theme—Stability and Change** What happens to your breathing rate when you are sleeping? Why?
2. **Theme—Systems and Interactions** People trapped in fires often die of smoke inhalation rather than from burns. How is smoke inhalation fatal?
3. **Physics Connection** Briefly describe how the larynx produces low and high sounds.
4. **Science and Society** Cigarette ad writers try to convince you that using their product will bring high-performance cars, exotic vacations, and the perfect mate into your life. How do ad writers aim their product at you, the adolescent?
5. **A Closer Look** How is a grasshopper's respiratory system different from yours? How is it similar?

Air: Molecules in Motion

In this unit, you investigated how the structure of an element's atoms determines how the element is classified and how it reacts with other elements to form molecules, such as the gases in Earth's atmosphere.

You also saw that your respiratory system interacts with the gases in Earth's atmosphere by taking in oxygen when you breathe in, and releasing carbon dioxide when you breathe out. The oxygen taken into your body during cellular respiration is very important because it allows cells to carry on life processes.

Try the exercises and activity that follow—they will challenge you to use and apply some of the ideas you learned in this unit.

CONNECTING IDEAS

1. The surface area of the palm of your hand is about 15 square inches. Air pressure is about 15 pounds per square inch. Calculate the amount of air pressure on your hand. Explain why you do not feel this pressure on your hand.

2. What are the most common gases in Earth's atmosphere? Which of these does the human body use? Describe several examples of how human activities affect the concentration of gases in Earth's atmosphere. How do you think human respiration might change if Earth's atmosphere were all oxygen?

Exploring Further ACTIVITY

What causes air to move?

What To Do

1. Draw a diagram of the respiratory system.

2. Use an arrow to show where cold air is heated before it reaches the lungs. What method of heat transfer is involved?

3. *In your Journal*, describe the process that enables your lungs to take in gases from the atmosphere. How is this process related to the process that causes winds?

Life at the Cellular Level

Using microscopes, you are about to discover the unseen, inner world of cells. You'll learn about chemical reactions that take place within the cell. You will realize how chemical reactions in nature enable life as we know it to continue.

Try It!

Have you thought about your skin lately? Is it dry and flaky or perhaps oily in some areas? Skin is generally taken for granted until it starts causing you problems. But what exactly is skin? What is skin made of?

What To Do

1. Find a partner to work with. Hold your index fingers about six inches in front of your faces and draw what you see on a sheet of paper.

2. Now place your fingers under a hand lens. Magnify the images of your fingers as much as the hand lens will allow. What do you see? Can you see any flakes of skin? What do you notice about the lines and rings that make up your fingerprints?

3. Rub your hands back and forth quickly over a dark sheet of paper and you may see some dead flakes of skin that fall off. Make a wet-mount slide using the flakes. Look at the slide under a microscope and describe what you see.

Try It Again

After you've learned more about cells, try this activity again and see if you can observe any more detail on your finger or in the flakes of skin that fall from it.

CHAPTER 17

BASIC UNITS OF LIFE

Chipmunk

Did you know that you began life as a single cell? That first cell then divided into two. Those two became four. The dividing continued on and on until that original cell had become about two trillion cells by the time you were born nine months later!

You're not the only thing made up of cells. All living things—from whales to chipmunks to blades of grass—are made up of these remarkable structures. Cells are so small that most of them can't be seen without the help of a microscope.

This chapter will take you on a voyage into the inner world of the basic unit of life—the cell. You will see how vital cells are to small organisms, as well as to large ones.

▶ ***In the activity on the next page, explore a model of living things.***

Did you ever wonder...

- ✓ How your body replaces the skin on a scraped knee?
- ✓ Why leaves are usually green?
- ✓ What makes a wooden bat strong?

You'll find the answers to these questions as you read this chapter.

Before you begin to study about the basic units of life, think about these questions and answer them *in your Journal*. When you finish the chapter, compare your Journal write-up with what you have learned.

Humpback whale

What are living things made of?

Nearly everything in our world is made up of many smaller parts.

What To Do

1. Take a look at the honeycomb in the photograph. What does the whole comb look like?

2. *In your Journal*, describe the individual structures that make up the honeycomb.

In many ways, the structures that form the honeycomb can serve as a model of the basic structure that makes up all living things.

Honeybees

17-1 The World of Cells

Section Objectives

- Identify cells as structures common to all living things.
- Conclude that different cells usually have different functions.
- Draw conclusions about why most cells are small.

Key Terms

cell

What Is a Cell?

When you first looked at the honeycomb in the Explore activity photograph, what did you notice about it? You may have noticed that it looked very organized because it is made of many small units that were about the same general size and shape. It was also easy to see each unit, wasn't it?

Living things, or organisms, are also made up of many small units. But, in most organisms, these units are so small in size, they aren't easy to see using only your eyes. You need a tool called a microscope to be able to see what these very small structures look like.

Find Out! ACTIVITY

What is everything made of?

What To Do

1. Look at several different types of materials to find out what they are made of.

2. Using the directions on page 619, make separate wet-mount slides of talcum powder, salt, and Elodea (an aquarium plant). Use one Elodea leaf for the wet mount. Your teacher can also give you a prepared stained slide of frog blood.

3. Carefully follow the directions given on page 619, on how to use a microscope. Look at each slide first under low, then high power on the microscope.

Conclude and Apply

1. Describe the appearance of each sample. How do they differ?

2. Which of the samples looks as if it is made up of many small organized units?

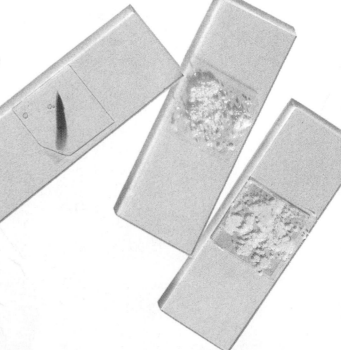

How were cells discovered?

Until the microscope was invented, no one had been able to see what living things were made of. In 1665, Robert Hooke, an English scientist, looked at a thin slice of cork under a microscope. The lenses of the microscope magnified the image of the cork, allowing Hooke to see what looked like a collection of little empty boxes. He called these boxes cells. At the time, he had no idea how important his discovery was. Over the next 200 years, lenses were improved and in 1838 and 1839, two German scientists, Matthias Schleiden and Theodor Schwann, both stated that the cell was the basic unit of all life. They had observed that both plants and animals are made up of cells. These observations, and those of others, have become part of what is known as the cell theory.

Of the samples you just looked at, you probably saw small organized units in the Elodea and blood and maybe even in the salt, but not in the talcum powder. Would you say that any of these samples were alive? Or were they alive at one time? How could you know? You would have to put them to some sort of test, wouldn't you? In order to know if these units were from a living thing, you would have to know if they came from something that had cells. You would also need to know if the organism could grow, reproduce, use food for energy, and respond to changes. These are features of living things. The salt and talcum powder you used were in the form of crystals. Although crystals grow, they do not show the rest of the features of living things. The units you saw in the Elodea and blood samples, however, are cells. A **cell** is the basic unit of life in all living things.

Connect to...
Earth Science

Many non-living things, such as icicles, crystals, and sand dunes, appear to grow. Prepare a poster that shows the processes involved in the growth of living things and the "growth" of nonliving things.

Figure 17-1

Ability to grow is a feature of living things. Salt crystals, like those used on pretzels, grow, but they do not show the rest of the features of living things. Is salt a living thing?

DID YOU KNOW?

A single yeast cell is an organism all by itself, but your body is made up of more than 10 trillion (10 000 000 000 000) cells, none of which can exist alone for very long.

Are All Cells Alike?

With the help of a microscope, you've been able to see the cells that make up Elodea and frog blood. Did these two types of cells look like each other? Are the cells that make up the flowers on a rosebush the same as the cells that make up the wings of a butterfly?

Find Out! ACTIVITY

Do all cells look the same?

In this activity, you will look at cells from different types of organisms.

What To Do

1. You will need prepared slides of guard cells on the surface of a leaf, human cheek cells, and yeast cells. These slides may have been stained with different colors so that the parts of the cells can be seen more easily.

2. Place each slide on the microscope stage and focus with the low-power objective in place. *In your Journal*, draw what you see on each slide and label your drawing.

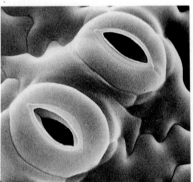

Guard cells

Conclude and Apply

1. How are the cells alike?

2. How do they differ?

Figure 17-2

The shape of a cell is often related to the job it does.

You've just observed an important fact about cells—cells come in different sizes and shapes. Your body contains many different kinds of cells. The shape of a cell may tell you something about the unique job of each cell. **Figure 17-2** shows you the unique shapes of nerve cells and plant stem cells. What do the traits of these cells help tell you about its job?

Nerve cell

A Notice that the nerve cell has extensions that look like electric wires. The job of nerve cells is to pass messages in the form of chemical impulses from nerve cell to nerve cell throughout the body.

Plant cell

B Various plant cells have different jobs. Two plant-cell jobs are to carry water throughout the plant and to collect sunlight and change it into food. Judging from the shape of the plant cell shown, which job do you think it does?

How Big Is a Cell?

Think back to any organisms you have seen on your way to school. Some of them, such as trees, dogs, or your classmates, are large. Others, like blades of grass, a mosquito, or a caterpillar, are quite small. Are their respective cells large and small as well?

Find Out! ACTIVITY

Does the size of a living organism tell you anything about the size of its cells?

What To Do

1. Your teacher will give you two slides. One slide has human cheek cells. The other slide is of Elodea cells.

2. Look at the cells with a microscope using low power for each slide. Notice the size and shape of each.

3. You must use the same power each time to be able to compare the cells. Draw two circles the exact same size *in your Journal.*

4. Then, draw each cell exactly as you see it in relation to the circle. Are the cells on each slide about the same size?

Conclude and Apply

1. What does the size of an organism tell you about the size of its cells?

The two types of cells you just looked at were about the same size. Yet one slide contained cells from a human being, while the other slide contained cells from a small plant. Bigger organisms do not have bigger cells. They just have a larger number of cells.

Is there some advantage to a cell being so small? Why, for instance, aren't you made up of just one large cell instead of trillions of tiny cells? Let's think for a minute about objects, their sizes, and distance.

Figure 17-3

What makes you bigger than a toad? Both you and a toad are made of cells. Are human cells bigger than toad cells, or do humans just have more cells? The answer is number, not size. Most of your cells are not any larger than the toad's cells. You just have a lot more of them.

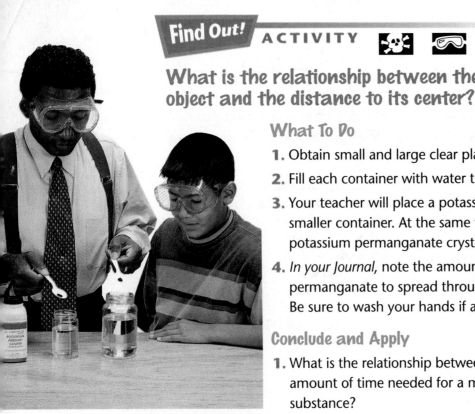

Find Out! ACTIVITY

What is the relationship between the size of an object and the distance to its center?

What To Do

1. Obtain small and large clear plastic containers.

2. Fill each container with water that is the same temperature.

3. Your teacher will place a potassium permanganate crystal in the smaller container. At the same time, your teacher will also place a potassium permanganate crystal in the larger container.

4. *In your Journal*, note the amount of time it takes for the potassium permanganate to spread throughout the water in each container. Be sure to wash your hands if any solution touches them.

Conclude and Apply

1. What is the relationship between the size of a substance and the amount of time needed for a material to spread through a substance?

Why Cells Divide

How does cell size in other living things compare? Surprisingly, a tiny mouse and a gigantic elephant have something in common with each other and with you. The cells in mice, elephants, and humans are all about the same size.

More than ten trillion cells make up your body. As you can imagine, each cell is very small. If you could line up 1000 of those cells, they would total less than 2 centimeters in length— only about the width of a thumbnail.

Why Small?

Whatever the size of the whole organism, the cell remains small. That's because it is important for cells to have as much surface area as possible. Through this surface area, cells absorb needed materials and give off wastes. A larger surface area allows more of this activity to go on. In addition, the smaller cell size means that the incoming materials have to travel a shorter distance to reach the center of the cell.

Surface to Volume

The diagram on the next page shows how surface area is related to volume. The first cube has a volume of 1 cubic centimeter (height × width × depth). Its surface area is 6

The greater the size of the container of water, the longer it took for the potassium permanganate to spread through it. As the size of an object increases, so does the distance from its sides to its center. Suppose the plastic containers you observed were cells. Materials might travel from the center of the smaller cell to its edges in a shorter length of time than materials travelling similarly in a larger cell. The ability of a cell to function well depends on the efficient flow of materials around it and into and out of it. Since materials travel at the same rate, it appears that materials may be supplied more efficiently in small cells than in larger ones.

Figure 17-4

Ostrich egg

A Bird egg yolks are the largest known cells. Ostrich egg yolks have a diameter of about 450 mm. The diameter of chicken egg yolks is about 45 mm.

B Because cell materials must travel further, they take longer to get to the cell part where they are needed in large cells than in small cells. Which cells— large or small— appear to be most efficient? Why?

Chicken egg yolk

square centimeters (height × width × 6 sides of the cube). Comparing the surface area to the volume produces a ratio of 6/1, or 6.

Using the same math on the second cube, which is 4 centimeters on each side, yields a surface area of 4 × 4 × 6, or 96, and a volume of 4 × 4 × 4, or 64. Thus, this cube has a smaller surface-to-volume ratio—94/64, or 1.5. Even though it is larger, the second cube has a relatively smaller surface-area-to-volume ratio than the first cube.

Now look what happens when the larger cube is divided into 64 small cubes. The large cube still has the same volume, 64, but it now has a total surface area of 384 (1 × 1 × 6 ×

64 cubes), and its surface-to-volume ratio increases from 1.5 to 6. The divided cube has a much greater surface area.

To get an idea of relative surface area, pretend that the large cube and the individual parts of the divided cube are gift boxes. Suppose that you are wrapping each gift box in fancy paper. You'd need a lot more paper to wrap all of the small boxes than to wrap the one large box. However, you could store either the one large

box or all of the small boxes in the same space because their volumes are equal.

What Do You Think?

Keeping in mind surface-to-volume ratio, why do you think it would take less time to digest food that is well chewed?

Volume	1	64	64
Surface area	6	96	384
Surface-to-volume ratio	6	1.5	6

Exploring Cell Size

In this activity, you will measure the size of a period at the end of a sentence, then compare the size of cells with the size of that period.

Problem

How many cells can fit on a sentence period?

Materials

newspaper	scissors
slide	slide cover
microscope	metric ruler
paper and pencil	flower petals
prepared slides of frog skin	

Safety Precautions

What To Do

1 Copy the data table *into your Journal*.

2 Cut out a piece of newspaper page that has a period on it.

3 Make a wet mount and locate the period under low power of your microscope.

4 Draw a circle with a diameter of exactly 100 mm to represent the field of view you see through the microscope.

5 Look through the eyepiece. *Observe* how much space the period takes up. Draw the period in the circle as it appears in your viewing field. If the period takes up half of the space in the eyepiece, it should take up half of the space in the circle. This is called drawing to scale.

6 *Measure* the width of the period in your drawing in millimeters and multiply it by

A

B

C

0.015. Your answer is the actual diameter of the period in millimeters. Record the data in the table.

7 Repeat Step 4. Now, *observe* frog skin cells under high power. Draw a frog skin cell to scale in your circle.

8 *Measure* the diameter of one frog skin cell in your drawing in millimeters and multiply by 0.0035. Record the data in the table.

9 Repeat Step 4. Observe the flower petal under high power. Draw a flower petal cell to scale in your circle. Measure the width and multiply by 0.0035. Record the data in the table.

The point of this pin, shown magnified, actually measures about 0.20 mm in diameter. Most cells are about 0.01 mm to 0.02 mm in diameter!

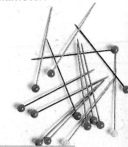

Data and Observations

Type of Cell	Drawing Measurement	Multiply By	Actual Diameter of Object Viewed
Period			
Frog Skin			
Flower Petal			

Analyzing

1. How many times larger is the period than the frog skin cell?

2. *Sequence* the cells studied in order from smallest to largest cell size.

Concluding and Applying

3. What do your observations tell you about the size of cells?

4. **Going Further** A compound light microscope can magnify an object up to 2000 times its normal size, while an electron microscope can magnify images more than 300 000 times. How do you think electron microscopes have helped researchers understand cells?

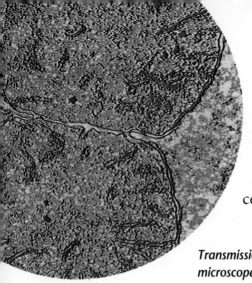

Transmission electron microscope (TEM) image

In the Investigate activity, you used a microscope to observe cells. Due to the invention and improvement of the microscope over the centuries, scientists are able to compare the cells of various organisms. They have discovered that while cells may vary in size and function, all cells have the same basic structure. Knowledge about cells was greatly advanced due to the development of the electron microscope. **Figure 17-5** shows the images of two different types of electron microscopes. In the next section, you will learn more about the features of cells.

Figure 17-5

A Development of the electron microscope greatly advanced the study of cells. The transmission electron microscope (TEM) is used to study the inside parts of cells, like the rat liver cell above. The TEM uses an electron gun to produce an electron image of the specimen. That image is then converted to a visual image, which people can understand.

B The scanning electron microscope (SEM) is used to study the details on the surfaces of objects, such as this insect. SEMs form and display an image of the specimen. If you wanted to learn about the texture of an eyelash, which microscope would you use?

Scanning electron microscope (SEM) image

check your UNDERSTANDING

1. How could you determine whether a green patch found on an orange is living or nonliving?

2. You are given two slides labeled "Rabbit cells." You examine them briefly and observe that they differ somewhat from each other in shape. Explain why two cells from the same animal might have different shapes.

3. Through which type of cell, a chicken egg yolk or an ostrich egg yolk, might material move more efficiently? Explain.

4. **Apply** In the Find Out activity on page 520, you compared the amount of time it took for potassium permanganate to spread throughout water in plastic containers of different sizes. While the size of the containers differed, the temperature of the water was the same. Now suppose you repeated the activity but filled the larger container with hot water and the smaller container with cool water. Would your results be the same or would they be different? Explain your answer.

17-2 ▸ The Inside Story of Cells

The Parts of a Cell

You've learned that all living things are composed of the same basic units—cells. As you've explored the world of cells, you've discovered that cells differ from one another in size, shape, and function. Even with these differences, however, most cells share some common traits. An understanding of these features will help you understand how a cell does its job.

Each different type of cell in your body has a specific job to do. Nerve cells transmit impulses. Muscle cells contract and cause bones to move.

A cell and its activities might be compared to a business that operates 24 hours a day, making different products. It operates inside a building. Only materials that are needed to make specific products are brought into the building. Finished products and waste products are then moved out onto loading docks to be carried away. A cell performs similar functions to that of a business, and it also has a barrier that encloses it. Try this next activity to see what that barrier is like.

Section Objectives
- Identify the parts of a typical cell.
- Describe the jobs of cell parts.
- Compare and contrast plant and animal cells.

Key Terms
cell membrane, cytoplasm, nucleus, chromosomes, mitochondria, cell wall, chloroplasts

Explore! ACTIVITY

What holds a cell together?

What To Do

1. Make a model of a cell using semisolid gelatin and a clear, plastic, resealable sandwich bag.

2. Fill the bag with the gelatin and close it.

3. Gently poke the center of the bag. *In your Journal*, describe what happens to the gelatin inside. Do the bag and its contents have a definite shape? Can you change the shape of the bag? Does the shape stay changed? What helps keep the shape of the bag?

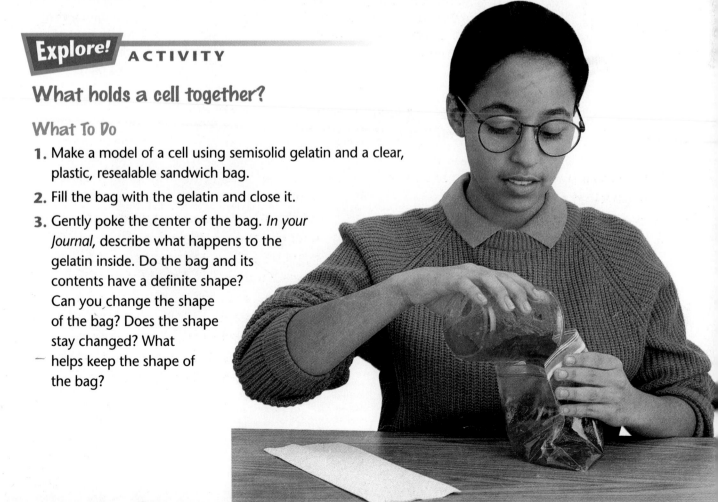

The cell is the basic unit of structure and function in all living things. It is the basic building block of organisms. Among the many-celled organisms, there are two basic cell types—the animal cell and the plant cell. Although these two types of cells share many common structures, there are a few exceptions. The following diagrams will help you to identify the parts of typical cells. Each cell part will then be discussed, comparing their respective jobs within the cell.

Figure 17-6

ANIMAL CELL

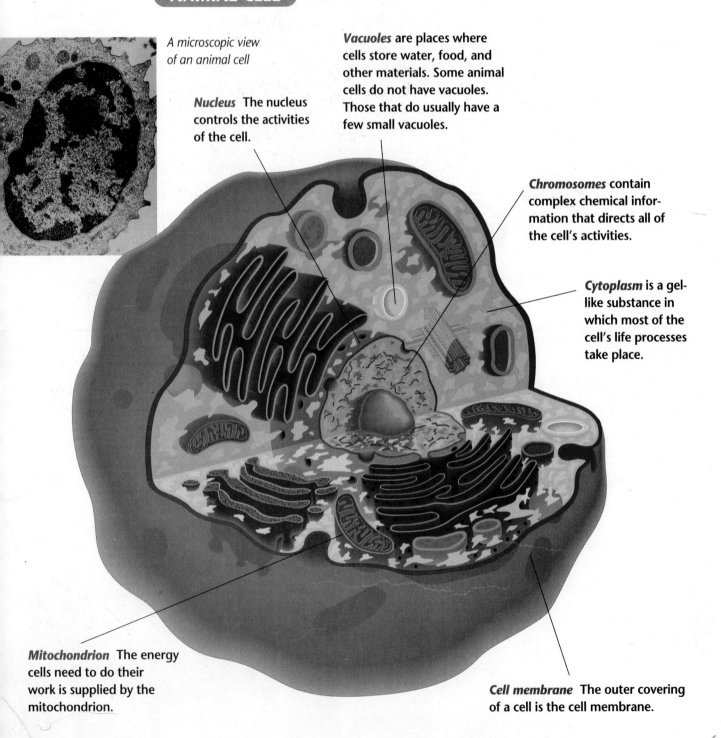

A microscopic view of an animal cell

Vacuoles are places where cells store water, food, and other materials. Some animal cells do not have vacuoles. Those that do usually have a few small vacuoles.

Nucleus The nucleus controls the activities of the cell.

Chromosomes contain complex chemical information that directs all of the cell's activities.

Cytoplasm is a gel-like substance in which most of the cell's life processes take place.

Mitochondrion The energy cells need to do their work is supplied by the mitochondrion.

Cell membrane The outer covering of a cell is the cell membrane.

Figure 17-7

Nucleus The nucleus controls the activities of the cell.

Cytoplasm is a gel-like substance in which most of the cell's life processes take place.

Chloroplasts allow plants to make their own food by converting light energy into chemical energy.

Chromosomes contain complex chemical information that directs all of the cell's activities.

Mitochondrion The energy cells need to do their work is supplied by the mitochondrion.

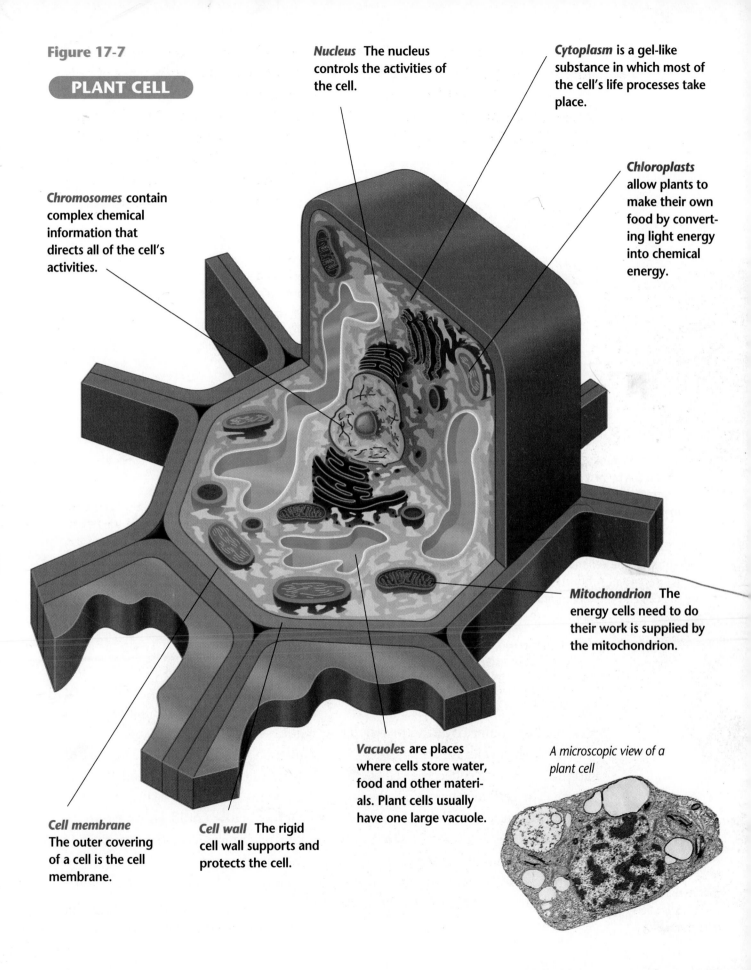

Vacuoles are places where cells store water, food and other materials. Plant cells usually have one large vacuole.

A microscopic view of a plant cell

Cell membrane The outer covering of a cell is the cell membrane.

Cell wall The rigid cell wall supports and protects the cell.

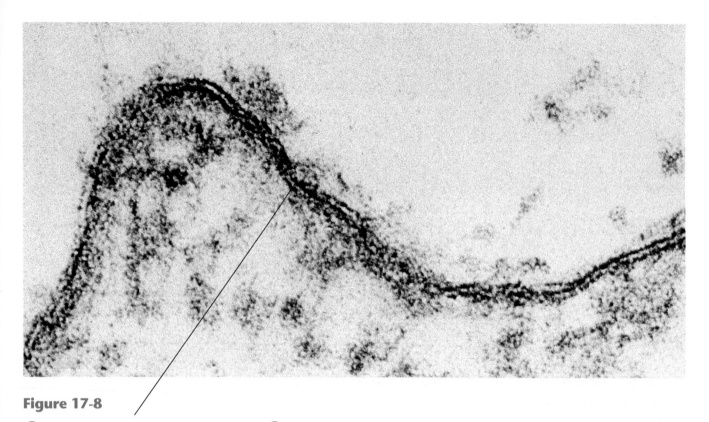

Figure 17-8

A The cell membrane contains the cell and is partly responsible for its shape. Because the membrane is flexible, it allows the shape of the cell to change under pressure. Food and oxygen enter the cell through the cell membrane. Water and other products made by the cell exit the membrane.

B A cell can be compared to a factory. Products going into a factory are regulated by the receiving department. Products leaving the building are regulated by the shipping department. Both of these jobs in a cell are carried out by the cell membrane.

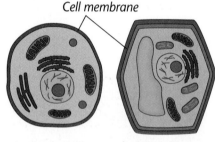

Cell membrane

Animal cell   *Plant cell*

■ Cell Membranes

In the model of a cell you made in the Explore activity, a plastic bag represented the outer covering or barrier of a cell. Most cells are surrounded by an outer covering called the cell membrane. The **cell membrane** is a flexible structure that forms the outer boundary of the cell. You can't see a cell membrane using a regular light microscope. However, by using chemical tests and the electron microscope, scientists have found that a cell membrane is a double-layered structure that surrounds the contents of the cell. In the Explore activity, you made a model of a cell using a plastic sandwich bag and gelatin. The part of the model that represented the cell membrane was only a single-layered structure. How could you have more accurately represented the structure of a cell membrane?

Figure 17-8 shows the cell membrane of a cell and tells about the important jobs it performs.

■ Cytoplasm

Think back to the photograph of the honeycomb you examined at the beginning of this chapter in the Explore activity. What filled each part of the comb? Honey, of course. What about cells? Are they filled with anything? In the Find Out activity that follows, you will discover the answer to this question.

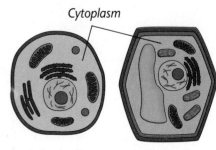

Find Out! ACTIVITY

What's inside cells?

What To Do

1. Take a piece of a leaf from a fresh red onion bulb. Bend it so that you can peel off a single, paper-thin layer from the inside of the leaf.

2. Prepare a wet-mount slide of this layer of cells.

3. Observe the sample under low power and make a drawing of what you see. If you watch long enough, you may be able to see something moving around inside each rectangular cell.

Conclude and Apply

1. How would you describe the material (cytoplasm) from looking at these cells?

The liquid, found in both plant and animal cells, is where many of the cell's activities take place. **Cytoplasm** is a gel-like material inside the cell membrane. **Figure 17-9** shows where cytoplasm is located within the cell.

Quite a large portion of the cell you observed is made up of colorless cytoplasm. Cytoplasm contains a large amount of water, but it also contains chemicals and cell structures that carry out life processes for the cell. Some structures found in the onion cell have a small amount of color. The large red storage area in the onion cell is called a vacuole. The gel-like cytoplasm constantly moves around the structures within the cell. What use does this movement probably serve for the cell?

Figure 17-9

Just as air surrounds the workers in a factory, cytoplasm surrounds the internal structures of the cell. Cytoplasm is a soft, gel-like substance in which most of the cell's life processes take place. Like air, cytoplasm is constantly moving.

Cytoplasm

Animal cell   *Plant cell*

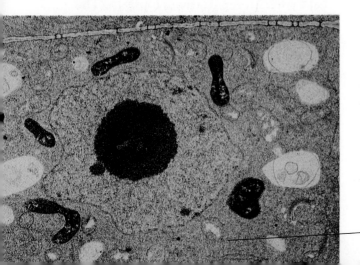

— *Cytoplasm*

■ Nucleus

Factories generally have a manager who directs everyday business for the company from a central office. A cell also has a command center that controls its activities. Just where is this center? What does it look like and what is it called?

Find Out! ACTIVITY

Where is the cell's command center located?

What To Do

1. Observe a layer of onion skin again, this time using a white onion.
2. Make a wet-mount slide of onion skin and look at it first under low power, then under high power.
3. With your teacher's help, let a small drop of iodine seep under the coverslip. **CAUTION:** *Iodine is poisonous. Wash your hands to remove any iodine that gets on your skin.* Look for a large round structure in the cytoplasm that takes on color. Draw what you observe *in your Journal.*
4. Now look at a prepared slide of an onion root tip under high power.

Conclude and Apply

1. What structure(s) in the cytoplasm became colored by iodine?
2. Did you see any movement in the living tissue?
3. How did your observations compare with the prepared, stained slide?

Nucleus

Figure 17-10

The nucleus contains genetic blueprints for operation of the cell. The nucleus has its own structures including the chromosomes.

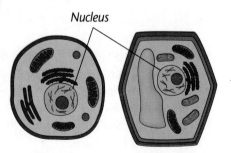

Nucleus

Animal cell   Plant cell

When you saw a large sphere in the cells you examined, you were looking at the nucleus of the cell. In many cells, the nucleus is the largest structure you can see in the cytoplasm. The **nucleus** of a cell is its command center—the structure that directs all the activities of the cell. It contains complex chemical information that directs the cell's activities, including its ability to reproduce. This material inside the nucleus is separated from the cytoplasm by a thin membrane.

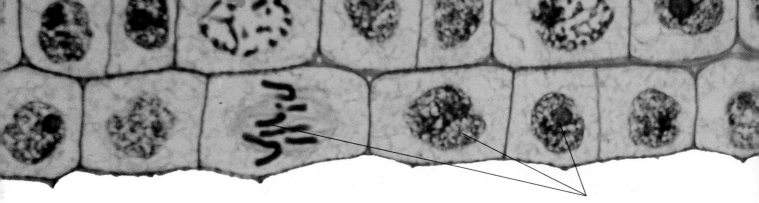

Chromosomes

Chromosomes

Chromosomes are threadlike structures made up of proteins and DNA, the molecules that control the activities of the cell. Look at **Figure 17-11**, and identify the nucleus and the chromosomes.

Chromosomes aren't visible all the time. When a cell is not reproducing, the nucleus looks grainy. The best time you can observe chromosomes is when a cell is dividing. What does this tell you about the cells you observed in the onion root tip?

Mitochondria

Almost any factory uses some type of machine to do work. The energy needed for these machines to run is supplied by a power plant located nearby. Cells do work, so they require energy, too. Inside each cell are structures that enable the cell to release energy obtained through food digestion.

Look at **Figure 17-12**. The round to rod-shaped structures you see are called mitochondria. **Mitochondria** are the power plants of a cell, which release energy needed for cell activities. Inside the mitochondria, molecules from food digestion are broken down to release energy that can be used for the activities of the cell.

Figure 17-11

Chromosomes take up most of the space of the nucleus. These long strands of material contain complex chemical information that controls all of the cell's activities including its ability to reproduce. Chromosomes are usually only visible when a cell is dividing.

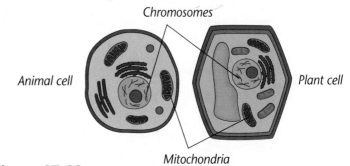

Chromosomes

Animal cell

Plant cell

Mitochondria

Figure 17-12

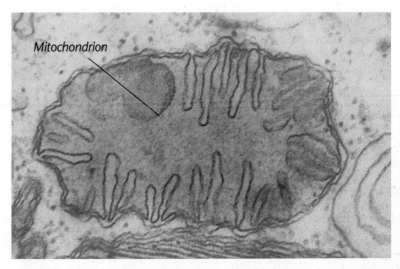

Mitochondrion

Power companies supply the energy for a factory to carry out its work. Mitochondria supply the energy for cells to do their work. Some cells use more energy than others because they are more active. Muscle cells have more mitochondria than do the cells that produce fingernails. Why do you think that is so?

Plant Cell Adaptations

In your trip through the structure of a cell, you have observed the cell membrane, cytoplasm, nucleus, chromosomes, and mitochondria of different cells. Animal cells contain all these structures. Plant cells, however, contain some additional cell parts. In the next activity, you will make a model of a plant cell to learn about these cell parts.

Explore! ACTIVITY

How do plant and animal cells differ?

What To Do

1. Take a clear food container and a plastic bag filled with semisolid gelatin.
2. Place the bag inside the container, pressing gently so that the plastic bag fits snugly up against the sides of the container.
3. *In your Journal*, record how the shape of the bag now compares with the shape of the container. If the bag were placed in a different type of container, would its shape change?

■ Cell Walls

Figure 17-13

Cell walls are usually rigid, but when a plant cell enlarges, its walls temporarily soften. Plant cells grow mostly in length and in the same direction as the vertical growth of stems and roots.

In your model, the plastic container represents an adaptation found in plant cells, fungi, and bacteria. This structure, the outermost rim of the cell, is called the cell wall. The **cell wall**, shown in **Figure 17-13**, is a rigid structure located outside the cell membrane that supports and protects the cell. Cell walls from dead plants are used as wood. If you play baseball, cell walls may have helped you "muscle" a ball over the pitcher's head. The wooden bat you may have used is made up of the dead cells from an ash tree. Cell walls remain strong even though the contents of the cells are no longer there. Just imagine what would happen if your baseball bat had been made from animal cells whose only outer covering was a flexible cell membrane.

Tiny openings, or pores, in the cell wall permit substances to pass through. In your model of the cell, which part represented the cell wall?

Cell wall

Plant cell

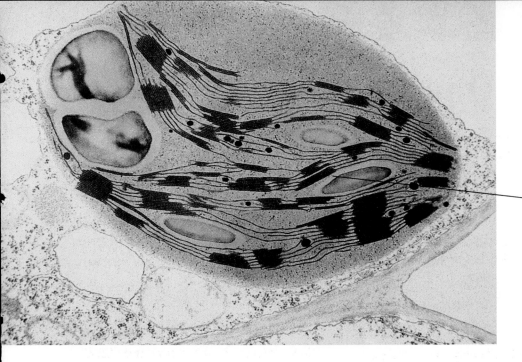

Figure 17-14

Chloroplasts are structures that contain chlorophyll, a green pigment that allows plants to make their own food by converting light energy into chemical energy in the form of a sugar called glucose.

Chloroplast

Plant cell

■ Chloroplasts

You already know that plant cells have a structural adaptation that animal cells do not, namely, a cell wall. But when you studied plant and animal cells under the microscope and compared their structures, you may have made another interesting discovery. Green plant cells have another structure that animal cells don't, chloroplasts.

Chloroplasts are small structures that contain chlorophyll, a green pigment that allows plants to make their own food. Most chloroplasts are located in the leaves of a plant. It is the green color of the chlorophyll that makes the leaves green.

You have now completed your journey through the major parts of plant and animal cells. The structures in these cells carry out certain life processes. In the next section, you will learn more about one of these processes—reproduction.

SKILLBUILDER

Making and Using Tables
Make a table that lists the parts of a cell and each of their jobs. If you need help, refer to the **Skill Handbook** on page 639.

check your UNDERSTANDING

1. Compare the job of a cell membrane with that of a cell wall.
2. What cell parts are found in green plant cells?
3. Describe the relationship that appears to exist between the job of a cell and the number of mitochondria it contains.
4. What cell parts are more clearly visible when a cell is dividing?
5. **Apply** Suppose a disease destroyed all the chloroplasts in a green plant. Explain what would happen to the plant and why.

17-3 When One Cell Becomes Two

Section Objectives
- Describe the process of mitosis and its end products.
- Give examples of instances where cell reproduction takes place.

Key Terms

mitosis

Change and Growth

What happens to the tiny green shoots that, in spite of traffic, push through the cracks in playgrounds and parking lots? They often grow tall and strong, and produce roots that are hard to pull out. Puppies grow too, maturing into full-grown adult dogs. A green and black banded caterpillar sealed inside a pale green cocoon emerges as an orange and black monarch butterfly. All living things change and grow, often right before your eyes. Are you also changing?

Besides growing taller, you can find other evidence that the cells in your body are increasing in number. When you cut yourself, you see

Figure 17-15

5 WEEKS

Pig weighs 11.5-13.5 kg (25-30 lb)

2 WEEKS

Piglet weighs 4.5 kg (10 lb)

NEWBORN

Newborn weighs 1.8 kg (4 lb)

A As pigs, humans, and other animals develop, many of their body cells increase in number, causing the animal to grow gradually larger.

dramatic evidence of cell reproduction. A cut is a break in your skin. Have you ever scraped your knee on the ground? As you know, when a cut occurs, blood initially flows through the opening. But in time, the tear in your skin is no longer visible.

Why? Your body actually repairs itself by sealing off the flow of blood and then producing new skin cells. The new cells fill the break in your skin as the dead cells are replaced. Cuts heal as new cells are produced.

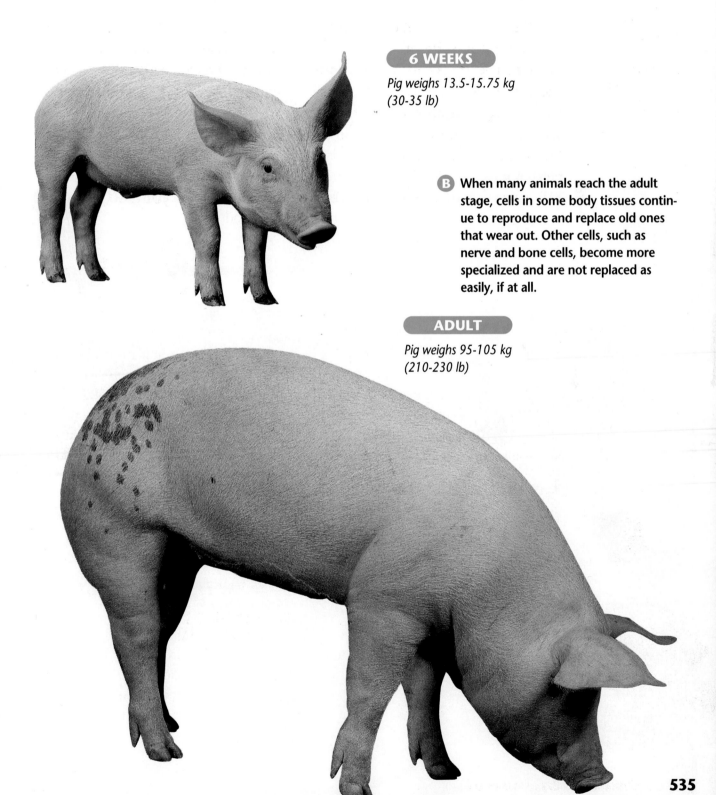

6 WEEKS

Pig weighs 13.5-15.75 kg (30-35 lb)

B When many animals reach the adult stage, cells in some body tissues continue to reproduce and replace old ones that wear out. Other cells, such as nerve and bone cells, become more specialized and are not replaced as easily, if at all.

ADULT

Pig weighs 95-105 kg (210-230 lb)

An Introduction to Cell Reproduction

In order to understand how your body makes new cells, you first need to review the features of a nucleus and chromosomes. In the following Find Out activity, you will take a closer look at these cell structures.

Find Out! ACTIVITY

When are chromosomes visible?

Chromosomes are generally visible only when a cell is undergoing reproduction. If you can see a cell's chromosomes, then the cell is probably reproducing.

What To Do

1. Examine a prepared slide of an onion root tip under both low and high power. Look at cells that are undergoing reproduction.

Physics CONNECTION

A magnified view of a spider's fangs

Light Microscope

It's easy to think of a microscope as a super magnifying glass, but a microscope is much more complex. Unlike a magnifying glass, which has only one lens, a microscope usually has at least three lenses and sometimes more. First, there is the lens closest to your eye, called the eyepiece. Then, there is the lens closest to the item you want to see, called the objective lens. Finally, there is the lens closest to the light source that illuminates the item so you can see it, called the condenser.

What Happens When You Look into a Microscope?

Light, from either a mirror or a built-in light bulb, passes through the condenser lens where it is intensified and

2. Make a drawing *in your Journal* of a cell that's not reproducing. Then make a drawing of a cell that is reproducing.

Conclude and Apply

1. How do your drawings differ?

2. What structures indicated that the cell was undergoing reproduction?

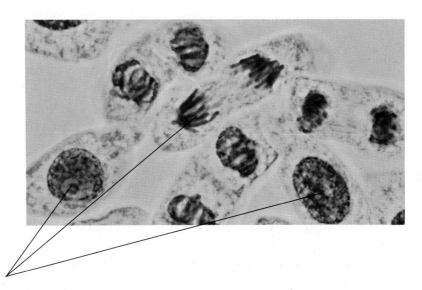

Onion root tip cell's chromosomes

Did you see chromosomes in the onion root tip cell? Chromosomes are threadlike structures located in the nucleus of the cell. In most cells, chromosomes play an important role in the reproduction of cells.

focused on the specimen you are looking at. The light then passes through the specimen and is collected by the objective lens, which shapes the light to form a magnified image of the specimen. That light image is then gathered by the eyepiece lens, which magnifies it again. Finally, the light carries the image into your eye, where it is projected on the layer at the back of your eye called the retina. As a result, you see an onion cell, a skin cell, bacteria, or whatever else you may be looking at through the microscope.

Magnification

Most microscopes actually have more than one objective lens. Usually, they have three objective lenses with different powers of magnification—10×, 40×, and 100×—meaning they enlarge the image of an item to 10 times, 40 times, or 100 times its natural size. Some microscopes also have changeable eyepiece lenses with different powers of magnification. If you multiply the power of the objective lens by the power of the eyepiece, you get the total magnification power of the microscope. For example, if your microscope has an eyepiece of 10 and objective lenses of 10×, 40×, and 100×, it can

magnify items from 100 to 1000 times their natural size!

What Do You Think?

The image produced by a microscope is backwards, like the reflection in a mirror, and upside down. For example, if you move a specimen slide to the right, the image you see through the eyepiece will look like it is moving to the left. Or if you move the slide down (toward you), the image will look like it is moving up (away from you). Why does this happen? Can you think of a way to correct the visual image you see so that it operates the same way as the real item?

How Body Cells Reproduce

Have you ever watched a magician at work? Objects seem to disappear or reappear with sleight of hand. Such tricks can even make one object appear to become two. When a cell reproduces, one cell becomes two identical cells. It's not magic, however—it's mitosis.

Mitosis is the process by which the nucleus of a cell divides to produce two nuclei, each with the same type and number of chromosomes

Figure 17-16

STAGE 1

Mitosis begins with the chromosomes becoming fully visible. Each chromosome makes a copy of itself. The identical chromosomes remain joined together as a pair. At this point, the nuclear membrane begins to disappear and threadlike spindle fibers form. The chromosome pairs attach to the spindle fibers.

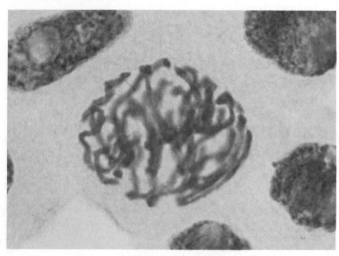

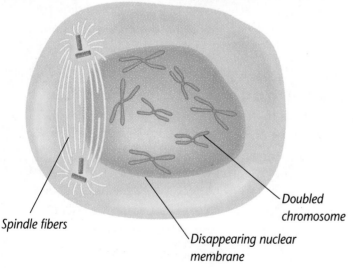

Spindle fibers

Disappearing nuclear membrane

Doubled chromosome

STAGE 2

The spindle fibers move all of the joined chromosome pairs to the center of the cell. The chromosome pairs line up along the middle of the cell.

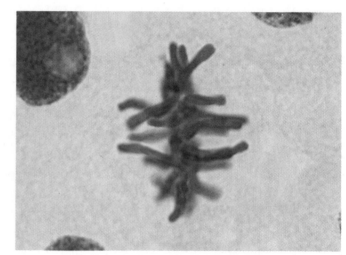

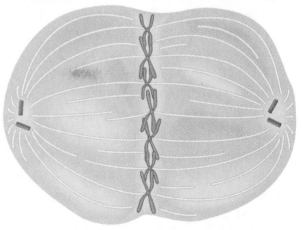

Chromosomes line up at equator

that the parent cell had. After the nucleus divides, the cytoplasm also usually separates. Follow the steps in **Figure 17-16** as this process is described.

Cell reproduction by mitosis has been taking place in your body from the moment you were conceived, and it continues even now. As you read this page, many cells in your body are dividing through mitosis. What evidence do you have that this is true?

All of your body cells reproduce by the same process—mitosis. But, the rate at which mitosis occurs in different types of cells may vary. In the next activity, you will observe the rate of mitosis in a young plant root.

STAGE 3

The chromosome pairs split apart. The spindle fibers seem to guide or pull the members of each chromosome pair to opposite ends of the cell.

STAGE 4

The spindle fibers disappear and the cytoplasm divides in half. The result is two new cells—each identical to the original cell. The process of mitosis has been called the dance of the chromosomes. Why do you think it might be called that?

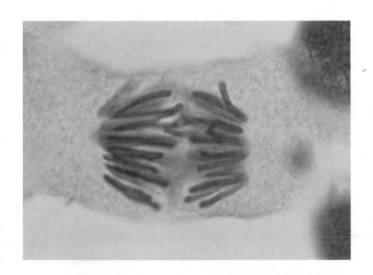

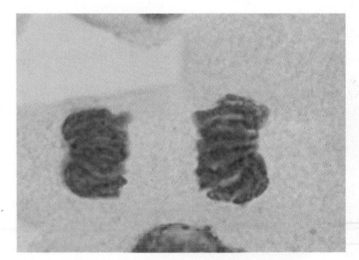

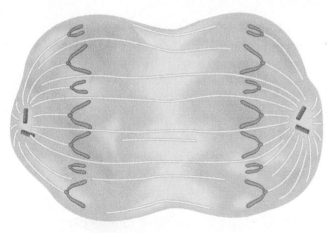

Chromosomes and their copies

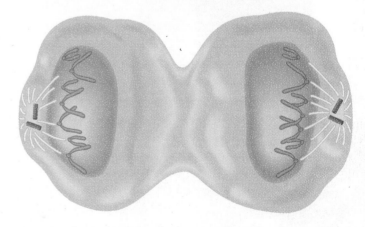

Cytoplasm divides in half

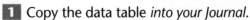

INVESTIGATE!

48-Hour Cell Reproduction

You have learned that cells reproduce through the process of mitosis. In the following activity, you will observe the average growth of young growing roots as an indirect measurement of how many new cells are formed during a 48-hour period.

Problem

What is the average growth rate of young, growing roots over a 48-hour period?

Materials

5 young corn seedlings	metric ruler
permanent marking pen (not water-soluble)	5 plastic bags
	labels
	paper towels

What To Do

1 Copy the data table *into your Journal*.

2 Label the five plastic bags (see photo **A**). Write "Seedling 1" on the first bag, and write "Seedling 2" on the second plastic bag. Continue labeling until all five bags have been identified.

3 Obtain five young corn seedlings from your teacher. On the first seedling, referred to as "Seedling 1", locate the growing root (see photo **B**).

4 Use the marking pen to then place a dot on the root 10 mm from the tip end. *Record* this measurement in the data table under "Original Length."

5 Wrap the seedling in a moist paper towel and place carefully into the plastic bag labeled "Seedling 1" (see photo **C**).

6 Repeat Steps 4 through 6 with the other four seedlings. Record each length in the table and place each wrapped seedling into the appropriate plastic bag.

A

B

C

7 After 48 hours, *measure* the length of each root from its tip to the dot you made. Record measurements in the table under "Final Length."

8 Subtract the original length from the final length. Record this measurement in the table under "Growth of Root."

9 Calculate the average growth of a root tip. Record this number in the table under "Average Growth of Roots."

Data and Observations

Seedling	Original Length (mm)	Final Length (mm)	Growth of Roots (mm)	Average Growth of Roots (mm)
1				
2				
3				
4				
5				

Analyzing

1. What evidence do you have that mitosis occurred in the corn roots?

2. Water is a nutrient needed by all living things. How did you supply the seedlings with the water they need to exist?

3. How much, on average, did the roots grow in 48 hours?

Concluding and Applying

4. *Predict* the amount of growth that would occur in an average corn root after a week.

5. Suppose you found that the length of the seedlings had not changed during the 48-hour period. *Hypothesize* about some possible explanations for this lack of growth.

6. **Going Further** Using similar steps, design an experiment to determine the effect of temperature on cell reproduction. Show your design to your teacher. If you are advised to revise your plan, be sure to check with your teacher again. Check for all safety concerns. Carry out your plan.

Cells That Reproduce Rapidly

In the Investigate activity, you observed growth in the corn seedlings' roots. This growth occurred due to mitosis, a process that occurs in most living cells. Through mitosis, the corn plants produced new cells that were identical to their parent cell.

Why do root cells of young plants divide through mitosis so rapidly? **Figure 17-17** may help you answer this question.

Once a new cell forms, how does it stay alive? How does a cell maintain itself within its environment? In Chapter 19, these questions will be answered as you discover how cells obtain the materials they need for life.

Figure 17-17

A A root grows longer because cells in a particular area at the end of the root are able to rapidly reproduce, and the new cells are able to grow slightly in length. If the growth area is damaged, the root cannot grow longer.

B The root-growth area is protected at the very tip of the root by a root cap. Root cap cells are easily rubbed off by soil particles, but these cells are constantly being replaced from within. Plant root cells, like human skin cells, are an example of cells with a rapid rate of mitosis.

check your UNDERSTANDING

1. How do the end products of mitosis compare with the original cell?
2. You know that each new nucleus produced by mitosis contains the same number of chromosomes as the original cell. A cell from the body of a frog contains a nucleus with 26 chromosomes. If one of these cells undergoes mitosis, how many chromosomes will be in each new cell produced? Explain your answer.
3. How could you tell whether or not a cell was undergoing the process of mitosis? Which specific structures are visible during this process?
4. **Apply** What cell process causes hair to constantly increase in length?

Technology Connection

Genetic Engineering

Today scientists are developing new and faster ways to improve herds and crops. The field is genetic engineering, which means the production of new genes by substituting or adding new genetic material to them. The changed genetic material is called "recombinant DNA".

How Does It Work?

Scientists decide on a goal—say, to protect a certain variety of crop plant from a certain kind of insect pest. First, they remove DNA from the bacteria that kills the pests. Then they coat tiny pieces of metal "bullets" with this bacterial DNA and shoot it into the crop plant's cells. As the treated plant cells reproduce, bacterial DNA becomes part of the new plant cells. When the pests feed on the products of these "new" plant cells, the pests die.

This technology can be used to improve and increase plant and animal production, size, resistance to disease, and other areas.

Genetic engineering can also be used to solve different types of problems. Mussels produce a sticky protein on their feet that helps them attach to rocks. Researchers have isolated the gene that controls the stickiness and have transferred the gene to bacteria and yeasts for mass production. The resulting glue works well in wet surroundings and is used in mouth, eye, and bone surgery.

What Do You Think?

The American Medical Association and the Food and Drug Administration have some serious concerns about these genetically engineered plants and animals. How will the body react to genetically engineered foods? How will these foods interfere with medical treatment the consumer might be taking? What if a "new" plant or animal escapes the lab, returns to the wild, and

Blue mussels

reproduces? What if genetic engineering were to be misused by a person or a group who wanted to change the human race according to his or her own ideas? How do scientists police genetic engineering?

These questions and more will have to be answered. Genetically engineered plants and animals are among us now and will be even more common soon.

Science *and* Society

Our Aging Population

How long can human beings live? Most gerontologists (scientists who study old age) think that the human body is designed to live no longer than 120 years. However, 110 years is probably the longest that anyone could hope to live—if he or she is extremely healthy and extremely lucky. Research in molecular biology has given some scientists reason to think we can extend the natural human life span to as long as 130 years! Nevertheless, our cells simply cannot continue to reproduce indefinitely. They wear out, and as a result, we get old and eventually die.

But even though we can't live forever, human beings in America are living longer than they ever have before. In 1900, the average American life expectancy was only 47 years. Today, life expectancy for the average American is 75 years. So, in less than one century, our life expectancy has increased by 28 years. That's pretty remarkable, considering that it took 2000 years for the average human life expectancy to increase from 25 years (the life expectancy when Julius Caesar was born in 100 B.C.E.) to 50 years.

When Are We Old?

Sixty-five may already be out-of-date as the dividing line between middle age and old age. After all, many older people don't begin to experience physical and mental decline until after age 75.

Why Are People in the United States Living Longer?

The main reason that people in the United States are living longer is that more people survive childhood. Before modern medicine changed the laws of nature with vaccines and antibiotics, many youngsters died of common childhood diseases such as measles and whooping cough. Now that the chances of dying young are much lower, the chances of living long are much higher due to better diets and health care.

Overall, our population is getting older. Fewer Americans are having children and

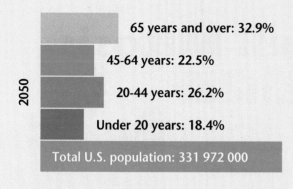

65 years and over: 32.9%

45-64 years: 22.5%

2050

20-44 years: 26.2%

Under 20 years: 18.4%

Total U.S. population: 331 972 000

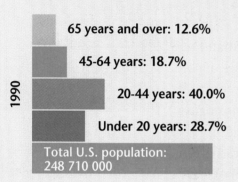

65 years and over: 12.6%

45-64 years: 18.7%

1990

20-44 years: 40.0%

Under 20 years: 28.7%

Total U.S. population:
248 710 000

more of them are living longer. Since 1950, the number of Americans who are 65 and older has more than doubled, to reach 28 million. Of that 28 million older Americans, 2.6 million are over the age of 85—four times as many as in 1950.

Twelve out of every 100 Americans are 65 years old or older. The United States Census Bureau predicts that percentage will reach as high as 25 out of every 100 by the year 2035. By the year 2050, more than one-third of our population may be over 65, and only about one-fifth will be under 20!

One reason for the graying of America is the baby boom that followed World War II. Between the mid-1940s and the mid-1960s, 76 million children were born in the United States—increasing our population by one-third. Starting in 2010, the first of the baby boom generation will reach 65, and by 2030, all of the surviving baby boomers will be 65

to 85 years old. By 2050, there will be only five people of traditional working age for every four people who are past 65, the age of retirement.

What Are the Consequences of a Gray America?

As American society continues to age, the shift in our population will have far-reaching effects on our economy and our way of life. Some people fear such changes will be for the worse. For example, money that should be used to provide an education for the young will be used instead to provide expensive medical care for the elderly. Also, working-age people will have to pay incredibly high taxes so the government can afford to pay Social Security benefits to the retired.

On the other hand, some people see opportunity, not disaster, in the changes caused by our aging population. Today, many men and women in their "golden years" are healthy and alert, still active, and young in outlook if not in years.

As our society ages, we will need the contributions of our millions of older citizens. And with long lives ahead of them, they will need to stay active and involved.

What Do You Think?

What changes might come about in American society as a result of the graying population? For example, do you think more people will work past the age of 65? What kinds of jobs might they have? What kinds of living arrangements will they have? Will they live with their adult children or perhaps with roommates or in senior citizen facilities? How will they get the medical care they need? Who will pay for it? As you look ahead, what effects do you think the aging of America will have on your life?

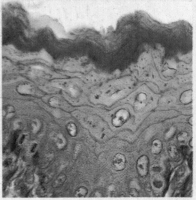

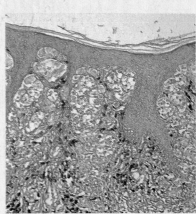

Health
CONNECTION

Skin Cell Mitosis and Cancer

Each kind of cell in our bodies that reproduces undergoes mitosis at its own particular rate. The rate at which a cell reproduces is part of the information stored in the nucleus of that kind of cell. Sometimes a cell is damaged, however, and some of the information stored in its nucleus becomes permanently changed. This change often affects how the cell grows and reproduces.

What Is a Tumor?

The original damaged cell and the damaged cells it produces through mitosis form a growing mass of tissue called a tumor. A tumor that is one centimeter across (about the size of a pea) can contain as many as one billion damaged cells!

Some tumors are benign, meaning the cells do not have the ability to invade other body tissues. Other tumors are malignant, meaning the cells are much more seriously damaged. They can invade other tissue and spread to other parts of the body. This is called cancer. Cancerous cells undergo mitosis in less than half the time of normal cells. Both kinds of tumors may grow very rapidly or very slowly, but most cancer tumors grow and spread quickly.

What Is Skin Cancer?

One of the most common kinds of cancer is skin cancer. The top photograph is a magnified section of normal skin. The bottom one shows a malignant tumor of the skin called a melanoma. Each year, more than 500 000 cases of skin cancer are reported!

The major cause of skin cancer is ultraviolet radiation from the sun. However, people can use proper sunscreen to prevent ultraviolet rays from damaging their skin cells.

You Try It!

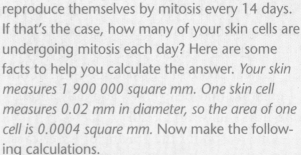

Your skin cells normally reproduce themselves by mitosis every 14 days. If that's the case, how many of your skin cells are undergoing mitosis each day? Here are some facts to help you calculate the answer. *Your skin measures 1 900 000 square mm. One skin cell measures 0.02 mm in diameter, so the area of one cell is 0.0004 square mm.* Now make the following calculations.

1. How many skin cells are present on your body? (Need help? Divide the area of one cell into the area of all of your skin.)
2. How many skin cells undergo mitosis each day? (Need help? Divide the number of days needed to reproduce by mitosis into the number of skin cells.)

Review the statements below about the big ideas presented in this chapter, and try to answer the questions. Then, re-read your answers to the Did You Ever Wonder questions at the beginning of the chapter. *In your Journal*, write a paragraph about how your understanding of the big ideas in the chapter has changed.

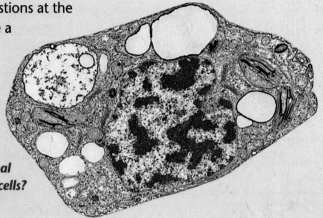

1 The cell is the basic unit of life for all living things. Most cells have a covering called a cell membrane. *What additional outer structure exists in plant cells?*

Nucleus

Animal cell

Plant cell

Mitochondria

2 A cell contains many structures that sustain its life. The nucleus directs the activities of the cell and contains information that controls the traits of an organism. Mitochondria release energy for the cell. *How do plant cells convert light energy into a more useable form of energy?*

3 Cells reproduce themselves through a process called mitosis. In mitosis, the nucleus of a cell divides so that each new cell has the same number of chromosomes as the parent cell. *What processes in the body give evidence that mitosis is taking place?*

   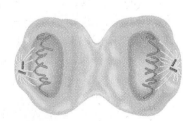

Using Key Science Terms

cell	cytoplasm
cell membrane	mitochondria
cell wall	mitosis
chloroplasts	nucleus
chromosomes	

For each set of terms below, explain the relationship that exists.
1. cell wall, cell membrane
2. chloroplasts, cell wall
3. chromosomes, mitosis
4. cytoplasm, mitochondria, chloroplasts
5. nucleus, chromosomes

Understanding Ideas

Answer the following questions in your Journal using complete sentences.
1. What characteristics determine if something is living or nonliving?
2. Which cell part is being compared with the following analogy?
   a. walls of a building from which a business operates
   b. manager who directs the business from a central office
   c. power plant that supplies energy to the business
3. Why can't animal cells make their own food?
4. How do you know that some of your body cells are reproducing?
5. What might a large number of mitochondria in a cell tell you about the cell's level of activity?

Developing Skills

Use your understanding of the concepts developed in this chapter to answer each of the following questions.
1. **Concept Mapping** Complete the following concept map of the basic units of life.

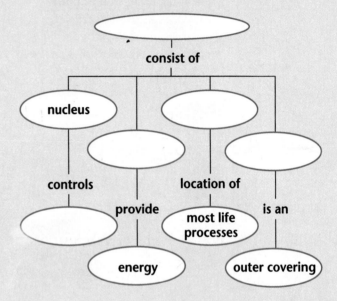

2. **Comparing and Contrasting** Compare and contrast plant and animal cells.
3. **Sequencing** Sequence the steps of mitosis.
4. **Making and Using Graphs** From the Investigate on pages 540-541, make a bar graph to represent the growth of each seedling.

Critical Thinking

In your Journal, *answer each of the following questions.*
1. Why is it important that each new cell produced by mitosis has the same number of chromosomes as the parent?

2. The figure shows a cell that is reproducing by mitosis. Carefully examine

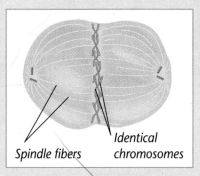

Spindle fibers   Identical chromosomes

what is occurring in the cell. Explain what will happen next in the cell as the mitosis process continues.

3. Has the total number of cells in your body changed since your birth? Has the structure of your individual cells changed during your lifetime? Explain your answer.

Problem Solving

Read the following paragraph and discuss your answers in a brief paragraph.

Sharlene is investigating the growth rate of various types of cells. One of the organisms she is studying is *E. coli*, a one-celled bacterium. Sharlene observes that this bacterium can double its size in about 30 minutes if the environmental conditions are suitable. She also observes that once the cell has grown to twice its original size, it divides to form two new cells.

1. Why does *E. coli* divide when it grows to twice its size rather than continue to grow as a single cell?

2. If *E. coli* can divide at such a rapid rate, why doesn't the population of this bacterium outnumber all other kinds of organisms?

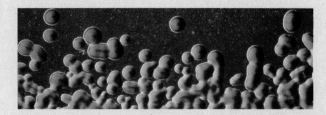

CONNECTING IDEAS

Discuss each of the following in a brief paragraph.

1. **Theme—Energy** How do chloroplasts produce food for plants?

2. **Theme—Scale and Structure** Explain the relationship between the size of a cell and the movement of materials through it.

3. **Theme—Scale and Structure** Cells that exist by themselves tend to be spherical in shape. Cells in many-celled organisms are often shaped like cubes or have other regular shapes. How might you explain the difference?

4. **Physics Connection** What is the magnification power of a microscope equipped with a 10X eyepiece and a 100X objective lens? How has the development of the microscope helped scientists understand the structure of cells?

5. **Health Connection** How is mitosis changed when cancer is present?

CHAPTER 18

Chemical Reactions

Did you ever wonder...

- ✓ Why most cars built today must use unleaded gasoline?
- ✓ Why chemicals with strange-sounding names are in your food?
- ✓ Why your body is warm?
- ✓ Why some things rust and others don't?

Before you begin to study about chemical reactions, think about these questions and answer them *in your Journal*. When you finish the chapter, compare your Journal write-up with what you have learned.

*I*magine what that tricycle once looked like and how it felt to ride it. Not long ago, the wheels probably glistened in the sun. Now much of the trike is coated with reddish-brown rust.

Rusting is just one of many kinds of chemical changes that go on around you. A hamburger's cooking, flowers' growing and blooming, and the burning of gasoline in an automobile are all actions during which the properties of substances change.

▶ **In this chapter, you will find out how chemical changes take place.**

Explore! ACTIVITY

What kinds of things rust?

Perhaps you have noticed that certain objects around you rust, and other objects don't ever rust at all. What is rust and why does it form?

What To Do

Record the following observations and the answers to the questions *in your Journal*.

1. Look for rust on objects at home, in school, and on your way to school. Make a list of these rusty objects.

2. Think about the items on your list. What do things that rust have in common?

3. Where does rust form? Do you notice more rust on objects that are indoors or outdoors? Why do you think this is so?

18-1

How Does Matter Change Chemically?

Section Objectives

- Describe materials before and after chemical changes.
- Recognize when chemical reactions have taken place.
- Identify and describe several chemical reactions.

Key Terms

chemical reaction

Observing Chemical Changes

You're already familiar with many changes around you. Melting is a common change. It is a physical change because the material that is changed stays the same material. Ice is frozen water, and when ice melts, it is still water.

If a different substance is produced by the change, the change is chemical. Burning wood turns to ashes. Rust forms on tools left in the rain. The paint on buildings fades. Plants and animals grow. How are these chemical changes similar? How are they different? This section will help you answer these questions.

Find Out! ACTIVITY

Are all chemical changes alike?

Chemical changes are all around you and you observe them every day, whether you realize it or not.

What To Do

You are going to observe several chemical changes.

1. Observe what happens when a piece of paper burns. *In your Journal*, list the changes that you and your classmates observe.

2. Watch what happens as a marshmallow burns. Again, list the changes you observe. Which changes are alike for the paper and the marshmallow? Which are different?

3. Next, observe how a banana changes over a period of a few days. Describe

any changes in the color, odor, and texture of the skin or the fruit inside.

Conclude and Apply

1. Compare and contrast the changes in the banana, the paper, and the marshmallow.

2. How do these changes differ from what you observe when you boil a pot of water?

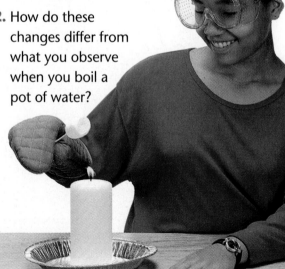

Chemical Reactions Around You

When a piece of paper burns, a banana ripens, or a bike rusts, the chemical and physical properties of the substance change. These changes may happen quickly or slowly. In each case, however, new substances are formed. A chemical reaction has taken place. A **chemical reaction** is a well-defined process that results in the formation of new substances having properties that are different from those of the original substances.

Have you ever noticed changes in a piece of newspaper? As is shown in **Figure 18-1**, the changes may be physical, but many are chemical changes caused by the reaction between substances in the air and in the paper. Whenever you see a cut apple turn brown, exhaust gases come out of a car's tailpipe, or a caterpillar change into a butterfly, you know that chemical reactions are taking place because new substances are formed.

Figure 18-1

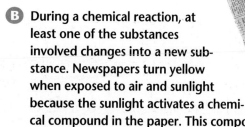

A Cutting, tearing, and crumpling change the newspaper's size, shape, and texture. These are physical changes and alter only the physical properties of the paper, not the paper itself. The newspaper *looks* different after you tear and crumple it, but it's still the same newspaper. No new substance is created.

B During a chemical reaction, at least one of the substances involved changes into a new substance. Newspapers turn yellow when exposed to air and sunlight because the sunlight activates a chemical compound in the paper. This compound reacts with the oxygen in the air, and it is believed that a new substance is formed. Because this new substance reflects yellow light and absorbs some other colors, the paper appears yellow.

C The burning of the paper is a chemical reaction because the oxygen in the air combines with substances in the newspaper. New gaseous and solid products and energy are produced. It is easy to see the changes in both the chemical and physical properties of a newspaper that has been burned.

Chemical Reactions Inside You

In the last section, you saw that chemical reactions take place around you all the time. Would you be surprised to find out that chemical reactions take place inside your body every moment of your life?

Find Out! ACTIVITY

Is oxygen changed inside your body?

You know you breathe in oxygen from the air around you. But what happens to that oxygen?

What To Do

1. Colorless limewater turns cloudy or milky in the presence of carbon dioxide gas. Test this by adding a few drops of colorless carbonated soft drink to a small amount of colorless limewater.

What We Breathe Can Destroy Bridges!

Of all the chemical reactions possible, corrosion probably receives more attention and costs more money than any other. Rust and other types of corrosion take their toll on bridges, overpasses, and ships. Corrosion occurs when metals, such as iron or steel, are affected by ordinary water and oxygen in the environment. If rain is acidic or if there are dissolved salts in the atmosphere, corrosion occurs even faster.

Rust Resisters

There are ways to protect metal from corrosion. Perhaps you've seen the overpasses along the expressway being painted. You may have coated your ice-skate blades or your bicycle chain with oil before you stored them for next season. Both of these methods of protection help to keep oxygen and water in the air from reaching the metal and causing corrosion.

2. Observe what happens when the bubbles of carbon dioxide in the soft drink come in contact with the limewater.

3. Now gently blow out through a straw into a glass half-filled with colorless limewater. **CAUTION:** *Be sure not to take in any limewater.*

4. *In your Journal,* describe the changes you observe in the limewater as you continue to blow out through the straw.

Conclude and Apply

1. How could you be sure that limewater does not turn cloudy when oxygen is present?

2. What can you infer from your observations?

3. Has a chemical reaction taken place?

Oxygen combines with food you have taken in. Through a series of chemical reactions called respiration, new substances, carbon dioxide and water, and energy are produced. It is this carbon dioxide you exhaled into the limewater. The energy sustains life.

At the same time, digestion takes place. During digestion, food is broken down by chemical reactions.

You already know that the reaction of some metals with oxygen can produce an oxide. For instance, if aluminum is exposed to air, a thin coating of aluminum oxide is formed. Unlike iron oxide, which is loose and dusty, aluminum oxide consists of very tightly packed units. These units are so tightly packed that the aluminum oxide actually protects the metal beneath from further reactions.

Galvanizing

Another method for protecting metals from corrosion relies on the element zinc. Perhaps you've heard of galvanized steel, as is shown in the photo. It's often used for garbage cans,

plumbing, and gutters. Galvanized steel is steel coated with a layer of zinc by electroplating or by applying molten zinc. The zinc slowly forms a zinc oxide coating that protects the iron or steel beneath it.

Magnesium sheets bolted to bridge pillars and ship hulls protect in the same way. Both magnesium and zinc are allowed to corrode in order to protect the structural metal beneath.

You Try It!

Design a sculpture of iron or steel using discarded items you might have at home or might find in an alley or vacant lot. Then tell how you might protect it from corrosion.

Describing Chemical Reactions

Remember how you described what happened to the marshmallow and the banana? You probably used words that told about changes in physical properties, such as color, shape, texture, and smell. How could you describe a rusting bicycle or a burning paper? When you say that paper burns and iron rusts, you are describing the chemical properties that change during chemical reactions. In **Figure 18-2**, you can clearly see what effect rusting had on the unprotected tool. The tool that was protected from rust still has its original properties.

How would you describe the chemical reactions that occur when a building is demolished by using explosives? It might appear that the substances haven't changed. You have brick or stone before and after the explosion. But what was the reaction that caused the building to collapse?

While descriptive words might describe what an explosion looks or sounds like, these words don't tell us much about the chemical reaction that takes place. The next section will help you describe the chemical reactions that take place around you.

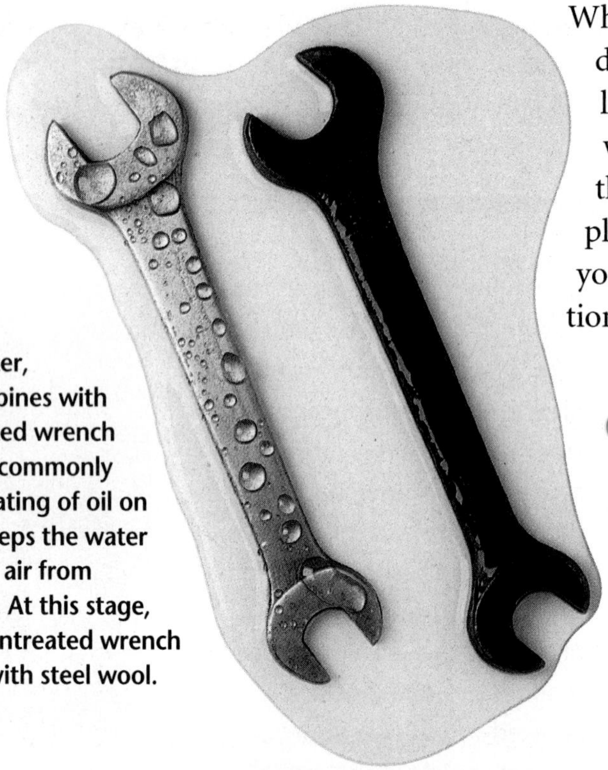

Figure 18-2

Two wrenches— one treated with a coating of oil and the other untreated—are left outside and forgotten. Rain collects in a puddle around the wrenches. The scene is set for chemical reaction.

A In the presence of water, oxygen in the air combines with the iron in the untreated wrench and forms iron oxide, commonly known as rust. The coating of oil on the treated wrench keeps the water and the oxygen in the air from reacting with the iron. At this stage, the rust layer on the untreated wrench could be scraped off with steel wool.

B Over time, the chemical reaction continues. More of the iron in the untreated wrench is changed into rust. What will eventually happen to the untreated wrench if it stays where it is? What will happen to the treated wrench?

check your UNDERSTANDING

1. List several ways that you can tell that a chemical change has taken place.
2. Name three chemical reactions that you read about in this section.
3. List two chemical changes not mentioned in this section. How did you decide that they were chemical rather than physical changes?
4. **Apply** When you dissolve sugar in water, does a chemical reaction take place? How do you know?

Word Equations

Writing Word Equations

Section Objectives
■ Distinguish between reactants and products.
■ Write word equations.

Key Terms
reactants
products

How might you describe the chemical reactions in respiration? You could describe changes in the physical and chemical properties of the substances in words. Another way is to write a word equation. For example, you could use a plus sign (+) to mean *and* and an arrow (→) to mean *produces*. Then, the word equation for respiration would look like this:

oxygen + food → carbon dioxide + water

In any chemical reaction, the substances that you start with are the **reactants**. The new substances formed by the reaction are the **products**. In the above equation, oxygen and food are the reactants, and carbon dioxide and water are products. Can you describe what is happening in another chemical reaction?

 Explore! **ACTIVITY**

Can we describe any chemical reaction?

What To Do
You will observe a chemical reaction and describe what is happening.

1. Drop a piece of freshly sandpapered magnesium ribbon into a small amount of white (distilled) vinegar.

2. Observe carefully for several minutes. Record your observations *in your Journal.*

3. How do you know a reaction is taking place? How can you keep the reaction going?

4. What do you need to know to describe the reactants and products?

Let's take this reaction step by step to see what happened. Vinegar contains acetic acid, which contains hydrogen. When the magnesium was placed in the vinegar, it reacted with the acetic acid. Bubbles of hydrogen gas were released. This is the word equation for the reaction:

magnesium + acetic acid →
magnesium acetate + hydrogen

What are the reactants in this reaction? What are the products?

This reaction has more than one reactant and more than one product. In another reaction, sugar, one reactant, can be heated until it breaks down into carbon and water, two products. When rust forms, iron and oxygen, two reactants, produce rust, one product. You can see that the reactions may vary in the number of reactants and the number of products. In general, any word equation can be written in the form:

$$\text{reactant(s)} \rightarrow \text{product(s)}$$

■ Acid—Base Reactions

Have you ever enjoyed an ice-cold glass of lemonade? Have you ever used a recipe that called for baking powder to make a cake rise? If so, you have used acids and bases.

In general, acids taste sour, react with metals, and contain hydrogen. Bases taste bitter, feel slippery, and are hydroxides.

Suppose you spill some household ammonia, ammonium hydroxide, on the kitchen counter. You wipe it up, but the counter still feels slippery. You try several different solutions, but you find that lemon juice removes the slippery feeling.

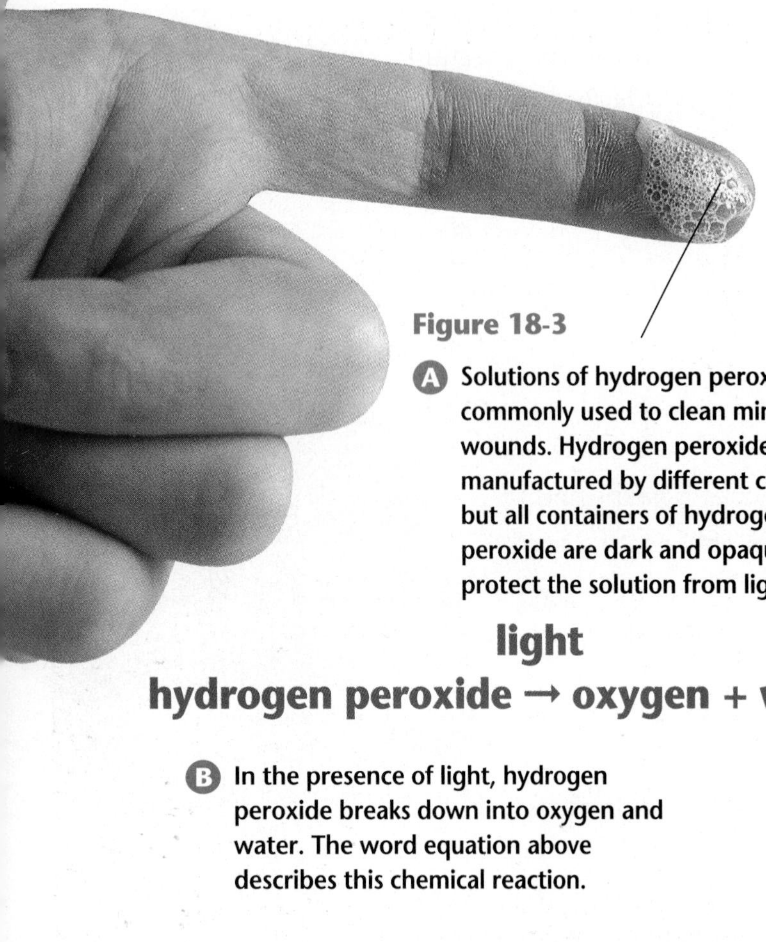

Figure 18-3

A Solutions of hydrogen peroxide are commonly used to clean minor wounds. Hydrogen peroxide is manufactured by different companies, but all containers of hydrogen peroxide are dark and opaque to protect the solution from light.

light
hydrogen peroxide → oxygen + water

B In the presence of light, hydrogen peroxide breaks down into oxygen and water. The word equation above describes this chemical reaction.

What has happened? Acids, such as the citric acid found in lemon juice, and bases, such as ammonium hydroxide, react together to form a salt and water:

acid + base → salt + water

For this particular reaction,

citric acid + ammonium hydroxide → ammonium citrate + water.

The water is formed from the hydrogen from the acid and the hydroxide from the base. The parts of the acid and base that are left over form the salt.

■ Other Reactions

Chemical reactions occur constantly around you. Several of these are explored in **Figures 18-3–18-5**. Whether treating a cut, watching the blasting off of the space shuttle, or exploring a cave, chemical reactions affect and control your life.

carbonic acid + calcium carbonate → calcium hydrogen carbonate

Figure 18-4

Ⓐ Limestone caves are largely the result of chemical reactions. The calcium carbonate of the limestone reacts with acids such as the carbonic acid in rainwater that trickles down through the ground. The reaction produces calcium hydrogen carbonate. The calcium hydrogen carbonate dissolves in the water and washes away easily, leaving empty caverns in the limestone.

Ⓑ The word equation above describes the most common chemical reaction that produces caves.

Figure 18-5

Ⓐ The fuel system of the Space Shuttle includes separate tanks of liquid hydrogen and liquid oxygen. When mixed in correct proportion and ignited, the hydrogen and oxygen react to provide energy. The reaction also produces water, seen here as steam.

liquid hydrogen + liquid oxygen → water (steam) + energy

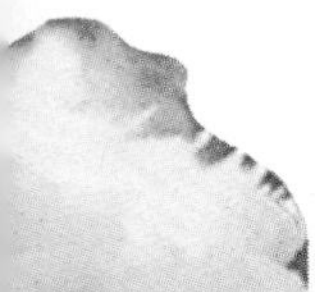

Ⓑ The chemical reaction created by the fuel system is described in the word equation above.

INVESTIGATE!

Describing Reactions

In this activity, you will compare the reaction of several metals with an acid to observe the results and describe what happens using word equations.

Problem
What metals will react with an acid?

Materials
3 test tubes	wooden splint
test-tube rack	15 mL dilute
goggles	hydrochloric acid
graduated cylinder	apron
small pieces of copper,	
zinc, and magnesium	

Safety Precautions

Use caution when using acid. Wear lab aprons and goggles at all times.

What To Do

1. Copy the data table *into your Journal.*
2. Put on goggles and an apron.
3. Set the three test tubes in a rack. Pour 5 mL of dilute hydrochloric acid, which contains hydrogen chloride, into each tube. **CAUTION:** *Handle acid with care. Immediately rinse away any spilled acid with plenty of water.*
4. Place a small piece of copper in the first tube, zinc in the second tube, and magnesium in the third tube.
5. Observe what happens in each tube and record your observations in the data table.
6. Have your teacher collect some of the gas from the test tube that contains the most bubbles. Bring a lighted splint near the gas. Record what you observe.

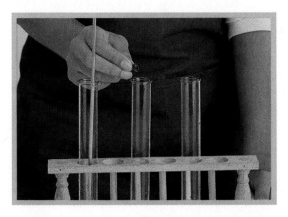

A

B

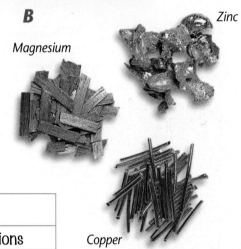

Magnesium

Zinc

Copper

Certain metals cause chemical reactions within your body that are essential for good heath. Copper helps prevent anemia, zinc helps convert nutrients into energy, and magnesium helps with respiration.

Data and Observations		
Tube	Substances Mixed	Observations
1	Hydrochloric Acid + Copper	
2	Hydrochloric Acid + Zinc	
3	Hydrochloric Acid + Magnesium	

Analyzing

1. What evidence of chemical reaction did you observe? Which metals reacted with the acid?

2. Write a word equation for each reaction that took place.

3. When ignited, hydrogen explodes with a "pop." What can you infer about the identity of the gas produced? Why?

Concluding and Applying

4. Predict which of these metals would be least affected by acid rain if this metal were used to build statues.

5. **Going Further** The method of displacement in this Investigate is the most common way to prepare large amounts of hydrogen for use in the laboratory. Which of the metals you tested would be best for this purpose? Why?

Reactions like those that you just investigated can be useful or destructive. For example, Figure 18-6 shows how ozone, a form of oxygen, is involved in both helpful and harmful chemical reactions. By being able to determine what products will be formed from certain reactions, we can predict the effects of some industrial processes on the environment or the effects of a new medicine on the body.

Review the word equations you studied in this section. Can you suggest other factors that play a part in determining whether chemical reactions will take place? In the next section, we'll look at the role played by energy in chemical reactions.

Figure 18-6

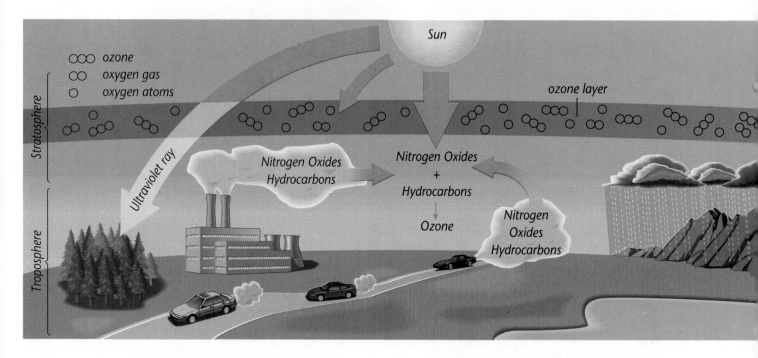

A The exhaust from cars and some industrial plants contains nitrogen oxides and hydrocarbons. These gases, in the presence of sunlight, may react with oxygen in the air to produce ozone. Ozone damages plants and reacts with body tissue in a harmful way.

B A layer of ozone is also created high in the stratosphere when ultraviolet rays from the sun react with regular oxygen molecules. The ozone layer absorbs most of the ultraviolet rays from the sun, which can cause sunburn and some forms of cancer.

check your UNDERSTANDING

1. Write a word equation to describe this chemical reaction: Iron and sulfur form iron sulfide.
2. Mercury(II) oxide breaks down when it is heated. Write a word equation for this reaction.
3. Mercury(II) oxide is a red, powdery substance. All substances that contain mercury, including mercury itself, are poisonous. Use this information to compare the properties of the reactants and products from Question 2.
4. **Apply** Many foods, such as tomato sauce, contain acids. What factors would you consider when choosing a container to cook or store such foods?

Chemical Reactions and Energy

18-3

Energy in Reactions

Section Objectives
- Relate how energy is involved in chemical reactions.
- Differentiate endothermic and exothermic reactions.

Key Terms
endothermic reaction
exothermic reaction

Have you ever seen a fireworks display on the Fourth of July? Brilliant colors and the sounds of exploding rockets fill the night sky. Did you know that these sights and sounds are caused by a series of chemical reactions? Although you can't actually see these reactions taking place, you can certainly observe the results! You've seen that chemical reactions produce new substances. In addition to new substances, light and sound are produced in the fireworks reaction. Where did this energy come from?

Explore! ACTIVITY

Does a rubber band have energy?

What To Do

1. Slip one end of a rubber band over a pencil.

2. Push the other end of the rubber band through a small hole in the center of an index card, as shown.

3. Hold the pencil flat against the back of the card.

4. Pull on the rubber band to stretch it a bit. Then, let it go and listen to the sound it makes.

5. Pull on the rubber band several more times. Each time, stretch the rubber band a little bit more.

6. Answer the following questions *in your Journal*. What happens to the sound? How do you know that a stretched rubber band has energy? Where does the energy come from?

563

Chemical Energy

The stretched rubber band in the Explore activity absorbs the energy you put in when you pull on the rubber band. When you let go, the potential energy of the rubber band is released and transformed into sound energy. There is a similar energy change in chemical reactions.

The substances in the fireworks in the rockets contain chemical potential

Figure 18-7

(A) Certain metals and metal salts each produce a flame that has a characteristic color. The substances take in energy from the flame and then release it in the form of light.

(B) Because each of these substances always produces the same color flame, scientists use a flame test to identify some unknown substances.

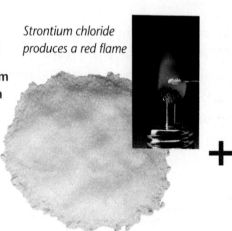

Strontium chloride produces a red flame

+

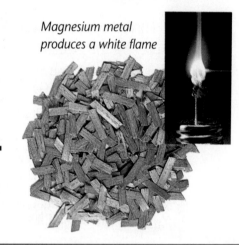

Magnesium metal produces a white flame

Life Science CONNECTION

Edible Fuel

Like automobiles, our bodies have efficient engines. If they get the fuel they need, they have a better chance of running at peak performance. One essential nutrient that provides chemical energy is the carbohydrate.

Where Are Carbohydrates Found?

Carbohydrates come in many shapes and sizes. They're in foods such as apples, pears, grapes, oatmeal, spaghetti, bread, corn, potatoes, tortillas, and rice. All carbohydrates are made of carbon, oxygen, and hydrogen. All sugars and starches are carbohydrates.

When you eat foods with sugar, such as refined white sugar, your body can quickly use the sugar as fuel to provide needed energy. Inside your body's cells, the sugar combines with oxygen. This chemical reaction, called respiration, provides quick energy.

energy that was stored when the substances were formed. When the rockets are ignited, chemical reactions take place. The chemical potential energy in the substances is released and changed into light, motion, and sound, as well as thermal energy.

Look back at the chemical reactions you studied in the last section. Notice how some of these reactions release energy while other reactions absorb energy.

Copper chloride produces a blue flame

C Makers of fireworks take advantage of the colored flames of certain metals and metal salts, like the three shown here, to make colorful fireworks.

Extended Energy

What can you eat if you need energy over a longer period of time? Strenuous activities require a lot of energy. If an athlete's muscles are to get the energy they need for a long race, runners must consume large amounts of carbohydrates. Athletes are counting on the starch in these foods to provide the fuel for respiration reactions throughout the event.

The starches in carbohydrates cannot provide quick energy because they are composed of several joined sugar molecules. There must be a chemical reaction to break apart the starch molecule. Then, the resulting sugar can be used by the cell for energy.

You Try It!

Test for starch in bread. Put on goggles and a lab apron. Add a few drops of iodine to two teaspoons of water and stir with a wooden splint. **CAUTION:** *Iodine is poisonous and stains. Do not taste food you have tested.*

Put a few drops of solution on a small piece of bread and observe what happens. Starch turns blue when tested with iodine.

Test some other foods, including spaghetti and apples, to see which contain starch.

Connect to...

Life Science

ADP and ATP are important biological compounds that help supply the energy needed to run many reactions in your body. Which molecule, ADP or ATP, stores more energy?

Chemical Reactions that Absorb Energy

Exploding fireworks give off a lot of energy. However, some reactions require a lot of energy to get them started and keep them going. Does the following equation look familiar?

$$\text{carbon dioxide + water} \xrightarrow{\text{light}} \text{sugar + oxygen}$$

The word *light* over the arrow means that light is necessary for this reaction to occur. You would read this equation, "In the presence of light, carbon dioxide and water produce sugar and oxygen." Recall that this photosynthesis reaction takes place only in the light. Green plants absorb energy from sunlight. This energy is changed into the chemical energy in sugar and in oxygen. If you keep a green plant in the dark for too long, it will eventually die.

The photosynthesis reaction involves the absorbing of energy. A chemical reaction in which energy is absorbed as the reaction continues is called an **endothermic reaction**. The refining of aluminum metal from its ore is also an endothermic reaction, as shown in **Figure 18-8**. What kind of energy is absorbed in this reaction?

Figure 18-8

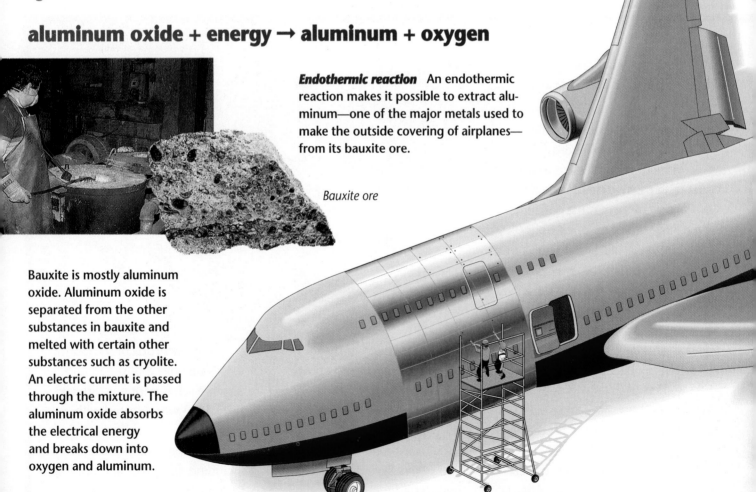

aluminum oxide + energy → aluminum + oxygen

Endothermic reaction An endothermic reaction makes it possible to extract aluminum—one of the major metals used to make the outside covering of airplanes—from its bauxite ore.

Bauxite ore

Bauxite is mostly aluminum oxide. Aluminum oxide is separated from the other substances in bauxite and melted with certain other substances such as cryolite. An electric current is passed through the mixture. The aluminum oxide absorbs the electrical energy and breaks down into oxygen and aluminum.

Chemical Reactions that Release Energy

Imagine that you've worked hard for several hours. When you eat, the chemical reactions of digestion release some of the chemical energy in food. This energy can be used by the body for movement or internal processes of the cells. The heat of your body is an example of chemical energy that has been changed to thermal energy.

A chemical reaction in which energy is released is called an **exothermic reaction**. The explosion of fireworks is an exothermic reaction that produces light, sound, and thermal energy. Think about the word equation for the burning of rocket fuel, as shown in **Figure 18-9**. You don't have to keep supplying energy for the reaction to continue.

In the activity that follows, you will determine whether a reaction is endothermic or exothermic.

Figure 18-9

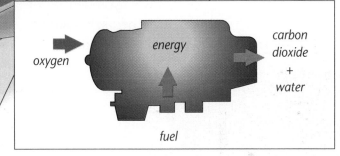

Exothermic reaction The process of burning jet fuel is an exothermic reaction—a reaction that releases energy. Do any substances used for fuels produce an endothermic reaction? Why?

(jet fuel) + oxygen → carbon dioxide + water + energy

Energy Changes

If you were told that your dinner was going to be liver and potatoes, you might not race to the dinner table. Do you ever wonder why we eat what we eat? In this activity, you will observe a chemical reaction involving food and measure and record any change in energy that takes place.

Problem

How can you tell if a reaction is exothermic or endothermic?

Materials

clock or watch with second hand

3% hydrogen peroxide solution

25-mL graduated cylinder

8 test tubes and rack

goggles

raw liver

apron

raw potato

thermometer

Safety Precautions

Wear a lab apron and goggles at all times.

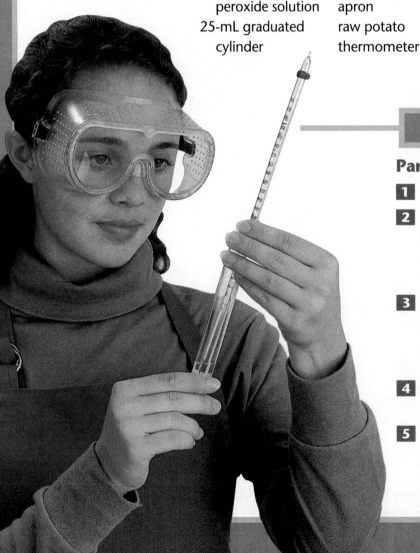

What To Do

Part A

1 Copy the data table *into your Journal.*

2 Put on goggles and an apron. Add 5 mL of hydrogen peroxide to one test tube. **CAUTION:** *Hydrogen peroxide can irritate skin and eyes and damage clothing.*

3 Insert the thermometer and record the starting temperature of the hydrogen peroxide (see photo **A**). **CAUTION:** *If using a mercury thermometer, handle carefully.*

4 Remove the thermometer. Add a small piece of liver (see photo **B**).

5 Record the temperature of the liver and hydrogen peroxide every 30 seconds for 6 minutes.

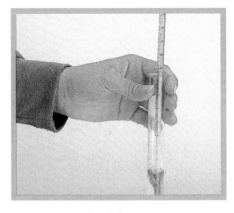

A

B

6 Repeat the procedure three more times. Use clean equipment and new materials each time.

7 Average the four trials in each column to complete your data table.

Part B

1 Make a new data table.

2 Repeat Part A using small pieces of potato. Record your observations.

Data and Observations										
		Temperature after adding Liver/Potato								
		Minutes								
Trial	Starting Temperature									
1										
2										
3										
4										
Total										
Average										

Analyzing

1. What evidence indicates that a chemical reaction took place?

2. Were the reactions exothermic or endothermic? How do you know?

3. Identify the variables in this experiment.

4. Where did the energy to start this reaction come from?

Concluding and Applying

5. Predict the effect of using smaller pieces of liver or potato.

6. **Going Further** Make a hypothesis about whether there is a relationship between how "fattening" a food is and how much energy it will release. Design an experiment to test your hypothesis.

Tracing Energy Changes

Making and Using Graphs

Make a graph of the data you collected in the Investigate. Plot the temperature against time, beginning with the starting temperature. Plot the points for the liver in one color and the potato in a different color. For each set of data, connect the dots using straight lines. What do these lines show? If you need help, refer to the **Skill Handbook** on page 640.

In the reactions you just observed, the chemical energy in hydrogen peroxide was released when the liver and the potato were added to it. The chemical energy was changed to thermal energy, as evidenced by the increase in the temperature over time.

Using information from this chapter,

Figure 18-10 traces the energy changes and identifies the endothermic and exothermic reactions that may occur on a camping trip. In addition to those shown in the figure, what other chemical reactions might occur on the trip?

Make a list of things that you do and things around you that involve chemical reactions. Try to trace the changes in chemical energy for each item on your list.

Figure 18-10

B You cook an egg for your breakfast.

A You strike a match to light your camp stove.

C You eat the egg and start off on a long hike. What endothermic and exothermic reactions occur in each of these tasks?

check your UNDERSTANDING

1. Describe the role of energy in the chemical reaction of baking a cake. Is the reaction endothermic or exothermic?

2. In writing a word equation for the burning of wood, where would you place thermal energy?

3. **Apply** Sometimes during thunderstorms, lightning may strike a tree and set it on fire. As you know, burning is a chemical reaction. Tell where the energy comes from to begin this reaction.

Speeding Up and Slowing Down Reactions

Speeding Up Reactions

Baking a cake involves a reaction that requires energy in order to take place. Some reactions, such as the breaking down of table salt, would never take place without a great deal of energy. Is there a way to speed up a chemical reaction without using lots of energy?

Find Out! ACTIVITY

Can a chemical reaction be made to go faster without adding energy?

Remember that hydrogen peroxide breaks down very slowly when exposed to light.

What To Do

1. Wearing goggles and an apron, pour about 5 mL of 3-percent hydrogen peroxide into each of two test tubes.

2. Very carefully, watch for any signs that a chemical reaction is taking place.

3. Use a small plastic spoon or a spatula to add a small amount of manganese dioxide to one of the test tubes. Record your observations *in your Journal.*

4. Light a wooden splint and blow it out.

5. Place the glowing splint just inside the mouth of the tube without the manganese dioxide. What happens?

6. Repeat with the test tube containing the manganese dioxide. What happens?

7. Heat this tube in a beaker of boiling water until no liquid is left. What do you see?

Conclude and Apply

1. Although oxygen doesn't burn, it must be present for burning to take place. How do you know oxygen was produced in this reaction?

2. What can you infer about the role of manganese dioxide in this reaction?

- Describe how a catalyst affects a chemical reaction.
- Explain how to control a chemical reaction with an inhibitor.

Key Terms
catalyst
inhibitor

The manganese dioxide in the Find Out activity helped the reaction take place and made the reaction go faster. However, the manganese dioxide was not permanently changed as a result of the reaction. The word equation for this reaction is:

manganese dioxide
hydrogen peroxide → water + oxygen

Any substance that speeds up a chemical reaction without being permanently changed is called a **catalyst**. Manganese dioxide is a catalyst in the breaking down of hydrogen peroxide. How do you know?

■ Enzymes

Catalysts are also involved in many of the chemical reactions that take place in organisms. These catalysts are protein substances called enzymes. **Figure 18-11** summarizes your body's production of enzymes and what these enzymes do. The digestion of food, for example, depends on enzymes. In this way, enzyme catalysts make possible the many chemical reactions that keep you alive.

Figure 18-11

Enzyme catalysts make possible the many chemical reactions that keep you alive.

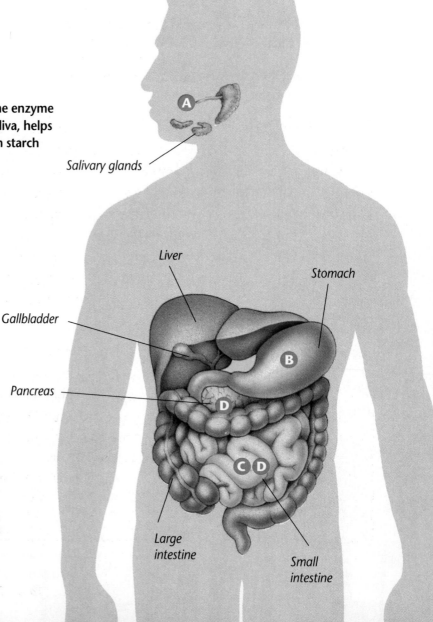

A *Amylase*, the enzyme found in saliva, helps break down starch into sugar.

Salivary glands

Liver

Stomach

B *Pepsin*, in the presence of the acid in your stomach, starts the digestion of protein.

Gallbladder

C *Trypsin* helps to continue protein digestion in your small intestine.

Pancreas

D *Lipase*, the enzyme that is produced in your pancreas, is secreted into your small intestine, where it breaks down fats.

Large intestine

Small intestine

Figure 18-12

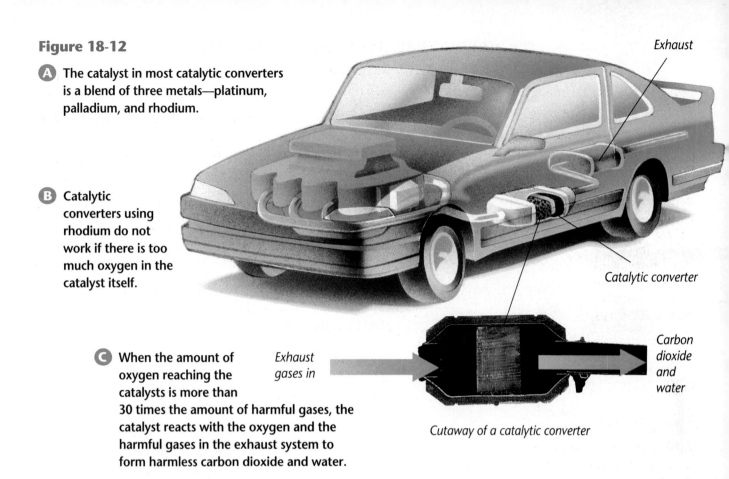

A The catalyst in most catalytic converters is a blend of three metals—platinum, palladium, and rhodium.

B Catalytic converters using rhodium do not work if there is too much oxygen in the catalyst itself.

C When the amount of oxygen reaching the catalysts is more than 30 times the amount of harmful gases, the catalyst reacts with the oxygen and the harmful gases in the exhaust system to form harmless carbon dioxide and water.

Exhaust

Catalytic converter

Exhaust gases in

Carbon dioxide and water

Cutaway of a catalytic converter

■ Catalytic Converters

Air pollution caused by automotive exhaust gases is a problem. This pollution is reduced by using catalysts to speed up the chemical reaction between oxygen and the harmful substances produced by cars. The reaction takes place inside a device called a catalytic converter.

In one type of converter, shown in **Figure 18-12**, air and exhaust gases are passed through a bed of small beads that are coated with the catalysts platinum, rhodium, and palladium. The harmful gases, under the influence of the catalyst, combine with oxygen to form harmless carbon dioxide and water.

How Do We Know?

The Role of Chlorophyll

One of the ways we know that the catalyst chlorophyll is necessary for photosynthesis is by studying organisms that lack chlorophyll. Nongreen plants and fungi get their nourishment by living on food produced by other organisms. When separated from their host organisms, nongreen plants soon die.

From experimental evidence, we know that chlorophyll alone cannot produce the photosynthesis reaction. When chlorophyll extracted from green plants is mixed with water and carbon dioxide and exposed to light, photosynthesis does not take place. The process is quite complex and not completely understood.

Slowing Down Reactions

Figure 18-13

A Bread slice 1

Bread slice 2

B Bread slice 1

Bread slice 2

C Bread slice 1

Bread slice 2

A The slice of bread on the left is made of flour, salt, and yeast. The one on the right is made from the same ingredients and a food preservative. Both slices are exposed to the air.

B After a few days, the slice without the preservative shows signs of mold. Preservatives inhibit the growth of mold on food.

C A few more days later and the slice without a preservative is almost totally covered with mold. Although the preservative inhibited mold growth in the other slice for a time, it too shows signs of mold.

Have you ever wanted to make a sandwich and discovered that the bread had molded? Or maybe you have wondered why some foods spoil more quickly than do others. Sometimes ingredients are added to food to slow down the rate at which foods combine with oxygen. Oxidation is a major cause of spoilage in foods.

Any substance that slows down a chemical reaction is called an **inhibitor**. Most preservatives that are added to foods are inhibitors. Foods containing inhibitors will spoil eventually, but inhibitors greatly decrease the rate at which this occurs. Some antibiotics also act as inhibitors by slowing down the action of those enzymes in the body that tend to help bacteria grow. Some paints are advertised as being rust inhibitors. How do you think these paints help keep rust from forming?

check your UNDERSTANDING

1. You want to slow down the following reaction:

   iron + oxygen → iron oxide

   Which would act as an inhibitor, oil or water?
2. When a rusty iron nail is added to a test tube containing hydrogen peroxide, bubbles quickly form. The nail undergoes no obvious change. What conclusion can you draw about the iron oxide (rust) that is on the nail?
3. **Apply** Enzymes are sometimes used in detergents to boost their cleaning power. What do you think that means?

EXPAND your view

Science and Society

What's In Your Food Besides Food?

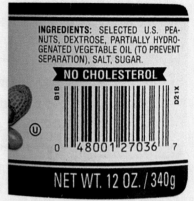

INGREDIENTS: SELECTED U.S. PEA-NUTS, DEXTROSE, PARTIALLY HYDRO-GENATED VEGETABLE OIL (TO PREVENT SEPARATION), SALT, SUGAR.
NO CHOLESTEROL
0 48001 27036 7
NET WT. 12 OZ. / 340g

When George Washington Carver first made peanut butter, he probably gathered the nuts, roasted them, mashed them, and spread them on bread—all within a day or two. Now the peanut butter may spend weeks on a grocer's shelf and months in your cupboard.

The peanut butter can readily be changed by reactions with oxygen in the air. To prevent chemical changes, food manufacturers add chemicals, called food additives, to food.

Food Additives

Salt was one of the first additives and was used to preserve meats and fish. Natural additives, such as salt and ascorbic acid (vitamin C), are still used today. The food industry, however, depends on hundreds of different chemicals to keep your food edible for a longer time.

There are also additives to improve the appearance or texture of food. Iodine in salt and vitamin D in milk are added to prevent diseases.

Regulating Additives

All these chemicals are regulated by the Food and Drug Administration (FDA). Occasionally, the FDA has approved additives that were later shown to cause cancer. There are additives that cause reactions ranging from mild to life-threatening for certain individuals. One is the flavor enhancer monosodium glutamate, known as MSG.

What Do You Think?

Make a list of your favorite foods. Are any of these foods available without additives? How much more would you be willing to pay for the additive-free item?

CAREER connection

A **food chemist** works to develop additives. Food chemists study chemistry, biology, and biochemistry.

Are You Too Awake?

The story goes that a monk in an Arabian monastery centuries ago observed goats in the field nibbling the berries from a coffee plant. The goats ran and played all night long without ever seeming to be tired. The monk decided to try the berries himself. He gathered some, added them to boiling water, and found that the resultant brew, which contained caffeine, did indeed make him more alert.

Effects of Caffeine

Whether that story is true or not, caffeine has been used for centuries as a stimulant. Caffeine is a combination of carbon, hydrogen, nitrogen, and oxygen. When caffeine is taken into the body, chemical changes take place that turn caffeine into other chemicals that interfere with your body's natural substances and stimulate the nerves.

The problems come when there is too much caffeine in the body and the nerves are too stimulated. The results can be inability to sleep, irregular heartbeat, nervousness, and high cholesterol.

Sources of Caffeine

Many products besides coffee contain caffeine. Tea, soft drinks, chocolate, cocoa, and several over-the-counter drugs contain fairly large amounts of caffeine. It is also hard to know how much caffeine you take into your

Average Amounts of Caffeine	
Coffee	80 mg-120 mg
Hot cocoa	1-8 mg
Tea	40 mg
Soft drinks	40 mg

body. For example, a cup of coffee can contain 29 milligrams of caffeine or 176 milligrams of caffeine, or any amount in between. The amount of caffeine depends in part on the way the coffee was prepared. Some researchers say that people can take up to 600 milligrams of caffeine per day without any harm being done. Others say that even smaller amounts can do damage.

What Do You Think?

The chart shows the average amounts of caffeine in a cup of four drinks. Keep a record of how much caffeine you take in a day from these sources. Would you be better off with less?

Technology
Connection

Steely Recipes

You've seen rust on steel bicycles and cars. You know rust forms when iron combines with oxygen. What is the relationship between iron and steel?

Pig Iron

Pig iron is made from two parts iron ore (iron oxide and sand), one part carbon in coke form, a "pinch" of limestone (calcium carbonate), and four parts hot air.

When heated with a limited amount of air, carbon combines with oxygen in the air to produce carbon monoxide. The carbon monoxide reacts with the iron oxide in the ore to produce carbon dioxide and pig iron. The sand from the ore combines with calcium oxide formed by the heated limestone and is easily removed as slag. Pig iron, however, is not very strong.

Steel

To produce steel, molten pig iron is placed in a converter, and forced through a large quantity of hot air. The oxygen in the air combines with the carbon in the iron to form carbon monoxide. Also produced is iron with less than 1 percent carbon—called steel.

Stainless steel and other special steels are made with molten pig iron, scrap iron, and powdered limestone. These are all placed in an oven lined with calcium oxide. Oxygen is added. A series of rapid exothermic reactions takes place that keeps the contents mixed and molten.

The tendency to corrode, as well as the strength of the steel, can be varied by adding nickel, chromium, or tungsten at the beginning of the process. Stainless steel contains from 12 to 30 percent chromium.

You Try It!

Look through newspaper ads and clip those that mention stainless, nickel, chromium, or tungsten steels. List the use of each type of steel.

Teens in SCIENCE

Cellular Fun

Have you ever wondered exactly why your doctor or dentist uses certain types of equipment?

Edie Shin, a 17-year-old high school senior in Orland Park, Florida, did more than wonder. "I noticed that my dentist always covered me with a lead apron before she took X rays of my mouth. I decided to find out why she takes such great precautions with X rays. In my chemistry class, we'd been talking about the effects of radiation on human cells. I wanted to find out just how harmful X rays can be."

Irradiating Cells

A local hospital gave Edie a supply of human cells that had come from the throat culture of a healthy 50-year-old man. Edie used the hospital's equipment to expose the throat cells to a minimum of 50 RADS of radiation every week for nearly a year. Each exposure equaled nearly 250 times the amount of radiation that you are exposed to during regular dental X rays.

Edie soon discovered that the cells she had irradiated looked very different. "Many cells died over the course of the experiment. But the cells that survived grew as much as ten times their normal size. Some had as many as six nuclei."

Results of Radiation

Edie came to the conclusion that when precautions such as using the lead apron are taken, normal dental X rays do not harm human cells. However, when human cells are exposed to high levels of radiation over a long period of time, a series of chemical reactions occur in the cellular water of normal cells. This can result in mutations.

At first, Edie wasn't sure what was going to happen. She found that, to her, the best thing about science was that the investigation and questioning were themselves rewards.

You Try It!

Make a list of any medical or dental equipment that you would like to understand better.

Choose one item from your list. Telephone your doctor's or dentist's office and ask him or her to explain why this equipment is used.

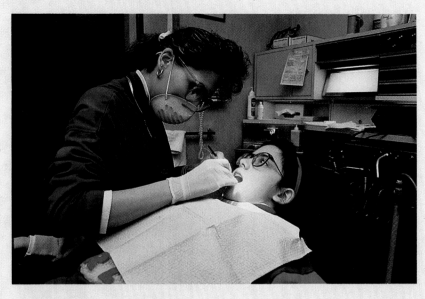

Review the statements below about the big ideas presented in this chapter, and try to answer the questions. Then, re-read your answers to the Did You Ever Wonder questions at the beginning of the chapter. *In your Journal*, write a paragraph about how your understanding of the big ideas in the chapter has changed.

1 A chemical reaction involves the changing of substances into other substances. *How does this change differ from a physical change?*

2 A word equation is a way to describe what happens in a chemical reaction. *What word equation describes the pictured reaction?*

3 Every chemical reaction involves changes in energy. Energy may be absorbed, as in an endothermic reaction. Or energy may be released, as in an exothermic reaction. *Is the pictured reaction endothermic or exothermic?*

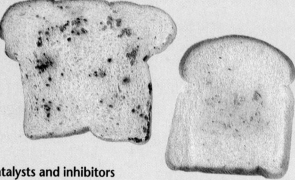

4 Catalysts and inhibitors help control the rate at which some chemical reactions take place. Catalysts and inhibitors themselves remain chemically unchanged at the end of the reaction. *Does the figure show the effect of a catalyst or does it show the effect of an inhibitor?*

Using Key Science Terms

catalyst   inhibitor
chemical reaction   product
endothermic reaction   reactant
exothermic reaction

For each term below, identify which key science term from the list is opposite in meaning.

1. reactant
2. endothermic reaction
3. catalyst

Use your knowledge of the key science terms to answer these questions.

4. Describe how reactants and products are a part of a chemical reaction.
5. Describe how catalysts and inhibitors affect a chemical reaction.

Understanding Ideas

Answer the following questions in your Journal using complete sentences.

1. What is the common reactant in the chemical reactions that take place when an apple turns brown, tools rust, or newspaper turns yellow?
2. Explain why it is necessary to have oxygen to digest food.
3. Differentiate an endothermic reaction and an exothermic reaction. What evidence do you have that respiration is an exothermic reaction?
4. What is an inhibitor? How might an inhibitor be useful in medicine?
5. Why are some products kept in dark glass containers?

Developing Skills

Use your understanding of the concepts developed in the chapter to answer each of the following questions.

1. **Concept Mapping** Create a concept map of chemical reactions using the following terms: *catalyst, chemical reactions, components, endothermic, energy, exothermic, inhibitor, product, rate, reactant.*

2. **Observing and Inferring** Continue to think about the Explore activity on page 551. Why do some iron products rust? Why don't other iron products rust? Make a list of factors that may have caused some products to rust faster than others.

3. **Recognizing Cause and Effect** Repeat the Find Out activity on page 554. Using two jars with one cup of distilled water in each, put the nozzle of a bicycle pump in one jar of water and gently pump air through it for 10 strokes. In the other jar, use the straw to gently blow air into the water for 10 seconds. Add 10 drops of bromothymol blue solution to each jar. What do you observe? What caused the color change?

4. **Sequencing** You know that burning is an exothermic reaction. If this is true, why doesn't toast continue to get darker after it is removed from the toaster?

5. **Interpreting Data** Two identical pieces of apple were left out in the air. One piece was first dipped in lemon juice. Based on the results in the table on the following page, do you think lemon juice

is a catalyst, or is it an inhibitor? Explain your reasoning.

Time	With Lemon Juice	Without Lemon Juice
10	no browning	edges brown
20	no browning	more browning
30	no browning	surface brown

Critical Thinking

Use your understanding of the concepts developed in the chapter to answer each of the following questions.

1. How do catalytic converters reduce air pollution?
2. Food eaten has chemical potential energy. Explain why athletes eat food high in carbohydrates before an event.
3. When water is broken down into hydrogen and oxygen, how do the products differ from the reactants?

4. What two factors might be responsible for bananas ripening more slowly if they are kept in the refrigerator?
5. If your doctor prescribed an inhibitor, how would it affect how your nerves transmit impulses across the synapse?

Problem Solving

Read the following problem and discuss your answers in a brief paragraph.

You are a highway engineer assigned to maintain your company's equipment in good condition.

1. How can you use your knowledge of chemical reactions to design a maintenance program that will protect the equipment from rust?
2. Your work site is near the sea. What other factors in the environment might you need to consider?

CONNECTING IDEAS

Discuss each of the following in a brief paragraph.

1. **Theme—Systems and Interactions** In photosynthesis, is sunlight a catalyst or a reactant?
2. **Theme—Systems and Interactions** When matter changes chemically, it is neither created nor destroyed; only its form is changed. Identify some chemical changes that you notice from day to day.
3. **Theme—Energy** Explain how gasoline has chemical potential energy.
4. **A Closer Look** Write a word equation for the burning of propane to form water and carbon dioxide. Be sure to indicate whether heat is needed for the reaction to proceed, or if the reaction gives off heat.
5. **Life Science Connection** What is the word equation for the chemical reaction that changes sugar to energy in the cell? Is the reaction exothermic or endothermic? Explain your answer.

CHAPTER 19

HOW CELLS DO THEIR JOBS

Did you ever wonder...

✓ **Why rice gets soft when it is cooked?**

✓ **Why you get hot when you run fast?**

✓ **How you can make a cup of tea without stirring?**

Before you begin to study about how cells do their jobs, think about these questions and answer them *in your Journal*. When you finish the chapter, compare your Journal write-up with what you have learned.

*H*ave you ever been swimming in the ocean? If so, you know that ocean water is quite different from water found in a lake or river. It's salty! Ocean water is about 3.5 percent salt, while freshwater bodies such as lakes may contain less than 0.005 percent salt.

You may know that it is deadly to place saltwater fish in a freshwater tank and freshwater fish in a saltwater tank. Why can some organisms only live in salt water? What happens to cells in different environments?

In Chapter 17, you learned that organisms are made of cells. Most cells are "on duty" 24 hours a day, every day, taking in nutrients and giving off products. How can cells do all the things they do? This chapter will help you find out.

▶ *In the activity on the next page, explore how salt affects living things.*

Explore! ACTIVITY

How does salt affect living things?

What To Do

1. Use a pair of scissors to cut a 6-cm piece from the green end of a green onion.

2. Cut one end of the section into thin strands.

3. Dip the cut end of the onion into a container of distilled water. Wait about four minutes and watch what happens. Record your observations *in your Journal*.

4. Take the onion and put it in a container of salt water.

5. *In your Journal* tell what happened to the strands of green onion? If the onion changed shape, what might have caused the change?

19-1 Traffic In and Out of Cells

Section Objectives

- Describe the function of the cell membrane.
- Explain how materials move in and out of cells.
- Compare and contrast osmosis and diffusion.

Key Terms

diffusion
osmosis

The Cell Membrane

You have now observed that onion strands soaked in salt water appear different from those soaked in distilled water. Somehow the salt in the salt water affected the cells. Did the salt coat the cells? Did it enter the cells? Did the water enter the cells? What caused the onion strands to change as they did in the presence of salt? To answer that question, you'll need to think back to Chapter 17, where you learned that all cells are covered by a thin cell membrane. The cell membrane gives the cell its shape. In order to live, a cell must obtain certain materials from its environment and release other materials. Given that a cell has a membrane, how is it possible for these materials to enter and leave the cell?

Find Out! ACTIVITY

What substances can pass through a barrier?

What To Do

1. Obtain a double layer of cheesecloth, a small amount of sand and gravel, a funnel, a stirring rod, and two glass jars.

2. Put the sand and gravel in one jar and add enough water to cover them by about 1 cm. Stir the mixture thoroughly.

3. Place the layers of cheesecloth inside the funnel.

4. While holding the funnel over an empty jar, pour your mixture through. Record your observations in your Journal.

5. Wait several minutes and remove the cheesecloth from the funnel. Inspect the cheesecloth's contents. Record your findings *in your Journal.*

Conclude and Apply

Describe what happened. What was the job of the cheesecloth?

The cell membrane

Even if you use a simple light microscope, such as the one in your classroom, you will not be able to see the details of a cell membrane's structure. How then do we know about the structure of the cell membrane?

One time or another, you've probably experienced the thrill of pulling and pushing metal objects with the invisible force supplied by a magnet. In the 1920s, scientists discovered that beams of tiny particles called electrons could be pushed or pulled with a very powerful magnet. Years later, researchers put this knowledge to use by building a new type of microscope called the electron microscope.

This microscope is much more powerful than a light microscope and can magnify an object over 1 000 000 times its normal size. Using it, we are able to see the microscopic structures of a cell membrane.

Figure 19-1

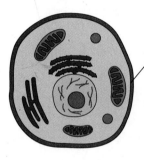

Animal cell

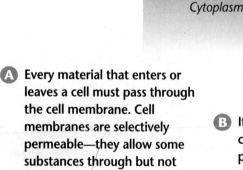

Cytoplasm

Proteins

Fat molecules

Cell membrane

A Every material that enters or leaves a cell must pass through the cell membrane. Cell membranes are selectively permeable—they allow some substances through but not others.

B If a cell membrane had human characteristics, you might say it was particular, welcoming some substances in and refusing others. Could cells exist if the membrane was permeable, that is, if it allowed all substances to pass through?

■ Modeling the Cell Membrane

You have just seen that all of the sand passed through the cheesecloth, while most of the gravel was held back. The thin cell membrane that covers every cell, shown in **Figure 19-1**, works in a similar way to the cheesecloth.

The cell membrane permits certain molecules to pass in or out, depending on the type and size of the molecules. Water, oxygen, and carbon dioxide molecules pass through the cell membrane easily while other substances, such as sugars or sodium, are stopped or slowed down. Entry of

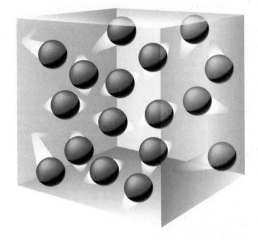

Figure 19-2

As molecules move, they bump into one another. The collision of two molecules causes both to change directions and move away from each other.

these kinds of substances may require energy on the part of the cell membrane to get them in or out of the cell, or may make use of special molecules in the cell membrane itself.

All matter is made up of molecules that are constantly moving. A diagram of molecular motion is shown in **Figure 19-2**. By bumping into each other and bouncing off, molecules move from an area where they are crowded together to places where there are fewer of them. Molecular motion like this occurs in the air and in the cytoplasm of your cells.

Explore! ACTIVITY

How do tea bags work?

Would you believe that a cup of tea can help you understand something about molecular motion? Try this activity.

What To Do

1. Place a wet tea bag in a clear glass of hot water. Without stirring, carefully watch where the tea color first appears. Wait two minutes, then describe the glass *in your Journal*.

2. Make an observation every 2 minutes for 10 minutes. What change in water color do you notice? How do you think the tea color got into the water?

In the Explore activity, you made a model that demonstrated molecular movement. The bag containing tea represented a cell membrane. When you placed the tea bag in the hot water, molecules that make up tea moved from inside the bag out into the water. Likewise, the water moved

through the bag to the tea leaves. Why did these molecules move? As you learned in Chapter 6, the process of convection helped the tea move from the tea bag and throughout the glass because the hot water was in motion. The movement of molecules was also involved.

Movement of Molecules

Molecules are in constant motion, causing many substances to move in and out of cells. This constant movement plays a role in changing the concentration of materials inside and outside the cells. **Figure 19-3** shows how the state of equilibrium is achieved when the concentrations of molecules inside and outside of the cell are not the same. When the concentrations become equal inside and outside of the cell, the molecules continue back and forth through the membrane at an equal rate in each direction.

■ Diffusion

The process by which the constant motion of molecules causes movement from an area of high concentration to an area of low concentration is called **diffusion**. In Chapter 14, you learned about the behavior of gas molecules, and in Chapter 16, you

DID YOU KNOW?

The word *cell* comes from the Latin word *cella*, which means small room.

Figure 19-3

Some molecules move from areas of high concentration to areas of low concentration, even when those areas are on opposite sides of a cell membrane.

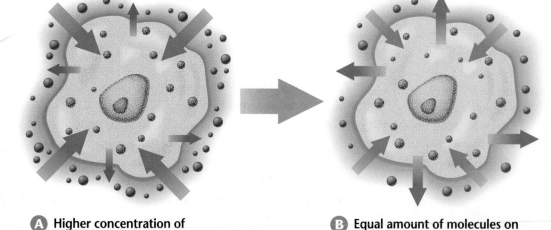

A Higher concentration of molecules outside the cell.

B Equal amount of molecules on both sides of the cell membrane.

When the concentrations of molecules are equal on both sides of the cell membrane, equilibrium exists.

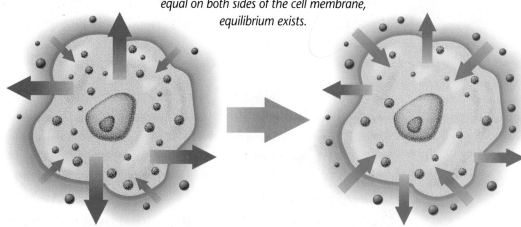

C Higher concentration of molecules inside the cell.

D Equal amount of molecules on both sides of the cell membrane.

learned how carbon dioxide and oxygen molecules are exchanged in the lungs by the process of diffusion. Whether diffusion involves gas molecules through air, or water molecules through a cell membrane, it occurs without the use of energy on the part of the cell.

Figure 19-4

When ink enters water, the ink molecules diffuse from areas of high concentration to areas of low concentration. The water molecules also move and become mixed with the ink molecules.

In time, the ink molecules—evenly dispersed with the water molecules—make the whole solution appear ink-colored.

Find Out! ACTIVITY

How does diffusion occur?

What To Do

You can observe diffusion in the following activity.

1. With your teacher's help, prepare a dialysis membrane bag according to your teacher's directions.
2. Place about 1/4 cup of cooked rice in the bag.
3. Place the bag into a 200-mL beaker of iodine solution.
4. Wait five minutes and look at the rice in the bag.

Conclude and Apply

1. *In your Journal*, describe any changes you see in the rice.
2. What evidence do you have that iodine molecules diffused into the bag?

In the Find Out activity, you observed the diffusion of iodine molecules through the bag into the rice. A change in the color of the rice gives you evidence that diffusion has occurred. What would happen if you soaked uncooked rice in a pot of water overnight? Diffusion would also occur. When the dry rice grains, containing no water molecules, are placed in a container filled with water, water molecules will pass from the area of high concentration to the area of low concentration. The fact that the rice grains plump up, get soft, and change color gives you evidence that water

Figure 19-5

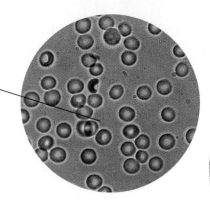

Ⓐ Blood cells gained water molecules and bulged.

Ⓑ Blood cells lost water molecules and shriveled.

has diffused into the grains. How does the amount of water in the pot before and after soaking indicate diffusion has occurred?

■ Osmosis: Diffusion of Water

Most cells live in an aqueous environment. In other words, they are bathed by fluids that are mostly water. This constant presence of water is important. All life processes in cells take place in water. If a cell does not receive an adequate supply of water, it will die because it cannot carry out its life processes.

Recall the Explore activity at the beginning of this chapter. You observed the onion section spread out like a fan in the distilled water. The change in the onion section was due to diffusion of water into the onion cells. When the onion was in the distilled water, there was a higher concentration of water molecules outside the onion cells than inside. As a result, water molecules diffused into the onion cells. A similar experiment was performed on the blood cells in **Figure 19-5**. When you placed the onion in salt water, the cells lost water. This time, water molecules moved out of the onion cells and into the surrounding water.

The diffusion of water through a cell membrane is called **osmosis**. This is illustrated in **Figure 19-6**. In the following Investigate, you will observe and measure osmosis.

Observing and Inferring

Make a chart of the observations you made during the last Find Out activity. Head one column *Before* and head a second column *After*. Make a third column headed Inference. Explain how the three columns are related. If you need help, refer to the **Skill Handbook** on page 642.

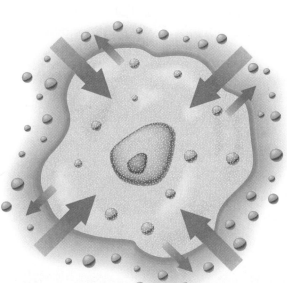

Figure 19-6

In osmosis, water molecules diffuse from an area of high concentration to an area of low concentration through a semipermeable membrane. Eventually equilibrium is reached, and then the number of water molecules moving into the cell becomes equal to the number moving out of the cell. Osmosis requires no energy use by the cell.

Eggs as Model Cells

A chicken egg can be used as a model cell because the yolk is actually a single large cell. The surrounding egg white, or albumin, contains water and several different proteins.

Problem

How can osmosis be measured? Can you design an experiment using an egg to show osmosis?

Materials

2 raw eggs	200 mL of syrup
400 mL of white vinegar	200 mL of distilled water
1 graduated cylinder	balance
paper towels	wax pencil
	2 250-mL glass jars with lids

Safety Precautions

Wear goggles when pouring liquids.

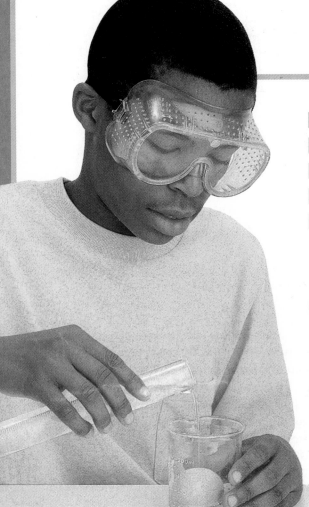

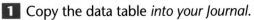

What To Do

1 Copy the data table *into your Journal*.

2 Use the wax pencil to label the jars A and B.

3 Place one egg in each of the jars (see photo **A**).

4 Add enough vinegar to each jar to cover the eggs.

5 After 24 hours, pour off the vinegar. *Observe* what has happened. Record your observations. Carefully remove the eggs from the jars, rinse them with water, and dry with a paper towel.

6 Find the mass of each dry egg. Record your findings in the table under "Original" mass of egg. Rinse the jars and dry them thoroughly. Return each egg to its original jar.

7 How is the concentration of water different in distilled water and syrup?
a: Add exactly 200 mL of distilled water to Jar A (see

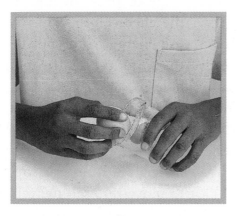

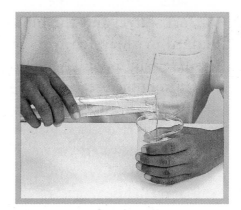

A

B

Data and Observations				
Egg in Solution	Mass of Egg		Volume of Liquid	
	Original	Final	Original	Final
Distilled Water (A)				
Syrup (B)				

photo **B**). *Hypothesize* what will happen to both the egg and the distilled water.
b: Add exactly 200 mL of syrup to Jar B. *Hypothesize* what will happen to both the egg and the syrup.

8 Allow each egg to remain in its jar for 24 hours.

9 After 24 hours, do the following:
a: Carefully remove the egg and dry it. **b:** Record the mass of the egg.
c: Measure and record the remaining liquid.

Analyzing

1. *In your Journal,* compare what happened to the mass of the egg in distilled water to what happened to the mass of the egg placed in syrup. Did the results support your hypothesis?

2. Why were the eggs placed in the vinegar at the beginning of the experiment?

3. What happened to the volume of distilled water in Jar A? Of syrup in Jar B? Did the results support your hypothesis?

Concluding and Applying

4. Can you *infer* that the egg membrane permitted any substance to pass through it? What evidence do you have that supports your conclusion?

5. What conclusions can you make about the process of osmosis?

6. **Going Further** If you put a freshwater fish in salt water or a saltwater fish in fresh water, the fish will die. Use your knowledge of osmosis to explain how this happens.

As you observed in the last activity, osmosis occurred in the eggs. For the same reason that the eggs gained or lost water, and the blood cells bulged or shriveled, you can now explain why people who get their water from the ocean remove the salt before drinking it. If you were stranded on a deserted island, why wouldn't you drink seawater? As you guessed, drinking seawater would actually cause you to lose water.

■ Active Transport

While water can diffuse through a cell membrane, certain materials require energy to pass through it. Think back to the Find Out activity with the cheesecloth. Some of the larger pieces of gravel were too large to pass through the holes in the cheesecloth. You would have to use energy from your body to force the large pieces through the small holes.

In the same way, the cell membrane uses energy to move large molecules, such as sugar molecules, through it. If materials require energy to move through the cell membrane, active transport occurs. You will learn more about how the cell membrane uses energy to move substances in the "A Closer Look" article below.

In this section, you have examined diffusion and osmosis, two important

The Cell Membrane

The key to understanding how the cell membrane works lies in its structure. Scientists now know that the cell membrane not only acts as a filter, but is also a very active structure.

Structure

The cell membrane looks somewhat like a double-layered cake. Each layer is made up of a sheet of fat molecules. Larger protein molecules, which play a key role in the working of the membrane, are embedded in these layers. This model, shown on page 593, is known as the fluid mosaic model.

Some substances, such as glucose, move across the membrane by diffusing through channels made by tube-shaped protein molecules.

Active Transport

Sometimes cells require nutrients that are not in higher concentration in their environment. If the concentration of a substance outside a cell is lower than inside, the cell will lose that substance to the outside by diffusion. Cell membranes need to allow certain molecules to move in the reverse direction—from areas of low to high concentration. This type of movement requires energy and is known as active transport.

processes that depend on the movement of molecules. Both diffusion and osmosis cause materials to move through the cell membrane without the help of energy, while active transport requires energy. Through these processes, living cells obtain the substances they need as well as eliminate other materials they produce. In the next section, you will learn about other life processes that occur in living cells.

check your UNDERSTANDING

1. Name two functions of the cell membrane.
2. How are osmosis and diffusion alike? How are they different?
3. A bottle of ammonia is left open in the back of a classroom. What causes the odor of ammonia to be detected in the front of the room after only several minutes?
4. **Apply** A plant cell is surrounded by a particular substance. If the plant cell itself contains a larger concentration of this same substance than is present outside the plant cell, in which direction would you expect diffusion of the substance to occur? Explain your answer.

In active transport, molecules called carrier proteins attach to the molecules of the substance to be transported. Energy released by the cell is transferred to the carrier protein, which then changes shape. This change in shape moves the molecules into the cell.

What Do You Think?

Based on the fluid mosaic model of a cell membrane, find out what is different about the cell membrane of a diabetic.

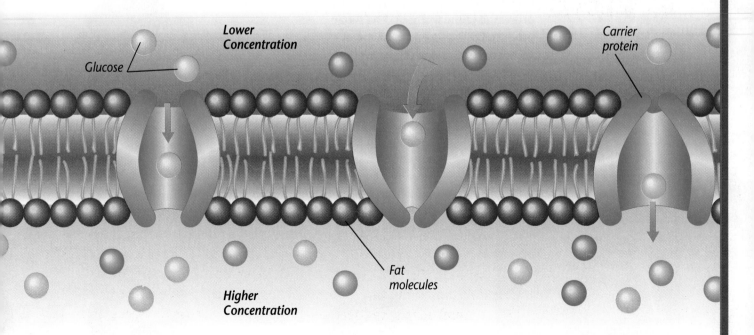

Lower Concentration

Glucose

Carrier protein

Fat molecules

Higher Concentration

19-2 | Why Cells Need Food

Section Objectives

- Explain the importance of energy to cells.
- Describe the process of respiration in terms of its products and reactants.
- Relate the number of mitochondria in different types of cells to their levels of activity.

Key Terms

respiration
fermentation

Cells and Energy

You may recall that energy can be found in many forms. If you have ever been to the ocean or a large lake on a windy day, you may have seen the motion of waves. This is an example of mechanical energy. Wet clothes hanging on a clothesline eventually dry due to thermal energy. Televisions and video games run on electrical energy.

When you think about the production of energy, you usually think of power plants. Power plants use energy-containing materials, such as oil, coal, water, or trash to produce the electrical energy that people use in their everyday activities.

Your cells, and the cells of other living organisms, also run on energy. Cells use this energy to carry out their life activities. At this very moment, your brain cells are using energy to allow you to read the words on this page. Muscle cells in your fingers are using energy to enable your fingers to turn the pages! Where does this energy come from? The original source of energy for the activities of living things is the sun. Think back to your earlier studies of plants and animals. **Figure 19-7** illustrates one path of energy transfer.

Figure 19-7

A Green plants convert light energy from the sun into sugars through the process of photosynthesis. The sugar produced contains a form of chemical energy. This same chemical energy is passed on to you through the food chain.

B A food chain is the feeding relationship that transfers energy through a community of producers, herbivores, and carnivores. In the food chain shown, which is the producer?

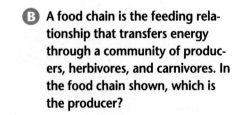

594

■ Respiration

Each of your cells changes chemical energy to other forms of energy through processes such as respiration. **Respiration** is a chemical process in which glucose molecules are broken down to release energy. In many ways, a cell can be compared to a power plant. Each cell requires fuel to convert energy. A summary of this chemical process of respiration is given in **Figure 19-8**.

Figure 19-8

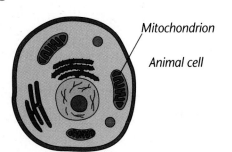

Mitochondrion

Animal cell

Organisms that depend on oxygen carry out respiration. Your brain cells, kidney cells, skin cells, and the cells in your big toe are using energy released during respiration. So are the leaves on the trees in the local park.

How can you tell if your body cells are producing energy? Feel your own forehead. It feels warm, doesn't it? What you are feeling is the heat energy produced as a product of the thousands of respiration reactions occurring in your body.

But what about plants? Plants don't feel warm. Do plants carry out respiration? In the following activity, you can prove to yourself that plants carry out respiration, and that this process converts one form of energy to another.

A Glucose is one fuel human cells use. Glucose molecules are broken apart into simpler molecules. These then enter the mitochondrion, where they combine with oxygen molecules to form water and carbon dioxide.

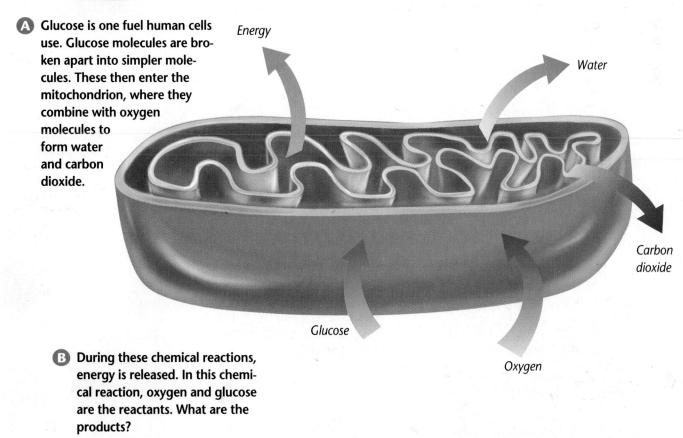

Energy

Water

Carbon dioxide

Glucose

Oxygen

B During these chemical reactions, energy is released. In this chemical reaction, oxygen and glucose are the reactants. What are the products?

Find Out! ACTIVITY

Does respiration release energy?

Thermal energy is a form of energy released as a product of respiration. In this activity, you will actually measure some of the energy released by respiration in beans!

What To Do

1. Obtain the following materials: one large beaker, two clear glass jars, two thermometers, two corks to fit glass jars or a large ball of cotton, 50 dry kidney beans, and 50 kidney beans that have soaked overnight.

2. Carefully place the soaked beans in one glass jar and label it.

3. Place 50 dry beans in the other glass jar.

4. Put a thermometer in each jar and seal with a large wad of cotton.

5. Take a temperature reading in each jar every half hour for three hours and record your observations *in your Journal*.

Conclude and Apply

1. Did the two different bottles have the same temperatures each time you took a reading?

2. What conclusions can you draw between your observations and your knowledge of respiration?

You saw evidence that the soaked beans released energy by respiration. You were able to measure the release of stored energy in the soaked beans by comparing the temperatures of the two treatments. Cells use the energy released by respiration in a variety of ways. Nerve cells need energy to transmit messages through the body. Plant cells need energy to form beautiful and complex flowers.

Although every living cell uses energy, the amount of energy one cell needs may differ from the amount of energy needed by a different cell. How does one cell have more energy available to it than another cell? One

596   Chapter 19   How Cells Do Their Jobs

answer lies in the number of mito-chondria found within the cell.

■ The Role of Mitochondria

As you recall, mitochondria are the sites of respiration. Not all cells contain the same number of mito-chondria, however. Why would there be more mitochondria present in the cytoplasm of brain cells than there are in the cytoplasm of skin cells? **Figure 19-9** addresses this question.

You have learned that energy is one product of respiration. Cells, like most factories, produce waste. The waste products of respiration are water and carbon dioxide. They are released from your body when you are exhaling. Nearly all organisms give off carbon dioxide as a result of respira-tion. However, the rate at which car-bon dioxide is given off differs from organism to organism. In the activity that follows, you will investigate how temperature affects the rate at which respiration occurs.

DID YOU KNOW?

Each heart muscle cell contains more than 3000 mito-chondria.

Figure 19-9

The number of mitochondria per cell varies from fewer than 100 to several thousand. The greater the activity and energy use of a cell, the greater the number of mito-chondria the cell contains.

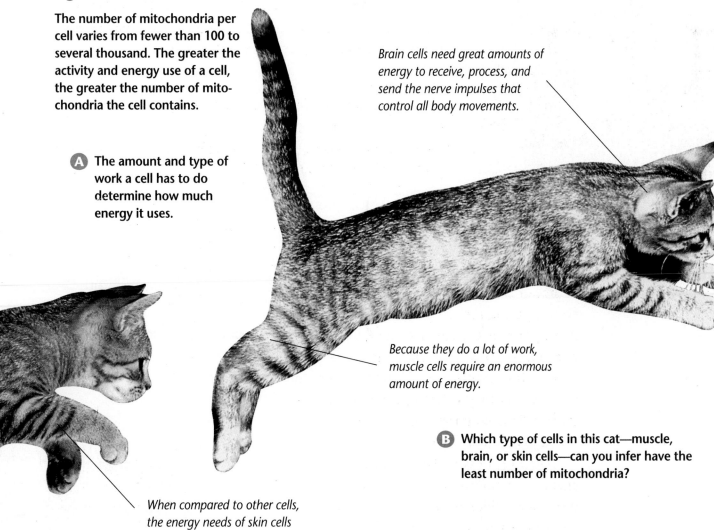

A The amount and type of work a cell has to do determine how much energy it uses.

Brain cells need great amounts of energy to receive, process, and send the nerve impulses that control all body movements.

Because they do a lot of work, muscle cells require an enormous amount of energy.

B Which type of cells in this cat—muscle, brain, or skin cells—can you infer have the least number of mitochondria?

When compared to other cells, the energy needs of skin cells are low.

Respiration and Temperature

In this activity, you will observe evidence of respiration in yeast cells. You will also relate temperature to the rate of a reaction.

Problem

How is respiration influenced by temperature?

Materials

2 rubber stoppers with plastic tubing inserted	tap water
	2 test tubes
20 mL 25% sucrose solution	metric ruler
	2 flasks
	yeast cubes
	watch or clock
	10-mL graduated cylinder
	glass-marking pencil

Safety Precautions

What To Do

1 Copy the data table *into your Journal.*

2 Pour 10 mL of the sucrose solution into each test tube.

3 Place the yeast into the test tubes and mix well.

4 Insert a rubber stopper into each test tube. The end of the plastic tube should be below the surface of the liquid. Use the figure as a guide.

5 a. Add enough cold water to a flask to reach a height of 3 cm. Label this flask "cold" (see photo *B*).
b. Label the second flask "warm" and repeat Step 5a using warm water.

6 Carefully place one test tube in each flask (see photo *C*).

7 *Measure* the height of the liquid in each plastic tube

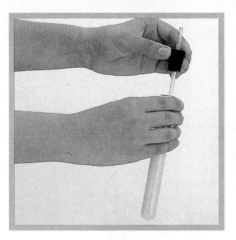

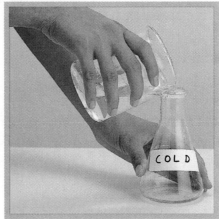

A　　　　　　　　**B**　　　　　　　　**C**

to the nearest millimeter. Position the ruler so that the 0.0 mm mark lines up with the bottom of the flask, as in the figure. Record your measurements in the table under "Starting Height."

8 Take measurements every 5 minutes for 20 minutes.

9 *Calculate* and record the total distance the yeast-water mixture moved. If the last reading was lower than the starting height, subtract this from your total.

Data and Observations						
	Starting Height	5 Mins.	10 Mins.	15 Mins.	20 Mins.	Total Distance
Cold						
Warm						

Analyzing

1. *In your Journal,* describe what gas is released by yeast cells as they carry out respiration.

2. Which tube showed the greater rise in the height of the liquid? In which tube was more gas produced?

Concluding and Applying

3. Do you think that temperature has an effect on the rate of respiration? What evidence do you have to support your statement?

4. Going Further What can you *infer* about the rate of respiration in a fish swimming in cold water compared to the same fish swimming in warm water?

As you saw in the Investigate, a relationship exists between temperature and the rate at which respiration occurs. As temperature increases, so does the amount of respiration that occurs in an organism. This is true for your body as well as yeast cells. Think about the last time you exercised. Strenuous physical activities such as running or swimming require a lot of energy. If your arm and leg muscles

Figure 19-10

In order for the lion's leg muscles to get the energy they need, fast and numerous respiration reactions must occur. These reactions, as well as the muscle activity, release heat, which raises the lion's body temperature. The increased body temperature helps maintain the rate of respiration needed.

Chemistry CONNECTION

Does Mother Nature's Math Add Up?

When a cow eats grass, the cells in its body obtain energy from the grass through the process of respiration.

Respiration

During this process, glucose molecules in the grass are broken down to release energy. The cow will use this energy to grow, produce a calf, and make milk. Respiration uses oxygen that has been delivered by the circulatory system to produce carbon dioxide and water, in addition to energy.

Respiration is a series of chemical reactions. In all chemical reactions, atoms are neither created nor destroyed. How can we be sure that Mother Nature's math adds up?

Chemical Equation of Respiration

The equation for the chemical reaction of respiration is illustrated on the next page.

The equation can also be written in such a way that we

are to get the energy they need, fast and numerous respiration reactions must occur. These reactions, as well as the muscle activity, release heat, which raises your body temperature. Your increased body temperature maintains the rate of respiration to continually supply your muscles with energy. Due to this cycle, your body gets the energy it needs so you can reach the finish line!

Figure 19-11

This lion has just stopped running and is panting. As the lion pants, water from its mouth evaporates. The evaporation process reduces body temperature. As the lion stands and pants, does its rate of respiration increase or decrease? Why?

can count up the atoms.

To find out if the math adds up, you only need to count up the atoms on both sides of the arrow.

Let's start on the left side of the arrow. Each carbon atom is represented by the letter C.

How many carbon atoms (C) are there?

How many hydrogen atoms (H) do you see?

How many oxygen atoms (O)?

How many atoms total are on the left side of the arrow?

Now let's look at the right side of the arrow. How many carbon atoms do you see? How many hydrogen atoms? How many oxygen atoms? How many atoms total?

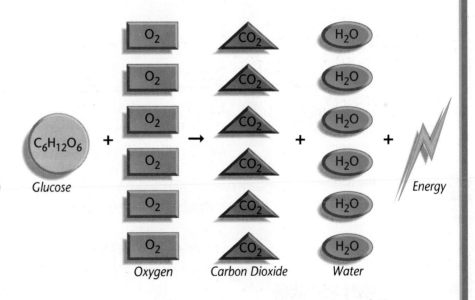

What Do You Think?

1. Is the sum of each kind of atom (C, H, O) on the left side of the arrow equal to the sum on the right side?

2. Does the total sum of atoms on the left side of the arrow equal the total sum of the atoms on the right side?

3. Were any atoms created or destroyed during respiration?

Figure 19-12

A At the start of the bread-making process, bakers mix flour, water, salt, and yeast. They often also add some sugar or certain enzymes that convert some of the starch in the flour into sugar.

B During fermentation, the yeast cells use sugars as food and give off alcohol and carbon dioxide gas as waste chemicals. Heat makes the trapped gas expand and stretch the dough. The bread rises.

C As the bread bakes, the alcohol evaporates. The bubbles of carbon dioxide, however, stay trapped. The spaces that the bubbles form give bread its light texture.

■ Fermentation

But do all cells undergo respiration? Sometimes during periods of strenuous activity, muscle cells run low on oxygen. The muscles begin to tire. You begin to breathe harder and faster in an effort to supply the needed oxygen. But your body has another method to continue supplying smaller amounts of energy. When oxygen levels are low, the muscle cells begin to release energy from glucose by fermentation.

Fermentation is a process that releases energy by breaking down glucose without the use of oxygen. Yeast and some bacteria also use fermentation to release energy. **Figure 19-12** demonstrates one use of fermentation. Certain cells, such as some kinds of bacteria, lack mitochondria and therefore, cannot obtain their energy through respiration.

In this section, you learned that living organisms have mechanisms for supplying themselves with the energy they require. Different types of cells have different energy needs. In the next section, you will see how these cells are organized in the body so that they can complete their jobs.

check your UNDERSTANDING

1. Why do cells need energy?
2. Name three products of respiration.
3. What two reactants are needed for cell respiration?
4. How does fermentation differ from respiration?

5. **Apply** After examining a muscle cell from your lower jaw and a skin cell under a microscope, you find that the jaw muscle cell contains more mitochondria than the skin cell. What can you infer about the energy requirements of the jaw muscle cell?

Special Cells with Special Jobs

19-3

A Variety of Cells

If you've ever used a tool kit, you know that there is nothing better than having the right tool for the right job. Some tools have flat and heavy parts for banging things, like a hammer. Others, such as screwdrivers, have long, thin parts for fitting into thin,

Figure 19-13

Your body contains many different kinds of cells, each with its own unique shape and job.

tight places. Still others, such as a saw, have specially shaped teeth for cutting things. There is a definite relationship between the size and shape of a tool and its job, isn't there? The same is true of cells. Like the tools in a tool kit, there is a relationship between the structure of a cell and its parts, and how it functions in the body. **Figure 19-13** demonstrates this relationship.

Section Objectives

■ Explain differences between types of cells and how their differences are related to cell functions.

■ Identify the levels of organization in life forms from cell to tissue, to organ, to organ system, to organism.

Key Terms

tissues, organ, organ systems, organism

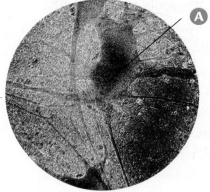

A Some nerve cells in your peripheral nervous system are very long. Their shape is useful for carrying messages long distances—for instance, from your spinal cord to the muscles in your feet.

Nerve cell

B Sperm cells have an arrowlike head and a long, thin tail. Their shape helps them swim through body fluids.

Sperm cell

C Some plant stem cells are long and hollow like drinking straws. Their shape helps them transport water and nutrients from the roots to the rest of the plant.

Plant cell

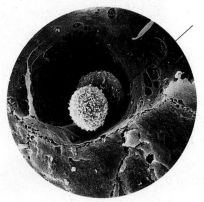

D White blood cells, which surround and destroy harmful bacteria in your body, change into many different shapes while performing their job. How do you think these traits help a white blood cell do its job?

White blood cell

Levels of Organization

Connect to...

Earth Science

Some of the oldest fossil organisms were composed of one–celled bacteria and algae. These organisms resemble modern bacteria and blue-green algae in size and shape. Draw a time line showing how many years ago they appeared on Earth, when Earth was formed, and the present.

The amoeba is a one-celled organism. The entire organism is composed of just one cell! The animal, plant, and fungus organisms that you are familiar with are all many-celled organisms. They contain more than one cell. One-celled organisms, however, still carry out the same life processes that occur in many-celled organisms such as your dog, your cat, and you.

Unlike one-celled organisms, the cells of many-celled organisms usually cannot function by themselves. Like parts in a machine, cells in your body work together to function effectively.

They are arranged in levels of organization. Each level is more organized than the one before.

What is meant by the phrase "levels of organization?" Your textbook shows different levels of organization. Letters of the alphabet are grouped together to form words. Words are grouped together in sentences. Many sentences arranged together are called paragraphs, and a group of paragraphs are organized into a story.

Cells in your body, like letters of the alphabet, are the most basic level of organization. Similar types of cells,

Figure 19-14

The cells of an organism—plant or animal—are arranged in levels of organization, much like letters of an alphabet are arranged in levels of organization to create a story. In a story, the levels are letters, words, sentences, paragraphs, and story.

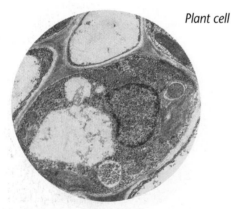

Plant cell

Ⓐ **Cells** are the most basic level of organization. Specific types of cells have specific jobs.

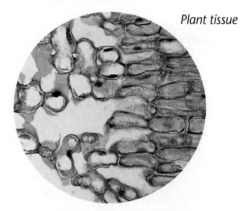

Plant tissue

Ⓑ **Tissues** Similar types of cells, working together to perform the same function, make up tissues.

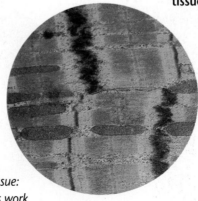

Animal cells and tissue: cardiac muscle cells work together to form heart tissue

working together to perform the same functions, are called **tissues**, like the words made up of letters.

Individual types of tissues usually are found with other types of tissue. An **organ** is a structure in the body made up of several different types of tissue that all work together to do a particular job, much like sentences made up of words. **Figure 19-14** shows the organization from cell to tissue to organ in a plant and the circulatory system in a person. The next level of organization in many-celled organisms like yourself is the organ system. **Organ systems** are simply groups of organs working together to perform a particular job, like the paragraphs that are groups of sentences.

The highest level of organization is an organism, like a bean plant, a frog, or even you. An **organism** is made up of several organ systems that work together, like paragraphs organized into a story. Each system plays a vital role in keeping the organism functioning normally. Can you think of other organisms? Think back to the organization of this book. Would the book provide as much information if there were no paragraphs or sentences? Just as a book needs parts to work together, so do living, many-celled organisms. Do you think you could be reading this book without a functioning nervous system?

*Plant organ:
tomato plant leaf*

*Plant organ system:
transport system—
roots, stems, leaves*

C *Organs* The third level of organization is organs—various types of tissue, all working together to perform a particular function.

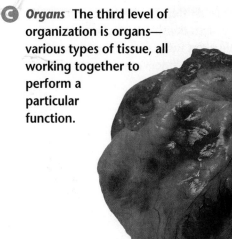

Animal organ: heart

D *Organ systems* are the next level of organization. Organ systems are groups of organs working together to perform a particular job. What is the next level of organization?

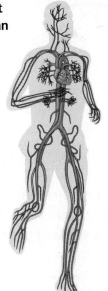

*Animal organ system:
circulatory system*

19-3   Special Cells with Special Jobs   **605**

In this chapter, you have seen that the structure of the cell membrane maintains the proper concentrations of molecules inside and outside the cell, so the cell can perform an important task: to provide usable forms of energy for life! You also observed that even though all cells in the body use energy, there are different types of cells for different jobs, and similar cells work together as a team to complete these jobs. **Figure 19-15** shows this same type of organization within a plant. Finally, you learned that all of the cells, tissues, organs, and organ systems in your body work together to form a whole, living organism.

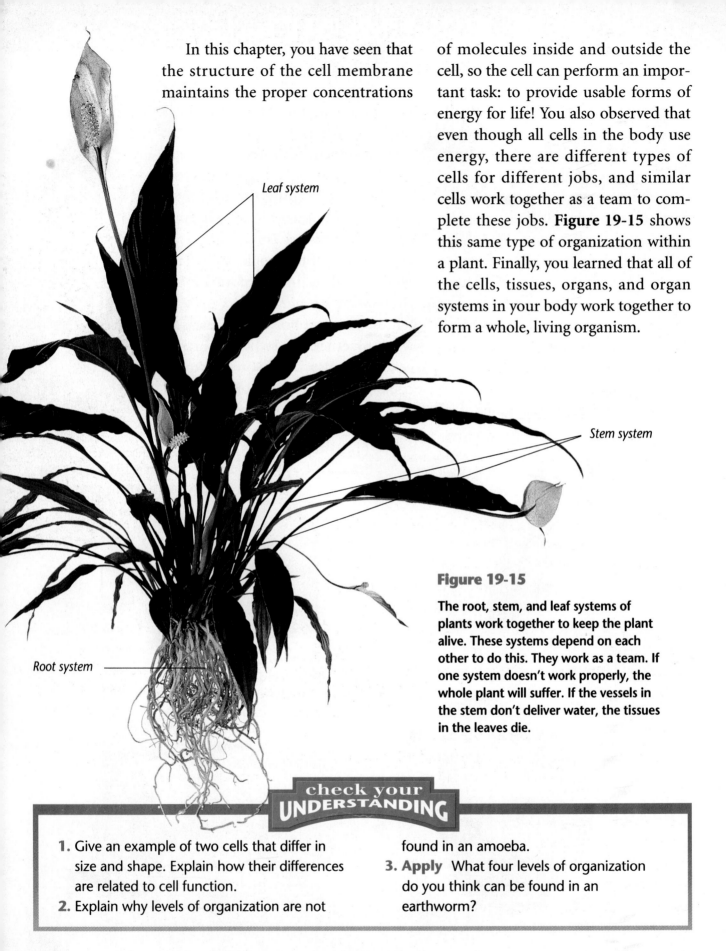

Leaf system

Stem system

Root system

Figure 19-15

The root, stem, and leaf systems of plants work together to keep the plant alive. These systems depend on each other to do this. They work as a team. If one system doesn't work properly, the whole plant will suffer. If the vessels in the stem don't deliver water, the tissues in the leaves die.

check your UNDERSTANDING

1. Give an example of two cells that differ in size and shape. Explain how their differences are related to cell function.
2. Explain why levels of organization are not found in an amoeba.
3. **Apply** What four levels of organization do you think can be found in an earthworm?

Science *and* Society

Cryogenics: Frozen and Hopeful

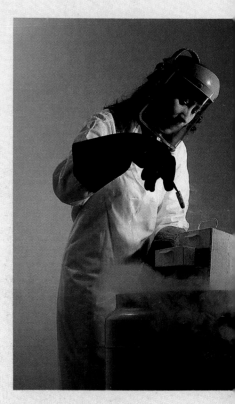

No longer just in science-fiction movies—you can now buy the treatment. Your body can be frozen in order to be revived later. It's called cryonic suspension.

No one so far has been removed from cryonic suspension and revived. Only hamsters and dogs have been kept frozen for brief periods of time and revived. The success rate is, however, improving.

But when human beings are cryonically suspended, by law, they have to have died first. That means their revival will have to wait until medical science can reverse death, if ever, as well as cure whatever disease the person died of. If they died of old age, their cryonic suspension will continue until medical science can both revive and rejuvenate them.

How Does It Work?

Minutes after death, ideally, the patient's body is connected to a heart-lung machine. This enables oxygenated blood to continue bathing body tissues—especially the brain. The patient's temperature is lowered rapidly. When the body reaches the cryonics lab, the body's blood is replaced by a nontoxic chemical solution that acts like antifreeze. It replaces water in the tissues so no ice crystals rupture cell membranes. Once prepared, the body is cooled to the temperature of dry ice and then immersed in a vat of liquid nitrogen at -196°C. At this temperature, decay is essentially nonexistent. The body will remain unchanged for hundreds of years.

Questions, Anyone?

Note that we've been saying the body. Should that be the patient? Does a dead person whose body is now preserved cryonically have rights? Do heirs inherit property and other goods, or can the person store them for future need?

Will the person's memories awaken with the body? How much time are we talking about here—hundreds of years? Will revived people be able to make a life for themselves?

What Do You Think?

Write a reaction paper on cryonic suspension. Discuss one of the questions above or one of your own.

Health CONNECTION

Shaping Up: You Can't Do It Overnight

Your life is full of activity—running for a bus, dancing, playing sports. You couldn't do any of these activities if the cells of your body didn't release energy.

Energy

Your cells release energy through the process of respiration, which takes place in the presence of oxygen. During activities, your cells receive plenty of oxygen through the working of your respiratory and circulatory systems.

Activities such as sprinting or lifting weights require so much energy that your heart and lungs cannot work fast enough to provide your muscle cells with enough oxygen. When this occurs, your muscle cells release energy from glucose without oxygen through fermentation.

In people who are out of shape, strenuous activities don't have to last for very long before fermentation takes over in muscle cells. During fermentation, your muscles begin to tire, because of the build-up of a substance in your muscles. It takes time for the circulatory system to carry away this product. Even the next day, you may feel as if

your muscles can barely move. Fermentation doesn't produce as much energy as respiration and your body quickly tires out.

Benefits of Exercise

Exercise can strengthen the muscle in the heart's left ventricle so more blood can be pumped to your cells per heartbeat. Regular exercise can also strengthen the muscles of respiration so more air can be moved through the lungs per breath.

Exercise can also improve the oxygen-carrying properties of blood cells and increase blood volume in the body.

You Try It!

Getting into shape does not happen overnight. To maintain fitness, exercise must be performed on a regular basis. Your physician, physical education teacher, or a fitness professional can help you design the right fitness program for you.

HOW IT WORKS

The Artificial Kidney Machine

Every 40 minutes, your entire blood supply circulates through your kidneys. The kidneys cleanse about 180 liters of blood every 24 hours, filtering waste products and water from your blood. As they do this, your kidneys produce about 2 liters of urine a day. When kidneys are diseased or damaged, water and nitrogen waste products can collect in the blood and cause a variety of unhealthy or even life-threatening conditions.

What is Hemodialysis?

An artificial-kidney machine duplicates some of the kidney's functions by removing waste products and excess water. During the process, called hemodialysis, a patient's blood circulates through a filter.

The actual filtering device is a hemodialyzer. A hemodialyzer resembles a tube, like the tube inside a roll of paper towels. The tube is clear, with a thick bundle of white, hairy-looking material inside. This material is the filtering membrane, and it filters substances very much like the cell membranes of kidney cells.

How Does a Hemodialyzer Work?

The filtering membrane separates the hemodialyzer into two compartments. Blood from the patient's artery flows through one compartment, while a cleansing fluid flows through the second compartment.

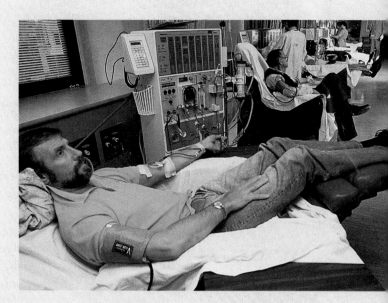

As blood circulates through the tubing, the blood with a high concentration of waste molecules diffuses through the membrane into the cleansing fluid. Here the concentration of waste molecules is very low. Fresh cleansing fluid is constantly added to the second compartment so that waste molecules continue to diffuse. The freshly cleansed blood is then returned to the patient.

A single treatment may take from two to four hours and usually needs to be repeated every two to three days. Although not a cure, it is a treatment that allows patients to live longer.

What Do You Think?

The dialyzer and the cell membrane have much in common. What characteristics do they have in common? What processes occur in both the dialyzer and the cell membrane?

eview the statements below about the big ideas presented in this chapter, and try to answer the questions. Then, re-read your answers to the Did You Ever Wonder questions at the beginning of the chapter. *In your Journal,* write a paragraph about how your understanding of the big ideas in the chapter has changed.

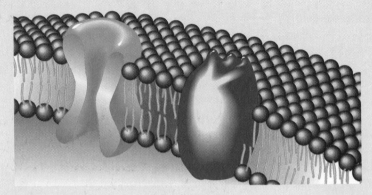

1 Cells carry out life processes with the help of the cell membrane. *What is the major function of the cell membrane?*

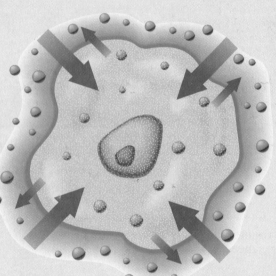

2 Some materials move through the cell membrane by the process of diffusion, in which molecules move from an area of high concentration to an area of lower concentration until equilibrium is reached. *What is osmosis?*

3 In the cells of most organisms, energy is released from glucose in the presence of oxygen by the process of respiration. *How do organisms release energy without oxygen?*

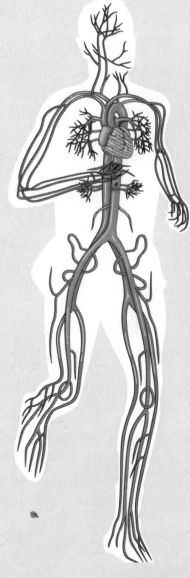

4 Most many-celled organisms are not just a collection of individual cells working by themselves. *Into what levels are these cells organized?*

Using Key Science Terms

diffusion	organ systems
fermentation	osmosis
organ	respiration
organisms	tissues

1. What are two ways molecules can reach equilibrium? How do these two ways differ?
2. How are the processes of fermentation and respiration alike? How are they different?
3. In what order do organ, organism, organ system, and tissue appear in the levels of organization? Briefly explain each term.

Understanding Ideas

Answer the following questions in your Journal *using complete sentences.*

1. How does respiration help an organism survive?
2. Would you expect to find more mitochondria in a more active cell or a less active cell? Why?
3. Do molecules stop moving through a cell membrane once equilibrium is reached? Explain your answer.
4. Name three types of tissue that are found in your body.
5. Why does your body get warm as you exercise?
6. In which direction do molecules flow during diffusion?

Developing Skills

Use your understanding of the concepts developed in this chapter to answer each of the following questions.

1. **Concept Mapping** Create a concept map of cell processes using the following processes: diffusion, osmosis, active transport, respiration, fermentation. Use additional terms as necessary.
2. **Observing and Inferring** Repeat the Explore activity on page 586 using a tea bag in a clear glass of room temperature water. Make an observation of the glass every two minutes for 20 minutes. How do your observations compare with those you made with the tea bag in hot water? What can you infer about the effect of hot water in this investigation?
3. **Predicting** Repeat the Find Out activity on page 596, adding water to the jar of dry beans. Predict what will happen to your temperature readings. What do the results of your temperature readings show?

Critical Thinking

In your Journal, *answer each of the following questions.*

1. In the first Investigate, you observed osmosis through an egg membrane. Do you think you would have obtained the same results if the shells had not been dissolved by the vinegar? Explain your answer.
2. Applying your knowledge of osmosis, explain how plant roots obtain water from the soil.
3. In snowy states, salt is used to melt ice on the roads. Explain what happens to many roadside plants as a result.
4. What do you think happens to substances that are not allowed to pass into your cells?
5. Why might a person feel very tired and weak after skipping several meals?

Problem Solving

Read the following problem and discuss your answers in a brief paragraph.

Chris made a salad of lettuce, tomatoes, carrots, and cucumbers. He seasoned the damp salad with herbs, salt, and pepper. Then he placed it in the refrigerator for a couple of hours.

When Chris returned, he took the salad from the refrigerator. The lettuce had wilted and the other vegetables were limp. He noticed that there was a liquid in the bottom of the bowl.

1. Where did the liquid in the bottom of the salad bowl come from?
2. Why did the lettuce wilt after having been left in the refrigerator for a couple of hours?

CONNECTING IDEAS

Discuss each of the following in a brief paragraph.

1. **Theme—Systems and Interactions** Why don't some cells release energy through respiration? What other process do they use to get energy?
2. **Theme—Energy** How do you think the energy requirements of a muscle cell compare to that of a skin cell? Explain your answer.
3. **Theme—Systems and Interactions** Describe how cells get the materials they need. Where do the nutrients, water, and oxygen come from?
4. **Health Connection** Sometimes when you exercise, your body is not able to provide enough oxygen to your muscle cells. What do you think happens then?
5. **Science and Society** How would your life change if you had to depend on hemodialysis?

Life at *the* Cellular *Level*

In this unit, you investigated how a microscope can be used to observe cells. You learned that chemical reactions occur in living and nonliving matter.

Try the exercises and activity that follow—they will challenge you to use and apply some of the ideas you learned in this unit.

CONNECTING IDEAS

1. Find a way to calculate the magnification of a hand lens and a bifocal lens. Use the magnifying power you calculate to determine how much larger a single cell would appear using both of these tools.

2. Remember the biosphere experiment you set up at the beginning of this book? What were some of the important factors you took into consideration when deciding what to place into your biosphere? How would you explain the outcome of your experiment using what you have learned about respiration and photosynthesis?

Exploring Further ACTIVITY

Where do you get your energy?

In the body, stored food is chemically combined with oxygen and energy is given off. How much energy is in a peanut? Let's burn one and see. Remember, a rise in temperature indicates energy is being given off. Although energy is required to start the burning reaction, energy does not have to be supplied to keep it going. The releasing of the chemical energy in the peanut keeps the reaction going.

What To Do

1. Get a ring stand; a ring; a utility clamp; a cork; a long straight pin; a small, empty can; aluminum foil; a thermometer; a peanut; water; and matches.

2. Set up your equipment as shown in the photograph. Place the cork and peanut 2 cm from the bottom of the can.

3. Pour 100 mL of water into the small can and record the water temperature.

4. Set fire to the peanut. **CAUTION:** *Use care around an open flame.*

5. What happened to the temperature of the water? Was energy present in the peanut?

APPENDICES

Table of Contents

International System of Units

The International System (SI) of Measurement is accepted as the standard for measurement throughout most of the world. Three base units in SI are the meter, kilogram, and second. Frequently used SI units are listed below.

Table A-1: Frequently used SI Units	
Length	1 millimeter (mm) = 1000 micrometers (µm) 1 centimeter (cm) = 10 millimeters (mm) 1 meter (m) = 100 centimeters (cm) 1 kilometer (km) = 1000 meters (m) 1 light-year = 9 460 000 000 000 kilometers (km)
Area	1 square meter (m^2) = 10 000 square centimeters (cm^2) 1 square kilometer (km^2) = 1 000 000 square meters (m^2)
Volume	1 milliliter (mL) = 1 cubic centimeter (cm^3) 1 liter (L) = 1000 milliliters (mL)
Mass	1 gram (g) = 1000 milligrams (mg) 1 kilogram (kg) = 1000 grams (g) 1 metric ton (g) = 1000 kilo grams (kg)
Time	1 s = 1 second

Temperature measurements in SI are often made in degrees Celsius. Celsius temperature is a supplementary unit derived from the base unit kelvin. The Celsius scale (°C) has 100 equal graduations between the freezing temperature (0°C) and the boiling temperature of water (100°C). The following relationship exists between the Celsius and kelvin temperature scales:

$$K = °C + 273$$

Several other supplementary SI units are listed below.

Table A-2: Supplementary SI Units			
Measurement	Unit	Symbol	Expressed in Base Units
Energy	Joule	J	$kg \cdot m^2/s^2$ or $N \cdot m$
Force	Newton	N	$kg \cdot m/s^2$
Power	Watt	W	$kg \cdot m^2/s^3$ or J/s
Pressure	Pascal	Pa	$kg/(m \cdot s^2)$ or N/m^2

°F	°C
210	100
200	90
190	
180	80
170	
160	70
150	
140	60
130	
120	50
110	
100	40
90	30
80	
70	20
60	
50	10
40	
30	0
20	
10	-10
0	
-10	-20

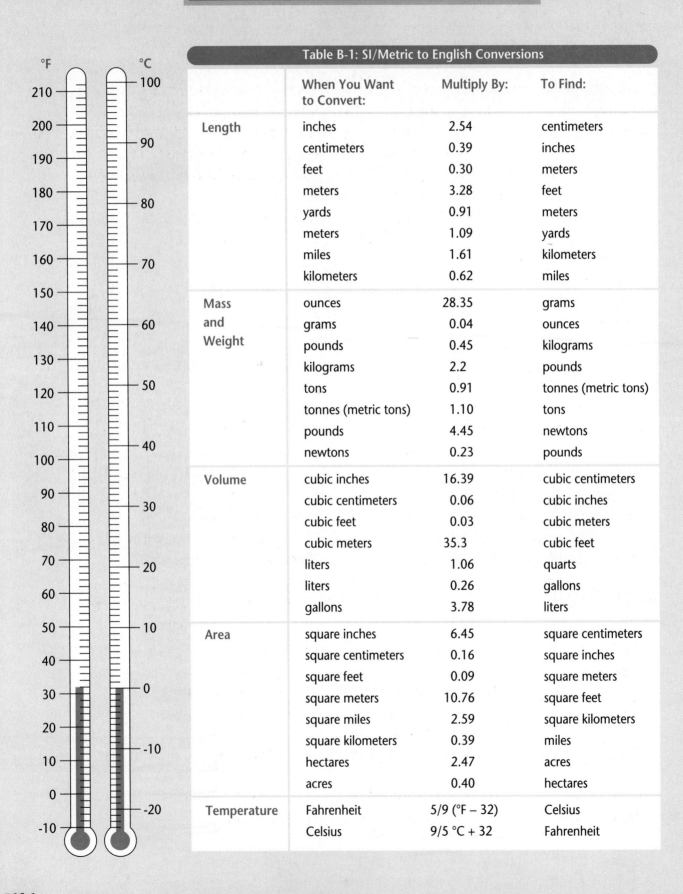

Table B-1: SI/Metric to English Conversions

	When You Want to Convert:	Multiply By:	To Find:
Length	inches	2.54	centimeters
	centimeters	0.39	inches
	feet	0.30	meters
	meters	3.28	feet
	yards	0.91	meters
	meters	1.09	yards
	miles	1.61	kilometers
	kilometers	0.62	miles
Mass and Weight	ounces	28.35	grams
	grams	0.04	ounces
	pounds	0.45	kilograms
	kilograms	2.2	pounds
	tons	0.91	tonnes (metric tons)
	tonnes (metric tons)	1.10	tons
	pounds	4.45	newtons
	newtons	0.23	pounds
Volume	cubic inches	16.39	cubic centimeters
	cubic centimeters	0.06	cubic inches
	cubic feet	0.03	cubic meters
	cubic meters	35.3	cubic feet
	liters	1.06	quarts
	liters	0.26	gallons
	gallons	3.78	liters
Area	square inches	6.45	square centimeters
	square centimeters	0.16	square inches
	square feet	0.09	square meters
	square meters	10.76	square feet
	square miles	2.59	square kilometers
	square kilometers	0.39	miles
	hectares	2.47	acres
	acres	0.40	hectares
Temperature	Fahrenheit	5/9 (°F − 32)	Celsius
	Celsius	9/5 °C + 32	Fahrenheit

APPENDIX C

Safety in the Science Classroom

1. Always obtain your teacher's permission to begin an investigation.
2. Study the procedure. If you have questions, ask your teacher. Understand any safety symbols shown on the page.
3. Use the safety equipment provided for you. Goggles and a safety apron should be worn when any investigation calls for using chemicals.
4. Always slant test tubes away from yourself and others when heating them.
5. Never eat or drink in the lab, and never use lab glassware as food or drink containers. Never inhale chemicals. Do not taste any substances or draw any material into a tube with your mouth.
6. If you spill any chemical, wash it off immediately with water. Report the spill immediately to your teacher.
7. Know the location and proper use of the fire extinguisher, safety shower, fire blanket, first aid kit, and fire alarm.
8. Keep materials away from flames. Tie back hair and loose clothing.
9. If a fire should break out in the classroom, or if your clothing should catch fire, smother it with the fire blanket or a coat, or get under a safety shower. NEVER RUN.
10. Report any accident or injury, no matter how small, to your teacher.

Follow these procedures as you clean up your work area.

1. Turn off the water and gas. Disconnect electrical devices.
2. Return all materials to their proper places.
3. Dispose of chemicals and other materials as directed by your teacher. Place broken glass and solid substances in the proper containers. Never discard materials in the sink.
4. Clean your work area.
5. Wash your hands thoroughly after working in the laboratory.

Table C-1: First Aid	
Injury	Safe Response
Burns	Apply cold water. Call your teacher immediately.
Cuts and bruises	Stop any bleeding by applying direct pressure. Cover cuts with a clean dressing. Apply cold compresses to bruises. Call your teacher immediately.
Fainting	Leave the person lying down. Loosen any tight clothing and keep crowds away. Call your teacher immediately.
Foreign matter in eye	Flush with plenty of water. Use eyewash bottle or fountain. Call your teacher immediately.
Poisoning	Note the suspected poisoning agent and call your teacher immediately.
Any spills on skin	Flush with large amounts of water or use safety shower. Call your teacher immediately.

APPENDIX D

Table D-1: Safety Symbols

Disposal Alert
This symbol appears when care must be taken to dispose of materials properly.

Animal Safety
This symbol appears whenever live animals are studied and the safety of the animals and the students must be ensured.

Biological Hazard
This symbol appears when there is danger involving bacteria, fungi, or protists.

Radioactive Safety
This symbol appears when radioactive materials are used.

Open Flame Alert
This symbol appears when use of an open flame could cause a fire or an explosion.

Clothing Protection Safety
This symbol appears when substances used could stain or burn clothing.

Thermal Safety
This symbol appears as a reminder to use caution when handling hot objects.

Fire Safety
This symbol appears when care should be taken around open flames.

Sharp Object Safety
This symbol appears when a danger of cuts or punctures caused by the use of sharp objects exists.

Explosion Safety
This symbol appears when the misuse of chemicals could cause an explosion.

Fume Safety
This symbol appears when chemicals or chemical reactions could cause dangerous fumes.

Eye Safety
This symbol appears when a danger to the eyes exists. Safety goggles should be worn when this symbol appears.

Electrical Safety
This symbol appears when care should be taken when using electrical equipment.

Poison Safety
This symbol appears when poisonous substances are used.

Plant Safety
This symbol appears when poisonous plants or plants with thorns are handled.

Chemical Safety
This symbol appears when chemicals used can cause burns or are poisonous if absorbed through the skin.

Care and Use of a Microscope

Coarse Adjustment *Focuses the image under low power*

Fine Adjustment *Sharpens the image under high and low magnification*

Arm *Supports the body tube*

Low-power objective *Contains the lens with low-power magnification*

Stage clips *Hold the microscope slide in place*

Base *Provides support for the microscope*

Eyepiece *Contains a magnifying lens you look through*

Body tube *Connects the eyepiece to the revolving nosepiece*

Revolving nosepiece *Holds and turns the objectives into viewing position*

High-power objective *Contains the lens with the highest magnification*

Stage *Platform used to support the microscope slide*

Diaphragm *Regulates the amount of light entering the body tube*

Light source *Allows light to reflect upward through the diaphragm, the specimen, and the lenses*

Care of a Microscope

1. Always carry the microscope holding the arm with one hand and supporting the base with the other hand.
2. Don't touch the lenses with your finger.
3. Never lower the coarse adjustment knob when looking through the eyepiece lens.
4. Always focus first with the low-power objective.
5. Don't use the coarse adjustment knob when the high-power objective is in place.
6. Store the microscope covered.

Using a Microscope

1. Place the microscope on a flat surface that is clear of objects. The arm should be toward you.
2. Look through the eyepiece. Adjust the diaphragm so that light comes through the opening in the stage.
3. Place a slide on the stage so that the specimen is in the field of view. Hold it firmly in place by using the stage clips.
4. Always focus first with the coarse adjustment and the low-power objective lens. Once the object is in focus on low power, turn the nosepiece until the high-power objective is in place. Use ONLY the fine adjustment to focus with the high-power objective lens.

Making a Wet Mount Slide

1. Carefully place the item you want to look at in the center of a clean glass slide. Make sure the sample is thin enough for light to pass through.
2. Use a dropper to place one or two drops of water on the sample.
3. Hold a clean coverslip by the edges and place it at one edge of the drop of water. Slowly lower the coverslip onto the drop of water until it lies flat.
4. If you have too much water or a lot of air bubbles, touch the edge of a paper towel to the edge of the coverslip to draw off extra water and force air out.

Animal Cell

Refer to this diagram of an animal cell as
you read cell parts and their jobs.

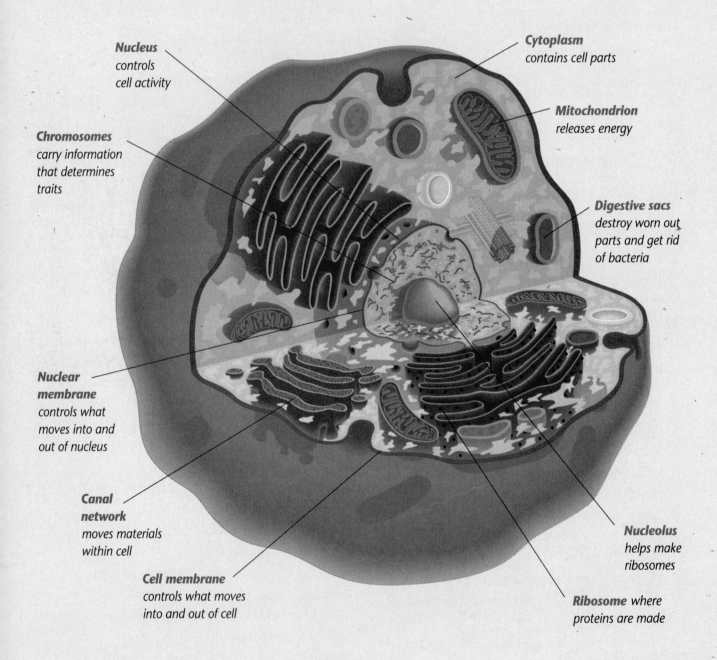

Nucleus
*controls
cell activity*

Cytoplasm
contains cell parts

Mitochondrion
releases energy

Chromosomes
*carry information
that determines
traits*

Digestive sacs
*destroy worn out
parts and get rid
of bacteria*

**Nuclear
membrane**
*controls what
moves into and
out of nucleus*

**Canal
network**
*moves materials
within cell*

Cell membrane
*controls what moves
into and out of cell*

Nucleolus
*helps make
ribosomes*

Ribosome *where
proteins are made*

Plant Cell

Refer to this diagram of a plant cell as you
read cell parts and their jobs.

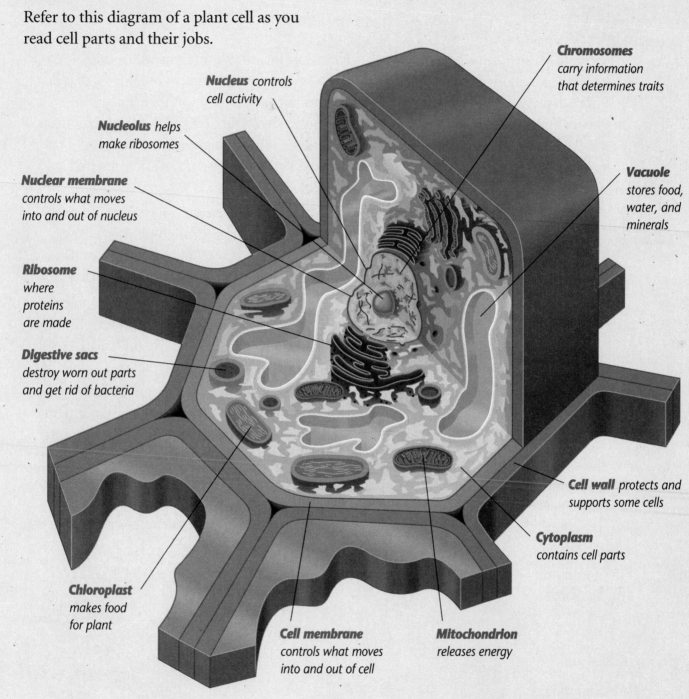

Nucleus controls
cell activity

Nucleolus helps
make ribosomes

Nuclear membrane
controls what moves
into and out of nucleus

Ribosome
where
proteins
are made

Digestive sacs
destroy worn out parts
and get rid of bacteria

Chloroplast
makes food
for plant

Cell membrane
controls what moves
into and out of cell

Mitochondrion
releases energy

Chromosomes
carry information
that determines traits

Vacuole
stores food,
water, and
minerals

Cell wall protects and
supports some cells

Cytoplasm
contains cell parts

Diversity of Life: Classification of Living Organisms

Scientists use a five-kingdom system for the classification of organisms. In this system, there is one kingdom of organisms, Kingdom Monera, which contains organisms that do not have a nucleus and lack specialized structures in the cytoplasm of their cells. The members of the other four kingdoms each have cells that contain a nucleus and structures in the cytoplasm that are surrounded by membranes. These kingdoms are Kingdom Protista, Kingdom Fungi, the Plant Kingdom, and the Animal Kingdom.

Kingdom Monera

Phylum Cyanobacteria one-celled prokaryotes; make their own food, contain chlorophyll, some species form colonies, most are blue-green

Bacteria one-celled prokaryotes; most absorb food from their surroundings, some are photosynthetic; many are parasites; round, spiral, or rod shaped

Kingdom Protista

Phylum Euglenophyta one-celled; can photosynthesize or take in food; most have one flagellum

Phylum Crysophyta most are one-celled; make their own food through photosynthesis; golden-brown pigments mask chlorophyll; diatoms

Phylum Pyrrophyta one-celled; make their own food through photosynthesis; contain red pigments and have two flagella; dinoflagellates

Phylum Chlorophyta one-celled, many-celled, or colonies; contain chlorophyll and make their own food; live on land, in fresh water or salt water; green algae

Phylum Rhodophyta most are many-celled and photosynthetic; contain red pigments; most live in deep saltwater environments; red algae

Phylum Phaeophyta most are many-celled and photosynthetic; contain brown pigments; most live in saltwater environments; brown algae

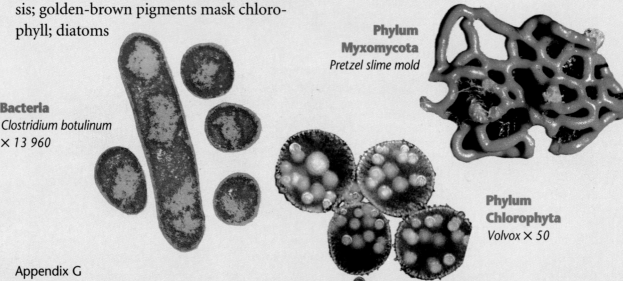

Bacteria
Clostridium botulinum
× 13 960

Phylum Myxomycota
Pretzel slime mold

Phylum Chlorophyta
Volvox × 50

APPENDIX G

Phylum Sarcodina one-celled; take in food; move by means of pseudopods; free-living or parasitic; sarcodines

Phylum Mastigophora one-celled; take in food; have two or more flagella; free-living or parasitic; flagellates

Phylum Ciliophora one-celled; take in food; have large numbers of cilia; ciliates

Phylum Sporozoa one-celled; take in food; no means of movement; parasites in animals; sporozoans

Phylum Myxomycota, Phylum Acrasiomycota one- or many-celled; absorb food; change form during life cycle; cellular and plasmodial slime molds

Kingdom Fungi

Phylum Zygomycota many-celled; absorb food; spores are produced in sporangia; zygote fungi

Phylum Ascomycota one- and many-celled; absorb food; spores produced in asci; sac fungi; yeast

Phylum Ascomycota
Yeast × 7800

Lichens
Old Man's Beard lichen

Phylum Basidiomycota many-celled; absorb food; spores produced in basidia; club fungi

Phylum Deuteromycota members with unknown reproductive structures; imperfect fungi

Lichens organism formed by symbiotic relationship between an ascomycote or a basidiomycote and a green alga or a cyanobacterium

Plant Kingdom
Spore Plants

Division Bryophyta nonvascular plants that reproduce by spores produced in capsules; many-celled; green; grow in moist land environments; mosses and liverworts

Division Lycophyta many-celled vascular plants; spores produced in cones; live on land; are photosynthetic; club mosses

Division Sphenophyta vascular plants with ribbed and jointed stems; scalelike leaves; spores produced in cones; horsetails

Division Pterophyta vascular plants with feathery leaves called fronds; spores produced in clusters of sporangia called sori; live on land or in water; ferns

Division Bryophyta
Liverwort

Seed Plants

Division Ginkgophyta deciduous gymnosperms; only one living species called the maidenhair tree; fan-shaped leaves with branching veins; reproduces with seeds; ginkgos

Division Cycadophyta palmlike gymnosperms; large compound leaves; produce seeds in cones; cycads

Division Coniferophyta deciduous or evergreen gymnosperms; trees or shrubs; needlelike or scalelike leaves; seeds produced in cones; conifers

Division Gnetophyta shrubs or woody vines; seeds produced in cones; division contains only three genera; gnetum

Division Anthophyta dominant group of plants; ovules protected at fertilization by an ovary; sperm carried to ovules by pollen tube; produce flowers and seeds in fruits; flowering plants

Animal Kingdom

Phylum Porifera aquatic organisms that lack true tissues and organs; they are asymmetrical and sessile; sponges

Phylum Cnidaria radially symmetrical organisms with a digestive cavity with one opening; most have tentacles armed with stinging cells; live in aquatic environments singly or in colonies; includes jellyfish, corals, hydra, and sea anemones

Phylum Platyhelminthes bilaterally symmetrical worms with flattened bodies; digestive system has one opening; parasitic and free-living species; flatworms

Phylum Cnidaria
Jellyfish

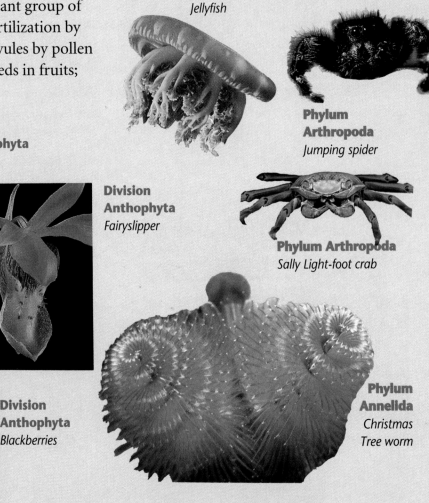

Phylum Arthropoda
Jumping spider

Division Coniferophyta
Slash Pine cones

Division Anthophyta
Fairyslipper

Phylum Arthropoda
Sally Light-foot crab

Division Anthophyta
Blackberries

Phylum Annelida
Christmas Tree worm

Phylum Nematoda round bilaterally symmetrical body; digestive system with two openings; some free-living forms but mostly parasitic; roundworms

Phylum Mollusca soft-bodied animals, many with a hard shell; a mantle covers the soft body; aquatic and terrestrial species; includes clams, snails, squid, and octopuses

Phylum Annelida bilaterally symmetrical worms with round segmented bodies; terrestrial and aquatic species; includes earthworms, leeches, and marine polychaetes

Phylum Arthropoda very large phylum of organisms that have segmented bodies with pairs of jointed appendages, and a hard exoskeleton; terrestrial and aquatic species; includes insects, crustaceans, spiders, and horseshoe crabs

Phylum Echinodermata saltwater organisms with spiny or leathery skin; water-vascular system with tube feet; radial symmetry; includes starfish, sand dollars, and sea urchins

Phylum Chordata organisms with internal skeletons, specialized body systems, and paired appendages; all at some time have a notochord, dorsal nerve cord, gill slits, and a tail; include fish, amphibians, reptiles, birds, and mammals

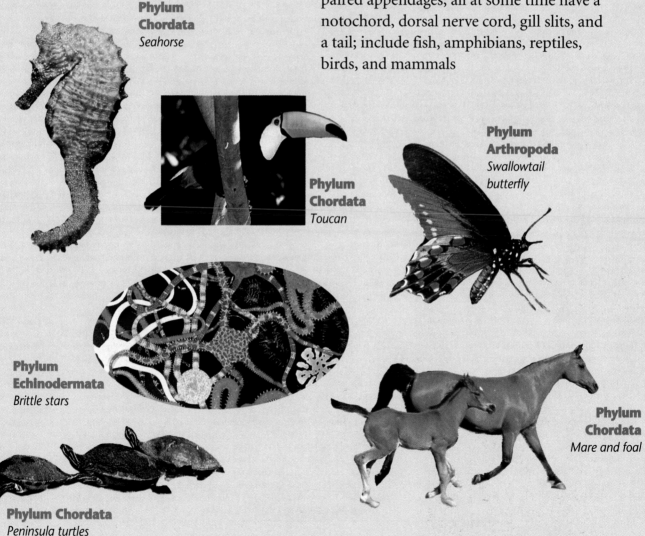

Phylum Chordata
Seahorse

Phylum Chordata
Toucan

Phylum Arthropoda
Swallowtail butterfly

Phylum Echinodermata
Brittle stars

Phylum Chordata
Mare and foal

Phylum Chordata
Peninsula turtles

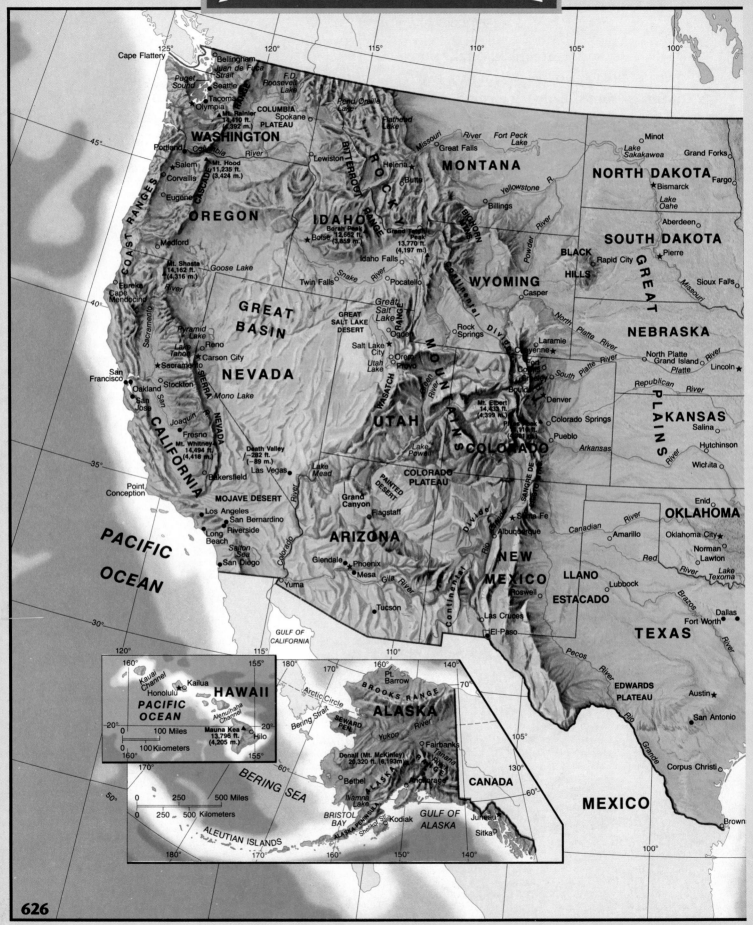

CANADA

Lake of the Woods

Red Lake

Lake Superior

MAINE

Moosehead Lake

Bangor

Mt. Washington 6,288 ft. (1,905 m.)

Augusta

Lewiston

MINNESOTA

Duluth

MICHIGAN

Lake Champlain

Burlington

Montpelier

N.H.

VT.

Portland

WISCONSIN

Green Bay

Appleton

Lake Michigan

Lake Huron

ADIRONDACK MTNS.

Hudson River

Concord

Manchester

MASS.

Cape Cod

Minneapolis

St. Paul

Mississippi

Madison

Milwaukee

Racine

Grand Rapids

Flint

Lansing

Detroit

Ann Arbor

Lake Ontario

Rochester

Utica

Syracuse

Albany

Springfield

Worcester

Boston

Providence

R.I.

Rochester

River

NEW YORK

Niagara Falls

Buffalo

Binghamton

Susquehanna River

Hartford

New Haven

CONN.

Sioux City

Dubuque

Rockford

Chicago

South Bend

Toledo

Cleveland

Erie

Lake Erie

Youngstown

Allentown

Newark

Yonkers

New York

N.J.

River

IOWA

Cedar Rapids

Davenport

Aurora

Gary

Hammond

Fort Wayne

Akron

Canton

PENNSYLVANIA

Philadelphia

Trenton

Camden

Wilmington

Omaha

Council Bluffs

Des Moines

ILLINOIS

Peoria

OHIO

Columbus

Pittsburgh

Wheeling

Harrisburg

Baltimore

MD.

DEL.

Dover

DELAWARE BAY

CENTRAL

LOWLAND

Muncie

Indianapolis

Dayton

Parkersburg

Cincinnati

WEST VIRGINIA

Arlington

Annapolis

Washington

D.C.

Topeka

Lawrence

Kansas City

Kansas City

Independence

Jefferson City

Springfield

Decatur

INDIANA

R.

Evansville

Ohio River

Frankfort

Lexington

Louisville

Charleston

Huntington

MOUNTAINS

Richmond

Newport News

Norfolk

ATLANTIC OCEAN

CHESAPEAKE BAY

East St. Louis

St. Louis

Wabash R.

KENTUCKY

VIRGINIA

Roanoke

Roanoke River

MISSOURI

Harry S. Truman Res.

Owensboro

River

Charleston

Greensboro

Durham

Raleigh

Cape Hatteras

Tulsa

Kerr Res.

R.S. Res.

Springfield

Cumberland

Knoxville

PLATEAU

Winston-Salem

Mt. Mitchell 6,684 ft. (2,037 m.)

ARKANSAS

Nashville

APPALACHIAN

Charlotte

NORTH CAROLINA

Lake Eufaula

Fort Smith

North Little Rock

Little Rock

Hot Springs

Memphis

Tennessee River

Chattanooga

Huntsville

Greenville

Spartanburg

Columbia

Pine Bluff

Mississippi R.

CUMBERLAND

Columbia

SOUTH CAROLINA

Charleston

Greenville

Chattahoochee

Atlanta

Augusta

Shreveport

Meridian

Jackson

Birmingham

Tuscaloosa

GEORGIA

Macon

Savannah

COASTAL

LOUISIANA

ALABAMA

Montgomery

Columbus

PLAIN

Toledo Bend Res.

Hattiesburg

Alabama R.

Albany

Sam Rayburn Reservoir

MISSISSIPPI

Mobile

Pensacola

Jacksonville

Houston

Baton Rouge

Lake Pontchartrain

Biloxi

Lafayette

New Orleans

Lake Charles

Lake Okeechobee

FLORIDA

Tallahassee

Orlando

Cape Canaveral

GULF OF MEXICO

St. Petersburg

Tampa

Palm Beach

Miami Beach

Miami

Cape Sable

Key West

Strait of Florida

THE BAHAMAS

CUBA

UNITED STATES

- ⊛ National capital
- ★ State capital
- ● Major city
- ○ Other city
- ▬ International boundary
- ▬ State boundary

0   100   200 Miles

0   100   200 Kilometers

Projection: Albers Equal Area

N

627

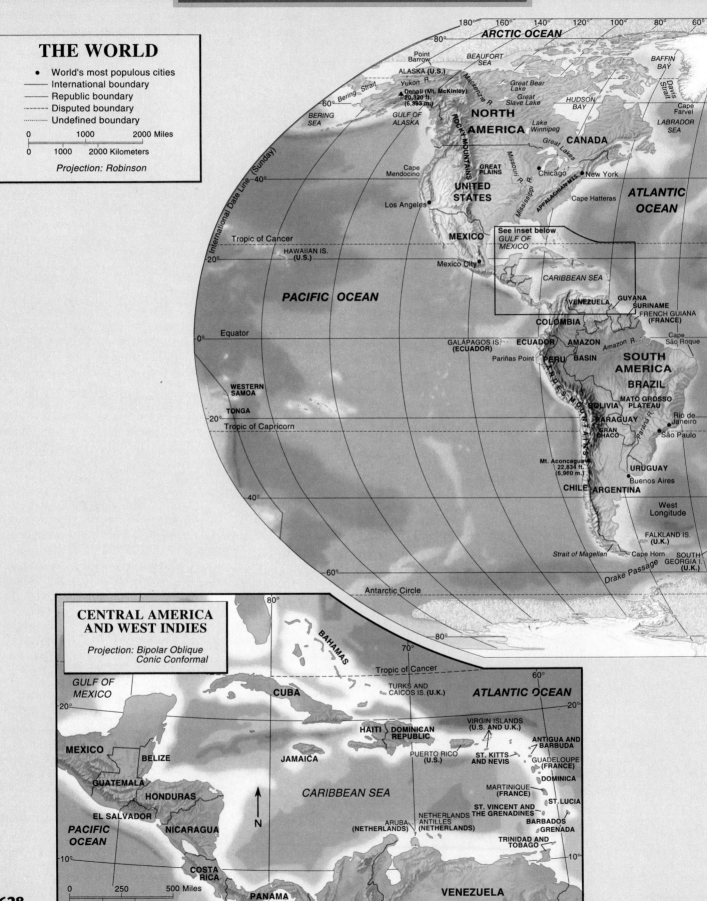

THE WORLD

- • World's most populous cities
- — International boundary
- — Republic boundary
- --- Disputed boundary
- ··· Undefined boundary

0   1000   2000 Miles
0   1000   2000 Kilometers

Projection: Robinson

ARCTIC OCEAN

Point Barrow

BEAUFORT SEA

ALASKA (U.S.)

Bering Strait

Denali (Mt. McKinley) 20,320 ft. (6,393 m.)

Yukon R.

BAFFIN BAY

Great Bear Lake

Great Slave Lake

HUDSON BAY

BAFFIN

Davis Strait

Cape Farvel

LABRADOR SEA

NORTH AMERICA

CANADA

BERING SEA

GULF OF ALASKA

ROCKY MOUNTAINS

Mackenzie R.

Lake Winnipeg

Great Lakes

Missouri R.

Cape Mendocino

GREAT PLAINS

Chicago

New York

UNITED STATES

APPALACHIAN MTS.

Mississippi R.

Cape Hatteras

ATLANTIC OCEAN

Los Angeles

International Date Line (Sunday)

MEXICO

See inset below GULF OF MEXICO

Tropic of Cancer

HAWAIIAN IS. (U.S.)

Mexico City

CARIBBEAN SEA

PACIFIC OCEAN

VENEZUELA   GUYANA   SURINAME

FRENCH GUIANA (FRANCE)

COLOMBIA

Equator

GALÁPAGOS IS. (ECUADOR)

ECUADOR

AMAZON

Amazon R.

Cape São Roque

Pariñas Point

PERU   BASIN

SOUTH AMERICA

WESTERN SAMOA

BRAZIL

ANDES MOUNTAINS

BOLIVIA

MATO GROSSO PLATEAU

TONGA

PARAGUAY

GRAN CHACO

Paraná R.

Rio de Janeiro

São Paulo

Tropic of Capricorn

Mt. Aconcagua 22,834 ft. (6,960 m.)

URUGUAY

Buenos Aires

CHILE   ARGENTINA

West Longitude

FALKLAND IS. (U.K.)

Strait of Magellan   Cape Horn

SOUTH GEORGIA I. (U.K.)

Drake Passage

Antarctic Circle

CENTRAL AMERICA AND WEST INDIES

Projection: Bipolar Oblique Conic Conformal

GULF OF MEXICO

BAHAMAS

CUBA

TURKS AND CAICOS IS. (U.K.)

ATLANTIC OCEAN

Tropic of Cancer

MEXICO

BELIZE

HAITI

DOMINICAN REPUBLIC

VIRGIN ISLANDS (U.S. AND U.K.)

ANTIGUA AND BARBUDA

JAMAICA

PUERTO RICO (U.S.)

ST. KITTS AND NEVIS

GUADELOUPE (FRANCE)

GUATEMALA

DOMINICA

HONDURAS

CARIBBEAN SEA

MARTINIQUE (FRANCE)

ST. LUCIA

EL SALVADOR

ST. VINCENT AND THE GRENADINES

BARBADOS

PACIFIC OCEAN

NICARAGUA

ARUBA (NETHERLANDS)

NETHERLANDS ANTILLES (NETHERLANDS)

GRENADA

TRINIDAD AND TOBAGO

COSTA RICA

0   250   500 Miles
0   250   500 Kilometers

PANAMA

VENEZUELA

COLOMBIA

GUYANA

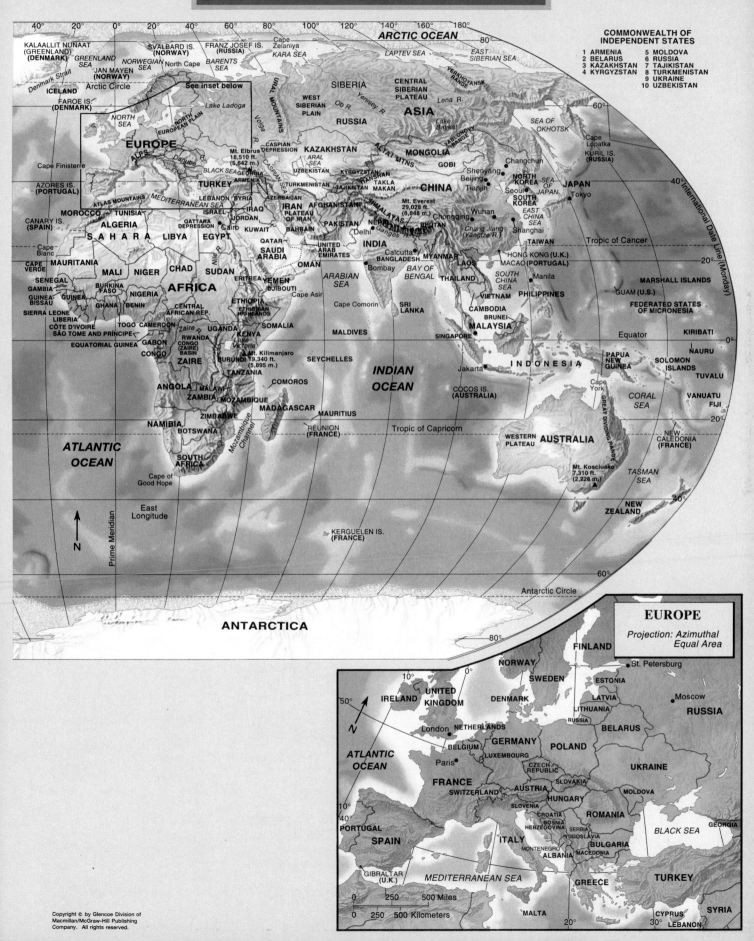

Periodic Table

Alkali Metals 1

Metallic Properties

1		
H		
Hydrogen		
1.007 94		

Alkaline Earth Metals 2

3	4
Li	**Be**
Lithium	Beryllium
6.941	9.012 182

11	12
Na	**Mg**
Sodium	Magnesium
22.989 77	24.305

Transition Elements

3	4	5	6	7	8	9
21	22	23	24	25	26	27
Sc	**Ti**	**V**	**Cr**	**Mn**	**Fe**	**Co**
Scandium	Titanium	Vanadium	Chromium	Manganese	Iron	Cobalt
44.955 91	47.88	50.9415	51.9961	54.9380	55.847	58.9332
39	40	41	42	43	44	45
Y	**Zr**	**Nb**	**Mo**	**Tc**	**Ru**	**Rh**
Yttrium	Zirconium	Niobium	Molybdenum	Technetium	Ruthenium	Rhodium
88.9059	91.224	92.9064	95.94	97.9072*	101.07	102.9055
71	72	73	74	75	76	77
Lu	**Hf**	**Ta**	**W**	**Re**	**Os**	**Ir**
Lutetium	Hafnium	Tantalum	Tungsten	Rhenium	Osmium	Iridium
174.967	178.49	180.9479	183.85	186.207	190.2	192.22
103	104	105	106	107	108	109
Lr	**Unq**	**Unp**	**Unh**	**Uns**	**Uno**	**Une**
Lawrencium	Unnilquadium	Unnilpentium	Unnilhexium	Unnilseptium	Unniloctium	Unnilennium
260.1054*	261*	262*	263*	262*	265*	266*

Potassium / Calcium row:

19	20
K	**Ca**
Potassium	Calcium
39.0983	40.078

37	38
Rb	**Sr**
Rubidium	Strontium
85.4678	87.62

55	56
Cs	**Ba**
Cesium	Barium
132.9054	137.33

87	88
Fr	**Ra**
Francium	Radium
223.0197*	226.0254

— Metallic properties —

Lanthanoid Series

57	58	59	60	61	62
La	**Ce**	**Pr**	**Nd**	**Pm**	**Sm**
Lanthanum	Cerium	Praseodymium	Neodymium	Promethium	Samarium
138.9055	140.12	140.9077	144.24	144.9128*	150.36

Actinoid Series

89	90	91	92	93	94
Ac	**Th**	**Pa**	**U**	**Np**	**Pu**
Actinium	Thorium	Protactinium	Uranium	Neptunium	Plutonium
227.0278*	232.0381	231.0359*	238.0289	237.0482	244.0642*

*Mass of isotope with longest half-life that is the most stable isotope of the element

Noble Gases
18

Halogens
17

Transition Elements

Nonmetallic properties

			13	14	15	16	17	18
								2 **He** Helium 4.002 602
			5 **B** Boron 10.811	6 **C** Carbon 12.011	7 N Nitrogen 14.0067	8 O Oxygen 15.9994	9 F Fluorine 18.998 403	10 Ne Neon 20.1797
			13 **Al** Aluminum 26.981 54	14 **Si** Silicon 28.0855	15 **P** Phosphorus 30.973 76	16 **S** Sulfur 32.07	17 Cl Chlorine 35.453	18 Ar Argon 39.948
10	11	12						
28 **Ni** Nickel 58.69	29 **Cu** Copper 63.546	30 **Zn** Zinc 65.39	31 **Ga** Gallium 69.723	32 **Ge** Germanium 72.61	33 **As** Arsenic 74.9216	34 **Se** Selenium 78.96	35 Br Bromine 79.904	36 Kr Krypton 83.80
46 **Pd** Palladium 106.42	47 **Ag** Silver 107.8682	48 **Cd** Cadmium 112.41	49 **In** Indium 114.82	50 **Sn** Tin 118.710	51 **Sb** Antimony 121.757	52 **Te** Tellurium 127.60	53 **I** Iodine 126.9045	54 Xe Xenon 131.29
78 **Pt** Platinum 195.08	79 **Au** Gold 196.9665	80 Hg Mercury 200.59	81 **Tl** Thallium 204.383	82 **Pb** Lead 207.2	83 **Bi** Bismuth 208.9804	84 **Po** Polonium 208.9824*	85 **At** Astatine 209.987 12*	86 Rn Radon 222.017*

Metals   Metalloids   Nonmetals

Lettering: ■ Solids   ☐ Synthetics (solid)   Liquids   Gases

63 **Eu** Europium 151.96	64 **Gd** Gadolinium 157.25	65 **Tb** Terbium 158.9253	66 **Dy** Dysprosium 162.50	67 **Ho** Holmium 164.9303	68 **Er** Erbium 167.26	69 **Tm** Thulium 168.9342	70 **Yb** Ytterbium 173.04
95 Am Americium 243.0614*	96 Cm Curium 247.0703*	97 Bk Berkelium 247.0703*	98 Cf Californium 251.0796*	99 Es Einsteinium 252.0828*	100 Fm Fermium 257.0951*	101 Md Mendelevium 258.0986*	102 No Nobelium 259.1009*

Minerals with Nonmetallic Luster

Mineral (formula)	Color	Streak	Hardness	Specific gravity	Crystal system	Breakage pattern	Uses and other properties
talc ($Mg_3Si_4O_{10}$ $(OH)_2$)	white, greenish	white	1	2.8	monoclinic	cleavage in one direction	easily cut with fingernail; used for talcum powder; soapstone; is used in paper and for tabletops
bauxite (hydrous aluminum compound)	gray, red, white, brown	gray	1-3	2.0-2.5	–	–	source of aluminum; used in paints, aluminum foil, and airplane parts
kaolinite ($Al_2Si_2O_5$ $(OH)_4$)	white, red, reddish brown, black	white	2	2.6	triclinic	basal cleavage	clays; used in ceramics and in china dishes; common in most soils; often microscopic-sized particles
gypsum ($CaSO_4$ • $2H_2O$)	colorless, gray, white, brown	white	2	2.3	monoclinic	basal cleavage	used extensively in the preparation of plaster of paris, alabaster, and dry wall for building construction
sphalerite (ZnS)	brown	pale yellow	3.5-4	4	cubic	cleavage in six directions	main ore of zinc; used in paints, dyes, and medicine
sulfur (S)	yellow	yellow to white	2	2.0	ortho-rhombic	conchoidal fracture	used in medicine, fungicides for plants, vulcanization of rubber, production of sulfuric acid
muscovite ($KAl_2(Al_3Si_3$ $O_{10})(OH)_2$)	white, light gray, yellow, rose, green	colorless	2.5	2.8	monoclinic	basal cleavage	occurs in large flexible plates; used as an insulator in electrical equipment, lubricant
biotite ($K(Mg,Fe)_3$ $(AlSi_3O_{10})$ $(OH)_2$)	black to dark brown	colorless	2.5	2.8-3.4	monoclinic	basal cleavage	occurs in large flexible plates
halite ($NaCl$)	colorless, red, white, blue	colorless	2.5	2.1	cubic	cubic cleavage	salt; very soluble in water; a preservative
calcite ($CaCO_3$)	colorless, white, pale blue	colorless, white	3	2.7	hexagonal	cleavage in three directions	fizzes when HCl is added; used in cements and other building materials
dolomite ($CaMg$ $(CO_3)_2$)	colorless, white, pink, green, gray, black	white	3.5-4	2.8	hexagonal	cleavage in three directions	concrete and cement, used as an ornamental building stone

Mineral (formula)	Color	Streak	Hardness	Specific gravity	Crystal system	Breakage pattern	Uses and other properties
fluorite (CaF_2)	colorless, white, blue, green, red, yellow, purple	colorless	4	3-3.2	cubic	cleavage	used in the manufacture of optical equipment; glows under ultraviolet light
limonite (hydrous iron oxides)	yellow, brown, black	yellow, brown	5.5	2.7-4.3	–	conchoidal fracture	source of iron; weathers easily, coloring matter of soils
hornblende ($(Ca,Na)_{2\text{-}3}$ $(Mg,Fe,Al,)_5$ $Si_6(Si,Al)_2$ $O_{22}(OH)_2$)	green to black	gray to white	5-6	3.4	monoclinic	cleavage in two directions	will transmit light on thin edges; 6-sided cross section
feldspar (orthoclase) $KAlSi_3O_8$	colorless, white to gray, green and yellow	colorless	6	2.5	monoclinic	two cleavage planes meet at 90° angle	insoluble in acids; used in the manufacture of porcelain
feldspar (plagioclase) ($NaAlSi_3O_8$) ($CaAl_2Si_2O_8$)	gray, green, white, pink	colorless	6	2.5	triclinic	two cleavage planes meet at 86° angle	used in ceramics; striations present on some faces
augite ((Ca,Na) (Mg,Fe,Al) (Al, Si)$_2$ O_6)	black	colorless	6	3.3	monoclinic	2-directional cleavage	square or 8-sided cross section
olivine ((Mg,Fe)$_2$ SiO_4)	olive green	colorless	6.5	3.5	ortho-rhombic	conchoidal fracture	gemstones, refractory sand
quartz (SiO_2)	colorless, various colors	colorless	7	2.6	hexagonal	conchoidal fracture	used in glass manufacture, electronic equipment, radios, computers, watches, gemstones
garnet ($(Mg,Fe,Ca)_3$ $(Al_2Si_3O_{12})$)	deep yellow-red, green, black	colorless	7.5	3.5	cubic	conchoidal fracture	used in jewelry, also used as an abrasive
topaz (Al_2SiO_4) ($F,OH)_2$)	white, pink, yellow, pale blue, colorless	colorless	8	3.5	ortho-rhombic	basal cleavage	valuable gemstone
corundum (Al_2O_3)	colorless, blue, brown, green, white, pink,	colorless	9	4.0	hexagonal	fracture	gemstones; ruby is red, sapphire is blue; industrial abrasive

APPENDIX L

Minerals with Metallic Luster

Mineral (formula)	Color	Streak	Hardness	Specific gravity	Crystal system	Breakage pattern	Uses and other properties
graphite (C)	black to gray	black to gray	1-2	2.3	hexagonal	basal cleavage (scales)	pencil lead, lubricants for locks, rods to control some small nuclear reactions, battery poles
silver (Ag)	silvery white, tarnishes to black	light gray to silver	2.5	10-12	cubic	hackly	coins, fillings for teeth, jewelry, silver plate, wires; malleable and ductile
galena (Pbs)	gray	gray to black	2.5	7.5	cubic	cubic cleavage perfect	source of lead, used in pipes, shields for X rays, fishing equipment sinkers
gold (Au)	pale to golden yellow	yellow	2.5-3	19.3	cubic	hackly	jewelry, money, gold leaf, fillings for teeth, medicines; does not tarnish
bornite (Cu_5FeS_4)	bronze, tarnishes to dark blue, purple	gray-black	3	4.9-5.4	tetragonal	uneven fracture	source of copper; called "peacock ore" because of the purple shine when it tarnishes
copper (Cu)	copper red	copper red	3	8.5-9	cubic	hackly	coins, pipes, gutters, wire, cooking utensils, jewelry, decorative plaques; malleable and ductile
chalcopyrite ($CuFeS_2$)	brassy to golden yellow	greenish black	3.5-4	4.2	tetragonal	uneven fracture	main ore of copper
chromite ($FeCr_2O_4$)	black or brown	brown to black	5.5	4.6	cubic	irregular fracture	ore of chromium, stainless steel, metallurgical bricks
pyrrhotite (FeS)	bronze	gray-black	4	4.6	hexagonal	uneven fracture	often found with pentlandite, an ore of nickel; may be magnetic
hematite (specular) (Fe_2O_3)	black or reddish brown	red or reddish brown	6	5.3	hexagonal	irregular fracture	source of iron; roasted in a blast furnace, converted to "pig" iron, made into steel
magnetite (Fe_3O_4)	black	black	6	5.2	cubic	conchoidal fracture	source of iron, naturally magnetic, called lodestone
pyrite (FeS_2)	light, brassy yellow	greenish black	6.5	5.0	cubic	uneven fracture	source of iron, "fool's gold," alters to limonite

634   Appendix K

SKILL HANDBOOK

Table of Contents

Organizing Information

Thinking Critically

Practicing Scientific Processes

Representing and Applying Data

Organizing Information

▶ Classifying

You may not realize it, but you make things orderly in the world around you. If you hang your shirts together in the closet, if your socks take up a particular corner of a dresser drawer, or if your favorite CDs are stacked together, you have used the skill of classifying.

Classifying is the process of sorting objects or events into groups based on common features. When classifying, first observe the objects or events to be classified. Then, select one feature that is shared by most members in the group but not by all. Place those members that share the feature into a subgroup. You can classify members into smaller and smaller subgroups based on characteristics.

How would you classify a collection of CDs? You might classify those you like to dance to in one subgroup and CDs you like to listen to in the next column, as in the diagram. The CDs you like to dance to could be subdivided into a rap subgroup and a rock subgroup. Note that for each feature selected, each CD only fits into one subgroup. Keep select-

ing features until all the CDs are classified. The diagram above shows one possible classification.

Remember, when you classify, you are grouping objects or events for a purpose. Keep your purpose in mind as you select the features to form groups and subgroups.

▶ Sequencing

A sequence is an arrangement of things or events in a particular order. A sequence with which you are most familiar is the use of alphabetical order. Another example of sequence would be the steps in a recipe. Think about baking chocolate chip cookies. Steps in the recipe have to be followed in order for the cookies to turn out right.

When you are asked to sequence objects or events within a group, figure out what comes first, then think about what should come second. Continue to choose objects or events until all of the objects you started out with are in order. Then, go back over the sequence to make sure each thing or event in your sequence logically leads to the next.

▶ Concept Mapping

If you were taking an automobile trip, you would probably take along a road map. The road map shows your location, your destination, and other places along the way. By looking at the map and finding where you are, you can begin to understand where you are in relation to other locations on the map.

A concept map is similar to a road map. But, a concept map shows relationships among ideas (or concepts) rather than places. A concept map is a diagram that visually shows how concepts are related. Because the concept map shows relationships among ideas, it can make the meanings of ideas and terms clear, and help you understand better what you are studying.

Network Tree Look at the concept map about Protists. This is called a network tree. Notice how some words are circled while others are written across connecting lines. The circled words are science concepts. The lines in the map show related concepts. The words written on the lines describe the relationships between concepts.

Network Tree

When you are asked to construct a network tree, write down the topic and list the major concepts related to that topic on a piece of paper. Then look at your list and begin to put them in order from general to specific. Branch the related concepts from the major concept and describe the relationships on the lines. Continue to write the more specific concepts. Write the relationships between the concepts on the lines until all concepts are mapped. Examine the concept map for relationships that cross branches, and add them to the concept map.

Events Chain An events chain is another type of concept map. An events chain map, such as the one on the effects of gravity, is used to describe ideas in order. In science, an

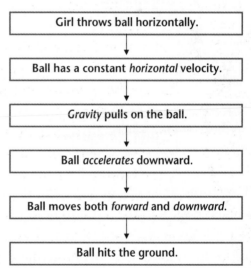

Events Chain

| Girl throws ball horizontally. |
| Ball has a constant *horizontal* velocity. |
| *Gravity* pulls on the ball. |
| Ball *accelerates* downward. |
| Ball moves both *forward* and *downward*. |
| Ball hits the ground. |

events chain can be used to describe a sequence of events, the steps in a procedure, or the stages of a process.

When making an events chain, first find the one event that starts the chain. This event is called the initiating event. Then, find the next event in the chain and continue until you reach an outcome. Suppose you are asked to describe what happens when someone throws a ball horizontally. An events chain map describing the steps might look like the one on page 637. Notice that connecting words are not necessary in an events chain.

Cycle Map A cycle concept map is a special type of events chain map. In a cycle concept map, the series of events does not produce a

Cycle Map

```
              Plants undergoing
              photosynthesis
        which has been              use
        released by
                                    carbon
        oxygen                      dioxide

        in the                      which is
        presence of                 released by
              respiration in
              animals and plants
```

final outcome. Instead, the last event in the chain relates back to the initiating event. Look at the cycle map for photosynthesis.

As in the events chain map, you first decide on an initiating event and then list each event in order. Since there is no outcome and the last event relates back to the initiating event, the cycle repeats itself. Look at the cycle map of insect metamorphosis.

Spider Map A fourth type of concept map is the spider map. This is a map that you can use for brainstorming. Once you have a central idea, you may find you have a jumble of ideas that relate to it, but are not necessarily clearly related to each other. By writing these

Spider Map

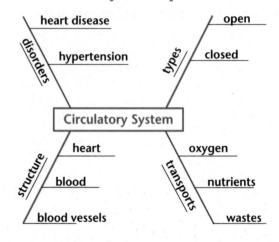

ideas outside the main concept, you may begin to separate and group unrelated terms so that they become more useful.

There is usually not one correct way to create a concept map. As you construct one type of map, you may discover other ways to construct the map that show the relationships between concepts in a better way. If you do discover what you think is a better way to create a concept map, go ahead and use the new way. Overall, concept maps are useful for breaking a big concept down into smaller parts, making learning easier.

▶ Making and Using Tables

Browse through your textbook, and you will notice tables in the text and in the activities. In a table, data or information is arranged in such a way that makes it easier for you to understand. Activity tables help organize the data you collect during an activity so that results can be interpreted more easily.

Parts of a Table   Most tables have a title. At a glance, the title tells you what the table is about. A table is divided into columns and rows. The first column lists items to be compared. In the table shown to the right, different magnitudes of force are being compared. The row across the top lists the specific characteristics being compared. Within the grid of the table, the collected data is recorded. Look at the features of the table in the next column.

What is the title of this table? The title is "Earthquake Magnitude." What is being compared? The distance away from the epicenter that tremors are felt and the average number of earthquakes expected per year are being compared for different magnitudes on the Richter scale.

Using Tables   What is the average number of earthquakes expected per year for an earthquake with a magnitude of 5.5 at the focus? Locate the column labeled "Average number expected per year" and the row "5.0 to 5.9." The data in the box where the column and row intersect is the answer. Did you answer "800"? What is the distance away from the epicenter for an earthquake with a

Earthquake Magnitude		
Magnitude at Focus	Distance from Epicenters that Tremors are Felt	Average Number Expected Per Year
1.0 to 3.9	24 km	>100 000
4.0 to 4.9	48 km	6200
5.0 to 5.9	112 km	800
6.0 to 6.9	200 km	120
7.0 to 7.9	400 km	20
8.0 to 8.9	720 km	<1

magnitude of 8.1? If you answered "720 km," you understand how to use the parts of a table.

Making Tables   To make a table, list the items to be compared down in columns and the characteristics to be compared across in rows. Make a table and record the data comparing the mass of recycled materials collected by a class. On Monday, students turned in 4 kg of paper, 2 kg of aluminum, and 0.5 kg of plastic. On Wednesday, they turned in 3.5 kg of paper, 1.5 kg of aluminum, and 0.5 kg of plastic. On Friday, the totals were 3 kg of paper, 1 kg of aluminum, and 1.5 kg of plastic. If your table looks like the one shown below, you are able to make tables to organize data.

Recycled Materials			
Day of Week	Paper (kg)	Aluminum (kg)	Plastic (kg)
Mon.	4	2	0.5
Wed.	3.5	1.5	0.5
Fri.	3	1	1.5

▶ Making and Using Graphs

After scientists organize data in tables, they may display the data in a graph. A graph is a diagram that shows how variables compare. A graph makes interpretation and analysis of data easier. There are three basic types of graphs used in science—the line graph, the bar graph, and the pie graph.

Line Graphs   A line graph is used to show the relationship between two variables. The variables being compared go on two axes of the graph. The independent variable always goes on the horizontal axis, called the *x*-axis. The dependent variable always goes on the vertical axis, called the *y*-axis.

Suppose a school started a peer study program with a class of students to see how science grades were affected.

Average Grades of Students in Study Program	
Grading Period	Average Science Grade
First	81
Second	85
Third	86
Fourth	89

You could make a graph of the grades of students in the program over the four grading periods of the school year. The grading period is the independent variable and is placed on the *x*-axis of your graph. The average grade of the students in the program is the dependent variable and would go on the *y*-axis.

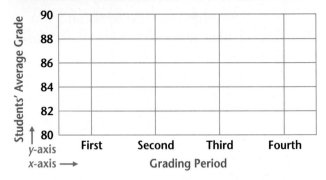

After drawing your axes, you would label each axis with a scale. The *x*-axis simply lists the four grading periods. To make a scale of grades on the *y*-axis, you must look at the data values. Since the lowest grade was 81 and the highest was 89, you know that you will have to start numbering at least at 81 and go through 89. You decide to start numbering at 80 and number by twos through 90.

Next, plot the data points. The first pair of data you want to plot is the first grading period and 81. Locate "First" on the *x*-axis and locate "81" on the *y*-axis. Where an imaginary vertical line from the *x*-axis and an imaginary horizontal line from the *y*-axis would meet, place the first data point. Place the other data points the same way. After all the points are plotted, connect them with straight lines.

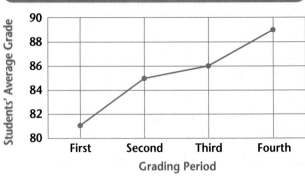

Bar Graphs Bar graphs are similar to line graphs. They compare data that do not continuously change. In a bar graph, vertical bars show the relationships among data.

To make a bar graph, set up the *x*-axis and *y*-axis as you did for the line graph. The data is plotted by drawing vertical bars from the *x*-axis up to a point where the *y*-axis would meet the bar if it were extended.

Look at the bar graph comparing the masses lifted by an electromagnet with different numbers of dry cell batteries. The *x*-axis is the number of dry cell batteries, and the *y*-axis is the mass lifted.

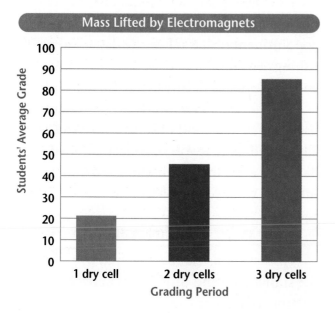

Pie Graphs A pie graph uses a circle divided into sections to display data. Each section represents part of the whole. All the sections together equal 100 percent.

Suppose you wanted to make a pie graph to show the number of seeds that germinated in a package. You would have to count the total number of seeds and the number of seeds that germinated out of the total.

You find that there are 143 seeds in the package. This represents 100 percent, the whole pie.

You plant the seeds, and 129 seeds germinate. The seeds that germinated will make up one section of the pie graph, and the seeds that did not germinate will make up the remaining section.

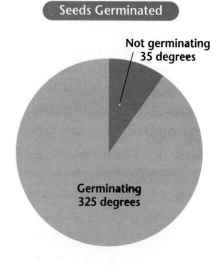

To find out how much of the pie each section should take, divide the number of seeds in each section by the total number of seeds. Then multiply your answer by 360, the number of degrees in a circle, and round to the nearest whole number. The section of the pie graph in degrees that represents the seeds germinated is figured below.

$$\frac{129}{143} \times 360 = 324.75 \text{ or } 325 \text{ degrees}$$

Plot this group on the pie graph using a compass and a protractor. Use the compass to draw a circle. Then, draw a straight line from the center to the edge of the circle. Place your protractor on this line and use it to mark a point on the edge of the circle at 325 degrees. Connect this point with a straight line to the center of the circle. This is the section for the group of seeds that germinated. The other section represents the group of 14 seeds that did not germinate. Label the sections of your graph and title the graph.

Processing Information Critically

▶ Observing and Inferring

Imagine that you have just finished a volleyball game. At home, you open the refrigerator and see a jug of orange juice on the back of the top shelf. The jug feels cold as you grasp it. Then you drink the juice, smell the oranges, and enjoy the tart taste in your mouth.

As you imagined yourself in the story, you used your senses to make observations. You used your sense of sight to find the jug in the refrigerator, your sense of touch when you felt the coldness of the jug, your sense of hearing to listen as the liquid filled the glass, and your senses of smell and taste to enjoy the odor and tartness of the juice. The basis of all scientific investigation is observation.

Scientists try to make careful and accurate observations. When possible, they use instruments, such as microscopes. Other instruments, such as thermometers or a pan balance, measure observations.

Measurements provide numerical data that can be checked and repeated.

When you make observations in science, you'll find it helpful to examine the entire object or situation first. Then, look carefully for details. Write down everything you see before using other senses to make additional observations.

Scientists often make inferences based on their observations. An inference is an attempt to explain or interpret observations or to say what caused what you observed. For example, if you observed a CLOSED sign in a store window around noon, you might infer the owner is taking a lunch break. But, it's also possible that the owner has a doctor's appointment or has taken the day off to go fishing. The only way to be sure your inference is correct is to investigate further.

When making an inference, be certain to use accurate data and observations. Analyze all of the data that you've collected. Then, based on everything you know, explain or interpret what you've observed.

▶ Comparing and Contrasting

Observations can be analyzed by noting the similarities and differences between two or more objects or events that you observe. When you look at objects or events to see how they are similar, you are comparing them. Contrasting is looking for differences in similar objects or events.

Suppose you were asked to compare and contrast the planets Venus and Earth. You would start by looking at what is known about these planets. Then, make two columns on a piece of paper and list ways the planets are similar in one column and ways

Comparison of Venus and Earth		
Properties	Earth	Venus
Diameter (km)	12 742	12 112
Average density (g/cm³)	5.5	5.3
Percentage of sunlight reflected	39	76
Daytime surface temperature	300	750
Number of satellites	1	0

they are different in the other.

Similarities you might point out are that both planets are similar in size, shape, and mass. Differences include Venus having a hotter surface temperature and a dense, cloudy atmosphere that reflects more sunlight than Earth. Also, Venus lacks a moon.

▶ Recognizing Cause and Effect

Have you ever watched something happen and then made a suggestion as to why or how it happened? If so, you have observed and inferred. The event is an effect, and the reason for the event is the cause.

Suppose that every time your teacher fed the fish in a classroom aquarium, she or he tapped the food container on the edge of the aquarium. Then, one day your teacher just happened to tap the edge of the aquarium with a pencil while making a point about an ecology lesson. You observed the fish swim to the surface of the aquarium to feed. What is the effect, and what would you infer to be the cause? The effect is the fish swimming to the surface of the aquarium. You might infer the cause to be the teacher tapping on the edge of the aquarium. In determining cause and effect, you have made a logical inference based on your observations.

Perhaps the fish swam to the surface because they reacted to the teacher's waving hand or for some other reason. When scientists are unsure of the cause of a certain event, they design controlled experiments to determine what causes the event. Although you have made a logical conclusion about the behavior of the fish, you would have to perform an experiment to be certain that it was the tapping that caused the effect you observed.

▶ Measuring in SI

The metric system is a system of measurement developed by a group of scientists in 1795. It helps scientists avoid problems by providing standard measurements that all scientists around the world can understand. A modern form of the metric system, called the International System, or SI, was adopted for worldwide use in 1960.

Metric Prefixes			
Prefix	Symbol	Meaning	
kilo-	k	1000	thousand
hecto-	h	100	hundred
deka-	da	10	ten
deci-	d	0.1	tenth
centi-	c	0.01	hundredth
milli-	m	0.001	thousandth

The metric system is convenient because unit sizes vary by multiples of 10. When changing from smaller units to larger units, divide by 10. When changing from larger units to smaller, you multiply by 10. For example, to convert millimeters to centimeters, divide the millimeters by 10. To convert 30 millimeters to centimeters, divide 30 by 10 (30 millimeters equals 3 centimeters).

Prefixes are used to name units. Look at the table for some common metric prefixes and their meanings. Do you see how the prefix *kilo-* attached to the unit *gram* is *kilogram*, or 1000 grams? The prefix *deci-* attached to the unit *meter* is *decimeter*, or one-tenth (0.1) of a meter.

Length You have probably measured lengths or distances many times. The meter is the SI unit used to measure length. A baseball bat is about one meter long. When measuring smaller lengths, the meter is divided into smaller units called centimeters and millimeters. A centimeter is one-hundredth (0.01) of a meter, which is about the size of the width of the fingernail on your ring finger. A millimeter is one-thousandth of a meter (0.001), about the thickness of a dime.

Most metric rulers have lines indicating centimeters and millimeters. The centimeter lines are the longer, numbered lines, and the shorter lines are millimeter lines. When using a metric ruler, line up the 0 centimeter mark with the end of the object being measured, and read the number of the unit where the object ends.

Surface Area Units of length are also used to measure surface area. The standard unit of area is the square meter (m²). A square that's one meter long on each side has a surface area of one square meter. Similarly, a square centimeter (cm²) is one centimeter long on each side. The surface area of an object is determined by multiplying the length times the width.

Volume The volume of a rectangular solid is also calculated using units of length. The cubic meter (m^3) is the standard SI unit of volume. A cubic meter is a cube one meter on each side. You can determine the volume of rectangular solids by multiplying length times width times height.

Liquid Volume During science activities, you will measure liquids using beakers and graduated cylinders marked in milliliters. A graduated cylinder is a cylindrical container marked with lines from bottom to top.

Liquid volume is measured using a unit called a liter. A liter has the volume of 1000 cubic centimeters. Since the prefix *milli-* means thousandth (0.001), a milliliter equals one cubic centimeter. One milliliter of liquid would completely fill a cube measuring one centimeter on each side.

Mass Scientists use balances to find the mass of objects in grams. You will use a beam balance similar to the one illustrated. Notice that on one side of the balance is a pan and on the other side is a set of beams. Each beam has an object of a known mass called a *rider* that slides on the beam.

Before you find the mass of an object, set the balance to zero by sliding all the riders back to the zero point. Check the pointer on the right to make sure it swings an equal distance above and below the zero point on the scale. If the swing is unequal, find and turn the adjusting screw until you have an equal swing.

Place an object on the pan. Slide the rider with the largest mass along its beam until the pointer drops below zero. Then move it back one notch. Repeat the process on each beam until the pointer swings an equal distance above and below the zero point. Add the masses on each beam to find the mass of the object.

You should never place a hot object or pour chemicals directly on the pan. Instead, find the mass of a clean beaker or a glass jar. Place the dry or liquid chemicals in the container. Then find the combined mass of the container and the chemicals. Calculate the mass of the chemicals by subtracting the mass of the empty container from the combined mass.

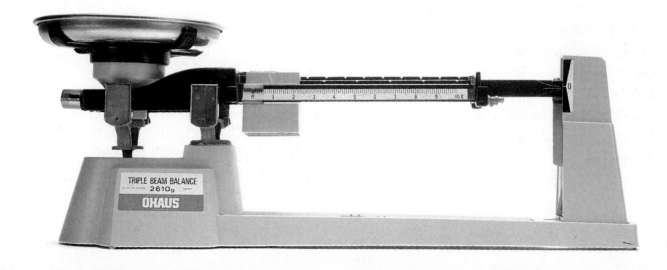

Practicing Scientific Methods

You might say that the work of a scientist is to solve problems. But when you decide how to dress on a particular day, you are doing problem solving, too. You may observe what the weather looks like through a window. You may go outside and see if what you are wearing is warm or cool enough.

Scientists use an orderly approach to learn new information and to solve problems. The methods scientists may use include observing, forming a hypothesis, testing a hypothesis, separating and controlling variables, and interpreting data.

▶ Observing

You observe all the time. Anytime you smell wood burning, touch a pet, see

lightning, taste food, or hear your favorite music, you are observing. Observation gives you information about events or things. Scientists try to observe as much as possible about the things and events they study so that they can know that what they say about their observations is reliable.

Some observations describe something using only words. These observations are called qualitative observations. If you were making qualitative observations of a dog, you might use words such as furry, brown, short-haired, or short-eared.

Other observations describe how much of something there is. These are quantitative observations and use numbers as well as words in the description. Tools or equipment are used to measure the characteristic being described. Quantitative observations of a dog might include a mass of 459 g, a height of 27 cm, ear length of 14 mm, and an age of 283 days.

▶ Using Observations to Form a Hypothesis

Suppose you want to make a perfect score on a spelling test. Begin by thinking of several ways to accomplish this. Base these possibilities on past observations. If you put each of these possibilities into sentence form, using the words if and then, you can form a hypothesis. All of the following are hypotheses you might consider to explain how you could score 100 percent on your test:

If the test is easy, then I will get a perfect score.

If I am intelligent, then I will get a perfect score.

Scientists make hypotheses that they can test to explain the observations they have made. Perhaps a scientist has observed that plants that receive fertilizer grow taller than plants that do not. A scientist may form a hypothesis that says: If plants are fertilized, then their growth will increase.

▶ Designing an Experiment to Test a Hypothesis

Once you state a hypothesis, you probably want to find out whether or not it explains an event or an observation. This requires a test. A hypothesis must be something you can test. To test a hypothesis, you design and carry out an experiment. Experiments involve planning and materials. Let's figure out how to conduct an experiment to test the hypothesis

stated before about the effects of fertilizer on plants.

First, you need to write out a procedure. A procedure is the plan that you follow in your experiment. A procedure tells you what materials to use and how to use them. In this experiment, your plan may involve using ten bean plants that are each 15 cm tall (to begin with) in two groups, Groups A and B. You will water the five bean plants in Group A with 200 mL of plain water and no fertilizer twice a week for three weeks. You will treat the five bean plants in Group B with 200 mL of fertilizer solution twice a week for three weeks.

You will need to measure all the plants in both groups at the beginning of the experiment and again at the end of the three-week period. These measurements will be the data that you record in a table. A sample table has been done for you. Look at the data in the table for this experiment. From the data, you can draw a conclusion and make a statement about your results. If the conclusion you draw from the data supports your hypothesis, then you can say that your hypothesis is

Growing Bean Plants		
Plants	Treatment	Height 3 Weeks Later
Group A	no fertilizer added to soil	17 cm
Group B	3 g fertilizer added to soil	31 cm

reliable. Reliable means that you can trust your conclusion. If it did not support your hypothesis, then you would have to make new observations and state a new hypothesis, one that you could also test.

▶ Separating and Controlling Variables

In the experiment with the bean plants, you made everything the same except for treating one group (Group B) with fertilizer. In any experiment, it is important to keep everything the same, except for the item you are testing. In the experiment, you kept the type of plants, their beginning heights, the soil, the frequency with which you watered them, and the amount of water or fertilizer all the same, or constant. By doing so, you made sure that at the end of three weeks, any change you saw was the result of whether or not the plants had been fertilized. The only thing that you changed, or varied, was the use of fertilizer. In an experiment, the one factor that you change (in this case, the fertilizer), is called the independent variable. The factor that changes (in this case, growth) as a result of the independent variable is called the dependent variable. Always make sure that there is only one independent variable. If you allow more than one, you will not know what causes any change you observe in the dependent variable.

Many experiments also have a control, a treatment that you can compare with the results of your test groups. In this case, Group A was the control because it was not treated with fertilizer. Group B was the test group. At the end of three weeks, you were able to compare Group A with Group B and draw a conclusion.

▶ Interpreting Data

The word *interpret* means to explain the meaning of something. Information, or data, needs to mean something. Look at the problem originally being explored and find out what the data shows. Perhaps you are looking at a table from an experiment designed to test the hypothesis: If plants are fertilized, then their growth will increase. Look back to the table showing the results of the bean plant experiment.

Identify the control group and the test group so you can see whether or not the variable has had an effect. In this example, Group A was the control and Group B was the test group. Now you need to check differences between the control and test groups. These differences may be qualitative or quantitative. A qualitative difference would be if the leaf colors of plants in Groups A and B were different. A quantitative difference would be the difference in numbers of centimeters of height among the plants in each group. Group B was in fact taller than Group A after three weeks.

If there are differences, the variable being tested may have had an effect. If there is no difference between the control and the test groups, the variable being tested apparently

had no effect. From the data table in this experiment on page 647, it appears that fertilizer does have an effect on plant growth.

▶ What is Data?

In the experiment described on these pages, measurements have been taken so that at the end of the experiment, you had something concrete to interpret. You had numbers to work with. Not every experiment that you do will give you data in the form of numbers. Sometimes, data will be in the form of a description. At the end of a chemistry experiment, you might have noted that one solution turned yellow when treated with a particular chemical, and another remained clear, like water, when treated with the same chemical. Data therefore, is stated in different forms for different types of scientific experiments.

▶ Are All Experiments Alike?

Keep in mind as you perform experiments in science, that not every experiment makes use of all of the parts that have been described on these pages. For some, it may be difficult to design an experiment that will always have a control. Other experiments are complex enough that it may be hard to have only one dependent variable. Real scientists encounter many variations in the methods that they use when they perform experiments. The skills in this handbook are here for you to use and practice. In real situations, their uses will vary.

Representing and Applying Data

▶ Interpreting Scientific Illustrations

As you read this textbook, you will see many drawings, diagrams, and photographs. Illustrations help you to understand what you read. Some illustrations are included to help you understand an idea that you can't see easily by yourself. For instance, we can't see atoms, but we can look at a diagram of an atom and that helps us to understand some things about atoms. Seeing something often helps you remember more easily. The text may describe the surface of Jupiter in detail, but seeing a photograph of Jupiter may help you to remember that it has cloud bands. Illustrations also provide examples that clarify difficult concepts or give additional information about the topic you are studying. Maps, for example, help you to locate places that may be described in the text.

Captions and Labels   Most illustrations have captions. A caption is a comment that identifies or explains the illustration. Diagrams, such as the one of the feather, often have labels that identify parts of the item shown or the order of steps in a process.

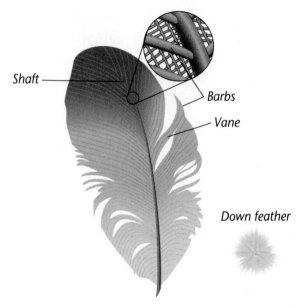

Shaft

Barbs

Vane

Down feather

Contour feather

Learning with Illustrations   An illustration of an organism shows that organism from a particular view or orientation. In order to understand the illustration, you may need to identify the front (anterior) end, tail (posterior) end, the underside (ventral), and the back (dorsal) side of the organism shown.

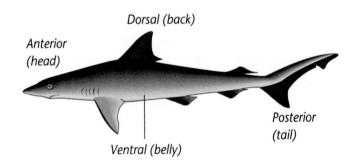

Dorsal (back)

Anterior (head)

Posterior (tail)

Ventral (belly)

You might also check for symmetry. Look at the illustration on the following page. A shark has bilateral symmetry. This means that drawing an imaginary line through the center of the animal from the anterior to posterior end forms two mirror images.

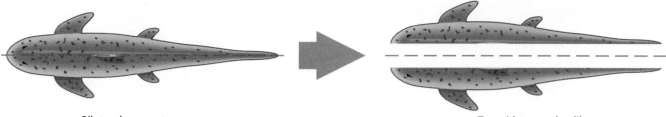

Bilateral symmetry

Two sides exactly alike

Radial symmetry is the arrangement of similar parts around a central point. An object or organism such as a hydra can be divided anywhere through the center into similar parts.

Some organisms and objects cannot be divided into two similar parts. If an organism or object cannot be divided, it is asymmetrical. Study the sponge. Regardless of how you try to divide a sponge, you cannot divide it into two parts that look alike.

Some illustrations enable you to see the inside of an organism or object. These illustrations are called sections.

Look at all illustrations carefully. Read captions and labels so that you understand exactly what the illustration is showing you.

▶ Making Models

Have you ever worked on a model car or plane or rocket? These models look, and sometimes work, just like the real thing, but they are usually much smaller than the real thing. In science, models are used to help simplify large processes or structures that may be difficult to understand. Your understanding of a structure or process is enhanced when you work with materials to make a model that shows the basic features of the structure or process.

In order to make a model, you first have to get a basic idea about the structure or process involved. You decide to make a model to show the differences in size of arteries, veins, and capillaries. First, read about these structures. All three are hollow tubes. Arteries are round and thick. Veins are flat and have thinner walls than arteries. Capillaries are very small.

Now, decide what you can use for your model. Common materials are often best and cheapest to work with when making models. Different

Butternut squash

Longitudinal section

Cross section

▶ Predicting

When you apply a hypothesis, or general explanation, to a specific situation, you predict something about that situation. First, you must identify which hypothesis fits the situation you are considering. People use prediction to make everyday decisions. Based on previous observations and experiences, you may form a hypothesis that if it is wintertime, then temperatures will be lower. From past experience in your area, temperatures are lowest in February. You may then use this hypothesis to predict specific temperatures and weather for the month of February in advance. Someone could use these predictions to plan to set aside more money for heating bills during that month.

▶ Sampling and Estimating

When working with large populations of organisms, scientists usually cannot observe or study every organism in the population. Instead, they use a sample or a portion of the population. Sampling is taking a small portion of organisms of a population for research. By making careful observations or manipulating variables with a portion of a group, information is discovered and conclusions are drawn that might then be applied to the whole population.

Scientific work also involves estimating. Estimating is making a judgment about the size of something or the number of something without actually measuring or counting every member of a population.

kinds and sizes of pasta might work for these models. Different sizes of rubber tubing might do just as well. Cut and glue the different noodles or tubing onto thick paper so the openings can be seen. Then label each. Now you have a simple, easy–to–understand model showing the differences in size of arteries, veins, and capillaries.

What other scientific ideas might a model help you to understand? A model of a molecule can be made from gumdrops (using different colors for the different elements present) and toothpicks (to show different chemical bonds). A working model of a volcano can be made from clay, a small amount of baking soda, vinegar, and a bottle cap. Other models can be devised on a computer.

Suppose you are trying to determine the effect of a specific nutrient on the growth of water lilies. It would be impossible to test the entire population of water lilies, so you would select part of the population for your experiment. Through careful experimentation and observation on a sample of the population, you could generalize the effect of the chemical on the entire population.

Here is a more familiar example. Have you ever tried to guess how many beans were in a sealed jar? If you did, you were estimating. What if you knew the jar of beans held one liter (1000 mL)? If you knew that 30 beans would fit in a 100–milliliter jar, how many beans would you estimate to be in the one–liter jar? If you said about 300 beans, your estimate would be close to the actual number of beans.

Scientists use a similar process to estimate populations of organisms from bacteria to buffalo. Scientists count the actual number of organisms in a small sample and then estimate the number of organisms in a larger area. For example, if a scientist wanted to count the number of microorganisms in a petri dish, a microscope could be used to

count the number of organisms in a one square millimeter sample. To determine the total population of the culture, the number of organisms in the square millimeter sample is multiplied by the total number of millimeters in the culture.

GLOSSARY

This glossary defines each key term that appears in **bold type** in the text. It also indicates the chapter number and page number where you will find the word used.

abyssal plain: flat plains on the ocean bottom; created by sediments from the continental shelves and slopes filling in the hills and valleys on the ocean floor. (Chap. 12, p. 378)

action force: the force you exert when you push on something; every action force has an equal and opposite reaction force that occurs at exactly the same time—for example, as you walk on the ground (action force), the ground pushes back at you (reaction force). (Chap. 1, p. 37)

alveoli: thin-walled balloon-like sacs within your lungs; each alveolus is surrounded by capillaries; oxygen diffuses from the alveoli into the capillaries and then into your red blood cells; at the same time, carbon dioxide diffuses from the capillaries into the alveoli and is exhaled from the lungs. (Chap. 16, p. 489)

artery: thick, muscular vessel that transports blood away from the heart; the right ventricle pumps oxygen-poor blood toward the lungs through the arteries, and the left ventricle pumps oxygen-rich blood toward the body cells through the arteries. (Chap. 3, p. 86)

asthma: lung disorder in which the bronchial tubes become constricted quickly; results in reduced flow of air to the lungs, shortness of breath, wheezing, and coughing; often an allergic or stress reaction. (Chap. 16, p. 502)

atherosclerosis: condition that results when arteries supplying oxygen and nutrients to the heart become clogged with fatty deposits and calcium buildup; if the clogging continues, the person may have a heart attack. (Chap. 3, p. 102)

atmosphere: layer of gases hundreds of kilometers thick that surrounds Earth; divided into the troposphere, stratosphere, mesophere, and thermosphere; made up of a mixture of solids, liquids, and gases such as oxygen, nitrogen, methane, and carbon dioxide. (Chap. 15, p. 456)

atom: smallest particle of an element; different atoms are needed to "build" various substances—for example, you'd need to chemically combine two atoms of the element oxygen and one atom of the element hydrogen to make one molecule of the compound water. (Chap. 14, p. 441)

atomic theory of matter: theory that all matter consists of atoms, all atoms of an element are identical, different elements have different atoms, and atoms maintain their properties in chemical reactions. (Chap. 14, p. 439)

balanced forces: forces whose actions cancel each other; for example, when equal upward and downward forces are exerted on the same object, the object does not accelerate. (Chap. 1, p. 35)

blood pressure: pressure created by the force of blood flowing against the inner walls of arteries, veins, and capillaries; in a healthy young person, normal systolic blood pressure is about 110-120 mm Hg and normal diastolic blood pressure is about 70-80 mm Hg. (Chap. 3, p. 95)

bone marrow: gel-like substance filling spaces within the bones; red marrow makes new blood cells and is found in spongy bone; yellow marrow is found in the long parts of bones and contains fat and some blood-cell producing components. (Chap. 7, p. 215)

Boyle's law: explains the relationship between pressure and the volume of a gas; states that the volume of a certain amount of gas is inversely proportional to the pressure, if the temperature remains constant. (Chap. 14, p. 432)

brain stem: part of the brain that controls involuntary body activities such as digestion, breathing, and the beating of your heart; all nerve impulses sent to and from the brain travel through the brain stem. (Chap. 8, p. 250)

buoyant force: upward force exerted by water equal to the weight of water the object is displacing. (Chap. 1, p. 44)

capillary: microscopic, thin-walled vessel through which exchanges between blood and tissues take place; form an extensive network connecting your arteries to your veins. (Chap. 3, p. 86)

cardiac muscle: muscle found only in the heart; pumps blood through the heart and to the cells of the body by rhythmically relaxing and contracting (Chap. 7, p. 226)

cartilage: rubbery material which first forms the skeletal system; later replaced by bone; the end of your nose and external parts of your ears are made of flexible cartilage; cartilage also helps reduce bone-on-bone friction at joints. (Chap. 7, p. 220)

catalyst: substance that speeds up a chemical reaction; examples include the body's enzyme catalysts and catalytic converters that convert harmful automotive gases to harmless carbon dioxide and water. (Chap. 18, p. 572)

cell: basic unit of structure and function in all living things; your body contains more than 10 trillion cells; each different type of cell has a specific job to do. (Chap. 17, p. 517)

cell membrane: flexible, double-layered, outer covering of most cells; surrounds the cell's cytoplasm; oxygen and food enter and water and other products leave the cell through the cell membrane. (Chap. 17, p. 528)

cell wall: adaptation of plants, fungi, and bacteria; the cell wall is the outermost rim of the cell, outside the cell membrane; provides support and protection for the cell. (Chap. 17, p. 532)

cellular respiration: process in which your body gets energy to operate; oxygen from the respiratory system combines with nutrients stored in your cells and releases energy, carbon dioxide, and water. (Chap. 16, p. 497)

cerebellum: part of the brain that coordinates speed and timing of muscle action and maintains balance; sends messages to your cerebrum, which processes the messages, then sends out impulses along motor nerves to activate the muscles needed to carry out specific actions. (Chap. 8, p. 246)

cerebrum: largest part of the brain; carries out complex functions such as memory, speech, and thought; processes messages from your cerebellum and directs muscles to carry out movements; receives nerve impulses and changes them into such sensations as sound and taste and smell. (Chap. 8, p. 245)

Charles' law: explains the relationship between temperature and the volume of a gas; states that gases increase or decrease their volume as the temperature rises and falls, provided pressure and amount of gas are held constant. (Chap. 14, p. 435)

chemical reaction: process in which substances are changed into other substances; involves changes in energy, which may be absorbed or released; for example, the chemical reactions of digestion release some of the chemical energy in food, which can be used for work by the body. (Chap. 18, p. 553)

chloroplasts: structures in the cytoplasm of green plant cells; contain chlorophyll, a green pigment that lets plants produce their own food by converting light energy into chemical energy in a sugar called glucose. (Chap. 17, p. 533)

chromosomes: threadlike structures found in the nucleus of plant and animal cells; made up of proteins and DNA, the molecules that control the cell's activities, including its reproduction; chromosomes can be seen only when a cell is dividing. (Chap. 17, p. 531)

cilia: tiny hairlike structures lining your nasal passages, trachea, and lungs; cilia beat in an upward direction, causing inhaled particles caught in mucus to move to the throat, where they are swallowed and broken down by stomach acids. (Chap. 16, p. 501)

cleavage: ability of a mineral to break along a smooth flat surface as a result of the orderly arrangement of the atoms making up its crystals; mica and barite have perfect cleavage. (Chap. 10, p. 311)

coinage metals: copper, silver, and gold, which have been used because they are malleable and easily stamped into coins; however, because the price of these metals has increased, gold and silver are no longer used in U.S. coins, and some U.S. pennies now contain zinc. (Chap. 9, p. 280)

compact bone: hard, thick, outer bone layer in which compounds of calcium and phosphorus are concentrated; protects internal organs, supplies support and a place for muscle attachment; contains blood vessels, bone cells, nerves, elastic fibers, and some spaces filled with bone marrow. (Chap. 7, p. 215)

compound machine: machines, such as fishing rods and bicycles, that are a combination of simple machines; compound machines make it possible to accomplish tasks that simple machines alone can't do. (Chap. 5, p. 167)

conduction: transfer of heat by two objects in physical contact; because wood is a poorer conductor of heat than metal, the handles of many pots and pans are made of wood. (Chap. 6, p. 191)

continental shelf: first part of the ocean floor after you leave the shore; formed of flat, gently slanted sections that extend into the ocean, then dip steeply down, forming a continental slope. (Chap. 12, p. 378)

convection: heat carried by a moving fluid; convection is a major cause of winds; many ocean currents result from convection. (Chap. 6, p. 192)

cystic fibrosis: lung disease that is passed genetically from parents to children; thick mucus blocks air passages of the respiratory system, causing lung damage, wheezing, and frequent lung infections. (Chap. 16, p. 502)

cytoplasm: gel-like, constantly moving material found inside the cell membrane of both plants and animals; most of the cell's life processes take place in the cytoplasm. (Chap. 17, p. 529)

diaphragm: thin sheet of muscle under your lungs; when you inhale, your diaphragm contracts, helping to increase the size of your chest cavity; when you exhale, your diaphragm relaxes, helping to reduce the size of your chest cavity. (Chap. 16, p. 492)

diffusion: process by which molecules move from an area of higher concentration to an area of lower concentration until equilibrium is reached; diffusion occurs without the use of energy by the cell. (Chap. 19, p. 587)

ductile: ability of an element to be pulled into a wire without breaking; most malleable metals are also ductile; copper, which is very ductile, is also an excellent conductor of electrical signals and is used to make electrical wire. (Chap. 9, p. 272)

effort force: the force applied to a machine; for example, when you are in a rowboat and use an oar, you are exerting an effort force on the oar. (Chap. 5, p. 150)

emphysema: lung disease in which the air passageways or alveoli are no longer able to expand or contract; the lungs become scarred and less oxygen goes into the bloodstream, so the heart must work harder, often resulting in heart problems as well. (Chap. 16, p. 503)

endothermic reaction: chemical reaction is which energy is absorbed as the reaction continues; takes place, for example, during the refining of aluminum from bauxite ore as electrical energy is absorbed and aluminum oxide separates into oxygen and aluminum. (Chap. 18, p. 566)

epicenter: point on Earth's surface directly above the focus; when primary and secondary seismic waves reach the epicenter, they generate surface waves that travel outward and cause great damage. (Chap. 2, p. 62)

exothermic reaction: chemical reaction in which energy is released; takes place, for example, during the explosion of fireworks, during which the chemical potential energy in the fireworks is released and changed into sound, light, and thermal energy. (Chap. 18, p. 567)

extrusive: igneous rock formed by lava on Earth's surface; extrusive igneous rock cools in air and moisture, forming minerals quickly that are much smaller than those in intrusive rock; rhyolite and basalt are examples. (Chap. 11, p. 333)

fault: fracture within Earth along which rock movement occurs; faults are caused by compression forces, which produce reverse faults, tension forces, which produce normal faults, or shearing forces, which produce slip-strike faults; earthquakes occur as a result of all three types of faults. (Chap. 2, p. 56)

fermentation: energy-releasing process that breaks down glucose without the use of oxygen; muscle cells release energy by fermentation when oxygen levels are low; bakers use fermentation by yeast to make bread rise. (Chap. 19, p. 602)

focus: point deep beneath Earth's surface where the sudden movement along a fault releases the energy that causes an earthquake. (Chap. 2, p. 61)

foliated: texture of metamorphic rocks whose mineral grains have been flattened and lined up in parallel bands; foliated rocks, such as slate, are easily separated along their foliation layers. (Chap. 11, p. 342)

force: a push or pull; more force is needed to move a large object than a small object; force equals mass times acceleration ($F = ma$); two types of forces are friction and gravity. (Chap. 1, p. 28)

fossil fuel: coal, natural gas, and oil formed millions of years ago from the remains of once-living organisms; contains chemical potential energy and when burned produces thermal energy; fossil fuels are nonrenewable natural resources. (Chap. 13, p. 397)

fracture: ability of a mineral to split into pieces with rough, jagged, or curved surfaces; quartz is a mineral with fracture. (Chap. 10, p. 311)

GLOSSARY

gem: valuable, rare mineral; examples include diamonds, sapphires, rubies, and emeralds; skilled stonecutters cut and grind facets into gemstones to bring out their beauty. (Chap. 10, p. 306)

generator: any machine that can convert kinetic energy to electrical energy; for example, a simple generator spins a coil of wire through a magnetic field, which causes the electrons in the wire to move, producing electricity. (Chap. 13, p. 394)

gills: main respiratory structures of most fish; when water passes over the gill filaments, oxygen diffuses from the water into the capillaries; at the same time, carbon dioxide moves from the capillaries into the water. (Chap. 16, p. 486)

hardness: property that can help identify a mineral; a measure of how easily a specific mineral can be scratched; the Mohs scale lists 10 minerals in order of hardness from 1 to 10. (Chap. 10, p. 310)

heat: energy in transit; heat is energy transferred from an object of higher temperature to an object of lower temperature by conduction, convection, or radiation. (Chap. 6, p. 190)

heat engine: inefficient means of doing work because most of the heat produced is transferred, wasting thermal energy; a car engine is an example of a heat engine. (Chap. 6, p. 201)

hemoglobin: oxygen-binding, iron-containing substance found in red blood cells; because of hemoglobin, red blood cells can transport oxygen from the lungs throughout your body and carry some carbon dioxide back to the alveoli. (Chap. 16, p. 494)

hormone: chemical messenger made by the endocrine glands, which are ductless and empty directly into the bloodstream; hormones are produced in one part of your body and cause change in another part of your body. (Chap. 8, p. 256)

hydroelectric: power plant that uses water power to generate electricity; hydroelectric energy is a clean, plentiful, renewable alternative to fossil fuels but ecosystems may be destroyed in power plant construction. (Chap. 13, p. 408)

hypertension (high blood pressure): disorder of the circulatory system that can result in organ damage; a known cause is atherosclerosis; hypertension places extra stress on the heart, which has to beat faster to get oxygen to tissues. (Chap. 3, p. 104)

igneous rock: forms when lava or magma cools and crystals grow together, creating solid igneous rock; two types of igneous rock are extrusive and intrusive. (Chap. 11, p. 332)

inclined plane: ramp or slope that reduces the force needed to lift an object; a more gradual inclined plane increases the distance but reduces the effort force needed to move an object; inclined planes are in everyday use—for example, ramps make buildings accessible to people in wheelchairs. (Chap. 5, p. 154)

inertia: tendency of an object to resist changes in motion; objects with large mass have great inertia and resist acceleration; as an object's inertia increases, the force needed to accelerate that object also increases. (Chap. 1, p. 23)

inhibitor: substance that slows down a chemical reaction; examples include most preservatives added to food, which slow the spoilage rate, and some antibiotics, which slow enzymatic body reactions that help bacteria grow. (Chap. 18, p. 574)

intrusive: igneous rock formed slowly from magma deep beneath Earth's crust; generally contains large, visible minerals; examples are granite and gabbro. (Chap. 11, p. 332)

joints: places where two or more bones of the skeleton join; movable joints allow actions such as bending your legs; immovable joints do not allow motion and form the bones of the skull; examples of movable joints are gliding joints and hinge joints. (Chap. 7, p. 222)

kinetic energy: the energy of motion; for example, as a roller coaster car rushes downhill, its kinetic energy increases; the amount of kinetic energy possessed by an object is never greater than the amount of work done on that object. (Chap. 4, p. 122)

law of conservation of energy: energy can change from one form to another, but it cannot be created or destroyed. (Chap. 4, p. 138)

lever: a bar that turns or pivots on a fulcrum; a lever is a simple machine that can exert a large resistance force over a short distance but only a small force over a long distance. (Chap. 5, p. 151)

ligaments: strong bands of tissue that hold bones together; injury to ligaments can result in sprains, often at the knees, ankles, and fingers. (Chap. 7, p. 224)

longshore current: flow of ocean water that approaches parallel to the shoreline; has enough mechanical energy to erode the shoreline and carry away tons of loose sediments. (Chap. 12, p. 364)

lung: the main organ of your respiratory system; exchange of oxygen and carbon dioxide takes place in your lungs in structures called alveoli; air moves in and out of the lungs through the bronchial tubes, which branch from the lower end of the trachea. (Chap. 16, p. 489)

lung cancer: cancer that causes the most deaths among men and women in the United States; inhaling tar from cigarette smoke is the largest contributing factor to lung cancer; cancer cells grow faster than normal cells and soon normal cells weaken and are no longer able to keep lung tissue healthy. (Chap. 16, p. 504)

malleable: ability of an element to be hammered or pressed into a thin sheet without breaking; most metals are malleable; gold, silver, and platinum are often used in making jewelry because they are so malleable. (Chap. 9, p. 272)

mechanical advantage (MA): the MA of a machine can be found by dividing the resistance force by the effort force; the larger the MA, the more helpful the machine. (Chap. 5, p. 159)

metalloids: elements with properties of both metals and nonmetals; boron and silicon are the two most common metalloids; boron and its compounds are used to make cleaning products and

rocket fuel; silicon is a semiconductor and is important in the computer and electronics industry. (Chap. 9, p. 290)

metals: groups of elements often having several properties in common, such as luster, hardness, ductility, malleability, and conductivity; examples are nickel, iron, and gold; examples of metals found in the body are calcium and iron. (Chap. 9, p. 272)

metamorphic rock: forms when heat or pressure or both are applied to any kind of rock; for example, the metamorphic rock slate forms when heat and pressure compact the minerals in the sedimentary rock shale. (Chap. 11, p. 340)

mid-ocean ridges: chains of underwater mountains alongside rift zones; often contain active volcanoes. (Chap. 12, p. 383)

mineral: inorganic, naturally occurring, crystalline structure with a unique chemical composition; a mineral can be an element or compound; examples are graphite, diamonds, and halite. (Chap. 10, p. 303)

mitochondria: power plants in the cell's cytoplasm in which energy is released for organisms to do their work; food molecules are broken down in the mitochondria and converted to forms the cell can use. (Chap. 17, p. 531)

mitosis: reproductive process of cells in which the cell nucleus divides so each new cell will have the same type and number of chromosomes as the parent cell; the original cell becomes two identical cells through mitosis. (Chap. 17, p. 538)

neuron: basic unit of the nervous system made up of a cell body, branching dendrites that carry electrical impulses to the cell body, and an axon that carries these messages away from the cell body; neurons are grouped in bundles called nerves. (Chap. 8, p. 242)

newton: standard unit of force, which is abbreviated N; 1 newton of force equals the amount of force needed to accelerate a 1-kg mass at 1 m/s^2. (Chap. 1, p. 35)

nonfoliated: texture of metamorphic rocks whose mineral grains have been changed, rearranged, or combined (but did not form parallel bands); such as marble (Chap. 11, p. 342)

nonmetals: most common nonmetals are gases, such as oxygen and nitrogen: solid nonmetals, such as sulfur, are dull, brittle, and poor conductors of heat and electricity; your body is composed mostly of non-metallic compounds, as is most living material. (Chap. 9, p. 282)

nonrenewable resource: any natural resource that people use up more quickly than it can be replaced by natural processes, or may never be replaced, or can be replaced only over a very long period of time; fossil fuels are nonrenewable resources. (Chap. 13, p. 403)

nucleus: membrane-enclosed command center in the cytoplasm of plant and animal cells; has chromosomes that contain complex chemical information that directs all the cell's activities, including its reproduction. (Chap. 17, p. 530)

organ: body structure made up of various types of tissue that all work together to perform a specific function; for example, your heart is an organ. (Chap. 19, p. 605)

organ systems: groups of organs that work together to perform a specific function; for example, your circulatory system is an organ system. (Chap. 19, p. 605)

organism: a living thing; organisms may be one-celled or many-celled. (Chap. 19, p. 605)

osmosis: diffusion of water through a semi-permeable cell membrane from an area of higher concentration to an area of lower concentration until equilibrium is reached; osmosis occurs without the use of energy by the cell. (Chap. 19, p. 589)

ozone: gas layer in the stratosphere that absorbs some of the harmful rays of the sun, helping to protect Earth from harmful radiation that can cause sunburn and skin cancer. (Chap. 15, p. 462)

pollution: any substance with the potential to damage the environment; pollution can be caused by such factors as burning of fossil fuels, oil spills, and industrial and medical wastes. (Chap. 12, p. 371)

potential energy: the stored energy of position; gravitational potential energy is stored when work lifts an object against the force of gravity; elastic potential energy is stored when work stretches or twists objects such as rubber bands or diving boards. (Chap. 4, p. 123)

power: power is the work done divided by the time it took to do it; the formula can be written as power = work/time. (Chap. 5, p. 168)

pressure: the force or weight acting on each unit of area; can be calculated by dividing the weight of an object by the surface area the object occupies; in contrast, water exerts pressure in all directions, and calculating water pressure depends on the depth of the water. (Chap. 1, p. 40)

prevailing westerlies: global wind system between 30° and 60° latitude; these winds are deflected from their north or south path by Earth's rotation; northern prevailing westerlies are responsible for much of the movement of weather in the United States and Canada. (Chap. 15, p. 474)

products: the new substances formed by any chemical reaction; citric acid + ammonium hydroxide → ammonium citrate + water is a word equation in which the products are ammonium citrate and water. (Chap. 18, p. 557)

pulley: a simple machine composed of a wheel with a rope or chain passing over it; a single fixed pulley changes the direction of the force applied to an object, but not the amount of the force; a single movable pulley increases the effect of the effort force and lessens the amount of effort you have to exert to get the job done, but does not change the direction of the force. (Chap. 5, p. 153)

pulse: rhythmic expansion and contraction of your arteries each time your heart beats; you can feel your pulse in your carotid artery and measure your heart rate. (Chap. 3, p. 91)

radiation: heat traveling across a space; does not need intermediate matter to transfer thermal energy; examples are heat from the sun and candles. (Chap. 6, p. 197)

reactants: substances you start with in any chemical reaction; citric acid + ammonium hydroxide → ammonium citrate + water is a word equation in which the reactants are citric acid and ammonium hydroxide. (Chap. 18, p. 557)

reaction force: the force that pushes back on you when you push on something; action-reaction forces occur in pairs, exert equal and opposite forces, and happen at exactly the same moment—for example, when you lean lightly against a parked car (action force), the car pushes lightly back at you (reaction force). (Chap. 1, p. 37)

reflex: automatic body response to an environmental stimuli that may harm you; your nervous system protects you by the whole reflex sequence—for example, instantly pulling your hand away from a pot of boiling water before you can even think about how hot it is. (Chap. 8, p. 254)

renewable resources: any natural resource that can be replaced by natural processes in less than a century; examples are trees and crops. (Chap. 13, p. 402)

resistance force: the force applied by a machine; for example, when you are in a rowboat and use an oar, you are exerting an effort force on the oar, which exerts a resistance force on the water and pushes the boat through the water. (Chap. 5, p. 150)

respiration: series of chemical reactions by which energy is released from glucose in the presence of oxygen; in your body, heat is a waste product of the thousands of respirations taking place in the mitochondria of your cells. (Chap. 19, p. 595)

rift zone: ocean region where the seafloor is spreading; magma oozes up from Earth's interior in rift zones; rift zones may become a future site for mining precious metals. (Chap. 12, p. 379)

rock: a mixture of one or more minerals or a mixture of mineraloids, glass, or organic particles. (Chap. 11, p. 331)

rock cycle: process by which the materials of Earth change to form different kinds of rocks; all rocks are in a constant state of change. (Chap. 11, p. 350)

screw: this simple machine is an inclined plane wound around a post; the ridges spiraling around a screw are called threads; these threads change the screwdriver's turning force into a downward force that helps lift the wood up around the screw. (Chap. 5, p. 156)

sedimentary rock: formed when any type of rock and plant and animal remains are weathered into sediments and then recombined to form rock by compaction, cementation, or precipitating out of solution; examples are limestone and sandstone. (Chap. 11, p. 343)

seismic waves: waves generated by earthquakes; primary and secondary seismic waves originate at the earthquake's focus, usually travel through Earth's

interior, and can be measured by a seismograph; surface seismic waves travel from the epicenter of the earthquake and cause the greatest damage. (Chap. 2, p. 61)

skeletal muscles: muscles that move bones; skeletal muscles work in pairs—when one skeletal muscle contracts, its partner relaxes—the biceps and triceps are examples; you can control the movement of these muscles. (Chap. 7, p. 226)

smog: type of air pollution caused by the burning of fossil fuels; harms people, making them more susceptible to lung disease and heart trouble; harms plants, preventing them from absorbing the carbon dioxide they need. (Chap. 15, p. 461)

smooth muscle: moving food through your digestive system is an example of work done by smooth muscles; smooth muscle is found in many places inside your body, but you do not control its actions. (Chap. 7, p. 226)

solar cell: converts sunlight into electricity; solar energy is clean, efficient, and renewable; however, solar energy is available only when there is sunlight, and solar cells are expensive to manufacture. (Chap. 13, p. 413)

spinal cord: a long cord that runs the length of the backbone and acts as a connection between the brain and nerves of the body; the spinal cord is protected by vertebrae and cartilage discs; your brain and spinal cord make up the central nervous system. (Chap. 8, p. 250)

spongy bone: inner bone layer containing many openings filled with bone marrow and tiny hard bone spikes made of minerals; found toward the ends of many compact bones; helps keep the skeleton lightweight and functions as shock absorber. (Chap. 7, p. 215)

streak: color of a mineral obtained when it is broken up and powdered or when a piece of the mineral is rubbed across a streak plate; a mineral's color can provide clues to its identity. (Chap. 10, p. 308)

synapse: a tiny space between neurons; electrical impulses from the axon of a neuron cause transmitting chemicals to cross the synapse and stimulate electrical impulses in the next neuron. (Chap. 8, p. 243)

target tissue: the specific tissue affected by the action of a hormone; for example, puberty occurs because the pituitary gland, an endocrine gland, releases

GLOSSARY

hormones that stimulate the sex organs in both males and females to produce sex hormones. (Chap. 8, p. 257)

tendons: elastic, strong tissue bands that attach skeletal muscles to bones at movable joints. (Chap. 7, p. 226)

thermal equilibrium: reached when two objects are in physical contact and the temperature of one is the same as the temperature of the other; if two objects in physical contact have different temperatures, transfer of thermal energy will continue until they are in thermal equilibrium. (Chap. 6, p. 186)

tissue: group of similar types of cells that work together to perform the same function. (Chap. 19, p. 605)

trachea: an air-conducting tube; a grasshopper has thousands of tracheal tubes that move air directly into all the cells of its body; in humans, the trachea is the windpipe, a sturdy tube supported by rings of cartilage. (Chap. 16, p. 485)

trade winds: global wind system; created by air sinking and returning to the equator; airplane pilots often ride the warm, steady trade winds to conserve fuel and increase speed. (Chap. 15, p. 473)

troposphere: atmospheric layer closest to the ground; we live in the troposphere; contains 75 percent of all atmospheric gases in addition to dust, ice, and water; clouds form and weather occurs in this layer. (Chap. 15, p. 462)

veins: elastic vessels that transport blood back to the heart; carbon dioxide-rich blood is returned to the right atrium by veins; oxygen-rich blood is returned to the left atrium by veins; veins contain one-way valves to prevent blood from flowing backward. (Chap. 3, p. 86)

vents: openings in Earth's surface through which volcanic material erupts; different types of volcanoes result from such factors as the number of vents and the type and temperature of the lava. (Chap. 2, p. 67)

watt (W): unit of power found by dividing the work done, in joules (J), by the number of seconds it took to do the work. (Chap. 5, p. 169)

wedge: inclined plane with a sharp, thin edge that cuts through a variety of materials; examples of this simple machine are knives, axes, and chisels. (Chap. 5, p. 157)

weight: the force with which an object is pulled by Earth's gravitational force; calculated by multiplying acceleration due to gravity times the object's mass. (Chap. 1, p. 36)

wheel and axle: a simple machine composed of a small wheel attached to the middle of a bigger wheel; a wheel and axle always rotate together; less effort force is needed to turn a large wheel than to turn a small wheel. (Chap. 5, p. 152)

work: the transfer of energy through both force and motion, with the force in the direction of the motion; work = force × distance ($W = F \times d$); unit for work can also be expressed as the newton • meter (N • m), which is also called a joule (J); 1 J is the work done when the force of 1 N acts through the distance of 1 m. (Chap. 4, p. 119)

This glossary defines each key term that appears in **bold type** in the text. It also indicates the chapter number and page number where you will find the word used.

abyssal plain/planicie abismal: superficie plana en las profundidades del océano la cual ha sido formada por los sedimentos acarreados por las corrientes marinas (Cap. 12, pág. 378)

action force/fuerza de acción: fuerza que resulta cuando empujas o halas algo (Cap. 1, pág. 37)

alveoli/alvéolos: manojos de pequeños saquitos con paredes delgadas localizados en las extremidades más angostas de los bronquiolos (Cap. 16, pág. 489)

arteries/arterias: vasos sanguíneos que llevan la sangre desde el corazón a las demás partes del cuerpo (Cap. 3, pág. 86)

asthma/asma: trastorno pulmonar caracterizado por falta de aliento, sibilancias o tos (Cap. 16, pág. 502)

atherosclerosis/aterosclerosis: condición en la cual se obstruyen las arterias coronarias debido a la acumulación de depósitos grasos y de calcio (Cap. 3, pág. 102)

atmosphere/atmósfera: capa de gases con un espesor de cientos de kilómetros que rodea la Tierra (Cap. 15, pág. 456)

atom/átomo: la partícula más pequeña de un elemento (Cap. 14, pág. 441)

atomic theory of matter/la teoría atómica de la materia: teoría que asevera que la materia está compuesta de pequeñas partículas llamadas átomos (Cap. 14, pág. 439)

balanced forces/fuerzas equilibradas: fuerzas que se anulan entre sí al actuar sobre un objeto (Cap. 1, pág. 35)

blood pressure/presión sanguínea: presión ejercida por la sangre contra las paredes internas de los vasos sanguíneos (Cap. 3, pág. 95)

bone marrow/médula ósea: sustancia gelatinosa que se halla dentro de los huesos en donde se forman las nuevas células sanguíneas (Cap. 7, pág. 215)

Boyle's law/ley de Boyle: dice que el volumen de cierta cantidad de gas es inversamente proporcional a la presión, si la temperatura permanece constante (Cap. 14, pág. 432)

brainstem/bulbo raquídeo: la parte del encéfalo que lo conecta a la médula espinal (Cap. 8, pág. 250)

buoyant force/fuerza boyante: fuerza ascendente que los fluidos ejercen sobre todos los objetos (Cap. 1, pág. 44)

capillaries/capilares: los vasos sanguíneos más finos que, en forma de red, conectan las arterias con las venas (Cap. 3, pág. 86)

cardiac muscle/músculo cardíaco: tipo de músculo que forma las paredes del corazón, el cual bombea la sangre a través del mismo y del resto del cuerpo (Cap. 7, pág. 226)

cartilage/cartílago: materia blanda y elástica, menos dura que el hueso (Cap. 7, pág. 220)

catalyst/catalizador: sustancia que acelera una reacción química, sin ser alterada permanentemente ella misma (Cap. 18, pág. 572)

cell/célula: la unidad básica de la vida en todos los organismos vivos (Cap. 17, pág. 517)

cell membrane/membrana celular: estructura flexible que forma el límite externo de la célula (Cap. 17, pág. 528)

cell wall/pared celular: estructura rígida ubicada fuera de la membrana celular, la cual da apoyo y protege la célula (Cap. 17, pág. 532)

cellular respiration/respiración celular: proceso en el cual el oxígeno se combina con los nutrimientos almacenados en las células para liberar energía, dióxido de carbono y agua (Cap. 16, pág. 497)

cerebellum/cerebelo: parte del encéfalo que coordina las acciones de todos tus músculos y mantiene el equilibrio (Cap. 8, pág. 246)

cerebrum/cerebro: la parte más grande del encéfalo, la cual interpreta los impulsos que le llegan de los nervios desde las diferentes partes del cuerpo (Cap. 8, pág. 245)

Charles' law/ley de Charles: dice que el volumen de los gases aumenta o disminuye a medida que la temperatura sube y baja, siempre y cuando se mantengan constantes la presión y la cantidad de gas (Cap. 14, pág. 435)

SPANISH GLOSSARY

chemical reaction/reacción química: proceso bien definido que resulta en la formación de nuevas sustancias que tienen propiedades diferentes de las de las sustancias originales (Cap. 18, pág. 553)

chloroplast/cloroplasto: pequeña estructura que contiene clorofila, un pigmento verde que permite que las plantas fabriquen su propio alimento (Cap. 17, pág. 533)

chromosome/cromosoma: estructura filamentosa compuesta de proteínas y DNA; molécula que controla las actividades celulares (Cap. 17, pág. 531)

cilia/cilios: estructuras filamentosas pequeñísimas que cubren el revestimiento húmedo de la tráquea y de los pulmones (Cap. 16, pág. 501)

cleavage/crucero: la propiedad de ciertos minerales de romperse a lo largo de superficies lisas y planas (Cap. 10, pág. 311)

coinage metals/metales de acuñación: metales que se usan en la fabricación de monedas (Cap. 9, pág. 280)

compact bone/hueso compacto: capa externa y gruesa que contiene grandes concentraciones de compuestos de calcio y fósforo, además de materias vivas y fibras elásticas (Cap. 7, pág. 215)

compound machine/máquina compuesta: es una combinación de máquinas simples, la cual permite realizar tareas que una máquina simple sola no puede realizar (Cap. 5, pág. 167)

conduction/conducción: proceso por el cual el calor se mueve a través de un material o de un material a otro (Cap. 6, pág. 191)

continental shelf/plataforma continental: primera área del océano que uno se encuentra al moverse mar adentro (Cap. 12, pág. 378)

convection/convección: transferencia de energía por el movimiento de un medio que transporta calor (Cap. 6, pág. 192)

cystic fibrosis/fibrosis cística: trastorno que afecta el sistema respiratorio al obstruir las vías respiratorias (Cap. 16, pág. 502)

cytoplasm/citoplasma: material gelatinoso que se encuentra en el interior de la membrana celular (Cap. 17, pág. 529)

diaphragm/diafragma: lámina muscular fina ubicada debajo de los pulmones (Cap. 16, pág. 492)

diffusion/difusión: proceso mediante el cual el movimiento constante de moléculas ocasiona el movimiento desde una región de mayor concentración hasta otra de menor concentración (Cap. 19, pág. 587)

ductile/dúctil: propiedad que poseen muchos metales para poder estirarse en forma de alambre sin romperse (Cap. 9, pág. 272)

effort force/fuerza de esfuerzo: fuerza que uno ejerce sobre una máquina (Cap. 5, pág. 150)

emphysema/enfisema: enfermedad que ocurre cuando las vías respiratorias o los alvéolos pierden la capacidad de expandirse y de contraerse (Cap. 16, pág. 503)

endothermic reaction/reacción endotérmica: reacción química en la cual se absorbe energía a medida que continúa la reacción (Cap. 18, pág. 566)

epicenter/epicentro: punto en la superficie terrestre que se encuentra directamente sobre el foco en un terremoto (Cap. 2, pág. 62)

exothermic reaction/reacción exotérmica: reacción química en la cual se libera energía (Cap. 18, pág. 567)

extrusive/extrusiva: roca ígnea que se forma de la lava que se enfría sobre la superficie terrestre (Cap. 11, pág. 333)

F

fault/falla: hendidura dentro de la Tierra donde ocurre un desplazamiento de rocas (Cap. 2, pág. 56)

fermentation/fermentación: proceso que libera energía al descomponer la glucosa, en ausencia del oxígeno (Cap. 19, pág. 602)

focus/foco: punto en el interior de la Tierra donde se originan las ondas sísmicas (Cap. 2, pág. 61)

foliated/foliada: roca metamórfica que posee una textura de granos aplanados y alineados en bandas paralelas (Cap. 11, pág. 342)

force/fuerza: un empujón o un halón (Cap. 1, pág. 28)

fossil fuel/combustible fósil: restos de plantas o animales antiguos que podemos quemar hoy en día para producir energía térmica (Cap. 13, pág. 397)

fracture/fractura: se dice que un mineral presenta una fractura cuando al romperse forma superficies curvas, ásperas o dentadas (Cap. 10, pág. 311)

SPANISH GLOSSARY

gem/gema: mineral valioso que es raro o muy difícil de obtener (Cap. 10, pág. 306)

generator/generador: cualquier máquina que convierte la energía cinética en energía eléctrica (Cap. 13, pág. 394)

gills/agallas: órganos respiratorios de algunos animales acuáticos a través de los cuales se extrae el oxígeno del agua (Cap. 16, pág. 486)

hardness/dureza: medida que se usa para determinar la facilidad o dificultad con que se puede rayar un mineral (Cap. 10, pág. 310)

heat/calor: energía que se transfiere de un objeto con mayor temperatura a uno de menor temperatura (Cap. 6, pág. 190)

heat engine/motor térmico: motor que usa combustible para producir energía térmica para realizar trabajo (Cap. 6, pág. 201)

hemoglobin/hemoglobina: sustancia de los glóbulos rojos sanguíneos que contiene hierro, el cual se enlaza fácilmente con el oxígeno (Cap. 16, pág. 494)

hormone/hormona: sustancia química fabricada por una glándula sin conductos en una parte del cuerpo, la cual produce cambios en otra parte del cuerpo. (Cap. 8, pág. 256)

hydroelectric/hidroeléctrico: que usa agua para generar electricidad (Cap. 13, pág. 408)

hypertension/hipertensión: trastorno del sistema circulatorio en el cual la presión sanguínea es más alta de lo normal. También llamada presión alta (Cap. 3, pág. 104)

igneous rock/roca ígnea: roca que se forma al enfriarse un material derretido (Cap. 11, pág. 332)

inclined plane/plano inclinado: una rampa o un plano inclinado que reduce la fuerza que necesitas ejercer para levantar un objeto (Cap. 5, pág. 154)

inertia/inercia: tendencia a resistir cambios en el movimiento (Cap. 1, pág. 23)

inhibitor/inhibidor: cualquier sustancia que aminora una reacción química (Cap. 18, pág. 574)

intrusive/intrusiva: roca ígnea que se forma del magma que se enfría debajo de la superficie terrestre (Cap. 11, pág. 332)

joint/articulación: área en el esqueleto donde dos o más huesos se unen (Cap. 7, pág. 222)

kinetic energy/energía cinética: energía de movimiento (Cap. 4, pág. 122)

law of conservation of energy/ley de conservación de la energía: ley que dice que la energía no se puede crear ni destruir (Cap. 4, pág. 138)

lever/palanca: una barra que da vueltas o gira sobre un punto llamado fulcro (Cap. 5, pág. 151)

ligament/ligamento: Banda fuerte de tejido que mantiene unidos a los huesos (Cap. 7, pág. 224)

longshore current/corriente de costa: flujo de agua del océano que corre cerca de la costa y paralelo a ella (Cap. 12, pág. 364)

lung cancer/cáncer del pulmón: ocurre cuando se dañan los cilios y los pulmones no se pueden defender contra las enfermedades (Cap. 16, pág. 504)

lungs/pulmones: ubicados en la cavidad torácica, son los órganos principales del sistema respiratorio (Cap. 16, pág. 489)

malleable/maleable: propiedad de algunos metales de poder martillarse o extenderse en planchas o láminas sin romperse (Cap. 9, pág. 272)

mechanical advantage/ventaja mecánica: la ventaja mecánica de una máquina te deja saber cuantas veces se multiplica la fuerza de esfuerzo (Cap. 5, pág. 159)

metal/metal: uno de los grupos de elementos más importantes, generalmente son sólidos brillantes, maleables, dúctiles que conducen el calor y la electricidad (Cap. 9, pág. 272)

metalloide/metaloide: elemento que posee características tanto de los metales como de los no metales (Cap. 9, pág. 290)

metamorphic rock/roca metamórfica: roca que se forma cuando el calor o la presión o ambos cambian la roca (Cap. 11, pág. 340)

mid-ocean ridge/dorsal medioceánica: cadena de montañas submarinas que se extiende a lo largo de la zona de cuencas profundas (Cap. 12, pág. 383)

mineral/mineral: estructura cristalina inanimada que se da en forma natural y que posee una composición definida. (Cap. 10, pág. 303)

mitochondria/mitocondria: son las centrales eléctricas de una célula; estructuras en donde se descomponen las moléculas de alimento y la energía química se convierte en formas que la célula puede usar (Cap. 17, pág. 531)

mitosis/mitosis: proceso mediante el cual el núcleo de una célula se divide para producir dos núcleos, cada uno con el mismo tipo y número de cromosomas que tenía la célula original (Cap. 17, pág. 538)

neuron/neurona: célula nerviosa que es la unidad básica del sistema nervioso (Cap. 8, pág. 242)

newton/newton: unidad de fuerza cuya abreviatura es N (Cap. 1, pág. 35)

nonfoliated/no foliada: roca metamórfica en que los granos minerales cambian, se combinan o se ordenan de manera diferente pero no forman bandas visibles (Cap. 11, pág. 342)

nonmetal/no metal: elemento sólido quebradizo y mal conductor de calor y de electricidad; los no metales también pueden ser gaseosos (Cap. 9, pág. 282)

nonrenewable resource/recurso no renovable: recurso que la gente usa mucho más rápidamente de lo que la naturaleza tarda en reemplazar (Cap. 13, pág. 403)

nucleus/núcleo: centro de comando de la célula que dirige todas las actividades celulares (Cap. 17, pág. 530)

organ/órgano: estructura del cuerpo formada por varios tipos diferentes de tejido que funcionan juntos para desempeñar una función específica (Cap. 19, pág. 605)

organ system/sistema de órganos: grupo de órganos que funcionan juntos para desempeñar una función específica (Cap. 19, pág. 605)

organism/organismo: está compuesto de un conjunto de órganos que funcionan juntos (Cap. 19, pág. 605)

osmosis/osmosis: difusión del agua a través de una membrana celular (Cap. 19, pág. 589)

ozone/ozono: gas que absorbe parte de la radiación dañina que proviene del Sol (Cap. 15, pág. 462)

pollution/contaminación: materiales o efectos indeseados o dañinos en el ambiente (Cap. 12, pág. 371)

potential energy/energía potencial: energía almacenada debido a la posición de un objeto (Cap. 4, pág. 123)

power/potencia: cantidad de trabajo realizado dividida entre el intervalo de tiempo (Cap. 5, pág. 168)

pressure/presión: peso o fuerza que actúa sobre cada unidad de superficie (Cap. 1, pág. 40)

prevailing westerlies/predominio vientos ponientes: vientos situados entre las latitudes de 30° y 60° (Cap. 15, pág. 474)

product/producto: sustancia nueva que se forma en una reacción química (Cap. 18, pág. 557)

pulley/polea: una rueda con una cuerda o cadena que pasa sobre la cadena (Cap. 5, pág. 153)

pulse/pulso: la expansión y contracción rítmica de una arteria (Cap. 3, pág. 91)

R

radiation/radiación: transferencia de energía térmica a través del espacio (Cap. 6, pág. 197)

reactant/reactivo: sustancia con la que comienzas una reacción química (Cap. 18, pág. 557)

reaction force/fuerza de reacción: fuerza que resulta en oposición directa a la fuerza de acción (Cap. 1, pág. 37)

reflex/reflejo: respuesta automática del cuerpo a un estímulo potencialmente peligroso (Cap. 8, pág. 254)

renewable resource/recurso renovable: recurso natural que se puede reemplazar, por medio de procesos naturales, en menos de 100 años (Cap. 13, pág. 402)

resistance force/fuerza de resistencia: fuerza aplicada por una máquina (Cap. 5, pág. 150)

respiration/respiración: proceso químico en el cual se descomponen las moléculas de glucosa con el fin de liberar energía (Cap. 19, pág. 595)

rift zone/zona de cuencas profundas: regiones en donde el suelo marino se está expandiendo (Cap. 12, pág. 379)

rock/roca: mezcla de uno o más minerales, de mineraloides, de vidrio o de partículas orgánicas (Cap. 11, pág. 331)

rock cycle/ciclo de las rocas: proceso mediante el cual las materias terrestres cambian para formar diferentes clases de rocas (Cap. 11, pág. 350)

screw/tornillo: un plano inclinado enrollado alrededor de un poste (Cap. 5, pág. 156)

sedimentary rock/roca sedimentaria: roca que se forma de sedimetos asentados que se vuelven a combinar para formar una roca sólida (Cap. 11, pág. 343)

seismic wave/onda sísmica: onda ocasionada por los terremotos (Cap. 2, pág. 61)

skeletal muscle/músculo del esqueleto: músculo que mueve los huesos (Cap. 7, pág. 226)

smog/smog: tipo de contaminación del aire que aparece como una niebla de humo (Cap. 15, pág. 461)

smooth muscle/músculo liso: músculo que se encuentra en muchas partes dentro de tu cuerpo, tales como el estómago y los intestinos. (Cap. 7, pág. 226)

solar cell/célula solar: célula que convierte la luz solar en electricidad (Cap. 13, pág. 413)

spinal cord/médula espinal: conducto largo que se extiende desde el bulbo raquídeo hasta la parte inferior de la espalda. (Cap. 8, pág. 250)

spongy bone/hueso esponjoso: parte del hueso que se parece a una esponja porque contiene muchos orificios pequeñísimos; se encuentra en los extremos de muchos huesos (Cap. 7, pág. 215)

streak/veta: es el color del mineral cuando se desmenuza y se pulveriza (Cap. 10, pág. 308)

synapse/sinapsis: espacio pequeño que se encuentra entre las neuronas y a través del cual se transmiten los impulsos nerviosos (Cap. 8, pág. 243)

target tissue/tejido asignado: tejido específico que es afectado por una hormona (Cap. 8, pág. 257)

tendon/tendón: banda fuerte y elástica de tejido (Cap. 7, pág. 226)

thermal equilibrium/equilibrio térmico: dos objetos que están en contacto y poseen la misma temperatura (Cap. 6, pág. 186)

tissue/tejido: tipos de células similares que funcionan en conjunto para desempeñar la misma función (Cap. 19, pág. 605)

trachea/tráquea: pasaje por el cual el aire entra y sale del cuerpo (Cap. 16, pág. 485)

trade winds/vientos alisios: vientos causados por el aire descendiente que regresa al ecuador (Cap. 15, pág. 473)

troposphere/troposfera: zona inferior de la atmósfera que es la capa más cercana al suelo (Cap. 15, pág. 462)

veins/venas: vasos sanguíneos que transportan la sangre de regreso al corazón desde los pulmones o el cuerpo (Cap. 3, pág. 86)

vent/chimenea: abertura por donde el magma fluye a la superficie terrestre como lava (Cap. 2, pág. 67)

wedge/cuña: un plano inclinado el cual utiliza el extremo afilado y angosto para cortar a través de materiales (Cap. 5, pág. 157)

weight/peso: fuerza de gravitación ejercida sobre ti o cualquier otro objeto (Cap. 1, pág. 36)

wheel and axle/rueda y eje: una rueda pequeña pegada al centro de una más grande (Cap. 5, pág. 152)

work/trabajo: energía que se transfiere a través de la fuerza y del movimiento (Cap. 4, pág. 119)

INDEX

The Index for *Science Interactions* will help you locate major topics in the book quickly and easily. Each entry in the Index is followed by the numbers of the pages on which the entry is discussed. A page number given in **boldface type** indicates the page on which that entry is defined. A page number given in *italic type* indicates a page on which the entry is used in an illustration or photograph. The abbreviation *act.* indicates a page on which the entry is used in an activity.

Credits

Illustrations

Jonathan Banchick 28, 31; **George Bucktell** 413; **John Edwards** 15, 172, 394-395, 408-409, 417, 573; **Chris Forsey/Morgan-Cain & Associates** 58, 59, 62-63, 66, 69, 70, 79, (b) 192-193, 318, 319, 325, 332-333, 350-351, 378-379, (b) 387, 397, 401; **Nancy Heim/158 Street Design Group** 89; **Tonya Hines** (b) 87, (b) 90, (t) 99, 100, 101, 102, (r) 110, 572; **Tom Kennedy/Romark Illustrations** 38, (r) 49, (t) 140; **Ruth Krabach** (b) 245, 247, (tl) 250; **Gina Lapurga** (bl) 250, (r) 255, (c) 262; **Ortelius Design** 626-627, 628-629; **Felipe Passalacqua** 222, 223, 514, 515; **Precision Graphics** 22-23, 27, 43, (l) 49, 82, 85, (t) 87, (t) 90, 93, 95, (l,c) 110, 124-125, 131, 138-139, (b) 140, 143, 145, 150-151, 154, 159, 160, 161, (b) 177, 187, 196-197, 198, 200, 201, 203, 207, 241, (t) 245, (r) 250, 257, 258, (tr, br) 262, 264, 276, 277, 285, 303, 340, 343, 344, 352, 357, 374, 392-393, 402-403, 405, 406, 418, 426, 432, 435, 437, 441, 444-445, 451, 463, 471, 472, (l) 479, 481, 484, 485, 487, 488, (t) 489, 493, 494, 501, 503, 508, 521, 526, 527, 528, 529, 530, 531, 532, 533, 538, 539, 547, 549, 562, 566-567, (l) 585, 586, 587, 589, (t) 595, 601, 605, (l,br) 610, 620 621, 630-631, 644, 650, 651; **Rolin Graphics Inc.** 47, (r) 213, 215, 224, 226, 227, 231, 235, 242-243, (l) 255, (tl,bl) 262, 364-365, (t) 387; **Doug Schneider** 648; **Jim Shough** 155, 156, (t) 177, (l) 213; **John Walter & Associates** 52, 78, (b) 99, 121, 142, 183, (t) 193, 403, 468-469, 473, 474, 475, (r) 479, 492, (r) 585, 593, (b) 595, (t,bc) 610.

Photographs

Mark Thayer Studio (t) 3, (b) 11, 34, (c,r) 40, 41, (t) 42, 44, (l) 49, (t) 103, (t) 116, 128, (b) 130, 131, 135, (t) 148, (t) 149, 151, 152, (t) 153, 156, 160, 161, (r) 164, 165, (br) 166, 166-167, (t) 174, (t) 177, (t) 180, (t,c) 183, (tl,bl) 186, (t) 191, (l) 207, (t) 211, 214, (b) 218, (b) 238-239, 256, 257, 268, (t) 269, (br) 273, 277, (t,c) 278, (t) 279, 280, 281, (b) 289, 292, (tr,c) 297, 299, (t,c) 302, (t) 303, 304, (tr) 305, (bl) 308, 308-309, (t) 309, (cl) 310, (bcl,bc,bcr,br) 311, (l) 313, 314, (tl,tr) 325, (l) 328, (c) 334-335, 337, (tl,bl) 338, 343, (t) 345, 352, 353, (b) 357, 359, (tl,bl) 366, (r) 367, 422-423, 424, (t) 425, (t) 429, (r)431, (l) 438, 441, 446, 457, 485, 499, (tl) 514, 516, 517, (t) 519, (t) 521, (b) 523, 542, 550-551, (t) 551, 553, 556, (l) 558, (b) 561, (tl, tr) 564, (tl,b) 565, (l,lc,rc) 570, 574, 576, (tl,bl,br) 579, (t) 582, (t) 588,(c) 602, 606, 611, (r) 636, (t) 645; **RMIP/Richard Haynes** 2, 4, 5, 6, 7, 8-9, 10, (t) 11, 12-13, 14, (t) 16, 19, (b) 21, 24, 25, 32, 33, 36, 39, 53, (b) 58, 60, 64, 65, 72, 76, 83, 84, 86, 92, 93, 97, 113, 115, (br) 117, (b) 119, (t) 123, 126, (b) 129, 132, 136, 137, (t) 145, (b) 149, (b) 153, (t) 157, 162, 163, (tr) 166, (l) 164, 170, (t) 171, (b) 177, 179, (b)181, 182, (bl) 183, 185, 194, (t) 207, (b) 211, 212, 216, 217, (t) 218, 219, 221, (r) 226, 227, 229, (t) 238, (t,b) 239, 244, 245, 248, 252, 253, 254, 258, 265, 267, (b) 269, (b) 272, 275, 278, 287, (b) 301, (b) 303, 316, (r) 317, (b) 329, 336, (t) 341, 344, (t) 346, 348, 361, (t) 363, 368, (t) 373, (t) 377, 380, (r) 391, 393, 398, (t) 399, 407, 410, 421, 423, (b) 425, 426, 428, 430, (l,c) 431, 434, 436, 442, 443, (b) 455, 459, 464, 466, 467, (t) 470, (t) 472, 483, 490, 491, 495, (b) 497, 502, 511, 513, (b) 515, (b) 519, 522, (t) 523, 525, 540, (l,r) 541, (b) 551, 560, (t) 561, 568, 569, (r) 570,

(b) 583, 584, 586, (b) 588, 590, 591, 596, 598, 599, 613, 647, 652; **Cover** (bk) Nicholas Devore/Photographer's Aspen, (tl) NASA, (tr) Glencoe file, (c) Chip Clarke, (b) Norbert Wu; **3,** (b) SuperStock; **16,** (bl) SuperStock; **17,** NASA; **18-19,** John Cleare/OffShoot Special Collections; **20,** (t) Scott McKiernan/Black Star, (b) Tom Sobolink/Black Star; **21,** (t) Studiohio; **26,** Ralph Brunke; **29,** Kenji Kerins; **30,** (t) Ed Degginger, (b) NASA; **31,** SuperStock; **35,** The Mary Evans Picture Library, London; **37,** Helen Marcus/Photo Researchers Inc.; **40,** (l) Carl Purcell, (lc) David Stocklein; **42,** (b) Stephen Frink/Waterhouse; **45,** Chris Sorenson; **46,** Robert Frerck/Odyssey; **48,** Studiohio; **49,** (c) David Stocklein, (r) Chris Sorenson; **51,** Fred Bodin; **52,** (t) Katsushika Hokusai/SuperStock; **52-53,** Francois Gohier/Photo Researchers Inc.; **54,** Kenji Kerins; **55,** (t) Dell Foute/Visuals Unlimited, (c) N.R. Rowan/Stock, Boston Inc., (b) James Sugar/Black Star; **56,** Herman Kokojan/Black Star; **57,** (t) Andrew Rankink/Tony Stone Worldwide, (b) David Young-Wolff/Photo Edit; **58,** (t) Greg Vaughn/Tom Stack & Associates; **59,** (l) Mike Andrews/Earth Scenes, (r) Kevin Schaefer/Tom Stack & Associates; **63,** Jose Fernandez/Woodfin Camp & Associates; **67,** Ken Ferguson; **68,** (l) Gregory Dimijian/Photo Researchers Inc., (r) Steve Lissau; **70,** (t) Nancy Cushing/Visuals Unlimited, (c) Krafft/Photo Researchers Inc., (b) D. Cavagnaro/Visuals Unlimited; **71,** (t) Forest Buchanan/Visuals Unlimited, (c) Paul Bierman/Visuals Unlimited, (b) Gary Braasch/Woodfin Camp & Associates; **74,** (l) Sid Balatan/Black Star, (r) Robert Frerck/Odyssey Productions; **75,** James Sugar/Black Star; **77,** Boyd Norton/Comstock; **79,** Gregory Dimijian/Photo Researchers Inc.; **82-83,** Baron Wolman; **89,** Custom Medical Stock; **91,** Studiohio; **94,** Kenji Kerins; **96,** Matt Meadows; **98,** L. Stein Mark/Custom Medical Stock; **100,** (t) Carl Roessler/Tony Stone Worldwide, (b) Stephen Dalton/Photo Researchers Inc.; **101,** Walter Harvey/Photo Researchers Inc.; **102,** Visuals Unlimited; **103,** (bl,br) W. Ober/Visuals Unlimited; **104,** Paul Barton/The Stock Market; **105,** Ed Kashi; **106,** Ed Kashi; **107,** (l) Courtesy of Dr. Kohman/SUNY; (r) Historical Picture Service; **109,** Courtesy of Tamika Walker; **110,** (t) Carl Roessler/Tony Stone Worldwide, (b) W. Ober/Visuals Unlimited; **114-115,** David Barnes/AllStock; **116-117,** Comstock; **117,** (t) David Madison; **118,** Studiohio; **119,** (t) Imageman/International Stock Photography; **120,** Ralph Brunke; **121,** Denver Bryan/Comstock; **122,** (l) William Sallaz/Duomo, (r) Tom Branch/Photo Researchers Inc. **123,** (b) Tom Bean; **125,** Erika Klass; **127,** Rhoda Sidney/Stock, Boston Inc.; **129,** (t) Ralph Brunke; **130,** (t) S. Tielemans/Duomo, (tc) Joe Strunk/Dr. Loren Winters; **133,** Ken Regan/Camera 5; **134,** Ken Ferguson; **138,** NASA; **139,** NASA; **141,** (l) Chris Sorenson, (r) Paul Sutton/Duomo; **144,** (t) The Niels Bohr Library at the National Institute of Physics, (b) North Wind Picture Archive/Alfred, Maine; **145,** (b) Rhoda Sidney/Stock, Boston Inc.; **147,** Bob Daemmrich/Stock, Boston Inc.; **148-149,** Dorothy Littel/Stock, Boston Inc.; **154,** Helmut Gritscher/Peter Arnold Inc.; **155,** Ken Ferguson; **157,** (c) Lauros-Giraudon/The Bridgeman Art Library, London, (b) Robert Frerck/Odyssey; **158,** Ken Ferguson; **168,** Peter Chapman; **169,** Richard Levine; **171,** (b) Wide World Photos; **173,** (t) R. & K.